HOLT
SCIENCE &
TECHNOLOGY

CALIFORNIA
Life
Science

HOLT, RINEHART AND WINSTON

A Harcourt Classroom Education Company

Austin • New York • Orlando • Atlanta • San Francisco • Boston • Dallas • Toronto • London

Staff Credits

Editorial

Robert W. Todd, Executive Editor

David F. Bowman, Managing Editor

Barbara Howell, Senior Editor

Charlotte Luongo, Annette Ratliff, Tracy Schagen, Laura Zapanta, Robin Goodman (Feature Articles)

ANNOTATED TEACHER'S EDITION

David Westerberg, Bill Burnside, Kelly Graham

ANCILLARIES

Jennifer Childers, Senior Editor

Erin Bao, Kristen Karns, Andrew Strickler, Clay Crenshaw, Wayne Duncan, Molly Frohlich, Amy James, Monique Mayer, Traci Maxwell

COPYEDITORS

Steve Oelenberger, Copyediting Supervisor

Suzanne Brooks, Brooke Fugitt, Tania Hannan, Denise Nowotny

EDITORIAL SUPPORT STAFF

Christy Bear, Jeanne Graham, Rose Segrest, Tanu'e White

EDITORIAL PERMISSIONS

Cathy Paré, Permissions Manager

Jan Harrington, Permissions Editor

Art, Design, and Photo

BOOK DESIGN

Richard Metzger, Art Director

Marc Cooper, Senior Designer

Sonya Mendeke, Designer

Alicia Sullivan (ATE), Cristina Bowerman (ATE), Eric Rupprath (Ancillaries)

IMAGE SERVICES

Elaine Tate, Art Buyer Supervisor

Kim Baker, Art Buyer

PHOTO RESEARCH

Tim Taylor, Senior Photo Researcher

Stephanie Friedman, Assistant Photo Researcher

PHOTO STUDIO

Sam Dudgeon, Senior Staff Photographer

Victoria Smith, Photo Specialist

DESIGN NEW MEDIA

Susan Michael, Art Director

DESIGN MEDIA

Joe Melomo, Art Director

Shawn McKinney, Designer

Production

Mimi Stockdell, Senior Production Manager

Beth Sample, Production Coordinator

Suzanne Brooks, Sara Carroll-Downs

Media Production

Kim A. Scott, Senior Production Manager

Nancy Hargis, Production Supervisor

Adriana Bardin, Production Coordinator

New Media

Jim Bruno, Senior Project Manager

Lydia Doty, Senior Project Manager

Jessica Bega, Project Manager

Armin Gutzmer, Manager Training and Technical Support

Cathy Kuhles, Nina Degollado

Design Implementation and Production

Mazer Corporation

For permission to reprint copyrighted material, grateful acknowledgment is made to the following source: sciLINKS is owned and provided by the National Science Teachers Association. All rights reserved.

Printed in the United States of America

ISBN 0-03-055639-2

8 9 10 11 048 05 04 03 02

Acknowledgments

Chapter Writers

Katy Z. Allen
Science Writer and Former Biology Teacher
Wayland, Massachusetts

Linda Ruth Berg, Ph.D.
Adjunct Professor–Natural Sciences
St. Petersburg Junior College
St. Petersburg, Florida

Leila Dumas
Former Physics Teacher
LBJ Science Academy
Austin, Texas

Jennie Dusheck
Science Writer
Santa Cruz, California

Mark F. Taylor, Ph.D.
Associate Professor of Biology
Baylor University
Waco, Texas

Lab Writers

Diana Scheidle Bartos
Science Consultant and Educator
Diana Scheidle Bartos, L.L.C.
Lakewood, Colorado

Carl Benson
Technology Coordinator
Plains High School
Plains, Montana

Charlotte Blassingame
Science Teacher and Dept. Chair
White Station Middle School
Memphis, Tennessee

Marsha Carver
Science Teacher and Dept. Chair
McLean County High School
Calhoun, Kentucky

Kenneth E. Creese
Science Teacher
White Mountain Junior High School
Rock Springs, Wyoming

Linda Culp
Science Teacher and Dept. Chair
Thorndale High School
Thorndale, Texas

James Deaver
Science Teacher and Dept. Chair
West Point High School
West Point, Nebraska

Frank McKinney, Ph.D.
Professor of Geology
Appalachian State University
Boone, North Carolina

Alyson Mike
Science Teacher
East Valley Middle School
East Helena, Montana

C. Ford Morishita
Biology Teacher
Clackamas High School
Milwaukie, Oregon

Patricia Morrell, Ph.D.
Assistant Professor, School of Education
University of Portland
Portland, Oregon

Hilary C. Olson, Ph.D.
Research Associate
Institute for Geophysics
The University of Texas
Austin, Texas

James B. Pulley
Science Teacher
Liberty High School
Liberty, Missouri

Denice Lee Sandefur
Science Teacher
Nucla High School
Nucla, Colorado

Patti Soderberg
Science Writer
The BioQUEST Curriculum Consortium
Beloit College
Beloit, Wisconsin

Phillip Vavala
Science Teacher and Dept. Chair
Salesianum School
Wilmington, Delaware

Albert C. Wartski
Biology Teacher
Chapel Hill High School
Chapel Hill, North Carolina

Lynn Marie Wartski
Science Writer and Former Science Teacher
Hillsborough, North Carolina

Ivora D. Washington
Science Teacher
Hyattsville Middle School
Hyattsville, Maryland

Academic Reviewers

David M. Armstrong, Ph.D.
Professor of Biology
University of Colorado
Boulder, Colorado

Alissa Arp, Ph.D.
Director and Professor of Environmental Studies
Romberg Tiburon Center
San Francisco State University
Tiburon, California

Russell M. Brengelman
Professor of Physics
Morehead State University
Morehead, Kentucky

Linda K. Butler, Ph.D.
Lecturer of Biological Sciences
The University of Texas
Austin, Texas

Barry Chernoff, Ph.D.
Associate Curator and Head
Division of Fishes
The Field Museum of Natural History
Chicago, Illinois

Donna Greenwood Crenshaw, Ph.D.
Research Associate
Department of Biology
Duke University
Durham, North Carolina

Hugh Crenshaw, Ph.D.
Assistant Professor of Zoology
Duke University
Durham, North Carolina

Joe W. Crim, Ph.D.
Professor of Biology
University of Georgia
Athens, Georgia

Andrew J. Davis, Ph.D.
Manager of ACE Science Center
Department of Physics
California Institute of Technology
Pasadena, California

Peter Demmin, Ed.D.
Former Science Teacher and Chair
Amherst Central High School
Amherst, New York

Gabriele F. Giuliani, Ph.D.
Professor of Physics
Purdue University
West Lafayette, Indiana

Joseph L. Graves, Jr., Ph.D.
Associate Professor of Life Sciences
Arizona State University West
Phoenix, Arizona

Laurie Jackson-Grusby, Ph.D.
Research Scientist and Doctoral Associate
Whitehead Institute for Biomedical Research
Massachusetts Institute of Technology
Cambridge, Massachusetts

William B. Guggino, Ph.D.
Professor of Physiology and Pediatrics
The Johns Hopkins University School of Medicine
Baltimore, Maryland

David Haig, Ph.D.
Assistant Professor of Biology
Department of Organismic and Evolutionary Biology
Harvard University
Cambridge, Massachusetts

John E. Hoover, Ph.D.
Associate Professor of Biology
Millersville University
Millersville, Pennsylvania

Joan E. N. Hudson, Ph.D.
Professor of Biology
Sam Houston State University
Huntsville, Texas

George M. Langford, Ph.D.
Professor of Biological Sciences
Dartmouth College
Hanover, New Hampshire

V. Patteson Lombardi, Ph.D.
Research Assistant Professor of Biology
Department of Biology
University of Oregon
Eugene, Oregon

William F. McComas, Ph.D.
Director of the Center to Advance Science Education
University of Southern California
Los Angeles, California

LaMoine L. Motz, Ph.D.
Coordinator of Science Education
Oakland County Schools
Waterford, Michigan

Acknowledgments (cont.)

Nancy Parker, Ph.D.
Associate Professor of Biology
Southern Illinois University
Edwardsville, Illinois

Barron S. Rector, Ph.D.
Associate Professor
Department of Rangeland
Ecology and Management
Texas A&M University
College Station, Texas

John Rigden, Ph.D.
Director of Special Projects
American Institute of
Physics
Colchester, Vermont

Miles R. Silman, Ph.D.
Assistant Professor of Biology
Wake Forest University
Winston-Salem, North
Carolina

Robert G. Steen, Ph.D.
Manager, Rat Genome Project
Whitehead Institute–Center
for Genome Research
Massachusetts Institute of
Technology
Cambridge, Massachusetts

Jack B. Swift, Ph.D.
Professor of Physics
The University of Texas
Austin, Texas

Martin VanDyke, Ph.D.
*Professor of Chemistry
Emeritus*
Front Range Community
College
Westminister, Colorado

E. Peter Volpe, Ph.D.
Professor of Medical Genetics
Mercer University School of
Medicine
Macon, Georgia

Harold K. Voris, Ph.D.
Curator and Head
Division of Amphibians and
Reptiles
The Field Museum of
Natural History
Chicago, Illinois

Peter Wetherwax, Ph.D.
Professor of Biology
Department of Education
University of Oregon
Eugene, Oregon

Mary Wicksten, Ph.D.
Professor of Biology
Texas A&M University
College Station, Texas

R. Stimson Wilcox, Ph.D.
Professor of Biology
Behavioral Ecology &
Communication of Animals
Binghamton University
Binghamton, New York

Conrad Zapanta, Ph.D.
Research Engineer
Sulzer Carbomedics, Inc.
Austin, Texas

Safety Reviewer

Jack Gerlovich, Ph.D.
Associate Professor
School of Education
Drake University
Des Moines, Iowa

Teacher Reviewers

Barry L. Bishop
Science Teacher and Dept. Chair
San Rafael Junior High
School
Ferron, Utah

Carol A. Bornhorst
Science Teacher and Dept. Chair
Bonita Vista Middle School
Chula Vista, California

Paul Boyle
Science Teacher
Perry Heights Middle School
Evansville, Indiana

Yvonne Brannum
Science Teacher and Dept. Chair
Hine Junior High School
Washington, D.C.

Gladys Cherniak
Science Teacher
St. Paul's Episcopal School
Mobile, Alabama

James Chin
Science Teacher
Frank A. Day Middle School
Newtonville, Massachusetts

Randy Christian
Science Teacher
Stovall Junior High School
Houston, Texas

Kenneth Creese
Science Teacher
White Mountain Junior High
School
Rock Springs, Wyoming

Linda A. Culp
Science Teacher and Dept. Chair
Thorndale High School
Thorndale, Texas

Georgiann Delgadillo
Science Teacher
East Valley Continuous
Curriculum School
Spokane, Washington

Alonda Droege
Biology Teacher
Evergreen High School
Seattle, Washington

Michael J. DuPré
Curriculum Specialist
Rush Henrietta Junior-Senior
High School
Henrietta, New York

Rebecca Ferguson
Science Teacher
North Ridge Middle School
North Richland Hills, Texas

Susan Gorman
Science Teacher
North Ridge Middle School
North Richland Hills, Texas

Karma Houston-Hughes
Science Teacher
Kyrene Middle School
Tempe, Arizona

Kerry A. Johnson
Science Teacher
Isbell Middle School
Santa Paula, California

Martha R. Kisiah
Science Teacher
Fairview Middle School
Tallahassee, Florida

Kathy LaRoe
Science Teacher
East Valley Middle School
East Helena, Montana

Jane M. Lemons
Science Teacher
Western Rockingham Middle
School
Madison, North Carolina

Scott Mandel, Ph.D.
*Director and Educational
Consultant*
Teachers Helping Teachers
Los Angeles, California

Maurine O. Marchani
Science Teacher and Dept. Chair
Raymond Park Middle
School
Indianapolis, Indiana

Jason P. Marsh
Biology Teacher
Montevideo High School
and Montevideo Country
School
Montevideo, Minnesota

Edith C. McAlanis
Science Teacher and Dept. Chair
Socorro Middle School
El Paso, Texas

Kevin McCurdy, Ph.D.
Science Teacher
Elmwood Junior High School
Rogers, Arkansas

Alyson Mike
Science Teacher
East Valley Middle School
East Helena, Montana

Gabriell DeBear Paye
Biology Teacher
West Roxbury High School
West Roxbury, Massachusetts

James B. Pulley
Former Science Teacher
Liberty High School
Liberty, Missouri

Terry J. Rakes
Science Teacher
Elmwood Junior High School
Rogers, Arkansas

Debra Sampson
Science Teacher
Booker T. Washington
Middle School
Elgin, Texas

Charles Schindler
Curriculum Advisor
San Bernardino City Unified
Schools
San Bernardino, California

**Acknowledgments
continue on page 690.**

Contents in Brief

Contents

 Unit 1 ··· **The Study of Living Things**

Unit 6 ··· **Ecology**

The more labs, the better!
Take a minute to browse the **LabBook** located at the end of this textbook. You'll find a wide variety of exciting labs that will help you experience science firsthand. But please don't forget to be safe. Read the "Safety First!" section before starting any of the labs.

Investigate!

Now is the time to Investigate!

Science is a process in which investigation leads to information and understanding. The **Investigate!** at the beginning of each chapter helps you gain scientific understanding of the topic through hands-on experience.

QuickLab

Not all laboratory investigations have to be long and involved.

The **QuickLabs** found throughout the chapters of this textbook require only a small amount of time and limited equipment. But just because they are quick, don't skimp on the safety.

MATH BREAK

Science and math go hand in hand.

The **MathBreaks** in the margins of the chapters show you many ways that math applies directly to science and vice versa.

APPLY

Science can be very useful in the real world.

It is interesting to learn how scientific information is being used in the real world. You can see for yourself in the **Apply** features. You will also be asked to apply your own knowledge. This is a good way to learn!

Connections

One science leads to another.
You may not realize it at first, but different areas of science are related to each other in many ways. Each **Connection** explores a topic from the viewpoint of another science discipline. In this way, areas of science merge to improve your understanding of the world around you.

 oceanography CONNECTION

 astronomy CONNECTION

 chemistry CONNECTION

 earth science CONNECTION

 environmental science CONNECTION

 physical science CONNECTION

 physics CONNECTION

Feature Articles

Feature articles for any appetite!
Science and technology affect us all in many ways. The following articles will give you an idea of just how interesting, strange, helpful, and action-packed science and technology are. At the end of each chapter, you will find two feature articles. Read them and you will be surprised at what you learn.

UNIT 1

The Study of Living Things

Life science is the study of living things—from the tiniest bacterium to the largest tree! In this unit, you will discover the similarities of all living things. You will learn about the tools life scientists use, and you'll learn to ask your own questions about the living world around you.

People have always searched for answers about life. This time-line includes a few of the many people who have studied living things through the centuries. And there's always more to be learned, so keep your eyes open.

2640 B.C.

Si Ling-Chi, Empress of China, observes silkworms in her garden and develops a process to cultivate them and make silk.

1944

Oswald T. Avery proposes that DNA is the material that carries genetic properties in living organisms.

1946

ENIAC, the first entirely electric computer, is built. It weighs 30 tons and takes up 450 m².

1967

The first successful human heart transplant is performed by Dr. Christian Barnard.

1970

Floppy disks for computer data storage are introduced.

1010

Arab physicist Ibn al Haytham discovers that vision is caused by the reflection of light from objects into the eye.

1590

Zacharius Jansen constructs the first microscope. It contains two lenses and a tube.

1685

Improvements to microscopes allow the first observation of red blood cells.

1914

George Washington Carver's studies on agriculture and soil conservation lead to research on peanuts.

1934

Dorothy Crowfoot Hodgkin uses X-ray techniques to determine protein structure.

1931

The first electron microscope is developed.

1983

Dian Fossey writes *Gorillas in the Mist,* a book about her research on mountain gorillas in Africa and her efforts to save them from poachers.

1984

A process known as DNA fingerprinting is developed by Alec Jeffries.

1998

In China, scientists discover a fossil of a dinosaur with feathers.

1 The World of Life Science

Imagine . . .

You are walking through a field with some classmates. Suddenly you notice that there are frogs hopping around all over the place! You and your classmates start catching the frogs with a net. As you lift the first frog from the net, you notice something weird. Its legs seem to be broken. You look at your friend's frog. It seems to be injured, too. So is another frog, and another! You look closer. A frog with no eyes? Wait a minute! These frogs aren't injured. They're deformed! What are these, aliens from outer space? a new species of frog?

Believe it or not, this really happened to a group of students from Le Sueur, Minnesota, during a visit to a wildlife refuge. About half of the frogs they collected were deformed. The students and their teacher were stunned by what they found. What could have caused these deformities? Was it just some weird natural phenomenon or were the frogs exposed to some sort of chemical made by people? The students gathered more information on the frogs and alerted local scientists to what they had found. Students and scientists from all over the country are now working together to solve the mystery of the freaky frogs.

The students, like almost all scientists, began their research by noticing something about the natural world and then asking questions about what they observed. In this chapter you will learn how questions fuel the study of science and how scientists go about finding answers to these questions.

What Do You Think?

In your ScienceLog, try to answer the following questions based on what you already know:

1. What tools do life scientists use?

2. What methods do scientists use to study life science?

3. Can anyone become a life scientist?

2. Study the picture of the fish below. Try to imagine how your five small shapes can be arranged to create the fish. Then test your idea. If necessary, make several tries. Hint: You may need to turn one or more shapes over. Record your solution in your ScienceLog.

Investigate!

Figure It Out

In this activity you will test your ability to do some of the things scientists do—make observations and use them to solve a puzzle.

Procedure

1. Fold a **square piece of paper** along the lines shown in the figure below. First fold the square in half. Fold it in half again. Then fold down the corners from A to B and from A to C. Unfold the paper. Using **scissors,** cut along the folds, indicated by dark lines in the figure below, to form five shapes.

Analysis

3. Did you figure out how to correctly arrange the small shapes just by making observations? What observations provided clues?

4. How did testing your ideas help you solve the puzzle?

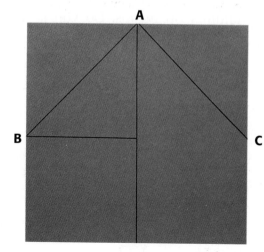

Asking About Life

It's summer. You are lying in the grass at the park, casually observing your surroundings. Three dogs are playing on your left. A bluebird is perched in the tree to your right. A few bumblebees are visiting nearby flowers. An ant makes off with a crumb from your sandwich. Suddenly a question pops into your head. "Why don't ants grow as big as people?" Then you think of another question. "Why do the bumblebees visit the purple flowers and not the white ones?" Finally you wonder, "Why are there no blue dogs?"

Congratulations! You have just taken the first steps toward becoming a life scientist. How did you do it? You observed the living world around you. You were curious, and you asked questions about your observations. After all, that's what science is all about. **Life science** is the study of living things.

NEW TERMS
life science

OBJECTIVES

- Explain the importance of asking questions in life science.
- Give three reasons why life science is beneficial to living things.

It All Starts with a Question

The world around you, near and far, is full of an amazing diversity of life. One-celled algae float unseen in ponds. Giant redwood trees seem to touch the sky. Forty-ton whales swim through the oceans. Tiny bacteria feed inside your intestines. Could you ever have thought up all of the living things, or organisms, that exist on Earth? For every organism that has ever lived, you could ask many questions about it, such as "How does it obtain food?" "Where does it live?" and "Why does it behave in a particular way?"

In Your Own Backyard Questions are easy to find. Take a look around your room, around your home, and around your neighborhood. What questions about life science can you think of? The student at left didn't have to look far to realize that he had questions about some very familiar organisms. Do you know the answer to any of these questions?

Touring the World Your neighborhood gives you just a taste of the questions that the world holds. The world is made up of many different places to live, such as deserts, oceans, forests, coral reefs, and tide pools. Just about anywhere you go on Earth, you will find some kind of living organism.

How do birds know where to go when they migrate?

Why do leaves change color in the fall?

How do fireflies make light?

Why do some plants eat bugs?

Why did the dinosaurs die out?

Looking for Answers

Close your eyes for a moment, and imagine a life scientist. What do you see? Is it someone in a laboratory, peering into a microscope? Which of the people in **Figure 1** do you think are scientists?

Figure 1 *Life scientists are people who ask many different kinds of questions.*

a Irene Duhart Long asks "How does the human body respond to space travel?"

b Geerat Vermeij, who is blind, asks "How have shells changed over time?"

c Irene Pepperberg asks "Are parrots smart enough to learn a language?"

Who? If you guessed that all of the people in Figure 1 are scientists, then you are right. Anyone can investigate the world around us. Women and men from any cultural or ethnic background can become life scientists.

Where? Doing investigations in a laboratory is an important part of life science, but life science can be studied in many other places too. Life scientists carry out investigations on farms, in forests, on the ocean floor—even in space. They work for businesses, hospitals, government agencies, and universities. Many are also teachers.

What? What a life scientist studies is determined by one thing—his or her curiosity. Life scientists specialize in many different areas of life science. They study how organisms function and behave and how organisms interact with each other and with their environment. Life scientists explore how organisms reproduce and how organisms pass traits from one generation to the next. Some life scientists investigate the origins of organisms and how organisms change over time.

Would you like to make a career out of learning about lizards? Turn to page 32 to read about someone who has.

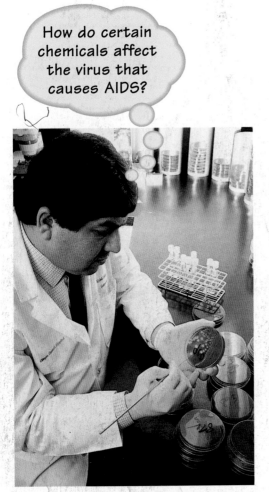

How do certain chemicals affect the virus that causes AIDS?

Figure 2 *Abdul Lakhani studies AIDS to find a cure for the disease.*

Which part of a person's genome is responsible for certain inherited diseases?

Why Ask Why?

What is the point of asking all these questions? Life scientists might find some interesting answers, but do any of the answers really matter? Will the answers affect *your* life? Absolutely! As you study life science, you will see how it affects you and all the living things around you.

Combating Disease Polio is a disease that affects the brain and nerves, causing paralysis. Do you know anyone who has had polio? Probably not. The polio virus has been eliminated from many areas of the world. But at one time it was much more common. In the 1950s, before life scientists discovered ways to prevent the spread of the polio virus, it infected 1 in every 3,000 Americans.

Today scientists continue to search for ways to fight diseases that have been around for a very long time, such as tuberculosis, as well as diseases that have emerged recently, such as acquired immune deficiency syndrome, or AIDS. The scientist in **Figure 2** is trying to learn more about AIDS, which now kills thousands of people every year. Life scientists have discovered how the virus that causes AIDS is carried from one person to another and how it affects the body. By learning more about AIDS, scientists may find a cure for this deadly disease.

Some diseases, such as cystic fibrosis, are inherited. They are passed from parents to children. Susumu Tonegawa, shown in **Figure 3,** is one of the many scientists worldwide who are studying the human genome. An organism's genome is inherited from its parents. The genome is the information in an organism's cells that controls the cells' activities. Mistakes in small parts of an organism's genome may cause the organism to be born with or to develop certain diseases. By learning about the human genome, scientists hope to find ways to cure or prevent inherited diseases.

Figure 3 *Susumu Tonegawa's work may help in the battle to fight inherited diseases.*

Protecting the Environment What environmental problems can you think of? If you were to make a list, it would probably be a long one. Most environmental problems are caused by people's misuse and improper disposal of natural resources. Understanding how we affect the world around us is the first step in finding solutions to problems such as pollution, deforestation, and the extinction of wildlife.

Why should we try to decrease the level of air and water pollution? Pollution can harm our health and the health of other animals and plants. Water pollution may be a cause of the frog deformities seen in Minnesota and other states. Oil pollution in oceans kills marine mammals, birds, and fish. By finding ways to decrease the amount of pollution we produce, we can help make the world a healthier place.

When we cut down trees to clear land for growing crops or to get lumber to build houses, we alter and sometimes destroy the habitat of other creatures. Dale Miquelle, shown in **Figure 4,** is part of a team of Russian and American scientists who are studying the Siberian tiger. Hunting and deforestation have almost caused the tigers to become extinct. By learning about the tigers' food and habitat needs, the scientists hope to develop a conservation plan that will ensure their survival.

Will whatever is causing the frogs to be deformed hurt me, too?

How much space does a tiger need in order to survive?

Figure 4 *To learn how much territory a Siberian tiger covers, Dale Miquelle tracks a tiger that is wearing a radio-transmitting collar.*

REVIEW

1. Describe life science.

2. What benefits to living things can life science provide?

3. Where do life scientists work? What do life scientists study?

4. Do you agree with the following statement? *The information learned by life scientists isn't very important.* Explain your answer.

5. **Apply** Take a look at the scene at right, and list five questions about the organisms shown. See if any of your classmates have the answers. Record the questions and answers in your ScienceLog.

Thinking Like a Life Scientist

OBJECTIVES

- Describe the scientific method.
- Evaluate the designs of experiments.
- Interpret the information in tables and graphs.
- Explain how scientific knowledge can change.

No matter where life scientists work or what questions they try to answer, life scientists all have two things in common. They are curious about the natural world, and they use similar methods to investigate it. Imagine that you are one of the students who discovered the deformed frogs discussed at the beginning of this chapter. If you wanted to investigate the cause of the frogs' deformities, where would you begin? Actually, you've already taken the first steps in the scientific process. You've made observations, and you've asked questions. What's next?

The Scientific Method

Most life scientists use the scientific method as the basis of their investigations. The **scientific method** is often described as a series of steps that is used to answer a question or solve a problem. **Figure 5** outlines the six steps of the scientific method. Take a moment to read each step.

- **Ask a question** based on observations.

- **Form a hypothesis,** which is a possible explanation for what you have observed.

- **Test the hypothesis** by conducting experiments.

- **Analyze the results** collected from experiments.

- **Draw conclusions** from the results of your experiment.

- **Communicate results** to other scientists.

Figure 5 *Life scientists often use the scientific method to solve problems and answer questions.*

Science Is a Creative Process After reading the steps of the scientific method, you may think that following each step in order will automatically produce the correct answer to your question or problem. But many questions cannot be answered that easily. Life scientists must use their imaginations to come up with explanations for what they have observed. They must also be creative when designing experiments to test their explanations. To find solutions, scientists may have to repeat steps of the scientific method or do them in a different order. In addition, every question doesn't necessarily require another experiment. Sometimes more observations are all that is needed to find an answer. And sometimes an answer cannot be found.

In the next few pages, you will revisit the mystery of the freaky frogs to see how the six steps of the scientific method were used in a real-life investigation.

Ask a Question Have you ever observed something out of the ordinary or not easily explained? The observation usually raises questions. If you are a scientist, the questions then need answers. Looking for answers often involves making more observations. Once the students from Le Sueur realized there was something wrong with the frogs, they decided they should continue their observations by collecting some data. The students began to make and record their observations, as shown in **Figure 6.** They counted how many deformed frogs and how many normal frogs they caught. They described the deformities as well as other characteristics of the frogs, such as their color. The students also photographed the frogs, took measurements, and wrote a thorough description of each frog.

Figure 6 *Collecting data was the first step in the students' investigation.*

In addition to collecting data on the frogs, the students collected data on other organisms living in the pond. They also conducted many tests on the pond water, measuring such things as the level of acidity. The students carefully recorded their data and observations. After all, they were scientists at work.

Observations can take many forms. They may be measurements of length, volume, temperature, time, or speed. They may describe how loud or soft a sound is or the color or shape of an organism. Observations may reveal the number of organisms in an area, the state of their health, or the pattern of their behavior. The range of observations a scientist can make is endless. But no matter what observations reveal, they are useful only if they are accurately made and recorded. A few of the tools that scientists use to make observations are shown in **Figure 7.**

Figure 7 *Microscopes, rulers, and thermometers are some of the many tools scientists use to collect information.*

Why did the chicken cross the highway? See page 33 to find out about "The Homesick Chicken," a science-fiction mystery.

Form a Hypothesis After making observations, scientists form one or more hypotheses. A **hypothesis** is a possible explanation or answer to a question. When scientists form hypotheses, they think logically and creatively and consider what they already know.

A hypothesis must be testable by experimentation. A hypothesis is not testable if no observations or information can be gathered or no experiment can be designed to test the hypothesis. Just because a hypothesis is not testable does not mean that it is wrong. It just means that there is no way to support or disprove the hypothesis.

Different scientists may have different hypotheses for the same problem. In the case of the frogs, the hypotheses shown below were formed. Which, if any, of these explanations was correct? To find out, each hypothesis would have to be tested.

Hypothesis 1 : The deformities were caused by one or more chemical pollutants in the water.

Hypothesis 2 : The deformities were caused by attacks from parasites or other frogs.

Hypothesis 3 : The deformities were caused by an increase in exposure to ultraviolet light from the sun.

✓ Self-Check

Which of the following statements is a hypothesis?

1. Deformed frogs have been found in the United States and Canada.
2. Insecticides and fertilizers caused the frog deformities.
3. Frogs can easily absorb pollutants through their skin.

(See page 636 to check your answers.)

Predictions

Before scientists can test a hypothesis, they must first make predictions. A prediction is a statement of cause and effect that can be used to set up a test for a hypothesis. Predictions are usually stated in an "If . . ., then . . ." format. For example, the following prediction was made for Hypothesis 3:

Hypothesis 3

Prediction: If an increase in exposure to ultraviolet light is causing the deformities, **then** some frog eggs exposed to ultraviolet light in a laboratory will develop into deformed frogs.

More than one prediction may be made for each hypothesis. Once predictions are made, scientists can design experiments to see which predictions, if any, prove to be true and support the hypothesis. On the following pages, you will learn how Hypothesis 3 was tested.

BRAIN FOOD

For any given set of facts, there are an infinite number of hypotheses that could explain them. To address this issue, the English philosopher William of Occam came up with a principle. This principle, called Occam's razor, states that the best explanation is usually the simplest.

You and a friend are walking through a heavily wooded park. Suddenly, you come upon a small area where all of the trees are lying on the ground. What knocked them down or caused them to fall over? Your friend thinks that extraterrestrials caused the trees to fall. Is your friend's hypothesis testable? In your ScienceLog, explain your answer. What other hypothesis can you come up with?

Test the Hypothesis After scientists make a prediction, they test the hypothesis. Scientists try to design experiments that will clearly show whether a particular factor was the cause of an observed outcome. A **factor** is anything in an experiment that can influence the experiment's outcome. Factors can be anything from temperature to the type of organism being studied.

Scientists strive to perform controlled experiments. A **controlled experiment** tests only one factor at a time. In a controlled experiment, there is a control group and one or more experimental groups. All of the factors for the control group and the experimental groups are the same except for one. The one factor that differs is called the **variable.** Because the variable is the only factor that differs between the control group and the experimental groups, scientists can be more certain that differences in the variable are the causes of any differences observed in the outcome of the experiment.

Designing a good experiment requires a lot of thought and planning. Let's see how an experiment might have been set up to test the prediction for Hypothesis 3: *If an increase in exposure to ultraviolet light is causing the deformities, **then** some frog eggs exposed to ultraviolet light in a laboratory will develop into deformed frogs.*

The first thing that needs to be identified is the variable. In this case, the variable is the amount of ultraviolet (UV) light exposure. The only factor that differs between the control group and the experimental groups is the length of time that frog eggs are exposed to UV light. This is shown in the table below.

All other factors, such as the kind of frog, the number of frog eggs in each aquarium, and the temperature of the water, should be the same in both the control group and the experimental groups.

Design of Experiment to Test the Effect of UV Light on Frogs

Group	Factors			
	Kind of frog	Number of eggs	Temperature of water	Variable: UV light exposure
#1 Control	leopard frog	100	25°C	0 days
#2 Experimental	leopard frog	100	25°C	15 days
#3 Experimental	leopard frog	100	25°C	24 days

As you can see from the table, each group in the experiment contains 100 eggs. Why is each group made up of so many individuals? Scientists always try to have many individuals in the control group and in the experimental group. The more organisms scientists test, the more certain scientists can be that differences in the outcome of an experiment are actually caused by differences in the variable and not by the natural differences between individuals. Repeating experiments is another way scientists support their conclusions about the effects of a variable. If an experiment produces the same results again and again, scientists can be more certain about the effect the variable has on the outcome of the experiment.

The experimental setup to test the prediction for Hypothesis 3 is illustrated in **Figure 8.**

Figure 8 *This controlled experiment was designed to find out whether UV light caused the frog deformities.*

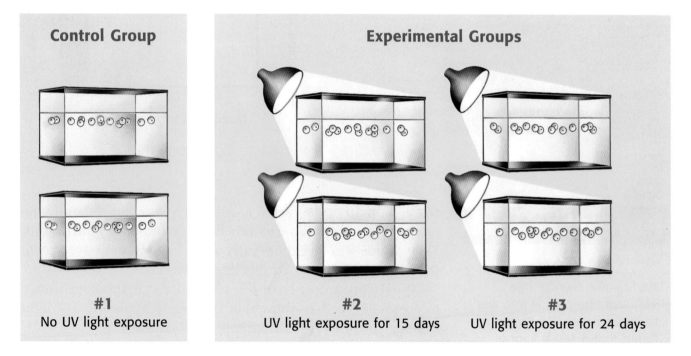

Control Group

Experimental Groups

#1
No UV light exposure

#2
UV light exposure for 15 days

#3
UV light exposure for 24 days

✔Self-Check

Henry is testing the effects of different antibacterial soaps on the growth of bacteria. His experiment contains several jars of the same strain of bacteria. Which of the jars described below is the control group?

1. To Jar A, Henry adds two drops of Supersoap.
2. To Jar B, Henry adds two drops of Anti-B Suds.
3. To Jar C, Henry adds no soap.

(See page 636 to check your answer.)

Analyze the Results A scientist's work does not end when an experiment is finished. Scientists must organize the data from the experiment so that the data can be analyzed. Scientists can organize data in several ways. They may put the data into a table, a graph, or a chart. The data collected from the UV-light experiment are shown below in **Figure 9.**

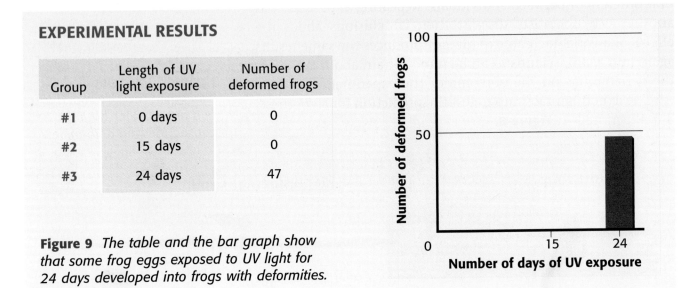

EXPERIMENTAL RESULTS

Group	Length of UV light exposure	Number of deformed frogs
#1	0 days	0
#2	15 days	0
#3	24 days	47

Figure 9 *The table and the bar graph show that some frog eggs exposed to UV light for 24 days developed into frogs with deformities.*

MATH BREAK

Averages

Finding the average of a group of numbers is one way to analyze data. Dr. Brown found that 3 seeds kept at 25°C sprouted in 8, 8, and 5 days. To find the average number of days that it took the seeds to sprout, she added 8, 8, and 5 and divided their sum by 3, the number of subjects (seeds) in the group.

$$\frac{(8 + 8 + 5)}{3} = \frac{21}{3} = 7 \text{ days}$$

Dr. Brown also found that 3 seeds kept at 30°C sprouted in 6, 5, and 4 days. What's the average number of days that it took these seeds to sprout?

Draw Conclusions After scientists have organized and analyzed the data from an experiment, they can draw conclusions. They decide whether the results of the experiment have shown that a prediction was correct or incorrect.

What conclusion have *you* reached about the data shown in **Figure 9?** Do they show that frog eggs exposed to UV light develop into deformed frogs?

The scientists who conducted the experiment concluded that Hypothesis 3 is supported by the tests. UV light exposure in the laboratory did cause deformities. The data also showed something else. The number of days that eggs were exposed to UV light was an important factor in the development of deformities.

When scientists find that a hypothesis is not supported by the tests, they must try to find another explanation for what they have observed. Proving that a hypothesis is wrong is just as helpful as supporting it. Why? Either way, the scientist has learned something, and that is the purpose of using the scientific method to investigate or answer a question.

The UV light experiment supports the hypothesis that the frog deformities were caused by exposure to UV light. Does this mean that UV light definitely caused the frogs living in the Minnesota wetland to be deformed? No, it does not. What does this experiment show about the two other hypotheses? Does it prove that the deformities were not caused by parasites or some substance in the pond water? No, it does not. The only thing this experiment shows is that UV light may be a cause of the deformities.

The other hypotheses about the frog deformities remain, and many scientists think that two or more factors could be interacting. Some scientists even speculate that different types of frog deformities may have different causes.

Puzzles as complex as the deformed-frog mystery are rarely solved with a single experiment. The quest for a solution may continue for years or even decades. As you can see, finding an answer doesn't always end an investigation. Often that answer begins another investigation.

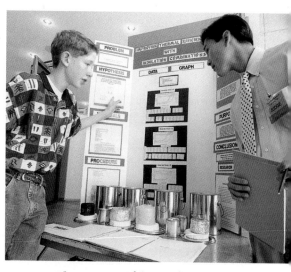

Figure 10 *This student scientist is communicating the results of his investigation at a science fair.*

Communicate Results In today's world, scientists form a global community. After scientists complete their investigations, they make a report and communicate their results to other scientists, as the student in **Figure 10** is doing. Some other scientists may repeat the experiments to see if they get the same results. The information in the report can also help scientists discover new questions and answers. New answers may strengthen scientific theories or show that the theories need to be altered. The paths from observations and questions to communicating results are shown in **Figure 11.**

Figure 11 *Scientific investigations do not always proceed from one step to the next. Sometimes steps can be skipped, and sometimes they must be repeated.*

Scientific Knowledge Changes

As you read earlier, there can be more than one prediction for a hypothesis. Each time a prediction is proven true, the hypothesis gains more support. A unifying explanation for a broad range of hypotheses and observations that have been supported by testing is a **theory.**

However, when scientists reexamine data or experimental results, they may arrive at different conclusions. Other times, new observations show that the old conclusions are wrong. Or, new observations just show that more research is needed.

The development of new technologies also leads to answers. **Technology** is the use of knowledge, tools, and materials to solve problems and accomplish tasks. By using new technology, scientists can get information that wasn't available before the technology was developed. For example, scientists have long wondered whether or not Neanderthals are the ancestors of humans. Neither Neanderthal fossils, which show what they looked like, nor dating techniques, which reveal when they lived, provided enough data to answer the question. The technology for comparing genetic information was developed recently. The scientist shown in **Figure 12** is using this technology to look for evidence of whether Neanderthals are our ancestors.

Life scientists are always asking new questions or looking at old questions from a different angle. As they find new answers, scientific knowledge continues to grow and change.

Figure 12 *Dr. Mark Stoneking is using modern techniques to find out if Neanderthals are our ancestors.*

Temperature (°C)	Time to double (minutes)
10	130
20	60
25	40
30	29
37	17
40	19
45	32
50	no growth

REVIEW

1. What are the six basic steps of the scientific method?

2. What causes scientific knowledge to change and grow?

3. **Applying Concepts** Design an experiment to test the following hypothesis: "Temperature affects how often crickets chirp." Begin by making a prediction using the "If..., then..." format.

4. **Graphing Data** The table at left gives information on the growth of a kind of bacteria that lives in your intestines. The table shows how long it takes for one bacterium to divide and become two bacteria. Plot this information on a graph, with temperature as the *x*-axis and the time to double as the *y*-axis. What temperature allows the bacteria to multiply in the least amount of time?

Tools of Life Scientists

Life scientists use various tools to aid them in their work. These tools are used to make observations and to gather, store, and analyze information.

Tools for Seeing

If you look at a jar of pond water, you may see some scum and a few creatures swimming around. But examine that same water under a microscope or with a hand lens, and presto!— a complex community of organisms suddenly appears.

In order to make accurate observations of organisms and parts of organisms that are too small to be seen with the naked eye, life scientists use tools that can magnify. People have used glass as a magnifier for almost 3,000 years. The magnifying tools available to a life scientist today include hand lenses and microscopes.

Compound Light Microscope One type of microscope that is commonly used today is the compound microscope, shown in **Figure 13**. The **compound light microscope** is made up of three main parts—a tube with lenses, a stage, and a light. Specimens viewed through a compound microscope are sometimes stained with special dyes, which enable the specimens to be seen more clearly.

Specimens are placed on the stage so that the light passes through them. The lenses, which are at each end of the tube, magnify the image of the specimen, making it appear larger than it actually is.

NEW TERMS

compound light microscope
electron microscope
meter
area
volume
mass
temperature

OBJECTIVES

- Describe the tools life scientists use for seeing.
- Explain how life scientists use computers.
- Explain the importance of the International System of Units.

MATH BREAK

Magnification

If you use a microscope to observe an object that is 0.2 mm long under 100× magnification, how large will the object appear to be?

Ocular lens

Objective lens

Stage

Light

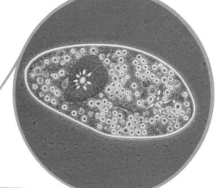

Figure 13 *A compound light microscope can produce an image of a specimen that is 1,000 times (1,000×) larger than the actual specimen. The paramecium has been magnified 200×.*

A hidden world all around you? See what it means on page 563 of your LabBook.

Electron Microscope **Electron microscopes** use tiny particles of matter called electrons to produce magnified images. The process that prepares specimens for viewing kills living specimens. Because of this, living specimens cannot be examined with an electron microscope. There are two kinds of electron microscopes used in life science: the transmission electron microscope and the scanning electron microscope.

Transmission electron microscopes can magnify specimens up to 200,000 times (200,000×) their actual size. The scanning electron microscope can produce images that are up to 100,000 times their actual size. The images electron microscopes produce are clearer and more detailed than those made by compound microscopes. Each kind of electron microscope is shown in **Figure 14** with a description of its specialized purpose and an example of the image that it can produce.

Figure 14 *The transmission electron microscope produces a greatly magnified image. The scanning electron microscope provides a clear view of surface features.*

Transmission Electron Microscope

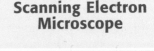

- Electrons pass through the specimen.
- A flat image is produced.

Paramecium (15,000×)

Scanning Electron Microscope

- Electrons bounce off the surface of the specimen.
- A three-dimensional (3-D) image is produced.

Paramecium (1500×)

Quick **Lab**

See for Yourself

Take a look at one of your fingernails. In your ScienceLog, draw and describe what you see. After you have done that, look at your nail with a hand lens. How does looking through a hand lens affect what you can see? Draw and describe how your nail looks when it is magnified.

Seeing Internal Structures Life scientists also use several tools to help them see internal structures of organisms. These tools help them to see inside organisms and to understand the chemical composition of materials.

For almost a century, X rays have provided pictures of internal body structures such as the bones, heart, and lungs. If you have ever broken a bone, you have had an X ray, such as the one shown in **Figure 15.** X rays have also been used to help life scientists learn about the structures of proteins, which are substances important to the life processes of every organism.

CT scans and MRI provide clearer and more detailed images of internal tissues than do X rays. In a CT (computed tomography) scan, such as the one shown in **Figure 16,** low-dosage X-ray beams are passed through the body at different angles. Often a dye is injected to help highlight the tissues. MRI (magnetic resonance imaging) uses short bursts of a magnetic field and produces images like the one shown in **Figure 17.** With CT scans and MRI, data are transferred to a computer that creates an image that an expert can interpret. Both of these techniques are especially useful for studying the brain and spinal tissue.

Computers

Since the first electronic computer was built in 1946, improvements in technology have made computers more powerful and easier to use. The amount of information that a computer can collect, store, organize, and analyze is enormous. Modern computers can complete billions of calculations in the same amount of time that it took early computers to do thousands. With the help of computers, life scientists are able to solve problems that they were not able to solve in the past.

Computers can be used to create graphs and solve complex mathematical problems. Life scientists also use computers to help them decide whether differences in experimental data are important. In addition, computers make it easy for scientists to share data and ideas with each other and to prepare reports and articles about their research.

Figure 15 *This X ray shows a broken forearm.*

Figure 16 *The internal tissues of the brain are shown in this computed tomography (CT) scan.*

Figure 17 *This image, showing blood circulation through the lungs, was produced with magnetic resonance imaging (MRI).*

Systems of Measurement

The ability to make accurate and reliable measurements is an important tool in science. Hundreds of years ago, different countries used different systems of measurement. These different systems used different standards to compare the properties of things. For example, at one time in England, the standard for 1 inch was three grains of barley arranged end to end. Even the units of the modern English system used today in the United States were once based on parts of the body, as shown in **Figure 18.** Such systems were not very reliable because they were based on objects that varied in size.

In the late 1700s, the French Academy of Sciences began to develop a global measurement system now known as the International System of Units, or SI. Today all scientists and almost all countries use this system. Using SI measurements helps scientists to share and compare their observations and results.

The table below contains the commonly used SI units for length, volume, mass, and temperature. Prefixes are used with these units to change them to larger or smaller units. For example, *kilo* means 1,000 times and *milli* indicates 1/1,000 times. The prefix used depends on the size of the object being measured. All units are based on the number 10, which makes conversions from one unit to another easy to do.

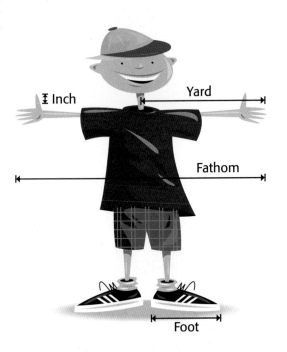

Figure 18 *The modern English system is widely used in the United States. The units, which are now standardized, were once based on parts of the human body.*

Common SI Units		
Length	**meter (m)**	
	kilometer (km)	1 km = 1,000 m
	decimeter (dm)	1 dm = 0.1 m
	centimeter (cm)	1 cm = 0.01 m
	millimeter (mm)	1 mm = 0.001 m
	micrometer (μm)	1 μm = 0.000001 m
	nanometer (nm)	1 nm = 0.000000001 m
Volume	**cubic meter (m^3)**	
	cubic centimeter (cm^3)	1 cm^3 = 0.000001 m^3
	liter (L)	1 L = 1 dm^3 = 0.001 m^3
	milliliter (mL)	1 mL = 0.001 L = 1 cm^3
Mass	**kilogram (kg)**	
	gram (g)	1 g = 0.001 kg
	milligram (mg)	1 mg = 0.000001 kg
Temperature	**Kelvin (K)**	
	Celsius (°C)	0°C = 273 K
		100°C = 373 K

The Long and the Short of It How long is a lizard? To describe a small lizard's length, a life scientist would probably use centimeters (cm). The basic unit of length in SI is the **meter** (m). SI prefixes are added to the basic unit to express very large or very small numbers. For example, 1 kilometer (km) equals 1,000 meters (m). One meter equals 100 centimeters, or 1,000 millimeters. So, if you divide 1 m into 1,000 parts, each part equals 1 mm. This means that 1 mm is one-thousandth of a meter. Although that seems pretty small, some organisms and structures are so tiny that even smaller units must be used. To describe the length of microscopic objects, micrometers (μm) or nanometers (nm) are used. In **Figure 20,** the scale compares the sizes of different organisms.

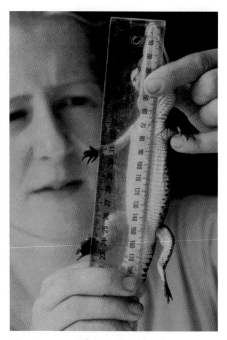

Figure 19 *This scientist is measuring a lizard's length using a metric ruler.*

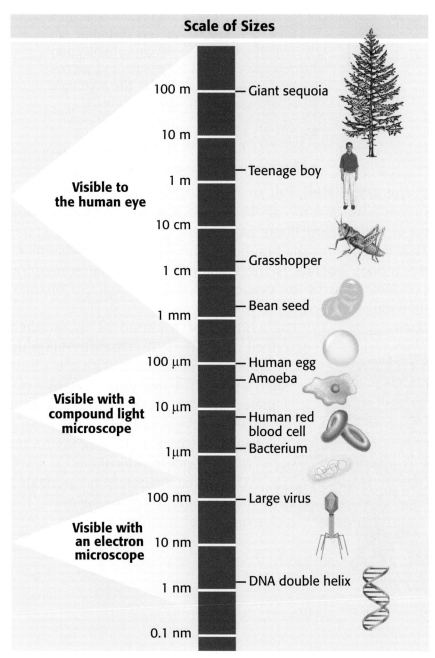

Scale of Sizes

100 m	Giant sequoia
10 m	
1 m	Teenage boy
10 cm	
1 cm	Grasshopper
1 mm	Bean seed
100 μm	Human egg
	Amoeba
10 μm	Human red blood cell
1 μm	Bacterium
100 nm	Large virus
10 nm	
1 nm	DNA double helix
0.1 nm	

Visible to the human eye

Visible with a compound light microscope

Visible with an electron microscope

Explore

Measure the width of your desk, but do not use a ruler or a tape measure. Pick an object to use as your unit of measurement. It could be a pencil, your hand, or anything else. Find how many units wide your desk is, and compare your measurement with those of your classmates. In your ScienceLog, explain why it is important to use standard units of measurement.

Figure 20 *This scale compares organisms that can be seen with the naked eye with organisms and structures that are microscopic.*

The World of Life Science   **23**

MATH BREAK

Finding Area

You can use the equation at right to find the area of any rectangular surface.

1. What is the area of a square with sides measuring 5 m?
2. What is the area of the top of your desk?
3. A rectangle has an area of 36 cm² and a length of 9 cm. What does its width measure?

Area How much carpet would it take to cover the floor of your classroom? Answering this question involves finding the area of the floor. **Area** is a measure of how much surface an object has.

Some quantities, such as area, can't be expressed with one measurement. That is, they are formed from combinations of two or more measurements. To calculate area, first measure the length and width, and then use the following equation:

$$\text{Area} = \text{length} \times \text{width}$$

The units for area are called square units, such as m², cm², and km². **Figure 21** will help you understand square units.

Figure 21 *The area of this rectangle is 20 cm². If you count the smaller squares within the rectangle, you'll count 20 squares that each measure 1 cm².*

Is the Glass Half Full or Half Empty? Suppose that some hippos born in a zoo are being relocated to their native habitat in Africa. How many hippos will fit into a moving crate? That depends on the volume of the crate and the volume of the hippos. **Volume** is the amount of space that something occupies, or as in the case of the crate, the amount of space that something contains.

The volume of a liquid is most often described using liters (L). One liter takes up the same amount of space as a cube whose sides are each 1 dm long. Just like the meter, the liter can be divided into smaller units. A milliliter (mL) is one-thousandth of a liter. A microliter (µL) is one-millionth of a liter. Graduated cylinders or graduated beakers are used to measure the volume of liquids.

The volume of a solid object, such as a crate, is described using cubic meters (m³). Smaller objects can be measured in cubic centimeters (cm³) or cubic millimeters (mm³). One cm³ is equal to one mL. To calculate the volume of a cube (or any other rectangular shape), multiply the length by the width by the height. In **Figure 22,** you can find the volume of the aquarium for yourself.

An object like a hippo or a rock has an irregular shape. If you multiplied its length, width, and height, you would not get a very accurate measure of its volume. One way to figure out the volume of an irregularly shaped object is to measure how much fluid the object displaces.

The girl in **Figure 23** is measuring the volume of a rock by placing it in a graduated cylinder that contains a known quantity of water. The rock displaces some water, which causes the level of the water to rise. The girl can figure out the volume of the rock by subtracting the volume of the water alone from the volume of the water and the rock. Then the volume of water in milliliters displaced by the rock must be converted to cm³.

Figure 22 *The volume of this aquarium is found by multiplying its length, width, and height. What is its volume?*

Figure 23 *This graduated cylinder contains 70 mL of water. After the rock was added, the water level moved to 80 mL. Because the rock displaced 10 mL of water, and because 1 mL = 1 cm³, the volume of the rock is 10 cm³.*

A Massive Undertaking **Mass** is the amount of matter that makes up an object. The kilogram (kg) is the basic unit for mass. The mass of a very large object, such as a hippo, is described using kilograms (kg) or metric tons. A kilogram equals 1,000 g; therefore, a gram is one-thousandth of a kilogram. A metric ton equals 1,000 kg. Grams are used to describe the mass of small objects. A medium-sized apple has a mass of about 100 g. As shown in **Figure 24,** mass can be measured with a balance.

Figure 24 *The mass of the apple equals the mass of the weights.*

Is It Hot Enough for You? How hot does it need to be to kill bacteria? To answer this question, a life scientist would measure the temperature at which bacteria die. **Temperature** is a measure of how hot or cold something is. You may not realize it, but the molecules that make up all matter are constantly moving. When energy is transferred to these molecules, they move even more, which causes the temperature to increase. Temperature, then, can also be defined as a measure of the average energy of the molecules of a substance.

You are probably used to describing temperature using degrees Fahrenheit (°F). Scientists commonly use degrees Celsius (°C), although Kelvins are the official SI units for temperature. You will use °C in this book. The thermometer in **Figure 25** shows the relationship between °F and °C.

°F	°C
212°F Water boils	100°C Water boils
98.6°F Normal body temperature	37°C Normal body temperature
32°F Water freezes	0°C Water freezes

Figure 25 *Water freezes at 0°C and boils at 100°C. Your normal body temperature is 37°C, which is equal to 98.6°F.*

Safety Rules!

Life science is exciting and fun, but it can also be dangerous. So don't take any chances! Always follow your teacher's instructions, and don't take shortcuts—even when you think there is little or no danger.

Before starting an experiment, get your teacher's permission and read the lab procedures carefully. Pay particular attention to safety information and caution statements. The diagram below shows the safety symbols used in this book. Get to know these symbols and what they mean. Do this by reading the safety information starting on page 556. **This is important!** If you are still unsure about what a safety symbol means, ask your teacher.

Stay on the safe side by reading the safety information on page 556.

This is a must before doing an experiment!

SAFETY SYMBOLS

Eye Protection

Clothing Protection

Hand Safety

Heating Safety

Electric Safety

Sharp Object

Chemical Safety

Animal Safety

Plant Safety

REVIEW

1. How is temperature related to energy?

2. If you were going to measure the mass of a fly, which metric unit would be most appropriate?

3. What are two benefits of using the International System of Units?

4. **Understanding Technology** What tool was used to produce the image at right? How can you tell?

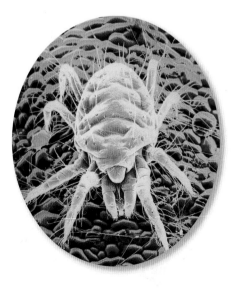

Chapter Highlights

Vocabulary

life science *(p. 6)*

Section Notes

• Life science is the study of living things. Observations of organisms often lead to questions. Questions fuel the study of life science.

• Anyone can become a life scientist. Life scientists work in many different places and investigate a wide variety of questions and problems.

• Life scientists help prevent and treat diseases and help solve environmental problems.

Vocabulary

scientific method *(p. 10)*

hypothesis *(p. 12)*

factor *(p. 14)*

controlled experiment *(p. 14)*

variable *(p. 14)*

theory *(p. 18)*

technology *(p. 18)*

Section Notes

• The scientific method is a series of steps that scientists use to answer a question or solve a problem.

• The parts of the scientific method are not always done in the same order. Steps are sometimes skipped or repeated.

• Scientists perform controlled experiments to test the effects of one factor at a time.

• Life scientists must make careful observations, record data accurately, and be creative in finding answers and designing experiments.

• A hypothesis, which is a possible explanation for what has been observed, must be testable.

☑ Skills Check

Math Concepts

UNIT CONVERSIONS Imagine that you are writing a paper on the Empire State Building, in New York City. One source in the library lists the height of the building as 381,000,000 micrometers tall. This is a very large number, so you'll probably want to convert it to a more manageable number by using meters instead of micrometers. As you can see in the table on page 22, 1 µm = 0.000001 m. To convert micrometers to meters, you multiply by 0.000001.

$$381{,}000{,}000 \times 0.000001 = 381 \text{ m}$$

Visual Understanding

HOW BIG? To review the sizes of things in relation to what can be seen with different types of microscopes, turn to pages 19 and 20. The Scale of Sizes, on page 23, will also help you to visualize sizes decribed using the metric system.

SAFETY FIRST! Make sure that you know and understand the different safety symbols shown on page 27.

SECTION 2

- A theory is a unifying explanation for a broad range of hypotheses and observations that have been supported by testing.

- Scientific knowledge is constantly changing and growing as scientists ask new questions, find different answers to the same questions, and use technologies that allow them to gather information in new ways.

Labs

Does It All Add Up? *(p. 560)*

Graphing Data *(p. 562)*

SECTION 3

Vocabulary

compound light microscope *(p. 19)*

electron microscope *(p. 20)*

meter *(p. 23)*

area *(p. 24)*

volume *(p. 24)*

mass *(p. 26)*

temperature *(p. 26)*

Section Notes

- Life scientists commonly use compound light microscopes and electron microscopes to make observations of organisms or parts of organisms that are too small to be seen with the naked eye.

- X rays, CT scans, and MRI are used by life scientists to view internal structures of organisms.

- Life scientists use computers to collect, store, organize, analyze, and share data.

- The International System of Units (SI), which is a simple and reliable system of measurement, is used by all scientists.

Labs

A Window to a Hidden World *(p. 563)*

---

 internetconnect

go.hrw.com **GO TO:** go.hrw.com

Visit the **HRW** Web site for a variety of learning tools related to this chapter. Just type in the keyword:

KEYWORD: HSTLIV

SCILINKS **GO TO:** www.scilinks.org

Visit the **National Science Teachers Association** on-line Web site for Internet resources related to this chapter. Just type in the *sci*LINKS number for more information about the topic:

TOPIC: Deformed Frogs	*sci*LINKS NUMBER: HSTL005
TOPIC: Careers in Life Science	*sci*LINKS NUMBER: HSTL010
TOPIC: Tools of Life Science	*sci*LINKS NUMBER: HSTL015
TOPIC: SI Units	*sci*LINKS NUMBER: HSTL020

Chapter Review

To complete the following sentences, choose the correct term from each pair of terms listed below:

1. The set of skills or steps that scientists use to answer questions is the ___?___. (*controlled experiment* or *scientific method*)

2. After recognizing a problem or asking a question, life scientists form one or more ___?___, which are possible explanations for what has been observed. (*predictions* or *hypotheses*)

3. In a controlled experiment, the ___?___ is the one factor that differs between the ___?___ and the experimental group. (*prediction, variable group* or *variable, control group*)

4. ___?___ is a measure of how much surface an object has. (*area* or *volume*)

5. Life scientists use ___?___ to describe the measurement of an object's mass. (*meters* or *grams*)

UNDERSTANDING CONCEPTS

Multiple Choice

6. Which of the following would *not* be an area of study in life science?
   a. studying how lions and hyenas interact
   b. measuring the rate at which bacteria divide
   c. comparing the reproduction of arctic plants with that of desert plants
   d. studying how volcanoes are formed

7. The steps of the scientific method
   a. must all be used in every scientific investigation.
   b. must always be used in the same order.
   c. are not always used in order.
   d. start with the development of a theory.

8. In a controlled experiment,
   a. a control group is compared with one or more experimental groups.
   b. there are at least two variables.
   c. all factors should be different.
   d. a variable is not needed.

9. When a scientist finds that a hypothesis is wrong, the scientist usually
   a. tries to find another explanation for what has been observed.
   b. stops studying science.
   c. feels that nothing valuable was learned.
   d. adds an additional variable to his or her experiment.

10. What tool would a life scientist use to get a three-dimensional image of a microscopic organism?
    a. CT scan
    b. X ray
    c. scanning electron microscope
    d. a hand lens

11. The International System of Units
    a. is based on standardized body measurements.
    b. contains units that are based on the number 10.
    c. is useful only for measuring lengths.
    d. is a device used to measure volume.

Short Answer

12. Why do hypotheses need to be testable?

13. What is a prediction?

14. Which SI units can be used to describe the measurement of volume? Which SI units can be used to describe the mass of an object?

Concept Mapping

15. Use the following terms to create a concept map: observations, predictions, questions, controlled experiments, variable, hypothesis.

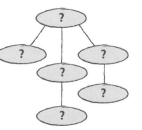

CRITICAL THINKING AND PROBLEM SOLVING

Write one or two sentences to answer the following questions:

16. In a controlled experiment, why should there be several individuals in the control group and several in each of the experimental groups?

17. A scientist who studies mice observes that on the day he feeds the mice vitamins with their meals they perform better in mazes. What hypothesis would you form to explain this phenomenon?

18. The volume of an egg and water in a graduated beaker is 200 mL. After the egg is removed, the volume of the water is found to be 125 mL. What is the volume of the egg in cm^3?

200 mL   125 mL

MATH IN SCIENCE

19. If you magnified a 5 μm long organism 1,000 ×, how long would that organism appear in millimeters (mm)?

Examine the illustration below of an experiment set up to test the following prediction: **If** bees are more attracted to yellow flowers than to red flowers, **then** bees will visit yellow flowers more often than they will visit red flowers.

11 visits   3 visits   11 visits

2 visits   9 visits   4 visits

20. How many total visits did the yellow flowers receive? How many total visits did the red flowers receive?

21. What is the average number of visits for yellow flowers? What is the average number of visits for red flowers?

22. In what ways might the experimental setup be an unreliable test of the prediction?

NOW What Do You Think?

Take a minute to review your answers to the ScienceLog questions on page 5. Have your answers changed? If necessary, revise your answers based on what you have learned since you began this chapter.

CAREERS

ZOOLOGIST

Eric Pianka became interested in lizards when he was 6 years old. "On a trip across the country with my family, I saw a big green lizard at a roadside park," Pianka explains. I tried to catch it, but all I got was the tail. At that moment, I knew I had to find out everything I could about the kind of life it led." Pianka is now a world-famous professor of zoology at the University of Texas, in Austin, Texas.

*O*ne of the things Eric Pianka likes best about his job is being in the wilderness and seeing things that few people have ever seen. "I've been almost everywhere! I've spent a lot of time studying deserts in the western United States. I've been to deserts in southern Africa, India, and Chile. My most current (and oldest) interest is in the deserts of Australia. I haven't had a chance to study the Brazilian Amazon yet, but that's my goal for the future!"

The Ecology of Desert Lizards

In his research as a zoologist, Pianka has focused on the ecology of desert lizards. He goes to a desert, collects lizards, and examines and classifies them. Then he compiles data and interprets it in books or papers. As Pianka puts it, "I try to answer questions like, Why are there more lizards in one place than in another? How do they react with each other and other species? How have they adapted to their environment?"

Recently, Pianka conducted a study to learn about the effects of wildfires on the ecology and diversity of lizard species. He hopes this work will show how lizard species adapted to the large-scale wildfires that at one time occurred regularly in desert areas but which today are usually controlled by humans.

Learning from Wildlife

Pianka believes that doing research on lizards and other animals may help us protect our environment. "Everyone always asks, 'Why lizards?' I turn the question around and say, 'Why you?' The general attitude is that everything on Earth has to somehow serve humans. By looking at how other species have lived and died and changed over millions of years, we can gain a better understanding of the world we live in."

▶ *The collared lizard lives in rocky regions of the southwestern United States.*

Be a Zoologist for a Day

▶ Select a common animal that lives in your area and that can be easily observed. Spend a couple of hours watching what it eats, what it does, and where it goes. Carefully document everything you observe. Did you discover anything you did not already know? Present your findings to the class.

Science Fiction

"The Homesick Chicken"

by Edward D. Hoch

OK, OK, why *did* the chicken cross the road? Oh sure, you know the answer to this old riddle, don't you? Or maybe you think you do! But "The Homesick Chicken," by Edward D. Hoch, may surprise you. That old chicken may not be exactly what it seems...

You see, one of the chickens at Tangaway Research Farms has escaped—not just flown the coop, mind you, but really escaped. It pecked a hole in a super-strength security fence and then crossed an eight-lane highway to get away. But after all that effort, it just stopped! It was found in a vacant lot across the highway from Tangaway, pecking away contentedly.

Barnabus Rex, a specialist in solving scientific riddles, is called in to work on the mystery. He is intrigued by this escaping chicken. Why would it go to all the trouble to peck through the tough security fence, risk being flattened on the superhighway, and then just stop when it got to the other side?

There are a few clues in the story. As you read it, maybe you can see what Mr. Rex sees. If you know anything about chickens, you might be able to solve the mystery. Escape to the *Holt Anthology of Science Fiction* and read "The Homesick Chicken."

2 It's Alive!! Or, Is It?

Imagine . . .

The Movile Cave, in Romania, is one of the spookiest, slimiest, and smelliest places on Earth. For more than 5 million years, the cave and its inhabitants were sealed off from the outside world. Many of the creepiest organisms known to science inhabit the Movile Cave. Poisonous water scorpions lurk in murky pools and breathe through snorkels attached to their stomach. With huge antennae, predatory centipedes zero in on smaller bugs and inject them with a paralyzing toxin. Ferocious wolf spiders move like lightning on long, spindly legs in pursuit of millipedes, pill bugs, and even their own young!

All living things use energy as they go about their activities. Almost all living things get their energy either directly or indirectly from the sun. But what about the inhabitants of the Movile Cave, a place where sunlight never enters? The supply of energy that fuels life in the Movile Cave comes from organisms that can't be seen. These microorganisms don't feed on other creepy crawlies; they feed on hydrogen sulfide. This chemical is abundant in the cave and fills the air with an overwhelming stench of rotten eggs. The energy that the microorganisms obtain from

hydrogen sulfide fuels their life processes. When the microorganisms are eaten, their energy is transferred to other organisms.

Using energy is just one of the characteristics of life. Read on to find out what all living things have in common.

What Do You Think?

In your ScienceLog, try to answer the following questions based on what you already know:

1. What characteristics do all living things have in common?

2. What do organisms need in order to stay alive?

Investigate!

Lights On!

Responding to change is a characteristic of living things. In this activity, you will work with a partner to see how eyes react to changes in light.

Procedure

1. Observe a classmate's eyes in a room with normal light. Find the pupil, which is the black area in the center of the colored part of the eye. Light enters the eye through the pupil. Notice the size of your classmate's pupils.

Pupil

2. Have your partner keep both eyes open and completely cover each one with a cupped hand so that no light can reach them. Wait about 1 minute.

3. Instruct your partner to quickly pull away both hands. Immediately look at the pupils. In your ScienceLog, record what happens to the pupils.

4. Now briefly shine a **flashlight** into your partner's eyes. In your ScienceLog, record the effect this has on the pupils. **Caution:** Do not use the sun as the source of the light.

5. Change places with your partner, and repeat the entire procedure so that he or she can observe how your eyes respond to changes in light.

Analysis

6. How did your partner's eyes respond to changes in the level of light?

7. How did changes in the size of your pupils affect your vision? What does this tell you about why pupils change size?

Characteristics of Living Things

NEW TERMS

cell
stimulus
homeostasis
asexual
  reproduction

sexual
  reproduction
DNA
heredity
metabolism

OBJECTIVES

■ List the characteristics of living things.

■ Distinguish between asexual reproduction and sexual reproduction.

■ Define and describe homeostasis.

While out in your yard one day, you notice something strange in the grass. It's slimy, bright yellow, and about the size of a dime. You have no idea what it is. Is it a plant part that fell from a tree? Is it alive? How can you tell?

Even though an amazing variety of living things exist on Earth, they are all alike in several ways. What does a dog have in common with a tree? What does a fish have in common with a mushroom? And what do *you* have in common with a slimy blob (also known as a slime mold)? Read on to find out about the six characteristics that all organisms share.

Slime mold

1 All Living Things Have Cells

Every living thing is composed of one or more cells. A **cell** is a membrane-covered structure that contains all of the materials necessary for life. The membrane that surrounds a cell separates the contents of the cell from the cell's environment.

Many organisms, such as those in **Figure 1,** are made up of only one cell. Other organisms, such as the monkeys and trees in **Figure 2,** are made up of trillions of cells. Most cells are too small to be seen with the naked eye.

All cells perform the basic functions of life. In an organism with many cells, cells may also perform specialized functions. For example, your nerve cells are specialized to transport signals, and your muscle cells are specialized for movement.

Figure 1 *Each of these organisms is made of only one cell.*

Figure 2 *Trillions of cells make up these organisms.*

2 All Living Things Sense and Respond to Change

All organisms have the ability to sense change in their environment and to respond to that change. When your pupils are exposed to light, they respond by becoming smaller. A change in an organism's environment that affects the activity of the organism is called a **stimulus** (plural *stimuli*).

Stimuli can be things such as chemicals, gravity, darkness, light, sounds, or tastes. Stimuli cause organisms to respond in some way. A gentle touch causes a response in the plant shown in **Figure 3.**

✓ Self-Check

Is your alarm clock a stimulus? Explain. *(See page 636 to check your answer.)*

Figure 3 The touch of an insect ... Venus' flytrap to ... leaves.

Homeostasi... ment may char... nal environment ... of organisms invol... tions that can occur ... The maintenance of a ... rna... **homeostasis** (HOH mee oh ... r sis).

Your body maintains a temperatu... you get hot, your body responds by ... cold, your muscles twitch in an attem... causes you to shiver. Whether you ar... your body is trying to return things ...

Another example of homeostasis ... stable amount of sugar in your blood. ... level in your blood rises. Your body responds by releasing a special compound that removes the sugar from your blood and stores it in your muscle cells and liver cells. When you have not eaten for a long time, your blood-sugar level begins to drop. Your body responds to this by releasing a different compound, which causes your muscles and liver to release sugar into your blood.

...eanography
NNECTION

...in the ice-cold ...tarctica make a ...eeze that keeps ...eezing.

3 All Living Things Reproduce

All organisms make other organisms like themselves. This is accomplished in one of two ways: by asexual reproduction or by sexual reproduction. In **asexual reproduction,** a single parent produces offspring that are identical to the parent. **Figure 4** shows an organism that reproduces asexually. Most single-celled organisms reproduce in this way. **Sexual reproduction,** however, almost always requires two parents to produce offspring that will share characteristics of both parents. Most animals and plants reproduce in this way. The bear cubs in **Figure 5** were produced sexually by their parents.

Figure 4 *The hydra is an animal that can reproduce asexually by forming buds that will break off and grow into new individuals. Can you find the buds on this hydra?*

Figure 5 *Like most animals, bears produce offspring by sexual reproduction.*

Figure 6 *Children resemble their parents because of heredity.*

4 All Living Things Have DNA

The cells of all living things contain a special molecule called **DNA** (**d**eoxyribo**n**ucleic **a**cid). DNA provides instructions for making molecules called *proteins*. Proteins take part in almost all of the activities of an organism's cells. Proteins also determine many of an organism's characteristics.

When organisms reproduce, they pass on copies of their DNA to their offspring. The transmission of characteristics from one generation to the next is called **heredity.** Offspring, such as the children in **Figure 6,** resemble their parents because of heredity.

5 All Living Things Use Energy

All organisms use energy to carry out the chemical activities of life. These chemical activities include such things as making food, breaking down food, moving materials into and out of cells, and building cells. An organism's **metabolism** is the total of all the chemical activities that it performs.

APPLY

been programmed to learn, that is, to get better and faster at solving problems over time. Do you think ... d become
as ... hey shoul
doi... alive? Why
So...

MATH BREAK

Body Proportions

As you have grown, your body's proportions have changed. When you were ... length of your head

(handwritten "Do →")

6 ... l **Dev**...

All li... ne cell o...
cells, ... n in singl...
orga... anisms r...
man...

I... ay also ...
and... rganisms...
Figu... ges in y...
life as you develop into an adult.

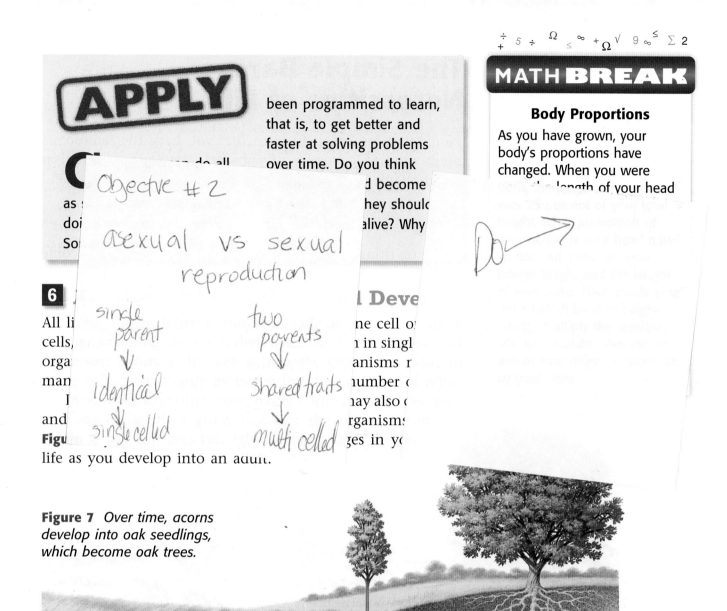

Figure 7 *Over time, acorns develop into oak seedlings, which become oak trees.*

REVIEW

1. What characteristics of living things does a river have? Is a river alive?

2. What does the fur coat of a bear have to do with homeostasis?

3. How is reproduction related to heredity?

4. **Applying Concepts** What are some stimuli in your environment? How do you respond to these stimuli?

Explore

Imagine that you have the ability to create a new organism. What would your organism be like? How would it display each of the characteristics of living things?

The Simple Bare Necessities of Life

OBJECTIVES

- Explain why organisms need food, water, air, and living space.
- Discuss how living things obtain what they need to live.

Would it surprise you to learn that you have the same basic needs as a tree, a frog, or a fly? In fact, almost every organism has the same basic needs: food, water, air, and living space.

Food

All living things must have food. This probably doesn't come as a surprise. Food provides organisms with the energy and raw materials needed to carry on life processes and to build and repair cells and body parts. But not all organisms get food in the same way. In fact, organisms can be grouped into three different categories based on how they get their food.

Some organisms, such as plants, are called **producers** because they can produce their own food. The plants in **Figure 8** are an example of producers. Like most producers, they use energy from the sun to make food from water and carbon dioxide. Some producers, like the microorganisms in Movile Cave, obtain energy and food from the chemicals in their environment.

Other organisms are called **consumers** because they must eat (consume) other organisms to get the food they need. The salamander in **Figure 8** is an example of a consumer. It gets the energy it needs by eating insects and other organisms.

Some consumers are decomposers. **Decomposers** are organisms that get their food by breaking down the nutrients in dead organisms or animal wastes. The fungus in **Figure 8** is absorbing nutrients from the dead plant material in the soil.

Figure 8 *The salamander and the fungus it is crawling on are consumers. The plants are producers.*

Water

You may have heard that your body is made up mostly of water. In fact, your cells and the cells of almost all living organisms are made up of approximately 70 percent water—even the cells of a cactus, a camel, and a dragonfly. The metabolism of organisms is dependent on water because most of the chemical reactions that take place in organisms involve water.

Organisms differ greatly in terms of how much water they need and how they obtain it. You could survive for only about 3 days without water. You obtain water from the fluids you drink and also from the food you eat. The desert-dwelling kangaroo rat never drinks. It gets all of its water from its food.

2 All Living Things Sense and Respond to Change

All organisms have the ability to sense change in their environment and to respond to that change. When your pupils are exposed to light, they respond by becoming smaller. A change in an organism's environment that affects the activity of the organism is called a **stimulus** (plural *stimuli*).

Stimuli can be things such as chemicals, gravity, darkness, light, sounds, or tastes. Stimuli cause organisms to respond in some way. A gentle touch causes a response in the plant shown in **Figure 3.**

✓ **Self-Check**

Is your alarm clock a stimulus? Explain. *(See page 636 to check your answer.)*

Figure 3 *The touch of an insect triggers the Venus' flytrap to quickly close its leaves.*

Homeostasis Even though an organism's external environment may change, the organism must maintain a stable internal environment to survive. This is because the life processes of organisms involve many different kinds of chemical reactions that can occur only in delicately balanced environments. The maintenance of a stable internal environment is called **homeostasis** (HOH mee OH STAY sis).

Your body maintains a temperature of about 37°C. When you get hot, your body responds by sweating. When you get cold, your muscles twitch in an attempt to generate heat. This causes you to shiver. Whether you are sweating or shivering, your body is trying to return things to normal.

Another example of homeostasis is the maintenance of a stable amount of sugar in your blood. After you eat, the sugar level in your blood rises. Your body responds by releasing a special compound that removes the sugar from your blood and stores it in your muscle cells and liver cells. When you have not eaten for a long time, your blood-sugar level begins to drop. Your body responds to this by releasing a different compound, which causes your muscles and liver to release sugar into your blood.

oceanography CONNECTION

Fish that live in the ice-cold waters off Antarctica make a natural antifreeze that keeps them from freezing.

3 All Living Things Reproduce

All organisms make other organisms like themselves. This is accomplished in one of two ways: by asexual reproduction or by sexual reproduction. In **asexual reproduction,** a single parent produces offspring that are identical to the parent. **Figure 4** shows an organism that reproduces asexually. Most single-celled organisms reproduce in this way. **Sexual reproduction,** however, almost always requires two parents to produce offspring that will share characteristics of both parents. Most animals and plants reproduce in this way. The bear cubs in **Figure 5** were produced sexually by their parents.

Figure 4 *The hydra is an animal that can reproduce asexually by forming buds that will break off and grow into new individuals. Can you find the buds on this hydra?*

Figure 5 *Like most animals, bears produce offspring by sexual reproduction.*

Figure 6 *Children resemble their parents because of heredity.*

4 All Living Things Have DNA

The cells of all living things contain a special molecule called **DNA** (**d**eoxyribo**n**ucleic **a**cid). DNA provides instructions for making molecules called *proteins*. Proteins take part in almost all of the activities of an organism's cells. Proteins also determine many of an organism's characteristics.

When organisms reproduce, they pass on copies of their DNA to their offspring. The transmission of characteristics from one generation to the next is called **heredity.** Offspring, such as the children in **Figure 6,** resemble their parents because of heredity.

5 All Living Things Use Energy

All organisms use energy to carry out the chemical activities of life. These chemical activities include such things as making food, breaking down food, moving materials into and out of cells, and building cells. An organism's **metabolism** is the total of all the chemical activities that it performs.

been programmed to learn, that is, to get better and faster at solving problems over time. Do you think computers could become so advanced that they should be considered alive? Why or why not?

Computers can do all kinds of things, such as storing information and doing complex calculations. Some computers have even

6 All Living Things Grow and Develop

All living things, whether they are made of one cell or many cells, grow during periods of their lives. Growth in single-celled organisms occurs as the cell gets larger. Organisms made of many cells grow mainly by increasing their number of cells.

In addition to getting larger, living things may also develop and change as they grow. Just like the organisms in **Figure 7,** you will pass through different stages in your life as you develop into an adult.

Figure 7 *Over time, acorns develop into oak seedlings, which become oak trees.*

REVIEW

1. What characteristics of living things does a river have? Is a river alive?

2. What does the fur coat of a bear have to do with homeostasis?

3. How is reproduction related to heredity?

4. **Applying Concepts** What are some stimuli in your environment? How do you respond to these stimuli?

Explore

Imagine that you have the ability to create a new organism. What would your organism be like? How would it display each of the characteristics of living things?

The Simple Bare Necessities of Life

Would it surprise you to learn that you have the same basic needs as a tree, a frog, or a fly? In fact, almost every organism has the same basic needs: food, water, air, and living space.

Food

All living things must have food. This probably doesn't come as a surprise. Food provides organisms with the energy and raw materials needed to carry on life processes and to build and repair cells and body parts. But not all organisms get food in the same way. In fact, organisms can be grouped into three different categories based on how they get their food.

Some organisms, such as plants, are called **producers** because they can produce their own food. The plants in **Figure 8** are an example of producers. Like most producers, they use energy from the sun to make food from water and carbon dioxide. Some producers, like the microorganisms in Movile Cave, obtain energy and food from the chemicals in their environment.

Other organisms are called **consumers** because they must eat (consume) other organisms to get the food they need. The salamander in **Figure 8** is an example of a consumer. It gets the energy it needs by eating insects and other organisms.

Some consumers are decomposers. **Decomposers** are organisms that get their food by breaking down the nutrients in dead organisms or animal wastes. The fungus in **Figure 8** is absorbing nutrients from the dead plant material in the soil.

Figure 8 *The salamander and the fungus it is crawling on are consumers. The plants are producers.*

Water

You may have heard that your body is made up mostly of water. In fact, your cells and the cells of almost all living organisms are made up of approximately 70 percent water—even the cells of a cactus, a camel, and a dragonfly. The metabolism of organisms is dependent on water because most of the chemical reactions that take place in organisms involve water.

Organisms differ greatly in terms of how much water they need and how they obtain it. You could survive for only about 3 days without water. You obtain water from the fluids you drink and also from the food you eat. The desert-dwelling kangaroo rat never drinks. It gets all of its water from its food.

Air

Air is a mixture of several different gases, including oxygen and carbon dioxide. Animals, plants, and most other living things need oxygen in order to stay alive. Oxygen is used in *respiration,* the chemical process that releases energy from food. Organisms that live on land get oxygen from the air. Organisms living in fresh water and salt water either take in dissolved oxygen from the water or come to the water's surface to get oxygen from the air. Some organisms, such as the European diving spider in **Figure 9,** go to great lengths to get oxygen.

Green plants, algae, and some bacteria also need carbon dioxide gas in addition to oxygen. The food these organisms produce is made from carbon dioxide and water by *photosynthesis,* the process that converts the energy in sunlight to energy stored in food.

Figure 9 *This spider surrounds itself with an air bubble so that it can obtain oxygen underwater.*

A Place to Live

All organisms must have a space to live in that contains all the things they need to survive. Some organisms, such as elephants, require a large amount of space. Other organisms, such as bacteria, may live their entire life in a single pore on the tip of your nose.

Because the amount of space on Earth is limited, organisms often compete with each other for food, water, and other necessities. Many animals, including the warbler in **Figure 10,** will claim a particular space and try to keep other animals away. Plants also compete with each other for living space and for access to water and sunlight.

Figure 10 *A warbler's song is more than just a pretty tune. The warbler is protecting its home by singing a message that tells other warblers to stay out of its territory.*

REVIEW

1. Why are decomposers categorized as consumers? How do they differ from producers?

2. Why are most cells 70 percent water?

3. **Making Inferences** Could life as we know it exist on Earth if air contained only oxygen? Explain.

4. **Identifying Relationships** How might a cave, an ant, and a lake meet the needs of an organism?

Is there life on Mars? Find out on page 50.

The Chemistry of Life

NEW TERMS

proteins   phospholipids
enzymes   nucleic acids
carbohydrates   ATP
lipids

OBJECTIVES

- Compare and contrast the chemical building blocks of cells.
- Explain the importance of ATP.

You know that all living things are made of cells, but what are cells made of? Everything, whether it is living or not, is made up of tiny building blocks called *atoms*. There are about 100 different kinds of atoms that combine in countless ways to make up everything that exists. Air, rocks, water, beagles, lima beans, and cells are all composed of a lot of atoms.

A substance made up of one type of atom is called an *element*. When two or more atoms join together, they form what's called a *molecule*. A molecule may be made of a single element or two or more different elements. Molecules found in living things are usually made of different combinations of six elements: carbon, hydrogen, nitrogen, oxygen, phosphorous, and sulfur.

Proteins, carbohydrates, lipids, nucleic acids, and ATP are compounds that are found in all cells. You will learn more about these compounds in this section.

Proteins

Almost all of the life processes of a cell involve proteins. After water, proteins are the most abundant materials in cells. **Proteins** are large molecules that are made up of subunits called *amino acids*.

Organisms break down the proteins in food to supply their cells with amino acids. These amino acids are then linked together to form new proteins. Some proteins are made up of only a few amino acids, while others contain more than 10,000 amino acids.

Proteins have many different functions. Some proteins form structures that are easy to see, like those in **Figure 11.** Other proteins are at work at the cellular level. The protein *hemoglobin* in red blood cells attaches to oxygen so that oxygen can be delivered throughout the body. Some proteins help protect cells from foreign materials. And special proteins called **enzymes** make many different chemical reactions in a cell occur quickly. Cells use enzymes to make the chemical compounds they need and to break down compounds for energy.

Figure 11 *Spider webs, feathers, and hair are all made of proteins.*

Carbohydrates

Carbohydrates are a group of compounds made of sugars. Cells use carbohydrates as a source of energy and for energy storage. When an organism needs energy, its cells break down carbohydrates to release the energy stored in the carbohydrates.

There are two types of carbohydrates, simple carbohydrates and complex carbohydrates. Simple carbohydrates are made of one sugar molecule or a few sugar molecules linked together. The sugar in fruits and the sugar that you may sprinkle on your cereal are examples of simple carbohydrates.

When an organism has more sugar than it needs, its extra sugar may be stored for later use in the form of complex carbohydrates. Complex carbohydrates are made of hundreds or thousands of sugar molecules linked together. Your body makes some complex carbohydrates and stores them in your liver. Plants, however, make the most complex carbohydrates. *Starch* is a complex carbohydrate that is made by plants. As shown in **Figure 12,** a potato plant stores its extra sugar as the starch in a potato. When you eat mashed potatoes or French fries, you are eating a potato plant's stored starch. Your body can then break down this complex carbohydrate to release the energy stored in it.

Special carbohydrates attached to proteins at the surface of your red blood cells determine what blood type you have.

Sugars

Starch

Figure 12 *Most sugars are simple carbohydrates. The extra sugar in a potato plant is stored in the potato as starch, a complex carbohydrate.*

Figure 13 *These are two common lipids used for cooking. Lard comes from animal fat, whereas the oil shown here comes from corn.*

Yeast cells get energy the same way other cells do. See for yourself on page 566 of the LabBook.

Lipids

Lipids are compounds that cannot mix with water. Lipids have many important functions in the cell. Like carbohydrates, some lipids store energy. Other lipids form the membranes of cells.

Fats and Oils Fats and oils are lipids that store energy. When an organism has used up most of its carbohydrates, it can obtain energy from these lipids. The structures of fats and oils are almost identical, but at room temperature most fats are solid and oils are liquid. Most of the lipids stored in plants are oils, while most of the lipids stored in animals are fats. Some sources of fats and oils that you may eat are shown in **Figure 13.**

Phospholipids All cells are surrounded by a structure called a *cell membrane*. **Phospholipids** are the molecules that form much of the cell membrane. As you read earlier, water is the most abundant material in a cell. When phospholipids are in water, the tails come together and the heads face out into the water. This happens because the head of a phospholipid molecule is attracted to water, while the tail is not. **Figure 14** shows how phospholipid molecules form two layers when they are in water.

Figure 14 *The contents of a cell are surrounded by a membrane of phospholipid molecules.*

Phospholipid molecule

Tail   Head

a *The head of a phospholipid molecule is attracted to water, but the tail is not.*

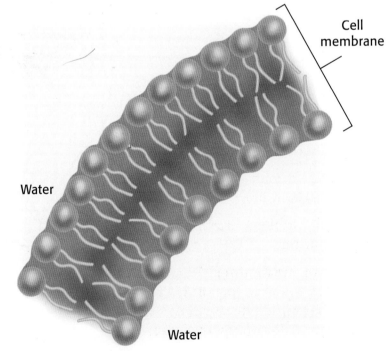

Cell membrane

Water

Water

b *When phospholipid molecules come together in water, they form two layers.*

Nucleic Acids

Nucleic acids are compounds made up of subunits called *nucleotides*. A nucleic acid may contain thousands of nucleotides. Nucleic acids are sometimes called the blueprints of life because they contain all the information needed for the cell to make all of its proteins.

DNA is a nucleic acid. As you learned earlier, a DNA molecule is like a recipe book titled *How to Make Proteins*. When a cell needs to make a certain protein, it gets information from DNA to direct how amino acids are hooked together to make that protein. You will learn more about DNA later.

The Cell's Fuel

Another molecule that is important to cells is ATP (**a**denosine **tri**phosphate). **ATP** is the major fuel used for all cell activities that require energy.

When food molecules, such as carbohydrates and fats, are broken down, some of the released energy is transferred to ATP molecules, as shown in **Figure 15.** The energy in carbohydrates and lipids must be transferred to ATP before the stored energy can be used by cells to fuel their life processes.

Energy in lipids and carbohydrates

ATP

Energy in adenosine triphosphate

Energy for a cell's activities

Figure 15 *The energy in the carbohydrates and lipids in food must be transferred to ATP molecules before cells can use the energy.*

REVIEW

1. What are the subunits of proteins? of starch? of DNA?

2. What do carbohydrates, fats, and oils have in common?

3. Are all proteins enzymes? Explain your answer.

4. **Making Predictions** What would happen to the supply of ATP in your cells if you did not eat enough carbohydrates? How would this affect your cells?

Chapter Highlights

SECTION 1

Vocabulary

cell (*p. 36*)

stimulus (*p. 37*)

homeostasis (*p. 37*)

asexual reproduction (*p. 38*)

sexual reproduction (*p. 38*)

DNA (*p. 38*)

heredity (*p. 38*)

metabolism (*p. 38*)

Section Notes

● All living things share the six characteristics of life.

● Organisms are made of one or more cells. Cells are structures that are the basic units of life.

● Organisms detect stimuli in their environment and respond to those stimuli.

● Organisms work to keep their internal environment stable so that the chemical activities of their cells are not disrupted. The maintenance of a stable internal environment is called homeostasis.

● Organisms reproduce and make more organisms like themselves. Offspring can be produced asexually or sexually.

● Offspring resemble their parents. The passing of characteristics from parent to offspring is called heredity.

● Organisms grow and may also change during their lifetime.

● Organisms use energy to carry out the chemical activities of life. Metabolism is the sum of an organism's chemical activities.

Labs

Roly-Poly Races (*p. 564*)

SECTION 2

Vocabulary

producers (*p. 40*)

consumers (*p. 40*)

decomposers (*p. 40*)

Section Notes

● Organisms must have food. Producers make their own food. Consumers eat other organisms for food. Decomposers break down the nutrients in dead organisms and animal wastes.

☑ Skills Check

Math Concepts

WHAT PERCENTAGE? In the Mathbreak on page 39, you determined the percentage of your height that is taken up by your head.

$$\frac{\text{head height}}{\text{total height}} \times 100\% = \begin{array}{l}\text{\% of total height} \\ \text{taken up by head}\end{array}$$

A woman who is 160 cm tall and has a head height of 20 cm has 12.5 percent of her height taken up by her head.

$$\frac{20 \text{ cm}}{160 \text{ cm}} \times 100\% = 12.5\%$$

Visual Understanding

SUGAR AND STARCH On page 43 you can find illustrations of sugar and starch. The hexagons in each illustration represent sugar molecules. Sugars are simple carbohydrates that are made of one or two sugar molecules. Starch is a complex carbohydrate made of many sugar molecules linked together. These illustrations help you see the difference in structure between simple and complex carbohydrates.

SECTION 2

- Organisms depend on water. Water is necessary for maintaining metabolism.

- Organisms need oxygen to release the energy contained in their food. Plants, algae, and some bacteria also need carbon dioxide.

- Organisms must have a place to live where they can obtain the things they need.

SECTION 3

Vocabulary

proteins (p. 42)

enzymes (p. 42)

carbohydrates (p. 43)

lipids (p. 44)

phospholipids (p. 44)

nucleic acids (p. 45)

ATP (p. 45)

Section Notes

- The compounds most important to life are proteins, carbohydrates, lipids, nucleic acids, and ATP.

- Cells use carbohydrates for energy storage. Carbohydrates are made of sugars.

- Lipids such as fats and oils store energy. The lipids that make cell membranes are phospholipids.

- Proteins are made up of amino acids and have many important functions. Enzymes are proteins that help chemical reactions occur quickly.

- Nucleic acids are made up of nucleotides. DNA is a nucleic acid that contains the information for making proteins.

- Cells use molecules of ATP to fuel their activities.

Labs

The Best-Bread Bakery Dilemma (p. 566)

---

 internet**connect**

 GO TO: go.hrw.com

Visit the **HRW** Web site for a variety of learning tools related to this chapter. Just type in the keyword:

KEYWORD: HSTALV

*SCi*LINKS℠
N S T A **GO TO:** www.scilinks.org

Visit the **National Science Teachers Association** on-line Web site for Internet resources related to this chapter. Just type in the *sci*LINKS number for more information about the topic:

TOPIC: Characteristics of Living Things	*sci*LINKS NUMBER: HSTL030
TOPIC: The Necessities of Life	*sci*LINKS NUMBER: HSTL035
TOPIC: The Chemistry of Life	*sci*LINKS NUMBER: HSTL040
TOPIC: Is There Life on Other Planets?	*sci*LINKS NUMBER: HSTL045

Chapter Review

To complete the following sentences, choose the correct term from each pair of terms listed below:

1. The process of maintaining a stable internal environment is known as __?__. *(metabolism* or *homeostasis)*

2. The resemblance of offspring to their parents is a result of __?__. *(heredity* or *stimuli)*

3. A __?__ obtains food by eating other organisms. *(producer* or *consumer)*

4. Starch is a __?__ and is made up of __?__. *(carbohydrate/sugars* or *nucleic acid/ nucleotides)*

5. Fats and oils are __?__ that store energy for an organism. *(proteins* or *lipids)*

UNDERSTANDING CONCEPTS

Multiple Choice

6. Cells are
   a. the structures that contain all the materials necessary for life.
   b. found in all organisms.
   c. sometimes specialized for particular functions.
   d. All of the above

7. Which of the following is a true statement about all living things?
   a. They cannot sense changes in their external environment.
   b. They reproduce.
   c. They do not need to use energy.
   d. They reproduce asexually.

8. Organisms must have food because
   a. food is a source of energy.
   b. food supplies cells with oxygen.
   c. organisms never make their own food.
   d. All of the above

9. A change in an organism's environment that affects the organism's activities is a
   a. response.   c. metabolism.
   b. stimulus.   d. producer.

10. Organisms store energy in molecules of
    a. nucleic acids.   c. lipids.
    b. phospholipids.   d. water.

11. The molecule that contains the information on how to make proteins is
    a. ATP.
    b. a carbohydrate.
    c. DNA.
    d. a phospholipid.

12. The subunits of nucleic acids are
    a. nucleotides.   c. sugars.
    b. oils.   d. amino acids.

Short Answer

13. What is the difference between asexual reproduction and sexual reproduction?

14. In one or two sentences, explain why living things must have air.

15. What is ATP, and why is it important to a cell?

Concept Mapping

16. Use the following terms to create a concept map: cell, carbohydrates, protein, enzymes, DNA, sugars, lipids, nucleotides, amino acids, nucleic acid.

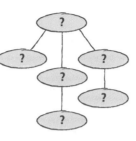

Write one or two sentences to answer the following questions:

17. A flame can move, grow larger, and give off heat. Is a flame alive? Explain.

18. Based on what you know about carbohydrates, lipids, and proteins, why is it important for you to eat a balanced diet?

19. Your friend tells you that the stimulus of music makes his goldfish swim faster. How would you design a controlled experiment to test your friend's claim?

MATH IN SCIENCE

20. An elephant has a mass of 3,900 kg. If 70 percent of the elephant's mass comes from water, how many kilograms of water does the elephant contain?

INTERPRETING GRAPHICS

Take a look at the pictures below, which show the same plant over a time span of 3 days.

Day 1

Day 2

Day 3

21. What is the plant doing?

22. What characteristic(s) of living things is the plant exhibiting?

NOW What Do You Think?

Take a minute to review your answers to the ScienceLog questions on page 35. Have your answers changed? If necessary, revise your answers based on what you have learned since you began this chapter.

Life on Mars?

In late 1996 the headlines read, "Evidence of Life on Mars." What kind of life? Aliens similar to those that we see in sci-fi movies? Some creature completely unlike any we've seen before? Not quite, but the story behind the headlines is no less fascinating!

An Unusual Spaceship

In 1996, a group of researchers led by NASA scientists studied a 3.8-billion-year-old meteorite named ALH84001. These scientists agree that ALH84001 is a potato-sized piece of the planet Mars. They also agree that it fell to Earth about 13,000 years ago. It was discovered in Antarctica in 1984. And according to the NASA team, ALH84001 brought with it evidence that life once existed on Mars.

Life-form Leftovers

On the surface of ALH84001, scientists found certain kinds of *organic molecules* (molecules of compounds containing carbon). These carbonate molecules are similar to those left behind when living things break down substances for food. And when these scientists examined the interior of the meteorite, they found the same organic

▲ *This scanning electron micrograph image of a tube-like structure found within meteorite ALH84001 is thought to be evidence of life on Mars.*

molecules throughout. Because these molecules were spread throughout the meteorite, scientists concluded the molecules were not contamination from Earth. The NASA team believes these organic leftovers are strong evidence that tiny organisms similar to bacteria once lived, ate, and died on Mars millions of years ago.

Dirty Water or Star Dust . . .

Many scientists disagree that ALH84001 contains evidence of Martian life. Some of them argue that the organic compounds are contaminants from Antarctic meltwater that seeped into the meteorite.

Others argue that the carbonate molecules were created by processes involving very high temperatures. These scientists think the compounds were formed during star formation and ended up on Mars when it became a planet. Other supporters of this theory believe the compounds were created during the formation of rocks on Mars. In either case, they argue, no life-forms could exist at such high temperatures, and these compounds could not be the result of living things.

The Debate Continues

Scientists continue to debate the evidence of ALH84001. They are looking for evidence specific to biological life, such as proteins, nucleic acids, and cellular walls. Other scientists are looking to Mars itself for more evidence. Some hope to find underground water that might have supported life. Others hope to gather soil and rock samples that might hold evidence that Mars was once a living planet. Until scientists have more evidence, the debate will continue.

Think About It

▶ If you went to Mars, what kinds of evidence would you look for to prove that life once existed there? How could the discovery of nucleic or amino acids prove life existed on Mars?

Science Fiction

"They're Made Out of Meat"

by Terry Bisson

Two space travelers millions of light-years from home are visiting an uncharted sector of the universe to find signs of life. Their mission is to contact, welcome, and log any and all beings in this quadrant of the universe. Once they discover a living being, they must find a way to communicate with it.

During their mission they encounter a life-form quite unlike anything they have ever seen before. These unusual beings can think and communicate. They have even built a few simple machines, so they aren't exactly pond scum.

Nevertheless, the explorers have very strong doubts about adding this new species to the list of known life-forms in the universe. The creatures are just too strange and, well, disgusting. They just don't fit on the list. Besides, with their limited abilities, it is unlikely they will make contact with any of the other life-forms that dwell elsewhere in the universe.

Perhaps it might be better if the explorers agreed to pretend they never encountered these beings at all. But the travelers' official duty is to contact and welcome all life-forms, no matter how ugly they are or what they are made of. Can they bring themselves to perform their official duty? Will anyone believe their story if they do?

You'll find out by reading Terry Bisson's short story "They're Made Out of Meat." This story is in the *Holt Anthology of Science Fiction*.

3 Light and Living Things

Babies being treated with fluorescent lights wear small eye patches to protect their eyes from light damage.

Strange but True!

What would you think if you walked into a hospital and saw the baby in the picture shown above? It looks like the baby is in a tanning booth! But this baby isn't getting a tan—he is being treated for a condition called jaundice (JAWN dis).

Jaundice occurs in some infants when bilirubin (BIL i ROO bin)—a pigment in healthy red blood cells—builds up in the bloodstream as blood cells break down. The excess bilirubin is then deposited in the skin, giving the skin a yellow-ish hue. Jaundice is not dangerous if treated quickly. If left untreated, it can lead to brain damage.

The excess bilirubin in the skin is best broken down by bright blue light. For this reason, hospitals hang special blue fluorescent lamps above the cribs of newborns needing treatment. Sometimes the blue light is balanced with light of other colors so that doctors and nurses can be sure the baby itself is not blue due to a lack of oxygen.

A more convenient form of treatment is offered by the "bili blanket," a soft pad made of fiber-optic materials connected to a light box that produces blue light. This special light-emitting blanket can be wrapped around the infant, and the newborn can even be picked up and cuddled during treatment.

Light treatment for babies with jaundice is just one of the important uses of light. In this chapter you will learn about the nature of light, how light waves interact, and other ways that light is important to your life.

Investigate!

Colors of Light

Blue light is used to treat babies with jaundice. When a baby is under blue light, however, it is difficult to see whether the baby is blue from a lack of oxygen or from the reflected blue lighting. To solve this problem, the blue light is mixed with other colors of light to produce white light. When this white light shines on a baby, doctors and nurses can see the baby's true color. In this activity you will study two types of white light.

Procedure

1. Turn on an **incandescent light bulb.** Hold a **diffraction grating** in front of one eye, and look through it toward the light bulb. Rotate the grating until you see colors on both sides of the light. Use a **piece of tape** to mark the top of the grating.

Paper with slit

Paper-towel tube

Diffraction grating

What Do You Think?

In your ScienceLog, try to answer the following questions based on what you already know:

1. What are electromagnetic waves?

2. What determines the color of an object?

3. How is a rainbow formed?

2. Tape a piece of **black construction paper** to one end of a **paper-towel tube** so that the paper covers the opening of the tube. Your teacher will cut a narrow slit in the center of the paper.

3. Tape the grating to the opposite end of the tube so that the top of the grating lines up vertically with the slit. You have now made your own spectroscope. Spectroscopes are used to separate light into its component colors. When you look through the spectroscope, you will see separated light on the sides of the tube.

4. Hold the spectroscope up to one eye and look at the light bulb. Describe what you see.

5. Repeat step 4 using a **fluorescent light bulb.** Describe what you see. How does it compare with what you saw when you looked at the incandescent light?

Analysis

6. Both incandescent light bulbs and fluorescent light bulbs produce white light. What did you learn about white light using the spectroscope?

The Electromagnetic Spectrum

NEW TERMS

wave
electromagnetic wave
wavelength
frequency
electromagnetic spectrum

OBJECTIVES

- Explain how electromagnetic waves differ from other waves.
- Describe the relationship between a wave's wavelength and its frequency.
- Describe the relationship between the energy of a wave and its wavelength and frequency.
- Identify ways visible light and ultraviolet light are helpful or harmful.

When you look around, you can see objects because light reflects off them. But if a bee looked at the same objects, it would see them differently, as shown in **Figure 1.** This is because bees can see a type of light that you can't see. This type of light is called ultraviolet light.

It might seem strange to you to call something you can't see *light,* because the light you are most familiar with is visible light. But ultraviolet light is very similar to visible light. Both visible light and ultraviolet light are types of electromagnetic waves. In this section, you will learn about electromagnetic waves and how they differ from other kinds of waves. You will also learn what makes one type of electromagnetic wave different from another.

Figure 1 *The petals of the flower on the right look solid yellow to you. But a bee looking at the same flower can see the ultraviolet markings that direct it to the center of the flower.*

Waves Carry Energy

When you think of waves, you probably think of water waves on an ocean or a lake. But there are many different types of waves. For example, everything you hear travels in a sound wave, earthquakes cause seismic waves, and the light that allows you to see is an electromagnetic wave. A **wave** is any disturbance that transmits energy through matter or space.

As a wave travels, its energy can cause matter to move. For example, the energy of waves on a pond causes the water to move up and down. The energy of the waves also moves anything floating on the water's surface. For example, boats and ducks bob up and down with waves, but they don't move in the same direction as the waves.

Energy is carried away from its source by a wave. However, the material through which the wave travels does not move with the energy. For example, sound waves often travel through air, but the air does not travel with the sound. If air traveled with sound, you would feel a rush of air every time you heard the phone ring! **Figure 2** illustrates how waves carry energy but not matter.

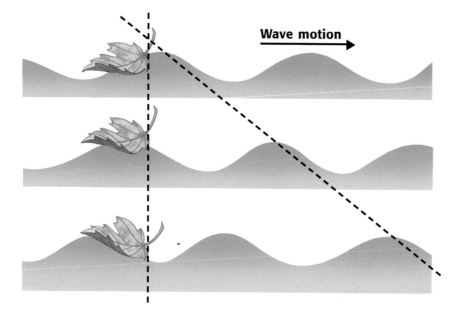

Figure 2 *The diagonal line shows the motion of a wave as it travels across a pond. The vertical line shows that the leaf floating on the surface does not move with the wave.*

Energy Transfer Through a Medium Some waves transfer energy through the vibration of the particles in a medium. A *medium* is a substance through which a wave can travel. A medium can be a solid, a liquid, or a gas.

When a particle vibrates, it has energy. It can pass its energy to a particle next to it. After the energy is transferred to the second particle, the second particle will vibrate and transfer energy to a third particle. In this way, energy is transmitted through a medium. Waves that require a medium are called *mechanical waves*. Water waves, sound waves, and seismic waves are examples of mechanical waves.

Energy Transfer Without a Medium Some waves can transfer energy without traveling through a medium. Visible light is an example of a wave that doesn't require a medium. Other examples include microwaves, which are used in microwave ovens; radio waves, which transmit TV and radio signals; and X rays, which are used by dentists and doctors. Waves that do not require a medium are called **electromagnetic waves,** or EM waves. Although electromagnetic waves do not require a medium, they can travel through substances such as air, water, and glass. However, they travel fastest through empty space.

Extra! Extra! Read all about how fireflies save people's lives! Turn to page 74.

Light and Living Things **55**

Electromagnetic Waves

You probably know that light travels faster than anything else in the universe. But did you know that all electromagnetic waves travel as fast as light? In the near-vacuum of space, the speed of light (and all other electromagnetic waves) is about 300,000,000 m/s. Electromagnetic waves travel slightly slower in air, glass, and other types of matter.

All electromagnetic waves are essentially the same. However, scientists have classified EM waves into different groups based on their wavelength and frequency. As shown in **Figure 3,** the **wavelength** of a wave is the distance between one point on a wave and the corresponding point on an adjacent wave. The **frequency** of a wave is the number of waves produced in a given amount of time. The wavelength and frequency of a wave partially determine how much energy is carried by the wave.

In general, waves with short wavelengths and high frequencies carry more energy than do waves with long wavelengths and low frequencies.

The entire range of EM waves is called the **electromagnetic spectrum.** The electromagnetic spectrum is arranged from long to short wavelength and from low to high frequency. The diagram below shows the different categories of waves in the electromagnetic spectrum. Two categories of EM waves that are important for the survival of life on Earth are visible light and ultraviolet light.

Figure 3 *At a given speed, the frequency increases as the wavelength decreases. Conversely, frequency decreases as the wavelength increases.*

Electromagnetic Spectrum

Decreasing wavelength ⟹

Increasing frequency ⟹

Radio waves
All radio and television stations broadcast radio waves.

Microwaves
Despite their name, microwaves have a relatively long wavelength.

Infrared waves
Infrared means "below red."

Visible Light *Visible light* is the narrow range of wavelengths and frequencies in the electromagnetic spectrum that humans can see. We see the different wavelengths as different colors, as shown in **Figure 4.** We see the longest wavelengths as red light and the shortest wavelengths as violet light. Because violet light has the shortest wavelength, it carries the most energy of the visible light waves. Blue light carries enough energy to cause the breakdown of bilirubin in the skin of newborn babies.

Figure 4 *White light, such as light from the sun, is visible light of all wavelengths combined. You see all the colors of visible light in a rainbow.*

Visible light provides the energy necessary for the chemical reactions known as photosynthesis—the process by which plants make their own food. Photosynthesis is important because the food produced by plants provides energy to almost every living organism on Earth.

The range of colors that makes up visible light is called the *visible spectrum.* To help you remember the order of the colors, you can use the imaginary name "Roy G. Biv." The letters in Roy's name represent the first letter of each color of visible light: **r**ed, **o**range, **y**ellow, **g**reen, **b**lue, **i**ndigo, and **v**iolet. When all the colors of visible light are combined, you see the light as white light. Sunlight and light from incandescent light bulbs and fluorescent light bulbs are examples of white light.

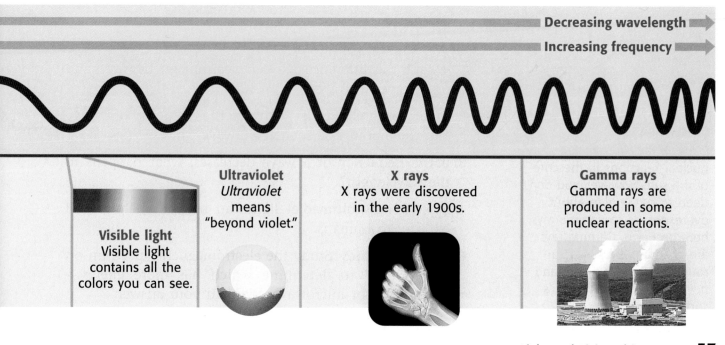

Decreasing wavelength

Increasing frequency

Visible light
Visible light contains all the colors you can see.

Ultraviolet
Ultraviolet means "beyond violet."

X rays
X rays were discovered in the early 1900s.

Gamma rays
Gamma rays are produced in some nuclear reactions.

Ultraviolet Light *Ultraviolet light* is the category of electromagnetic waves just beyond visible light. Approximately 10 percent of the energy from the sun is in the form of ultraviolet light. Ultraviolet waves have shorter wavelengths and higher frequencies than visible light waves have. Therefore, ultraviolet waves carry more energy than visible light waves carry. This greater amount of energy affects us in both positive and negative ways.

On the positive side, ultraviolet light is used to kill bacteria on food and surgical instruments. In addition, limited exposure to ultraviolet light is beneficial to your body. When exposed to ultraviolet light, skin cells produce vitamin D, a substance necessary for the absorption of calcium by the intestines. Without calcium, your teeth and bones would be very weak.

On the negative side, overexposure to ultraviolet light can cause sunburn, skin cancer, damage to the eyes, and wrinkles. Fortunately, much of the ultraviolet light from the sun does not reach the surface of the Earth. But you should still protect yourself against the ultraviolet light that does reach you. To do so, you should use sunscreen with a high SPF (**s**un **p**rotection **f**actor) and wear sunglasses that block out ultraviolet light, like the person on the right in **Figure 5.** You need this protection even on overcast days because ultraviolet light can travel through clouds.

Figure 5 *Sunburn not only is painful but also can lead to wrinkles and skin cancer later in life.*

astronomy
CONNECTION

Gamma rays are produced by nuclear reactions in the core of the sun. However, you don't need to be worried about overexposure to gamma rays here on Earth. Gamma rays are absorbed by gases surrounding the sun's core and never even reach the sun's surface.

REVIEW

1. What is the difference between electromagnetic waves and other types of waves?

2. What is the relationship between the frequency of a wave and the amount of energy the wave carries?

3. If the frequency of a wave decreases, what happens to the wavelength?

4. Explain how ultraviolet light can be both helpful and harmful to humans.

5. **Using Graphics** Study the electromagnetic spectrum on pages 56–57 to determine which has more energy—visible light or microwaves. Explain your answer.

Reflection, Absorption, and Scattering

NEW TERMS

reflection   scattering
law of reflection transmission
absorption   pigment

OBJECTIVES

- Compare regular reflection with diffuse reflection.
- Describe absorption and scattering of light.
- Explain how the color of an object is determined.
- Compare the primary colors of light with the primary pigments.

You're walking outside in the dark, and you hear something rustling in the bushes. You shine your flashlight in the direction of the sound, and you see two glowing eyes. Startled at first, you realize that it is just a cat. Why do the cat's eyes seem to glow in the dark?

Cats have a special layer of cells in the back of their eyes that reflects light. This layer helps the cat see better by giving its eyes another chance to detect the light. Crocodiles, deer, and sharks also have this kind of reflective layer in their eyes. Reflection is just one of the ways light waves interact. In this section you will learn about three different interactions of light waves—reflection, absorption, and scattering.

Reflection

Reflection occurs when light or any other wave bounces off an object. When you see yourself in a mirror, you are actually seeing light that has been reflected twice—first from you and then from the mirror. Reflection enables you to see objects that don't produce their own light. When light strikes an object, some of the light reflects off it and is detected by your eyes.

If light is reflecting off you and off the objects around you, why can't you see your reflection on a wall? To answer this question, you must first learn about the law of reflection.

Figure 6 The Law of Reflection

The beam of light traveling toward the mirror is called the *incident beam.*

A line perpendicular to the mirror's surface is called the *normal.*

The beam of light reflected off the mirror is called the *reflected beam.*

The angle between the incident beam and the normal is called the *angle of incidence.*

The angle between the reflected beam and the normal is called the *angle of reflection.*

The Law of Reflection Light reflects from surfaces the same way that a ball bounces off the ground. If you throw the ball straight down against a smooth surface, it will bounce straight up. If you bounce it at an angle, it will bounce away at an angle. This is an example of the law of reflection. The **law of reflection** states that the angle of incidence is equal to the angle of reflection. *Incidence* is the falling of a beam of light on a surface. **Figure 6** illustrates this law.

Types of Reflection So back to the question, "Why can you see your reflection in a mirror but not in a wall?" The answer has to do with how smooth the reflecting surface is. If the reflecting surface is very smooth, like a mirror or polished metal, light beams reflect off all points of the surface at the same angle. This is known as *regular reflection*. If the reflecting surface is slightly rough, like a wall, light beams hit the surface and reflect at many different angles. This is known as *diffuse reflection*. **Figure 7** illustrates the difference between the two types of reflection.

Figure 7 Regular Reflection Versus Diffuse Reflection

Regular reflection occurs when light beams are reflected at the same angle. When your eye detects the reflected beams, you can see a reflection on the surface.

Diffuse reflection occurs when light beams reflect at many different angles. You can't see a reflection because not all of the reflected light is detected by your eyes. The light that is detected by your eyes allows you to see the surface.

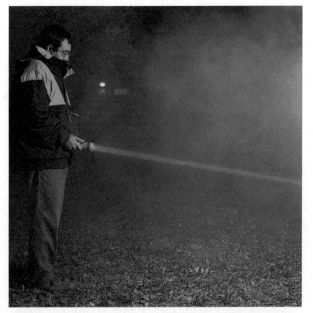

Figure 8 *A beam of light becomes dimmer partially because of absorption and scattering.*

Absorption and Scattering

You have probably noticed that when you use a flashlight, objects that are closer to you appear brighter than objects that are farther away. The light appears to weaken the farther it travels from the flashlight. This happens partially because the beam spreads out and partially because of absorption and scattering.

Absorption is the transfer of energy carried by light waves to particles in matter. When you shine a flashlight in the air, the air particles absorb some of the energy from the light. This causes the light to become dim, as shown in **Figure 8**. The farther the light travels from the flashlight, the more it is absorbed by air particles. This is one reason why the light becomes dimmer the farther it travels.

Scattering is the release of light energy by particles of matter that have absorbed extra energy. When light is released, it scatters in all directions. Light from a flashlight is scattered out of the beam by air particles. This scattered light allows you to see objects outside the beam. However, because light is scattered out of the beam, the beam becomes dimmer.

Scattering makes the sky blue. Light with shorter wavelengths is scattered more than light with longer wavelengths. Sunlight is made up of many different colors of light, but blue light (which has a very short wavelength) is scattered more than any other color. So when you look at the sky, you see a background of blue light. You can learn more about the scattering of light by doing the QuickLab at right.

Light and Color

Have you ever wondered what gives an object its color? You already know that white light is made of all the colors of light. But when you see fruit in white light, you see color. Strawberries are red, limes are green, and bananas are yellow. Why aren't they all white? To answer this question, you must first learn how light interacts with matter.

Light and Matter When light strikes any form of matter, it can interact with the matter in three different ways—it can be reflected, absorbed, or transmitted. You already learned about reflection and absorption. **Transmission** is the passing of light through matter. You see the transmission of light all the time. All of the light that reaches your eyes is transmitted through air. Light can interact with matter in several ways at the same time, as shown in **Figure 9.**

QuickLab

Scattering Milk

1. Fill a clear **2 L bottle** with **water.**

2. Turn the lights off, and shine a **flashlight** through the water. Look at the water from all sides of the bottle. In your ScienceLog, describe what you see.

3. Add a few drops of **milk** to the water, and shake the bottle to mix it up.

4. Repeat step 2. Describe any color changes. If you don't see any, add more milk until you do.

5. How is the water-and-milk mixture like air particles in the atmosphere? Write your answer in your ScienceLog.

Figure 9 *Light is transmitted, reflected, and absorbed when it strikes the glass in a window.*

You can see the glass and your reflection in it because light is **reflected** off the glass.

You can see objects outside because light is **transmitted** through the glass.

The glass feels warm when you touch it because some light is **absorbed** by the glass.

Colors of Objects How does the interaction of light with matter determine an object's color? You already know that the color of light is determined by the wavelength of the light wave. Red has the longest wavelength, violet has the shortest, and other colors have wavelengths in between.

The color of an object is determined by the color of light that reaches your eyes. The light can reach your eyes after being reflected off an object or after being transmitted through an object.

When white light strikes a colored object, some colors of light are absorbed and some are reflected. Only the light that is reflected can reach your eyes and be detected. Therefore, the colors of light that are reflected by an object determine the color you see. For example, if your sweater reflects blue light and absorbs all other colors, you will see that the sweater is blue. Another example is shown in **Figure 10**.

Figure 10 *When white light shines on a strawberry, only red light is reflected. All other colors of light are absorbed. Therefore, the strawberry looks red to you.*

If green objects reflect green light and red objects reflect red light, what colors of light are reflected by the cow shown at left? Remember that white light includes all colors of light. So white objects—such as the white hair in the cow's hide—appear white because all the colors of light are reflected. On the other hand, black is the absence of color. When light strikes a black object, all the colors are absorbed.

✔Self-Check

If blue light shines on a white sheet of paper, what color does the paper appear to be? *(See page 636 to check your answer.)*

Mixing Colors of Light

In order to get white light, you need to combine all colors of light, right? Well, that's one way of doing it. You can also get white light by adding just three colors of light together—red, blue, and green—as shown in **Figure 11.** In fact, these three colors can be combined in different ratios to produce all colors of visible light. Red, blue, and green are therefore called the *primary colors of light.*

When colors of light combine, more wavelengths of light are present. Therefore, combining colors of light is called color addition. When two primary colors are added together, a *secondary color* is produced. The secondary colors are cyan (blue plus green), magenta (blue plus red), and yellow (red plus green). In Figure 11, the secondary colors appear between the primary colors.

BRAIN FOOD

The colors you see on a color television are produced by color addition of the primary colors of light. A television screen is made up of tiny light-emitting dots called pixels. Each pixel can glow red, blue, or green. The colors emitted by the pixels add together to produce the different colors you see on the screen.

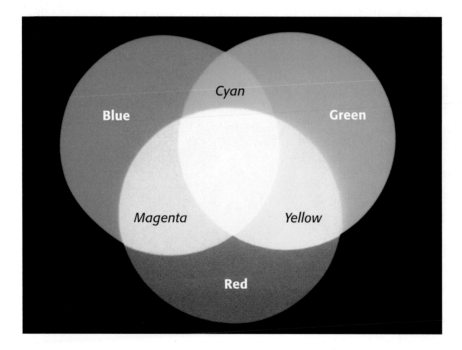

Figure 11 *Primary colors—written in bold—combine to produce white light. Secondary colors—written in italics—are the result of two primary colors added together.*

APPLY

Magda is in charge of the lighting for the school play. She has checked the prop room and found spotlights that produce three different colors of light—red, blue, and green. She knows she also needs cyan, magenta, yellow, and white spotlights. There is no more money in the budget to buy new spotlights. What can she do to obtain each of these colors?

Mixing Colors of Pigment

If you have ever tried mixing paints in art class, you know that you can't make white paint by mixing red, blue, and green paint. The processes of mixing paint and mixing light are different because paint contains pigments. A **pigment** is a material that gives a substance its color by absorbing some colors of light and reflecting others.

Almost everything contains pigments. In fact, pigments give objects color by reflecting and absorbing light. Chlorophyll and melanin are examples of pigments. Chlorophyll gives plants a green color, and melanin gives your skin its color.

Each pigment absorbs at least one color of light. When you mix pigments together, more colors of light are absorbed, or subtracted. Therefore, mixing colors of pigments is called color subtraction. The *primary pigments* are yellow, cyan, and magenta. They can be combined to produce any other color. In fact, all the colors in this book were produced by using just the primary pigments and black ink. The black ink was used to provide contrast to the images. **Figure 12** shows how the four pigments combine to produce many different colors.

Figure 12 *The picture of the balloon on the left was made by overlapping cyan ink, magenta ink, yellow ink, and black ink.*

Cyan

Magenta

Yellow

Black

When is science class like art class? When you use paints to mix colors on page 568 of the LabBook.

REVIEW

1. Explain the difference between absorption and scattering.

2. Plants must get the energy they need to live from the sun. Why is it an advantage for plant cells to contain chlorophyll?

3. **Applying Concepts** Explain what happens to the different colors of light when white light shines on a violet object.

4. **Making Inferences** Explain why you can see your reflection on a spoon but not on a piece of cloth.

Refraction

NEW TERMS

refraction   convex lens
lens   concave lens

OBJECTIVES

- Define *refraction.*
- Explain how refraction can separate white light into different colors of light.
- Describe the differences between convex lenses and concave lenses.
- Identify examples of lenses used in your everyday life.

Do you know someone who wears glasses or contact lenses? Do you wear them yourself? Approximately 37 percent of people in the United States wear glasses or contact lenses to correct problems with their vision. If you examine different pairs of glasses, you might notice differences in the lenses in the frames. For example, some lenses are thicker in the middle than at the edges, while other lenses are thinner in the middle than at the edges.

Your eyes have lenses too. When you see something, light produced by or reflected off an object enters your eye through the pupil, passes through your cornea and lens, and forms an image on the back surface of your eye, the retina. Why are the cornea and lens of the eye important for forming images on the retina? To find the answer, you need to learn about the way light travels and what happens to it when it passes from one type of matter into another.

Rays Show the Path of Light Waves

Like all waves, light waves travel from their source in all directions. If you could trace the path of one wave as it traveled away from a light source, you would find that the path is a straight line. Because light waves travel in straight lines, you can show the path and the direction of a light wave with an arrow called a *ray.* **Figure 13** shows some rays coming from a light bulb.

Although light waves normally travel in straight lines, light waves can change direction when they interact with matter. For example, light waves change direction when they reflect off an object. Light waves also change direction and speed when they pass from one medium, such as air, into another medium, such as glass.

Figure 13 *Rays from this light bulb show the path and direction of the light waves produced by the bulb.*

Refraction

Refraction is the bending of a wave as it passes at an angle from one medium to another. Refraction of light waves occurs because the speed of light varies depending on the material through which the waves are traveling. In a vacuum (a place in which there is no matter), light travels at 300,000,000 m/s, but it travels slower through matter. When a wave enters a new medium at an angle, the part of the wave that enters first begins traveling at a different speed from the rest of the wave. **Figure 14** shows how a light beam is bent by refraction.

If light passes into a medium where the speed of light is slower, the light bends away from the boundary between the media.

Light in →

If light passes into a medium where the speed of light is faster, the light bends toward the boundary.

Figure 14 *Light travels slower through glass than through air. Therefore, light refracts as it passes at an angle from air to glass or from glass to air.*

Refraction and Color Separation When light is refracted, the amount that the light bends depends on its wavelength. Light waves with short wavelengths are bent more than light waves with long wavelengths. You have already learned that white light is composed of all the colors of visible light. You also know that the different colors correspond to different wavelengths. Because of this, white light can be separated into different colors during refraction, as shown in **Figure 15.** Color separation during refraction is partially responsible for the formation of rainbows. Rainbows are created when sunlight is refracted by water droplets.

Figure 15 *A prism is a piece of glass that separates white light into the colors of visible light by refraction.*

Light passing through a prism is refracted twice—once when it enters and once when it exits.

Violet light, which has a short wavelength, is refracted more than red light, which has a long wavelength.

You can see the colors of the rainbow when white light is separated by a prism.

Lenses Refract Light

What do cameras, binoculars, telescopes, movie projectors, and your eyes have in common? They all contain lenses. A **lens** is a curved, transparent object that refracts light. Lenses are classified by their shape. The two types of lenses are convex lenses and concave lenses.

Convex Lenses A lens that is thicker in the middle than at the edges is a **convex lens.** When light rays enter a convex lens, they always refract toward the center. The amount of refraction depends on the curvature of the lens, as shown in **Figure 16.** Light rays that pass through the center of a lens are not refracted.

A convex lens can focus the light that enters it. Because of this, convex lenses are used in cameras, telescopes, movie projectors, and in glasses for people who are farsighted. Your eye has a convex lens that focuses light by changing its shape, as shown in **Figure 17.**

Figure 16 *Refraction of light rays through convex lenses depends on lens curvature.*

Figure 17 *Incoming light rays are refracted by the cornea and the lens. The size of the pupil determines the amount of light entering the eye. The light rays converge at the retina, forming an image.*

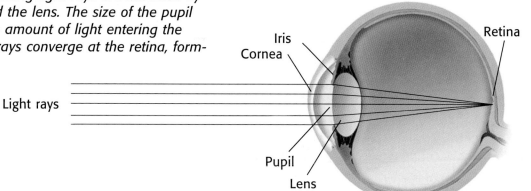

Light rays

Iris
Cornea
Pupil
Lens
Retina

Concave Lenses A **concave lens** is a lens that is thinner in the middle than at the edges. Light rays passing through concave lenses always bend away from each other toward the edges of the lens, as shown in **Figure 18.** Concave lenses are commonly used in glasses that correct the vision of people who are nearsighted. Concave lenses can also be used in combination with other lenses in telescopes. The combination of lenses helps produce clearer images of distant objects.

Figure 18 *Light passing through a concave lens is refracted outward.*

Optical Instruments

Optical instruments are technological devices that use arrangements of mirrors and lenses to help people make observations. Some optical instruments help people see objects that are very far away, and some help people see objects that are very small. The optical instrument that you are probably most familiar with is the camera.

Smile for the Camera! The way a camera works is similar to the way your eye works. A camera has a lens that focuses light and an opening that lets light in. The main difference between a camera and your eye is that the lens in a camera can be moved back and forth to focus light, while the lens in your eye changes shape when focusing is needed. **Figure 19** shows the parts of a camera and their functions.

Figure 19 *Cameras are useful for permanently recording images as photographs.*

The *shutter* opens and closes to allow light into the camera. The speed at which the shutter opens and closes controls how much light enters the camera. The longer the shutter is open, the more light that enters the camera.

The *film* is coated with chemicals that react when struck by light. Light focused by the lens strikes the film to form an image.

The *lens* of a camera is a convex lens that focuses light on the film. Moving the lens back and forth focuses light from objects at different distances.

The *aperture* is an opening that lets light into the camera. The larger the aperture is, the more light that enters the camera.

✓ Self-Check

What parts of the human eye correspond to the following parts of a camera?

a. the aperture **b.** the lens **c.** the film

(See page 636 to check your answers.)

Telescopes Astronomers use telescopes to study objects in space, such as the moon, planets, and stars. Telescopes are classified as either refracting or reflecting. Refracting telescopes use lenses to collect light, while reflecting telescopes use mirrors. **Figure 20** illustrates how simple refracting and reflecting telescopes work.

Figure 20 *Both refracting and reflecting telescopes are used to see objects that are far away.*

A **refracting telescope** has two convex lenses. Light enters through the objective lens and forms an image. This image is then magnified by the eyepiece lens. You see this magnified image when you look through the eyepiece lens.

A **reflecting telescope** has a curved mirror that collects and focuses light to form an image. The light strikes a flat mirror that directs the light to the convex eyepiece lens, which magnifies the image.

Light Microscopes Simple light microscopes are similar to refracting telescopes. They have two convex lenses—an objective lens, which is close to the object being studied, and an eyepiece lens, which you look through. The difference between microscopes and telescopes is that microscopes are used to see magnified images of tiny, nearby objects rather than images of large, distant objects. More-complex light microscopes have several lenses to increase magnification and reduce distortion.

REVIEW

1. What is refraction?

2. Why can you see the colors of the rainbow when white light refracts through a prism?

3. How do convex lenses differ from concave lenses?

4. **Comparing Concepts** Explain how a simple light microscope is similar to a refracting telescope.

Chapter Highlights

SECTION 1

Vocabulary

wave *(p. 54)*

electromagnetic wave *(p. 55)*

wavelength *(p. 56)*

frequency *(p. 56)*

electromagnetic spectrum
(p. 56)

Section Notes

• A wave is a disturbance that transmits energy through matter or space.

• Waves that require a medium are called mechanical waves. Waves that do not require a medium are called electromagnetic waves.

• All EM waves travel at the speed of light. EM waves differ only by their wavelength and frequency.

• The frequency of a wave increases as its wavelength decreases.

• The energy of a wave is partially determined by its wavelength and frequency.

• The entire range of EM waves is called the electromagnetic spectrum.

• Visible light is the narrow range of wavelengths that humans can see. Different wavelengths are seen as different colors.

• Ultraviolet light is useful for killing bacteria and for producing vitamin D in the body, but overexposure can cause health problems.

SECTION 2

Vocabulary

reflection *(p. 59)*

law of reflection *(p. 59)*

absorption *(p. 60)*

scattering *(p. 61)*

transmission *(p. 61)*

pigment *(p. 64)*

Section Notes

• You can see an image reflected from a surface during regular reflection but not during diffuse reflection.

• Absorption and scattering of light are two reasons why light beams become weaker with distance.

• Light can interact with matter by reflection, absorption, or transmission.

☑ Skills Check

Visual Understanding

THE ELECTROMAGNETIC SPECTRUM The entire range of electromagnetic waves is called the electromagnetic spectrum. The EM waves are arranged from long to short wavelength or from low to high frequency in the electromagnetic spectrum. Study the diagram on the bottom of pages 56–57 to review the different categories of electromagnetic waves in the electromagnetic spectrum.

LIGHT AND MATTER Light can interact with matter in three different ways—light can be reflected, absorbed, or transmitted. These three interactions are illustrated in Figure 9 on page 61.

SECTION 2

- An object's color is determined by the color of light it reflects.

- The primary colors of light are red, blue, and green. All three primary colors of light combine by color addition to produce white light.

- Pigments give objects color. Pigments combine by color subtraction.

- The primary pigments are yellow, cyan, and magenta. They can be combined to produce any other color.

Labs

Mixing Colors *(p. 568)*

SECTION 3

Vocabulary

refraction *(p. 66)*

lens *(p. 67)*

convex lens *(p. 67)*

concave lens *(p. 67)*

Section Notes

- Light beams are bent during refraction.

- The amount of refraction depends on the wavelength of the light. Because of this, light can be separated into different colors by refraction.

- A lens is a curved, transparent object that refracts light. Lenses may be convex or concave.

- A convex lens is thicker in the middle than at the edges. A convex lens can focus the light that enters it.

- A concave lens is thinner in the middle than at the edges. Light passing through a concave lens bends toward the edges of the lens.

- Cameras, telescopes, and microscopes are optical instruments that contain lenses.

---

 internet connect

 GO TO: go.hrw.com

Visit the **HRW** Web site for a variety of learning tools related to this chapter. Just type in the keyword:

KEYWORD: HSTLLT

*sci*LINKS. **NSTA** **GO TO:** www.scilinks.org

Visit the **National Science Teachers Association** on-line Web site for Internet resources related to this chapter. Just type in the *sci*LINKS number for more information about the topic:

TOPIC: The Electromagnetic Spectrum — *sci*LINKS NUMBER: HSTL705
TOPIC: Ultraviolet Light — *sci*LINKS NUMBER: HSTL710
TOPIC: Colors — *sci*LINKS NUMBER: HSTL715
TOPIC: Lenses — *sci*LINKS NUMBER: HSTL720

Chapter Review

To complete the following sentences, choose the correct term from each pair of terms listed below:

1. Convex lenses focus light by __?__. (*reflection* or *refraction*)

2. Light travels through an object during __?__. (*absorption* or *transmission*)

3. The distance between one point on a wave and the corresponding point on an adjacent wave is the __?__ of the wave. (*wavelength* or *frequency*)

4. A lens that is thinner in the middle than at the edges is a __?__. (*convex lens* or *concave lens*)

5. Visible light is a type of __?__. (*electromagnetic wave* or *mechanical wave*)

UNDERSTANDING CONCEPTS

Multiple Choice

6. What color of light is produced when red light is added to green light?
   a. cyan
   b. blue
   c. yellow
   d. white

7. You can see yourself in a mirror because of
   a. absorption.
   b. scattering.
   c. regular reflection.
   d. diffuse reflection.

8. Prisms produce rainbows through
   a. reflection.
   b. refraction.
   c. absorption.
   d. scattering.

9. As the wavelength of a wave increases, the frequency
   a. decreases.
   b. increases.
   c. remains the same.
   d. increases, then decreases.

10. Refraction occurs when a light wave enters a new medium at an angle because
    a. the frequency changes.
    b. light becomes a mechanical wave.
    c. the speed of light changes depending on the medium.
    d. None of the above

11. Waves transfer
    a. matter.
    b. energy.
    c. particles.
    d. water.

12. A simple refracting telescope has
    a. a convex lens and a concave lens.
    b. a mirror and a concave lens.
    c. two convex lenses.
    d. two concave lenses.

Short Answer

13. Name two ways electromagnetic waves differ from each other.

14. Describe the law of reflection.

15. Describe the difference between convex and concave lenses.

Concept Mapping

16. Use the following terms to create a concept map: light, color, absorption, matter, reflection, transmission, scattering.

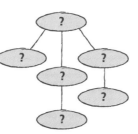

Write one or two sentences to answer the following questions:

17. Both radio waves and gamma rays are types of electromagnetic waves. Exposure to radio waves does not harm the human body, whereas exposure to gamma rays can be extremely dangerous. What is the difference between these types of EM waves? Why are gamma rays more dangerous?

18. If you compare clothes that are worn in the summer with clothes that are worn in the winter, you will notice that most summer clothes are often white or light colored but most winter clothes are black or dark colored. Using your knowledge of how the colors of objects are determined, try to explain this trend.

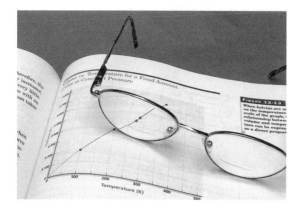

19. Sometimes people are both nearsighted and farsighted. They wear glasses called bifocals, which contain two different kinds of lenses. Why are two kinds of lenses necessary?

20. What's inside each mystery box? The only clues you have are the light rays that enter and leave each box.

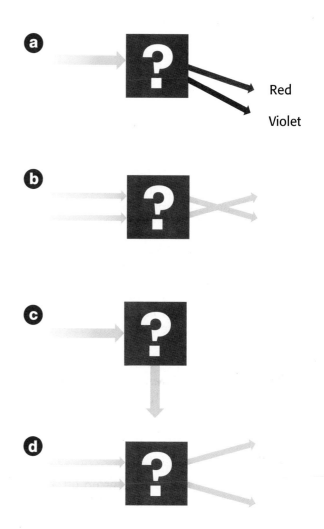

NOW What Do You Think?

Take a minute to review your answers to the ScienceLog questions on page 53. Have your answers changed? If necessary, revise your answers based on what you have learned since you began this chapter.

Science, Technology, and Society

Fireflies Light the Way

Just as beams of light from coastal lighthouses warn boats of approaching danger, scientists are using the light of an unlikely source—fireflies—to warn food inspectors of life-threatening bacterial contamination! Thousands of people die each year from meat contaminated with bacteria. The light from fireflies is being used to study several diseases, waste-water treatment, and environmental protection as well!

Nature's Guiding Light

A number of organisms, including some fishes, squids, beetles, and bacteria, emit light. Fireflies, in particular, use this light to attract mates. How do these organisms use energy to emit light?

Remarkably, all of these organisms use a substance called *luciferin* and an enzyme called *luciferase* to make light. Luciferase uses the energy from *adenosine triphosphate* (ATP) to break down luciferin to produce light in the form of a glow or flash. Fireflies are very effective light bulbs. Nearly 100 percent of the energy they get from ATP is given off as light. This is much more than the 10 percent of energy given off by electrical light bulbs in the form of light; the other 90 percent is heat!

Harnessing Life's Light

How have scientists harnessed the firefly's ability to produce light to find bacteria? Researchers have found the gene responsible for making luciferase. Scientists have taken the gene from fireflies that makes luciferase and have inserted it into a virus that preys on bacteria. The virus isn't harmful to humans and is mixed into meat. When the virus infects the bacteria, it transfers the gene into the genetic machinery of the bacteria. This bacteria then produces luciferase and glows in the presence of luciferin.

▲ *You might see fireflies clustered around a tree.*

This process is being used to find a number of dangerous bacteria that contaminate foods, including *Salmonella* and *E. coli*. These bacteria are responsible for thousands of deaths each year. Not only is the test effective, it is fast. Before researchers developed this test, it took up to 3 days to determine whether bacteria had contaminated food. By that time, the food was already at the grocery store!

Think About It!

▶ Fireflies use ATP as an energy source to emit light. Plants use the energy from light to produce ATP. Plants can then use this ATP at a later time as an energy source! What color of light would you hypothesize gives plants the most energy? Investigate, and see if your hypothesis is right!

EYE ON THE ENVIRONMENT

Light Pollution

At night, large cities are often visible from far away. Soft light from windows outlines buildings. Bright lights from stadiums and parking lots shine like beacons. Scattered house lights twinkle like jewels. The sight is stunning!

Unfortunately, astronomers consider these lights a form of pollution. Light pollution is reducing our ability to see beyond our atmosphere. Astronomers around the world are losing their ability to see through our atmosphere into space.

Sky Glow

Twenty years ago, stars were very visible above even large cities. The stars are still there, but now they are obscured by city lights. This glow, called sky glow, is created when light reflects off dust and other particles suspended in the atmosphere. Even remote locations around the globe are affected by light pollution. Sky glow affects the entire atmosphere to some degree.

The majority of light pollution comes from outdoor lights such as headlights, street lights, porch lights, and bright parking-lot and stadium lights. Other sources include forest fires and gas burn-offs in oil fields. Air pollution makes the situation even worse, adding more particles to the air so that there is even greater reflection.

A Light of Hope

Unlike other kinds of pollution, light pollution has some simple solutions. In fact, light pollution can be cleaned up in as little time as it takes to turn off a light! While turning off most city lights is impractical, several simple strategies can make a surprising difference. For example, using covered outdoor lights keeps the light angled downward, preventing most of the light from reaching particles in the sky. Also, using motion-sensitive lights and

▲ *Lights from cities can be seen from space, as shown in this photograph taken from the space shuttle* Columbia. *Bright, uncovered lights (inset) create a glowing haze in the night sky above most cities in the United States.*

timed lights helps eliminate unnecessary light. Many of these strategies also save money by saving energy.

Astronomers hope that public awareness will help improve the visibility of the night sky in and around major cities. Some cities, including Boston and Tucson, have already made some progress in reducing light pollution. Scientists have projected that if left unchecked, light pollution will affect every observatory on Earth within the next decade.

See for Yourself

▶ With your parents' permission, go outside at night and find a place where you can see the sky. Count the number of stars you can see. Now turn on a flashlight or porch light. How many stars can you see now? Compare your results. How much was your visibility reduced?

UNIT 2

Cells

Cells are everywhere. Even though most can't be seen with the naked eye, they make up every living thing. Your body alone contains trillions of cells.

In this unit, you will learn about cells. You will learn the difference between animal cells, plant cells, and bacterial cells. You'll learn about the different parts of a cell and see how they work together.

Cells were discovered in 1665, and since then we have learned a lot about cells and the way they work. This timeline shows some of the discoveries that have been made along the way, but there is still a lot to learn about the fascinating world of cells!

1665
Robert Hooke discovers cells after observing a thin piece of cork under a microscope.

1620
The Pilgrims settle Plymouth Colony.

1937
The Golden Gate Bridge opens in San Francisco.

1873
Anton Schneider observes and accurately describes mitosis.

1952
Martha Chase and Alfred Hershey demonstrate that DNA, found in the nucleus of cells, is the hereditary material.

1941
George Beadle and Edward Tatum discover that genes control the chemical reactions in cells by directing protein production.

1831
Robert Brown discovers the nucleus in a plant cell.

1838
Matthias Schleiden discovers that all plant tissue is made up of cells.

1839
Theodor Schwann shows that all animal tissue is made up of cells.

1861
The American Civil War begins.

1858
Rudolf Virchow determines that all cells are produced from cells.

1971
Lynn Margulis proposes a theory about the origin of cell organelles.

1956
The manufacture of protein in the cell is found to occur in ribosomes.

1997
A sheep named Dolly becomes the first animal to be cloned from a single cell.

4 Cells: The Basic Units of Life

What If . . . ?

Imagine this scene from a horror film. A young man sits down to dinner to find that his mother has made asparagus again. The young man eats the dreaded asparagus stalks. Later, he finds out that instead of being digested, one of the stalks has taken up residence inside his body and is very much alive! Too horrifying to think about? What if the asparagus began to do wonderful things for the young man, such as giving him more energy than he ever dreamed possible? Lynn Margulis, a scientist, thinks that something similar may have happened to certain one-celled organisms that lived more than a billion years ago, giving rise to the kinds of cells that we are made of today.

According to Margulis's theory, about 1.2 billion years ago, some larger cells began eating smaller cells for dinner. Like the white blood cell on this page, these larger cells trapped the smaller cells with extensions of their cell body. But some of these smaller cells resisted being digested. In fact, they began to do very well in their new homes.

The larger cells also benefited from their new guests. The smaller cells released large amounts of energy from food taken in by the larger cells. Other kinds of small cells used the energy in sunlight to make enough food to feed themselves and the larger cell. The energy-producing structures of most cells, including yours, are thought to have descended from these smaller cells. In this chapter, you will learn more about cells and their structures.

What Do You Think?

In your ScienceLog, try to answer the following questions based on what you already know:

1. What is a cell, and where are cells found?

2. Why are there cells, and why are they so small?

Investigate!

What Are You Made Of?

As you have already learned, all living things are made of cells, including you! What do some of your cells look like? Do this activity to find out.

Procedure

1. Wear goggles, protective gloves, and an apron throughout this experiment. Have your teacher place a drop of **methylene blue stain** on your **plastic microscope slide.**
   Caution: Be careful not to get this stain on your skin or clothing. If this happens, rinse it off immediately, and call your teacher.

2. *Gently* scrape the inside of your cheek with the blunt end of a **toothpick.**

3. Stir the scraped material into the drop of stain. **Caution:** Don't put the toothpick back in your mouth! Throw away the toothpick as your teacher directs.

4. Place a **plastic coverslip** on top of the drop, as shown below.

5. Place the slide on your **microscope,** and try to find the cells. In your ScienceLog, draw a picture of what you see.

Analysis

6. What do your cheek cells look like? Are they all the same?

7. Do you think all of the cells in your body look like this? Explain your answer.

Organization of Life

Imagine that you are going on a trip to Mars. In your suitcase, you should pack everything you will need in order to survive. What would you pack? To start, you'd need food, oxygen, and water. And that's just the beginning. You would probably need a pretty big suitcase, wouldn't you? Actually, you have all of these items inside your body's cells. A cell is smaller than the period at the end of this sentence, yet a single cell has all the items necessary to carry out life's activities.

Every living thing has at least one cell. Many living things exist as a single cell, while others have trillions of cells. To get an idea of what a living thing with nearly 100 trillion cells looks like, just look in the mirror!

Cells: Starting Out Small

Most cells are too small to be seen without a microscope, but you might have one of the world's largest cells in your refrigerator. To find out what it is, see **Figure 1.** The first cell of a chicken is yellow with a tiny white dot in it, and it is surrounded by clear, jellylike fluid called egg white. The white dot divides over and over again to form a chick. The yellow yolk (from the first cell) and the egg white provide nutrients for the developing chick's cells. Like a chicken, you too began as a single egg cell. Look at **Figure 2** to see some of the early stages of your development.

Not all of your cells look or act the same. You have about 200 different kinds of cells, and each type is specialized to do a particular job. Some are bone cells, some are blood cells, and others are skin cells. When someone looks at all of those cells together, they see you.

Figure 1 *The first cell of a chicken is one of the largest cells in the world.*

Figure 2 *You began as a single cell. But after many cell divisions, you are now made of about 100 trillion cells.*

24 hours

40 hours

6 days

4 months

Tissues: Cells Working in Teams

When you look closely at your clothes, you can see that threads have been grouped together (woven) to make cloth that has a function. In the same way, cells are grouped together to make a tissue that has a function. A **tissue** is a group of cells that work together to perform a specific job in the body. The material around and between the cells is also part of the tissue. Some examples of tissues in your body are shown in **Figure 3**.

Organs: Teams Working Together

When two or more tissues work together to perform a specific job, the group of tissues is called an **organ.** Some examples of organs are your stomach, intestines, heart, lungs, and skin. That's right; even your skin is an organ because it contains different kinds of tissues. To get a closer look, see **Figure 4.**

Plants also have different kinds of tissues that work together. A leaf is a plant organ that contains tissue that traps light energy to make food. Other examples of plant organs are stems, roots, and leaves.

Fat

Muscle

Red blood cells

Figure 3 *Blood, fat, and muscle cells are just a few of the many cells that make tissues in your body.*

BRAIN FOOD

The part of the skin, hair, and nails that you can see is dead tissue! Isn't it strange to think that we put so much effort into making sure our dead cells look nice?

Figure 4 *The skin is the body's largest organ. An average-sized person's skin has a mass of about 4.5 kg.*

chemistry
CONNECTION

On the surface of every person's cells are special proteins that act like identification cards. When a person gets an organ transplant, the cells of the new organ must have most of the same "ID cards" as the person's cells. If too many are different, the person's body will try to reject the new organ.

Explore

Think about how a school system is organized. The school system's job is to educate students at all levels. The different schools (elementary, middle, and high school) are like the different organs within an organ system. Groups of teachers at each school work together to teach a specific grade level of students. If each group of teachers at a school can be thought of as tissue performing a particular function, what would that make each individual teacher? What other examples can you use to represent the parts of an organ system? Explain your answer.

Organ Systems: A Great Combination

Organs work together in groups to perform particular jobs. These groups are called **organ systems.** Each system has a specific job to do in the body. For example, your digestive system's job is to break down food into very small particles so it can be used by all of your body's cells. Your nervous system's job is to transmit information back and forth between your brain and the other parts of your body. Organ systems in plants include leaf systems, root systems, and stem systems, as shown in **Figure 5.**

Your body has several organ systems. The digestive system is shown in **Figure 6.** Each organ in the digestive system has a job to do. A particular organ is able to do its job because of the different tissues within it.

The organs in an organ system depend on each other. If any part of the system fails, the whole system is affected. And failure of one organ system can affect other organ systems. Just think of what would happen if your digestive system stopped converting food to energy. None of the other organ systems would have energy to function.

Figure 5 *Plants have organ systems too. For example the stem system includes the stems and branches.*

Figure 6 *The digestive system is one of the 11 main organ systems. It is made of different organs, which in turn are made of different tissues.*

82 Chapter 4

Organisms: Independent Living

Anything that can live on its own is called an **organism.** All organisms are made up of at least one cell. If a single cell is living on its own, it is called a **unicellular** organism. Most unicellular organisms are so small that you need to use a microscope to see them. Some different kinds of unicellular organisms are shown in **Figure 7.**

You are a **multicellular** organism. This means that you can exist only as a group of cells and that most of your cells can survive only if they remain a part of your body. When you fall down on a sidewalk and scrape your knee, the cells you leave behind on the sidewalk are not able to live on their own. **Figure 8** shows how your cells work together to make a multicellular organism.

Figure 7 *Unicellular organisms come in a wide variety of shapes and sizes.*

Cell
Human heart muscle cell

Tissue
Human heart tissue

Organ
Human heart

Organism
Made of many organ systems

Organ system

Figure 8 *Multicellular organisms are made of many cells that work together in tissues and organs.*

The Big Picture

Although unicellular organisms and multicellular organisms can live on their own, they usually do not live alone. Organisms interact with each other in many different ways.

Populations A group of organisms that are of the same kind and that live in the same area make up a **population.** All of the ladybird beetles living in the forest shown in **Figure 9** make up the ladybird beetle population of that forest. All of the red oak trees make up the forest's red oak population.

Figure 9 *A population is made up of all of the individuals of the same kind that live in the same area.*

Communities Two or more different populations living in the same area make up a **community.** The populations of foxes, oak trees, lizards, flowers, and other organisms in a forest are all part of a forest community, as shown in **Figure 10.** Your hometown is a community that includes all of the people, dogs, cats, and other organisms living there.

Ecosystems The community and all of the nonliving things that affect it, such as water, soil, rocks, temperature, and light, make up an **ecosystem.** Ecosystems on land are called *terrestrial* ecosystems, and they include forests, deserts, prairies, and your own backyard. Ecosystems in water are called *aquatic* ecosystems, and they include rivers, ponds, lakes, oceans, and even aquariums. The community in Figure 10 lives in a terrestrial ecosystem.

Figure 10 *The fox, flowers, and trees are all part of a forest community.*

REVIEW

1. Complete the following sentence: *Cells* are related to ? in the same way that ? are related to *organ systems.*

2. How do the cells of unicellular organisms differ from the cells of multicellular organisms?

3. **Applying Concepts** Use the picture of an aquarium at left to answer the following questions:

   a. How many *different* kinds of organisms are visible?

   b. How many populations are visible?

   c. How many communities are visible?

The Discovery of Cells

NEW TERMS

cell theory
cell membrane
organelles
cytoplasm
surface-to-
volume ratio

nucleus
prokaryotic
eukaryotic
bacteria

OBJECTIVES

- State the parts of the cell theory.
- Explain why cells are so small.
- Calculate a cell's surface-to-volume ratio.
- List the advantages of being multicellular.
- Explain the difference between prokaryotic cells and eukaryotic cells.

Most cells are so tiny that they are not visible to the naked eye. So how did we find out that cells are the basic unit of all living things? What would make someone think that a rabbit or a tree or a person is made up of tiny parts that cannot be seen? Actually, the discovery of cells happened by accident because the first person to see cells was not even looking for them.

Seeing the First Cells

In 1665, a British scientist named Robert Hooke was trying to find something interesting that he could show to other scientists at a meeting. Earlier, he had built a crude compound microscope (one with several glass lenses) that allowed him to look at very tiny objects. One day he decided to look at a thin slice of cork, a soft plant tissue found in the bark of trees like the ones shown in **Figure 11.** To his amazement, the cork looked like hundreds of little boxes, which he described as looking like a honeycomb. He named these tiny boxes *cells,* which means "little rooms" in Latin.

Although Hooke did not realize it, these boxes were actually the outer layers of the cork cells that were left behind after the cells died. Later, he looked at thin slices of carrots, ferns, and other plants and saw that they too were made of tiny cells. He saw that some of them were even filled with "juice" (those were living cells). Hooke's microscope and drawings of cork cells are shown in **Figure 12.**

Hooke also used his microscope to look at feathers, fish scales, and the eyes of house flies, but he spent most of his time looking at plants and fungi. Since plant and fungal cells had walls that were easier to see, Hooke thought that cells were found only in those types of organisms and not in animals.

Figure 11 *Cork is a soft material found in trees. Cork cells were the first cells seen with a microscope.*

Figure 12 *This is the compound microscope that Hooke used to see the first cells. Hooke made a drawing of the cork cells that he saw.*

Seeing Cells in Other Life-Forms

In 1673, a few years after Hooke made his observations, a Dutch merchant named Anton van Leeuwenhoek (LAY vuhn hook) used one of his own hand-made microscopes to get a closer look at pond scum, similar to that shown in **Figure 13.** He was amazed to see many small creatures swimming around in the slimy ooze; he named the creatures *animalcules,* which means "little animals."

Leeuwenhoek, shown in **Figure 14,** also looked at blood he took from different animals and tartar he scraped off their teeth and his own. He observed that blood cells in fish, birds, and frogs are oval-shaped, while those in humans and dogs are flatter. He was the first person to see bacteria, and he discovered that the yeasts used to make bread dough rise are actually unicellular organisms.

Figure 13 *Leeuwenhoek saw unicellular organisms similar to these, which are found in pond scum.*

"I didn't clean my teeth (on purpose) for three days running, and then took the stuff . . . above my front teeth; and I mixed it with . . . spit and fair rain-water; and I found a few living animalcules in it too."

**Figure 14
Anton van Leeuwenhoek**

Elephant-sized "animalcules"? Find out for yourself on LabBook page 570!

The Cell Theory

After Hooke first saw the cork cells, almost two centuries passed before anyone realized that cells are present in *all* living things. Matthias Schleiden, a German scientist, looked at many slides of plant tissues and read about what other scientists had seen under the microscope. In 1838, he concluded that all plant parts are made of cells.

The next year, Theodor Schwann, a German scientist who studied animals, stated that all animal tissues are made of cells. Not long after that, Schwann wrote the first two parts of what is now known as the **cell theory:**

- **All organisms are composed of one or more cells.**
- **The cell is the basic unit of life in all living things.**

About 20 years later, in 1858, Rudolf Virchow, a German doctor, saw that cells could not develop from anything except other cells. He then wrote the third part of the cell theory:

- **All cells come from existing cells.**

Cell Similarities

Cells come in many different shapes and sizes and perform a wide variety of functions, but they all have the following things in common:

Cell Membrane All cells are surrounded by a **cell membrane.** This membrane acts as a barrier between the inside of the cell and the cell's environment. It also controls the passage of materials into and out of the cell. **Figure 15** shows the outside of a cell.

Figure 15 *The cell membrane holds the contents of the cell together.*

Hereditary Material Part of the cell theory states that all cells are made from existing cells. When new cells are made, they receive a copy of the hereditary material of the original cells. This material is *DNA* (deoxyribonucleic acid). It controls all of the activities of a cell and contains the information needed for that cell to make new cells.

Cytoplasm and Organelles All cells have chemicals and structures that enable the cell to live, grow, and reproduce. The structures are called **organelles.** Although all cells have organelles, they don't all have the same kind. Some organelles are surrounded by membranes, but others are not. The cell in **Figure 16** has membrane-covered organelles. The chemicals and structures of a cell are surrounded by fluid. This fluid and almost everything in it are collectively called the **cytoplasm** (SIET oh PLAZ um).

Organelles

Cytoplasm

Figure 16 *This cell has many organelles. Some of the organelles are surrounded by a membrane.*

Small Size Almost all cells are too small to be seen with the naked eye. You are made up of 100 trillion cells, and it would take 50 cells just to cover up the dot on the letter *i.*

Self-Check

Why do all cells need DNA? *(See page 636 to check your answer.)*

Giant Amoeba Eats New York City

This is not a headline you are likely to see in any newspaper. Why not? It's because amoebas consist of only a single cell. Most amoebas can't even grow large enough to be seen without a microscope. That's because as a cell gets larger, more materials must be able to move into and out of the cell through the cell membrane. The bigger the cell is, the more food and oxygen it needs and the more waste it produces.

To keep up with these demands, a growing cell needs a larger surface area through which it exchanges waste products and nutrients. As the cell's volume increases, its outer surface grows too. But there is a problem. The volume of a cell (the amount a cell will hold) increases at a faster rate than the area of its outer surface. Therefore, if a cell gets too large, its surface will have too few openings to allow enough materials into and out of it.

To understand why the volume of a cell increases faster than its surface area, look at the surface-to-volume ratio of the cells in **Figure 17.** The **surface-to-volume ratio** is the area of a cell's outer surface in relationship to its volume. As you can see, the surface-to-volume ratio decreases as cell size increases.

Figure 17 *The large cell has a smaller surface-to-volume ratio than the small cell. Increasing the number of cells but not their size maintains a high surface-to-volume ratio.*

Surface-to-Volume Ratio

Each side of this cell is 1 unit long.	Each side of this cell is 2 units long.	The sides of each of these 8 cells are 1 unit long.
The surface area of one side is **1 square unit.** (1 × 1 = 1)	The surface area of one side is **4 square units.** (2 × 2 = 4)	The combined surface area of these 8 cells is **48 square units.** (8 × 6 square units = 48)
The surface area of the cell is **6 square units.** (1 × 1 × 6 = 6)	This cell has a surface area of **24 square units.** (2 × 2 × 6 = 24)	The combined volume of these cells is **8 cubic units.** (8 × 1 cubic unit = 8)
The volume of this cell is **1 cubic unit.** (1 × 1 × 1 = 1)	The volume of this larger cell is **8 cubic units.** (2 × 2 × 2 = 8)	The surface-to-volume ratio of these cells is 48:8, or **6:1.**
The surface-to-volume ratio of this cell is **6:1.**	The surface-to-volume ratio of this cell is 24:8, or **3:1.**	

The Benefits of Being Multicellular Do you understand now why you are made up of many tiny cells instead of just one or a few very large cells? A single cell as big as you and shaped like you would have an incredibly small surface-to-volume ratio. The cell could not survive because its outer surface would be too small to allow in the materials it would need. Multicellular organisms grow by producing more small cells, not larger cells. An elephant's cells are the same size as yours; the elephant just has more of them.

In addition to being able to grow larger, multicellular organisms are able to do lots of other things because they are made up of different kinds of cells. Just as there are teachers who are specialized to teach, doctors and nurses who are specialized to help sick people, and mechanics who are specialized to work on cars, different cells are specialized to perform different jobs. A single cell cannot do all the things that many different cells can do. Having many different cells that are specialized for specific jobs allows multicellular organisms to perform more functions than unicellular organisms.

The different kinds of cells can form tissues and organs with different functions. Because people have specialized cells, such as bone cells, muscle cells, eye cells, and brain cells, they can sit in chairs, walk, run, watch a movie, think about what they see, and do other activities. If you enjoy doing many different things, then be glad you are not a single cell.

Figure 18 *An elephant is larger than a human because it has more cells, not larger cells.*

Surface-to-Volume Ratio

The shape of a cell can affect its surface-to-volume ratio. Examine the cells below, and answer the questions that follow:

1. What is the surface area of Cell A? of Cell B?
2. What is the volume of Cell A? of Cell B?
3. Which of the two cells pictured here has the greater surface-to-volume ratio?

Imagine that you are the lucky recipient of a pet paramecium, a type of unicellular organism. In order to properly care for your new pet, you have to figure out how much you need to feed it. The dimensions of your paramecium are roughly 125 μm × 50 μm × 20 μm. If seven food molecules can enter through each square micrometer of surface every minute, how many molecules can your pet eat in 1 minute? If your pet needs one food molecule per cubic micrometer of volume every minute to survive, how much would you have to feed it every minute?

Self-Check

1. As a cell grows larger, what happens to its surface-to-volume ratio?

2. What does a eukaryotic cell have that a prokaryotic cell does not?

(See page 636 to check your answer.)

The many different kinds of cells that exist can be divided into two groups. As you have already learned, all cells have DNA. In one group, cells have a **nucleus,** which is a membrane-covered organelle that holds the cells' DNA. In the other group, the cells' DNA is not contained in a nucleus. Cells that do not have a nucleus are **prokaryotic** (proh KAR ee AH tik), and cells that have a nucleus are **eukaryotic** (yoo KAR ee AH tik).

Prokaryotic Cells Prokaryotic cells (also called **bacteria**) are the world's smallest cells. They are called *prokaryotic* because they do not have a nucleus (*prokaryotic* means "before nucleus" in Greek). A prokaryotic cell's DNA is one long, circular molecule shaped sort of like a rubber band.

Bacteria do not have any membrane-covered organelles, but they do have tiny, round organelles called ribosomes. These organelles work like little factories to make proteins.

Most bacteria are covered by a hard cell wall outside a softer cell membrane. Think of the membrane pressing against the wall as an inflated balloon pressing against the inside of a glass jar. But unlike the balloon and jar, the membrane and the wall allow food and waste molecules to pass through. **Figure 19** shows a generalized view of a prokaryotic cell.

Bacteria were probably the first type of cells on Earth. Some scientists think they have existed for at least 3.8 billion years. The oldest fossils of bacteria ever found are estimated to be 3.5 billion years old.

*Quick*Lab

Do Bacteria Taste Good?

If they're the kind found in yogurt, they taste great! Using a **cotton swab,** put a small dot of **yogurt** on a **microscope slide.** Add a drop of **water** to the yogurt, and use the cotton swab to stir. Add a **coverslip,** and examine the slide using a **compound microscope.** Focus with the low-power objective lens, then the medium-power lens, and finally the high-power lens. Draw what you see.

The masses of rod-shaped cells are called *Lactobacillus.* These bacteria feed on the sugar in milk (lactose) and convert it into lactic acid. Lactic acid causes fluid milk to thicken, which makes yogurt!

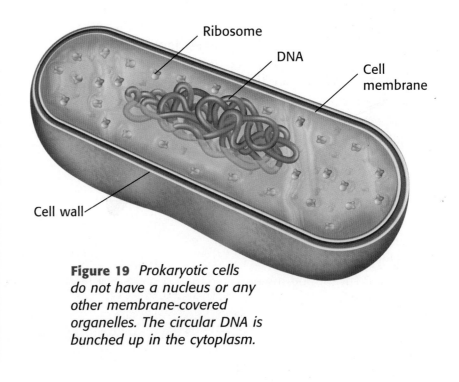

Figure 19 *Prokaryotic cells do not have a nucleus or any other membrane-covered organelles. The circular DNA is bunched up in the cytoplasm.*

Eukaryotic Cells Eukaryotic cells are more complex than prokaryotic cells. Although most eukaryotic cells are about 10 times larger than prokaryotic cells, they still have a high enough surface-to-volume ratio to survive. Fossil evidence suggests that eukaryotic cells first appeared about 2 billion years ago. All living things that are not bacteria are made of one or more eukaryotic cells. This includes plants, animals, fungi, and protists.

Eukaryotic cells have a nucleus (*eukaryotic* means "true nucleus" in Greek) and many other membrane-covered organelles. An advantage of having the cell divided into compartments is that it allows many different chemical processes to occur at the same time. A generalized eukaryotic cell is shown in **Figure 20.**

There is more DNA in eukaryotic cells than there is in prokaryotic cells, and it is stored in the nucleus. Instead of being circular, the DNA molecules in eukaryotic cells are linear.

All eukaryotic cells have a cell membrane, and some of them have a cell wall. Those that have cell walls are found in plants, fungi, and some unicellular organisms. The cell walls of eukaryotes are chemically different from the cell walls of bacteria. The tables below summarize the differences between eukaryotic and prokaryotic cells.

Nucleus

Figure 20 *Eukaryotic cells contain a nucleus and many other organelles.*

PROKARYOTIC CELLS	EUKARYOTIC CELLS
No nucleus	Nucleus
No membrane-covered organelles	Membrane-covered organelles
Circular DNA	Linear DNA
Bacteria	All other cells

across the sciences
CONNECTION

A new way to cure sick cells? See page 104.

REVIEW

1. What are the three parts of the cell theory?

2. What do all cells have in common?

3. What are two advantages of being multicellular?

4. If a unicellular organism has a cell wall, ribosomes, and circular DNA, is it eukaryotic or prokaryotic?

5. **Applying Concepts** Which has the greater surface-to-volume ratio, a tennis ball or a basketball? Explain your answer. What could be done to increase the surface-to-volume ratio of both?

Eukaryotic Cells: The Inside Story

For a long time after the discovery of cells, scientists did not really know what cells were made of. Cells are so small that the details of their structure could not be seen until better methods of magnifying and staining were developed. We now know that cells are very complex, especially eukaryotic cells. Everything, from the structures covering the cells to the organelles inside them, performs a task that helps to keep the cells alive.

Holding It All Together

All cells have outer coverings that separate what is inside the cell from what is outside the cell. One kind of covering, called the cell membrane, surrounds all cells. Some cells have an additional layer outside the cell membrane called the cell wall.

Cell Membrane All cells are covered by a cell membrane. The job of the cell membrane is to keep the cytoplasm inside, to allow nutrients in and waste products out, and to interact with things outside the cell. In **Figure 21,** you can see a close-up view of the cell membrane of a cell that has had its top half cut away.

Phospholipids

Figure 21 *A cell membrane surrounds all cells. Phospholipid molecules form the cell membrane.*

Cell Wall The cells of plants and algae have a hard cell wall made of cellulose. The **cell wall** provides strength and support to the cell membrane. When too much water enters or leaves a plant cell, the cell wall can prevent the membrane from tearing. The strength of billions of cell walls in plants enables a tree to stand tall and its limbs to defy gravity. When you are looking at dried hay, sticks, and wooden boards, you are seeing the cell walls of dead plant cells. The cells of fungi, such as mushrooms, toadstools, mold, and yeasts, have cell walls made of a chemical similar to that found in the hard covering of insects. **Figure 22** shows a cross section of a generalized plant cell and a close-up view of the cell wall.

The Cell's Library

The largest and most visible organelle in a eukaryotic cell is the nucleus. The word *nucleus* means "kernel" or "nut" (maybe it does look sort of like a nut inside a piece of candy). As you can see in **Figure 23,** the nucleus is covered by a membrane through which materials can pass.

The nucleus has often been called the control center of the cell. As you know, it stores the DNA that has information on how to make all of the cell's proteins. Almost every chemical reaction that is important to the cell's life involves some kind of protein. Sometimes a dark spot can be seen inside the nucleus. This spot is called a *nucleolus,* and it looks like a small nucleus inside the big nucleus. The nucleolus stores the materials that will be used later to make ribosomes in the cytoplasm.

Cell wall

Cell membrane

Figure 22 *The cell wall surrounds the cell membrane. In plant cells, the cell wall is made of cellulose fibers.*

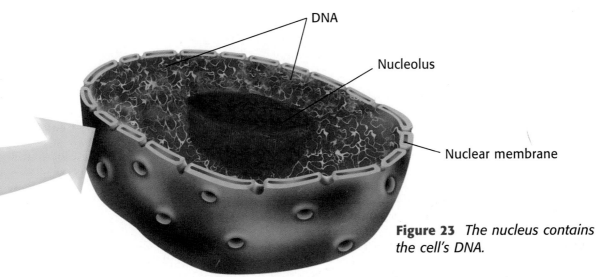

DNA

Nucleolus

Nuclear membrane

Figure 23 *The nucleus contains the cell's DNA.*

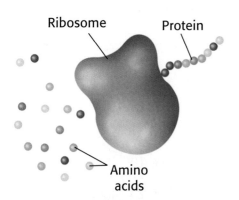

Ribosome   Protein

Amino acids

Figure 24 *Amino acids are hooked together at ribosomes to make proteins.*

✓ Self-Check

What is the difference between a cell wall and a cell membrane? *(See page 636 to check your answer.)*

Ribosome

Endoplasmic reticulum

Figure 25 *The ER is made up of flattened compartments and tubes. Ribosomes are attached to some of the ER.*

Mitochondria

Endoplasmic reticulum

Protein Factories

Proteins, the building blocks of all cells, are made up of chemicals known as *amino acids*. These amino acids are hooked together to make proteins at very small organelles called **ribosomes.** Ribosomes are the smallest but most abundant organelles and are shown in **Figure 24.** *All* cells have ribosomes because all cells need protein to live. Unlike most other organelles, ribosomes are not covered with a membrane.

The Cell's Delivery System

Eukaryotic cells have an organelle called the endoplasmic (EN doh PLAZ mik) reticulum (ri TIK yuh luhm), which is shown in **Figure 25.** The **endoplasmic reticulum,** or ER, is a membrane-covered compartment that makes lipids and other materials for use inside and outside the cell. It is also the organelle that breaks down drugs and certain other chemicals that could damage the cell. The ER is also the internal delivery system of a cell. Substances in the ER can move from one place to another through its many tubular connections, sort of like cars moving through tunnels.

The ER looks like flattened sacks stacked side by side or a cloth folded back and forth. Some ER may be covered with ribosomes that make its surface look rough. The proteins made at those ribosomes pass into the ER. Later the proteins are released from the ER for use elsewhere.

The Cell's Power Plants

In today's world, we use many sources of energy, such as oil and gas, coal, nuclear power, and even garbage. We need this energy to do all sorts of things, such as heat our homes, fuel our cars and buses, and cook our food. Cells also need energy to function and live. Where do they get it?

Mitochondria Inside all cells, food molecules are "burned" (broken down) to release energy. The energy is transferred to a special molecule that the cell uses to get work done. As you learned earlier, this molecule is called ATP.

ATP can be made at several locations in eukaryotic cells, but most of it is produced at bean-shaped organelles called **mitochondria** (MIET oh KAHN dree uh), shown in **Figure 26.** These organelles are surrounded by two membranes. The inner membrane, which has many folds in it, is where most of the ATP is made. Mitochondria can work only if they have oxygen. The reason you breathe air is to make sure your mitochondria have the oxygen they need to make ATP. Highly active cells, such as those in the heart and liver, may have thousands of mitochondria, while other cells may have only a few.

Figure 26 *Mitochondria have two membranes. The inner membrane has many folds.*

Figure 27 *Chloroplasts, found in plant cells, also have two membranes. The inner membrane forms stacks of flattened sacs.*

Chloroplasts Plants and algae have an additional kind of energy-converting organelle, called a **chloroplast,** which is shown in **Figure 27.** The word *chloroplast* means "green structure." As you can see, it also has two membranes and structures that look like stacks of coins. These are flattened, membrane-covered sacs that contain an important chemical called chlorophyll. Chlorophyll is what makes chloroplasts green. It is also what makes a chloroplast a power plant for the cell. The energy of sunlight is trapped by chlorophyll and used to make sugar. This process is called *photosynthesis.* The sugar that is produced is used by mitochondria to make ATP. You will learn more about photosynthesis in a later chapter.

Small prokaryotic cell

DNA of large cell

Large prokaryotic cell

Mitochondria

DNA enclosed in nucleus

Small prokaryotic cell that can photosynthesize

Chloroplast

Figure 28 *Mitochondria and chloroplasts may have originated from energy-producing ancestors that were engulfed by larger cells.*

Endosymbiotic Theory Many scientists believe that mitochondria and chloroplasts originated as prokaryotic cells that were "eaten" by larger cells. Instead of being digested, the bacteria survived. This theory on the origins of mitochondria and chloroplasts is called the endosymbiotic (EN doh sim bie AHT ik) theory.

What evidence do scientists have that this is how these two organelles came to be? The first piece of evidence is that mitochondria and chloroplasts are about the same size as bacteria. The second is that both are surrounded by *two membranes*. If the theory is correct, the outer membrane was created when the bacteria were engulfed by the larger cells. Other evidence that supports this theory is that mitochondria and chloroplasts have the same kind of ribosomes and circular DNA as bacteria. They also divide like bacteria. **Figure 28** shows how bacteria might have become the ancestors of mitochondria and chloroplasts.

The Cell's Packaging Center

When proteins and other materials need to be processed and shipped out of a eukaryotic cell, the job goes to an organelle called the **Golgi complex.** This structure is named after Camillo Golgi, the Italian scientist who first identified it.

The Golgi complex looks like the ER, but it is located closer to the cell membrane. The Golgi complex of a cell is shown in **Figure 29.** Lipids and proteins from the ER are delivered to the Golgi complex, where they are modified for different functions. The final products are enclosed in a piece of the Golgi complex's membrane that pinches off to form a small compartment. This small compartment transports its contents to other parts of the cell or outside of the cell.

Golgi complex

Figure 29 *The Golgi complex processes, packages, and transports materials sent to it from the ER.*

The Cell's Storage Centers

All eukaryotic cells have membrane-covered compartments called **vesicles.** Some of them form when part of the membrane pinches off the ER or Golgi complex. Others are formed when part of the cell membrane surrounds an object outside the cell. This is how white blood cells engulf other cells in your body, as shown in **Figure 30.**

Vacuoles Most plant cells have a very large membrane-covered chamber called a **vacuole.** You can see a vacuole in **Figure 31.** Vacuoles are storage containers for water and other liquids. Vacuoles that are full of water help support the cell. Some plants wilt when their cell vacuoles lose water. If you want crispy lettuce for a salad, all you need to do is fill up the vacuoles with water. This can be done by leaving the lettuce in a bowl of clean water overnight. Have you ever wondered what makes roses red and violets blue? It is a colorful liquid stored inside vacuoles. Vacuoles also contain the sour and sweet juices you associate with lemons, oranges, and other fruits.

Some unicellular organisms that live in freshwater environments have a problem with too much water entering the cell. They have a special structure called a contractile vacuole that can squeeze excess water out of the cell. It works in much the same way that a pump removes water from inside a boat.

Figure 30 *The smaller cell is a yeast cell that is being engulfed by a white blood cell.*

Vacuole

Figure 31 *This plant cell's vacuole is the large structure in the middle of the cell shown in blue. Vacuoles are usually the largest organelles in a plant cell.*

Vesicle
with food

Lysosome

Packages of Destruction

What causes most of the cells of a caterpillar to dissolve into ooze inside a cocoon? What causes the tail of a tadpole to shrink and then disappear? Lysosomes, that's what!

Lysosomes are special vesicles in animal cells that contain enzymes. When a cell engulfs a particle and encloses it in a vesicle, lysosomes bump into these vesicles and pour enzymes into them. This is illustrated in **Figure 32.** The particles in the vesicles are digested by the enzymes.

Lysosomes destroy worn-out or damaged organelles. They also get rid of waste materials and protect the cell from foreign invaders.

Sometimes lysosome membranes break, and the enzymes spill into the cytoplasm, killing the cell. This is what must happen for a tadpole to become a frog. Lysosomes cause the cells in a tadpole's tail to die and dissolve as the tadpole becomes a frog. Lysosomes played a similar role in your development! Before you were born, lysosomes caused the destruction of cells that formed the webbing between your fingers. Lysosome destruction of cells may also be one of the factors that contribute to the aging process in humans.

Figure 32 *This lysosome is pouring enzymes into a vesicle that contains food particles. Once digested, the food molecules are released into the cytoplasm so that they can be used by the cell.*

Organelles and Their Functions

Nucleus contains the cell's DNA and is the control center of the cell	**Chloroplasts** make food using the energy of sunlight
Ribosomes the site where amino acids are hooked together to make proteins	**Golgi complex** processes and transports materials out of the cell
Endoplasmic reticulum makes lipids, breaks down drugs and other substances, packages up proteins for release from the cell	**Vacuole** stores water and other materials
Mitochondria break down food molecules to make ATP	**Lysosomes** digest food particles, wastes, cell parts, and foreign invaders

Plant or Animal?

How can you tell the difference between a plant cell and an animal cell? They both have a cell membrane, and they both have nuclei, ribosomes, mitochondria, endoplasmic reticula, Golgi complexes, and lysosomes. But plant cells have things that animal cells do not have: a cell wall, chloroplasts, and a large vacuole. You can see the differences between plant and animal cells in **Figure 33.**

Figure 33 *Animal and plant cells have some structures in common, but they also have some that are unique.*

Found in Plant and Animal Cells

Animal cell

Cell membrane	Mitochondria
Nucleus	Golgi complex
Ribosomes	Lysosomes

Found Only in Plant Cells

Plant cell

Cell wall

Large vacuoles

Chloroplasts

REVIEW

1. How does the nucleus control the cell's activities?

2. Which of the following would not be found in an animal cell: mitochondria, cell wall, chloroplast, ribosome, endoplasmic reticulum, Golgi complex, vacuole, DNA, chlorophyll?

3. Use the following words in a sentence: oxygen, ATP, breathing, and mitochondria.

4. **Applying Concepts** Suppose you are assigned the job of giving new names to different things in a city but the new names have to be parts of a eukaryotic cell. Write down some things you would see in a city, and assign them the name of a cell part that is most appropriate to their function. Explain your choices.

Chapter Highlights

Vocabulary

tissue (p. 81)

organ (p. 81)

organ systems (p. 82)

organism (p. 83)

unicellular (p. 83)

multicellular (p. 83)

population (p. 83)

community (p. 84)

ecosystem (p. 84)

Section Notes

- The cell is the smallest unit of life on Earth. Organisms can be made up of one or more cells.

- In multicellular organisms, groups of cells can work together to form tissue. Organs are formed from different tissues and work together with other organs in organ systems.

- The same kind of organisms living together in the same place at the same time make up a population. Different populations living together in the same area make up a community. An ecosystem includes the community and an area's nonliving parts, such as the water and soil.

Vocabulary

cell theory (p. 86)

cell membrane (p. 87)

organelles (p. 87)

cytoplasm (p. 87)

surface-to-volume ratio (p. 88)

nucleus (p. 90)

prokaryotic (p. 90)

eukaryotic (p. 90)

bacteria (p. 90)

Section Notes

- The cell theory states that all organisms are made of cells, the cell is the basic unit of life, and all cells come from other cells.

- All cells have a cell membrane, DNA, cytoplasm, and organelles. Most cells are too small to be seen with the naked eye.

☑ Skills Check

Math Concepts

SURFACE-TO-VOLUME RATIO You can determine the surface-to-volume ratio of a cell or other object by dividing surface area by the volume. To determine the surface-to-volume ratio of the rectangle at left, you must first determine the surface area. Surface area is the total area of all the sides. This rectangle has two sides with an area of 6 cm × 3 cm, two sides with an area of 3 cm × 2 cm, and two sides with an area of 6 cm × 2 cm.

6 cm

2 cm

3 cm

surface area = 2(6 cm × 3 cm) + 2(3 cm × 2 cm)
+ 2(6 cm × 2 cm) = 72 cm^2

Next you need to find the volume. The volume is determined by multiplying the length of the three sides.

volume = 6 cm × 3 cm × 2 cm = 36 cm^3

To find surface-to-volume ratio, you divide the surface area by the volume:

$$\frac{72}{36} = 2$$

So the surface-to-volume ratio of this rectangle is 2:1.

- Materials that cells need to take in or release must pass through the cell membrane.

- The surface-to-volume ratio is a comparison of the cell's outer surface to the cell's volume. A cell's surface-to-volume ratio decreases as the cell grows.

  - Eukaryotes have linear DNA enclosed in a nucleus and membrane-covered organelles. Prokaryotic cells have circular DNA and organelles that are not covered by membranes.

Labs

Elephant-Sized Amoebas *(p. 570)*

Vocabulary

cell wall *(p. 93)*

ribosomes *(p. 94)*

endoplasmic reticulum *(p. 94)*

mitochondria *(p. 95)*

chloroplast *(p. 95)*

Golgi complex *(p. 96)*

vesicles *(p. 97)*

vacuole *(p. 97)*

lysosomes *(p. 98)*

Section Notes

- All cells have a cell membrane that surrounds the contents of the cell. Some cells have a cell wall outside their membrane.

- The nucleus is the control center of the eukaryotic cell. It contains the cell's DNA.

- Ribosomes are the sites where amino acids are strung together to form proteins.

Ribosomes are not covered by a membrane.

- The endoplasmic reticulum (ER) and the Golgi complex are membrane-covered compartments in which materials are made and processed before they are transported to other parts of the cell or out of the cell.

- Mitochondria and chloroplasts are energy-producing organelles.

- Vesicles and vacuoles are membrane-covered compartments that store material. Vacuoles are found in plant cells. Lysosomes are vesicles found in animal cells.

Labs

Cells Alive! *(p. 572)*
Name That Part! *(p. 573)*

14106545

---

  internetconnect

 GO TO: go.hrw.com

Visit the **HRW** Web site for a variety of learning tools related to this chapter. Just type in the keyword:

KEYWORD: HSTCEL

SCI LINKS **NSTA** **GO TO:** www.scilinks.org

Visit the **National Science Teachers Association** on-line Web site for Internet resources related to this chapter. Just type in the *sci*LINKS number for more information about the topic:

TOPIC: Organization of Life	*sci*LINKS NUMBER: HSTL055
TOPIC: Populations, Communities, and Ecosystems	*sci*LINKS NUMBER: HSTL060
TOPIC: Prokaryotic Cells	*sci*LINKS NUMBER: HSTL065
TOPIC: Eukaryotic Cells	*sci*LINKS NUMBER: HSTL070

Chapter Review

USING VOCABULARY

To complete the following sentences, choose the correct term from each pair of terms listed below:

1. The cell wall of plant cells is made of __?__. (*lipids* or *cellulose*)

2. Having membrane-covered organelles is a characteristic of __?__ cells. (*prokaryotic* or *eukaryotic*)

3. The information for how to make proteins is located in the __?__. (*Golgi complex* or *nucleus*)

4. The two organelles that can generate ATP in a plant cell are __?__ and __?__. (*chloroplasts/ER* or *mitochondria/ chloroplasts*)

5. Vesicles that will transport materials out of the cell are formed at the __?__. (*Golgi complex* or *cell membrane*)

UNDERSTANDING CONCEPTS

Multiple Choice

6. Which of the following is *not* found in animal cells?
   a. cell wall
   b. cell membrane
   c. lysosomes
   d. vesicle

7. Different __?__ work together in an organ.
   a. organ systems
   b. tissues
   c. organisms
   d. prokaryotes

8. Which of the following refers to all of the organisms in a particular area?
   a. population
   b. ecosystem
   c. community
   d. organelles

9. The scientist who said that all cells come from cells was named
   a. Virchow.
   b. Schleiden.
   c. Hooke.
   d. Schwann.

10. Which of the following are *not* covered by a membrane?
    a. Golgi complex
    b. mitochondria
    c. ribosomes
    d. none of the above

11. Which of the following contain enzymes that can break down particles in vesicles?
    a. mitochondria
    b. endoplasmic reticulum
    c. lysosomes
    d. none of the above

Short Answer

12. Why are most cells so small?

13. What five characteristics of mitochondria suggest that they may have originated as bacteria?

14. In your own words, list the three parts of the cell theory.

Concept Mapping

15. Use the following terms to create a concept map: ecosystem, cells, organisms, Golgi complex, organ systems, community, organs, endoplasmic reticulum, nucleus, population, tissues.

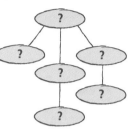

CRITICAL THINKING AND PROBLEM SOLVING

Write one or two sentences to answer the following questions:

16. Explain how the nucleus can control what happens in a lysosome.

17. Even though cellulose is not made at ribosomes, explain how ribosomes in a plant cell are important to the formation of a cell wall.

MATH IN SCIENCE

18. Assume that three food molecules per cubic unit of volume per minute is required for the cell below to survive. If one molecule can enter through each square unit of surface per minute, this cell is
    a. too big and would starve.
    b. too small and would starve.
    c. at a size that would allow it to survive.

3

3   2

INTERPRETING GRAPHICS

Look at the cell diagrams below, and answer the questions that follow:

Cell A

19

Cell B

21

19. Name the organelle labeled "19" in Cell A.

20. Is Cell A a bacterial cell, a plant cell, or an animal cell? Explain your answer.

21. What is the name and function of the organelle labeled "21" in Cell B?

22. Is Cell B a prokaryotic cell or a eukaryotic cell? Explain your answer.

NOW What Do You Think?

Take a minute to review your answers to the ScienceLog questions on page 79. Have your answers changed? If necessary, revise your answers based on what you have learned since you began this chapter.

Battling Cancer with Pigs' Blood and Laser Light

What do you get when you cross pigs' blood and laser beams? Would you believe a treatment for cancer? Medical researchers have developed an effective new cancer treatment called *photodynamic therapy,* or PDT. It combines high-energy laser beams with a light-sensitive drug derived from pigs' blood to combat the deadly disease.

▲ *Blood from pigs provides substances used to help treat cancer.*

Pigs' Blood to the Rescue

The first step in PDT involves a light-sensitive substance called *porphyrin.* Porphyrins are natural chemicals found in red blood cells that bind to lipoproteins, which carry cholesterol in our blood. They are important because they can absorb energy from light. All cells use lipoproteins to make their cell membranes. But cells that divide quickly, like cancer cells, make membranes faster than normal cells. Since they use more lipoproteins, they also accumulate more porphyrins. Scientists have developed a synthetic porphyrin, called Photofrin®, made from natural porphyrins found in pigs' blood. When Photofrin is injected into a patient's bloodstream, it acts the same way natural porphyrins do—it becomes part of the cell membranes formed by cancer cells. A short time later, the patient visits a surgeon's office for step two of PDT, zapping the diseased tissue with a laser beam.

Hitting the Target

A surgeon threads a long, thin laser-tipped tube into the cancerous area where the Photofrin has accumulated. When the laser beam hits the cancerous tissue, Photofrin absorbs the light energy. Then, in a process similar to photosynthesis, Photofrin releases oxygen. The type of oxygen released damages the proteins, lipids, nucleic acids, and other components of cancer cells. This damage kills off cancer cells in the treated area but doesn't kill healthy cells. Photofrin is more sensitive to certain wavelengths of light than are natural porphyrins. And the intense beam of laser light can be precisely focused on the cancerous tissue without affecting nearby healthy tissue.

An Alternative?

PDT is an important medical development because it kills cancer cells without many of the harmful side effects caused by other cancer therapies, such as chemotherapy. However, PDT does have some side effects. Until the drug wears off, in about 30 days, the patient is susceptible to severe sunburn. Researchers are working to develop a second-generation drug, called BPD (benzoporphyrin derivative), that will have fewer side effects and respond to different wavelengths of lasers. BPD is also being tested for use in certain eye diseases and as a treatment for psoriasis.

Find Out for Yourself

▶ Do some research to find out why scientists used pigs' blood to create Photofrin.

The Scrape of the Future

What did you do the last time you scraped your knee? You probably put a bandage on it, and before you realized it your knee was as good as new. Basically, bandages serve as barriers that help prevent infection and further injury. But what if there were such a thing as a living bandage that actually helped your body heal? It sounds like science fiction, but it's not!

▲ *Dr. Daniel Smith holds the GEBB that he designed.*

The Main Factor

An injury to the skin, such as a scraped knee, triggers skin cells to produce and release a steady stream of proteins that heal the injury. These naturally occurring proteins are called *human growth factors,* or just *growth factors.* Growth factors specialize in rebuilding the body. Some reconstruct connective tissue that provides structure for new skin, some help rebuild blood vessels in a wounded area, and still others stimulate the body's immune system. Thanks to growth factors, scraped skin usually heals in just a few days.

Help from a Living Bandage

Unfortunately, healing isn't always an easy, natural process. Someone with a weakened immune system may be unable to produce enough growth factors to heal a wound properly. For example, someone with severe burns may have lost the ability in the burned area to produce the proteins necessary to rebuild healthy tissues. In these cases, using manufactured human growth factors can greatly assist the healing process.

Recent advances in bioengineering can help people whose immune system prevents them from healing naturally. The Genetically Engineered Biological Bandage (GEBB) is a special bandage that is actually a bag of living skin cells taken from donors. The cells' DNA is manipulated to produce human growth factors. The GEBB is about 1 cm thick and consists of three layers: a thin gauze layer; a thin, permeable artificial membrane; and a dome-shaped silicone bag containing the growth factors. The bandage is applied to the wound just as a normal bandage is, with the gauze layer closest to the injury. The growth factors leave the silicone bag through the membrane and pass through the gauze into the wound. There they act on the wound just as the body's own growth factors would.

Time-Release Formula

The GEBB also helps heal wounds more quickly. It maximizes the effectiveness of growth hormones by releasing them at a constant rate over 3 to 5 days.

Because the GEBB imitates the body's own healing processes, other versions of the living bandage will likely be used in the future to treat a variety of wounds and skin conditions, such as severe acne.

Think About It

▶ Can you think of other advances in medical technology, such as eyeglasses or a hearing aid, that mimic or enhance what the human body does naturally?

5 The Cell in Action

Happy 140th Birthday!

What If . . . ?

How long would you like to live? What if you could live to be 120 years old? or 150 and beyond? Since ancient times, people have searched in vain for a magical fountain or potion that could give them eternal youth. No one has yet found the secret of immortality, but scientists have recently made a startling discovery that may help extend people's lives.

In January of 1998, researchers at the University of Texas reported that they had found an enzyme in the body that acts like a "cellular fountain of youth." In the laboratory, the enzyme enables human cells to stay young and multiply long past the time when cells would normally stop dividing and die. Researchers hope that the enzyme can someday be used to understand and treat certain cancers and other incurable diseases. Although the so-called immortalizing enzyme won't help people live forever, it may help them live longer, healthier lives.

Every living thing is made of cells. In this chapter you will learn how cells grow and how they make more cells. You will also learn how cells transport materials and obtain the energy they need to survive.

What Do You Think?

In your ScienceLog, try to answer the following questions based on what you already know:

1. How do water, food, and wastes get into and out of a cell?

2. How are food molecules used by a cell?

3. How does one cell produce many cells?

Cells in Action

Yeast are unicellular fungi that are frequently used in cooking. Yeast cells feed on sugar. They break down sugar molecules to release energy. This energy keeps them alive.

When yeast cells release energy from sugar, a gas called carbon dioxide (CO_2) is produced. CO_2 bubbles make bread dough rise. The amount of CO_2 produced depends on how much sugar is broken down.

Procedure

1. From your teacher, get a **small plastic cup** that contains 10 mL of a **yeast-and-water mixture.**

2. Next fill a **small test tube** with 4 mL of a **sugar solution** that has also been prepared by your teacher. Pour it into the cup containing the yeast-and-water mixture. Thoroughly mix the two liquids with a **stirring rod.**

3. Pour the contents of the small plastic cup back into the small test tube.

4. As shown in the figure below, place a slightly **larger test tube** over the small test tube. The top of the small test tube should touch the bottom of the large test tube.

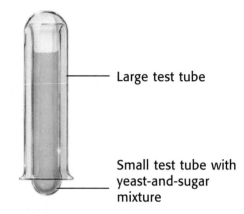

Large test tube

Small test tube with yeast-and-sugar mixture

5. Quickly turn the tubes over. As shown below, most of the yeast-and-water mixture should still be contained in the small test tube. Some of the mixture will be in the larger test tube. Use a **ruler** to measure the height of the fluid in the large test tube.

6. Place the test tubes in a **test-tube stand,** and do not disturb them for 20 minutes. After 20 minutes, measure the height of the liquid in the outer test tube again.

Analysis

7. What is the difference between the first height measurement and the second?

8. What do you think caused the change in the height of the fluid?

Exchange with the Environment

NEW TERMS

diffusion   active transport

osmosis   endocytosis

passive transport exocytosis

OBJECTIVES

- Explain the process of diffusion.
- Describe how osmosis occurs.
- Compare and contrast passive transport and active transport.
- Explain how large particles get into and out of cells.

What would happen to a factory if its power were shut off or its supply of raw materials never arrived? What if the factory weren't able to get rid of its garbage? If a factory doesn't have power or raw materials and is filling up with trash, it will stop functioning. Just like a factory, a cell must be able to obtain energy and raw materials and get rid of wastes.

The exchange of materials between a cell and its environment takes place at the cell's membrane. Before reading about how materials move into and out of the cell, you need to understand diffusion, a process that affects the movement of particles.

What Is Diffusion?

What will happen if you pour dye into a container of solid gelatin? At first, it will be easy to see where the gelatin ends and the dye begins. But over time the line between the two layers will become blurry, as shown in **Figure 1.** Why does this happen? The dye and the gelatin, like all matter, are made up of tiny particles. The particles of matter are always moving and colliding with each other. The mixing of the different particles causes the layers to blur. This occurs whether matter is in the form of a gas, a liquid, or a solid.

Figure 1 *The particles of the dye and the gelatin slowly begin to mix because of diffusion.*

Quick Lab

Bead Diffusion

Arrange three groups of **colored beads** on the bottom of a **plastic bowl.** Each group should have five beads of the same color. Stretch some **clear plastic wrap** tightly over the top of the bowl. Gently shake the bowl for 10 seconds while watching the beads. How is the scattering of the beads like the diffusion of particles? How is it different from the diffusion of particles?

Particles naturally travel from areas where they are crowded to areas where they are less crowded. This kind of movement is called diffusion. **Diffusion** is the movement of particles from an area where their concentration is high to an area where their concentration is low. This movement can occur across cell membranes or outside of cells. Organisms, or their cells, do not need to use any energy for diffusion of particles to occur.

Diffusion of Water All organisms need water to live. The cells of living organisms are surrounded by and filled with fluids that are made mostly of water. The diffusion of water through the cell membrane is so important to life processes that it has been given a special name—**osmosis.**

Water, like all matter, is made up of small particles. Pure water has the highest possible concentration of water particles. To lower this concentration, you simply mix water with something else, such as food coloring, sugar, or salt. **Figure 2** shows what happens when osmosis occurs between two different concentrations of water.

The Cell and Osmosis As you have learned, water particles will move from areas of high concentration to areas of lower concentration. This concept is especially important when you look at it in relation to your cells.

For example, **Figure 3** shows the effects of different concentrations of water on a red blood cell. As you can see, osmosis takes place in different directions depending on the concentration of water surrounding the cell. Fortunately for you, your red blood cells are normally surrounded by blood plasma, which is made up of water, salts, sugars, and other particles in the same concentration as they exist inside the red blood cells.

The cells of plants also take in and release water by osmosis. This is why a wilted plant or even a wilted stalk of celery will become firm again if given water.

✓ Self-Check

What would happen to a grape if you placed it in a dish of pure water? What would happen to it if you soaked it in water mixed with a large amount of sugar? *(See page 636 to check your answer.)*

Figure 2 *This container is divided by a barrier. Particles of water are small enough to pass through the barrier, but the particles of food coloring are not.*

❶ The side of the container with pure water has the higher concentration of water.

❷ During osmosis, water particles move to where they are less concentrated.

ⓐ This cell has a normal shape because the concentration of water in the cell is the same as the concentration outside the cell.

ⓑ This cell is in pure water. It is gaining water because the concentration of water particles is lower inside the cell than outside.

Figure 3 *The shape of these red blood cells is affected by the concentration of water outside the cell.*

Moving Small Particles

Many particles, such as water and oxygen, can diffuse directly through the cell membrane, which is made of phospholipid molecules. These particles can slip through the molecules of the membrane in part because of their small size. However, not all of the particles a cell needs can pass through the membrane in this way. For example, sugar and amino acids aren't small enough to squeeze between the phospholipid molecules, and they are also repelled by the phospholipids in the membrane. They must travel through protein "doorways" located in the cell membrane in order to enter or leave the cell.

Particles can travel through these proteins either by passive transport or by active transport. **Passive transport,** shown in **Figure 4,** is the diffusion of particles through the proteins. The particles move from an area of high concentration to an area of low concentration. The cell does not need to use any energy to make this happen.

Active transport, shown in **Figure 5,** is the movement of particles through proteins against the normal direction of diffusion. In other words, particles are moved from an area of low concentration to an area of high concentration. The cell must use energy to make this happen. This energy comes from the molecule ATP, which stores energy in a form that cells can use.

Help solve The Perfect Taters Mystery on page 574 of the LabBook!

PASSIVE TRANSPORT

Cell membrane

A particle in an area of high concentration diffuses through a protein.

Figure 4 *In passive transport, particles travel through proteins from areas of high concentration to areas of low concentration.*

ACTIVE TRANSPORT

ATP

Energy from ATP is used to move a particle through a protein against the direction of diffusion.

Figure 5 *In active transport, cells use energy to move particles from areas of low concentration to areas of high concentration.*

Moving Large Particles

Diffusion, passive transport, and active transport are good methods of moving small particles into and out of cells, but what about moving large particles? The cell membrane has two ways of accomplishing this task: *endocytosis* and *exocytosis*. In **endocytosis,** the cell membrane surrounds a particle and encloses it in a vesicle. This is how large particles, such as other cells, can be brought into a cell, as shown in **Figure 6.**

Figure 6 Endocytosis *means "within the cell."*

❶ The cell comes into contact with a particle.

❷ The cell membrane begins to wrap around the particle.

❸ Once the particle is completely surrounded, a vesicle pinches off.

When a large particle must be removed from the cell, the cell uses a different process. In **exocytosis,** vesicles are formed at the endoplasmic reticulum or Golgi complex and carry the particles to the cell membrane, as shown in **Figure 7.**

❶ Large particles that must leave the cell are packaged in vesicles.

❷ The vesicle travels to the cell membrane and fuses with it.

❸ The cell releases the particles into its environment.

Figure 7 Exocytosis *means "outside the cell."*

REVIEW

1. During diffusion, do particles move from areas of low concentration to areas of high concentration or from areas of high concentration to areas of low concentration?

2. How does a cell take in large particles? How does a cell expel large particles?

3. **Making Inferences** The transfer of glucose into a cell does not require ATP. What type of transport supplies a cell with glucose? Explain your answer.

Cell Energy

Why do you get hungry? Feeling hungry is your body's way of telling you that your cells need energy. Your cells and the cells of all organisms use energy to carry out the chemical activities that allow them to live, grow, and reproduce.

From Sun to Cell

Nearly all of the energy that fuels life comes from the sun. How do your cells get this energy? They get it from the food you eat. Like many other kinds of organisms, you must eat plants or organisms that have eaten plants. This is because plants are able to capture light energy from the sun and change it into food through a process called **photosynthesis.** *Photosynthesis* means "made by light." The food that plants make supplies them with energy and also becomes a source of energy for the organisms that eat the plants. Without plants and other producers, consumers would not be able to live.

Photosynthesis Plants have molecules in their cells that absorb the energy of light. These molecules are called *pigments.* Chlorophyll, the main pigment used in photosynthesis, gives plants their green color. In the cells of plants, chlorophyll is found in chloroplasts, which are shown in **Figure 8.**

Plants use the energy captured by chlorophyll to change carbon dioxide (CO_2) and water (H_2O) into food. The food that is produced is the simple sugar glucose ($C_6H_{12}O_6$). Glucose is a carbohydrate. When plants make glucose, they are converting the sun's energy into a form of energy that can be stored. The energy in glucose is used by the plant's cells, and some of it may be stored in the form of other carbohydrates or lipids. Photosynthesis also produces oxygen (O_2). The process of photosynthesis can be summarized by the following equation:

NEW TERMS
photosynthesis
cellular respiration
fermentation

OBJECTIVES
- Describe the processes of photosynthesis and cellular respiration.
- Compare and contrast cellular respiration and fermentation.

Plant Cell

Chloroplast

$$6CO_2 + 6H_2O + \text{light energy} \longrightarrow C_6H_{12}O_6 + 6O_2$$

Carbon dioxide   Water   Glucose   Oxygen

Figure 8 *During photosynthesis, plant cells use the energy in sunlight to make food (glucose) from carbon dioxide and water. Photosynthesis takes place in chloroplasts.*

Getting Energy from Food

Although your cells get the energy they need from food, cells can't directly use a banana or a slice of pizza for energy. The food you eat has to be broken down so that the energy it contains can be converted into a form your cells can use. In fact, all organisms must break down food molecules in order to release the energy stored in food. There are two ways to do this. One way uses oxygen and is called **cellular respiration.** The other way does not use oxygen and is called **fermentation.**

Cellular Respiration   The word *respiration* means "breathing," but cellular respiration is not the same thing as breathing even though they are closely related. Breathing supplies your cells with the oxygen they need to perform cellular respiration. Breathing also rids your body of carbon dioxide, which is a waste product of cellular respiration.

Most organisms, such as the cow in **Figure 9,** use cellular respiration to obtain energy that is stored in food. During cellular respiration, food (glucose) is broken down into CO_2 and H_2O, and energy is released. A lot of the energy is stored in the form of ATP. As you have learned, ATP is the molecule that supplies energy to fuel the activities of cells. Most of the energy released, however, is in the form of heat. In some organisms, including yourself, this heat helps to maintain the body's temperature.

In the cells of plants, animals, and other eukaryotes, cellular respiration takes place in mitochondria. The process of cellular respiration is summarized in the following equation:

$$C_6H_{12}O_6 + 6O_2 \longrightarrow 6CO_2 + 6H_2O + \text{energy (ATP)}$$

| Glucose | Oxygen | Carbon dioxide | Water |

Does the equation for respiration remind you of the equation for photosynthesis? Look at the diagram on the following page to see how photosynthesis and respiration are related.

Explore

List five foods you have eaten in the last 24 hours that were originally part of another organism. Write down the names of those organisms. Which were producers? Which were consumers, like you?

across the sciences
CONNECTION

Can the energy produced by cells be used to make electricity? Find out on page 124.

Mitochondria

Animal Cell

Figure 9 *The mitochondria in the cells of this cow will use cellular respiration to release the energy stored in the grass.*

The Cell in Action   **113**

Photosynthesis and Respiration: What's the Connection?

ATP

Photosynthesis
Light energy, carbon dioxide, and water are used to make glucose in chloroplasts. Oxygen is released.

Light Energy

$$CO_2 + H_2O$$

Chloroplast

Mitochondrion

$$C_6H_{12}O_6 + O_2$$

Cellular Respiration
Oxygen and the energy in glucose are used to make ATP. ATP is a molecule that stores energy in a form that cells can use. ATP is produced by mitochondria. Carbon dioxide and water are also released. Cellular respiration occurs in both plant and animal cells.

You have been given the assignment of restoring life to a barren island. What types of organisms would you put on the island? If you want to have animals on the island, what other organisms must be on the island as well? Explain your answer.

Figure 10 *When no oxygen is present, muscle cells use fermentation to make ATP from sugar. Lactic acid is also produced and may cause the muscles to "burn" when exercising.*

Fermentation Have you ever run so far that you started to feel a burning sensation in your muscles? Well, sometimes your muscle cells can't get the oxygen they need to produce ATP by cellular respiration. When this happens, they use the process of fermentation. Fermentation leads to the production of a small amount of ATP and products from the partial breakdown of glucose.

There are two major types of fermentation, as described in **Figure 10** and **Figure 11**. The first type occurs in your muscles. It produces lactic acid, which contributes to muscle fatigue after strenuous activity. This type of fermentation also occurs in the muscle cells of other animals and in some types of fungi and bacteria. The second type of fermentation occurs in certain types of bacteria and in yeast.

Figure 11 *Yeast cells make carbon dioxide and alcohol during the fermentation of sugar. The carbon dioxide causes bubbles to form in bread.*

REVIEW

1. Why are producers important to the survival of all other organisms?

2. How do the processes of photosynthesis and cellular respiration relate to each other?

3. What does breathing have to do with cellular respiration?

4. How are respiration and fermentation similar? How are they different?

5. **Identifying Relationships** In which cells would you expect to find the greater number of mitochondria: cells that are very active or cells that are not very active? Why?

earth science
CONNECTION

When the Earth was young, its atmosphere lacked oxygen. The first forms of life used fermentation to gain energy. After organisms evolved the ability to photosynthesize, about 3 billion years ago, the oxygen they produced was added to the atmosphere.

The Cell Cycle

In the time that it takes you to read this sentence, your body will have produced millions of new cells! Why does your body need to produce so many new cells? As with all other multicellular organisms, producing new cells allows you to grow and replace cells that have died. For example, the environment in your stomach is so acidic that the cells lining it must be replaced every week!

The Life of a Cell

As you grow from an infant to an adult, you pass through different stages in life. Similarly, your cells pass through different stages in their life cycle. The life cycle of a cell is known as the **cell cycle.**

The cell cycle begins when the cell is formed and ends when the cell divides and forms new cells. Before a cell divides, it must make a copy of its DNA and other materials that are needed to carry out the processes of life. As you have read, DNA contains the information that tells a cell how to make proteins. The DNA of a cell is organized into structures called **chromosomes.** In some organisms, chromosomes also contain protein. Copying chromosomes ensures that each new cell will have all of the necessary tools for survival.

How does a cell make more cells? Well, that depends on whether the cell is prokaryotic or eukaryotic.

Making More Prokaryotic Cells As you learned earlier, prokaryotic cells (bacteria) and their DNA are not very complex. Bacteria have ribosomes and a single, circular chromosome, but they don't have any membrane-covered organelles. Because of this, division in bacteria is fairly simple. This simple type of cell division is called **binary fission,** which means "splitting into two parts." Each of the resulting cells contains one copy of the DNA. Some of the bacteria in **Figure 12** are undergoing binary fission.

$$\div \quad 5 \div \quad \Omega \quad \leq \quad \infty \quad +\Omega \quad \sqrt{} \quad 9 \quad \infty \quad \leq \quad \Sigma \quad 2$$

MATH BREAK

Cell Multiplication

It takes Cell *A* 6 hours to complete its cell cycle and produce two cells. The cell cycle of Cell *B* takes 8 hours. How many more cells would be formed from Cell *A* than from Cell *B* in 24 hours?

Figure 12 *Bacteria reproduce by pinching in two.*

Eukaryotic Cells and Their DNA Eukaryotic cells are usually much larger and more complex than prokaryotic cells. Because of this, eukaryotic cells have a lot more DNA. The chromosomes of eukaryotes contain DNA and proteins.

The number of chromosomes in the cells of eukaryotes differs from one kind of organism to the next and has nothing to do with the complexity of an organism. For example, fruit flies have 8 chromosomes, potatoes have 48, and humans have 46. **Figure 13** shows the 46 chromosomes of a human body cell lined up in pairs. These pairs are made up of similar chromosomes known as **homologous** (hoh MAHL uh guhs) **chromosomes.**

Making More Eukaryotic Cells The eukaryotic cell cycle includes three main stages. In the first stage, the cell grows and copies its organelles and chromosomes. During this time, the strands of DNA and proteins are like loosely coiled pieces of thread. After each chromosome is duplicated, the two copies are held together at a region called the **centromere** and are called **chromatids.** The chromatids each twist and coil and condense into an X shape, as shown in **Figure 14.** After this happens, the cell enters the second stage of the cell cycle.

In the second stage, the chromatids separate. The complicated process of chromosome separation is **mitosis.** Mitosis ensures that each new cell receives a copy of each chromosome. Mitosis can be divided into four phases, as shown on the following pages.

In the third stage of the cell cycle, the cell divides and produces two cells that are identical to the original cell. The process of cell division will be discussed after mitosis has been described.

Figure 13 *Human body cells have 46 chromosomes, or 23 pairs of homologous chromosomes.*

Chromatids

Centromere

Figure 14 *Two strands of DNA and protein coiled together to form this duplicated chromosome, which consists of two chromatids.*

Self-Check

After duplication, how many chromatids are there in a pair of homologous chromosomes? *(See page 636 to check your answer.)*

Mitosis and the Cell Cycle

The diagram below shows the cell cycle and the phases of mitosis in an animal cell. Although mitosis is a continuous process, it can be divided into the four phases that are shown and described. As you know, different types of living things have different numbers of chromosomes. In this diagram, only four chromosomes are shown to make it easier to see what's happening.

Before mitosis begins, the chromosomes and other cell materials are copied. The pair of *centrioles,* which are two cylindrical structures, are also copied. Each chromosome now consists of two chromatids.

Mitosis Phase 1

Mitosis begins. The nuclear membrane breaks apart. Chromosomes condense into rodlike structures. The two pairs of centrioles move to opposite sides of the cell. Fibers form between the two pairs of centrioles and attach to the centromeres.

Mitosis Phase 2

The chromosomes line up along the equator of the cell.

Mitosis Phase 3

The chromatids separate and are pulled to opposite sides of the cell by the fibers attached to the centrioles.

Mitosis Phase 4

The nuclear membrane forms around the two sets of chromosomes, and they unwind. The fibers disappear. Mitosis is completed.

Once mitosis is completed, the cytoplasm splits in two. This process is called **cytokinesis**. The result is two identical cells that are also identical to the original cell from which they were formed. After cytokinesis, the cell cycle is complete, and the new cells are at the beginning of their next cell cycle.

More About Cytokinesis In animal cells and other eukaryotes that do not have cell walls, division of the cytoplasm begins at the cell membrane. The cell membrane begins to pinch inward to form a groove, which eventually pinches all the way through the cell, and two daughter cells are formed. Cytokinesis in an animal cell is shown above.

Eukaryotic cells that have a cell wall, such as the cells of plants, algae, and fungi, do things a little differently. In these organisms, a *cell plate* forms in the middle of the cell and becomes the new cell membranes that will separate the two new cells. After the cell is split in two, a new cell wall forms between the two membranes. Cytokinesis in a plant cell is shown in **Figure 15.**

Cell plate

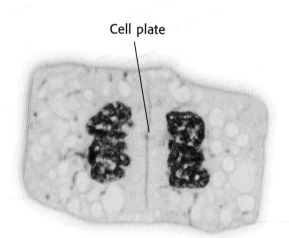

Figure 15 *When plant cells divide, a cell plate forms in the middle and grows toward the edge until the cell is split in two.*

REVIEW

1. How are binary fission and mitosis similar? How are they different?

2. Why is it important for chromosomes to be copied before cell division?

3. How does cytokinesis differ in animals and plants?

4. **Applying Concepts** What would happen if cytokinesis occurred without mitosis?

Chapter Highlights

Vocabulary

diffusion *(p. 108)*

osmosis *(p. 109)*

passive transport *(p. 110)*

active transport *(p. 110)*

endocytosis *(p. 111)*

exocytosis *(p. 111)*

Section Notes

- A cell can survive only if food molecules are taken into the cell and waste materials are removed. Materials enter and leave the cell by passing through the cell membrane. The cell membrane allows some materials to pass through but prevents others.

- A cell does not need to use energy to move particles from regions of high concentration to regions of low concentration. This type of movement is called diffusion.

- Osmosis is the diffusion of water through a membrane.

- Some substances enter and leave a cell by passing through proteins. During passive transport, substances diffuse through proteins. During active transport, substances are moved from areas of low concentration to areas of high concentration. The cell must supply energy for active transport to occur.

- Particles that are too large to pass easily through the membrane can enter a cell by a process called endocytosis. Large particles can leave a cell by exocytosis.

Labs

The Perfect Taters Mystery *(p. 574)*

☑ Skills Check

Math Concepts

CELL CYCLE It takes 4 hours for a cell to complete its cell cycle and produce 2 cells. How many cells can be produced from this cell in 12 hours? First you must determine how many cell cycles will occur in 12 hours:

12 hours/4 hours = 3

The number of cells doubles after each cycle:

Cycle 1   1 cell × 2 = 2 cells

Cycle 2   2 cells × 2 = 4 cells

Cycle 3   4 cells × 2 = 8 cells

Therefore, after 3 cell cycles (12 hours), 8 cells will have been produced from the original cell.

Visual Understanding

MITOSIS The process of mitosis can be confusing, but looking at illustrations can help. Look at the illustrations of the cell cycle on pages 118 and 119. Read the label for each phase, and look at the illustrations and photographs for each. Look for the cell structures that are described in the label. Trace the movement of chromosomes through each step. By carefully studying the labels and pictures, you can better understand mitosis.

SECTION 2

Vocabulary

photosynthesis *(p. 112)*
cellular respiration *(p. 113)*
fermentation *(p. 113)*

Section Notes

- The sun is the ultimate source of almost all energy needed to fuel the chemical activities of organisms. Most producers use energy from sunlight to make food during the process known as photosynthesis. This food then becomes a source of energy for the producers and for the consumers that eat the producers.

- Cells use cellular respiration or fermentation to release the energy from food to make ATP. Cellular respiration requires oxygen, but fermentation does not.

Labs

Stayin' Alive *(p. 576)*

SECTION 3

Vocabulary

cell cycle *(p. 116)*
chromosome *(p. 116)*
binary fission *(p. 116)*
homologous chromosomes *(p. 117)*
centromere *(p. 117)*
chromatids *(p. 117)*
mitosis *(p. 117)*
cytokinesis *(p. 119)*

Section Notes

- The life cycle of a cell is called the cell cycle. The cell cycle begins when the cell is formed and ends when the cell divides to produce two new cells. Prokaryotic cells produce new cells by binary fission. Eukaryotic cells produce new cells by mitosis and cytokinesis.

- Before mitosis, the chromosomes are copied. During mitosis, chromatids separate, and two new nuclei are formed. During cytokinesis, the cell divides.

🔲 internet**connect**

 GO TO: go.hrw.com

Visit the **HRW** Web site for a variety of learning tools related to this chapter. Just type in the keyword:

KEYWORD: HSTACT

 GO TO: www.scilinks.org

Visit the **National Science Teachers Association** on-line Web site for Internet resources related to this chapter. Just type in the *sci*LINKS number for more information about the topic:

TOPIC: Cell Energy	*sci*LINKS NUMBER: HSTL080
TOPIC: Photosynthesis	*sci*LINKS NUMBER: HSTL085
TOPIC: The Cell Cycle	*sci*LINKS NUMBER: HSTL090
TOPIC: Microbes	*sci*LINKS NUMBER: HSTL095

The Cell in Action **121**

Chapter Review

To complete the following sentences, choose the correct term from each pair of terms listed below:

1. The diffusion of water through the cell membrane is called __?__. (*osmosis* or *active transport*)

2. A cell can remove large particles during __?__. (*exocytosis* or *endocytosis*)

3. Plants use __?__ to make glucose. (*cellular respiration* or *photosynthesis*)

4. During __?__, food molecules are broken down to form CO_2 and H_2O and release large amounts of energy. (*cellular respiration* or *fermentation*)

5. In eukaryotes, __?__ creates two nuclei, and __?__ creates two cells. (*cytokinesis* or *mitosis*)

UNDERSTANDING CONCEPTS

Multiple Choice

6. When particles are moved through a membrane from a region of low concentration to a region of high concentration, the process is called
   a. diffusion.
   b. passive transport.
   c. active transport.
   d. fermentation.

7. An organism with chloroplasts is a
   a. consumer.   c. producer.
   b. prokaryote.   d. centromere.

8. What is produced by mitosis?
   a. two identical cells
   b. two nuclei
   c. chloroplasts
   d. two different cells

9. Before the energy in food can be used by a cell, it must first be transferred to molecules of
   a. proteins.
   b. carbohydrates.
   c. DNA.
   d. ATP.

10. Which one of the following does not perform mitosis?
    a. prokaryotic cell
    b. human body cell
    c. eukaryotic cell
    d. plant cell

11. Which of the following would form a cell plate during the cell cycle?
    a. human cell
    b. prokaryotic cell
    c. plant cell
    d. all of the above

Short Answer

12. What cell structures are needed for photosynthesis? for respiration?

13. How many chromatids are present in a chromosome at the beginning of mitosis?

14. What are the three stages of the cell cycle in a eukaryotic cell?

Concept Mapping

15. Use the following terms to create a concept map: chromosome duplication, cytokinesis, prokaryote, mitosis, cell cycle, binary fission, eukaryote.

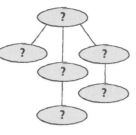

19. A cell has six chromosomes at the beginning of its cell cycle. How many chromatids will line up at the equator of the cell during mitosis?

CRITICAL THINKING AND PROBLEM SOLVING

Write one or two sentences to answer the following questions:

16. Which one of the plants below was given water mixed with salt, and which one was given pure water? Explain how you know, and be sure to use the word *osmosis* in your answer.

INTERPRETING GRAPHICS

Look at the cell below to answer the following questions:

20. Is the cell prokaryotic or eukaryotic?

21. In what stage of the cell cycle is this cell?

22. How many chromatids are present? How many pairs of homologous chromosomes are present?

23. How many chromosomes will be present in each of the new cells after the cell divides?

17. Why would your muscle cells need to be supplied with more food when there is a lack of oxygen than when there is plenty of oxygen present?

18. A parent cell has 10 chromosomes before dividing.
    a. Will the cell go through binary fission or mitosis and cytokinesis to produce new cells?
    b. How many chromosomes will each new cell have after the parent cell divides?

NOW What Do You Think?

Take a minute to review your answers to the ScienceLog questions on page 107. Have your answers changed? If necessary, revise your answers based on what you have learned since you began this chapter.

Electrifying News About Microbes

Your car is out of fuel, and there isn't a service station in sight. No problem! Your car's motor runs on electricity supplied by trillions of micro-organisms—and they're hungry. You pop a handful of sugar cubes into the tank along with some fresh water, and you're on your way. The microbes devour the food and produce enough electricity to get you home safely.

A "Living" Battery

Sound far-fetched? Peter Bennetto and his team of scientists at King's College, in London, don't think so. Chemists there envision "living" batteries that will someday operate everything from wristwatches to entire towns. Although cars won't be using batteries powered by bacteria anytime soon, the London scientists have demonstrated that microorganisms can convert food into usable electrical energy. One test battery that is smaller than 0.5 cm^2 kept a digital clock operating for a day.

Freeing Electrons

For nearly a century, scientists have known that living things produce and use electric charges. But only in the last few decades have they figured out the chemical processes that produce these tiny electric charges. As part of their normal activities, living cells break down starches and sugars, and these chemical reactions release electrons. Scientists produce electricity by harvesting these free electrons from single-celled organisms, such as bacteria.

Bennetto and his colleagues have developed a list of foods that matches the carbohydrates, such as table sugar and molasses, with the microorganisms that digest them the most efficiently. Bennetto explains that there are lazy bacteria and efficient bacteria. An efficient microbe can convert more than 90 percent of its food into compounds that will fuel an elec-

▲ *Bacteria like this can convert carbohydrates to electrical energy.*

tric reaction. A less-efficient microbe converts 50 percent or less of its food into electron-yielding compounds.

Feed Them Leftovers

One advantage that batteries powered by microbes have over generators is that microbes do not require nonrenewable resources, such as coal or oil. Microbes can produce electricity by consuming pollutants, such as certain byproducts from the milk and sugar industries. And since the microorganisms reproduce constantly, no battery charging is necessary; just give the battery a bacteria change from time to time. For now, the London scientists are content to speculate on the battery's potential. Other specialists, such as electrical engineers, are needed to make this technology practical.

Project Idea

▶ Imagine that you manage a government agency and you are asked to provide funds for research on batteries powered by microbes. Think of some of the benefits of developing "living batteries." Are there any problems you can think of? As a class, decide whether you would fund the research.

Science Fiction

"Contagion"

by Katherine MacLean

A quarter mile from their spaceship, the *Explorer*, a team of doctors walk carefully along a narrow forest trail. Around them, the forest looks like an Earth forest in the fall—the leaves are green, copper, purple, and fiery red. But it isn't fall. And the team is not on Earth.

Minos is enough like Earth to be the home of another colony of humans. But Minos might also be home to unknown organisms that could cause severe illness or death among the *Explorer*'s crew. These diseases might be enough like Earth diseases to be contagious, yet just different enough to be extremely difficult to treat.

Something large moves among the shadows —it looks like a man. When he suddenly steps out onto the trail, he is taller than any of them, lean and muscled, and darkly tanned with bright red hair. Even more amazing, he speaks.

"Welcome to Minos. The mayor sends greetings from Alexandria."

And so we, and the crew of the *Explorer*, meet red-haired Patrick Mead. According to Patrick, there was once a colony of humans on Minos. About two years after the colony arrived, a terrible plague swept through the colony and killed everyone except the Mead family. But, Patrick tells them, the plague has never come back and there are no other contagions on Minos.

Or are there? What has Patrick hidden from the crew of the *Explorer*? Read Katherine MacLean's "Contagion" in the *Holt Anthology of Science Fiction* to find out.

UNIT 3

Heredity, Evolution, and Classification

The differences and similarities among living things are the subject of this unit. You will learn how characteristics are passed from one generation to another, how living things are classified based on their characteristics, and how these characteristics help living things survive. Scientists have not always understood these topics, and there is still much to be learned. This timeline will give you an idea of some things that have been learned so far.

1753

Carolus Linnaeus publishes the first of two volumes containing the classification of all known species.

1951

Rosalind Franklin photographs DNA.

1953

James Watson and Francis Crick figure out the structure of DNA.

1960

Louis and Mary Leakey discover fossil bones of the human ancestor *Homo habilis* in Olduvai Gorge, Tanzania.

1969

Apollo 11 lands on the moon. Neil Armstrong becomes the first person to walk on the lunar surface.

1859

Charles Darwin suggests that natural selection is a mechanism of evolution.

1860

Abraham Lincoln is elected the 16th president of the United States.

1865

Gregor Mendel publishes the results of his studies of genetic inheritance in pea plants.

1930

The planet Pluto is discovered.

1905

Nettie Stevens describes how sex is determined by the X and Y chromosomes.

1990

Ashanti DeSilva is given genetically engineered white blood cells to combat disease.

1974

Donald Johanson discovers a fossilized skeleton of one of the first hominids.

2000

The Human Genome Project has identified thousands of human genes and is scheduled to decode the entire human genome by 2003.

6 Heredity

Would You Believe . . . ?

It all started in ancient China. A fisherman caught an unusual carp. Usually these small freshwater fish are drab colored, but this one had a pale golden hue. It was too pretty to eat, so the fisherman took the fish home as a pet.

Months later, the fisherman caught another gold-tinged carp. He kept the two fish in the same bowl. When the fish reproduced, the offspring were even more brightly colored than their parents. The first goldfish had been born!

In the years that followed, people throughout China began keeping and breeding the new, orange-colored pets. Many became goldfish matchmakers, choosing only the most handsome mates for their favorite fish. With each generation of hatchlings, the fish looked more and more distinctive. By A.D. 1500, when the first shipments of goldfish arrived in Japan, goldfish no longer resembled carp. In fact, they were so regal looking that the commoners in Japan were forbidden to keep these animals as pets.

Without knowing it, these early goldfish breeders were using the principles of genetics to create many new kinds of goldfish. In this chapter you will learn about heredity, the passing on of traits from parents to offspring. You'll discover the principles that allowed beautiful goldfish to be bred from rather plain-looking carp.

What Do You Think?

In your ScienceLog, try to answer the following questions based on what you already know:

1. Why don't all humans look exactly alike?

2. What determines whether a human baby will be a boy or a girl?

Investigate!

Clothing Combos

Do you look like your father or your mother? Do you look like your sister or your brother? You may. But chances are you look quite different. Even though you are different, you share some characteristics with your siblings and your parents.

In this activity you will investigate how different characteristics can be combined to make something special and unique, just like you are.

Procedure

1. Your teacher will provide **three boxes.** One box contains **five hats.** One box contains **five gloves,** and one box contains **five scarves.**

2. Without looking in the boxes, five of your classmates will select one hat, one scarf, and one glove. They will put the items on and model them for the class. Then they will put the clothing back into the boxes for the next five students. This process will continue until all students have made their selections.

3. Record the clothing combination you selected in your ScienceLog.

Analysis

4. Were any of the combinations the same? How many different combinations did you have in your class?

5. Do you think you saw all of the possible combinations? Explain your answer.

6. Choose a partner. Using the pieces of clothing you and your partner selected from the box, how many different combinations could you make by giving a third person one hat, one glove, and one scarf? You may want to make a chart like the one below to help you figure it out.

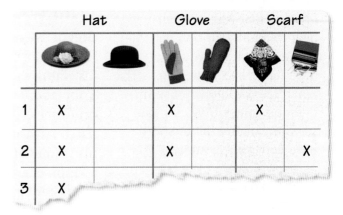

	Hat		Glove		Scarf	
1	X			X		X
2	X			X			X
3	X						

7. Considering what you have learned from this Investigate, why do you think parents often have children who look very different from each other?

Mendel and His Peas

NEW TERMS

heredity
self-pollinating plant
true-breeding plant
dominant trait
recessive trait
genes

alleles
Punnett square
genotype
phenotype
probability

OBJECTIVES

■ Explain the experiments of Gregor Mendel.

■ Explain how genes and alleles are related to genotypes and phenotypes.

■ Use the information found in a Punnett square.

If you could travel the world, you would find that there is no one else exactly like you. You are unique. But what sets you apart? If you look around your classroom, you'll see that you share many physical characteristics with your classmates. For example, you all have skin instead of scales, feet instead of hooves, and a noticeable lack of antennae. You are a human being very much like all your fellow human beings.

Yet you are different from everyone else in many ways. The people who you most resemble are your parents and your brothers and sisters. But you probably don't look exactly like them either. Do you have any ideas why this is so?

Why Don't You Look Like a Rhinoceros?

The answer to this question is simple: Neither of your parents is a rhinoceros. But there's more to this answer than meets the eye. As it turns out, **heredity,** or the passing of traits from parents to offspring, is a very complicated subject. For example, you might have curly hair, while both your parents have straight hair. You might have blue eyes, even though both your parents have brown eyes. How does this happen? People have investigated this question for a long time. About 150 years ago, some very important experiments were performed that helped scientists begin to find some answers. The person who performed these experiments was Gregor Mendel.

Explore

Imagine that you are planning to meet your pen pal at the airport, but you two have never met in person. What traits would you use to describe yourself? Would you say that you are tall or short, have curly hair or straight hair, have brown eyes or green eyes? Make a list. Which of these traits do you think you inherited? Put a check mark next to these traits on your list.

Who Was Gregor Mendel?

Gregor Mendel was born in 1822 in Heinzendorf, Austria. Growing up on his family's farm, Mendel learned a lot about cultivating flowers and fruit trees. As a boy, he was fascinated with nature. After completing his studies at a university, he entered a monastery. He worked in the monastery garden, where he was able to use plants to study the way traits are passed from parents to offspring. **Figure 1** shows an illustration of Mendel in the monastery garden.

Figure 1 Gregor Mendel

Unraveling the Mystery

Mendel was both observant and curious. From his experiences breeding plants, he knew that sometimes the patterns of inheritance seemed simple and sometimes they did not. Mendel wanted to find out why.

Mendel was interested in the way traits are passed from parents to offspring. For example, sometimes a trait that appeared in one generation did not show up in any of the offspring in the next generation. In the third generation, though, the trait showed up again. Mendel noticed patterns such as this in people, plants, and many other living things.

To simplify his investigation, Mendel decided to study only one kind of organism. He had already done studies using the garden pea plant, so he chose the garden pea plant again as his subject.

How Do You Like Your Peas? Garden peas were a good choice for several reasons. These plants grow quickly, they are usually self-pollinating, and they come in many varieties. A **self-pollinating plant** contains both male and female reproductive structures, like the flower in **Figure 2**. Therefore, pollen from one flower or plant can fertilize the eggs of the same flower or the eggs of another flower on the same plant. In order to understand Mendel's experiments, you need to understand the parts of a flower and how fertilization takes place in plants. **Figure 3** illustrates this.

Figure 2 *This photograph of a flower shows the male and female reproductive structures.*

Figure 3 *During pollination, pollen containing sperm from the anthers (male) is transferred to the stigma (female). Fertilization occurs when a sperm from the pollen travels through the stigma and enters the egg in an ovule.*

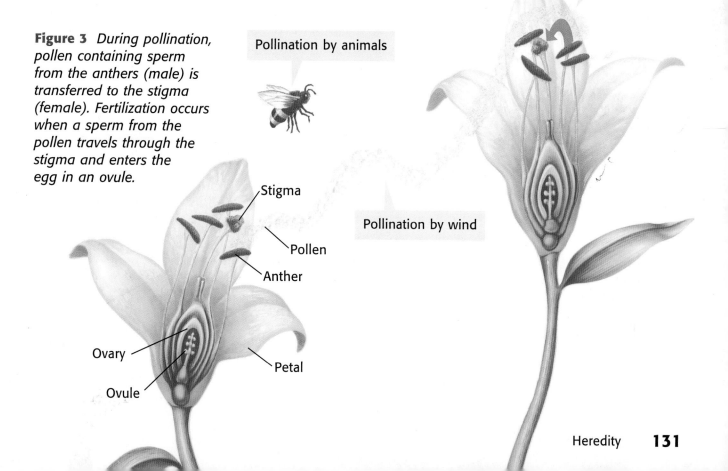

Pollination by animals

Self-pollination

Pollination by wind

Stigma

Pollen

Anther

Ovary

Petal

Ovule

Peas Be My Podner

To keep things simple, Mendel chose to study only one characteristic, such as plant height or pea color, at a time. That way, he could understand the results. Mendel chose plants that had two forms for each of the characteristics that he studied. For example, for the characteristic of plant height, one form always produced tall plants, and the other form always produced short plants. For the characteristic of flower color, Mendel selected a plant that always produced purple flowers and another plant that always produced white flowers. Purple and white are the two forms (or traits) for the characteristic of flower color. Some of the characteristics investigated by Mendel are shown in **Figure 4.** The two different traits of each characteristic are also shown.

True-Breeding Plants Mendel was very careful to use plants that were true breeding for each of the traits he was studying. When a **true-breeding plant** self-pollinates, it will always produce offspring with the same trait the parent plant has. For example, a tall true-breeding plant will always produce offspring that are tall.

Mendel decided to find out what would happen if he crossed two plants that had different forms of a single trait. To do this, he used a method known as *cross-pollination*. In cross-pollination, the anthers of one plant are removed so that the plant cannot self-pollinate. Then pollen from another plant is used to fertilize the plant without anthers. This way, Mendel could select which pollen would fertilize which plant. This technique is illustrated in **Figure 5.**

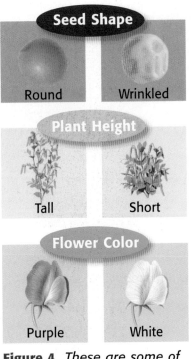

Figure 4 *These are some of the plant characteristics that Mendel studied.*

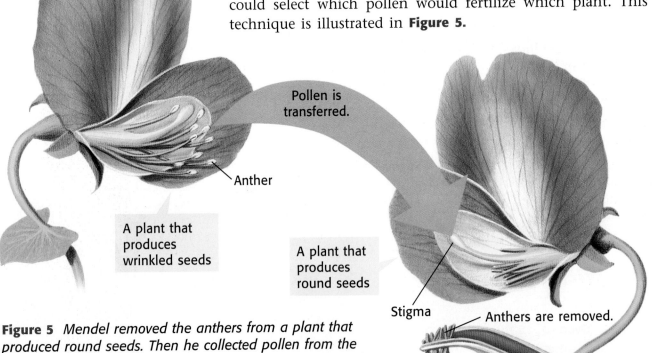

Pollen is transferred.

Anther

A plant that produces wrinkled seeds

A plant that produces round seeds

Stigma

Anthers are removed.

Figure 5 *Mendel removed the anthers from a plant that produced round seeds. Then he collected pollen from the anthers of a plant that produced wrinkled seeds and used the pollen to fertilize the plant that produced round seeds.*

Mendel's First Experiment

In his first experiment, Mendel performed crosses to study seven different characteristics. Each of the crosses was between the two traits of each characteristic. The results of the cross between plants that produce round seeds and plants that produce wrinkled seeds are shown in **Figure 6.** The offspring from this cross are known as the *first generation*. Do the results surprise you? What do you think happened to the trait for wrinkled seeds?

Mendel got similar results for each of the crosses that he made. One trait always appeared, and the other trait seemed to vanish. Mendel chose to call the trait that appeared the **dominant trait.** The other trait seemed to recede into the background, so Mendel called this the **recessive trait.** To find out what might have happened to the recessive trait, Mendel decided to perform another experiment.

Mendel's Second Experiment

Mendel allowed the first generation from each of the seven crosses to self-pollinate. This is also illustrated in Figure 6. This time the plant with the dominant trait for seed shape (which is round) was allowed to self-pollinate. As you can see, the recessive trait for wrinkled seeds showed up again.

Mendel performed this same experiment on the two traits of each of the seven characteristics. No matter which characteristic Mendel investigated, when the first generation was allowed to self-pollinate, the recessive trait reappeared.

Figure 6 *A plant that produces wrinkled seeds is fertilized with pollen from a plant that produces round seeds.*

Parent generation

Pollen transfer

First generation
All round seeds

Growth

First generation
A seed grows into a mature plant that is allowed to self-pollinate.

Second generation
For every three round seeds, there is one wrinkled seed.

Bug Builders, Inc., needs your help to design some new bugs. Turn to page 578 of the LabBook.

A Different Point of View

Mendel then did something that no one else had done before: He decided to count the number of plants with each trait that turned up in the second generation. He hoped that this might help him explain his results. Take a look at Mendel's actual results, shown in the table below.

Mendel's Results

Characteristic	Dominant trait		Recessive trait		Ratio
Flower color	705 purple		224 white		?
Seed color	6,002 yellow		2,001 green		?
Seed shape	5,474 round		1,850 wrinkled		?
Pod color	428 green		152 yellow		?
Pod shape	882 smooth		299 bumpy		?
Flower position	651 along stem		207 at tip		?
Plant height	787 tall		277 short		?

÷ 5 ÷ Ω ≤ ∞ + Ω √ 9 ≤ Σ 2

MATH BREAK

Understanding Ratios

A ratio is a way to compare two numbers by using division. In Mendel's results, the ratio of plants with purple flowers to plants with white flowers can be written as 705 to 224, or 705:224. This ratio can be reduced, or simplified, by dividing the first number by the second as follows:

$$\frac{705}{224} = \frac{3.15}{1}$$

which is the same thing as a ratio of 3.15:1.

This means that for every three plants that produce purple flowers, there will be roughly one plant that produces white flowers. Following is another problem for you to try:

In a box of chocolates, there are 18 nougat-filled chocolates and 6 caramel-filled chocolates. What is the ratio of nougat-filled chocolates to caramel-filled chocolates?

As you can see, the recessive trait showed up again, but not as often as the dominant trait showed up. Mendel decided to calculate the *ratio* of dominant traits to recessive traits for each characteristic. Follow in Mendel's footsteps by calculating the dominant-to-recessive ratio for each characteristic. (If you need help, check out the MathBreak at left.) Can you find a pattern among the ratios?

A Brilliant Idea

Mendel realized that his results could be explained only if each plant had two sets of instructions for each characteristic. Each parent would donate one set of instructions to the offspring. These sets of instructions are now known as **genes.** The fertilized egg would then have two forms of the same gene for every characteristic—one from each parent. The two forms of a gene are known as **alleles.**

The Proof Is in the Punnett Square To understand how Mendel came to his conclusions, we'll use a diagram known as a Punnett square. A **Punnett square** is a tool used to visualize all the possible combinations of alleles from the parents. Dominant alleles are symbolized with capital letters, and recessive alleles are symbolized with lowercase letters. Therefore, the alleles for a true-breeding purple-flowered plant are written as *PP.* The alleles for a true-breeding white-flowered plant are written as *pp.* The cross between these two parent plants, as shown in **Figure 7,** is then written as *PP* × *pp.* The inside of the square contains the allele combinations that could occur in the offspring. The inherited combination of alleles is known as the offspring's **genotype.**

As the Punnett square in Figure 7 shows, all the offspring from this cross had the same genotype: *Pp.* What would these plants look like? An organism's inherited appearance is known as its **phenotype.** The dominant allele, *P,* in each genotype ensures that all the offspring will be the same phenotype; that is, they will be purple-flowered plants. The recessive allele, *p,* ensures that instructions for making white-flowered plants will be passed on to the next generation.

A true-breeding white flower *(pp)*

A true-breeding purple flower *(PP)*

Figure 7 *When an organism breeds true for a trait, each allele for that trait must carry the same instructions. The possible allele combinations in the offspring for this cross are all the same:* Pp.

How to Make a Punnett Square

To make a Punnett square, draw a square, and divide the inside of the square into four sections. Next, write the letters that represent alleles from one parent along the top of the box. Write the letters that represent alleles from the other parent along the side of the box.

The cross shown in the Punnett square at right is between a plant that produces only round seeds, *RR,* and a plant that produces only wrinkled seeds, *rr.* Follow the arrows to see how the inside of the box was filled in. The resulting alleles inside the box show all the possible genotypes for the offspring from this cross. What would be the phenotypes for these offspring?

	R	*R*
r	*Rr*	*Rr*
r	*Rr*	*Rr*

A self-pollinating purple flower

Male alleles

Female alleles

P   P

P   PP   Pp

p   pP   pp

Figure 8 *This Punnett square shows the possible results from the cross* **Pp** × **Pp.**

More Evidence In Mendel's second experiment, he allowed the first-generation plants to self-pollinate. The results of this experiment can also be shown using a Punnett square. **Figure 8** shows a self-pollination cross of a first-generation plant with the genotype *Pp*. The parental alleles in the cross indicate that the egg and sperm can contain either a *P* allele or a *p* allele.

What might the genotypes of the offspring be? Notice that one square shows the *Pp* combination, while another shows the *pP* combination. These are exactly the same genotype, even though the letters are written in a different order. The other possible genotypes in the offspring are *PP* and *pp*. The combinations *PP*, *Pp*, and *pP* have the same phenotype—purple flowers—because they each contain at least one dominant allele (*P*). Only one combination, *pp*, produces plants with white flowers. The ratio of dominant to recessive is 3:1, just as Mendel calculated from his data.

Quick Lab

Take Your Chances

Imagine that you have two guinea pigs you would like to breed. Each has brown fur and the genotype *Bb.* What are the chances that their offspring will have white fur with the genotype *bb?* Try this experiment to find out. Stick a piece of **masking tape** on both sides of **two quarters.** Label one side of each quarter with a capital *B* and the other side with a lowercase *b.* Toss both coins 50 times, making note of your results each time. How many times did you get the *bb* combination? Now try 50 more tosses. How many times did the *bb* combination appear in the second 50 tosses? What is the probability that the next toss will result in *bb?*

What Are the Chances?

It's important to understand that offspring are equally likely to inherit either allele from either parent. Think of a coin toss. There's a 50 percent chance you'll get heads and a 50 percent chance you'll get tails. Like the toss of a coin, the chance of inheriting one allele or another is completely random. To predict the likelihood that a certain genotype will be inherited, the laws of probability must be considered.

Probability The mathematical chance that an event will occur is known as **probability.** Probability is usually expressed as a fraction or percentage. If you toss a coin, the probability of tossing tails is $\frac{1}{2}$. This means that half the number of times you toss a coin, you will get tails. To express probability as a percentage, divide the numerator of the fraction by the denominator, and then multiply the answer by 100.

$$\frac{1}{2} \times 100 = 50\%$$

To find the probability that you will toss two heads in a row, multiply the probability of the two events.

$$\frac{1}{2} \times \frac{1}{2} = \frac{1}{4}$$

The percentage would be $1 \div 4 \times 100$, which equals 25 percent.

APPLY

A curly eared cat, like the one at right, mated with a cat that had normal ears. If half the kittens had the genotype **Cc** and curly ears, and the other half had the genotype **cc** and normal ears, which was the allele for curly ears?

What was the genotype of each parent? (Hint: Use a Punnett square to fill in the genotypes of the offspring, and then work backward.)

Genotype Probability The same method is used to calculate the probability that an offspring will inherit a certain genotype. For a pea plant to inherit the white flower trait, it must receive a **p** allele from each parent. There is a 50 percent chance of inheriting either allele from either parent. So the probability of inheriting two **p** alleles is $\frac{1}{2} \times \frac{1}{2}$, which equals $\frac{1}{4}$, or $1 \div 4 \times 100$, which is 25 percent.

Gregor Mendel—Gone but Not Forgotten Good ideas are often overlooked or misunderstood when they first appear. This was the fate of Gregor Mendel's ideas. In 1865, he published his findings for the scientific community. Unfortunately, his work didn't get much attention. It wasn't until after his death almost 30 years later that Mendel finally got the recognition he deserved. Once Mendel's ideas were rediscovered and understood, the door was opened to modern genetics.

chemistry CONNECTION

Round seeds may look more appealing, but wrinkled seeds taste sweeter. The dominant allele for seed shape, **R,** causes starch (which is a storage molecule for sugar) to be stored in the seed. This makes the seed plump and round. Seeds with the genotype **rr** do not make or store this starch. This makes the seed wrinkled, and because the sugar has not been converted into starch, the seed tastes sweeter.

REVIEW

1. The allele for a cleft chin, **C,** is dominant among humans. What would be the results from a cross between a woman with the genotype **Cc** and a man with the genotype **cc**? In your ScienceLog, create a Punnett square showing this cross.

2. Of the possible combinations you found in question 1, what is the ratio of offspring with a cleft chin to offspring without a cleft chin?

3. **Applying Concepts** The Punnett square at right shows the possible combinations of alleles for fur color in rabbits. Black fur, **B,** is dominant over white fur, **b.** Given the combinations shown, what are the genotypes of the parents?

	?	?
?	**Bb**	**Bb**
?	**Bb**	**Bb**

Meiosis

NEW TERMS

sex cells
homologous chromosomes
meiosis
sex chromosomes

OBJECTIVES

■ Explain the difference between mitosis and meiosis.

■ Describe how Mendel's ideas are supported by the process of meiosis.

■ Explain the difference between male and female sex chromosomes.

In the early 1900s, scientists began doing experiments similar to those done by Gregor Mendel. Excited by their findings, they searched for similar results obtained by others. They came across Mendel's forgotten paper and realized that their discoveries were not new; Mendel had made the same observation 35 years earlier. However, genes were still a mystery. Where were they located, and how did they pass information from one cell to another? Understanding reproduction was the first step in finding the answers to these questions.

Two Kinds of Reproduction

From earlier studies, you know that there are two types of reproduction: asexual reproduction and sexual reproduction. In *asexual reproduction,* only one parent cell is needed for reproduction. First, the internal structures of the cell are copied by a process known as mitosis. The parent cell then divides, producing new cells that are exact copies of the parent cell. Most single-celled organisms reproduce in this way. Most of the cells in your body also divide this way.

A different type of reproduction is used to make a new human being or a new pea plant. In *sexual reproduction,* two parent cells join together to form a new individual. The parent cells, known as **sex cells,** are different from ordinary body cells. Human body cells, for example, normally have 46 chromosomes (or 23 pairs), as shown in **Figure 9.** The chromosomes in each pair are called **homologous** (hoh MAHL uh guhs) **chromosomes.** But human sex cells have only 23 chromosomes—half the usual number. Male sex cells are called *sperm.* Female sex cells are called *eggs,* or ova. Each sperm and each egg has only one of the chromosomes from a homologous pair.

Figure 9 *Human body cells have 46 chromosomes, or 23 pairs of chromosomes. One member of a pair of homologous chromosomes is shown at right. Homologous chromosomes are usually the same size and shape.*

Less Is More Why is it important that sex cells have half the usual number of chromosomes? When an egg and a sperm join to form a new individual, each parent donates one half of a homologous pair of chromosomes. This ensures that the offspring will receive a normal number of chromosomes in each body cell. Each body cell must have an entire set of 46 chromosomes in order to grow and function properly.

Meiosis to the Rescue Sex cells are made during meiosis, a type of copying process that is different from mitosis. **Meiosis** (mie OH sis) produces new cells with half the usual number of chromosomes. When the sex cells are made, the chromosomes are copied once, and then the nucleus divides twice. The resulting sperm and eggs have half the number of chromosomes found in a normal body cell.

Meanwhile, Back at the Lab

What does all this have to do with the location of genes? Not long after Mendel's paper was rediscovered, a young graduate student named Walter Sutton made an important observation. Sutton was studying sperm cells in grasshoppers. Sutton knew of Mendel's studies, which showed that the egg and sperm must each contribute the same amount of information to the offspring. That was the only way the 3:1 ratio found in the second generation could be explained. Sutton also knew from his own studies that although eggs and sperm were different, they did have something in common: their chromosomes were located inside a nucleus. Using his observations of meiosis, his understanding of Mendel's work, and some creative thinking, Sutton proposed something very important:

Genes are located on chromosomes!

And Sutton was correct, as it turned out. The steps of meiosis are outlined on the next two pages. First, let's review mitosis so that you can compare the two processes.

Mitosis Revisited

1 Inside a typical cell: each of the long strands (chromosomes) makes a copy of itself.

2 Each chromosome consists of two identical copies called chromatids. The chromosomes thicken and shorten.

3 The nuclear membrane dissolves. The chromosomes line up along the equator (center) of the cell.

4 The chromatids pull apart.

5 The nuclear membrane forms around the separated chromatids. The chromosomes unwind, and the cell divides.

6 The result: two identical copies of the original cell.

Meiosis in Eight Easy Steps

The diagram on these two pages shows each stage of meiosis. Read about each step as you look at the diagram. Different types of living things have different numbers of chromosomes. In this diagram, only four chromosomes are shown.

One pair of homologous chromosomes

1 Before meiosis begins, the chromosomes are in a threadlike form. Each chromosome makes an identical copy of itself, forming two exact halves called *chromatids.* The chromosomes then thicken and shorten into a form that is visible under a microscope. The nuclear membrane disappears.

Two chromatids

2 Each chromosome is now made up of two chromatids, the original and an exact copy. Similar chromosomes pair with one another, forming *homologous chromosome pairs.* The paired homologous chromosomes line up at the equator of the cell.

3 The chromosomes separate from their homologous partners and move to opposite ends of the cell.

4 The nuclear membrane re-forms, and the cell divides. The paired chromatids are still joined.

Each cell contains one member of each homologous chromosome pair. The chromosomes are not copied again between the two cell divisions.

6 The chromosomes line up at the equator of each cell.

7 The chromatids pull apart and move to opposite ends of the cell. The nuclear membrane forms around the separated chromosomes, and the cells divide.

 The result: Four new cells have formed from the original single cell. Each new cell has half the number of chromosomes present in the original cell.

✓ Self-Check

1. How many chromosomes are in the original single cell?

2. How many homologous pairs are shown?

3. How many times do the chromosomes make copies of themselves? How many times do cells divide during meiosis?

4. How many chromosomes are present in each cell at the end of meiosis? at the end of mitosis?

5. Which separate first, the chromatids or the homologous chromosomes?

(See page 636 to check your answers.)

Meiosis and Mendel

As Walter Sutton realized, the steps in meiosis support and explain Mendel's findings. To see what happens to a pair of homologous chromosomes during meiosis and fertilization, producing Mendel's results, examine **Figure 10** below. The cross shown in the diagram is between a plant that is true breeding for round seeds and a plant that is true breeding for wrinkled seeds.

Peas aren't the only organisms used to study genetics. Read Lab Rats with Wings on page 149.

Figure 10 *The process of meiosis explains Mendel's findings.*

Following meiosis, each sperm cell contains a recessive allele for wrinkled seeds and each egg cell contains a dominant allele for round seeds.

Fertilization of any egg by any sperm results in the same genotype (*Rr*) and the same phenotype (round). This is exactly what Mendel found in his studies.

Male Parent In the plant cell nucleus below, each homologous chromosome has an allele for seed shape and each allele carries the same instructions: to make wrinkled seeds.

Female Parent In the plant cell nucleus below, each homologous chromosome has an allele for seed shape and each allele carries the same instruction: to make round seeds.

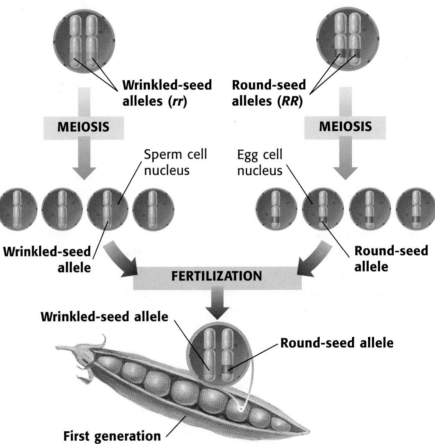

Wrinkled-seed alleles (*rr*)

Round-seed alleles (*RR*)

MEIOSIS

MEIOSIS

Sperm cell nucleus

Egg cell nucleus

Wrinkled-seed allele

Round-seed allele

FERTILIZATION

Wrinkled-seed allele

Round-seed allele

First generation

QuickLab

Round or Wrinkled

Draw a Punnett square for the cross **RR** × **rr,** shown in Figure 10. Then draw another Punnett square for the first-generation cross, **Rr** × **Rr.** How many genotypes are possible from the first cross? How many are possible from the second cross? What are they? What are the phenotypes from the second cross?

Each fertilized egg in the first generation contained one dominant allele and one recessive allele for seed type. Only one genotype was possible, because all sperm formed during meiosis contained the wrinkled-seed allele. All eggs contained the round-seed allele. When the first generation was allowed to self-pollinate, the possible genotypes changed. There are three genotype possibilities for this cross. What are they? Perform the QuickLab at left to find out.

Male or Female?

There are many ways that different kinds of organisms become male or female. To see how this happens in humans, examine **Figure 11,** and then look back at Figure 9, on page 138. Each photograph shows the chromosomes present in the body cells of a human. Which chromosome photograph is from a female, and which is from a male? Here's a hint: Females have 23 matched pairs, while males have 22 matched pairs and one unmatched pair.

Sex Chromosomes The last pair of chromosomes shown in Figure 11 are known as sex chromosomes. **Sex chromosomes** carry genes that determine a very important characteristic—whether the offspring is male or female. In humans, females have two X chromosomes (the matching pair), and males have one X chromosome and one Y chromosome (the unmatched pair). The chromosomes in Figure 11 are from a male, and the chromosomes in Figure 9 are from a female.

During meiosis, one of each of the chromosome pairs ends up in a sex cell. This is also true of the sex chromosomes X and Y. For example, females have two X chromosomes in each body cell. When meiosis produces the egg cells, each egg contains one X chromosome. Males have both an X chromosome and a Y chromosome in each body cell. During meiosis, these chromosomes separate, so each sperm cell contains either an X or a Y chromosome. Egg and sperm combine to form either the XX or XY combination. This is illustrated in **Figure 12.**

Figure 11 *Are these chromosomes from a male or female? How can you tell?*

50%
females

50%
males

Figure 12 *If an egg is fertilized by a sperm containing an X chromosome, the offspring will be a female. If the sperm contains a Y chromosome, the offspring will be male.*

REVIEW

1. Explain the difference between sex cells and sex chromosomes.

2. If there are 14 chromosomes in pea plant cells, how many chromosomes are present in a sex cell of a pea?

3. **Interpreting Illustrations** Examine the illustration at right. Does it show a stage of mitosis or meiosis? How can you tell?

Chapter Highlights

SECTION 1

Vocabulary

heredity (*p. 130*)

self-pollinating plant (*p. 131*)

true-breeding plant (*p. 132*)

dominant trait (*p. 133*)

recessive trait (*p. 133*)

genes (*p. 135*)

alleles (*p. 135*)

Punnett square (*p. 135*)

genotype (*p. 135*)

phenotype (*p. 135*)

probability (*p. 136*)

Section Notes

- Heredity is the passing on of traits from parents to offspring.

- Traits are inherited forms of characteristics.

- Gregor Mendel used pea plants to study heredity.

- Mendel's pea plants were self-pollinating. They contained both male and female reproductive structures. They were also true breeding, always producing offspring with the same traits as the parents.

- Offspring inherit two sets of instructions for each characteristic, one set from each parent.

- The sets of instructions are known as genes.

- Different versions of the same gene are known as alleles.

- If both the dominant allele and the recessive allele are inherited for a characteristic, only the dominant allele is expressed.

- Recessive traits are apparent only when two recessive alleles for the characteristic are inherited.

- A genotype is the combination of alleles for a particular trait.

- A phenotype is the physical expression of the genotype.

- Probability is the mathematical chance that an event will occur. It is usually expressed as a fraction or as a percentage.

Labs

Bug Builders, Inc. (*p. 578*)

Tracing Traits (*p. 580*)

☑ Skills Check

Math Concepts

RATIOS A jar contains 24 green marbles and 96 red marbles. There are 4 red marbles for every 1 green marble.

$$\frac{96}{24} = \frac{4}{1}$$

This can also be written as follows:

4:1

Visual Understanding

PUNNETT SQUARES

A Punnett square can help you visualize all the possible combinations of alleles passed from parents to offspring. See page 135 to review how Punnett squares are made.

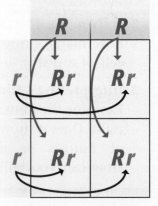

Vocabulary

sex cells (*p. 138*)

homologous chromosomes (*p. 138*)

meiosis (*p. 139*)

sex chromosomes (*p. 143*)

Section Notes

- Genes are located on chromosomes.

- Most human cells contain 46 chromosomes, or 23 pairs.

- Each pair contains one chromosome donated by the mother and one donated by the father. These pairs are known as homologous chromosomes.

- Meiosis produces sex cells, eggs and sperm.

- Sex cells have half the usual number of chromosomes.

- Sex chromosomes contain genes that determine an offspring's sex.

- Females have two X chromosomes, and males have one X chromosome and one Y chromosome.

internetconnect

go.hrw.com **GO TO:** go.hrw.com

Visit the **HRW** Web site for a variety of learning tools related to this chapter. Just type in the keyword:

KEYWORD: HSTHER

SCiLINKS **GO TO:** www.scilinks.org

Visit the **National Science Teachers Association** on-line Web site for Internet resources related to this chapter. Just type in the *sci*LINKS number for more information about the topic:

TOPIC:	*sci*LINKS NUMBER:
TOPIC: Gregor Mendel	*sci*LINKS NUMBER: HSTL105
TOPIC: Heredity	*sci*LINKS NUMBER: HSTL110
TOPIC: Dominant and Recessive Traits	*sci*LINKS NUMBER: HSTL115
TOPIC: Cell Division	*sci*LINKS NUMBER: HSTL120

Chapter Review

To complete the following sentences, choose the correct term from each pair of terms listed below:

1. Sperm and eggs are known as __?__. (*sex cells* or *sex chromosomes*)

2. The __?__, the expression of a trait, is determined by the __?__, the combination of alleles. (*genotype* or *phenotype*)

3. __?__ produces cells with half the normal number of chromosomes. (*Meiosis* or *Mitosis*)

4. Different versions of the same genes are called __?__. (*sex cells* or *alleles*)

5. A __?__ plant can pollinate its own eggs. (*self-pollinating* or *true-breeding*)

UNDERSTANDING CONCEPTS

Multiple Choice

6. Genes are found on
   a. chromosomes.
   b. alleles.
   c. proteins.
   d. anthers.

7. The process that produces sex cells is
   a. mitosis.
   b. photosynthesis.
   c. meiosis.
   d. probability.

8. The passing of traits from parents to offspring is
   a. probability.
   b. heredity.
   c. recessive.
   d. meiosis.

9. If you cross a white flower (with the genotype *pp*) with a purple flower (with the genotype *PP*), the possible genotypes in the offspring are:
   a. *PP* and *pp*.
   b. all *Pp*.
   c. all *PP*.
   d. all *pp*.

10. For the above cross, what would the phenotypes be?
    a. all white
    b. all tall
    c. all purple
    d. $\frac{1}{2}$ white, $\frac{1}{2}$ purple

11. In meiosis,
    a. the chromosomes are copied twice.
    b. the nucleus divides once.
    c. four cells are produced from a single cell.
    d. All of the above

12. Probability is
    a. always expressed as a ratio.
    b. a 50% chance that an event will occur.
    c. the mathematical chance that an event will occur.
    d. a 3:1 chance that an event will occur.

Short Answer

13. Which sex chromosomes do females have? Which do males have?

14. In your own words, give a one- or two-sentence definition of the term *recessive trait*.

15. How are sex cells different from other body cells?

Concept Mapping

16. Use the following terms to create a concept map: meiosis, eggs, cell division, X chromosome, sex cells, sperm, mitosis, Y chromosome.

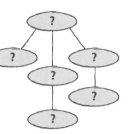

CRITICAL THINKING AND PROBLEM SOLVING

Write one or two sentences to answer the following questions:

17. If a child has blue eyes and both her parents have brown eyes, what does that tell you about the trait for blue eyes? Explain your answer.

18. Why is meiosis important for sexual reproduction?

19. Gregor Mendel used only true-breeding plants. If he had used plants that were not true breeding, do you think he would have discovered dominant and recessive traits? Why or why not?

MATH IN SCIENCE

20. Assume that Y is the dominent allele for yellow seeds and y is the recessive allele for green seeds. What is the probability that a pea plant with the genotype Yy crossed with a pea plant with the genotype yy will have offspring with the genotype yy?

INTERPRETING GRAPHICS

Examine the Punnett square below, and then answer the following questions:

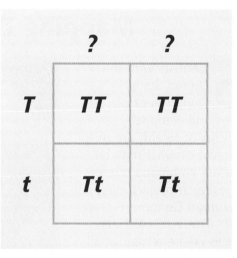

21. What is the unknown genotype?

22. If T represents the allele for tall pea plants, and t represents the allele for short pea plants, what is the phenotype of each parent and of the offspring?

23. If each of the offspring were allowed to self-fertilize, what are the possible genotypes in the next generation?

24. What is the probability of each genotype in item 23?

NOW What Do You Think?

Take a minute to review your answers to the ScienceLog questions on page 129. Have your answers changed? If necessary, revise your answers based on what you have learned since you began this chapter.

Science, Technology, and Society

Mapping the Human Genome

Scientists with the United States Department of Energy and National Institutes of Health are in the midst of what may be the most ambitious scientific research project ever—the Human Genome Project (HGP). These researchers want to create a map of all the genes found on human chromosomes. The body's complete set of genetic instructions is called the genome. Scientists hope this project will provide valuable information that may help prevent or even cure many genetic diseases.

◀ *This scientist is performing one of the many steps involved in the research for the Human Genome Project.*

Whose Genes Are These?

You might be wondering whose genome the scientists are decoding. Actually, it doesn't matter because each person is unique in only about 1 percent of his or her genetic material. The scientists' goal is to identify how tiny differences in that 1 percent of DNA make each of us who we are, and to understand how some changes can cause disease.

Genetic Medicine

The tiny changes that can cause disease, called mutations, are often inherited. Once scientists determine the normal order of our genes, doctors may be able to use this information to help detect mutations in patients. Then doctors would be able to warn patients of an increased risk of a disease before any symptoms appear! For example, a doctor's early warning about a genetic risk of high cholesterol would give a person a chance to eat healthier and exercise more before any serious symptoms were detectable.

Advancing Technology

The technology used in the HGP is constantly changing. Scientists make thousands of copies of genes and use them to make a detailed analysis of the chromosomes.

Scientists organizing the HGP hope to have a complete and accurate sequence of the human genome—estimated to have between 50,000 and 100,000 genes—by 2003. One day in the future, scientists may even be able to provide people with a healthy gene to replace a mutated one. This technique, called gene therapy, may eventually be the cure for many genetic diseases.

What Do You Think?

▶ Despite the medical advancements the Human Genome Project will bring, many people continue to debate ethical, social, and legal issues surrounding this controversial project. Look into these issues, and discuss them with your classmates!

Health

Lab Rats with Wings

What's less than 1 mm in length, can be extremely annoying when buzzing around your kitchen, and sometimes grows legs out of its eyes? The answer is *Drosophila melanogaster*—better known as the fruit fly because it feeds on fruit. This tiny insect has played a big role in helping us understand many illnesses, especially those that occur at certain stages of human development. Scientists use fruit flies to find out more about diseases and disorders such as cancer, Alzheimer's disease, muscular dystrophy, and Down's syndrome.

Why a Fly?

Fruit flies are some scientists' favorite research animal. Scientists can raise several generations of fruit flies in just a few months. Because fruit flies have only a two-week life cycle, scientists can alter a fruit-fly gene as part of an experiment and then see the results very quickly.

Another advantage to using these tiny animals is their small size. Thousands of fruit flies can be raised in a relatively small space. Researchers can afford to buy and maintain

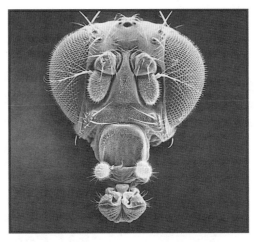

▲ *This is what a normal fruit fly looks like under a scanning electron microscope.*

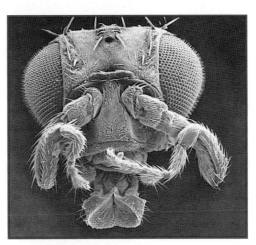

▲ *This fruit fly has legs growing out of its eyes!*

a variety of fruit fly strains to use in experiments.

Comparing Codes

Another important reason for using these "lab rats with wings" is that their genetic code is relatively simple and well understood. Fruit flies have 12,000 genes, whereas humans have more than 70,000. Nonetheless, many fruit-fly genes are similar in function to human genes, and scientists have learned to manipulate them to produce genetic mutations. Scientists who study these mutations gain valuable information about genetic mutations in humans. Without fruit flies, some human genetic problems that we now have important information about—such as basal cell carcinoma cancer—might have taken many more years and many more dollars to study.

Where Do You Draw the Line?

▶ Do you think it is acceptable for scientists to perform research on fruit flies? What about on rats, mice, and rabbits? Have a debate with your classmates about conducting scientific experiments on other species.

7 Genes and Gene Technology

POLICE LINE - DO NOT CROSS

4801 INDUSTRIAL BLVD.

WITNESSES: NONE

EVIDENCE: BLOOD SAMPLE

POSSIBLE ENTRY:
BROKEN SE WINDOW

The City

THE HOMETOWN GAZETTE · Monday

Weather Watch
Sunny during the day.
Much darker at night.

Accused Pleads Innocent
DNA Test Pending

The defendant has always maintained his innocence. He said he is confident the police will ___ late him.

Juvenile Court

Three Alarm Fire Totals Store

Supreme Court

What If . . . ?

Imagine that you are wrongly accused of a crime. A witness at the scene picks you out of a lineup. Your blood type matches blood found at the scene. You were really at home when the crime occurred, but you have no way to prove it. However, there is a witness that can help you—your DNA. DNA is a substance found in nearly every one of your cells.

A technique known as DNA fingerprinting can produce an image of the patterns made by your DNA. Unless you have an identical twin, your DNA fingerprint is like no one else's and can be used to identify you. But what is DNA? Why is yours unique? What does DNA have to do with who you are? In this chapter you will learn the answers to these questions.

What Do You Think?

In your ScienceLog, try to answer the following questions based on what you already know:

1. Why don't all humans look exactly alike?

2. What are genes? Where are they found?

3. How does knowing about DNA help scientists treat diseases?

Fingerprint Your Friends

One common method of identification is fingerprinting. Does it really work? Are everyone's fingerprints different? Try this activity to find out.

Procedure

1. Rub a **piece of charcoal** back and forth across a **piece of tracing paper.** Rub the tip of one of your fingers on the charcoal mark. Then place a **small piece of transparent tape** over the charcoal on your finger. Remove the tape, and stick it on a **piece of white paper.** Do the same for the rest of your fingers.

2. Observe the patterns with a **magnifying lens.** What kinds of patterns do you see? The fingerprint patterns shown at right are the most common found among humans. Is the pattern the same on each of your fingers?

Analysis

3. Compare your fingerprints with those of your classmates. How many of each type do you see? Do any two people in your class have the same prints? Try to explain your findings.

 Whorl

 Arch

 Loop

What Do Genes Look Like?

NEW TERMS

DNA	thymine
nucleotide	guanine
adenine	cytosine

OBJECTIVES

- Describe the basic structure of the DNA molecule.
- Explain how DNA molecules can be copied.
- Explain some of the exceptions to Mendel's heredity principles.

Scientists know that traits are determined by genes and that genes are passed from one generation to another. Scientists also know that genes are located on chromosomes, structures in the nucleus of most cells. Chromosomes are made of **DNA,** short for deoxyribonucleic (dee AHKS ee RIE boh noo KLAY ik) acid, and protein. But which type of material makes the genes? Scientists debated this issue for 50 years.

The Pieces of the Puzzle

The gene material must be able to carry out two functions. First it must be able to supply complex instructions for cell processes and for building cell structures. Second it must be able to be copied each time a cell divides, so that each cell contains an identical set of genes. This ensures that the hereditary information can be passed to the next generation. Early studies of DNA suggested that DNA was a very simple molecule. Because of this, most scientists thought protein was the probable carrier of hereditary information. After all, proteins are complex molecules.

In the 1940s, however, two surprising experiments showed that genes of bacteria and viruses are made of DNA. How could something so simple hold the key to making and directing a living organism? To find the answer to this question, let's take a closer look at the subunits that make up a DNA molecule.

Nucleotides—The Subunits of DNA DNA is made of only four subunits, which are known as **nucleotides.** Each nucleotide that makes up a DNA molecule consists of three different types of material: a sugar, a phosphate, and a base. Nucleotides are identical except for the type of base present. The four bases are **adenine, thymine, guanine,** and **cytosine,** and they each have a slightly different shape. The bases are usually referred to by the first letters in their names, **A, T, G,** and **C. Figure 1** shows diagrams of the four nucleotides. Can you imagine how they might fit together?

Figure 1 *Each nucleotide is made up of a sugar, a phosphate, and a base. There are four different bases.*

Adenine (A)

Nucleotide

Thymine (T)   Guanine (G)   Cytosine (C)

Chargaff's Rules In the 1950s, a biochemist named Erwin Chargaff was studying samples of DNA from different organisms. He found that the amount of adenine in the DNA always equals the amount of thymine, and the amount of guanine always equals the amount of cytosine. His findings, now known as Chargaff's rules, are represented as follows:

$$A = T \text{ and } G = C$$

At the time, no one knew quite what to make of Chargaff's findings. How could Chargaff's rules help solve the mysteries of DNA's structure? Read on to find out.

A Picture of DNA

More clues came from the laboratory of British scientist Maurice Wilkins. There, chemist Rosalind Franklin, shown in **Figure 2,** was able to create images of DNA molecules. The process that she used to create the image shown in **Figure 3** is known as X-ray diffraction. In this process, X rays bombard the DNA molecule. When the X ray hits a particle within the molecule, the ray bounces off the particle. This creates a pattern that is captured on film. The images that Franklin created suggested that DNA has a spiral shape.

Eureka!

Two other young scientists, James Watson and Francis Crick, shown in **Figure 4,** were also investigating the mystery of DNA's structure. Based on the work of others, Watson and Crick built models of DNA using simple materials, such as labeled pieces of cardboard. After seeing the X-ray images of DNA made by Rosalind Franklin, Watson and Crick put it all together. In a stroke of brilliance, they concluded that DNA resembles a twisted ladder shape known as a *double helix*. Watson and Crick used their DNA model to predict how DNA is copied. Upon making the discovery, Crick is said to have exclaimed, "We have discovered the secret of life!"

Figure 2 Rosalind Franklin, 1920–1958

Figure 3 *This special X-ray photograph is a picture of DNA taken by Rosalind Franklin.*

Figure 4 *This photo shows James Watson, on the left, and Francis Crick, on the right, with their model of DNA.*

DNA Structure

The twisted ladder, or double helix, shape is represented at left in **Figure 5.** As you can see in **Figure 6,** the two sides of the ladder are made of alternating sugar molecules and phosphate molecules. The rungs of the ladder are composed of a pair of nucleotide bases. Adenine on one side always pairs up with thymine on the other side. Guanine always pairs up with cytosine in the same way. How might this structure explain Chargaff's findings?

Figure 5 *The structure of DNA can be compared to a twisted ladder.*

Figure 6 *In a DNA molecule, the bases must pair up in a certain way. If a mistake happens and the bases do not pair up correctly, the gene will not carry the correct information.*

If you took all the DNA in your body from all of your cells and stretched it out end to end, it would extend about 610 million kilometers. That's long enough to stretch from Earth to the sun and back—twice!

Making Copies of DNA

What's so great about DNA? The Watson-Crick model explains how DNA molecules are copied. Because adenine always bonds with thymine, and guanine always bonds with cytosine, the bases on one side of the molecule become a template, or pattern, for the other side. One side, then, is *complementary* to the other. For example, a sequence such as ACCG would have the sequence TGGC added to form a new complementary side. The other side is copied in the same way. This creates two identical molecules of DNA.

As illustrated in **Figure 7,** the DNA molecule is split down the middle where the two bases meet. Then each side of the ladder is able to pair up with additional nucleotides in the nucleus.

MATH **BREAK**

Genes and Bases

A human being has about 100,000 genes. If there are about 30,000 bases in each human gene, about how many bases are in all the genes?

Old   New   New   Old

✓ Self-Check

What would the complementary strand of DNA be for the following sequence of bases? ACCTAGTTG *(See page 636 to check your answer.)*

Figure 7 *The illustration on the left shows the DNA molecule separating down the middle in order to make a copy of itself. Each half of the original molecule serves as a template along which a new complementary strand forms. The photograph at right shows a DNA molecule that has separated. It is magnified to about 1 million times the actual width of DNA.*

From Trait to Gene

The Watson-Crick model also explains how DNA can contain so much information. The bases on one side of the molecule can be put in any order, allowing for an enormous variety of genes. Each gene consists of a string of bases. The order of the bases gives the cell information about how to make each trait.

Putting It All Together DNA functions in the same way for all organisms, from bacteria to mosquitoes to whales to humans. DNA unites us all, and at the same time, it makes each of us unique. The journey from trait to DNA base is illustrated in the diagram on these two pages.

3
A cross section of your skin reveals many different types of cells.

2
. . . magnified 10 times

1
The skin of your forehead . . .

4
A typical skin cell is about 0.0025 cm in diameter.

8
A single loop
of DNA . . .

7
Each chromosome
contains an enormous
amount of DNA.

9
. . . contains
even more
coils.

6
Each chromosome
is made of protein
and DNA.

10
Each strand of
DNA contains
two halves that are
connected down the
center and twisted
like a spiral
staircase.

5
Each skin cell
contains 46
chromosomes.

S C . . . G S
P P
S G . . . C S
P P
S T . . . A S
P P
S C . . . G S
P P
S A . . . T S

DNA
on trial?
Read all about it
on page 172.

More News About Traits

As you may have already discovered, things are often more complicated than they first appear to be. Such is the case with Mendel's findings that you learned about in the previous chapter. Mendel uncovered the basic principles of how genes are passed on from one generation to the next. But as scientists learned more about heredity, they began to find exceptions to Mendel's principles. A few of these exceptions are explained in the following paragraphs.

Incomplete Dominance   In his studies with peas, Mendel found that different traits did not blend together to produce an in-between form. Since then, researchers have found that sometimes one trait is not completely dominant over another. These traits do not blend together, but each allele has its own degree of influence. This is known as *incomplete dominance*. One example of this is the snapdragon flower. **Figure 8** shows a cross between a true-breeding red snapdragon (R^1R^1) and a true-breeding white snapdragon (R^2R^2). As you can see, all of the possible phenotypes for their offspring are pink because both alleles of the gene have some degree of influence.

Figure 8 *The snapdragon provides a good example of incomplete dominance.*

One Gene Can Influence Many Traits Sometimes one gene influences more than one trait. An example of this phenomenon is shown by the white tiger at right. The white fur is caused by a single gene, but this gene influences more than just fur color. Do you see anything else unusual about the tiger? If you look closely, you'll see that the tiger has blue eyes. Here the gene that controls fur color also influences eye color.

A C G T
Learn the DNA alphabet on page 582.

Many Genes Can Influence a Single Trait

Some traits, such as the color of your skin, hair, and eyes, are the result of several genes acting together. That's why it's difficult to tell if a trait is the result of a dominant or recessive gene. As shown in **Figure 9,** you may have blue eyes, but they are probably a slightly different shade of blue than the blue eyes of a classmate. Different combinations of alleles result in slight differences in the amount of pigment present.

The Importance of Environment It's important to remember that genes aren't the only influences on your development. Many things in your environment also influence how you grow and develop. Consider the importance of a healthy diet, exercise, and examples set by family and friends. For example, your genes may determine that you can grow to be tall, but you must receive the proper nutrients as you grow in order to reach your full potential height. You may have inherited a special talent, but you need to practice. Dancer Tatum Harmon, shown below, is practicing to develop her talent.

Figure 9 *At least two genes, each showing incomplete dominance, determine human eye color. That's why so many shades of a color are possible.*

Tatum Harmon practices in a studio at the Alvin Ailey American Dance Theater, where she is a student.

REVIEW

1. List and describe the parts of a nucleotide.

2. Which bases pair together in a DNA molecule?

3. What shape was suggested by Rosalind Franklin's X-ray images?

4. Explain what is meant by the statement, "DNA unites all organisms."

5. **Doing Calculations** If a sample of DNA were found to contain 20 percent cytosine, what percentage of guanine would be in this sample? Why?

How DNA Works

Scientists knew that the order of the bases formed a code that somehow told each cell what to do. The next step in understanding DNA involved breaking this code.

NEW TERMS

ribosome   mutagen
mutation   pedigree

OBJECTIVES

- Explain the relationship between genes and proteins.
- Outline the basic steps in making a protein.
- Define *mutation,* and give an example of it.
- Evaluate the information given in a pedigree.

Genes and Proteins

Scientists discovered that the bases in DNA read like a book, from one end to the other and in one direction only. The bases **A, T, G,** and **C** form the alphabet of the code. Groups of three bases code for a specific amino acid. For example, the three bases **CCA** code for the amino acid proline. The bases **AGC** code for the amino acid serine. As you know, proteins are made up of long strings of amino acids. This is illustrated in **Figure 10.** The order of the bases determines the order of amino acids in a protein. Each gene is a set of instructions for making a protein.

NUCLEUS

A copy of a portion of the DNA molecule, where a particular gene is located, is made and transferred outside of the cell nucleus.

This single strand is a copy of one strand of the original DNA.

Base

Each group of three bases codes for one amino acid.

Figure 10 *A gene is a section of DNA that contains instructions for stringing together amino acids to make a protein.*

Why Proteins? You may be wondering, "What do proteins have to do with who I am or what I look like?" Proteins are found throughout cells. They act as chemical messengers, and they help determine how tall you will grow, what colors you can see, and whether your hair is curly or straight. Human cells contain about 100,000 genes, and each gene spells out sequences of amino acids for specific proteins. Proteins exist in an almost limitless variety. The human body contains about 50,000 different kinds of proteins. Proteins are the reason for the multitude of different shapes, sizes, colors, and textures found in living things, such as antlers, claws, hair, and skin.

The Making of a Protein

As explained on the previous page, the first step in making a protein is to copy the section of the DNA strand containing a gene. A copy of this section is made with the help of copier enzymes. Messenger molecules take the genetic information from the sections of DNA in the nucleus out into the cytoplasm.

In the cytoplasm, the copy of DNA is fed through a kind of protein assembly line. The "factory" where this assembly line exists is known as a **ribosome.** The copy is fed through the ribosome three bases at a time. Transfer molecules act as translators of the message contained in the copy of DNA. Each transfer molecule picks up a specific amino acid from the cytoplasm; the amino acid is determined by the order of the bases the transfer molecule contains. Like pieces of a puzzle, bases on the transfer molecule then match up with bases on the copy of DNA inside the ribosome. The transfer molecules then drop off their amino acid "suitcases," which are strung together to form a protein. This process is illustrated in **Figure 11.**

✓ Self-Check

1. How many amino acids are present in a protein that requires 3,000 bases in its code?
2. Explain how proteins influence how you look.

(See page 636 to check your answers.)

Figure 11 *The diagram below shows how a protein is made. The order of the bases on the copy of DNA determines which amino acids are transferred to the ribosome.*

RIBOSOME

Copy of DNA ▶

❶ A copy of the DNA strand is fed through the ribosome.

❷ Transfer molecules deliver amino acids from the cytoplasm of the cell to the ribosome.

❸ The amino acids are dropped off at the ribosome.

❹ The amino acids are joined together in a long chain to make a protein.

▲ Growing protein chain ▶

6th amino acid

5th amino acid

4th amino acid

3rd amino acid

2nd amino acid

1st amino acid

CYTOPLASM

Original sequence

a Base pair replaced

b Base pair added

c Base pair removed

Figure 12 *The original base-pair sequence at the top has been changed to illustrate (a) substitution, (b) insertion, and (c) deletion.*

earth science
CONNECTION

The layer of ozone in the Earth's atmosphere helps shield the planet's surface from incoming ultraviolet radiation. Ultraviolet radiation is known to cause mutations in skin cells that can lead to skin cancer. Each year more than 750,000 people get some form of skin cancer. Scientists fear that damage to the ozone layer may greatly increase the number of skin cancers each year.

Changes in Genes

Imagine that you've been invited to ride on a brand-new roller coaster at the state fair. Just before you climb into the front car, you are informed that some of the metal parts on the coaster have been replaced by parts made of a different substance. Would you still want to ride on this roller coaster?

Perhaps a better, stronger metal was substituted. Or perhaps another metal with identical properties was used. The third possibility is that a material not suited to the job was used. Imagine what would happen if cardboard were used instead of metal!

Mistakes like these occur in DNA frequently. They are known as **mutations.** Mutations occur when there is a change in the order of the bases in an organism's DNA. Sometimes a base is left out; this is known as a *deletion*. Or an extra base might be added; this is known as an *insertion*. The most common error occurs when an incorrect base replaces a correct base. This is known as a *substitution*. **Figure 12** illustrates these three types of mutations.

Mistakes Happen Fortunately, repair enzymes are continuously on the job, patrolling the DNA molecule for errors. When an error is found, it is usually repaired. But occasionally the repairs are not completely accurate, and the mistakes become part of the genetic message. As with the roller coaster, there are three possible consequences to changes in DNA: an improvement, no change at all, or a harmful change. If the correct protein is not made, the results can be fatal. If the damage occurs in the sex cells, the mistake can be passed from one generation to the next.

How Can DNA Become Damaged? In addition to random errors that occur when DNA is copied, damage can be caused by physical and chemical agents known as **mutagens.** A mutagen is anything that can cause a mutation in DNA. Examples of mutagens include high-energy radiation from X rays and ultraviolet radiation. Ultraviolet radiation is the type of energy in sunlight that is responsible for suntans and sunburns. Examples of chemical mutagens include asbestos and chemicals found in cigarette smoke.

An Example of a Substitution

Consider the DNA sequence containing the three bases **GAA**. **GAA** are the three letters that give the instructions: "Put glutamic acid here." If a mistake occurs and the sequence is changed to **GTA**, a completely different message is sent: "Put valine here."

This simple change just described can cause the disease *sickle cell anemia*. Sickle cell anemia is a disease that affects red blood cells. When valine is substituted for glutamic acid in a blood protein, as shown in **Figure 13,** the red blood cells become distorted into a sickle shape.

The sickled cells are not as good as normal red blood cells at carrying oxygen through the body. They are also more likely to get stuck in blood vessels, causing painful and dangerous clots.

Quick **Lab**

Mutations

The sentence below contains all 3-letter words, but has experienced a mutation. See if you can find the mutation and correct it.

THE IGR EDC ATA TET HEB IGB ADR AT

What kind of mutation did you find? Now what does the sentence say?

Figure 13 *The simple change of one base leads to the disease called sickle cell anemia.*

Genetic Counseling

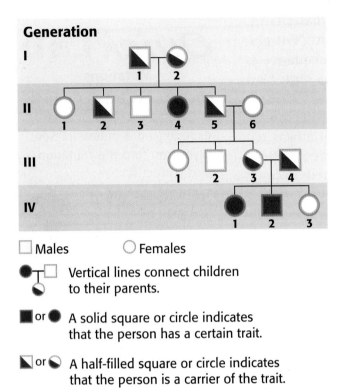

Generation

□ Males   ○ Females

Vertical lines connect children to their parents.

■ or ● A solid square or circle indicates that the person has a certain trait.

◣ or ◐ A half-filled square or circle indicates that the person is a carrier of the trait.

Figure 14 *Cystic fibrosis is a recessive hereditary disease that affects the respiratory system. A pedigree for cystic fibrosis is shown above.*

Most hereditary disorders, such as sickle cell anemia, are recessive disorders. This means that the disease occurs only when a child inherits a defective gene from both parents. Some people, called carriers, have only one allele for the disease. Carriers of the gene may pass it along to their children without knowing that they have the mutated gene.

Genetic counseling provides information and counseling to couples who wish to have children but are worried that they might pass a disease to their children. Genetic counselors often make use of a diagram known as a **pedigree,** which is a tool for tracing a trait through generations of a family. By making a pedigree, it is often possible to predict whether a person is a carrier of a hereditary disease. In **Figure 14,** the trait for the disease cystic fibrosis is tracked through four generations. Each generation is numbered with Roman numerals, and each individual is numbered with Arabic numerals. The symbols used in a pedigree are explained in Figure 14.

The pedigree at right shows the recessive trait of nearsightedness in Jane's family. Jane, her parents, and her brother all have normal vision. Which individuals in the pedigree are nearsighted? What are the possible genotypes of Jane's parents? Jane has two possible genotypes. What are they? Jane is planning to marry a person who has normal vision but carries the trait for nearsightedness. Work two Punnett squares to show the possible genotypes of Jane's future children.

REVIEW

1. List the three types of mutations. How do they differ?

2. What type of mutation causes sickle cell anemia?

3. **Applying Concepts** Mutations can occur in sex cells or in body cells. In which cell type might a mutation be passed from generation to generation? Explain.

Applied Genetics

NEW TERMS
genetic engineering
recombinant DNA
DNA fingerprinting
Human Genome Project

OBJECTIVES
- Define *genetic engineering*.
- List some of the benefits of combining the DNA of different organisms.

For thousands of years, humans have been aware of the benefits of selective breeding. In selective breeding, organisms with certain desirable characteristics are mated. You probably have enjoyed the benefits of selective breeding, although you may not have realized it. For example, you may have eaten an egg from a chicken that was bred to produce a large number of eggs. Or perhaps you've eaten wheat that was selectively bred to resist pests and disease. Your pet dog might even be a result of selective breeding. Some kinds of dogs, for example, have a thick coat so that they can retrieve game in icy waters.

Designer Genes

Scientists now have the ability to manipulate individual genes using a technique known as genetic engineering. Like all types of engineering, genetic engineering puts scientific knowledge to practical use. Basically, **genetic engineering** allows scientists to transfer genes from one organism to another. Genetic engineering is already used to manufacture proteins, repair damaged genes, and identify individuals who may carry an allele for a disease. Some other uses are shown in **Figure 15.**

Figure 15 *Some of the many examples of genetic engineering are shown below.*

a A sheep called Dolly was the first successfully cloned mammal.

b The photograph above shows cotton bolls from two different plants. The one on the right has been genetically altered to resist pests.

c This electron micrograph shows plastic granules produced inside a plant cell.

d Scientists added a gene found in fireflies to this tobacco plant. The plant now produces an enzyme that causes the plant to glow.

Human chromosome 2

Insulin gene transferred

Bacterial DNA

Gene for replication

Recombinant DNA introduced into bacteria

Bacteria culture producing insulin

Figure 16 *The gene that produces insulin in humans is found on chromosome 2. A copy is transferred to a piece of bacterial DNA. The bacteria containing the recombinant DNA will produce insulin.*

Living Factories

The structure of DNA is the same in all living organisms. In fact, the sameness of the DNA structure allows genes from one organism to work in another. When genes from one organism are put into another using genetic engineering, the resulting DNA is known as **recombinant DNA.** But why would we want scientists to do this?

One answer is that recombinant DNA can be used to treat diseases. The disease called diabetes, for example, is treated with a product made by using recombinant DNA. People with diabetes are unable to produce enough of the hormone insulin (a protein). Without sufficient insulin, most diabetics would die. To make the recombinant DNA, scientists insert a normal human insulin gene into the DNA of certain bacteria. The bacteria become insulin factories, producing insulin in very large amounts. This process is shown in **Figure 16.**

DNA Fingerprints

At the beginning of this unit, you were asked to imagine that you had been wrongly accused of a crime. The only "witness" in your defense was your DNA. As you have learned, each person's DNA is unique.

In the laboratory, DNA fragments are separated from each other based on their size. The patterns formed by the fragments can then be

Cellmark Diagnostics

Figure 17 *The dark bands are DNA fragments. The location of the dark bands is different in everyone.*

compared. You can see an example of these fragments in **Figure 17.** Comparing the fragments from different individuals is known as DNA analysis, or **DNA fingerprinting.** It is impossible for two people to have the same DNA fingerprint unless they are identical twins.

✓ Self-Check

Explain what is meant by living factories when referring to recombinant DNA. *(See page 636 to check your answer.)*

The Big Picture

Scientists know a lot about certain genes, such as the location and mutation of the gene that causes sickle cell anemia. **Figure 18** shows one of the results of DNA research. But there is still much to learn about genes that control other diseases and characteristics. The goal of an ambitious project known as the **Human Genome Project** is to create a map that shows the location and the DNA sequence of all our genes.

Scientists hope that the knowledge gained from this project will help them develop more-effective therapies for diseases. They have already identified genes associated with colon cancer and juvenile glaucoma. The Human Genome Project will take many years and millions of dollars to complete.

Select 10 scenic or human-interest pictures from magazines or newspapers. Select one or two items in the pictures that are now or someday might be affected by DNA technology. State whether DNA technology will help or harm the subject and whether the change will be beneficial or harmful to society.

Chromosome 7

Figure 18 *The girl in this picture is receiving therapy for cystic fibrosis. The gene was identified, and a therapy was developed through DNA technology.*

REVIEW

1. How is genetic engineering different from selective breeding?

2. What are some benefits of genetic engineering?

3. Why would it be an advantage to produce human insulin inside a bacterium?

4. **Understanding Technology** Describe how your DNA can be used to identify you.

Chapter Highlights

Vocabulary

DNA (p. 152)

nucleotide (p. 152)

adenine (p. 152)

thymine (p. 152)

guanine (p. 152)

cytosine (p. 152)

Section Notes

- Proteins are made up of long strings of amino acids.

- DNA is made up of long strings of nucleotides.

- Chromosomes are made of protein and DNA.

- The DNA molecule looks like a twisted ladder. The rungs of the ladder are made of base pairs, either adenine and thymine, or cytosine and guanine.

- DNA carries genetic information in the order of the nucleotide bases.

- DNA can be copied because one strand of the molecule serves as a template for the other side.

Vocabulary

ribosome (p. 161)

mutation (p. 162)

mutagen (p. 162)

pedigree (p. 164)

Section Notes

- A gene is a set of instructions for assembling a protein.

- Each group of three bases in a gene codes for a particular amino acid.

- Genes can become mutated when the order of the bases is changed.

Labs

Base-Pair Basics (p. 582)

☑ Skills Check

Math Concepts

THE GENETIC CODE The MathBreak on page 155 asks you to calculate the number of bases in all of your genes. If there are about 30,000 bases in each gene and there are 100,000 genes, then multiply to find the answer.

$$30{,}000 \times 100{,}000 = 3{,}000{,}000{,}000$$

So, there are about 3 billion bases in all of your genes.

Visual Understanding

COPIES OF DNA Look at Figure 10 on page 160. You can see the nucleus and the pores in its membrane. The copy of DNA emerges through these pores on its way to deliver its coded message to the ribosomes. Why does DNA send a copy out of the nucleus to relay its message? The answer is that DNA is much more protected from factors that might cause a mutation if it stays inside the nucleus. The messenger copy may encounter bad luck, but the master DNA usually stays very safe!

Vocabulary

genetic engineering *(p. 165)*

recombinant DNA *(p. 166)*

DNA fingerprinting *(p. 166)*

Human Genome Project *(p. 167)*

Section Notes

- People have used selective breeding for thousands of years to cross plants to produce bigger crops. People have also been selectively breeding animals with desireable traits for thousands of years.

- Genetic engineering allows scientists to change an organism's DNA to give the organism new characteristics.

- The goal of the Human Genome Project is to map the location of all human genes.

---

internet **connect**

GO TO: go.hrw.com

Visit the **HRW** Web site for a variety of learning tools related to this chapter. Just type in the keyword:

KEYWORD: HSTDNA

SCILINKS
NSTA

GO TO: www.scilinks.org

Visit the **National Science Teachers Association** on-line Web site for Internet resources related to this chapter. Just type in the *sci*LINKS number for more information about the topic:

TOPIC: DNA	*sci*LINKS NUMBER: HSTL130
TOPIC: Genes and Traits	*sci*LINKS NUMBER: HSTL135
TOPIC: Genetic Engineering	*sci*LINKS NUMBER: HSTL140
TOPIC: DNA Fingerprinting	*sci*LINKS NUMBER: HSTL145

Chapter Review

USING VOCABULARY

To complete the following sentences, choose the correct term from each pair of terms listed below:

1. A protein is a long string of ___?___.
   A strand of DNA is a long string of ___?___.
   (*amino acids* or *nucleotides*)

2. A disorder, such as cystic fibrosis, is known as ___?___ if the child must receive an allele for the disease from each parent in order to have the disease. (*dominant* or *recessive*)

3. A change in the order of bases in DNA is called a ___?___. (*mutation* or *mutagen*)

4. ___?___ is used to compare the DNA of different individuals. (*Genetic engineering* or *DNA fingerprinting*)

5. A ___?___ is a physical or chemical agent that causes damage to DNA. (*mutagen* or *pedigree*)

UNDERSTANDING CONCEPTS

Multiple Choice

6. In a DNA molecule, which of the following bases pair together?
   a. adenine and cytosine
   b. thymine and adenine
   c. thymine and guanine
   d. cytosine and thymine

7. A gene is
   a. a set of instructions for each trait.
   b. instructions on how to make a protein.
   c. a portion of a strand of DNA.
   d. All of the above

8. DNA
   a. is made up of three subunits.
   b. has a structure like a twisted ladder.
   c. cannot be repaired if it is mutated.
   d. All of the above

9. In incomplete dominance,
   a. a single gene controls many traits.
   b. genes for a trait are all recessive.
   c. each allele for a trait has its own degree of influence.
   d. the environment controls the genes.

10. Watson and Crick
    a. studied the amounts of each base in DNA.
    b. took X-ray pictures of DNA.
    c. made models to determine DNA structure.
    d. discovered that genes were located on chromosomes.

11. Which of the following is NOT a step in making a protein?
    a. Copies of DNA are taken to the cytoplasm.
    b. Transfer molecules deliver amino acids to the nucleus.
    c. Amino acids are joined together at the ribosome to make a protein.
    d. A copy of the DNA is fed through the ribosome.

Short Answer

12. What would the complementary strand of DNA be for the following sequence of bases?

    C T T A G G C T T A C C A

13. How does DNA copy itself? Draw a picture to help explain your answer.

14. If the DNA sequence TGAGCCATGA is changed to TGAGCACATGA, what kind of mutation has occurred?

Concept Mapping

15. Use the following terms to create a concept map: bases, adenine, thymine, nucleotides, guanine, DNA, cytosine.

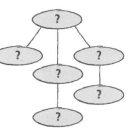

CRITICAL THINKING AND PROBLEM SOLVING

Write one or two sentences to answer the following questions:

16. If neither parent shows signs of having sickle cell anemia, does this fact guarantee that their children will not contract the disease? Explain.

17. How many amino acids does this DNA sequence code for?

    T C A G C C A C C T A T G G A

18. Bacteria grow easily and multiply rapidly. Why are bacteria good factories for making genetically engineered proteins?

MATH IN SCIENCE

19. The goal of the Human Genome Project is to discover all of the human genes. Scientists estimate that there are 100,000 human genes. In 1998, 38,000 genes had been discovered. How many more genes must the Human Genome Project discover?

20. If scientists find 6,000 genes each year, how many years will it take to finish the project?

21. Of the 38,000 genes discovered, 7,000 have been mapped to their chromosome location. What percentage of the discovered genes have been mapped?

INTERPRETING GRAPHICS

Examine the pedigree for albinism shown below, and then answer the following questions. You may need to use a Punnett square to answer some of these questions. (Albinism is a trait among individuals who produce no pigment in their skin, hair, or eyes.)

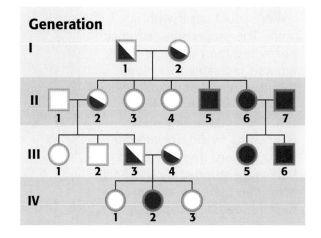

22. How many males are represented on this pedigree? How many females?

23. How many individuals in Generation II had albinism? How many were carriers of the trait?

24. Do you think albinism is a dominant trait or a recessive trait? Explain.

NOW What Do You Think?

Take a minute to review your answers to the ScienceLog questions on page 151. Have your answers changed? If necessary, revise your answers based on what you have learned since you began this chapter.

DNA on Trial

The tension in the courtroom was so thick you could cut it with a knife. The prosecuting attorney presented the evidence: "DNA analysis indicates that blood found on the defendant's shoes matches the blood of the victim. The odds of this match happening by chance are one in 20 million." The jury members were stunned by these figures. Can there be any doubt that the defendant is guilty?

Next Defendant: DNA

Court battles involving DNA fingerprinting are becoming more and more common. Traditional fingerprinting has been used for more than 100 years, and it has been an extremely important identification tool. Recently, many people have claimed that DNA fingerprinting, also called DNA profiling, will replace the traditional technique. The DNA profiling technique has been used to clear thousands of wrongly accused or convicted individuals. However, the controversy begins when the evidence is used to try to prove a suspect's guilt.

Room for Reasonable Doubt

Critics claim that the DNA fingerprinting process allows too much room for human error.

▲ *This forensic scientist is gathering dead skin cells from an article of clothing in hopes of collecting samples of DNA.*

Handling samples from a crime scene can be tricky—a sample may have been removed from a small area beneath a victim's fingernail or scraped off a dirty sidewalk. Contamination by salt, chemicals, denim, or even a lab person's sneeze can affect the accuracy of the results.

Much of the controversy about DNA fingerprinting surrounds the interpretation of the results. The question becomes, "How likely is it that someone in addition to the suspect also has that same DNA profile?" Answers can range from one in three to one in 20 million, depending on the person doing the interpreting, the sample size, and the process used.

Critics also point out that the results may be calculated without regard for certain factors. For instance, individuals belonging to certain ethnic groups are likely to share more characteristics of their DNA with others in their group than with people outside the group.

Beyond a Reasonable Doubt

Those who support DNA evidence point out that the analysis is totally objective because the labs that do the DNA analysis receive samples labeled in code. The data either clear or incriminate a suspect. Moreover, DNA evidence alone is rarely used to convict a person. It is one of several forms of evidence, including motive and access to the crime scene, used to reach a verdict.

Supporters of DNA fingerprinting say that checks and balances in laboratories help prevent human errors. In addition, recent efforts to standardize both evidence gathering and interpretation of samples have further improved results.

What Do You Think?

▶ Should DNA fingerprinting be admitted as evidence in the courtroom? Do some additional research, and decide for yourself.

Science Fiction

"Moby James"

by Patricia A. McKillip

Rob Trask has a problem. It's his older brother, James. Rob is convinced that James is not his real brother. Rob and his family live on a space station, and he just knows that his real brother was sent back to Earth. This person who claims to be James is really either some sort of mutant irradiated plant life or a mutant pair of dirty sweat socks.

Now Rob has another problem—his class is reading Herman Melville's novel *Moby Dick.* At first, Rob just can't get interested in the story. But as he reads more and more, Rob becomes entranced by the story of Captain Ahab and his quest for revenge against the great white whale Moby Dick. Moby Dick had taken something from Ahab—his leg—and Ahab wants to make the whale pay!

Suddenly Rob realizes that his brother is a great white mutant whale—Moby James. As Rob follows Ahab on his search for Moby Dick, Rob begins to understand what he must do to get his real brother back again. So he watches Moby James, trying to catch James in some mistake that will reveal him for the mutant he is. Once Rob catches the fake James, he will be able to get the real James back again.

To find out if Rob is successful in his quest to find his real brother, read "Moby James" in the *Holt Anthology of Science Fiction.*

8 The Evolution of Living Things

CENOZOIC TIMES

SECTION A

Main Street 6
Law & Order 9
Obituaries 11

COMMUNITY NEWS • Saturday : June 21

Large Bird Terrorizes Countryside!

Panic Possible

Farmers in the local area reported yesterday seeing a fantastic creature dashing through the trees and trampling crops in their fields. The creature has been described as weighing about 400 lb (about 182 kg), ...ing about 7 ft (over 2 m) tall, with a huge head, ...ngs, an enormous beak, and ferocious claws.

...ave been no casualties reported, ... acres of corn that was ready for ...appeared! Tracks left behind by ...are all over the former corn ...corn cobs litter the ground,
...say.

The local agriculture agent reports, "This could be the worst disaster to our corn harvest since the heat wave 10 years ago when all the corn popped in the field." Anyone spotting this creature should stay inside and contact the local ...

Artist's rendering of marauding monster

Barbecue Planned : Court News

What If . . . ?

The time is 50 million years ago. The place is a swamp in North America. Imagine yourself trekking through the steamy swamp, sidestepping snakes and spiders. Suddenly, out of the trees dashes a 182 kg giant with a huge head, a thick neck, and long, muscular legs.

What is this beast? A velociraptor? A giant sloth? A prehistoric bear? None of the above. It's a *Diatryma*, a kind of flightless bird that was common during the Cenozoic era of prehistory, 57 to 35 million years ago! *Diatryma* stood over 2 m tall and had an enormous beak and sharp claws.

Scientists know about *Diatryma* from many fossils dug up in Wyoming, New Mexico, and New Jersey. *Diatryma* was probably forced out of existence by large mammals. Though the monster bird is long gone, smaller versions of it live in poultry coops around the world. *Diatryma*, its fossils indicate, was a distant cousin of the present-day chicken!

Fossils reveal what extinct organisms looked like. They also provide clues about *evolution*—the process by which animals and other living things gradually change over time. What other evidence is there that evolution takes place? How does evolution happen? These are some of the questions you will explore in this chapter.

Investigate!

What Do You Think?

In your ScienceLog, try to answer the following questions based on what you already know:

1. What is evolution?

2. What role does the environment play in the survival of an organism?

3. How do fossils help scientists study changes in organisms?

Making a Fossil

In this activity, you and a classmate will work together to make two different types of fossils.

Procedure

1. The class will be divided into pairs of students. You and your partner will receive **a paper cup, a paper plate, modeling clay, some petroleum jelly,** and a small item, such as **a leaf, a shell,** or **a tiny toy dinosaur.** Put your names on your cups.

2. Pat some modeling clay into the bottom of the paper plate. Press the item into the clay, and then remove it as carefully as possible so that an impression of the object remains in the clay.

3. Pat some clay into the bottom of the cup. Rub petroleum jelly on the item, and place it in the bottom of the cup. (Do not press it into the clay this time.)

4. Have your teacher pour some **plaster of Paris** into the plate and the cup so that the clay and the object are covered. Place them where your teacher instructs, and allow the plaster to dry overnight.

5. The next day, carefully tear the paper plate and cup from the hardened plaster. Remove the clay and the object. You have now made two

different kinds of fossils. The two kinds of fossils are a *mold* and a *cast.* A mold is a cavity (imprint) that is the shape of an organism. A cast is a mold filled in with sediment.

Analysis

6. Identify each of your fossils as a mold or a cast.

7. Which of these organisms—a clam, a jellyfish, a crab, and a mushroom—would make good fossils? Which kind of fossil (mold or cast) would you expect to find? Which would not make good fossils? Explain your answers.

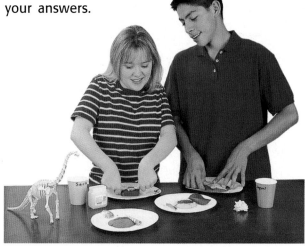

Change Over Time

NEW TERMS

adaptation   fossil
species   fossil record
evolution   vestigial structure

OBJECTIVES

- Explain how fossils provide evidence that organisms have evolved over time.
- Identify three ways that organisms can be compared to support the theory of evolution.

If someone asked you to describe a frog, you might say that a frog has long hind legs, eyes that bulge, and a habit of croaking from time to time. Then you might start to think about some of the differences among frogs—differences that set one kind of frog apart from another. Take a look at **Figures 1, 2,** and **3** on this page. These frogs look different from each other, yet they all inhabit a tropical rain forest. Read about each frog below, and you will discover that their differences are more than skin deep.

Figure 2 *The smoky jungle frog survives by hiding in dead leaves on the forest floor and blending into the background.*

Figure 3 *The strawberry dart-poison frog hops around on the forest floor during the day. Its bright coloring warns predators that it is poisonous.*

Figure 1 *The red-eyed tree frog survives by hiding among a tree's leaves during the day and coming out only at night.*

Differences Among Organisms

As you can see, these three frogs have different adaptations that enable them to survive. An **adaptation** is a hereditary characteristic that helps an organism survive and reproduce in its environment. Adaptations can include structures and behaviors for finding food, for protection, and for moving from place to place.

Living things that share the same characteristics and adaptations may be members of the same species. A **species** is a group of organisms that can mate with one another to produce fertile offspring. For example, all red-eyed tree frogs are members of the same species and can mate with one another to produce more red-eyed tree frogs.

BRAIN FOOD

Native tribes in Central America rub the poison from the strawberry dart-poison frog on their arrow tips before hunting. The poison helps to paralyze their prey.

Do Species Change Over Time? These frogs are just a few of the millions of different species that share the Earth with us. The species on Earth today range from bacteria that lack cell nuclei to multicellular fungi, plants, and animals. Have these same species always existed on Earth?

Earth is a very old planet. Scientists estimate that it is 4.6 billion years old. The planet itself has changed a great deal during that long period of time. Fossil evidence shows that living things have changed as well. Since life first appeared on Earth, a great number of species have died out and have been replaced by newer species. **Figure 4** shows some of the different life-forms that have existed during Earth's history.

What causes species to change? Scientists think that newer species have descended from older species through the process of evolution. **Evolution** is the process by which populations accumulate inherited changes over time. Because of evolution, scientists think that all living things, from daisies to crocodiles to humans, share a common ancestor.

Figure 4 *This spiral diagram represents many changes in life on Earth since the formation of the planet 4.6 billion years ago.*

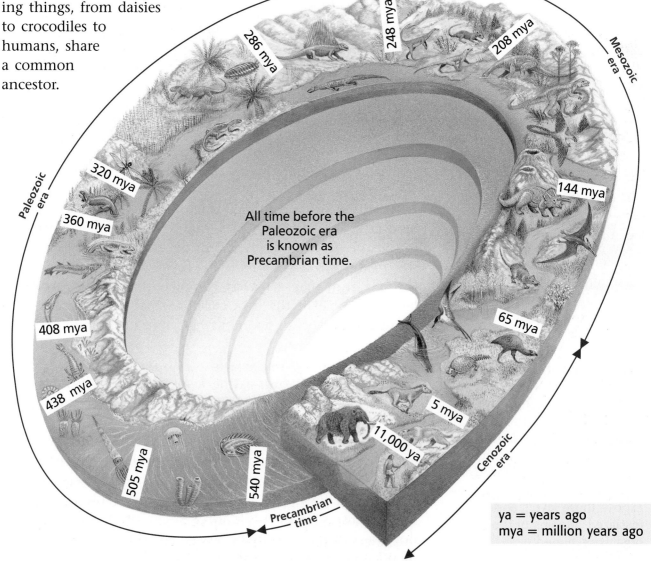

286 mya

248 mya

208 mya

Mesozoic era

320 mya

144 mya

360 mya

All time before the Paleozoic era is known as Precambrian time.

Paleozoic era

408 mya

65 mya

438 mya

5 mya

505 mya

540 mya

11,000 ya

Cenozoic era

Precambrian time

ya = years ago
mya = million years ago

The Evolution of Living Things   **177**

Evidence of Evolution: The Fossil Record

Evidence that living things evolve comes from many different sources. This evidence includes fossils as well as comparisons among different groups of organisms.

Fossils The outermost layer of the Earth is known as the *crust*. A large part of the crust is arranged in layers, with different kinds of rock and soil stacked on top of one another. These layers are formed when sediments, particles of sand, dust, or soil, are carried by wind and water and are deposited in an orderly fashion. Older layers are deposited before newer layers and are buried deeper within the Earth. **Fossils,** the solidified remains or imprints of once-living organisms, are found in these layers. Fossils, like those pictured in **Figure 5,** can be of complete organisms, parts of organisms, or just a set of footprints.

Figure 5 The fossil on the left is of a trilobite, an ancient aquatic animal related to the crab. It lived about 500 million years ago. The fossils on the right are of seed-ferns that lived about 300 million years ago.

earth science CONNECTION

Fossils are usually found in layered rock, called sedimentary rock. Sedimentary rock usually forms when rock is broken into sediment by wind, water, and other means. The wind and water move the sediment around and deposit it. Over time, layers of sediment pile up to great heights. Lower layers are compressed and changed into rock. Many years later, geologic forces may expose these layers and the fossilized remains of the organisms buried with them.

Fossils are usually formed when a dead organism is covered by a layer of sediment. Over time, more sediment settles on top of the organism. Minerals in the sediment may seep into the organism, gradually replacing the organism with stone. Or, the organism may rot away completely after being covered, leaving a hole in the rock called a *mold*. Fossils are usually formed on the ocean floor, in swamps, in mud, and in tar pits.

Reading the Fossil Record Fossils provide a historical sequence of life known as the **fossil record.** The fossil record, in turn, supplies evidence about the order in which evolutionary changes have occurred. Fossils found in the upper, or newer, layers of the Earth's crust tend to resemble present-day organisms. This similarity indicates that the fossilized organisms were close relatives of present-day organisms. The deeper in the Earth's crust fossils are found, the less they look like present-day organisms. These fossils are of earlier forms of life that may now be extinct. The fossil record also shows how environmental conditions on Earth may have changed over time.

Gaps in the Fossil Record If every organism that lived left an imprint behind, the fossil record would resemble a very large evolutionary family tree. **Figure 6** shows a hypothetical fossil record in which all relationships between organisms are clearly mapped.

Although scientists have collected thousands of fossils, a large number of gaps remain in the current fossil record, as shown in **Figure 7.** This is because specific conditions are necessary for fossils to form. Organisms without hard body parts are not usually preserved in the fossil record. Most fossilized organisms had skeletons or shells. The skeleton or shell must be buried in sediment that is very fine. Also, oxygen—which promotes decay—cannot be present. If oxygen is present, much of the organism will not fossilize. However, very few places are free of oxygen. Because the conditions needed for fossils to form are rare, fossils are often difficult to find.

Vestigial Structures Whales are the largest organisms in the ocean. They consume tons of plankton each day and are similar in shape to fish. Yet whales are *mammals*—warmblooded animals that breathe air, give live birth, and produce milk for their young. Although modern whales do not have hind limbs and feet, there are remnants of hind-limb bones embedded deep inside their bodies, as shown in **Figure 8.** These remnants of once-useful structures are known as **vestigial structures.** Scientists think that over millions of years, whales evolved from doglike land dwellers into sea-dwelling organisms. But scientists have not had the fossil evidence to support their ideas—until now. Read the following case study to learn the story of whale evolution.

The Fossil Record

Figure 6 *This is the way the fossil record might appear if fossils from every species had been found.*

The Fossil Record

Figure 7 *Scientists have been able to complete small sections of the fossil record.*

Figure 8 *Remnants of hind-limb bones are embedded deep inside the whale's body.*

Case Study: Evolution of the Whale

Scientists hypothesize that whales evolved from land-dwelling mammals like *Mesonychid* (muh ZOH ni kid), shown below, which *returned* to the ocean about 55 million years ago. During the 1980s and 1990s, several fossils of whale ancestors were discovered. These discoveries support a theory of whale evolution.

55 million years ago
Mesonychid

Ambulocetus (AM byoo loh SEE tuhs), pictured below, lived in coastal waters. *Ambulocetus* had shorter legs than *Mesonychid*, but it still had feet and toes that could support its weight on land. Although *Ambulocetus* had a tail, scientists think it kicked its legs like an otter in order to swim and used its tail for balance.

50 million years ago
Ambulocetus

46 million years ago
Rodhocetus

Forty-six million years ago, *Rodhocetus* (roh doh SEE tuhs) appeared in the fossil record. This animal more closely resembled modern whales, but it had hind limbs and feet that it retained from its land-dwelling ancestor. Because of its short legs, *Rodhocetus* was restricted to a crocodile-like waddle while on land. Unlike the legs of *Ambulocetus*, these legs were not necessary for swimming. Instead, *Rodhocetus* depended on its massive tail to propel it through the water. While *Ambulocetus* probably pulled itself onto land every night, *Rodhocetus* probably spent most of its time in the water.

Prozeuglodon (pro ZOO gloh dahn), which appeared in the fossil record 6 million years after *Rodhocetus*, was well adapted for life at sea. Although it still had a pair of very small legs, *Prozeuglodon* lived only in the water.

BRAIN FOOD

During their early development, modern whale embryos have four limbs. The rear limbs disappear before birth, and the front limbs develop into flippers.

40 million years ago
Prozeuglodon

Evidence of Evolution: Comparing Organisms

Evidence that life has evolved also comes from comparisons of different groups of organisms. On the following pages, the different kinds of evidence that support the theory of evolution are discussed in greater detail.

Human arm

Cat leg

Dolphin flipper

Bat wing

Figure 9 *The bones in the front limbs of these animals are similar, even though the limbs are used in different ways. In the figure, the most similar bones are shown in the same color.*

Comparing Skeletal Structures

What does your arm have in common with the front leg of a cat, the front flipper of a dolphin, or the wing of a bat? At first glance, you might think that they have little in common. After all, these structures don't look very much alike and are not used in the same way. If you look under the surface, however, the structure and order of the bones in the front limbs of these different animals, shown in **Figure 9,** are actually similar to the structure and order of the bones found in your arm.

The similarities indicate that animals as different as a cat, a dolphin, a bat, and a human are all related by a common ancestor. The evolutionary process has modified these bones over millions of years to perform specified functions.

Comparing DNA from Different Species Scientists hypothesize that if all organisms living today evolved from a common ancestor, they should all have the same kind of genetic material. And in fact they do. From microscopic bacteria to giant polar bears, all organisms share the same genetic material—DNA.

In addition, scientists hypothesize that species which appear to be close relatives should have greater similarities in their DNA than species that appear to be distant relatives. For example, chimpanzees and gorillas appear to be close relatives. Chimpanzees and toucans appear to be distant relatives. The DNA of chimpanzees is, in fact, more similar to the DNA of gorillas than to the DNA of toucans.

Comparing Embryonic Structures Can you tell the difference between a chicken, a rabbit, and a human? It's pretty easy when you compare adults from each species. But what about comparing members of these species before they are born? Look at the left side of **Figure 10,** which depicts the very early embryos of a chicken, a rabbit, and a human.

All the organisms shown in the figure are *vertebrates*, or animals that have a backbone. Early in development, human embryos and the embryos of all other vertebrates are similar. These early similarities are evidence that all vertebrates share a common ancestor. Although the embryos look similar to each other in very early stages, none of them look like their adult forms. Embryo development has evolved over millions of years causing the embryonic structures to grow into many different species of vertebrates. The changes in the process of embryo development therefore produce animals as different as a chicken and a human.

Figure 10 *The embryos of different vertebrates are very similar during the earliest stages of development.*

REVIEW

1. How does the fossil record suggest that species have changed over time?

2. How do the similarities in the forelimb bones of humans, cats, dolphins, and bats support the theory of evolution?

3. **Interpreting Graphics** The photograph at right shows the layers of sedimentary rock exposed during the construction of a road. Imagine that a species which lived 200 million years ago is found in the layer designated as *b*. Its ancestor, which lived 201 million years ago, would most likely be found in which layer, *a* or *c*? Explain your answer.

How Does Evolution Happen?

The early 1800s was a time of great scientific discovery. Geologists realized that the Earth is much older than anyone had previously thought. Evidence showed that gradual processes had shaped the Earth's surface over millions of years. Fossilized remains of bizarre organisms were found. Fossils of familiar things were also found, but some of them were in unusual places. For example, fish fossils, like the one pictured in **Figure 11,** and shells were found on the tops of mountains. The Earth suddenly seemed to be a place where great change was possible. Many people thought that evolution occurs, but no one had been able to determine *how* it happens—until Charles Darwin.

NEW TERMS

trait
selective breeding
natural selection
mutation

OBJECTIVES

- Describe the four steps of Darwin's theory of evolution by natural selection.
- Explain how mutations are important to evolution.

Charles Darwin

In 1831, 21-year-old Charles Darwin, shown in **Figure 12,** had just graduated from college. Like many young people just out of college, Darwin didn't know what he wanted to do with his life. His father wanted him to become a doctor. Unfortunately, Darwin was sickened by watching surgery. Although he eventually earned a degree in theology, he was *really* interested in natural science—the study of plants and animals.

Figure 11 *This fossil of a fish was discovered on top of a mountain.*

Darwin chose not to pursue a career in religion. Instead, he was able to talk his father into letting him sign on for a 5-year voyage around the world. He served as the naturalist (a scientist who studies nature) on a British naval ship, the HMS *Beagle*. During this voyage, Darwin made observations that later became the foundation for his theory of evolution by natural selection.

Figure 12 *Charles Darwin, shown at far left, sailed around the world on a ship very similar to this one.*

Darwin's Excellent Adventure

As the HMS *Beagle* made its way around the world, Darwin collected thousands of plant and animal samples and kept detailed notes of his observations. The *Beagle*'s journey is charted in **Figure 13.** During the journey, the ship visited the Galápagos Islands, shown below, which are 965 km (600 mi) west of Ecuador, a country in South America.

Figure 13 *The course of the HMS* Beagle *is noted by the red line.*

Darwin's Finches

Darwin observed that the animals and plants on the Galápagos Islands were very similar, yet not identical, to the animals and plants on the nearby South American mainland. For example, he noted that the finches living on the Galápagos Islands differed slightly from the finches in Ecuador. The finches on the islands were different not only from the mainland finches but also from each other. As you can see in **Figure 14,** the birds differed from each other mainly in the shape of their beaks and in the food they ate.

The large ground finch has a heavy, strong beak adapted for cracking big, hard seeds. This finch's beak works like a nutcracker.

The cactus finch has a tough beak that is good for eating cactus and its nectar. It works like a pair of needle-nosed pliers.

The warbler finch's small, pointed beak is adapted for probing into cracks and crevices to obtain small insects. This beak works like a pair of tweezers.

Figure 14 *The beaks of these three species of finches from the Galápagos Islands are adapted to the different ways the finches obtain food.*

Darwin Does Some Thinking

Darwin's observations raised questions that he couldn't easily answer, such as, "Why are the finches on the islands similar but not identical to the finches on the mainland?" and "Why do the finches from different islands differ from one another?" Darwin thought that perhaps all the finches on the Galápagos Islands descended from finches on the South American mainland. The original population of finches may have been blown from South America to the Galápagos Islands by a storm. Over many generations, the finches that survived may have adapted to various ways of living on the Galápagos Islands.

After Darwin returned to England, he spent many years working on his theory of how evolution happens. During this period, he pulled together many ideas from a variety of sources.

Have you ever heard of a bank that has no money, only seeds? Read about it on page 198.

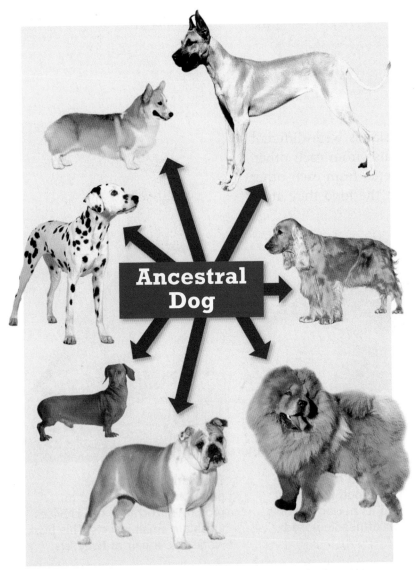

Figure 15 *Dogs are a good example of how selective breeding works. Over the past 12,000 years, dogs have been selectively bred to produce more than 150 different breeds.*

Darwin Learned from Farmers and Animal and Plant Breeders

In Darwin's time, many varieties of farm animals and plants had been selectively produced. Farmers chose certain **traits,** distinguishing qualities such as plump corn kernels, and bred only the individuals that had the desired traits. This procedure is called **selective breeding** because humans, not nature, select which traits will be passed along to the next generation. Selective breeding in dogs, shown in **Figure 15,** has exaggerated certain traits to produce more than 150 different breeds.

In your studies of genetics and heredity, you learned that a great variety of traits exists among individuals in a species. Darwin was impressed that farmers and breeders could direct and shape these traits and make such dramatic changes in animals and plants in just a few short generations. He thought that wild animals and plants could change in a similar way but that the process would take much longer because variations would be due to chance.

Darwin Learned from Geologists

Geologists told Darwin that they had evidence that the Earth was much older than anyone had imagined. He learned from reading *Principles of Geology*, by Charles Lyell, that Earth had been formed by natural processes over a long period of time. Lyell's data were important because Darwin thought that populations of organisms changed very slowly, requiring a lot of time.

Darwin Learned from the Work of Thomas Malthus In his *Essay on the Principle of Population*, Malthus proposed that humans have the potential to reproduce beyond the capacity of their food supplies. However, he also recognized that death caused by starvation, disease, and war affects the size of human populations. Malthus's thoughts are represented in **Figure 16.**

Darwin realized that other animal species are also capable of producing too many offspring. For these animal species, starvation, disease, and predators affect the size of their populations. Only a limited number survive to reproduce. Thus, there must be something special about the survivors. What traits make them better equipped to survive and reproduce? Darwin reasoned that the offspring of the survivors inherit traits that help them survive in their environment.

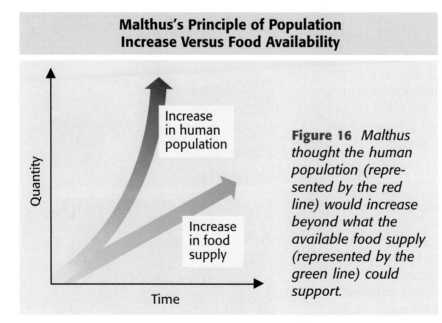

Malthus's Principle of Population Increase Versus Food Availability

Increase in human population

Increase in food supply

Quantity

Time

Figure 16 *Malthus thought the human population (represented by the red line) would increase beyond what the available food supply (represented by the green line) could support.*

Quick Lab

Could We Run out of Food?

Malthus thought we could. Do the following activity to better understand Malthus's hypothesis. Get **2 empty egg cartons** and a **bag of rice.** Label one carton "Food supply" and the second carton "Population growth." In the Food supply carton, place one grain of rice in the first cup. Increase the amount by one in each subsequent cup. Each grain represents a unit of food. In the Population growth carton, place one grain of rice in the first cup, and double the number of grains of rice in each subsequent cup. This rice represents people.

1. How many "people" are there in the last cup?
2. How many units of food are there in the last cup?
3. What conclusion can you draw?

Natural Selection

In 1858, about 20 years after he returned from his voyage on the HMS *Beagle*, Darwin received a letter from a naturalist named Alfred Russel Wallace. Wallace had independently arrived at the same theory of evolution that Darwin had been working on for so many years. Darwin and Wallace discussed their research and made plans to present their findings at a meeting later in the year. Then, in 1859, Darwin published his own results in his book called *On the Origin of Species by Means of Natural Selection*. Darwin theorized that evolution occurs through a process he called **natural selection.** This process, examined below, is divided into four parts.

Natural Selection in Four Steps

1 Overproduction Each species produces more offspring than will survive to maturity.

2 Genetic Variation The individuals in a population are slightly different from one another. Each individual has a unique combination of traits, such as size, color, and the ability to find food. Some traits increase the chances that the individual will survive and reproduce. Other traits decrease the chances of survival. These variations are genetic and can be inherited.

3 Struggle to Survive A natural environment does not have enough food, water, and other resources to support all the individuals born. In addition, many individuals are killed by other organisms. Only some of the individuals in a population survive to adulthood.

4 Successful Reproduction Successful reproduction is the key to natural selection. The individuals that are well adapted to their environment, that is, those that have better traits for living in their environment, are more likely to survive and reproduce. The individuals that are not well adapted to their environment are more likely to die early or produce few offspring.

Imagine that your grandfather has owned a kennel for more than 50 years but has never sold a dog. He cares for the dogs and keeps them in one large pen. Originally there were six labs, six terriers, and six pointers. There are now 76 dogs, and you are surprised that only a few look like pointers, labs, and terriers. The other dogs look similar to each other but not to any of the specific breeds. Your grandfather says that over the past 50 years each generation has looked less like the generation that preceded it.

By the time you visited the kennel, what may have happened to make most of the dogs look similar to each other but not to any specific original breed? Base your answer on what you've learned about selective breeding in this section.

More Evidence of Evolution

One of the observations on which Darwin based his theory of evolution by natural selection is that parents pass traits to their offspring. But Darwin did not know *how* inheritance occurs or *why* individuals vary within a population.

During the 1930s and 1940s, biologists combined the principles of genetic inheritance with Darwin's theory of evolution by natural selection. This combination of principles explained that the variations Darwin observed within a species are caused by **mutation,** or changes in a gene.

Since Darwin's time, new evidence has been collected from many fields of science. Although scientists recognize that other mechanisms may also play a part in the evolution of a species, the theory of evolution by natural selection provides the most thorough explanation for the diversity of life on Earth.

REVIEW

1. Why are some animals more likely to survive to adulthood than other animals?

2. **Summarizing Data** What did Darwin think happened to the first small population of finches that reached the Galápagos Islands from South America?

3. **Doing Calculations** A female cockroach can produce 80 offspring at a time. If half of the offspring were female, and each female produced 80 offspring, how many cockroaches would there be in 3 generations?

Natural Selection in Action

Footprints across time! Who do they belong to? Look on page 584 in your LabBook.

The theory of natural selection explains how a population changes over many generations in response to its environment. In fact, members of a population tend to be well adapted to their environment because natural selection is continuously taking place.

Insecticide Resistance To keep crops safe from certain insects, some farmers use a wide variety of chemical insecticides. However, some insecticides that worked well in the past are no longer as effective. For example, the boll weevil is becoming increasingly hard to control because it has developed a genetic resistance to many insecticides. The boll weevil isn't the only insect that has developed a resistance. In the 50 years that insecticides have been widely used, more than 500 species of insects have developed resistance to certain insecticides.

Insects quickly develop resistance to insecticides because they produce many offspring and usually have short generation times. A **generation time** is the period between the birth of one generation and the birth of the next generation. Follow the process in **Figure 17** to see how a common household pest, the cockroach, has evolved to become resistant to certain insecticides.

Diseases, such as tuberculosis, are also becoming more resistant to the antibiotics that were once very effective against them.

Figure 17 *Variety in a population's characteristics helps ensure that some individuals will be able to survive a change in the environment.*

1 When an effective insecticide is used on a population of insects, most of the insects are killed, but a few may survive. These survivors have genes that make them resistant to the insecticide.

2 The survivors then reproduce, passing the insecticide-resistance genes to their offspring.

3 In time, the replacement population of insects is made up mostly of individuals that have the insecticide-resistance genes.

4 Ultimately, when the same kind of insecticide is used on the insects, only a few are killed because the overall population has become resistant to that insecticide.

Adaptation to Pollution   There are two color variations among European peppered moths, as shown in **Figure 18.** Before 1850, the dark peppered moth was considered rare. The pale peppered moth was much more common. After the 1850s, however, dark peppered moths became more abundant in heavily industrialized areas.

Figure 18
Against a dark tree trunk (left), the pale peppered moth stands out. Against a light tree trunk (below), the dark peppered moth stands out.

✓ Self-Check

Match each statement (1–4) about the peppered moth population with the appropriate step (a–d) in natural selection.

1. Moths that live to maturity may mate and produce offspring.

2. A population of peppered moths contains some light-colored moths and some dark-colored moths.

3. Many moths do not survive because they are eaten by birds.

4. Peppered moths lay many eggs.

   a. Genetic variation

   b. Successful reproduction

   c. Overproduction

   d. Struggle to survive

(See page 636 to check your answers.)

What caused this change in the peppered moth population? Several species of birds eat peppered moths that rest on tree trunks. Before the 1850s, the trees had a gray appearance, and pale peppered moths blended into their surroundings. Dark peppered moths were easier for the birds to see and were eaten more frequently. After the 1850s, soot and smoke from newly developing industrial areas blackened nearby trees. The dark peppered moths became less visible on the dark tree trunks. The pale peppered moths stood out against the dark background and became easy prey for the birds. More dark moths survived and produced more dark offspring. Thus, the population changed from mostly light-colored moths to mostly dark-colored moths.

Formation of New Species

The process of natural selection can explain how a species can evolve into a new species. A portion of a species' population can become separated from the original population. Over time, the two populations can become so different that they can no longer interbreed. This process is called **speciation**. One way that speciation can occur is shown in the following three steps:

1. Separation The process of speciation often begins when a portion of a population becomes isolated. **Figure 19** shows some of the ways this can happen. A newly formed canyon, mountain range, or lake are a few of the ways that populations can be divided.

Figure 19 *Populations can become separated in a variety of ways.*

2. Adaptation If a population has been divided by one of the changes illustrated above, the environment may also change. This is where natural selection comes in. As the environment changes, so may the population that lives there. Over many generations, the separated groups may adapt to better fit their environment, as shown in **Figure 20.** If the environmental conditions are different for each of the groups, the adaptations in the groups may also be different.

Figure 20 *When a single population becomes divided, the groups may evolve separately and may form separate species.*

3. Division Over many hundreds, thousands, or even millions of generations, the two groups of a population may become so different that they can no longer interbreed, even if the geographical barrier is removed. At this point, the two groups are no longer the same species. Scientists think that the finches on the Galápagos Islands evolved by these three basic steps. **Figure 21** illustrates how this might have happened.

Figure 21 *The finches on the Galápagos Islands might have evolved into different species by the process depicted below.*

1 Some finches left the mainland and reached one of the islands (separation).

2 The finches reproduced and adapted to the environment (adaptation).

3 Some finches flew to a second island (separation).

4 The finches reproduced and adapted to the different environment (adaptation).

5 Some finches flew back to the first island but could no longer interbreed with the finches there (division).

6 This process may have occurred over and over again as the finches flew to the other islands.

REVIEW

1. Why did the number of dark peppered moths increase after the 1850s?

2. What factor indicates that a population has evolved into two separate species?

3. **Applying Concepts** Most cactuses have spines, which are leaves modified to protect the plant. The spines cover a juicy stem that stores water. Explain how cactus leaves and stems might have changed through the process of natural selection.

Chapter Highlights

Vocabulary

adaptation *(p. 176)*

species *(p. 176)*

evolution *(p. 177)*

fossil *(p. 178)*

fossil record *(p. 178)*

vestigial structure *(p. 179)*

Section Notes

- Evolution is the process by which populations change over time. Those changes are inherited. Over many generations, newer species may replace older species through the process of evolution.

- Evidence of a common ancestor for all organisms is provided by the following: the fossil record, comparisons of skeletal structures found in related species, comparisons of the embryos of distantly related vertebrates, and the presence of DNA in all living organisms.

- Species that are closely related have DNA that is more alike than DNA of distantly related species.

Labs

Mystery Footprints *(p. 584)*

Vocabulary

trait *(p. 186)*

selective breeding *(p. 186)*

natural selection *(p. 188)*

mutation *(p. 189)*

Section Notes

- Charles Darwin developed an explanation for evolution after years of studying the organisms he observed on the voyage of the *Beagle*.

- Darwin's study was influenced by the concepts of selective breeding, the age of the Earth, and the idea that some organisms are better equipped to survive than others.

- Darwin explained that evolution occurs through natural selection. Natural selection can be divided into four parts:

☑ Skills Check

Math Concepts

MALTHUS'S PRINCIPLE The graph on page 187 shows two types of growth. The straight line represents an increase in which the same number is added to the previous number, as in 3, 4, 5, 6, . . ., where 1 is added to each number.

The curved line represents an increase in which each number is multiplied by the same factor, as in 2, 4, 8, 16, . . ., where each number is multiplied by 2. As you can see on the graph, the curved line increases at a much faster rate than the straight line.

Visual Understanding

SKELETAL STRUCTURE Figure 9 on page 182 illustrates skeletal evidence for evolution. The similar limb bone structure of humans, cats, dolphins, and bats indicates that these animals come from a common ancestor. By looking at same-colored bones, you can see how the early mammalian skeletal structure has evolved in certain species to help with specialized tasks such as flying and swimming.

(1) Each species produces more offspring than will survive to reproduce.

(2) Individuals within a population are slightly different from one another.

(3) Individuals within a population compete with one another for limited resources.

(4) Individuals that are better equipped to live in an environment are more likely to survive and reproduce.

- Evolution is explained today by combining the principles of natural selection with the principles of genetic inheritance.

Labs

Survival of the Chocolates
(p. 587)

Vocabulary

generation time *(p. 190)*
speciation *(p. 192)*

Section Notes

- Natural selection allows a population to adapt to changes in environmental conditions.

- Evidence of natural selection can be seen by studying generations of organisms that

have developed resistance to an insecticide or antibiotic.

- Natural selection also explains how one species may evolve into another through the process of speciation.

Labs

Out-of-Sight Marshmallows
(p. 586)

GO TO: go.hrw.com

GO TO: www.scilinks.org

Visit the **HRW** Web site for a variety of learning tools related to this chapter. Just type in the keyword:

KEYWORD: HSTEVO

Visit the **National Science Teachers Association** on-line Web site for Internet resources related to this chapter. Just type in the *sci*LINKS number for more information about the topic:

TOPIC: Species and Adaptation	*sci***LINKS NUMBER:** HSTL155
TOPIC: The Fossil Record	*sci***LINKS NUMBER:** HSTL160
TOPIC: The Galápagos Islands	*sci***LINKS NUMBER:** HSTL165
TOPIC: Darwin and Natural Selection	*sci***LINKS NUMBER:** HSTL170

Chapter Review

USING VOCABULARY

To complete the following sentences, choose the correct term from each pair of terms listed below:

1. One species evolves into another through the process of __?__. *(adaptation* or *speciation)*

2. A group of similar organisms that can mate with one another to produce off-spring is known as a __?__. *(fossil* or *species)*

3. A(n) __?__ helps an organism survive better in its environment. *(adaptation* or *vestigial structure)*

4. __?__ is the process by which populations change over time. *(Natural selection* or *Evolution)*

5. In __?__, humans select traits that will be passed from one generation to another. *(selective breeding* or *natural selection)*

6. A change in a gene at the DNA level is called a __?__. *(mutation* or *trait)*

UNDERSTANDING CONCEPTS

Multiple Choice

7. Although Darwin did not realize it, the variations he observed among the individuals of a population of finches were caused by
   a. genetic resistance.   c. fossils.
   b. mutations.   d. selective breeding.

8. The theory of evolution combines the principles of
   a. natural selection and artificial selection.
   b. natural selection and genetic resistance.
   c. selective breeding and genetic inheritance.
   d. natural selection and genetic inheritance.

9. Fossils are commonly found in
   a. sedimentary rock.
   b. igneous rock.
   c. granite.
   d. loose sand or granite.

10. A human's arm, a cat's front leg, a dolphin's front flipper, and a bat's wing
    a. have similar kinds of bones.
    b. are used in similar ways.
    c. share many similarities with insect wings and jellyfish tentacles.
    d. have nothing in common.

11. The fact that all organisms have DNA as their genetic material is evidence that
    a. natural selection occurred.
    b. all organisms descended from a common ancestor.
    c. selective breeding takes place every day.
    d. genetic resistance rarely occurs.

12. Darwin thought the common ancestor of the Galápagos finches came from
    a. Africa.   c. South America.
    b. North America.   d. Australia.

13. What body part of the Galápagos finches appears to have been most modified by natural selection?
    a. their webbed feet
    b. their beaks
    c. the bone structure of their wings
    d. the color of their eyes

Short Answer

14. Describe the four parts of Darwin's theory of evolution by natural selection.

15. How do the fossils of whales provide evidence that whales have evolved over millions of years?

16. What might account for gaps in the fossil record?

Concept Mapping

17. Use the following terms to create a concept map: struggle to survive, genetic variation, Darwin, overproduction, natural selection, and successful reproduction.

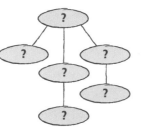

CRITICAL THINKING AND PROBLEM SOLVING

Write one or two sentences to answer the following questions:

18. In selective breeding, humans influence the course of evolution. What determines the course of evolution in natural selection?

19. Many forms of bacteria evolve resistance to antibiotics, drugs that kill disease-causing bacteria. Based on what you know about how insects evolve to resist insecticides, suggest how bacteria might evolve to resist antibiotics.

20. The two species of squirrels shown below live on opposite sides of the Grand Canyon, in Arizona. The two squirrels look very similar, but they cannot interbreed to produce offspring. Explain how a single species of squirrel might have become two species.

INTERPRETING GRAPHICS

Use the following graphs to answer questions 21, 22, and 23:

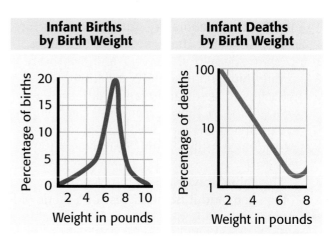

Infant Births by Birth Weight

Percentage of births / Weight in pounds

Infant Deaths by Birth Weight

Percentage of deaths / Weight in pounds

21. What is the most common birth weight?

22. What birth weight has the highest survival rate?

23. How do the principles of natural selection help explain why there are more deaths among babies with low birth weights than among babies of average birth weights?

NOW What Do You Think?

Take a minute to review your answers to the ScienceLog questions on page 175. Have your answers changed? If necessary, revise your answers based on what you have learned since you began this chapter.

EYE ON THE ENVIRONMENT

Saving at the Seed Bank

A very unusual laboratory can be found in Fort Collins, Colorado. There, sealed in test tubes, locked in specialized drawers, and even frozen in liquid nitrogen at −196°C, are hundreds of thousands of seeds and plants. Although in storage for now, these organisms may hold the keys to preventing worldwide famine or medicine shortage in the future. Sound serious? Well, it is.

This laboratory is called the National Seed Storage Lab, and it is the largest of a worldwide network of seed banks. The seeds and plant cuttings stored within these seed banks represent almost every plant grown for food, clothing, and medicine.

▲ *To protect tomorrow's wheat fields, we need the genetic diversity of crops stored in seed banks.*

No More Pizza!

Imagine heading out for pizza only to discover a sign on the door that says, "Closed today due to flour shortage." Flour shortage? How can that be? What about burritos? When you get to the burrito stand, the sign is the same, "Closed due to flour shortage." Think this sounds far-fetched?

Well, it really isn't.

If wheat crops around the world are ruined by a disease, we could have a flour shortage. And the best way to fight such devastation, and even prevent it, is by breeding new varieties. Through the process of selective breeding, many plants have been improved to increase their yields and their resistance to disease and insects. But to breed new crops, plant breeders need lots of different genetic material. Where do they get this genetic material? At the seed bank, of course!

Why We'll Never Know

But what if some plants never make it to the seed bank? We have the new and improved varieties, so why does it matter if we keep the old ones? It matters because these lost varieties often have important traits, like resistance to disease and drought, that might come in handy in the future. Once a variety of plant is improved, demand for the old variety can dwindle to nothing. If an old variety is no longer grown, it may become extinct if not placed in the seed bank. In fact, many varieties of plants have already been lost forever. We'll never know if one of those lost varieties was capable of resisting a severe drought.

It's All in the Bank

Fortunately, seed banks have collected seeds and plants for more than a century. They preserve the genetic diversity of crop plants while allowing farmers to grow the most productive varieties in their fields. As long as there are seed banks across the globe, it is unlikely that there will be a flour shortage. Let's go out for pizza!

Going Further

▶ Many seed banks are in jeopardy. Why? Find out by doing research to learn more about the complicated and costly process of operating a seed bank.

Science Fiction

"The Anatomy Lesson"

by Scott Sanders

You know what it's like. You have an important test tomorrow, or your semester project is due, and you've forgotten your book or just run out of clay. Suddenly things seem very serious.

That's the situation a certain medical student faces in Scott Sanders's "The Anatomy Lesson." The student needs to learn the bones of the human body for an anatomy exam the next day. After arriving at the anatomy library to check out a skeleton-in-a-box, the student finds the skeletons have all been checked out. Without bones to assemble as practice, the student knows passing the exam will be impossible. So the student asks the librarian to look again. Sure enough, the librarian finds one last box. And that's when things start to get strange.

There are too many bones. They are the wrong shape. They don't fit together just right. Somebody must be playing a joke! The bones fit together, sort of—but not in any way that helps the medical student get ready for the exam. When the student complains to the librarian, the librarian isn't very sympathetic. It seems she has other things on her mind. Now the student is really worried.

Find out what this medical student and a quiet librarian have in common. And find out how they will never be the same after "The Anatomy Lesson." You can read it in the *Holt Anthology of Science Fiction*.

CHAPTER 9 The History of Life on Earth

Imagine . . .

One day you and your friends learn about a secret underground passage that leads into an old abandoned mansion, and you set out to find it. As you walk across a field in search of the passage, you stumble across a large hole in the ground between the roots of a dead tree. Could this be it?

One by one, you and your friends squeeze down into the hole. You slide and tumble down the sloping tunnel and finally land. Dusting yourself off, you turn on your flashlight to get a better look around. Instead of finding a passage to an abandoned mansion, you and your friends find yourselves in an immense cavern. Painted high on the cavern's walls are pictures of bulls, cows, horses, and stags. You get the feeling these images have been here for a very long time.

What were the paintings intended to portray? Why were they painted deep within a cavern far from daylight?

This adventure actually occurred in southern France in the late 1940s. Four teenage boys went hunting for a secret passageway to the old manor of Lascaux. Instead of finding a passageway, they stumbled onto a 17,000-year-old connection with our distant ancestors, the Cro-Magnons. Three of the adventurers are shown below talking to their teacher.

In this chapter, you will learn more about the activities, culture, and evolution of humans. You will also learn about the evidence scientists have of the development of many different life-forms from the time when Earth was very young.

Timeline of Earth's History

To help you understand the great length of time involved in the Earth's history, make a timeline. You will need a **pencil,** a **metric ruler,** and a **strip of adding machine paper** 46 cm long.

Procedure

1. Starting on the right-hand side of the paper, measure off 10 cm sections. Make a large mark with your pencil to indicate each section. Divide each 10 cm section into ten 1 cm sections. (Each 1 cm represents 100 million years.)

2. Label each 10 cm section in order from top to bottom as follows: 1 bya (1 billion years ago), 2 bya, 3 bya, and 4 bya. The timeline begins at 4.6 bya.

3. Some of the important events of the Earth's history are listed below. Label them on your timeline.

   a. At the left-hand end of the paper (4.6 bya), write "The origin of the Earth."

   b. From the right-hand side of the paper, measure off 35 cm, and mark the end point (3.5 bya) with your pencil. Write "The earliest cells appear."

What Do You Think?

In your ScienceLog, try to answer the following questions based on what you already know:

1. How can you tell how old a fossil is?

2. How long did dinosaurs roam the Earth?

3. What two characteristics make humans different from other animals?

   c. Dinosaurs first appeared on Earth about 215 million years ago. Then about 65 million years ago, they became extinct. How would you measure this? If 100 million years = 1 cm, then 65 million years = ? Again, from the top of the right-hand side of your paper, measure off this length, and mark the end point with "Extinction of the dinosaurs."

   d. About 100,000 years ago, humans with modern features appeared. Mark this event on your timeline. (Hint: 10 million years = 1 mm. So 100,000 years ago would be a small fraction of 1 mm.)

   e. Continue to mark events on your timeline as you learn about them in this chapter.

Analysis

4. The Lascaux cave paintings were done more than 17,000 years ago. Compare that length of time with the length of time Earth existed before the beginning of life.

5. Compare the length of time dinosaurs roamed the Earth with the length of time humans have existed.

The History of Life on Earth   **201**

Evidence of the Past

Like detectives at the scene of a crime, some scientists look for clues to help them reconstruct what happened in the past. These scientists are called paleontologists. **Paleontologists,** like Paul Sereno, shown in **Figure 1,** use fossils to reconstruct the history of life millions of years before humans existed. Fossils show us that life on Earth has changed a great deal. They also provide us with clues to how those changes occurred.

NEW TERMS

paleontologist
fossils
rock cycle
relative dating
half-life
absolute dating
geologic time scale
extinct
mass extinction
Pangaea
plate tectonics

OBJECTIVES

- Describe two methods that scientists use to determine the age of fossils in sedimentary rock.
- Describe the geologic time scale and the information it provides scientists.
- Describe the possible causes of mass extinctions.
- Explain the theory of plate tectonics.

Fossils

Fossils are traces or imprints of living things—such as animals, plants, bacteria, and fungi—that are preserved in rock. Fossils are usually formed when a dead organism is covered by a layer of sediment. These sediments may later be pressed together to form sedimentary rock. Sedimentary rock, along with igneous and metamorphic rock, make up the rock cycle. The **rock cycle** is the process by which one rock type changes into another. **Figure 2** shows one way fossils can be formed in sedimentary rock.

Figure 1 *In 1995, paleontologist Paul Sereno found this enormous fossil skull of a dinosaur in the Sahara Desert. This dinosaur may have been the largest land predator that has ever existed!*

Figure 2 *Look at the pictures below to see one way fossils can form.*

1 An organism dies and becomes buried in sediment.

2 The organism gradually dissolves, leaving a hollow impression, or mold, in the sediment.

3 Over time, the mold fills with sediment that forms a cast of the original organism.

The Age of Fossils

When paleontologists find a fossil, how do they determine its age? They can use one of two methods: relative dating or absolute dating.

Relative Dating A cross section of sedimentary rock shows many layers. The oldest layers are on the bottom, and the newer layers are on the top. If fossils are found in the rock, a scientist could start at the bottom and work upward to examine a sequence of fossils in the order that the organisms existed. This method of ordering fossils to determine their age is known as **relative dating.**

Absolute Dating How can scientists estimate the age of a fossil? The answer lies in the tiny particles called *atoms* that make up all the matter in the universe. Atoms are made of different kinds of particles that are even smaller. These smaller particles are held together by strong forces. If these forces cannot hold the atom together, the atom is unstable. Unstable atoms break down by releasing a few of their particles. This is called *radioactive decay*. The atom then becomes stable, but it also becomes a different kind of atom.

Each kind of unstable atom decays at its own rate. The time it takes for half of the unstable atoms in a sample to decay is its **half-life.** Half-lives range from fractions of a second to billions of years. By measuring the ratio of unstable atoms to stable atoms, scientists can estimate the age of a rock sample and the fossil it contains. This method is called **absolute dating.** Follow the steps in **Figure 3** to see how unstable atoms in a rock break down.

Bananabana bobana is a rare fossil! Turn to page 588 in your LabBook to see it.

Figure 3 Sometimes volcanic rock will cover an organism buried in sediment just below the surface. By finding the age of this volcanic rock, scientists can get a good idea about the age of the fossil.

A. The unstable atoms in the sample of volcanic rock have a half-life of 1.3 billion years. The sample contained 4 mg of unstable atoms when the rock formed.

B. After 1.3 billion years, or one half-life, only 2 mg of the unstable atoms will be left in the rock, and 2 mg of its stable decay product will have formed.

C. After another 1.3 billion years (two half-lives), there will only be 1 mg of the unstable atoms and 3 mg of the decay atoms.

D. How many milligrams of unstable atoms are left after 3 half-lives?

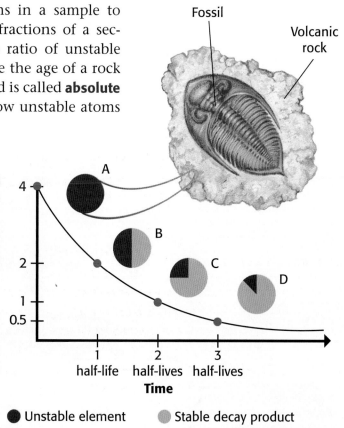

The Geologic Time Scale

When you consider important events that have happened during your lifetime, you usually recall each event in terms of the day, month, or year in which it occurred. These divisions of time make it easier to recall when you were born, when you kicked the winning soccer goal, or when you started the fifth grade. Because the span of time is so great from the formation of the Earth to now, scientists also use a type of calendar to divide the Earth's long history into very long units of time.

The calendar scientists use to outline the history of life on Earth is called the **geologic time scale,** shown in the table at left. After a fossil is dated using relative and absolute dating techniques, a paleontologist can place the fossil in chronological order with other fossils. This forms a picture of the past that shows how organisms have changed over time.

Divisions in the Geologic Time Scale Paleontologists have divided the time scale into large blocks of time called *eras*. Each era has been subdivided into smaller blocks of time as paleontologists have continued to find more fossil information.

Eras are characterized by the type of animal that dominated the Earth at the time. For instance, the Mesozoic era—dominated by dinosaurs and other reptiles—is referred to as the Age of Reptiles. The end of each era is marked by the extinction of certain organisms. The next section analyzes the different eras of the geologic time scale in greater detail.

The Geologic Time Scale

Era	Period	MYA	Representative Organisms
CENOZOIC	Quaternary	1.8	
	Tertiary	65	
MESOZOIC	Cretaceous	144	
	Jurassic	206	
	Triassic	248	
PALEOZOIC	Permian	290	
	Carboniferous	354	
	Devonian	417	
	Silurian	443	
	Ordovician	490	
	Cambrian	540	
PRECAMBRIAN		4,600	

Figure 4 *A meteorite hit the Earth about 65 million years ago. Climate changes resulting from the impact may have caused the extinction of the dinosaurs.*

Mass Extinctions Some of the important divisions in the geologic time scale are marked by events that caused many animal and plant species to die out completely, or become **extinct.** Once a species is extinct, it does not reappear. There have been several periods in the Earth's history when a large number of species died out at the same time. These periods of large-scale extinction are called **mass extinctions.**

Scientists are not sure what causes mass extinctions. They may result from major changes in Earth's climate or atmosphere. Some scientists think the mass extinction of dinosaurs and other species occurred after a meteorite struck Earth, as depicted in **Figure 4.** The collision may have caused a brief change in climate or atmospheric composition, leading to the death of many species. There may be other causes of global environmental changes that lead to mass extinctions. For example, movements of continents may cause changes in climate. Read on to find out how this is possible.

Scientists estimate that only a small fraction ($1/20$ of 1 percent) of all the species that have ever existed on Earth are living today. All the other species existed in the past and then became extinct.

✔ Self-Check

Ten grams of an unstable atom were present in a rock when the rock solidified. In grams, how much of these atoms will be present after one half-life? How much of the unstable atoms will be present after two half-lives? *(See page 636 to check your answers.)*

The Changing Earth

Do you know that dinosaur fossils have been found on Antarctica? Antarctica, now frozen, must have once had a warm climate to support these large reptiles. How could this be? The answer is that Antarctica was once located nearer the equator!

Many species of mammals that carry their young in pouches (marsupials) are found in Australia. There are a few marsupial species in South America and only one species in North America. Why are there so many marsupial species in Australia? The answer is that Australia moved away from other landmasses before other mammals evolved and began to compete with marsupials for food and space. Major changes in the Earth's biological environment may have been caused by major changes in the Earth's geological environment.

Pangaea If you take a look at a map of the world, you might notice that the shapes of the continents seem to resemble pieces of a puzzle. If you could move the pieces around, you might find that some of them almost fit together. A similar thought occurred to the German scientist Alfred Wegener in the early 1900s. He proposed that long ago the continents were part of one great landmass surrounded by a single gigantic ocean. Wegener called that single landmass **Pangaea,** meaning "all Earth."

Wegener thought our present continents were once part of one great supercontinent for three reasons. First, the shapes of the continents seemed to "fit" together. Second, fossils of plants and animals discovered on either side of the Atlantic Ocean were very similar. Third, Wegener noticed that glaciers had existed in places that now have very warm climates. **Figure 5** shows how the continents may have formed from Pangaea.

About 245 million years ago, the continents were one giant landmass called Pangaea. The grey outlines indicate where the continents are today.

About 180 million years ago, Pangaea began to divide into two pieces: Laurasia and Gondwanaland.

Even as recently as 65 million years ago, the location of Earth's tectonic plates was very different from their current location.

Figure 5 *Because the continents are moving 1–10 cm per year, the continents will be arranged very differently in 150 million years.*

Do the Continents Move? In the mid-1960s, J. Tuzo Wilson thought that huge pieces of the Earth's crust are driven back and forth by forces within the planet. Each piece of crust is called a *tectonic plate*. Wilson's theory is called **plate tectonics.**

According to Wilson, the outer crust of the Earth is broken into seven large, rigid plates and several smaller ones, shown in **Figure 6.** The continents and oceans ride on top of these plates. The motion of the plates causes continents to move, leading to the separation of some species.

Adaptation in Slow Motion
Although tectonic plates move very slowly, the motion affects living organisms. Living things usually have time to adapt (through evolution) to the changes brought about by moving continents. This is why living things are well adapted to the environment they live in. In the same location, however, you may find fossil evidence of very different organisms that could not survive the changes. For example, seashells are found on some mountaintops! Finding such fossils far above sea level is also evidence that the movement of tectonic plates forced previously buried rocks to the Earth's surface.

Figure 6 *Scientists think that the tectonic plates, outlined above, have been slowly rearranging the continents since the crust cooled billions of years ago.*

REVIEW

1. What information does the geologic time scale provide, and what are the major divisions of time?

2. What is one possible cause of mass extinctions?

3. Explain one way that geological changes in the Earth can cause plants and animals to change.

4. What is the difference between relative dating and absolute dating of fossils?

5. **Understanding Concepts** Fossils of *Mesosaurus*, a small aquatic lizard, shown at right, have been found only in Africa and South America. Using what you know about plate tectonics, how would you explain this finding?

Eras of the Geologic Time Scale

Look at the photograph of the Grand Canyon shown in **Figure 7.** If you look closely, you will notice that the walls of the canyon are layered with different kinds and colors of rocks. The deeper you go down into the canyon, the older the layer of rocks. It may surprise you to learn that each layer of the Grand Canyon was once the top layer. Billions of years ago the bottom layer was on top! Billions of years from now the layer that is now on top may have many layers on top of it.

Each layer tells a story about what was happening on Earth when that layer was on top. The story is told mainly by the types of rocks and fossils found in the layer. In studying these different rocks and fossils, scientists have divided geologic history into four eras: Precambrian time, the Paleozoic era, the Mesozoic era, and the Cenozoic era.

Figure 7 *Each rock layer of the Grand Canyon is like a page in the "history book of the Earth."*

Figure 8 *The animal that left this Precambrian fossil lived in shallow ocean waters.*

Precambrian Time

If you journey to the bottom of the Grand Canyon, you will find rocks between 1 and 2 billion years old! These rocks formed during the geologic era known as **Precambrian time,** a time prior to 540 million years ago when only very primitive organisms lived. Most of these organisms didn't have hard body parts, so only a few fossils from this time exist. One is shown in **Figure 8.**

The Early Earth Scientists hypothesize that life began when conditions were quite different from the Earth's current environment. These conditions included an atmosphere that lacked oxygen but was rich in other gases, such as carbon monoxide, carbon dioxide, hydrogen, and nitrogen. Also, the early Earth, as illustrated in **Figure 9,** was a place of great turmoil. Meteorites crashed into the Earth's surface. Violent thunderstorms and volcanic eruptions were constant on the young planet. Intense radiation, including ultraviolet radiation from the sun, bombarded the Earth's surface.

Figure 9 *The early Earth was a violent place.*

How Did Life Begin? Scientists hypothesize that under these conditions, life developed from nonliving matter. In other words, life started from the chemicals that already existed in the environment. These chemicals included water, clay, dissolved minerals in the oceans, and the gases present in the atmosphere. The energy present in the early Earth caused these chemicals to react with one another, forming the complex molecules that made life possible.

Scientists further hypothesize that for millions of years these molecules floated in the oceans and joined together to form larger molecules. These larger molecules reacted with each other, forming more-complicated structures. The molecules developed into cell-like structures that eventually became the first true cells. **Figure 10** shows a fossil of this type of cell. Scientists think it is a **prokaryote,** a cell without a nucleus. The first prokaryotes were **anaerobic,** which means they did not need and could not tolerate free oxygen. Organisms that need oxygen could not have survived on early Earth because the planet lacked free oxygen. Many anaerobic prokaryotes still live on Earth today in places without free oxygen.

Figure 10 *Fossilized prokaryotes (such as the circular structure in the photograph) lead scientists to think that life first appeared on Earth in the form of prokaryotes more than 3.5 billion years ago.*

Figure 11 *Cyanobacteria are the simplest living organisms that photosynthesize.*

environmental science
CONNECTION

Ozone depletion in the upper atmosphere is a serious problem. Industrial chemicals, such as those used to cool refrigerators and air conditioners, are slowly destroying the ozone layer in the Earth's upper atmosphere. Because of ozone depletion, all living things are exposed to higher levels of radiation, which can cause skin cancer. Some countries have outlawed ozone-depleting chemicals.

Figure 13 *This fossilized eukaryotic cell is about 800 million years old.*

The Earth's First Pollution—Oxygen! More than 3 billion years ago, prokaryotic organisms called cyanobacteria appeared in the fossil record. Cyanobacteria, pictured in **Figure 11,** are photosynthetic organisms, which means that they use energy from sunlight to produce sugars and starches. One of the byproducts of this process is oxygen. As cyanobacteria carried out photosynthesis, they released oxygen gas into the oceans. After hundreds of millions of years, the cyanobacteria had created enough oxygen that some could escape from the ocean into the atmosphere. Photosynthesis continued to increase the amount of oxygen in the atmosphere. But for 1 to 2 billion years, oxygen levels were probably only a small fraction of today's concentration.

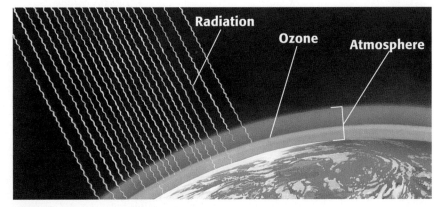

Figure 12 *Oxygen from photosynthesis formed ozone, which helps to absorb ultraviolet radiation.*

As the atmosphere filled with oxygen, some of the oxygen molecules recombined to form a layer of ozone in the upper atmosphere, as shown in **Figure 12. Ozone** is a gas that absorbs ultraviolet radiation from the sun. Ultraviolet radiation damages DNA but is absorbed by water. Before ozone formed, therefore, all life was restricted to the oceans. But the new ozone layer acted as a shield, blocking out most of the ultraviolet radiation. This brought radiation levels on Earth's surface down to a level that allowed life to move onto dry land.

After a long period of time, about 2 billion years, more-complex life-forms appeared in the fossil record. These organisms, known as **eukaryotes,** are much larger than prokaryotes, and they contain a central nucleus and a complicated internal structure. A fossilized eukaryote is shown in **Figure 13.** Scientists think that over the past 1.5 billion years, eukaryotic cells have evolved together to form organisms that are composed of many cells. Scientists think the first single-celled eukaryote evolved over 2 billion years ago and is the ancestor of all plants and animals that exist today. The first multicellular eukaryotic organisms are called *metazoans.* They evolved in the late Precambrian era.

The Paleozoic Era

The **Paleozoic era** began about 540 million years ago and ended about 248 million years ago. *Paleozoic* comes from the Greek words meaning "ancient life." Considering how long Precambrian time lasted, the Paleozoic era was relatively recent. Rocks from the Paleozoic era are rich in fossils of animals such as sponges, corals, snails, clams, squids, and trilobites. Fishes, the earliest animals with backbones, also appeared during this era, and ancient sharks became abundant. Some Paleozoic organisms are shown in **Figure 14.**

The Greening of the Earth During the Paleozoic era, plants, fungi, and air-breathing animals colonized dry land over a period of 30 million years. Plants provided the first land animals with food and shelter. By the end of the Paleozoic era, forests of giant ferns, club mosses, horsetails, and conifers covered much of the Earth. All major plant groups except for flowering plants appeared during this era.

Creepers Crawl onto Land Fossils indicate that crawling insects were some of the first animals to appear on land. They were followed by large salamander-like animals. Near the end of the Paleozoic era, reptiles, winged insects, cockroaches, and dragonflies appeared.

The largest mass extinction known occurred at the end of the Paleozoic era, about 248 million years ago. As many as 90 percent of all marine species died out.

Figure 14 *Organisms that appeared in the Paleozoic era include the first reptiles, amphibians, fishes, worms, and ferns.*

Self-Check

Place the following events in chronological order:

a. The ozone layer formed, and living things moved onto dry land.

b. Gases in the atmosphere and minerals in the oceans combined to form small molecules.

c. The first prokaryotic, anaerobic cells appeared.

d. Cyanobacteria appeared.

(See page 636 to check your answer.)

The Mesozoic Era

The **Mesozoic era** began about 248 million years ago and lasted about 183 million years. *Mesozoic* comes from the Greek words meaning "middle life." Scientists think that, after the extinctions of the Paleozoic era, a burst of evolution occurred among the surviving reptiles, resulting in many different species. Therefore, the Mesozoic era is commonly referred to as the Age of Reptiles.

Life in the Mesozoic Era Dinosaurs are the most well known of the reptiles that evolved during the Mesozoic era. Dinosaurs dominated the Earth for about 150 million years. (Consider that humans and their ancestors have been around for only about 4 million years.) Dinosaurs had a great variety of physical characteristics, such as duck bills and projecting spines. In addition to dinosaurs, there were giant marine lizards that swam in the ocean. The first birds also appeared during the Mesozoic era. The most important plants during the early part of the Mesozoic era were cone-bearing seed plants, which formed large forests. Flowering plants appeared later in the Mesozoic era. Some of the organisms that appeared during the Mesozoic era are shown in **Figure 15.**

A Bad Time for Dinosaurs At the end of the Mesozoic era, 65 million years ago, dinosaurs and many other animal and plant species became extinct. What happened to the dinosaurs? According to one hypothesis, a large meteorite hit the Earth and generated giant dust clouds and enough heat to cause worldwide fires. The dust and smoke from these fires blocked out much of the sunlight, causing many plants to die out. Without enough plants to eat, the plant-eating dinosaurs died out. As a result, the meat-eating dinosaurs that fed on the plant-eating dinosaurs died. Global temperatures may have dropped for many years. Only a few organisms, including some small mammals, were able to survive.

Figure 15 *The Mesozoic era ended with the mass extinction of most of the large animals, such as the ankylosaurs and aquatic plesiosaurs shown above. Survivors included small mammals and* Archaeopteryx.

The Cenozoic Era

The **Cenozoic era** began about 65 million years ago and continues today. *Cenozoic* comes from the Greek words meaning "recent life." Scientists have more information about the Cenozoic era than about any of the previous eras because fossils from the Cenozoic era are embedded in rock layers that are close to the Earth's surface. This makes them easier to find. During the Cenozoic era, many kinds of mammals, birds, insects, and flowering plants appeared. Some organisms that appeared in the Cenozoic era are shown in **Figure 16.**

A Good Time for Large Mammals The Cenozoic era is sometimes referred to as the Age of Mammals. Mammals came to dominate the Cenozoic era much as reptiles dominated the Mesozoic era. Early Cenozoic mammals were small forest dwellers. Larger mammals appeared later. Some of these larger mammals had long legs for running, teeth that were specialized for eating different kinds of food, and large brains. Cenozoic mammals include mastodons, saber-toothed cats, camels, giant ground sloths, and small horses.

Figure 16 *We live in the Cenozoic era, but humans are very recent arrivals on Earth.*

REVIEW

1. What is the main difference between the atmosphere 3.5 billion years ago and the atmosphere today?

2. How do prokaryotic cells and eukaryotic cells differ?

3. Explain why cyanobacteria are so important to the development of new life-forms.

4. **Identifying Relationships** Match the organisms to the time period in which they first appeared.

   1. eukaryotes   a. Precambrian time
   2. dinosaurs   b. Paleozoic era
   3. fishes   c. Mesozoic era
   4. flowering plants   d. Cenozoic era
   5. birds

across the sciences
CONNECTION

Fossils are usually found in sedimentary rock. To find out how this rock forms, turn to page 224.

Human Evolution

NEW TERMS

primate   australopithecine
prosimian   Neanderthal
hominid   Cro-Magnon

OBJECTIVES

- Discuss the shared characteristics of primates.
- Describe what is known about the differences between hominids.

At the beginning of this chapter, you learned about the Cro-Magnon people who created beautiful and mysterious cave paintings more than 17,000 years ago. From fossils, we know that these people were very much like ourselves. Other, older fossils of human-like beings have also been found.

After studying thousands of fossilized skeletons and other evidence, scientists theorize that humans evolved over millions of years from a distant ancestor that is also common to apes and monkeys. This common ancestor is thought to have lived more than 30 million years ago. How did we get from that distant ancestor to who we are today? This section presents some of the evidence that has been gathered so far.

Figure 17 *This orangutan and baby, the gorilla, and the chimpanzee have the characteristics that make them nonhuman primates, including opposable big toes!*

Primates

To understand human evolution, we must first understand the characteristics that make us human beings. Humans are classified as primates. **Primates** are a group of mammals that includes humans, apes, monkeys, and prosimians. Primates have the characteristics illustrated below and in **Figure 17**.

Characteristics of Primates

Most primates have five flexible fingers—four fingers plus an opposable thumb.

This opposable thumb enables primates to grip objects. All primates except humans also have opposable big toes.

Both eyes are located at the front of the head, providing **binocular,** or three-dimensional, vision. Each eye sees a slightly different image of the same scene. The brain merges these two images to create one three-dimensional image.

Based on physical and genetic similarities, the closest living relative of humans is thought to be the chimpanzee. This conclusion does not mean that humans descended from chimpanzees. Rather, it means that humans and chimpanzees share a common ancestor. The ancestor of humans is thought to have diverged from the ancestor of the chimpanzee about 7 million years ago. Since then, humans and chimpanzees have evolved along different paths.

Despite the similarities among humans, apes, and monkeys, humans are assigned to a family separate from other primates, called **hominids.** The word *hominid* refers specifically to humans and their human-like ancestors. The main characteristic that distinguishes hominids from other primates is the ability to walk upright on two legs as the main way of moving around. Walking on two legs is called *bipedalism.* Examine **Figure 18** to see some skeletal similarities and differences between hominids and other primates. Except for present-day humans, all hominid species are now extinct.

Explore

Tape your thumbs to the side of your hands so they cannot be used. Attempt each of the tasks listed below.

- Pick up a piece of chalk, and write your name on the board.
- Sharpen a pencil.
- Cut a circle out of a piece of paper using scissors.
- Tie your shoelaces.
- Button several buttons.

After each attempt, answer the following questions:

a. Was the task more difficult with or without an opposable thumb?

b. How did you have to change your usual technique in order to complete this task?

c. Without an opposable thumb, do you think you would carry out this task on a regular basis? Why?

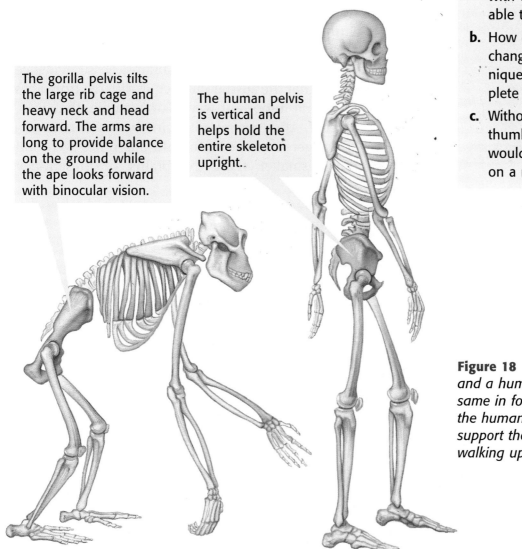

The gorilla pelvis tilts the large rib cage and heavy neck and head forward. The arms are long to provide balance on the ground while the ape looks forward with binocular vision.

The human pelvis is vertical and helps hold the entire skeleton upright.

Figure 18 *The bones of a gorilla and a human are basically the same in form and function, but the human pelvis is designed to support the internal organs while walking upright.*

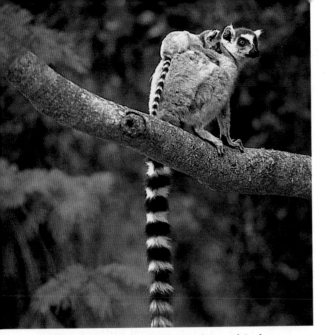

Figure 19 *Prosimians, such as this lemur, hunt in trees for insects and small animals.*

Hominid Evolution

The first primate ancestors appeared during the Cenozoic era, 55 million years ago, and evolved in several directions. These ancestors are thought to have been mouse-like mammals that were active during the night, lived in trees, and ate insects. When the dinosaurs died out, these mammals survived and gave rise to the first primates called **prosimians,** which means "before monkeys." Only a few species survive today. They include lorises and lemurs, such as the one pictured in **Figure 19.** How long after prosimians appeared did the first hominid appear? No one has been able to answer that question, but paleontologists have discovered fossil bones of hominids that date back to 4.4 million years ago.

Australopithecines Paleontologists think hominid evolution began in Africa. Among the oldest hominids are **australopithecines.** The word *Australopithecus* (aw STRAL uh PITH i kus) means "southern man ape." These early hominids had long arms, short legs, and small brains. Fossil evidence shows that the australopithecines differed from apes in several important ways. For example, they were bipedal. Also, australopithecine brains were generally larger than ape brains, although they were still much smaller than the brains of present-day humans.

In 1976, paleoanthropologist Mary Leakey discovered a series of footprints in Tanzania. Mary Leakey and the footprints are pictured in **Figure 20.** By determining the age of the rock containing the prints, she learned that the footprints were more than 3.6 million years old. The footprints indicated that a group of three hominids had walked in an upright position across the wet volcanic-ash-covered plain. Their fossilized footprints are additional evidence of bipedalism among human ancestors. After examining these footprints in Laetoli, Tanzania, Mary Leakey thought the people who made them had paused in midstride. She wrote, "This motion [this pausing], so intensely human, transcends time. A remote ancestor—just as you or I—experienced a moment of doubt."

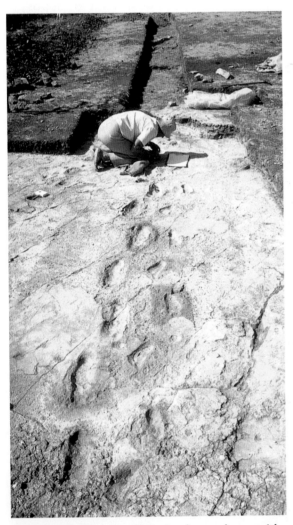

Figure 20 *Mary Leakey is shown here with the 3.6-million-year-old footprints.*

Lucy In 1979, a group of fossils was discovered in Ethiopia. Included in this group was the most complete skeleton of an australopithecine ever found. Nicknamed Lucy, this australopithecine lived about 2 million years ago. **Figure 21** shows Lucy's skeleton. Lucy had a sturdy body and stood upright, but her brain was about the size of a chimpanzee's. Fossil discoveries like this one demonstrate that upright posture evolved long before the brain enlarged.

A Face Like Ours Hominids with more human-like facial features appeared approximately 2.3 million years ago, probably evolving from australopithecine ancestors. This species is known as *Homo habilis*. Its skull is shown in **Figure 22.** Fossils of *Homo habilis* have been found along with crude stone tools. This has led scientists to think that these hominids fashioned and used tools for scraping meat out of animal carcasses. About 2 million years ago, *Homo habilis* was replaced by its larger-brained descendant, *Homo erectus,* pictured in **Figure 23.** *Homo erectus* was larger than *Homo habilis*. *Homo erectus* had a thick skull, a large brow ridge, a low forehead, and a very small chin.

Fossil evidence shows that *Homo erectus* may have lived in caves, built fires, and wore clothing. They successfully hunted large animals and butchered them using tools made of flint and bone. The appearance of *Homo erectus* marks the beginning of the expansion of human populations across the globe. *Homo erectus* survived for more than 1 million years, which is longer than any other species of human has lived, including present-day humans. These very adaptable humans disappeared about 200,000 years ago. This is about the time present-day humans, called *Homo sapiens,* first appear in the fossil record.

Although *Homo erectus* migrated across the globe, it is thought that *Homo sapiens* evolved in Africa and then migrated to Asia and Europe.

Figure 21 *Lucy's pelvis indicated that she walked upright.*

Figure 22 Homo habilis *is called handy man because this group of hominids made stone tools.*

Figure 23 Homo erectus *lived about 2 million years ago and may have looked like the sculpture at left.*

Figure 24 *Neanderthals had heavy brow ridges, like* Homo erectus, *but a larger brain than modern humans.*

Neanderthals In the Neander Valley, in Germany, fossils were discovered that belonged to a group of hominids referred to as **Neanderthals** (nee AN duhr TAHLS). They lived in Europe and western Asia beginning about 230,000 years ago. Short and sturdy, the Neanderthals had heavy brow ridges, like apes have, and brains that were larger than the brains of present-day humans.

By studying Neanderthal camps, scientists have learned that Neanderthals hunted large animals, made fires, and wore clothing. There is evidence that they also cared for the sick and elderly and buried their dead, sometimes placing food, weapons, and possibly even flowers with the dead bodies. Pictured in **Figure 24** is an artist's idea of how a Neanderthal might have looked. About 30,000 years ago, Neanderthals disappeared; nobody knows what caused their extinction.

Some scientists think the Neanderthals are a separate species, *Homo neanderthalensis*, from present-day humans, *Homo sapiens*. Other scientists think Neanderthals are a race of *Homo sapiens*. There is not yet enough evidence to fully answer this question.

Quick **Lab**

Neanderthal Tools

Neanderthals made sophisticated spear points and other stone tools. Examine the Neanderthal tools below. Each of these tools was specialized for a particular task. Can you suggest what each stone tool was used for?

Cro-Magnons In 1868, fossil skulls were found in caves in southwestern France. The skulls were about 35,000 years old, and they belonged to a group of *Homo sapiens* with modern features, called **Cro-Magnons.** Cro-Magnons may have existed in Africa 100,000 years ago and migrated from Africa about 40,000 years ago, coexisting with Neanderthals. Compared with Neanderthals, Cro-Magnons had a smaller and flatter face, and their skull was higher and more rounded, like an artist has modeled in **Figure 25.** The only significant physical difference between Cro-Magnons and present-day humans is that Cro-Magnons had thicker and heavier bones. In all important ways, Cro-Magnons were the first modern humans.

Figure 25 *This is an artist's idea of how a Cro-Magnon woman may have looked.*

The chapter introduction discussed the cave paintings made by Cro-Magnons. These paintings are the earliest known examples of human art. In fact, Cro-Magnon culture is marked by an amazing diversity of artistic efforts, including cave paintings, sculptures, and engravings, as shown in **Figure 26.** The preserved villages and burial grounds of Cro-Magnon groups also show that they had a complex social organization.

New Evidence of Human Evolution
Although we know a great deal about our hominid ancestors, much remains to be understood. Each fossil discovery causes great excitement and raises new questions, such as, "Where did *Homo sapiens* evolve?" Current evidence suggests that *Homo sapiens* evolved in Africa. "Which australopithecine gave rise to humans?" Some scientists think *Australopithecus afarensis* is the ancestor of all hominids, including present-day humans. **Figure 27** shows two different interpretations of hominid evolution.

Figure 27 *These evolutionary trees represent two hypotheses of how* Homo sapiens *descended from australopithecines.*

REVIEW

1. Identify three characteristics of primates.

2. Compare *Homo habilis* with *Homo erectus.* What made the two species different from one another?

3. What evidence suggests Neanderthals were like present-day humans?

4. **Inferring Conclusions** Imagine you are a paleontologist excavating an ancient campsite. What might you conclude about the people who used the site if you found the charred bones of large animals and various stone blades among human fossils?

The History of Life on Earth   **219**

Chapter Highlights

SECTION 1

Vocabulary

paleontologist *(p. 202)*

fossil *(p. 202)*

rock cycle *(p. 202)*

relative dating *(p. 203)*

absolute dating *(p. 203)*

half-life *(p. 203)*

geologic time scale *(p. 204)*

extinct *(p. 205)*

mass extinction *(p. 205)*

Pangaea *(p. 206)*

plate tectonics *(p. 207)*

Section Notes

- Paleontologists are scientists who study fossils.

- The age of a fossil can be determined using relative dating and absolute dating. Relative dating is an estimate based on the known age of the sediment layer in which the fossil is found. Absolute dating measures the rate of decay of the unstable elements found in the rock surrounding the fossil.

- The geologic time scale is a calendar scientists use to outline the history of Earth and life on Earth.

- Many species existed for a few million years and then became extinct. Mass extinctions have occurred several times in Earth's history.

Labs

Dating the Fossil Record *(p. 588)*

The Half-life of Pennies *(p. 591)*

SECTION 2

Vocabulary

Precambrian time *(p. 208)*

prokaryote *(p. 209)*

anaerobic *(p. 209)*

ozone *(p. 210)*

eukaryote *(p. 210)*

Paleozoic era *(p. 211)*

Mesozoic era *(p. 212)*

Cenozoic era *(p. 213)*

Section Notes

- Precambrian time includes the formation of the Earth, the beginning of life, and the evolution of simple multi-cellular organisms.

☑ Skills Check

Math Concepts

HALF-LIFE To understand half-life better, imagine that you have $10.00 in your pocket. You determine that you are going to spend half of all the money you have in your possession every 30 minutes. How much will you have after 30 minutes? ($5.00) How much will you have after another 30 minutes? ($2.50) How much will you have after 3 hours? (a little more than 15¢)

Visual Understanding

THE GEOLOGIC TIME SCALE You have probably seen old movies or cartoons that show humans and dinosaurs inhabiting the same environment. Can this be possible? Dinosaurs and humans did not exist at the same time. Dinosaurs became extinct 65 million years ago. Humans and their ancestors have been around for less than 4 million years. Review the Geologic Time Scale on page 204.

- The Earth is about 4.6 billion years old. Life formed from nonliving matter on the turbulent early Earth.

- The first cells, prokaryotes, were anaerobic. Later, photosynthetic cyanobacteria evolved and caused oxygen to enter the atmosphere.

- During the Paleozoic era, animals appeared in the oceans, and plants and animals colonized the land.

- Dinosaurs and other reptiles roamed the Earth during the Mesozoic era. Flowering plants, birds, and primitive mammals also appeared.

- Primates evolved during the Cenozoic era, which extends to the present day.

Vocabulary

primate *(p. 214)*

hominid *(p. 215)*

prosimian *(p. 216)*

australopithecine *(p. 216)*

Neanderthal *(p. 218)*

Cro-Magnon *(p. 218)*

Section Notes

- Humans, apes, and monkeys are primates. Primates are distinguished from other mammals by their opposable thumbs and binocular vision.

- Hominids, a subgroup of primates, include humans and their human-like ancestors. The oldest known hominids are australopithecines.

- Hominids that had more human features include *Homo habilis, Homo erectus,* and *Homo sapiens.*

- Neanderthals were a species of humans that disappeared about 30,000 years ago.

- Cro-Magnon culture was very sophisticated. Cro-Magnons did not differ very much from present-day humans.

---

internet connect

 GO TO: go.hrw.com

Visit the **HRW** Web site for a variety of learning tools related to this chapter. Just type in the keyword:

KEYWORD: HSTHIS

 GO TO: www.scilinks.org

Visit the **National Science Teachers Association** on-line Web site for Internet resources related to this chapter. Just type in the *sci*LINKS number for more information about the topic:

TOPIC: Evidence of the Past	*sci*LINKS NUMBER: HSTL180
TOPIC: Mass Extinctions	*sci*LINKS NUMBER: HSTL185
TOPIC: The Geologic Time Scale	*sci*LINKS NUMBER: HSTL190
TOPIC: Human Evolution	*sci*LINKS NUMBER: HSTL195
TOPIC: Birds and Dinosaurs	*sci*LINKS NUMBER: HSTL200

Chapter Review

USING VOCABULARY

To complete the following sentences, choose the correct term from each pair of terms listed below:

1. During the __?__ of the Earth's history, life is thought to have originated from nonliving matter. *(Precambrian time period or Paleozoic era)*

2. The Age of Mammals refers to the __?__. *(Mesozoic era or Cenozoic era)*

3. The Age of Reptiles refers to the __?__. *(Paleozoic era or Mesozoic era)*

4. Plants colonized dry land during the __?__. *(Precambrian time or Paleozoic era)*

5. The most ancient hominids are called __?__. *(Neanderthals or australopithecines)*

UNDERSTANDING CONCEPTS

Multiple Choice

6. Scientists estimate the age of the Earth to be about
   a. 10 billion years.
   b. 4.6 billion years.
   c. 3.8 billion years.
   d. 4.4 million years.

7. The first cells appeared over
   a. 10 billion years ago.
   b. 4.6 billion years ago.
   c. 3.5 billion years ago.
   d. 4.4 million years ago.

8. How is the age of a fossil estimated?
   a. by using the geologic time scale
   b. by measuring unstable elements in the rock that holds the fossil
   c. by studying the relative position of continents
   d. by measuring the amount of oxygen in the fossil rock

9. Plants and air-breathing animals appeared during this time period.
   a. Precambrian time
   b. Paleozoic era
   c. Mesozoic era
   d. Cenozoic era

10. These hominids made sophisticated tools, hunted large animals, wore clothing, and cared for the sick and elderly. Their extinction is a mystery.
   a. australopithecines
   b. hominids in the genus *Homo*
   c. Neanderthals
   d. Cro-Magnons

Short Answer

11. What kinds of information do fossils provide about the evolutionary history of life?

12. Name at least one important biological event that occurred during each of the following geologic eras: Precambrian time, Paleozoic era, Mesozoic era, and Cenozoic era.

13. Why are there usually more fossils from the Cenozoic era than from other geologic eras?

Concept Mapping

14. Use the following terms to create a concept map: Earth's history, humans, Paleozoic era, dinosaurs, Precambrian time, cyanobacteria, Mesozoic era, land plants, Cenozoic era.

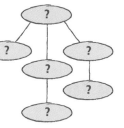

CRITICAL THINKING AND PROBLEM SOLVING

Write one or two sentences to answer the following questions:

15. Why do scientists think the first cells were anaerobic?

16. List three evolutionary changes in early hominids that led to the rise of modern humans.

MATH IN SCIENCE

17. A rock containing a newly discovered fossil is found to contain 5 g of an unstable form of potassium and 5 g of the stable element formed from its decay. If the half-life of the unstable form of potassium is 1.3 billion years, how old is the rock? What can you infer about the age of the fossil?

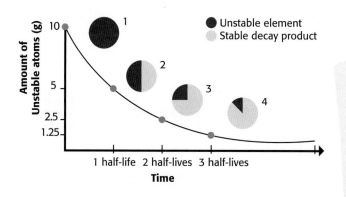

INTERPRETING GRAPHICS

The figure below illustrates the evolutionary relationships between different primate groups. The lower a line branches off, the earlier the event occurred. Examine the figure, and answer the questions that follow.

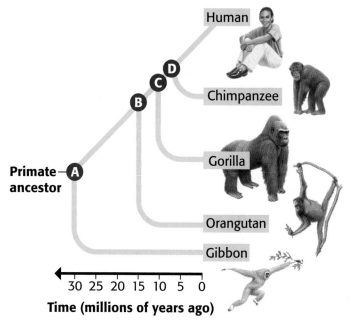

18. Which letter represents the time when humans and gorillas took different evolutionary paths?

19. About how many millions of years ago did orangutans diverge from the human evolutionary line?

20. Which group of apes has been separated from the human line of evolution for the longest period of time?

NOW What Do You Think?

Take a minute to review your answers to the ScienceLog questions on page 201. Have your answers changed? If necessary, revise your answers based on what you have learned since you began this chapter.

Windows into the Past

When you think about the history of life on Earth, you may not think of rocks. After all, rocks are nonliving! What can they tell you about life? It may surprise you to learn that a great deal of what we know about life on Earth has been provided by rocks. How? It just so happens that life-forms have been fossilized between layers of rock for million of years—maybe even since life first appeared on Earth. And finding these fossils is like finding an old snapshot of ancient life-forms.

Layers of Rock

Fossils are most likely to be found in sedimentary rock. This is a type of rock that forms as exposed rock surfaces are worn away by wind, rain, and ice. The particles from these rock surfaces then collect in low-lying areas. As these layers build up, their combined weight compacts the particles, and chemical reactions cement them together. After thousands of years, the layers of particles become solid rock—and so do parts of any organism that has been trapped in the layers.

The Rock Cycle

The illustration at right shows how sedimentary rock forms. It also shows how igneous rock and metamorphic rock form. Notice that sedimentary and metamorphic rock can melt and become igneous rock; this happens deep underground. Can you see why fossils would not normally be found in igneous rock?

The rock cycle is a continuous process. All three kinds of rock eventually become another type of rock. Fortunately for life scientists, this process can take millions of years. If this process happened more quickly—and sedimentary rock became either metamorphic or igneous rock at a faster pace—our fossil record would be much shorter. We may not have found out about the dinosaurs!

Cycle This!

▶ Suppose you found several fossils of the same organism. You found some fossils in very deep layers of sedimentary rock and some fossils in very shallow layers of sedimentary rock. What does this say about the organism?

▼ *The Rock Cycle*

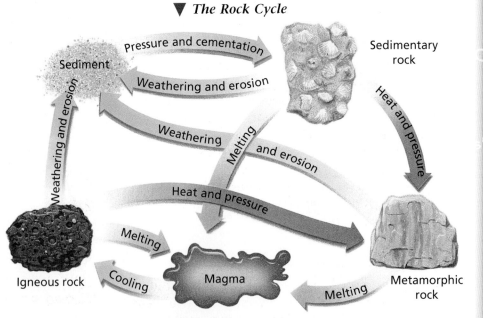

Pressure and cementation

Sediment

Weathering and erosion

Sedimentary rock

Weathering and erosion

Weathering

Melting and erosion

Heat and pressure

Heat and pressure

Melting

Igneous rock

Cooling

Magma

Melting

Metamorphic rock

CAREERS

PALEOBOTANIST

In school **Bonnie Jacobs** was fascinated by fossils, ancient cultures, and geology. "I have always had an interest in ancient things," she says. To pursue her interests, Jacobs became a paleobotanist. "A paleobotanist is someone who studies fossil plants," she explains. "That means you study fossilized leaves, wood, pollen, flower parts, or anything else that comes from a plant."

Bonnie Jacobs teaches and does research at Southern Methodist University, in Dallas, Texas. As a paleobotanist, she uses special "snapshots" that let her "see" back in time. If you look at these snapshots, you might see an ancient grassland, desert, or rain forest. Jacobs's snapshots might even give you a glimpse of the place where our human family may have started.

Fossil Plants and Ancient Climates

Jacobs and other paleobotanists study present-day plant species and how they grow in different climates. Plants that grow in warm, wet climates today probably grew in the same kind of climate millions of years ago. So when Jacobs finds ancient plant fossils that are similar to plants that exist today, she can determine what the ancient climate was like. But her fossils give more than just a climate report.

Plants and . . . Ancient Bones

Because some of these same plant fossils are found in rocks that also contain bits of bone—some from human ancestors—they may hold clues to human history. "Ideas about the causes of human evolution have a lot to do with changes in the landscape," Jacobs explains. "For instance, many scientists who study human evolution assumed that there was a big change from forested to more-open environments just before the origin of the human family. That assumption needs to be tested. The best way to do that is to go back to the plants themselves."

It's an Adventure!

In doing her research, Jacobs has traveled to many different places and worked with a wide variety of people. "Kiptalam Chepboi, a colleague we worked with in Kenya, grew up in the area where we do fieldwork. He took me to a sweat-bee hive. Sweat bees don't sting. You can take a honeycomb out from under a rock ledge, pop the whole thing in your mouth, and suck out the honey without worrying about getting stung. That was one of the neatest things I did out there."

Making a Modern Record

▶ Make your own plant fossil. Press a leaf part into a piece of clay. Fill the depression with plaster of Paris. Then write a report describing what the fossil tells you about the environment it came from.

▲ *Fossilized Leaves*

10 Classification

This Really Happened . . .

Skunks have been thrown out of their family. It wasn't their awful smell that got them thrown out, though. It was their DNA.

Skunks were once thought to be most closely related to weasels, ferrets, minks, badgers, and otters. Those furry, short-legged, long-bodied, meat-eating mammals are grouped together in a family called Mustelidae (moo STEL i dee). *Mustelidae* is from the Latin word for "mouse." Skunks were classified along with weasels and ferrets because they all share several physical characteristics with mice, such as short, round ears and short legs.

However, a researcher at the University of New Mexico's Museum of Southwestern Biology discovered that the DNA of skunks is very different from the DNA of the other members of Mustelidae. By comparing the DNA of different species, scientists can tell how closely related the species are. The DNA of two closely related animals—a house cat and a tiger, for example—are more similar than the DNA of two animals that are distantly related—such as a house cat and a chicken.

So where does that leave the little striped stinkers? Right in their own, newly created scientific family—Mephitidae (me FIT i dee). *Mephitid* is from the Latin word that means "bad odor!"

In this chapter you will learn why scientific names are important and how scientists classify organisms. You will also learn about the six major kingdoms into which all organisms are classified.

What Do You Think?

In your ScienceLog, try to answer the following questions based on what you already know:

1. What is classification?

2. How do people use classification in their everyday lives?

3. Why do scientists classify living things?

Investigate!

Classifying Shoes

In this activity, you will work in small groups to develop a system of classification for shoes.

Procedure

1. Gather **10 different shoes** from members of the class, a secondhand store, or a garage sale. Use a **black marker** to label the sole of each shoe with a number (1 through 10), and place the shoes on a table in the classroom.

2. Form small groups. In your ScienceLog, make a table similar to the one shown below. Make your own list of characteristics using the table as an example. Complete the chart, and then fill it in by describing each shoe.

Characteristics of Shoes

	Left or right	Boy's or girl's	Laced or slip-on	Color	Size
1.					
2.					
3.					
4.					
5.					

3. Use the information in the chart to make a key that can be used to identify each shoe. Your key should be a list of steps. Each step should contain two descriptive statements about the shoes that lead you to another set of statements. For example, step one might be:

1. **a.** This is a red sandal.   **Shoe #4**
   b. This is not a red sandal. **Go to step 2.**

Each set of statements should eliminate more shoes until only one shoe exactly fits the description, such as in (a) above. Check the number on the sole of the shoe to see if you are correct.

4. When all the groups have finished, exchange keys with members of another group. See if you can use their key to identify the shoes.

Analysis

5. How was it helpful to list the characteristics of the shoes before making the key?

6. Were you able to identify the shoes using another group's key? If not, what problems did you have?

Classification: Sorting It All Out

NEW TERMS

classification   family
kingdom   genus
phylum   species
class   dichotomous key
order   taxonomy

OBJECTIVES

- Explain the importance of having scientific names for species.
- List the seven levels of classification.
- Explain how scientific names are written.
- Describe how dichotomous keys help in identifying organisms.

Imagine that you live in a tropical rain forest and are responsible for getting your own food, shelter, and clothing from the forest. If you are going to survive, you will need to know which plants you can eat and which are poisonous. You will need to know which animals to eat and which will eat you if you aren't careful. You will need to organize the living things around you into categories—you will need to classify them. **Classification** is the arrangement of organisms into orderly groups based on their similarities.

Why Classify?

For thousands of years, humans have classified different kinds of organisms based on their usefulness. For example, the Chácabo people of Bolivia, like the family shown in **Figure 1,** know of 360 species of plants in the forest where they live, and they have uses for 305 of those plants. How many plants can you name that are useful in your life?

Biologists also classify organisms—both living and extinct. Why do they do this? There are millions of different species of living things in the world. Making sense of the sheer number and diversity of living things requires classification. As you know, scientists look for answers to questions. Classifying living things makes it easier for biologists to find the answers to many important questions, including the following:

- How many known species are there?
- What are the characteristics of these species?
- What are the relationships between these species?

In order to classify an organism, a biologist must use a system that groups organisms according to shared characteristics and their relationships between one another. There are seven levels of classification used by biologists—kingdom, phylum, class, order, family, genus, and species.

Figure 1 *The Chácabo people have a great amount of knowledge about their environment.*

Levels of Classification

Each organism is classified into one of several **kingdoms,** which are the largest, most general groups. All the organisms in a kingdom are then sorted into several *phyla* (singular, **phylum**). The members of one phylum are more like each other than they are like members of another phylum. Then all the organisms in a given phylum are further sorted into **classes.** Each class is subdivided into one or more **orders,** orders are separated into **families,** families are sorted into *genera* (singular, **genus**), and genera are sorted into **species.**

Examine **Figure 2** to follow the classification of the ordinary house cat from kingdom Animalia to species *Felis domesticus.*

Figure 2 *Kingdom Animalia contains all species of animals, while species* Felis domesticus *contains only one.*

Kingdom Animalia contains all the different phyla of animals.

Phylum Chordata contains animals with a hollow nerve cord.

Class Mammalia contains only animals that have a backbone and nurse their young.

Order Carnivora contains animals with a backbone that nurse their young and whose ancestors had special teeth for tearing meat.

Family Felidae contains animals with a backbone that nurse their young, have well-developed claws and special teeth for tearing meat, and are cats.

Genus *Felis* contains animals that have characteristics of the previous classifications, but they can't roar; they can only purr.

Species *Felis domesticus* contains only one kind of animal, the common house cat. This cat has characteristics of all the levels of classification above it, but it has other characteristics that make it unique.

Explore

A mnemonic device is a tool to help you remember something. It could be a word, a sentence that contains clues, or even a string tied around your finger!

One way to remember the levels of classification is to use a mnemonic device like this sentence: **K**ing **P**hillip **C**ame **O**ver **F**or **G**rape **S**oda.

Invent your own mnemonic device for the levels of classification using words that are meaningful to you.

What Is the Basis for Classification?

Carolus Linnaeus (lin AY uhs), pictured in **Figure 3,** was a Swedish physician and botanist who lived in the 1700s. Linnaeus founded **taxonomy,** the science of identifying, classifying, and naming living things.

Linnaeus attempted to classify all known organisms only by their shared characteristics. But this method changed after the publication of Darwin's theory of evolution by natural selection. Scientists began to recognize that evolutionary changes form a line of descent from a common ancestor. Taxonomy changed to include these new ideas about evolutionary relationships.

Today's taxonomists still classify organisms based on presumed evolutionary relationships. Species with a recent common ancestor can be classified together. For example, the platypus, brown bear, lion, and house cat are related because they are thought to have an ancestor in common—an ancient mammal. Because of this relationship, all four animals are grouped into the same class—Mammalia.

A brown bear, lion, and house cat are more closely related to each other than to the platypus. They are all mammals, but the platypus lays eggs, unlike the bear, lion, and house cat. Brown bears, lions, and house cats share a different common ancestor—an ancient carnivore. Thus, the brown bear, lion, and house cat are classified into the same order—Carnivora.

The close evolutionary relationship between lions and house cats is shown by the branching diagram in **Figure 4.** The characteristics listed on the arrow pointing to the right are the characteristics that make the next animal unique. The house cat and the platypus share the characteristics of hair and mammary glands. But they are different in many ways. For example, the house cat can purr. The branch that leads to lions is closest to the branch that leads to house cats. The lion and the house cat are closely related because they share the most recent common ancestor—an ancient cat.

Figure 3 *Carolus Linnaeus classified more than 7,000 species of plants.*

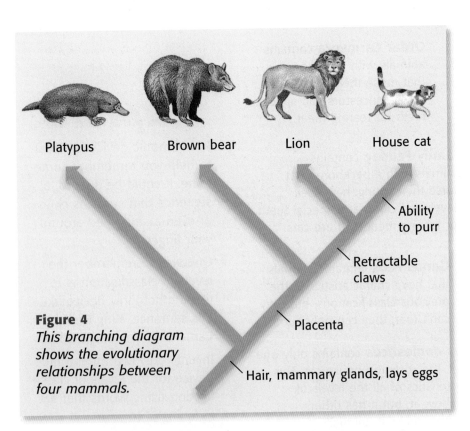

Platypus Brown bear Lion House cat

Ability to purr

Retractable claws

Placenta

Hair, mammary glands, lays eggs

Figure 4
This branching diagram shows the evolutionary relationships between four mammals.

Naming Names

By classifying organisms, biologists are also able to give them scientific names. A scientific name is always the same for a specific organism no matter how many common names it might have.

Before Linnaeus's time, scholars used Latin names up to 12 words long to identify species. Linnaeus simplified the naming of organisms by giving each species a two-part scientific name. The first part of the name identifies the genus, and the second part identifies the species. The scientific name for the Indian elephant, for example, is *Elephas maximus*. No other species has this name, and all scientists know that *Elephas maximus* refers to the Indian elephant. The first person to describe a new species gives it a scientific name.

It's All Greek (or Latin) to Me Scientific names might seem difficult to understand because they are in Latin or Greek. Most scientific names, however, are actually full of meaning. Take a look at **Figure 5.** You probably already know this animal's scientific name. It's *Tyrannosaurus rex*, of course! In this scientific name, the first word is a combination of two Greek words meaning "tyrant lizard," and the second word is Latin for "king." The genus name always begins with a capital letter, and the species name begins with a lowercase letter. Both words are underlined or italicized. You may have heard *Tyrannosaurus rex* called *T. rex*. This is acceptable in science as long as the genus name is spelled out the first time it is used. The species name is incomplete without the genus name or its abbreviation.

Come aboard the starship USS *Adventure*! Turn to page 594 in your LabBook.

Quick Lab

Evolutionary Diagrams

A branching evolutionary diagram can be constructed to trace the lineage of a species even though some of its ancestors exist only as fossils.

A branching evolutionary diagram can also be used to show evolutionary relationships between different phylums of organisms.

Construct a diagram similar to the one on page 230. Use a frog, a snake, a kangaroo, and a rabbit. What do you think is one major evolutionary change between one organism and the next? Write them on your diagram.

Figure 5
You would never call Tyrannosaurus rex *just* rex!

Why Are Scientific Names So Important? Examine the cartoon in **Figure 6.** What name do you have for the small black and white and sometimes smelly animal pictured? The skunk is called by several common names in English and has even more names—at least one name in every language! All of these common names can cause quite a bit of confusion for biologists who want to discuss the skunk. Biologists from different parts of the world who are interested in skunks need to know that they are all talking about the same animal, so they use its scientific name, *Mephitis mephitis*. All known living things have a two-part scientific name.

Figure 6 *Using an organism's two-part scientific name is a sure way for scientists to know they are discussing the same organism.*

When and where did the first bird live? Find out about the debate on page 244.

Dichotomous Keys

Taxonomists have developed special guides known as **dichotomous keys** to aid in identifying unknown organisms. A dichotomous key consists of several pairs of descriptive statements that have only two alternative responses. From each pair of statements, the person trying to identify the unknown organism chooses the appropriate statement. From there, the person is directed to another pair of statements. By working through the statements in the key, the person can eventually identify the unknown organism. Using the simple dichotomous key on the next page, try to identify the two animals shown.

Dichotomous Key to 10 Common Mammals in the Eastern United States

1. a. This mammal flies. Its hand is formed into a wing.	**Little brown bat**
b. This mammal does not fly.	**Go to step 2**
2. a. This mammal has a naked (no fur) tail.	**Go to step 3**
b. This mammal doesn't have a naked tail.	**Go to step 4**
3. a. This mammal has a short, naked tail.	**Eastern mole**
b. This mammal has a long, naked tail.	**Go to step 5**
4. a. This mammal has a black mask across its face.	**Raccoon**
b. This mammal does not have a black mask across its face.	**Go to step 6**
5. a. This mammal has a tail that is flattened and shaped like a paddle.	**Beaver**
b. This mammal has a tail that is not flattened or shaped like a paddle.	**Opossum**
6. a. This mammal is brown with a white underbelly.	**Go to step 7**
b. This mammal is not brown with a white underbelly.	**Go to step 8**
7. a. This mammal has a long, furry tail that is black on the tip.	**Longtail weasel**
b. This mammal has a long tail without much fur.	**White-footed mouse**
8. a. This mammal is black with a narrow white stripe on its forehead and broad white stripes on its back.	**Striped skunk**
b. This mammal is not black with white stripes.	**Go to step 9**
9. a. This mammal has long ears and a short, cottony tail.	**Eastern cottontail**
b. This mammal has short ears and a medium-length tail.	**Woodchuck**

REVIEW

1. Why do scientists use scientific names for organisms?

2. Explain the two parts of a scientific name.

3. List the seven levels of classification.

4. Describe how a dichotomous key helps to identify unknown organisms.

5. Interpreting Illustrations Study the figure at right. Which plant is the closest relative of the hibiscus? Which plant is most distantly related to the hibiscus? Which plants have seeds?

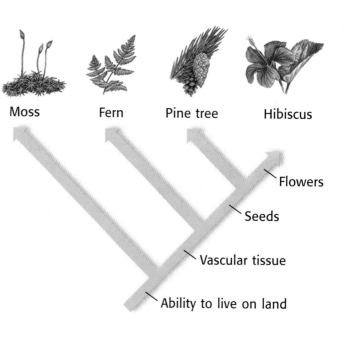

Moss   Fern   Pine tree   Hibiscus

Flowers

Seeds

Vascular tissue

Ability to live on land

The Six Kingdoms

For hundreds of years, all living things were classified as either plants or animals. These two kingdoms, Plantae and Animalia, worked just fine until organisms like the species *Euglena*, shown in **Figure 7,** were discovered. If you were a taxonomist, how would you classify such an organism?

What Is It?

As you know, organisms are classified by their characteristics. Being the excellent taxonomist that you are, you decide to list the characteristics of *Euglena*:

- *Euglena* are a species of single-celled organisms that live in pond water.
- *Euglena* are green and, like most plants, can make their own food through photosynthesis.

"This is easy!" you think to yourself. "*Euglena* are plants." Not so fast! There are other important characteristics to consider:

- *Euglena* can move about from place to place by whipping their "tails," called flagella.
- Sometimes *Euglena* use food obtained from other organisms.

You know that plants don't move around and usually do not eat other organisms. Does this mean that *Euglena* are animals? As you can see, neither category seems to fit. Scientists ran into the same problem, so they decided to add another kingdom for classifying organisms such as *Euglena*. This kingdom is known as Protista.

More Kingdoms As scientists continued to learn more about living things, they added kingdoms in order to account for the differences and similarities between organisms. Currently, most scientists agree that the six-kingdom classification system works best. There is still some disagreement, however, and still more to be learned. In the following pages, you will learn more about each of the kingdoms.

Figure 7 *How would you classify this organism?* Euglena, *shown here magnified 1,000 times, has characteristics of both plants and animals.*

BRAIN FOOD

If a *Euglena*'s chloroplasts are shaded from light or removed, it will begin to hunt for food like an animal. If the chloroplasts are shaded long enough, the chloroplasts degenerate and never come back.

The Two Kingdoms of Bacteria

Bacteria are extremely small single-celled organisms. Bacteria are different from all other living things in that they are *prokaryotes*, organisms that do not have nuclei. Many biologists divide bacteria into two kingdoms, **Archaebacteria** (AHR kee bak TEER ee uh) and **Eubacteria** (YOO bak TEER ee uh).

Archaebacteria have been on Earth at least 3 billion years. The prefix *archae* comes from a Greek word meaning "ancient." Today you can find archaebacteria living in places where most organisms could not survive. **Figure 8** shows a hot spring in Yellowstone National Park. The yellow and orange rings around the edge of the hot spring are formed by the billions of archaebacteria that live there.

Most of the other thousands of kinds of bacteria are eubacteria. These microscopic organisms live in the soil, in water, and even on and inside the human body! For example, the eubacterium *Escherichia coli*, pictured in **Figure 9,** is present in great numbers in human intestines, where it produces vitamin K. Another kind of eubacterium converts milk to yogurt, and yet another species causes ear and sinus infections and pneumonia.

Figure 8 *The Grand Prismatic Spring, in Yellowstone National Park, contains water that is about 90°C (194°F). The spring is home to archaebacteria that thrive in its hot water.*

Figure 9 E. coli *shown on the point of a pin are seen with a scanning electron microscope. These eubacteria live in the intestines of animals, where they decompose undigested food.*

Figure 10 *This* Paramecium *usually moves about rapidly.*

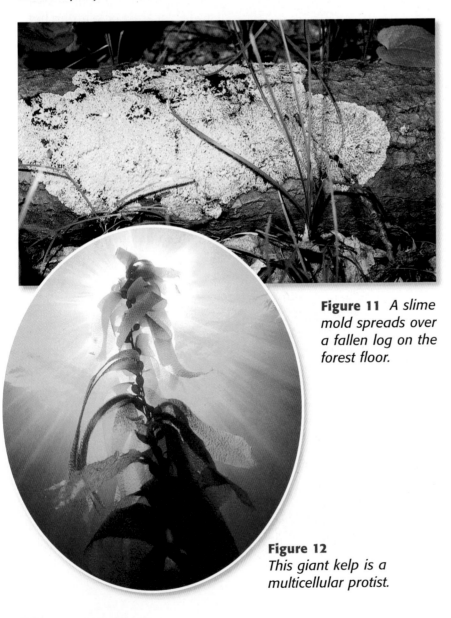

Figure 11 *A slime mold spreads over a fallen log on the forest floor.*

Figure 12
This giant kelp is a multicellular protist.

Kingdom Protista

Members of the kingdom **Protista,** commonly called protists, are single-celled or simple multicellular organisms. Unlike bacteria, protists are *eukaryotes,* organisms that have cells with a nucleus and membrane-bound organelles. Kingdom Protista contains all eukaryotes that are not plants, animals, or fungi. Scientists think the first protists evolved from ancient bacteria about 2 billion years ago. Much later, protists gave rise to plants, fungi, and animals as well as to modern protists.

As you can see, kingdom Protista contains many different kinds of organisms. Protists include protozoa, which are animal-like protists; algae, which are plantlike protists; and slime molds and water molds, which are fungus-like protists. *Euglena,* which were discussed earlier, are also members of kingdom Protista, as are the *Paramecium* and the slime mold pictured in **Figures 10** and **11.** Most protists are single-celled organisms, but some are multicellular, such as the giant kelp shown in **Figure 12.**

Self-Check

1. How are the two kingdoms of bacteria different from all other kingdoms?

2. How would you distinguish Protista from the two kingdoms of bacteria?

(See page 636 to check your answers.)

Kingdom Plantae

Although plants vary remarkably in size and form, most people easily recognize the members of kingdom **Plantae.** Plants are complex multicellular organisms that are usually green and use the sun's energy to make sugar by a process called *photosynthesis.* The giant sequoias and flowering plants shown in **Figures 13** and **14** are examples of the different organisms classified in the kingdom Plantae.

MATH BREAK

Building a Human Chain Around a Giant Sequoia

How many students would it take to join hands and form a human chain around a giant sequoia that is 30 m in circumference? Assume for this calculation that the average student can extend his or her arms about 1.3 m. NOTE: You can't have a fraction of a student, so be sure to round up your answer to the nearest whole number.

environmental science CONNECTION

Giant sequoia trees are very rare. They grow only in California and are a protected species. Some of them are over 3,000 years old.

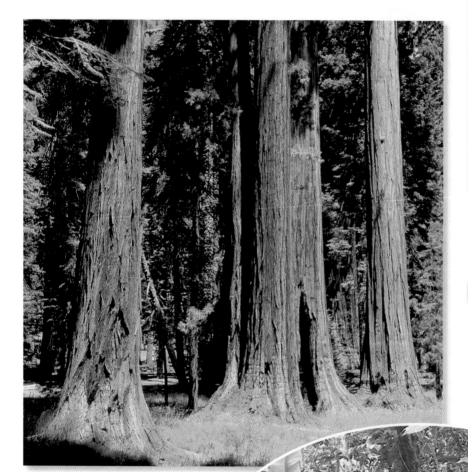

Figure 13 *A giant sequoia can measure 30 m around its base and can grow to more than 91.5 m tall.*

Figure 14 *Plants such as these are common in the rain forest.*

Kingdom Fungi

Molds and mushrooms are examples of the complex multicellular members of the kingdom **Fungi.** Fungi (singular, *fungus*) were originally classified as plants, but fungi do not obtain nutrients by photosynthesis. Moreover, fungi do not have many animal characteristics. Because of their unusual combination of characteristics, fungi are classified in a separate kingdom.

Fungi do not perform photosynthesis, as plants do, and they do not eat food, as animals do. Instead, fungi absorb nutrients from their surroundings after breaking them down with digestive juices. **Figure 15** shows a pretty but deadly mushroom, and **Figure 16** shows black bread mold (a fungus) growing on a piece of bread. Have you ever seen this type of mold on bread?

Figure 15 *This beautiful mushroom of the genus* Amanita *is poisonous.*

Figure 16 *This black bread mold growing on a piece of bread can be dangerous if you inhale the spores. Some molds are very dangerous, and other molds produce life-saving antibiotics, such as penicillin.*

Imagine that you and a friend are walking through the forest and you come upon the organism shown at right. You think it is a plant, but it doesn't look like any plant you have ever seen. It has a flower and seeds, very small leaves, and roots that are growing into a rotting log. But this organism is white from its roots to its petals. To which kingdom do you think this organism belongs? What characteristic is your answer based on? What additional information would you need in order to give a more accurate answer?

Kingdom Animalia

Animals are complex multicellular organisms that belong to the kingdom **Animalia.** Most animals can move about from place to place and have nervous systems that help them sense and react to their surroundings. At the microscopic level, animal cells differ from those of fungi, plants, most protists, and bacteria because animal cells lack cell walls. **Figure 17** shows some members of the kingdom Animalia.

Figure 17 *The kingdom Animalia contains many different organisms, such as eagles, tortoises, and dolphins.*

1. Name the six kingdoms.

2. Which of the six kingdoms include prokaryotes, and which include eukaryotes?

3. Explain the different ways plants, fungi, and animals obtain nutrients.

4. **Applying Concepts** Use the information in the evolutionary diagram of primates at right to answer the following questions: Which primate shares the most traits with humans? Do lemurs share the distinguishing characteristics listed at point *D* with humans? What characteristic do baboons have that lemurs do not have? Explain your answers.

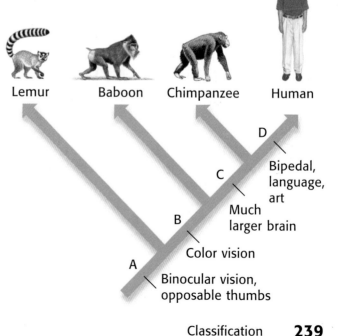

Lemur   Baboon   Chimpanzee   Human

D

C

Bipedal, language, art

Much larger brain

B

Color vision

A

Binocular vision, opposable thumbs

Chapter Highlights

Vocabulary

classification *(p. 228)*

kingdom *(p. 229)*

phylum *(p. 229)*

class *(p. 229)*

order *(p. 229)*

family *(p. 229)*

genus *(p. 229)*

species *(p. 229)*

taxonomy *(p. 230)*

dichotomous key *(p. 232)*

Section Notes

- Classification refers to the arrangement of organisms into orderly groups based on their similarities and evolutionary relationships.

- Biologists classify organisms in order to organize the number and diversity of living things and to give them scientific names.

- A scientific name is always the same for a specific organism, no matter how many common names it has.

- The classification scheme used today is based on the work of Carolus Linnaeus, a scientist who lived in the 1700s. Linnaeus founded the science of taxonomy, in which organisms are described, named, and classified.

- Today organisms are classified using a seven-level system of organization. The seven levels are kingdom, phylum, class, order, family, genus, and species. The genus and species of an organism compose its two-part scientific name.

- Dichotomous keys help to identify organisms.

- Modern classification schemes include evolutionary relationships.

Labs

Shape Island *(p. 592)*

☑ Skills Check

Math Concepts

LARGE ORGANISMS The rounding-off rule states: If the number you wish to round is greater than or equal to the midpoint, round the number to the next greater number.

Sometimes when you are working with objects instead of numbers, you have to use a different rule! The MathBreak on page 237 asks you to round up your answer even though the answer includes a fraction that is less than halfway to the next number. Why is that? The answer is that if you don't round up, you won't have enough students to encircle the tree.

Visual Understanding

LEVELS OF CLASSIFICATION If you are still a little unsure about how organisms are grouped into levels of classification, turn back to page 229. Review Figure 2. Notice that the broadest, most inclusive level is kingdom. For example, all animals are grouped into kingdom Animalia. From there, the groups become more and more specific until only one animal is included under the level of species. Working from species up, notice that more and more animals are included in the group as you move toward the level of kingdom.

Vocabulary

bacteria (p. 235)

Archaebacteria (p. 235)

Eubacteria (p. 235)

Protista (p. 236)

Plantae (p. 237)

Fungi (p. 238)

Animalia (p. 239)

Section Notes

• At first, living things were classified as either plants or animals. As scientists discovered more about living things and discovered more organisms, new kingdoms were added that were more descriptive than the old two-kingdom system.

• Most biologists recognize six kingdoms—Archaebacteria, Eubacteria, Protista, Plantae, Fungi, and Animalia.

• Bacteria are prokaryotes, single-celled organisms that do not contain nuclei. The organisms of all other kingdoms are eukaryotes, organisms that have cells with nuclei.

• Archaebacteria have been on Earth for about 3 billion years and can live where most other organisms cannot survive.

• Most bacteria are eubacteria and live almost everywhere. Some are harmful, and some are beneficial.

• Plants, most fungi, and animals are complex multicellular organisms. Plants perform photosynthesis. Fungi break down material outside their body and then absorb the nutrients. Animals eat food, which is digested inside their body.

Labs

Voyage of the USS *Adventure* (p. 594)

---

internet**connect**

 GO TO: go.hrw.com

Visit the **HRW** Web site for a variety of learning tools related to this chapter. Just type in the keyword:

KEYWORD: HSTCLS

 GO TO: www.scilinks.org

Visit the **National Science Teachers Association** on-line Web site for Internet resources related to this chapter. Just type in the *sci*LINKS number for more information about the topic:

TOPIC: The Basis for Classification	***sci*LINKS NUMBER:** HSTL205
TOPIC: Levels of Classification	***sci*LINKS NUMBER:** HSTL210
TOPIC: Dichotomous Keys	***sci*LINKS NUMBER:** HSTL215
TOPIC: The Six Kingdoms	***sci*LINKS NUMBER:** HSTL220

Chapter Review

USING VOCABULARY

To complete the following sentences, choose the correct term from each pair of terms listed below:

1. Linnaeus founded the science of __?__. (*DNA analysis* or *taxonomy*)

2. All of the organisms classified into a single kingdom are then divided into one of several __?__. (*phyla* or *classes*)

3. The narrowest level of classification is the __?__. (*genus* or *species*)

4. Linnaeus began naming organisms using __?__. (*two-part scientific names* or *evolutionary relationships*)

5. Archaebacteria and eubacteria are __?__. (*prokaryotes* or *eukaryotes*)

UNDERSTANDING CONCEPTS

Multiple Choice

6. When scientists classify organisms, they
   a. arrange them in orderly groups.
   b. give them many common names.
   c. decide whether they are useful.
   d. ignore evolutionary relationships.

7. When the seven levels of classification are listed from broadest to narrowest, which level is in the fifth position?
   a. class
   b. order
   c. genus
   d. family

8. The scientific name for the European white water lily is *Nymphaea alba*. What is the genus to which this plant belongs?
   a. *Nymphaea*   c. water lily
   b. *alba*   d. alba lily

9. "Kings Play Chess On Fine-Grained Sand" is a mnemonic device that helps one remember
   a. the scientific names of different organisms.
   b. the six kingdoms.
   c. the seven levels of classification.
   d. the difference between prokaryotic and eukaryotic cells.

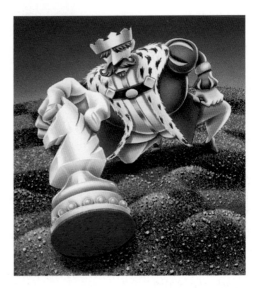

10. Most bacteria are classified in which kingdom?
    a. Archaebacteria   c. Protista
    b. Eubacteria   d. Fungi

11. What kind of organism thrives in hot springs and other extreme environments?
    a. archaebacteria   c. protists
    b. eubacteria   d. fungi

Short Answer

12. Why is the use of scientific names so important in biology?

13. List two kinds of evidence used by modern taxonomists to classify organisms based on evolutionary relationships.

14. Is a eubacterium a type of eukaryote? Explain your answer.

Concept Map

15. Use the following terms to create a concept map: kingdom, fern, lizard, Animalia, Fungi, algae, Protista, Plantae, mushroom.

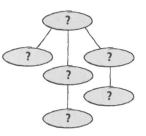

CRITICAL THINKING AND PROBLEM SOLVING

Write one or two sentences to answer the following questions:

16. How are the levels of classification related to evolutionary relationships among organisms?

17. Explain why two species that belong to the same genus, such as white oak *(Quercus alba)* and cork oak *(Quercus suber),* also belong to the same family.

18. What characteristic do the members of all six kingdoms have in common?

MATH IN SCIENCE

19. Scientists estimate that millions of species are yet to be discovered and classified. If only 1.5 million, or 10 percent, of species have been discovered and classified, how many species do scientists think exist on Earth?

20. Sequoia trees can grow to more than 90 m in height. There are 3.28 ft per meter. How many feet are in 90 m?

INTERPRETING GRAPHICS

The diagram below illustrates the evolutionary relationships among several plants.

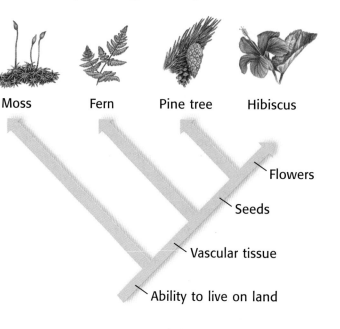

Moss   Fern   Pine tree   Hibiscus

Flowers
Seeds
Vascular tissue
Ability to live on land

21. Which plant is the closest relative to the common ancestor of all plants?

22. Using the diagram, name at least one characteristic that distinguishes each plant from its ancestors.

23. Which plant is most distantly related to the pine tree?

24. Where on this evolutionary diagram would you place algae? Explain your answer.

NOW What Do You Think?

Take a minute to review your answers to the ScienceLog questions on page 227. Have your answers changed? If necessary, revise your answers based on what you have learned since you began this chapter.

It's a Bird, It's a Plane, It's a *Dinosaur*?

Think about birds. Parrots, pigeons, buzzards, emus . . . they're everywhere! But once there were no birds. So where did they come from? When did birds evolve? Was it 225 million years ago, just 115 million years ago, or somewhere in between? No one really knows for sure, but the topic has fueled a long-standing debate among scientists.

The debate began when the fossil remains of a 150-million-year-old dinosaur with wings and feathers—*Archaeopteryx*—were found in Germany in 1860 and 1861.

▲ Archaeopteryx *was the first true bird.*

Birds Are Dinosaurs!

Some scientists think that birds evolved from small, carnivorous dinosaurs like *Velociraptor* about 115 million to 150 million years ago. Their idea relies on similarities between modern birds and these small dinosaurs. Particularly impor-

tant are the size, shape, and number of toes and "fingers"; the location and shape of the breastbone and shoulder; the presence of a hollow bone structure; and the development of wrist bones that "flap" for flight. To many scientists, all this evidence is overwhelming. It can lead to only one conclusion: Modern birds are descendants of dinosaurs.

No They Aren't!

"Not so fast!" say a smaller but equally determined group of scientists who think that birds developed 100 million years before *Velociraptor* and its relatives. They point out that all these dinosaurs were ground dwellers and were the wrong shape and size for flying. They would never get off the ground! Further, these dinosaurs lacked at least one of the bones necessary for flight in today's birds.

This "birds came before dinosaurs" idea rests on fossils of *thecodonts,* small tree-dwelling reptiles that lived about 225 million years ago. One thecodont, a small, four-legged tree dweller called *Megalancosaurus,* had the right bones and body shape—and the right center of gravity—for flight. The evidence is clear, say these scientists, that birds flew long before dinosaurs even existed!

▲ *This small tree-dwelling reptile,* Megalancosaurus, *may have evolved into the birds we know today.*

So Who Is Right?

Both sides are debating fossils 65 million years to 225 million years old. Some species left many fossils, while some left just a few. In the last few years, new fossils discovered in China, Mongolia, and Argentina have just added fuel to the fire. So scientists will continue to study the available evidence and provide their educated guesses. Meanwhile, the debate rages on!

Compare for Yourself

▶ Find photographs of *Sinosauropteryx* and *Archaeopteryx* fossils, and compare them. How are they similar? How are they different? Do you think birds could be modern dinosaurs? Debate your idea with someone who holds the opposite view.

WEIRD SCIENCE

LOBSTER-LIP LIFE-FORM

Have you ever stopped to think about lobsters' lips? Did you even know that lobsters have lips? Oddly enough, they do. And even stranger, scientists have found a tiny animal living on lobsters' lips. Surprised? Although scientists noticed this little critter about 30 years ago, they had never studied it closely. When they finally did, they were astounded! This tiny life-form is different from anything else in the world. Meet *Symbion pandora.*

▲ *Although scientists knew of* Symbion pandora's *existence for 30 years, they did not realize how unusual it was.*

A Little Weird

What makes *Symbion pandora* so unusual? As if spending most of its life on lobster lips isn't strange enough, *S. pandora* also seems to combine the traits of very different animals. Here are some of its strange characteristics:

- **Life stages:** *S. pandora*'s life cycle involves many different *stages,* or body forms. The stages are very different from each other. For instance, at certain times in its life, *S. pandora* can swim around, while at other times, it can exist only by attaching to a lobster's mouth.
- **Dwarf males:** Male *S. pandora* are much smaller than the females. Thus, they are called *dwarf males.*

- **Feeding habits:** Dwarf males don't eat; they can only find a female, reproduce, and then die!
- **Budding:** Many individuals are neither male nor female. These animals reproduce through a process called *budding.* In budding, a new, complete animal can sprout out of the adult. In turn, the new offspring can reproduce in the same way.
- **Disappearing guts:** When an adult starts to form a new bud, its digestive and nervous systems disappear! Part of these guts help make the new bud. Then the adult forms new digestive and nervous systems to replace the old ones.

How Unusual Is It?

When scientists discover a new plant or animal, they may conclude that it represents a new species within an existing genus. In that case scientists make up a name for the new species. Usually, the person who finds the new organism gets to name it. If the new organism is *very* unusual, scientists may place it not only in a new species but also in a new genus.

   S. pandora is so unusual that it was placed not only in a new species and a new genus, but also in a new family, a new order, a new class, and even a new phylum! Such a scientific discovery is extremely rare. In fact, when this discovery was made, in 1995, it was announced in newspapers all over the world!

Where Would You Look?

▶ *S. pandora* was first noticed more than 30 years ago, but no one realized how unusual it was until scientists studied it. Scientists estimate that we've identified less than 10 percent of Earth's organisms. Find out about other new animal species that have been discovered within the last 10 years. Where are some places you would look for new species?

245

UNIT 4

Plots → Plants

You are probably familiar with plants. Even in the city, you can see trees and grass and flowers. But do you know how important plants are? When plants make food for themselves, they provide oxygen and food for other living things.

Throughout history, people have been trying to understand plants, and in this unit you will join them. You'll learn how plants grow, reproduce, and make their own food. Read on to discover other fascinating things about plants.

250 B.C.
Mayan farmers build terraces to control the flow of water to their crops.

1931
Barbara McClintock discovers that new varieties of corn are created when a plant's genes exchange information.

1940
The first electron-microscope image of a chloroplast is taken.

1580

Prospero Alpini discovers that plants have both male and female structures.

1763

Joseph Kohlreuter studies pollination in plants.

1776

The Declaration of Independence is signed.

1891

The zipper is invented.

1837

Chlorophyll is found to be necessary for photosynthesis.

1996

A genetically engineered cotton crop that is resistant to insects is introduced.

1983

HIV, the virus responsible for AIDS, is isolated.

1967

Taxol, an extract from the bark of the Pacific yew tree, is shown to be an effective anticancer drug.

11 Introduction to Plants

This Really Happened . . .

A lone scientist trudges through a remote rain forest. Peering into a steep, narrow canyon, he notices something unusual. On closer inspection, he discovers that it is a species of tree that has survived from the days when *Tyrannosaurus rex* and *Velociraptor* walked the Earth!

No, this isn't a scene out of *Jurassic Park.* This really happened in an Australian rain forest in 1994. The scientist's name was David Noble. He discovered a tree species that dates back to the Cretaceous period, between 144 million and 65 million years ago.

The trees, called Wollemi pines, have large bladelike leaves and knobby brown bark. They grow as tall as 35 m, and their trunks can grow as wide as 1 m.

Since the discovery of the trees, scientists at the Royal Botanic Gardens in Sydney, Australia, have been planting seeds of the Wollemi pines and growing seedlings. Soon Wollemi pines will be made available to gardeners so they can transform their yards into their own Cretaceous parks.

In this chapter, you will learn more about the mysterious world of plants. You will see that plants are complex life-forms that challenge our understanding of nature.

2 c. of flour

1 tsp. of salt

1 tsp. of baking soda

$1\frac{1}{2}$ c. of sugar

1 tsp. of vanilla

2 eggs

2 c. of chocolate chips

$\frac{1}{2}$ c. of margarine

Investigate!

Cookie Calamity

One morning, a bakery receives an order for hundreds of chocolate chip cookies that must be made as soon as possible. When the baker goes to get the ingredients for the cookies, he finds that the bakery has run out of all the ingredients that come directly and indirectly from plants. Can he still make the cookies?

Procedure

1. Examine the ingredients listed in the cookie recipe.

2. Determine which ingredients come from plants, either directly or indirectly.

3. Identify the plant or plants involved in each ingredient.

Analysis

4. Suppose the recipe called for butter instead of margarine. Would that be of any help to the baker? Why or why not?

5. If you took all the plant ingredients out of chocolate chip cookies, what would you be eating?

Introduction to Plants **249**

What Makes a Plant a Plant?

NEW TERMS

cuticle   vascular plant
sporophyte   gymnosperm
gametophyte   angiosperm
nonvascular plant

OBJECTIVES

- Identify the characteristics that all plants share.
- Discuss the origin of plants.
- Explain how the four main groups of plants differ.

Imagine spending a day without anything made from plants. Not only would it be impossible to make chocolate chip cookies, it would be impossible to do many other things, too. You couldn't wear jeans or any clothes made of cotton or linen. You couldn't use any furniture constructed of wood. You couldn't write with wooden pencils or use paper in any form, including money. You couldn't eat anything because almost all food is made from plants or from animals that eat plants. Spending a day without plants would be very hard to do. In fact, life as we know it would be impossible if plants did not exist!

Plant Characteristics

As you can see, plants come in many different shapes and sizes. What do cactuses, water lilies, ferns, and all other plants have in common? Although one plant may seem very different from another, all plants share certain characteristics.

Sugar maple

Plants Make Their Own Food One thing that you have probably noticed about plants is that most of them are green. This is because plant cells have chloroplasts. As you learned earlier, chloroplasts are organelles that contain the green pigment *chlorophyll*. Chlorophyll absorbs light energy from the sun. Plants then use this energy to make food molecules, such as glucose. You may recall that this process is called *photosynthesis*.

Plants Have a Cuticle A **cuticle** is a waxy layer that coats the surface of stems, leaves, and other plant parts exposed to air. Most plants live on dry land, and the cuticle is an adaptation that helps keep plants from drying out.

Water lily

Fern

Prickly pear cactus

Plant Cells Have Cell Walls Plant cells are surrounded by a cell membrane and a rigid cell wall. The cell wall lies outside the cell membrane, as shown in **Figure 1.** The cell wall helps support and protect the plant. Cell walls contain complex carbohydrates and proteins that form a hard material. When the cell reaches its full size, a tough, woody, secondary cell wall may develop. Once it is formed, a plant cell can grow no larger.

Plants Reproduce with Spores and Sex Cells A plant's life cycle can be divided into two parts. Plants spend one part of their lives in the stage that produces spores and the other part in the stage that produces sex cells (egg and sperm cells). The spore-producing stage is called a **sporophyte** (SPOH roh FIET). The stage that produces egg cells and sperm cells is called a **gametophyte** (guh MEET oh FIET). A diagram of the plant life cycle is shown in **Figure 2.**

Spores and sex cells are tiny reproductive cells. Spores that land in a suitable environment, such as damp soil, can grow into new plants. In contrast, sex cells cannot grow directly into new plants. Instead, a male sex cell (sperm cell) must join with a female sex cell (egg cell). The fertilized egg that results may grow into a new plant.

Cell membrane
Cell wall

Figure 1 *In addition to the cell membrane, a cell wall surrounds plant cells.*

Figure 2 Plant Life Cycle

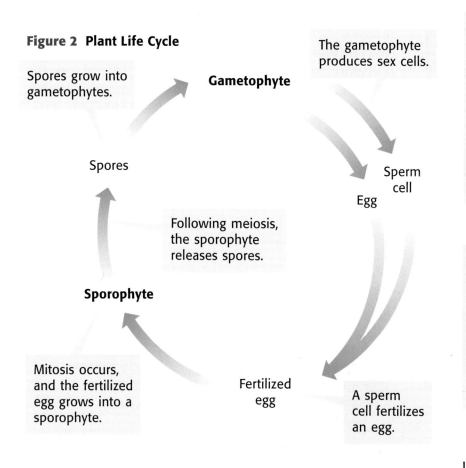

Spores grow into gametophytes.

Gametophyte

The gametophyte produces sex cells.

Spores

Sperm cell

Egg

Following meiosis, the sporophyte releases spores.

Sporophyte

Mitosis occurs, and the fertilized egg grows into a sporophyte.

Fertilized egg

A sperm cell fertilizes an egg.

Explore

Think about how plants are a part of your everyday life. List 10 ways that you use plants or plant products. Compare your list with those of your classmates, and see how your lists are similar or different.

Did you know that many medicines come from plants? Turn to p. 277 to read about a scientist who studies how people use plants to treat diseases.

Ancient green algae

Green algae   Plant

Figure 3 *The similarities between modern green algae and plants are evidence that both may have originated from an ancient species of green algae.*

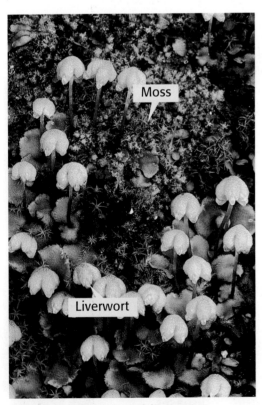

Moss

Liverwort

Figure 4 *Mosses and liverworts do not have conducting tissues.*

The Origin of Plants

If you were to travel back in time 440 million years, Earth would seem like a strange, bare, and unfriendly place. For one thing, no plants lived on land. Where did plants come from? What organisms were the ancestors of plants?

Take a look at the photographs in **Figure 3.** On the left is an organism called green algae. As you can see, plants and green algae are similar in color. Their similarities go beyond their color, however. For example, both green algae and plants contain the same kind of chlorophyll and have similar cell walls. They both store their energy in the form of starch. Like plants, green algae also have a two-part life cycle. What do these similarities suggest? Scientists think that ancient green algae that lived in the oceans were the ancestors of all plants as well as the ancestors of green algae that live today.

How Are Plants Classified?

There are more than 260,000 species of plants living on Earth today. Although all plants share the basic characteristics discussed earlier, they can be divided into two groups—vascular plants and nonvascular plants.

Plants Without "Plumbing" The nonvascular plants, mosses and liverworts, are shown in **Figure 4. Nonvascular plants** have no "plumbing," or pipes to transport water and nutrients. They depend on the processes of diffusion and osmosis to move materials from one part of the plant to another. Although diffusion and osmosis are slow processes, they supply the cells of mosses and liverworts with the materials the cells need to live. This is possible because nonvascular plants are small. If they were large—the size of trees, for example—there would be no way to deliver the needed materials to all the cells by diffusion and osmosis.

✓ Self-Check

One way plants and green algae differ is that cells of green algae do not have a cuticle surrounding them. Why do plants need a cuticle, while algae do not?
(See page 636 to check your answer.)

Plants with "Plumbing" Vascular plants do not rely solely on diffusion and osmosis to deliver needed materials to all the cells. That's because **vascular plants** have tissues made of cells that deliver needed materials throughout a plant, much as pipes deliver water to faucets in your home. Because vascular tissues can carry needed materials long distances within the plant body, vascular plants can be almost any size. Some vascular plants are tiny, but others may be quite large.

Vascular plants can be divided into two groups—plants that produce seeds and plants that do not. Plants that do not produce seeds include ferns, horsetails, and club mosses. Plants that produce seeds also fall into two groups—those that produce flowers and those that do not. Nonflowering plants are called **gymnosperms** (JIM noh SPUHRMZ). Flowering plants are called **angiosperms** (AN jee oh SPUHRMZ).

The four main groups of living plants—(1) mosses and liverworts; (2) ferns, horsetails, and club mosses; (3) gymnosperms; and (4) angiosperms—are shown in **Figure 5.**

MATH BREAK

Practice with Percents

The following list gives an estimate of the number of species in each plant group:

Mosses and liverworts	15,000
Ferns, horsetails, and club mosses	12,000
Gymnosperms	760
Angiosperms	235,000

What percentage of plants do not produce seeds?

Figure 5 The Main Groups of Living Plants

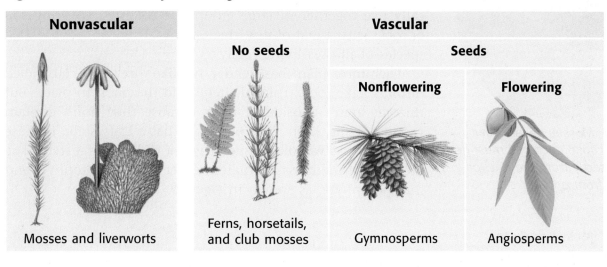

REVIEW

1. What are two characteristics that all plants have in common?

2. What type of organism is thought to be the ancestor of all plants? Why?

3. How are ferns, horsetails, and club mosses different from angiosperms?

4. **Applying Concepts** How would you decide whether an unknown organism is a type of green algae or a plant?

Seedless Plants

As you have just learned, there are two groups of plants that don't make seeds. One group of seedless plants is the non-vascular plants, mosses and liverworts. The other group is made up of several vascular plants—ferns, horsetails, and club mosses.

NEW TERMS
rhizoids
rhizome

OBJECTIVES

- Describe the features of mosses and liverworts.
- Describe the features of ferns, horsetails, and club mosses.
- Explain how plants without seeds are important to humans and to the environment.

Mosses and Liverworts

Even though plants are all around us, it is easy to overlook the nonvascular plants. Mosses and liverworts are small, growing on soil, the bark of trees, and rocks. Because they lack a vascular system, these plants usually live in places that are always wet. Each cell of the plant must absorb water by osmosis directly from the environment or from a neighboring cell.

Mosses and liverworts don't have true stems, roots, or leaves. They do, however, have structures that carry out the same activities of stems, roots, and leaves.

Rock-to-Rock Carpeting Mosses, shown in **Figure 6,** typically live together in large groups, or colonies, covering soil or rocks with a mat of tiny green plants. There are about 9,000 species of mosses living today.

Each moss plant has slender, hairlike threads of cells called **rhizoids.** Like roots, rhizoids help hold the plant in place. But rhizoids aren't considered roots because they don't contain vascular tissue. Each moss plant also has a leafy stalk. Because the stalk lacks vascular tissue, it is not considered a stem. The life cycle of the moss alternates between the gametophyte and the sporophyte, as shown in **Figure 7.**

Figure 6 *Mosses never grow large because each cell must get water directly from the environment or from another cell.*

Figure 7 Moss Life Cycle

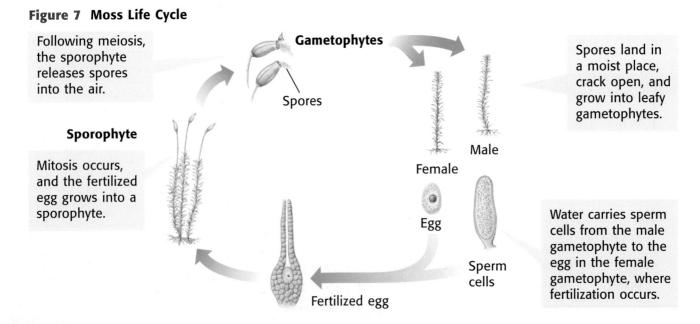

Following meiosis, the sporophyte releases spores into the air.

Gametophytes

Spores

Spores land in a moist place, crack open, and grow into leafy gametophytes.

Sporophyte

Mitosis occurs, and the fertilized egg grows into a sporophyte.

Male

Female

Egg

Sperm cells

Water carries sperm cells from the male gametophyte to the egg in the female gametophyte, where fertilization occurs.

Fertilized egg

Liverworts Like mosses, liverworts are small, non-vascular plants that usually live in damp or moist places. About 6,000 liverwort species exist today. Liverworts have a life cycle similar to that of mosses. The gametophytes of liverworts can be leafy and mosslike or broad and flattened, like those shown in **Figure 8.** Rhizoids extend out of the lower side of the liverwort body and help anchor the plant.

The Importance of Mosses and Liverworts
Although nonvascular plants are small, they play an important role in the environment. They are usually the first plants to inhabit a new, bare environment, such as newly exposed rock. When mosses and liverworts covering a rock die, they form a thin layer of soil in which new plants, including more mosses and liverworts, can grow. The mosses and liverworts cover the new soil and help hold it in place. This reduces soil erosion. Mosses also provide nesting materials for birds.

Peat mosses are the most important mosses to humans. Peat mosses grow in bogs and other wet places. In certain locations, such as Ireland, dead peat mosses have built up in bogs as thick deposits. This peat can be taken from the bog, dried, and burned as a fuel.

Ferns, Horsetails, and Club Mosses

Unlike most of their modern descendants, ancient ferns, horsetails, and club mosses grew to be quite tall. The first forests were made up of stands of 40 m high club mosses, 18 m high horsetails, and 8 m high ferns. **Figure 9** shows how these forests may have looked. These ancient plants had vascular systems and could therefore grow taller than non-vascular plants.

Figure 8 *This liverwort has a broad, flattened gametophyte. The sporophyte looks like a tiny palm tree or umbrella.*

Figure 9 *Vascular tissue allowed the ancestors of modern ferns, horsetails, and club mosses to grow tall.*

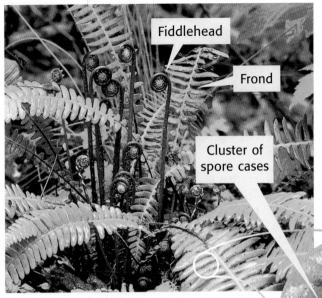

Fiddlehead

Frond

Cluster of spore cases

Figure 10 *This plant is a fern sporophyte. It produces spores in spore cases on the underside of the leaflike fronds. Fiddleheads grow into new fronds.*

Self-Check

Why are some vascular plants large, while nonvascular plants are always small? *(See p. 636 to check your answer.)*

Ferns Ferns grow in many places, from the cold Arctic to warm, humid tropical forests. Today there are about 11,000 species of ferns. Although most ferns are relatively small plants, some tree ferns in the tropics grow as tall as 23 m.

Figure 10 shows a typical fern. Most ferns have an underground stem, called a **rhizome,** that produces wiry roots and leaves called *fronds*. Young fronds are tightly coiled. They are called *fiddleheads* because they look like the end of a violin, or fiddle.

Like the life cycles of all other plants, the life cycle of ferns is divided into two parts. The stage that you are probably most familiar with is the sporophyte, shown in **Figure 11**. The fern gametophyte is a tiny plant about the size of half of one of your fingernails. It is green and flat, and it is usually shaped like a tiny heart. The fern gametophyte has male structures that produce sperm cells and female structures that produce eggs. Like mosses, ferns need water to transport sperm cells to the eggs. If a thin film of water is on the ground, the sperm cells can swim through it to an egg.

Figure 11 Fern Life Cycle

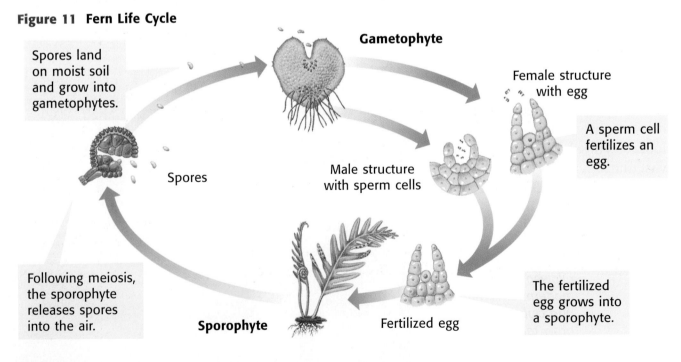

Spores land on moist soil and grow into gametophytes.

Gametophyte

Female structure with egg

Spores

Male structure with sperm cells

A sperm cell fertilizes an egg.

Following meiosis, the sporophyte releases spores into the air.

Sporophyte

Fertilized egg

The fertilized egg grows into a sporophyte.

Horsetails Horsetails were common plants millions of years ago, but only about 15 species have survived to the present. Modern horsetails, shown in **Figure 12,** are small vascular plants usually less than 1.3 m tall. They grow in wet, marshy places. They are called horsetails because some species resemble a bushy horse's tail. Their stems are hollow and contain silica. Because of this, they feel gritty. In fact, pioneers of the early United States called horsetails "scouring rushes" and used them to scrub pots and pans. The life cycle of horsetails is similar to that of ferns.

Club Mosses Club mosses, shown in **Figure 13,** are small plants, about 25 cm tall, that grow in woodlands. Despite their name, club mosses are not actually mosses. Unlike true mosses, club mosses have vascular tissue. Like horsetails, club mosses were common plants millions of years ago. About 1,000 species of club mosses exist today.

The Importance of Seedless Vascular Plants Seedless vascular plants play important roles in the environment. Like mosses and liverworts, the ferns, horsetails, and club mosses help to form soil. They also hold the soil in place, preventing soil erosion.

Ferns are popular as houseplants because of their beautiful leaves. The fiddleheads of some ferns are harvested in early spring, cooked, and eaten.

For humans, some of the most important seedless vascular plants lived and died about 300 million years ago. The remains of these ancient ferns, horsetails, and club mosses formed coal, a fossil fuel that we now extract from the Earth's crust.

Figure 12 *The cone-like tips of horsetails contain spores.*

REVIEW

1. What is the connection between coal and seedless vascular plants?

2. How are horsetails and club mosses similar to ferns?

3. List two ways that seedless vascular plants are important to the environment.

4. **Making Predictions** If mosses and ferns lived in an environment that suddenly experienced a drought, which plants would probably be the most affected? Explain your answer.

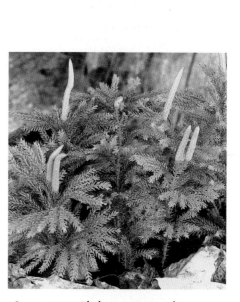

Figure 13 *Club mosses release spores from their conelike tips.*

Plants with Seeds

The plants that you are probably most familiar with are the seed plants. The plants on this page are all seed plants. Do they look familiar to you?

Peaches

As you read earlier, there are two groups of vascular plants that produce seeds—the gymnosperms and the angiosperms. Gymnosperms are trees and shrubs that produce seeds in cones or fleshy structures on stems. Pine, spruce, fir, and ginkgo trees are examples of gymnosperms. Angiosperms, or flowering plants, produce their seeds within a fruit. Peach trees, grasses, oak trees, rose bushes, cactuses, and buttercups are all examples of angiosperms.

Characteristics of Seed Plants

Like all other plants, seed plants alternate between two stages. Part of their life cycle is the sporophyte stage, and part is the gametophyte stage. But seed plants differ from all other plants in the following ways:

- Seed plants produce seeds, structures in which young sporophytes are nourished and protected.

- Unlike the gametophytes of seedless plants, the gametophytes of seed plants do not live independently of the sporophyte. Gametophytes of seed plants are tiny and are always found protected in the reproductive structures of the sporophyte.

- The male gametophytes of seed plants do not need water to travel to the female gametophytes. Male gametophytes develop inside tiny structures that can be transported by the wind or by animals. These dustlike structures are called **pollen.**

The above characteristics allow seed plants to live just about anywhere. Because of this, seed plants are the most successful and common plants on Earth today.

English elm

Desert yucca

What's So Great About Seeds?

A seed develops after fertilization, the union of an egg and a sperm cell, takes place. A seed is made up of three parts: a young plant (the sporophyte), stored food, and a tough seed coat that surrounds and protects the young plant. These parts are shown in **Figure 14.**

Did you know that seeds like to travel far from home? See how on page 598 of your LabBook.

Figure 14 *A seed contains stored food and a young plant. A seed is surrounded and protected by a seed coat.*

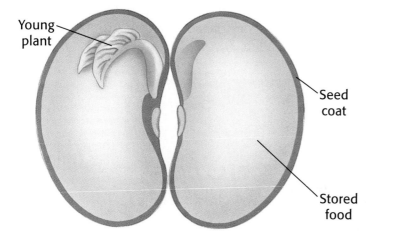

Young plant

Seed coat

Stored food

Plants that reproduce by seeds have several advantages over spore-forming seedless plants, such as ferns. For example, the young plant within a seed is composed of many cells. The young plant is well developed and has a small root, a small stem, and tiny leaves. In contrast, the plant spore is a single cell.

When a seed *germinates,* or begins to grow, the young plant is nourished by the food stored in the seed. By the time the young plant uses up these food reserves, it is able to make all the food it needs by photosynthesis. In contrast, the gametophyte that develops from a spore must be in an environment where it can begin photosynthesis as soon as it begins to grow.

environmental science
CONNECTION

Animals need plants to live, and some plants need animals, too. These plants produce seeds with tough seed coats that can't begin to grow into new plants until they have been eaten by an animal. When the seed is exposed to the acids and enzymes of the animal's digestive system, the seed coat wears down. After the seed passes out of the animal's digestive tract, it is able to absorb water, germinate, and grow.

APPLY

During the summer, Patrick and his sister love to sit out on the porch munching away on juicy watermelon. One year they held a contest to see who could spit the seeds the farthest. The next spring, Patrick noticed some new plants growing in their yard. When he examined them closely, he realized little watermelons were growing on the plants. Patrick and his sister had no idea that they were starting a watermelon garden. Think about the eating habits of animals in the wild such as squirrels and birds. How might they start a garden?

Gymnosperms: Seed Plants Without Flowers

The gymnosperms include several plants that are record-holders in the plant kingdom. The oldest living trees are bristlecone pines, gymnosperms that live in parts of California, Nevada, and Utah. One living bristlecone pine tree was found to be 4,900 years old! There are four groups of gymnosperms: conifers, ginkgoes, cycads, and gnetophytes (NEE toh FIETS). The seeds of gymnosperms are not enclosed in a fruit. The word *gymnosperm* is Greek for "naked seed." Examples of the four groups are shown in **Figure 15.**

Figure 15 *Gymnosperms are seed plants that do not produce flowers or fruits.*

The **conifers,** with about 550 species, make up the largest group of gymnosperms. Most conifers are evergreen and keep their needle-shaped leaves all year. Conifer seeds develop in cones. Pines, spruces, firs, and hemlocks are examples of conifers.

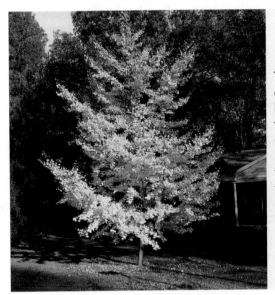

The **ginkgoes** contain only one living species, the ginkgo tree. Ginkgo seeds are produced in fleshy structures that are attached directly to branches.

The **cycads** were more common millions of years ago. Today there are only about 140 species. These plants grow in the tropics. Like seeds of conifers, seeds of cycads develop in cones.

The **gnetophytes** consist of about 70 species of very unusual plants. This gnetophyte is a shrub that grows in dry areas. Its seeds are formed in cones.

Gymnosperm Life Cycle The gymnosperms that are most familiar to you are probably the conifers. The name *conifer* comes from Greek and Latin words that mean "carry cones." Conifers have two kinds of cones—male and female. These are shown in **Figure 16.** Male spores are produced in the male cones, and female spores are produced in the female cones. The spores develop into gametophytes. The male gametophytes are pollen, dustlike particles that produce sperm cells. The female gametophyte, inside the scale of the female cone, produces eggs. Wind carries pollen from the male cones to the female cones on the same plants or on different plants. The transfer of pollen is called **pollination.**

After the egg is fertilized, it develops into a seed within the female cone. When the seed is mature, it is released by the cone and falls to the ground. The seed then germinates and grows into a new tree. The life cycle of a pine tree is shown in **Figure 17.**

The Importance of Gymnosperms The most economically important group of gymnosperms are the conifers. People harvest conifers and use the wood for building materials and paper products. Pine trees produce a sticky fluid called resin, which is used to make soap, turpentine, paint, and ink.

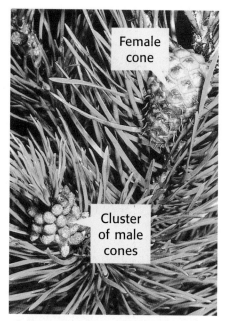

Figure 16 *A pine tree has male cones and female cones.*

Figure 17 Pine Life Cycle

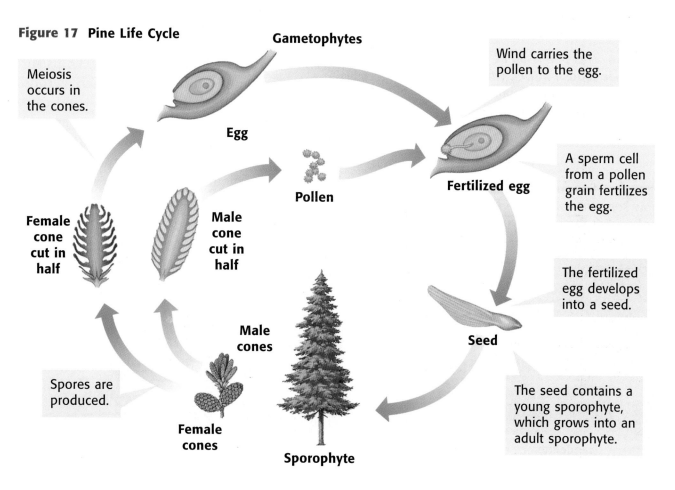

Meiosis occurs in the cones.

Gametophytes

Egg

Wind carries the pollen to the egg.

Pollen

Fertilized egg

A sperm cell from a pollen grain fertilizes the egg.

Female cone cut in half

Male cone cut in half

The fertilized egg develops into a seed.

Seed

Spores are produced.

Male cones

Female cones

Sporophyte

The seed contains a young sporophyte, which grows into an adult sporophyte.

Angiosperms: Seed Plants with Flowers

Flowering plants, or angiosperms, are the most successful plants today. Angiosperms can be found in almost every environment on land. There are at least 235,000 species of flowering plants, many more than all other plant species combined. Angiosperms come in a wide variety of sizes and shapes, from dandelions and water lilies to prickly-pear cactuses and oak trees.

All angiosperms are vascular plants that produce flowers and fruits. Tulips and roses are examples of flowering plants with large flowers. Other flowering plants, such as grasses and maple trees, have small flowers. After fertilization, angiosperms produce seeds within fruits. Peaches, lemons, and grapes are fruits, as are tomatoes, cucumbers, and many other foods we think of as vegetables.

What Are Flowers and Fruits For? Flowers and fruits are adaptations that help angiosperms reproduce. Some angiosperms depend on the wind for pollination, but other angiosperms have flowers that attract animals. As shown in **Figure 18,** when animals visit different flowers, they may carry pollen from flower to flower. Plants with flowers that are pollinated by animals don't need to make as much pollen as plants that are pollinated by wind. Why do you suppose this is?

Apples, tomatoes, and pumpkins may be ingredients in some of your favorite foods. However, fruits do more than just taste great—they also help to ensure that seeds survive as they are transported to areas where new plants can grow. Fruits surround and protect seeds. Some fruits and seeds, such as those shown in **Figure 19,** have structures that help the wind carry them short or long distances. Other fruits may attract animals that eat the fruits and discard the seeds some distance from the parent plant. Prickly burrs are fruits that are carried from place to place by sticking to the fur of animals or to the clothes and shoes of people.

Genetically altered fruit? Find out more on page 276.

Figure 18 *This bee is on its way to another squash flower, where it will leave some of the pollen it is carrying.*

Figure 19 *Special structures allow some fruits and seeds to float or drift through the air.*

Dandelion

Maple

Milkweed

Monocots and Dicots Angiosperms are divided into two classes—monocots and dicots. The two classes differ in the number of cotyledons in their seeds. A **cotyledon** (КАНТ uh LEED uhn) is a seed leaf found inside a seed. Monocot seeds have one cotyledon, and dicot seeds have two cotyledons. Other differences between monocots and dicots are summarized in **Figure 20.** Monocots include grasses, orchids, onions, lilies, and palms. Dicots include roses, cactuses, sunflowers, peanuts, and peas.

The Importance of Angiosperms

Flowering plants provide animals that live on land with the food they need to survive. A deer nibbling on meadow grass is using flowering plants directly as food. An owl that consumes a field mouse is using flowering plants indirectly as food because the field mouse ate seeds and berries.

Humans depend on flowering plants and use them in many ways. All of our major food crops, such as corn, wheat, and rice, are flowering plants. Some flowering plants, such as oak trees, are used to make furniture and toys. Others, such as cotton and flax, supply fibers for clothing and rope. Flowering plants are used to make many medicines as well as cork, rubber, and perfume oils.

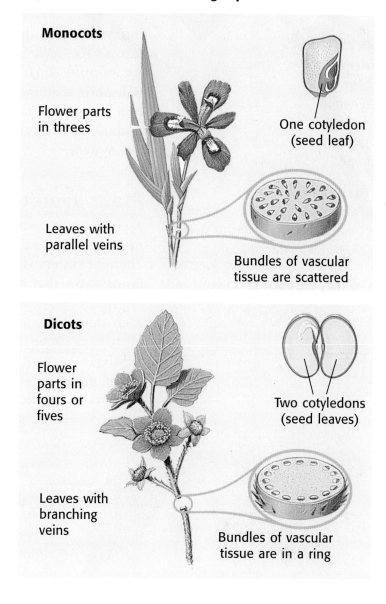

Figure 20 Two Classes of Angiosperms

Monocots

Flower parts in threes

Leaves with parallel veins

One cotyledon (seed leaf)

Bundles of vascular tissue are scattered

Dicots

Flower parts in fours or fives

Leaves with branching veins

Two cotyledons (seed leaves)

Bundles of vascular tissue are in a ring

REVIEW

1. What are two differences between a seed and a spore?

2. Briefly describe the four groups of gymnosperms. Which group is the largest and most economically important?

3. How do monocots and dicots differ from each other?

4. **Identifying Relationships** In what ways are flowers and fruits adaptations that help angiosperms reproduce?

The Structures of Seed Plants

Did you know that you have something in common with plants? You have different body systems that carry out a variety of functions. For example, your cardiovascular system transports materials throughout your body, and your skeletal system provides support and protection. Similarly, plants have systems too—a root system, a shoot system, and a reproductive system.

NEW TERMS

xylem	sepals
phloem	petals
epidermis	stamen
taproot	pistil
fibrous root	stigma
stomata	ovary

OBJECTIVES

■ Describe the functions of roots.
■ Describe the functions of stems.
■ Explain how the structure of leaves is related to their function.
■ Identify the parts of a flower and their functions.

Plant Systems

A plant's root system and shoot system supply the plant with needed resources that are found underground and aboveground. The root system is made up of roots. The shoot system is made up of stems that bear leaves, cones, flowers, or fruits.

The root system and the shoot system are dependent on each other. The vascular tissues of the two systems are connected, as shown in **Figure 21.** There are two kinds of vascular tissue—xylem (ZIE luhm) and phloem (FLOH em). **Xylem** transports water and minerals through the plant. **Phloem** transports sugar molecules. Xylem and phloem are found in all parts of vascular plants.

The Root of the Matter

Because most roots are underground, many people do not realize how extensive a plant's root system can be. For example, a 2.5 m tall corn plant can have roots that grow 2.5 m deep and 1.2 m out away from the stem!

Root Functions The main functions of roots are as follows:

- **Roots supply plants with water and dissolved minerals that have been absorbed from the soil.** These materials are transported throughout the plant in the xylem.

- **Roots support and anchor plants.** Roots hold plants securely in the soil.

- **Roots often store surplus food made during photosynthesis.** This food is produced in the leaves and transported as sugar in the phloem to the roots. There the surplus food is usually stored as sugar or starch.

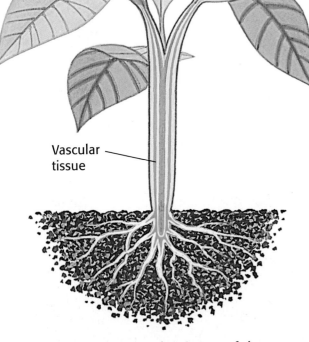

Vascular tissue

Figure 21 *The vascular tissues of the roots and shoots are connected.*

Root Structure The structures of a root are shown in **Figure 22.** Like the cells in the outermost layer of your skin, the layer of cells that covers the surface of roots is called the **epidermis.** Some cells of the root epidermis extend out from the root. These cells, which are called *root hairs,* increase the amount of surface area through which roots can absorb water and minerals.

After water and minerals are absorbed by the epidermis, they diffuse into the center of the root, where the vascular tissue is located. Roots grow longer at their tips. A group of cells called the *root cap* protects the tip of a root and produces a slimy substance that makes it easier for the root to grow through soil.

Root Types There are two types of roots—taproots and fibrous roots. Examples of each are shown in **Figure 23.**

A **taproot** consists of one main root that grows downward, with many smaller branch roots coming out of it. Taproots can usually obtain water located deep underground. Dicots and gymnosperms have taproots.

A **fibrous root** has several roots of the same size that spread out from the base of the stem. Fibrous roots typically obtain water that is close to the soil surface. Monocots have fibrous roots.

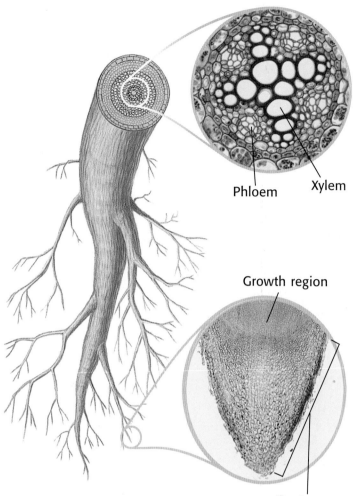

Phloem   Xylem

Growth region

Root cap

Figure 22 *The structures of a root are labeled above.*

Taproot

Taproots

Fibrous roots

Figure 23 *The onion has a fibrous root. The dandelion has a taproot. Carrots have an enlarged taproot that stores food.*

What's the Holdup?

As shown in **Figure 24,** stems vary greatly in shape and size. Stems are usually located aboveground, although many plants have underground stems.

Stem Functions A stem connects a plant's roots to its leaves and flowers and performs these main functions:

• **Stems support the plant body.** Leaves are arranged on stems so that each leaf can absorb the sunlight it needs for photosynthesis. Stems hold up flowers and display them to pollinators.

• **Stems transport materials between the root system and the shoot system.** Xylem carries water and dissolved minerals upward from the roots to the leaves and other shoot parts. Phloem carries the glucose produced during photosynthesis to roots and other parts of the plant.

• **Some stems store materials.** For example, the stems of the plants in **Figure 25** are adapted for water storage.

Figure 24 The stalks of daisies and the trunks of trees are stems.

Daisy

Valley oak

BRAIN FOOD

Root or shoot? Even though potatoes grow in the ground, they're not roots. The white potato is an underground stem adapted to store starch.

Baobab tree

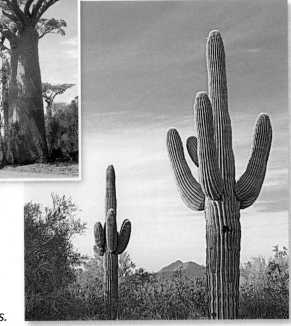

Saguaro cactus

Figure 25 Baobab trees store large quantities of water and starch in their massive trunks. Cactuses store water in their thick, green stems.

Stem Structures

Look at the two groups of plants on this page. What is the difference between the stems of the plants in each group?

Herbaceous Stems The plants in Group A have stems that are soft, thin, and flexible. These stems are called *herbaceous* stems. Examples of plants with herbaceous stems include wildflowers, such as clovers and poppies, and many vegetable crops, such as beans, tomatoes, and corn. Some plants with herbaceous stems live only 1 or 2 years. A cross section of one kind of herbaceous stem is shown at right.

Woody Stems The trees and shrubs in Group B have rigid stems made of wood and bark. Their stems are called *woody* stems. If a tree or a shrub lives in an area with cold winters, the plant has a growing period and a dormant period.

At the beginning of each growing period in the spring, large xylem cells are produced. As fall approaches, the plants produce smaller xylem cells, which appear darker than the larger xylem cells. In the fall the plants stop producing new cells. When the growing season begins again in the spring, large xylem cells are made. Then another ring of dark cells is made. A ring of dark cells surrounding a ring of light cells make up a growth ring.

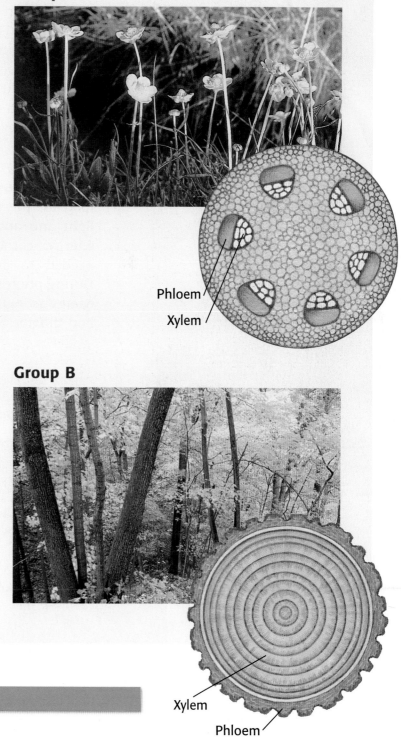

Group A

Phloem

Xylem

Group B

Xylem

Phloem

REVIEW

1. What are three functions of roots?

2. What are three functions of stems?

3. **Applying Concepts** Suppose the cross section of a tree reveals 12 light-colored rings and 12 dark-colored rings. How many years of growth are represented?

Mimosa

A Plant's Food Factories

Leaves vary greatly in shape and size. They may be round, narrow, heart-shaped, or fan-shaped. The raffia palm, shown in **Figure 26,** has leaves that may be 6 times longer than you are tall. A leaf of the duckweed, a tiny aquatic plant shown in Figure 26, is so small that several can fit on your fingernail.

Sweet gum

Leaf Function The main function of leaves is to make food for the plant. Leaves capture the energy in sunlight and absorb carbon dioxide from the air. Light energy, carbon dioxide, and water are needed to carry out photosynthesis. During photosynthesis, plants use light energy to make food (sugar) from carbon dioxide and water.

Eucalyptus

Figure 26 *Even though the leaves of these plants are very different, they serve the same purpose.*

Raffia palm

Duckweed

Turn to page 596 to find out whether there's more to leaves than meets the eye.

✔ Self-Check

How is the function of stems related to the function of leaves? *(See page 636 to check your answers.)*

Leaf Structure The structure of leaves is related to their main function—photosynthesis. **Figure 27** shows a cutaway view of a small block of leaf tissue. The top and bottom surfaces of the leaf are covered with a single layer of cells called the epidermis. Light can easily pass through the thin epidermis to the leaf's interior. Notice the tiny pores in the epidermis. These pores, called **stomata** (singular, *stoma*), allow carbon dioxide to enter the leaf. *Guard cells* open and close the stomata.

The middle of a leaf, which is where photosynthesis takes place, has two layers. The upper layer is the *palisade layer*, and the lower layer is the *spongy layer*. Cells in the palisade layer are elongated. These cells contain many chloroplasts, the green organelles that carry out photosynthesis. Cells in the spongy layer are spread farther apart than cells in the palisade layer. The air spaces between these cells allow carbon dioxide to diffuse more freely throughout the leaf.

The veins of a leaf contain xylem and phloem surrounded by supporting tissue. Xylem transports water and minerals to the leaf. Phloem conducts the sugar made during photosynthesis from the leaf to the rest of the plant.

Leaf Adaptations Some leaves have functions other than photosynthesis. For example, the leaves on a cactus plant are modified as spines. These hard, pointed leaves discourage animals from eating the succulent cactus stem. **Figure 28** shows leaves with a most unusual function. The leaves of a sundew are modified to catch insects. Sundews grow in soil that does not contain enough of the mineral nitrogen to meet the plants' needs. By catching and digesting insects, a sundew is able to meet its nitrogen requirement.

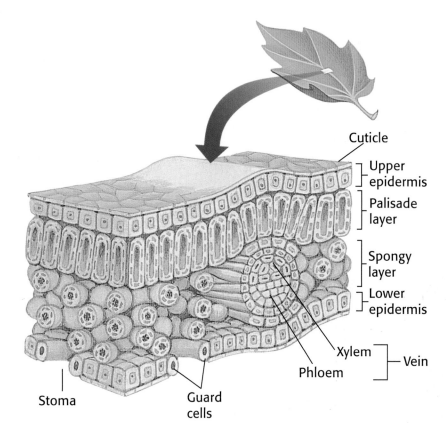

Figure 27 *Leaves have several layers of cells.*

Figure 28 *This damselfly is trapped in the sticky fluid of a sundew flower.*

Flowers

Most people admire the beauty of flowers, such as roses or lilies, without stopping to think about *why* plants have flowers. As you read earlier, flowers are adaptations for sexual reproduction. Flowers come in many different shapes, colors, and fragrances that attract pollinators or catch the wind. Flowers usually contain the following parts: sepals, petals, stamens, and one or more pistils. The flower parts are usually arranged in rings around the central pistil. **Figure 29** shows the parts of a typical flower.

Orchid

Petal

Stamen { Anther
Filament

Sepal

Stigma] Pistil
Style
Ovary

Ovule

Figure 29 *The stamens, which produce pollen, and the pistil, which produces eggs, are surrounded by the petals and the sepals.*

See how to build a flower of your very own on page 599.

Sepals make up the bottom ring of flower parts. They are often green like leaves. The main function of sepals is to cover and protect the immature flower when it is a bud. As the blossom opens, the sepals fold back so that the petals can enlarge and become visible.

Petals are broad, flat, and thin, like sepals, but they vary in shape and color. Petals may attract insects or other animals to the flower. These animals help plants reproduce by transferring pollen from flower to flower.

SECTION 3

Vocabulary

pollen *(p. 258)*
pollination *(p. 261)*
cotyledon *(p. 263)*

Section Notes

- Seed plants are vascular plants that produce seeds. The sperm cells of seed plants develop inside pollen.

- Gymnosperms are seed plants that produce their seeds in cones or in fleshy structures attached to branches. The four groups of gymnosperms are conifers, ginkgoes, cycads, and gnetophytes.

- Angiosperms are seed plants that produce their seeds in flowers. The two groups of flowering plants are monocots and dicots.

Labs

Travelin' Seeds *(p. 598)*

SECTION 4

Vocabulary

xylem *(p. 264)*
phloem *(p. 264)*
epidermis *(p. 265)*
taproot *(p. 265)*
fibrous root *(p. 265)*
stomata *(p. 269)*
sepals *(p. 270)*
petals *(p. 270)*
stamen *(p. 271)*
pistil *(p. 271)*
stigma *(p. 271)*
ovary *(p. 271)*

Section Notes

- Roots generally grow underground. Roots anchor the plant, absorb water and minerals, and store food.

- Stems connect roots and leaves. Stems support leaves and other structures; transport water, minerals, and food; and store water and food.

- The main function of leaves is photosynthesis. Leaf structure is related to this function.

- Flowers usually have four parts—sepals, petals, stamens, and one or more pistils. Stamens produce sperm cells in pollen. The ovary in the pistil contains ovules. Each ovule contains an egg. Ovules become seeds after fertilization.

Labs

Leaf Me Alone! *(p. 596)*
Build a Flower *(p. 599)*

---

 internetconnect

 GO TO: go.hrw.com

Visit the **HRW** Web site for a variety of learning tools related to this chapter. Just type in the keyword:

KEYWORD: HSTPL1

SciLINKS
NSTA **GO TO:** www.scilinks.org

Visit the **National Science Teachers Association** on-line Web site for Internet resources related to this chapter. Just type in the *sci*LINKS number for more information about the topic:

TOPIC: Plant Characteristics	*sci*LINKS NUMBER: HSTL280
TOPIC: How Are Plants Classified?	*sci*LINKS NUMBER: HSTL285
TOPIC: Seedless Plants	*sci*LINKS NUMBER: HSTL290
TOPIC: Plants with Seeds	*sci*LINKS NUMBER: HSTL295
TOPIC: The Structure of Seed Plants	*sci*LINKS NUMBER: HSTL300

Chapter Review

USING VOCABULARY

To complete the following sentences, choose the correct term from each pair of terms listed below:

1. The ___?___ is a waxy layer that coats the surface of stems and leaves. *(stomata* or *cuticle)*

2. During the plant life cycle, eggs and sperm cells are produced by the ___?___. *(sporophyte* or *gametophyte)*

3. In vascular plants, ___?___ conducts water and minerals, and ___?___ conducts food molecules, such as sugar. *(xylem/phloem* or *phloem/xylem)*

4. Seedless vascular plants include ferns, horsetails, and ___?___. *(club mosses* or *liverworts)*

5. A ___?___ is a seed leaf found inside a seed. *(cotyledon* or *sepal)*

6. In a flower, the ___?___ are the male reproductive structures. *(pistils* or *stamens)*

UNDERSTANDING CONCEPTS

Multiple Choice

7. Which of the following plants is nonvascular?
   a. fern
   b. moss
   c. conifer
   d. monocot

8. Coal formed millions of years ago from the remains of
   a. nonvascular plants.
   b. flowering plants.
   c. green algae.
   d. seedless vascular plants.

9. The largest group of gymnosperms is the
   a. conifers.
   b. ginkgoes.
   c. cycads.
   d. gnetophytes.

10. Roots
    a. absorb water and minerals.
    b. store surplus food.
    c. anchor the plant.
    d. All of the above

11. Woody stems
    a. are soft, green, and flexible.
    b. include the stems of daisies.
    c. contain wood and bark.
    d. All of the above

12. The veins of a leaf contain
    a. xylem and phloem.
    b. stomata.
    c. epidermis and cuticle.
    d. xylem only.

13. In a flower, petals function to
    a. produce ovules.
    b. attract pollinators.
    c. protect the flower bud.
    d. produce pollen.

14. Monocots have
    a. flower parts in fours or fives.
    b. two cotyledons in the seed.
    c. parallel veins in leaves.
    d. All of the above

Short Answer

15. Why are there no large moss plants?

16. What advantages does a seed have over a spore?

17. How is water important to the reproduction of mosses and ferns?

Concept Map

18. Use the following terms to create a concept map: nonvascular plants, vascular plants, xylem, phloem, ferns, seeds in cones, plants, gymnosperms, spores, angiosperms, seeds in flowers.

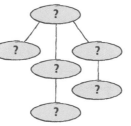

CRITICAL THINKING AND PROBLEM SOLVING

Write one or two sentences to answer the following questions:

19. Plants that are pollinated by wind produce much more pollen than plants that are pollinated by animals. Why do you suppose this is so?

20. If plants did not possess a cuticle, where would they have to live? Why?

21. Grasses do not have strong aromas or bright colors. How might this be related to the way these plants are pollinated?

22. Imagine that a seed and a spore are beginning to grow in a deep, dark crack in a rock. Which reproductive structure—the seed or the spore—is more likely to survive and develop into an adult plant after it begins to grow? Explain your answer.

MATH IN SCIENCE

23. One year a maple tree produced 1,056 seeds. If only 15 percent of those seeds germinated and grew into seedlings, how many seedlings would there be?

INTERPRETING GRAPHICS

24. Examine the cross section of the flower to answer the following questions:
    a. Which letter corresponds to the structure in which pollen is produced? What is the name of this structure?
    b. Which letter corresponds to the structure that contains ovules? What is the name of this structure?

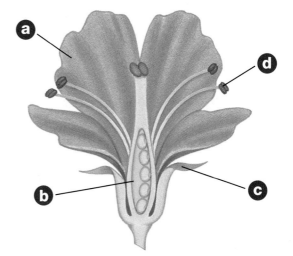

25. In a woody stem, a ring of dark cells and a ring of light cells represent one year of growth. Examine the cross section of a tree trunk below, and determine the age of the tree.

NOW What Do You Think?

Take a minute to review your answers to the ScienceLog questions on page 249. Have your answers changed? If necessary, revise your answers based on what you have learned since you began this chapter.

Science, Technology, and Society

Supersquash or Frankenfruit?

The fruits and vegetables you buy at the supermarket may not be exactly what they seem. Scientists may have genetically altered these foods to make them look and taste better, contain more nutrients, and have a longer shelf life.

From Bullets to Bacteria

Through genetic engineering, scientists are now able to duplicate one organism's DNA and place a certain gene from the DNA into the cells of another species of plant or animal. This technology enables scientists to give plants and animals a new trait. The new trait is then passed along to the organism's offspring and future generations.

Scientists alter plants by inserting a gene with a certain property into a plant's cells. The DNA is usually inserted by one of two methods. In one method, new DNA is first placed inside a special bacterium, and the bacterium carries the DNA into the plant cell. In another method, microscopic particles of metal coated with the new DNA are fired into the plant cells with a special "gene gun."

High-Tech Food

During the past decade, scientists have inserted genes into more than 50 different kinds of plants. In most cases, the new trait from the inserted gene makes the plants more disease resistant or more marketable in some way. For example, scientists have added genes from a caterpillar-attacking bacterium to cotton, tomato, and potato plants. The altered plants produce proteins that kill the crop-eating caterpillars. Scientists are also trying to develop genetically altered peas and red peppers that stay sweeter longer. A genetically altered tomato that lasts longer and tastes better is already in many supermarkets. One day it may even be possible to create a caffeine-free coffee bean.

Are We Ready?

As promising as these genetically engineered foods seem to be, they are not without controversy. Some scientists are afraid that genes introduced to crop plants could be released into the environment or that foods may be changed in ways that endanger human health. For example, could people who are allergic to peanuts become sick from eating a tomato plant that contains certain peanut genes? All of these concerns will have to be addressed before the genetically altered food products are widely accepted.

Find Out for Yourself

▶ Are genetically altered foods controversial in your area? Survey a few people to get their opinions about genetically altered foods. Do they think grocery stores should carry these foods? Why or why not?

◀ *A scientist uses a "gene gun" to insert DNA into plant cells.*

CAREERS

ETHNOBOTANIST

Paul Cox is an *ethnobotanist.* He travels to remote places to look for plants that can help cure diseases. He seeks the advice of shamans and other native healers in his search. In 1984, Cox made a trip to Samoa to observe healers. While there he met a 78-year-old Samoan healer named Epenesa. She was able to identify more than 200 medicinal plants, and she astounded Cox with her knowledge. Epenesa had an accurate understanding of human anatomy, and she dispensed prescriptions with great care and accuracy.

In Samoan culture, the healer is one of the most valued members of the community. After all, the healer has the knowledge to treat diseases. In some cases, Samoan healers know about ancient treatments that Western medicine has yet to discover. Recently, some researchers have turned to Samoan healers to ask them about their medical secrets.

Blending Polynesian and Western Medicine

After Cox spent months observing Epenesa as she treated patients, Epenesa gave him her prescription for yellow fever—a tea made from the wood of a rain-forest tree. Cox brought the yellow-fever remedy to the United States, and in 1986 researchers at the National Cancer Institute (NCI) began studying the plant. They found that the plant contains a virus-fighting chemical called *prostratin.* Further research by NCI indicates that prostratin may also have potential as a treatment for AIDS.

Another compound from Samoan healers treats inflammation. The healers apply the bark of a local tree to the inflamed skin. When a team of scientists evaluated the bark, they found that the healers were absolutely correct. The active compound in the bark, *flavanone,* is now being researched for its medicinal properties. Some day Western doctors may prescribe medicine containing flavanone.

Preserving Their Knowledge

When two of the healers Cox observed in Samoa died in 1993, generations of medical knowledge died with them. The healers' deaths point out the urgency of recording the ancient wisdom before all of the healers are gone. Cox and other ethnobotanists must work hard to gather information from healers as quickly as they can.

The Feel of Natural Healing

▶ The next time you have a mosquito bite or a mild sunburn, consider a treatment that comes from the experience of Native American healers. Aloe vera, another plant product, is found in a variety of lotions and ointments. Find out how well it works for you!

▶ *These plant parts from Samoa may one day be used in medicines to treat a variety of diseases.*

12 Plant Processes

Strange but True!

It's war every day in the cornfield. When beet armyworm caterpillars attack the corn, the corn fights back. The corn somehow manages to send out SOS signals. Soon, an air force of wasps swoops in, attacks the caterpillars, and saves the day!

How can a plant send out a distress signal? Beet armyworm caterpillars are a nasty pest in many cornfields in the United States. When a corn plant is being munched on by a caterpillar, chemicals in the mouth of the caterpillar cause the corn plant to release a second chemical into the air. Female parasitic wasps sense the corn's response and make a beeline for the infested plant.

Like an airborne cavalry, the wasps dive for the caterpillars and lay eggs under their skin. The eggs hatch in a short time, and the wasp larvae devour the insides of the caterpillars.

Jim Tumlinson, the scientist who discovered this partnership between corn and wasps, says it probably occurred by chance. Many plants release special chemicals when attacked by pests. The parasitic wasps have a natural attraction for the chemical released by corn plants.

Tumlinson hopes to breed other plants so that they release insect-attracting chemicals. Attracting plant-friendly wasps could decrease the need for poisonous pesticides.

Making and releasing special chemicals are processes that occur in many plants. In this chapter you will learn about other plant processes, such as reproduction in flowering plants, photosynthesis, responses to the environment, and plant growth.

Investigate!

Observing Plant Growth

When planting a garden, you bury seeds in the ground, water them, and then wait for tiny sprouts to poke through the soil. What happens to the seeds while they're underneath the soil? How do seeds grow into plants?

Procedure

1. Your instructor will supply you with the materials you need: a **clear 2 L soda bottle** with its top half cut off, **potting soil,** three or four **bean seeds,** and **aluminum foil.**

2. Fill the soda bottle to within 8 cm of the top with potting soil.

3. Press the seeds into the soil and against the wall of the soda bottle, as shown above. The top of the seeds should be level with the surface of the potting soil. Add an additional 5 cm of potting soil.

4. Cover the sides of the soda bottle with the aluminum foil to keep out light.

5. Water the seeds with about **60 mL of water.** Add more water whenever the top 1 cm of the soil is completely dry.

6. Once every day, remove the aluminum foil from the soda bottle for a few minutes and check on your seeds. Keep a record in your ScienceLog of how the seeds grow.

Analysis

7. How long did it take for the seeds to start growing? How many seeds grew?

8. Where does the energy come from that the seeds use to start their growth?

The Reproduction of Flowering Plants

NEW TERMS
dormant

OBJECTIVES
- Describe the roles of pollination and fertilization in sexual reproduction.
- Describe how fruits are formed from flowers.
- Explain the difference between sexual and asexual reproduction in plants.

If you went outside right now and made a list of all the different kinds of plants you could see, most of the plants on your list would probably be flowering plants. Flowering plants are the largest and the most diverse group of plants in the world. Their success is partly due to their flowers, which are adaptations for sexual reproduction. During sexual reproduction, an egg is fertilized by a sperm cell. In flowering plants, fertilization takes place within the flower and leads to the formation of one or more seeds within a fruit.

How Does Fertilization Occur?

In order for fertilization to occur, sperm cells must be able to reach eggs. The sperm cells of a flowering plant are contained in pollen grains. Pollination occurs when pollen grains are transported from anthers to stigmas. This action starts fertilization, as shown in **Figure 1.** After the pollen lands on the stigma, a tube grows from the pollen grain through the style to the ovary. Inside the ovary are ovules. Each ovule contains an egg.

Figure 1 *Fertilization occurs after pollination.*

Sperm cells within the pollen grain move down the pollen tube and into an ovule. Fertilization occurs as one of the sperm cells fuses with the egg inside the ovule.

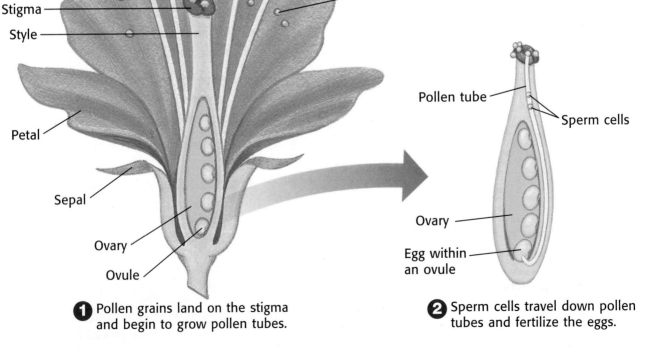

Anther

Stigma

Style

Petal

Sepal

Ovary

Ovule

Pollen

Pollen tube

Sperm cells

Ovary

Egg within an ovule

❶ Pollen grains land on the stigma and begin to grow pollen tubes.

❷ Sperm cells travel down pollen tubes and fertilize the eggs.

From Flower to Fruit

After fertilization takes place, the ovule develops into a seed that contains a tiny, undeveloped plant. The ovary surrounding the ovule develops into a fruit. **Figure 2** shows how the ovary and ovules of a flower develop into a fruit and seeds.

Figure 2 *Fertilization leads to the development of fruit and seeds.*

Each ovule within the flower's ovary contains a fertilized egg.

A mature plant produces the flower. Pollination and fertilization take place.

The ovary becomes the fruit. When the fruit ripens, the seeds are dispersed.

Petals and stamens fall away.

Each ovule becomes a seed containing a tiny plant. If a seed sprouts, or begins to grow, it will become a new plant.

Will mutant mustard take over the world? Turn to page 298 to find out.

✓ Self-Check

How many fruits and seeds could develop from a flower with one ovary containing six ovules? *(See page 636 to check your answer.)*

Familiar Fruits

At the same time that ovules are developing into the seeds, the ovary is developing into the fruit. As the fruit swells and ripens, it holds and protects the developing seeds. Look below to see which parts of the fruits shown developed from a flower's ovary and ovules.

From ovules

From ovary

Tomato

From ovary

From ovules

Orange

From ovary

From ovule

Avocado

Quick Lab

Thirsty Seeds

1. Obtain **12 dry bean seeds, 2 Petri dishes,** a **wax pencil,** and **water** from your teacher.

2. Fill one Petri dish two-thirds full of water and add six seeds. Label the dish with your name and "Water."

3. Add the remaining seeds to the dry Petri dish. Label this dish with your name and "Control."

4. Allow the seeds that are in water to soak overnight.

5. The next day, compare the size of the two sets of seeds. Write your observations in your ScienceLog.

6. What caused the size of the seeds to change? Why might this be important to the seed's survival?

Seeds Become New Plants

Once a seed is fully developed, the young plant inside the seed stops growing. The seed may become dormant. When seeds are **dormant,** they are inactive. Dormant seeds can often survive long periods of drought or freezing temperatures. Some seeds need extreme conditions such as cold winters or even forest fires to break their dormancy.

When a seed is dropped or planted in an environment that has water, oxygen, and a suitable temperature, the seed sprouts. Each plant species has an ideal temperature at which most of its seeds will begin to grow. For most plants, the ideal temperature for growth is about 27°C (80.6°F). **Figure 3** shows the *germination,* or sprouting, of a bean seed and the early stages of growth in a young bean plant.

Figure 3 *Sexual reproduction produces seeds that grow into new plants.*

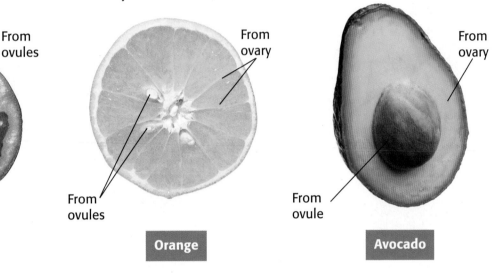

Other Methods of Reproduction

Many flowering plants can also reproduce asexually. Asexual reproduction in plants does not involve the formation of flowers, seeds, and fruits. In asexual reproduction, a part of a plant, such as a stem or root, produces a new plant. Several examples of asexual reproduction are shown below in **Figure 4**.

Figure 4 *Asexual reproduction can occur in several different ways. Some examples are shown here.*

a Potato tubers are underground stems that are swollen with stored food. The "eyes" of potatoes are buds that can grow asexually into new plants.

b The strawberry plant produces runners, which are stems that run horizontally along the ground. Buds along each runner grow into new plants that root in the ground.

c This kalanchoe plant produces plantlets, tiny plants along the margins of its leaves. The young plantlets eventually fall off the mother plant and root in the soil as separate plants.

REVIEW

1. How does pollination differ from fertilization?

2. Which part of a flower develops into a fruit?

3. **Relating Concepts** What do flowers and runners have in common? How are they different?

4. **Identifying Relationships** When might asexual reproduction be important for the survival of some flowering plants?

The Ins and Outs of Making Food

Plants do not have lungs, but they need air just like you. Air is a mixture of oxygen, carbon dioxide, and other gases. Plants must have carbon dioxide to carry out photosynthesis, which is the way they make their own food.

What Happens During Photosynthesis?

Plants need sunlight to produce food. During photosynthesis, the energy in sunlight is used to make food in the form of sugar ($C_6H_{12}O_6$) from carbon dioxide (CO_2) and water (H_2O). How does this happen?

Capturing Light Energy Plant cells have organelles called chloroplasts. Chloroplasts contain **chlorophyll,** a green pigment. Chlorophyll absorbs light energy. You may not know it, but sunlight is actually a mixture of all the colors of the rainbow. **Figure 5** shows how light from the sun can be separated into different colors when passed through a triangular piece of glass called a prism. Chlorophyll absorbs most of the colors in light, but not green. Plants look green because chlorophyll reflects green light.

White light

Prism

Figure 5 *Plants look green to us because green is reflected by the leaves. The other colors of light are absorbed by the chlorophyll in plant cells.*

Making Sugar The light energy absorbed by chlorophyll is used to split water (H_2O) into hydrogen (H) and oxygen (O). The hydrogen is then combined with carbon dioxide (CO_2) from the air surrounding the plant to make sugar ($C_6H_{12}O_6$). Oxygen is given off as a byproduct. The process of photosynthesis is summarized in the following chemical equation:

$$6CO_2 + 6H_2O \xrightarrow{\text{light energy}} C_6H_{12}O_6 + 6O_2$$

The equation shows that it takes six molecules of carbon dioxide and six molecules of water to produce one molecule of glucose and six molecules of oxygen. The process is illustrated in **Figure 6.**

The energy stored in food molecules is used by plant cells to carry out their life processes. Within each living cell, sugar and other food molecules are broken down in a process called cellular respiration. **Cellular respiration** converts the energy stored in food into a form of energy that cells can use. During this process, the plant uses oxygen and releases carbon dioxide and water.

LabBook

What do plants produce that is necessary for life as we know it? Find out on page 600 of your LabBook.

Figure 6 *During photosynthesis, plants take in carbon dioxide and water and absorb light energy. They make sugar and release oxygen.*

Light energy

Carbon dioxide

Oxygen

Sugar is made in the leaves.

Water

✓ **Self-Check**

What is the original source of the energy stored in the sugar produced by plant cells? *(See page 636 to check your answers.)*

Gas Exchange

All aboveground plant surfaces are covered by a cuticle. The cuticle is a waxy layer that doesn't allow gases or water to pass through. How does a plant obtain carbon dioxide through this barrier? Carbon dioxide enters the plant's leaves through the **stomata** (singular *stoma*). A stoma is an opening in the leaf's epidermis and cuticle. Each stoma is surrounded by two *guard cells,* which act like double doors opening and closing the gap. You can see open and closed stomata in **Figure 7.** The function of stomata is shown in action in **Figure 8.**

When the stomata are open, carbon dioxide diffuses into the leaf. At the same time, the oxygen produced during photosynthesis diffuses out of the leaf cells. The oxygen then moves into the spaces between the cells and out of the leaf through the stomata.

When the stomata are open, water vapor also exits the leaf. The loss of water from leaves is called **transpiration.** Most of the water absorbed by a plant's roots is needed to replace water lost during transpiration. When a plant wilts, it is usually because more water is being lost through its leaves than is being absorbed by its roots.

Closed stoma

Open stoma

Figure 7 *When light is available and photosynthesis can occur, the stomata are usually open. When it's dark, photosynthesis can't occur. Carbon dioxide is not needed, and the stomata close to conserve water.*

Figure 8 *Plants take in carbon dioxide and release oxygen and water through the stomata in their leaves.*

Cuticle

Vein

Guard cells

Stoma

CO_2 enters through stoma

H_2O and O_2 leave through stoma

REVIEW

1. What three things do plants need to carry out photosynthesis?

2. Why must plant cells carry out cellular respiration?

3. **Identifying Relationships** How are the opening and closing of stomata related to transpiration? When does transpiration occur?

Plant Responses to the Environment

NEW TERMS

tropism
phototropism
gravitropism
evergreen
deciduous

OBJECTIVES

- Describe how plants may respond to light and gravity.
- Explain how some plants flower in response to night length.
- Describe how some plants are adapted to survive cold weather.

MATH BREAK

Bending by Degrees

Suppose a plant has a positive phototropism and bends toward the light at a rate of 0.3 degrees per minute. How many hours will it take the plant to bend 90 degrees?

What happens when you get really cold? Do your teeth chatter as you shiver uncontrollably? If so, your brain is responding to the stimulus of cold by causing your muscles to twitch rapidly and generate heat. Anything that causes a reaction in an organ or tissue is a stimulus. Do plant tissues respond to stimuli? They sure do! Examples of stimuli to which plants respond include light, gravity, changing seasons, and even being eaten.

Plant Tropisms

Some plants respond to an environmental stimulus, such as light or gravity, by growing in a particular direction. Growth in response to a stimulus is called a **tropism.** Tropisms are either positive or negative, depending on whether the plant grows toward or away from the stimulus. Plant growth toward a stimulus is a positive tropism. Plant growth away from a stimulus is a negative tropism. Two examples of tropisms are phototropism and gravitropism.

Sensing Light If you place a houseplant so that it gets light from only one direction, such as from a window, the shoot tips bend toward the light. A change in the growth of a plant that is caused by light is called **phototropism.** As shown in **Figure 9,** the bending occurs when cells on one side of the shoot grow longer than cells on the other side of the shoot.

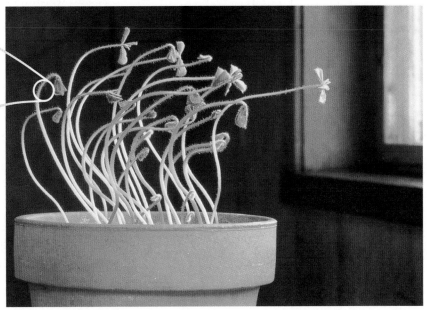

Figure 9 *The plant cells on the dark side of the shoot grow longer than the cells on the other side. This causes the shoot to bend toward the light.*

Which Way Is Up? When the growth of a plant changes direction in response to the direction of gravity, the change is called **gravitropism.** The effect of gravitropism is demonstrated by the plants in **Figure 10.** A few days after a plant is placed on its side or turned upside down, the roots and shoots show a change in their direction of growth. Most shoot tips have negative gravitropism—they grow upward, away from the center of the Earth. In contrast, most root tips have positive gravitropism—they grow downward, toward the center of the Earth.

Figure 10 *Gravity is a stimulus that causes plants to change their direction of growth.*

a To grow away from the pull of gravity, this plant has grown upward.

b This plant has recently been upside down. The newest growth is pointing downward.

Quick **Lab**

Which Way Is Up?

Will a potted plant grow sideways? You will need **several potted plants** to find out. Use **duct tape** to secure **cardboard** around the base of each plant so that the soil will not fall out. Turn the plants on their sides and observe what happens over the next few days. Record your observations in your ScienceLog. Describe two stimuli that might have influenced the direction of growth. How might gravitropism benefit a plant?

Self-Check

1. Use the following terms to create a concept map: tropism, stimuli, light, gravity, phototropism, and gravitropism.

2. Imagine a plant in which light causes a negative phototropism. Will the plant bend to the left or to the right when light is shining only on the plant's right side?

(See page 636 to check your answers.)

Seasonal Responses

What would happen if a plant living in an area that has severe winters flowered in December? Do you think the plant would be able to successfully produce seeds and fruits? If your answer is no, you're correct. If the plant produced any flowers at all, the flowers would probably freeze and die before they had the chance to produce mature seeds. Plants living in regions with cold winters can detect the change in seasons. How do plants do this?

As Different as Night and Day Think about what happens as the seasons change. For example, what happens to the length of the days and the nights? As autumn and winter approach, the days get shorter and the nights get longer. The opposite happens when spring and summer approach.

The difference between day length and night length is an important environmental stimulus for many plants. This stimulus can cause plants to begin reproducing. Some plants flower only in late summer or early autumn, when the night length is long. These plants are called short-day plants. Examples of short-day plants include poinsettias (shown below in **Figure 11**), ragweed, and chrysanthemums. Other plants flower in spring or early summer, when night length is short. These plants are called long-day plants. Clover, spinach, and lettuce are examples of long-day plants.

earth science CONNECTION

The seasons are caused by Earth's tilt and its orbit around the sun. We have summer when the Northern Hemisphere is tilted toward the sun and the sun's energy falls more directly on the Northern Hemisphere. While the Northern Hemisphere experiences the warm season, the Southern Hemisphere experiences the cold season. The opposite of this occurs when the Northern Hemisphere is tilted away from the sun.

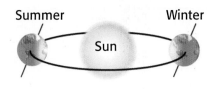

Figure 11 *Night length determines when poinsettias flower.*

Early summer

Night length

Day length

a In the early summer, night length is short. At this time, poinsettia leaves are all green, and there are no flowers.

Late fall

Night length

Day length

b Poinsettias flower in the fall, when nights are longer. The leaves surrounding the flower clusters turn red. Professional growers use artificial lighting to control the timing of the color change.

One fall afternoon, Holly looks into her backyard. She notices that a tree that was full of leaves the week before is now completely bare. What caused the tree to drop all its leaves? Holly came up with the following hypothesis:

> Each leaf on the tree was able to sense day length. When the day length became short enough, each leaf responded by falling.

Design an experiment that would test Holly's hypothesis.

Seasonal Changes in Leaves All trees lose their leaves at some time. Some trees, such as pine and magnolia, shed some of their leaves year-round so that some leaves are always present on the tree. These trees are called **evergreen.** Evergreen trees have leaves adapted to survive throughout the year.

Other trees, such as the maple tree in **Figure 12,** are **deciduous** and lose all their leaves at the same time each year. Deciduous trees usually lose their leaves before winter begins. In tropical climates that have wet and dry seasons, deciduous trees lose their leaves before the dry season. Having bare branches during the winter or during the dry season may reduce the water lost by transpiration. The loss of leaves helps plants survive low temperatures or long periods without rain.

Figure 12 *The leaves of some deciduous trees, like the maple shown here, change from green to orange in autumn. In winter, the maple is bare.*

As shown in **Figure 13,** leaves often change color before they fall. As autumn approaches, chlorophyll, the green pigment used in photosynthesis, breaks down. As chlorophyll is lost from leaves, other yellow and orange pigments are revealed. These pigments were always present in the leaves but were hidden by the green chlorophyll. Some leaves also have red pigments, which also become visible when chlorophyll is broken down.

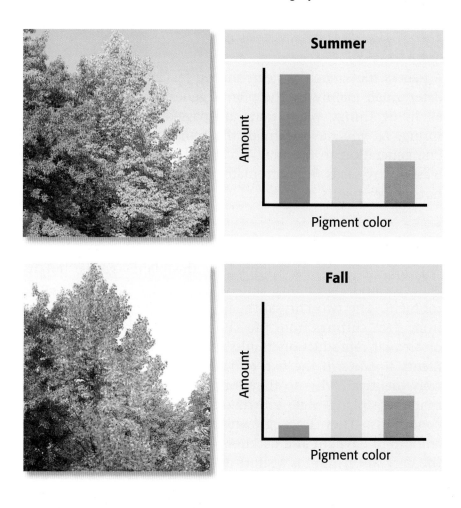

Figure 13 *The breakdown of chlorophyll in the autumn is a seasonal response in many trees. As the amount of chlorophyll in leaves decreases, other pigments become visible.*

Explore

Fallen leaves can cause a real mess on lawns. A mat of decaying leaves can block out the sun and air needed by the grass. Some people work hard to remove the leaves, but with landfills filling up across the nation, residents are encouraged to compost their leaves instead of disposing of them like trash. Many towns instruct residents on how to compost leaves and lawn clippings. Do library research to find out how composting helps the environment. Make a report and present it to your class. Include information about your community's approach to dealing with pesky fallen leaves.

REVIEW

1. What are the effects of the tropisms caused by light and gravity?

2. What is the difference between a short-day plant and a long-day plant?

3. How does the loss of leaves help a plant survive winter or long periods without rain?

4. **Applying Concepts** If a plant does not flower when exposed to 12 hours of daylight but does flower when exposed to 15 hours of daylight, is it a short-day plant or a long-day plant?

Plant Growth

OBJECTIVES
- Discuss how heredity affects plant growth.
- Discuss how a plant's environment affects its growth.
- Explain what plant hormones are and what they do.

All living things grow. You're growing right now. When you're older, you will reach a certain height and stop growing. Many plants, however, can keep growing for as long as they live. A plant's growth is affected by its genes, environment, and hormones.

Heredity

A plant's traits, such as heart-shaped leaves or red flowers, are determined mainly by the plant's genes, or its DNA. As with all living things, plant traits are passed from parent to offspring. As you have learned, the transmission of traits from one generation to the next is called heredity. Heredity is the reason why seeds from a tomato grow into tomato plants and not pepper plants.

Environment

A plant's traits are determined by the plant's genes, but its behavior and appearance can be affected by the plant's environment. The two chrysanthemums in **Figure 14** were grown from stem cuttings from the same parent plant. This method of asexual reproduction results in offspring plants that have identical genes. If the two chrysanthemum plants are genetically identical, why do they look so different? The answer is that these plants were grown under different environmental conditions. They were grown in a greenhouse where the amount of daylight and darkness could be adjusted. Recall that the chrysanthemum is a short-day plant. The chrysanthemum that flowered experienced short days and long nights. The chrysanthemum that did not flower experienced long days and short nights.

The amount of daylight and darkness is just one of many environmental factors that can affect a plant's growth. Other factors include the amount of water a plant receives and the kind of soil a plant grows in.

Figure 14 *Although these plants are genetically identical, they look different because they were grown under different conditions.*

Plant Hormones

Heredity and environment affect a plant's production of hormones. **Hormones** are chemical messengers that carry information from one part of an organism to another. They are produced in small amounts, but they have a strong effect on the organism. A plant hormone is produced in a specific part of a plant, such as the shoot tips. The hormone then moves through the plant and causes a response in all parts of the plant it contacts.

Auxin Life scientists have identified at least five major plant hormones. One of these is auxin (AWK sin). Auxin, a hormone produced in shoot tips, has many effects on plant growth. For example, auxin is the hormone involved in phototropism. When a plant is exposed to light from one direction, auxin travels from the shoot tip to the shaded side of a stem. It causes the cells on that side of the stem to grow longer. As you saw earlier, this causes the stem to bend toward the light.

Gibberellin Another important plant hormone is gibberellin (jib uhr ELL in). Like auxin, gibberellin affects plant growth in many ways. The plants in **Figure 15** are the same species, but gibberellin was applied to the plants on the right, causing them to grow very tall. Gibberellin also causes flower stalks to grow long.

People sometimes apply plant hormones to plants to make them grow in desirable ways. For example, some farmers spray grape stems with gibberellin. This hormone causes the stems that bear flowers to grow longer and the fruits they produce to grow larger.

Did you know that plant hormones are in the air? Many plants release a hormone gas called ethylene when their fruits begin to ripen. This hormone gas then triggers nearby fruits to release more ethylene and ripen at a faster rate. Scientists have developed ways for fruit growers to control ethylene gas so that their fruits won't ripen until they reach the grocery store.

Figure 15 *The plants on the right have greatly elongated stems because they were sprayed with gibberellin. The plants on the left show normal growth.*

> ### REVIEW
>
> 1. Discuss how a plant's heredity and environment affect its growth.
>
> 2. Hormones are chemical messengers. Describe a "message" that auxin sends.
>
> 3. **Analyzing Relationships** How are phototropism and a plant's production of auxin related?
>
> 4. **Applying Concepts** What might cause a tree to have a nearly horizontal trunk with vertical branches?

Chapter Highlights

SECTION 1

Vocabulary

dormant *(p. 282)*

Section Notes

- Sexual reproduction in flowering plants requires pollination and fertilization. Fertilization is the joining of an egg and a sperm cell.

- After fertilization has occurred, the ovules develop into seeds that contain plant embryos. The ovary develops into a fruit.

- Once seeds mature, they may become dormant. Seeds sprout when they are in an environment with the proper temperature and the proper amounts of water and oxygen.

- Many flowering plants can reproduce asexually without flowers.

SECTION 2

Vocabulary

chlorophyll *(p. 284)*
cellular respiration *(p. 285)*
stomata *(p. 286)*
transpiration *(p. 286)*

Section Notes

- During photosynthesis, leaves absorb sunlight and form the sugar glucose from carbon dioxide and water.

- During cellular respiration, a plant uses oxygen and releases carbon dioxide and water. Glucose is converted into a form of energy that cells can use.

- Plants take in carbon dioxide and release oxygen and water through stomata in their leaves.

Labs

Food Factory Waste *(p. 600)*
Weepy Weeds *(p. 602)*

✓ Skills Check

Visual Understanding

PIE CHART A pie chart is a great visual for illustrating fractions without using numbers. Each pie chart on page 289 represents a 24-hour period. The blue area represents the fraction of time in which there is no sunlight, and the gold area represents the fraction of time in which there is light. As shown by the chart, early summer is about $\frac{2}{3}$ day and $\frac{1}{3}$ night.

BAR GRAPHS As shown on page 291, bar graphs are often used to compare numbers. The graph at right compares the success rate of flower seeds from five seed producers. As shown by the bar height, company D, at about 88%, had the highest rate of success.

Seed Germination

Vocabulary

tropism *(p. 287)*

phototropism *(p. 287)*

gravitropism *(p. 288)*

evergreen *(p. 290)*

deciduous *(p. 290)*

Section Notes

- A tropism is plant growth in response to an environmental stimulus, such as light or gravity. Plant growth toward a stimulus is a positive tropism. Plant growth away from a stimulus is a negative tropism.

- Phototropism is growth in response to the direction of light. Gravitropism is growth in response to the direction of gravity.

- The change in the amount of daylight and darkness that occurs with changing seasons often controls plant reproduction.

- Evergreen plants have leaves adapted to survive throughout the year. Deciduous plants lose their leaves before cold or dry seasons. The loss of leaves helps deciduous plants survive low temperatures and dry periods.

Vocabulary

hormones *(p. 293)*

Section Notes

- Heredity and environmental factors interact to control plant growth.

- Plant hormones also influence plant growth. Plant hormones are chemical messengers that regulate plant growth. They are produced in one part of the plant and influence all parts of the plant they contact. Two important plant hormones are auxin and gibberellin.

- Auxin is the plant hormone responsible for phototropism. Gibberellin affects the length of plant shoots.

---

internet**connect**

GO TO: go.hrw.com

Visit the **HRW** Web site for a variety of learning tools related to this chapter. Just type in the keyword:

KEYWORD: HSTPL2

GO TO: www.scilinks.org

Visit the **National Science Teachers Association** on-line Web site for Internet resources related to this chapter. Just type in the *sci*LINKS number for more information about the topic:

TOPIC: Reproduction of Plants	***sci*LINKS NUMBER:** HSTL305
TOPIC: Photosynthesis	***sci*LINKS NUMBER:** HSTL310
TOPIC: Plant Tropisms	***sci*LINKS NUMBER:** HSTL315
TOPIC: Plant Growth	***sci*LINKS NUMBER:** HSTL320

Chapter Review

To complete the following sentences, choose the correct term from each pair of terms listed below:

1. After seeds develop fully, and before they sprout, they may become ___?___. *(deciduous* or *dormant)*

2. During ___?___, energy from sunlight is used to make sugar. *(photosynthesis* or *phototropism)*

3. The loss of water through stomata is called ___?___. *(transpiration* or *tropism)*

4. A change in plant growth in response to the direction of light is called ___?___. *(gravitropism* or *phototropism)*

5. Plants that have leaves year-round are ___?___. *(deciduous* or *evergreen)*

UNDERSTANDING CONCEPTS

Multiple Choice

6. The cells that open and close the stomata are the
   a. guard cells.
   b. xylem cells.
   c. cuticle cells.
   d. mesophyll cells.

7. Plant cells need carbon dioxide, which is used for
   a. cellular respiration.   c. fertilization.
   b. phototropism.   d. photosynthesis.

8. When chlorophyll breaks down,
   a. pollination occurs.
   b. other pigments become visible.
   c. red pigments disappear.
   d. photosynthesis occurs.

9. Which of the following sequences shows the correct order of events that occur after an insect brings pollen to a flower?
   a. germination, fertilization, pollination
   b. fertilization, germination, pollination
   c. pollination, germination, fertilization
   d. pollination, fertilization, germination

10. When the amount of water transpired from a plant's leaves is greater than the amount absorbed by its roots,
   a. the cuticle conserves water.
   b. the stem exhibits positive gravitropism.
   c. the plant wilts.
   d. the plant recovers from wilting.

11. The plant hormone that causes stems to grow very long is
   a. auxin.   c. gibberellin.
   b. glucose.   d. chlorophyll.

Short Answer

12. What is the relationship between transpiration, the cuticle, and the stomata?

13. What is the stimulus in phototropism? What is the plant's response to the stimulus?

14. Give an example of a positive tropism and a negative tropism.

Concept Mapping

15. Use the following terms to create a concept map: plantlets, flower, seeds, ovules, plant reproduction, asexual, runners.

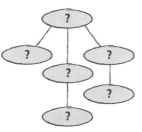

CRITICAL THINKING AND PROBLEM SOLVING

Write one or two sentences to answer the following questions:

16. Many plants that live in regions that experience severe winters have seeds that will not germinate at any temperature unless the seeds have been exposed first to a long period of cold. How might this characteristic help new plants survive?

17. If you wanted to make poinsettias bloom and turn red in the summer, what would you have to do?

18. What benefit is there for a plant's shoots to have positive phototropism? What benefit is there for its roots to have positive gravitropism?

MATH IN SCIENCE

19. If a particular leaf has a surface area of 8 cm^2, what is its surface area in square millimeters? (Hint: 1 cm^2 = 100 mm^2.)

20. Leaves have an average of 100 stomata per square millimeter of surface area. How many stomata would you expect the leaf in question 19 to possess?

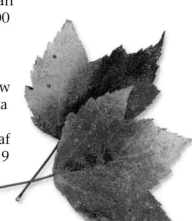

INTERPRETING GRAPHICS

Look at the illustrations below, and then answer the questions that follow. The illustration shows part of an experiment on phototropism in young plants. In part (1), the young plants have just been placed in the light after being in the dark. The shoot tip of one plant is cut off. The other tip is not cut. In part (2), the plants from part (1) are exposed to light from one direction.

Light rays

21. Why did the plant with the intact tip bend toward the light?

22. Why did the plant with the removed tip remain straight?

NOW What Do You Think?

Take a minute to review your answers to the ScienceLog questions found on page 279. Have your answers changed? If necessary, revise your answers based on what you have learned since you began this chapter.

MUTANT MUSTARD

The tiny mustard flowers grown by Elliot Meyerowitz are horribly deformed. You may think they are the result of a terrible accident, but Meyerowitz created these mutants on purpose. In fact, he is very proud of these flowers because they may help him solve an important biological mystery.

▲ *Elliot Meyerowitz, shown here in his laboratory, has raised about a million individual specimens of a mustard variety known as* Arabidopsis thaliana.

Normal and Abnormal Flowers

Normally, mustard flowers have four distinct parts that are arranged in a specific way. Many of the plants grown by Meyerowitz and his colleagues, however, are far from normal. Some have leaves in the center of their flowers. Others have seed-producing ovaries where the petals should be. At first glance, the arrangement of the parts seems random, but the structure of each flower has actually been determined by a small number of genes.

A Simple Model

After many years of careful studies, Meyerowitz and his colleagues have identified most of the genes that control the mustard flower's development. With this information, Meyerowitz has discovered patterns that have led to a surprisingly simple model. The model

points to just three classes of genes that determine what happens to the various parts of a flower as it develops. He learned that if one or more of those gene classes is inactivated, a mutant mustard plant results.

Pieces of an Old Puzzle

By understanding how genes shape the growth of flowers, Meyerowitz hopes to add pieces to a long-standing puzzle involving the origin of flowering plants. Scientists estimate that flowers first appeared on Earth about 125 million years ago and that they quickly spread to become the dominant plants on Earth. By studying which genes produce flowers in present-day plants, Meyerowitz and his colleagues hope to learn how flowering plants evolved in the first place.

Meyerowitz's mutant plants are well qualified to add to our understanding of the genetic makeup of plants. But don't look for these mustard plants in your local flower shop. These strange mutants won't win any prizes for beauty!

▲ *Meyerowitz alters the genes of a mustard plant so that it develops a mutant flower. The inset shows a normal flower.*

Think About It

▶ As you learned, it is possible to genetically change a plant. What are some possible risks of such a practice?

EYE ON THE ENVIRONMENT

A Rainbow of Cotton

Think about your favorite T-shirt. Chances are, it's made of cotton and brightly colored. The fibers in cotton plants, however, are naturally white. They must be dyed with chemicals—often toxic ones—to create the bright colors seen in T-shirts and other fabrics. To minimize the use of toxic chemicals, an ingenious woman named Sally Fox had an idea: What if you could grow the cotton *already colored*?

Learning from the Past

Cotton fibers come from the plant's seed pods, or *bolls.* Bolls are a little bigger than a golf ball and open at maturity to reveal a fuzzy mass of fibers and seeds. Once the seeds are removed, the fibers can be twisted into yarn and used to make many kinds of fabric. Sally Fox began her career as an *entomologist,* a scientist who studies insects. She first found out about colored cotton while studying pest resistance. Although most of the cotton grown for textiles is white, different shades of cotton have been harvested by Native Americans for centuries. These types of cotton showed some resistance to pests but had fibers too short to be used by the textile industry.

In 1982, Fox began the very slow process of crossbreeding different varieties of cotton to produce strains that were both colored *and* long-fibered. Her cotton is registered under the name FoxFibre® and has earned her high praise.

Solutions to Environmental Problems

The textile industry is the source of two major environmental hazards. The first hazard is the dyes used for cotton fabrics. The second is the pesticides that are required for growing cotton. These pesticides, like the dyes, can cause damage to both living things and natural resources, such as water and land.

Fox's cotton represents a solution to both of these problems. First, since the cotton is naturally colored, no dyes are necessary. Second, the native strains of cotton from which she bred her plants passed on their natural pest resistance. Thus, fewer pesticides are necessary to grow her cotton successfully.

Sally Fox's efforts demonstrate that with ingenuity and patience, science and agriculture work together in new ways to offer solutions to environmental problems.

▲ *Sally Fox in a Field of Colored Cotton*

Some Detective Work

▶ Like Fox's cotton, many types of plants and breeds of domesticated animals have been created through artificial selection. Do research to find out where and when your favorite fruit or breed of dog was first established.

299

UNIT 5

Animals

Have you ever been to a zoo or watched a wild-animal program on television? If so, you have some idea of the many different types of animals found on Earth—from tiny insects to massive whales.

Animals are fascinating, in part because of their variety in appearance and behavior. They also teach us about ourselves because we humans are also classified as animals. Humans have always observed and interacted with their fellow animals.

In this unit you will learn about many different types of animals, maybe even some that you never knew existed. So get ready for an animal adventure!

1610
Galileo uses a compound microscope to study insect anatomy.

1680
The dodo, a flightless bird, becomes extinct.

1960
Jane Goodall, an English zoologist, begins her research on chimpanzees in Tanzania.

1935
Francis B. Summer studies the protective coloration of fish.

1987
The last wild California condor is captured in an effort to save the species from extinction.

1983
The U.S. Space Shuttle *Challenger* is launched with Sally Ride, the first American woman in space, on board.

1693
John Ray correctly identifies whales as mammals.

1761
The first veterinary school is founded in Lyons, France.

1775
J. C. Fabricius develops a system for the classification of insects.

1882
Research on the ship *The Albatross* helps to increase our knowledge of marine life.

1827
John James Audubon publishes the first edition of *Birds of North America*.

1839
The first bicycle is constructed.

1995
Fourteen Canadian gray wolves are reintroduced to Yellowstone National Park.

1998
Keiko, the killer-whale star of the movie *Free Willy*, is taught to catch fish so that he can be released from captivity.

13 Animals and Behavior

This Really Happened . . .

Robert S. Ridgely and Lelis Navarette are ornithologists, people who study birds. In November 1997, they were hiking in the Andes mountains of Ecuador and recording bird songs. Suddenly they heard a sound that was a cross between the hoot of an owl and the bark of a dog. Even though they both had spent a lot of time in the woods, neither of the scientists had ever heard such a sound before.

What was in the woods? Some strange animal? They kept hiking, and almost 40 minutes later, they heard the sound again. This time, Ridgely, shown below, taped the sound and quickly played it back. The creature answered and came rushing through the woods toward them. It was a bird! But neither of the experts had ever seen a bird like it.

It turned out to be a species that no one had ever seen before! The bird is about 25 cm long, with long legs and a short tail. It has a broad white stripe across its face and a crown of black. It hops on the forest floor and eats large insects. So far, the bird does not have a name, but Ridgely and Navarette have been studying it and will name it soon.

For centuries, people like Robert Ridgely and Lelis Navarette have used their powers of observation to study animals and their behavior. We now know of over 1 million animal species, and we have learned much about how animals live and interact with other animals. But there are always more discoveries to be made! So the next time you take a walk outside, keep your eyes and ears open. You never know what you may find!

What Do You Think?

In your ScienceLog, try to answer the following questions based on what you already know:

1. What characteristics make an animal different from a plant?

2. How do animals know when to migrate?

Investigate!

Go on a Safari!

You don't have to travel far to see interesting animals. You can see ants walking along a sidewalk. Look for flowers, and you'll probably see bees. Turn over some soil, and you may find earthworms. Look up and you will see birds. If you are near a stream, you may see fish and salamanders and maybe a few mosquitoes. And don't forget household pets!

Procedure

1. Go outside and find **two different animals** to observe, or use the animals that your teacher supplies.

2. Without disturbing the animals, sit quietly and watch them for a few minutes from a distance. You may want to use **binoculars** or a **magnifying lens** to help you get a closer look. **Caution:** Always be careful around animals that may bite or sting.

3. Write down everything you notice about each animal. What kind of animal is it? What does it look like? You may want to draw a picture of it. How big is it? What is it doing? Why? Is it moving? How does it move? Is it eating? What is it eating?

Analysis

4. Compare the two animals you studied. How are they similar? How are they different?

5. How do the animals move? Do the ways they move give you clues about how they defend themselves or communicate with other animals?

6. Can you tell what each animal eats? What characteristics of these animals help them find or catch food?

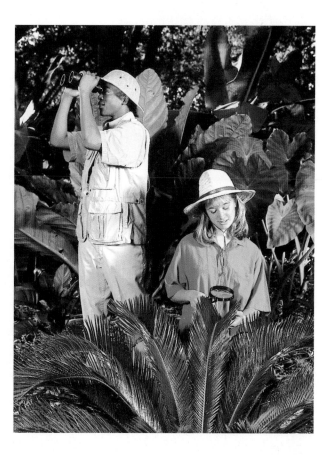

What Is an Animal?

What do you think of when you hear the word *animal*? You may think of your dog or cat. You may think about giraffes or grizzly bears or other creatures you've seen in zoos or on television. But would you think about a sponge? Natural bath sponges, like the one in **Figure 1,** are the remains of an animal that lived in the ocean!

Animals come in many different shapes and sizes. Some have four legs and fur, but most do not. Some are too small to be seen without a microscope, and others are bigger than a car. But they are all part of the fascinating world of animals.

The Animal Kingdom

Scientists have named over 1 million species of animals. How many different kinds of animals do you see in **Figure 2**? It may surprise you to learn that in addition to sponges, sea anemones and corals are also animals. So are spiders, fish, birds, and dolphins. Slugs, whales, kangaroos, and humans are animals too. Scientists have divided all these animal species into about 35 phyla and classes.

Most animals look nothing like humans. However, we do share characteristics with a group of animals called vertebrates. Any animal with a skull and a backbone is a **vertebrate.** Vertebrates include fish, amphibians, reptiles, birds, and mammals.

Figure 1 *This natural sponge used to be alive.*

Figure 2 *All of the living things in this picture are classified as animals. Do they look like animals to you?*

Even though you are probably most familiar with vertebrates, we are definitely the minority among living things. Less than five percent of known animal species are vertebrates. Take a look at **Figure 3.** As you can see, the great majority of animal species are insects, snails, jellyfish, worms, and other **invertebrates,** animals without backbones. In fact, one-fourth of all animal species are beetles!

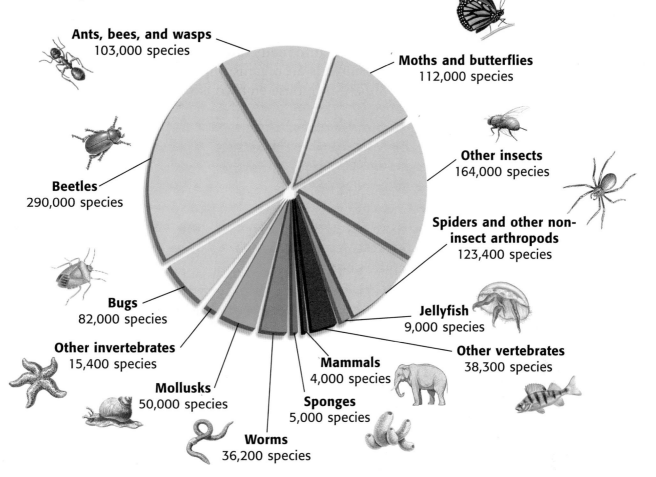

Ants, bees, and wasps
103,000 species

Moths and butterflies
112,000 species

Other insects
164,000 species

Beetles
290,000 species

Spiders and other non-insect arthropods
123,400 species

Bugs
82,000 species

Jellyfish
9,000 species

Other invertebrates
15,400 species

Mammals
4,000 species

Other vertebrates
38,300 species

Mollusks
50,000 species

Sponges
5,000 species

Worms
36,200 species

That's an Animal?

Sponges don't look like other animals. Indeed, until about 200 years ago, most people thought sponges were plants. Earthworms don't look anything like penguins, and no one would confuse a frog for a lion. So why do we say all these things are animals? What determines whether something is an animal, a plant, or something else?

There is no single answer. But all animals share characteristics that set them apart from all other living things.

Animals have many cells. All animals are **multicellular,** which means they are made of many cells. Your own body contains about 13 trillion cells. Animal cells are eukaryotic, and they do not have cell walls. Animal cells are surrounded by cell membranes only.

Figure 3 *This pie chart shows the major phyla and subgroups of the animal kingdom. Notice that most of the species are insects.*

Figure 4 *Several sperm surround an egg. Only one sperm can fuse with the egg to form a new individual.*

✓ **Self-Check**

Why are humans classified as vertebrates? *(See page 636 to check your answer.)*

Figure 6 *Like most other animals, sharks have organs for digestion, circulation, and reproduction.*

Animals usually reproduce by sexual reproduction. Animals make sex cells, eggs or sperm. When an egg and a sperm come together at fertilization, they form the first cell of a new individual. **Figure 4** shows an egg surrounded by sperm during fertilization. Some animals, like sponges and starfish, can also reproduce asexually, by budding and division.

Animals develop from embryos. The fertilized egg cell divides into many different cells to form an embryo. An **embryo** is an organism in the earliest stage of development. A mouse embryo is shown in **Figure 5.**

Head — — Tail

— Hind leg

— Front leg

Figure 5   A Mouse Embryo

Animals have many specialized parts. An animal's body has distinct parts that do different things. When a fertilized egg cell divides into many cells to form an embryo, the cells become different from each other. Some may become skin cells. Others may become muscle cells, nerve cells, or bone cells. These different kinds of cells arrange themselves to form **tissues,** which are collections of similar cells. For example, muscle cells form muscle tissue, and nerve cells form nervous tissue.

Most animals also have organs. An **organ** is a combination of two or more tissues. Your heart, lungs, and kidneys are all organs. All animals, including the shark shown in **Figure 6,** have different organs for different jobs.

Animals move. Most animals can move from place to place. As shown in **Figure 7,** they fly, run, swim, and jump. While it's true that other organisms move, animals are more likely to move quickly in a single direction. Some animals do not move much, though. Sea anemones and clams, for example, attach to rocks or the ocean floor and wait for food to arrive. But most animals are active.

Figure 7 *Animals move in many different ways.*

Animals are consumers. Animals cannot make their own food. All animals survive by eating other organisms, parts of other organisms, or the products of other organisms. In other words, animals are consumers. A **consumer** is an organism that eats other organisms. This trait sets animals, such as the panda in **Figure 8,** apart from plants. Except for the Venus' flytrap and a handful of other plants, plants do not eat other living things. Plants make their own food.

Animal food is as varied as animals themselves. Rabbits and caterpillars eat plants. Lions and spiders eat other animals. Reindeer eat lichens. Mosquitoes drink blood. Butterflies drink nectar from flowers.

Figure 8 *This giant panda is eating bamboo leaves.*

REVIEW

1. What characteristics separate animals from plants?

2. How are tissues and organs related?

3. **Interpreting Illustrations** What characteristics of the chameleon shown at far right tell you it is an animal?

Animal Behavior

In the last section, you learned the characteristics that help us recognize an animal. One characteristic of animals is that they move. Animals jump, run, fly, dart, scurry, slither, and glide. But animals don't move just for the sake of moving. They move for a reason. They run from enemies. They climb for food. They build homes. Even the tiniest mite can actively stalk its dinner, battle for territory, or migrate. All of these activities are known as behavior.

Survival Behavior

In order to stay alive, an animal has to do many things. It must find food and water, avoid being eaten, and have a place to live. Animals have many behaviors that help them accomplish these tasks.

Looking for Lunch Animals use many different methods to find or catch food. Owls swoop down on unsuspecting mice. Bees fly from flower to flower collecting nectar. Koala bears climb trees to get eucalyptus leaves. Jellyfish harpoon and lasso their prey with their tentacles. Some animals, such as the chimpanzee shown in **Figure 9,** use tools to get dinner. Whatever the meal of choice, animals have adapted to their surroundings so that they can obtain the most food using the least amount of energy.

How to Avoid Being Eaten Animals that eat other animals are known as **predators.** The animal being eaten is the **prey.** At any given moment, an animal *diner* can become another animal's *dinner.* Therefore, animals looking for food often have to think about other things besides which food looks or tastes the best. Animals will pass up a good meal if it's too dangerous to get. But being careful is just one method of defense. Keep reading to find out what other things animals do to stay alive.

NEW TERMS

predator
prey
camouflage
innate behavior
learned behavior
migrate

hibernation
estivation
biological clock
circadian rhythm
navigate
landmark

OBJECTIVES

- Explain the difference between learned and innate behavior.
- Explain the difference between hibernation and estivation.
- Give examples of how a biological clock influences behavior.
- Describe circadian rhythms.
- Explain how animals navigate.

Figure 9 *Chimpanzees make and use tools in order to get ants and other food out of hard-to-reach places.*

Hiding Out One way to avoid being eaten is to be hard to see. A rabbit often "freezes" so that its natural color blends into a background of shrubs or grass. Blending in with the background is called **camouflage.** Many animals mimic twigs, leaves, stones, bark, and other materials in their environment. The insect called a walking stick looks just like a twig. Some walking sticks even sway a bit, as though a breeze were blowing. See **Figure 10** for another example of camouflage.

In Your Face The horns of a bull and the spines of a porcupine clearly signal trouble to a potential predator, but other defenses may not be as obvious. For example, animals may defend themselves with chemicals. The skunk and the bombardier beetle both spray predators with irritating chemicals. Bees, ants, and wasps inject a powerful acid into their attackers. The skin of both the South American dart-poison frog and the hooded pitohui bird of New Guinea contains a deadly toxin. Any predator that eats, or even tries to eat, one of these animals will likely die.

Animals with a chemical defense need a way to warn predators that they should look elsewhere for a meal. Their chemical weapons are often advertised by the animal's outer covering, which has a bright design called *warning coloration*, as shown in **Figure 11.** Predators will avoid any animal with the colors and patterns they associate with pain, illness, or other unpleasant experiences. The most common warning colors are vivid shades of red, yellow, orange, black, and white.

Figure 10 *This is a picture of a caterpillar camouflaged as a twig. Can you find the caterpillar?*

Octopuses are camouflage experts. They can change the color of their entire body in less than 1 second.

Figure 11 *The warning coloration of the hooded pitohui warns predators that it is poisonous. The yellow and black stripes of the stinging yellow jacket are another example.*

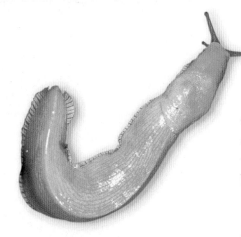

Figure 12 *Eating banana slugs, like this one, or not eating them is an innate behavior in garter snakes.*

What did the bumblebee do to Aunt Flossie? Find out on page 606.

Figure 13 *When researchers began throwing sweet potatoes on an island beach, Japanese macaques got a tasty, but sandy, snack. One monkey washed the sand off in the water. Others watched her, and now all of the macaques on the island wash their sweet potatoes.*

Why Do They Behave That Way?

How do animals know when a situation is dangerous? How do predators know which warning coloration to avoid? Sometimes animals instinctively know what to do, but sometimes they have to learn. Biologists call these two kinds of animal behavior innate behavior and learned behavior.

It's in the Genes Behavior that doesn't depend on learning or experience is known as **innate behavior.** Innate behaviors are influenced by genes. As described in **Figure 12,** snakes inherit preferences for certain types of food. Banana slugs are a favorite food for garter snakes on the California coast, but garter snakes from inland regions will not eat them. Humans inherit genes that give us the ability to walk. Puppies inherit the tendency to chew, bees the tendency to fly, and earthworms the tendency to burrow.

Some innate behaviors are present at birth. Newborn whales all have the innate ability to swim. Other innate behaviors develop months or years after birth. For example, the tendency of a bird to sing is innate. But a bird does not sing until it is nearly grown.

Animal School Just because a behavior is innate does not mean that it cannot be modified. Learning can change innate behavior. **Learned behavior** is behavior that has been learned from experience or from observing other animals. Humans inherit the tendency to speak. But the language we speak is not inherited. We might learn English, Spanish, Chinese, or Tagalog.

Humans are not the only animals that modify inherited behaviors through learning. Nearly all animals can learn. For example, many young animals learn by watching their parents. **Figure 13** shows a monkey that learned a new behavior by observation.

REVIEW

1. How do innate behavior and learned behavior differ?

2. **Applying Concepts** How does the effectiveness of warning coloration for protection depend on learning?

Seasonal Behavior

In many places, animals must deal with the winter hardships of little food and bitter cold. Some avoid winter by traveling to places that are warmer. Others collect and store food. Frogs bury themselves in mud, insects burrow into the ground, and some animals hibernate.

World Travelers When food is scarce because of winter or drought, many animals migrate. To **migrate** is to travel from one place to another and back again. Animals migrate to find food, water, or safe nesting grounds. Whales, salmon, bats, and even chimpanzees migrate. Each winter, monarch butterflies, shown in **Figure 14,** gather in central Mexico from all over North America to wait for spring. And each year, birds in the Northern Hemisphere fly thousands of kilometers south. In the spring, they return north to nest.

Slowing Down Some animals deal with food and water shortages by hibernating. **Hibernation** is a period of inactivity and decreased body temperature that some animals experience in winter. Hibernating animals survive on stored body fat. Many animals hibernate, including mice, squirrels, skunks, and bears. While an animal hibernates, its temperature, heart rate, and breathing rate drop. Some hibernating animals drop their body temperature to a few degrees above freezing and do not wake for weeks at a time. Other animals, like the polar bears in **Figure 15,** do not enter deep hibernation. Their body temperature does not drop as severely, and they sleep for shorter periods of time.

Winter is not the only time resources can be scarce. Many desert squirrels and mice experience a similar internal slowdown in the hottest part of the summer, when they run low on water and food. This period of reduced activity in the summer is called **estivation.**

Figure 14 *When the monarchs gather in Mexico, there can be as many as 4 million butterflies per acre. That's some family reunion!*

Don't wake the bats!

Read about the effects of humans on bat hibernation on page 322.

Figure 15 *Polar bears and other bears do not enter deep hibernation and are able to respond if threatened. However, they have periods of inactivity in which they do not eat, their body functions slow down, and they move very little.*

Quick Lab

How Long Is a Minute?

Do you have an internal clock that helps you keep track of time? Pair up with a classmate. Your partner will start a **stopwatch** and say, "Go." When you think a minute has passed, say, "Stop!" Check the time. Try several times, and keep a record of your results. Then trade places and let your partner try. Were the recorded times close to a minute? Did your performance improve? Try again, using your pulse or your breathing as a guide. Were these times closer? Do you think you have an internal clock? Explain.

✔ Self-Check

Is hibernation controlled by a circadian rhythm? Explain. *(See page 636 to check your answer.)*

The Rhythms of Life

Humans need clocks and calendars to tell us when to get up and go to school, when to get to the movie, and when to shop for someone's birthday present. Other animals also need to know when to get up in the morning, when to store food, and when to fly south for the winter. The clocks and calendars that animals use are called biological clocks. A **biological clock** is the internal control of natural cycles. Animals may use clues from their surroundings, such as the length of the day and the temperature, to set their clocks.

Some biological clocks keep track of very small amounts of time. Other biological clocks control daily cycles. These daily cycles are called **circadian rhythms.** *Circadian* means "around the day." Most animals wake up at about the same time each day and get sleepy at about the same time each night. This is an example of a circadian rhythm.

Some biological clocks control even longer cycles. Seasonal cycles are nearly universal among animals. Animals hibernate at certain times of the year and breed at other times. Animals know when to stockpile food to prepare for the winter. And every spring, migrating birds head north. Biological clocks control all of these cycles.

How Do Animals Find Their Way?

If you were planning a trip, you'd probably consult a map. If you were hiking, you might rely on a compass or trail markers to find your way. When it's time to migrate, how do animals, such as the arctic terns in **Figure 16,** know which way to go? They must **navigate,** or find their way from one place to another.

Figure 16 *Arctic terns are known for long-distance travel. Each year, these small birds make a 38,000 km round trip from the Northern Hemisphere to Antarctica.*

When people travel to places that are in a different time zone, they frequently suffer from "jet lag." Here's an example: New York time is 6 hours behind Paris time. A traveler from New York who is staying in Paris is suffering from jet lag. She goes to bed at 10 P.M., Paris time, but she wakes up at midnight, unable to fall back asleep. She lies awake all night and finally falls asleep at about 6 A.M., one hour before her alarm rings. How might circadian rhythms explain her jet lag? When it is 10 P.M. in Paris, what time is it in New York? Turn to the Math Concept on page 318 if you need help.

Take a Left at the Post Office For short trips, many animals, including humans, navigate by using landmarks. **Landmarks** are fixed objects that an animal uses to find its way. For example, once you see the corner gas station six blocks from your house, you know how to go the rest of the way. The gas station is a landmark for you.

Bees and pigeons have a kind of mental map of landmarks in their home territory. Birds use mountain ranges, rivers, and coastlines to find their way home. Humans and other animals also navigate short distances by using a mental image of an area. Not all landmarks are visual. Blind people can navigate precisely through a familiar house because they know where everything is and how long it takes to cross a room. Pigeons navigate in their home area based on smell as well as sight.

Compass Anyone? Like human sailors, animals use the position of the sun and stars as a map. But some animals, such as migratory birds, have other methods of finding their way. They navigate using the Earth's magnetic field. You can read about this in the physical science connection at right.

physical science CONNECTION

Earth's iron core acts as a giant magnet, with a magnetic north pole and a magnetic south pole. The strength and direction of the Earth's magnetic field varies from place to place, and many birds use this variation as a map. Migratory birds have tiny crystals of magnetite, the same kind of material from which magnets are made, in their heads above their nostrils. Biologists think that magnetite, found in the rock above, somehow moves or stimulates nerves so that a bird knows its position on Earth.

REVIEW

1. Why do animals migrate?

2. What are three methods animals use to navigate?

3. How are hibernation and estivation similar? How are they different?

4. **Applying Concepts** Some research suggests that jet lag can be overcome by getting plenty of exposure to sunlight in the new time zone. Why might this method work?

Living Together

NEW TERMS
social behavior
communication
territory
pheromone

OBJECTIVES

- Discuss ways that animals communicate.
- List the advantages and disadvantages of living in groups.

Most animals do not live alone; they associate with other animals. When animals interact, it may be in large groups or one on one. Animals may work together, or they may compete with one another. All of this behavior is called social behavior. **Social behavior** is the interaction between animals of the same species. Whether friendly or hostile, all social behavior requires communication.

Communication

Imagine what life would be like if people could not talk or read. There would be no telephones, no televisions, no books, and no Internet. The world would certainly be a lot different! Language is an important way for humans to communicate. In **communication,** a signal must travel from one animal to another, and the receiver of the signal must respond in some way.

Communication helps animals live together, find food, avoid enemies, and protect their homes. Animals communicate to warn others of danger, to identify family members, to frighten predators, and to find mates. Some of the most dramatic uses of communication are courtship displays. *Courtship* is special behavior by animals of the same species that leads to mating. **Figure 17** shows two cranes performing a courtship display.

Animals also communicate to protect their living space. Many animals defend a **territory,** an area that is occupied by one animal or a group of animals and that other members of the species are excluded from. Many species, such as the wolves in **Figure 18,** use their territories for mating, finding food, and raising young.

Figure 17 *Japanese ground cranes perform an elaborate courtship dance.*

Figure 18 *These wolves are howling to discourage neighboring wolves from invading their territory.*

How Do Animals Communicate?

Animals communicate by signaling intentions and information to other animals through smell, sound, vision, and touch. Most animal signals tend to be simple compared with those that we use. But no matter which signal is used, it must convey specific information.

Do You Smell Trouble? One method of communication is chemical. Even one-celled organisms communicate with one another by means of chemicals. In animals, these chemicals are called **pheromones** (FER uh MOHNZ).

Ants and other insects secrete a variety of pheromones. For example, alarm substances released into the air alert other members of the species to danger. Trail substances are left along a path so that others can follow to find food and return to the nest. Recognition odors on an ant's body announce which colony an ant is from. Such a message signals both friends and enemies, depending on who is receiving the message.

Figure 19 *Queen butterflies use pheromones as part of their courtship display.*

Many animals, including vertebrates, use pheromones to attract or influence members of the opposite sex. Amazingly, elephants and insects use some of the same pheromones to attract mates. Queen butterflies, like the one in **Figure 19,** use pheromones during their courtship displays.

Do You Hear What I Hear? Animals also communicate by making noises. Wolves howl. Dolphins and whales use whistles and complex clicking noises to communicate with others. Male birds may sing songs in the spring to claim their territory or attract a mate.

Sound is a signal that can reach a large number of animals over a large area. Elephants communicate with other elephants kilometers away using rumbles at a frequency too low for most humans to hear, as described in **Figure 20.** Humpback whales sing songs that can be heard for kilometers.

Figure 20 *Elephants communicate with low-pitched sounds that humans cannot hear. When an elephant is communicating this way, the skin on its forehead flutters.*

Figure 21 *Dogs prick up their ears and wag their tails when they are happy. When they want to play, they drop down on their forelegs. And they lay back their ears when they are uneasy.*

Showing Off Many forms of communication are visual. When we wink at a friend or frown at an opponent, we are communicating with *body language.* Other animals are no different. **Figure 21** shows some of the body language dogs use.

An animal that wants to scare another animal may do something that makes it appear larger. It may ruffle its feathers or fur or open its mouth and show its teeth. Visual displays are also important in courtship. Fireflies blink complex signals in the dark to attract one another.

Getting in Touch An animal may also use touch to communicate, like the honeybee. A honeybee that finds a patch of flowers rich in nectar returns to its hive to tell fellow workers where the flowers are. Inside the dark hive, the bee communicates by performing a complex figure-eight dance, as shown below, which the other bees learn by observation and touch.

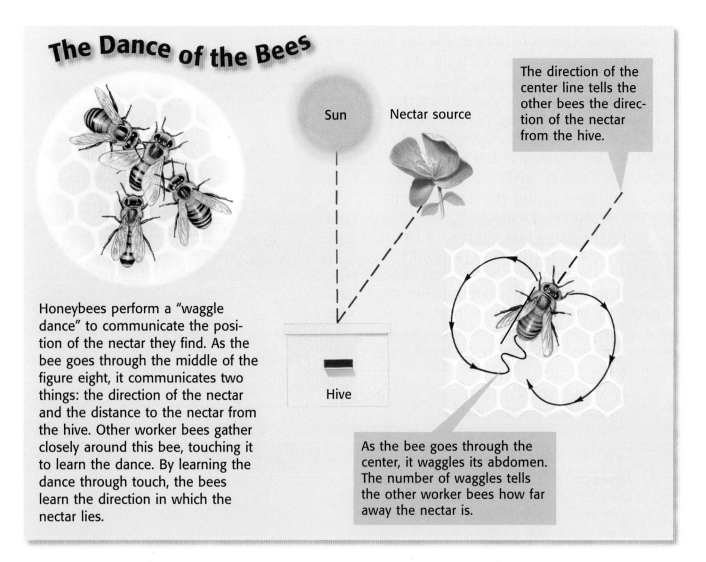

The Dance of the Bees

Honeybees perform a "waggle dance" to communicate the position of the nectar they find. As the bee goes through the middle of the figure eight, it communicates two things: the direction of the nectar and the distance to the nectar from the hive. Other worker bees gather closely around this bee, touching it to learn the dance. By learning the dance through touch, the bees learn the direction in which the nectar lies.

Sun

Nectar source

Hive

The direction of the center line tells the other bees the direction of the nectar from the hive.

As the bee goes through the center, it waggles its abdomen. The number of waggles tells the other worker bees how far away the nectar is.

Part of the Family

Tigers live alone. Except for the time a mother tiger spends with her cubs, a tiger meets other tigers rarely and for not much longer than it takes to mate. Yet the tiger's closest relative, the lion, is rarely alone. Lions live in tightly knit groups called prides. The members of a pride sleep together, hunt together, and raise their cubs together. **Figure 22** shows two lions at work. Why do some animals live in groups, while others live apart?

Figure 22 *This pair of lions is cooperating to hunt down a gazelle.*

The Benefits of Living in a Group Living with other animals is much safer than living alone. Large groups of animals can quickly spot a predator or other dangers, and groups of animals can cooperate to defend themselves. For example, if a predator threatens them, a herd of musk oxen will form a circle with their young in the middle and their horns pointed outward. Honeybees attack by the thousands when another animal tries to take their honey. Five thousand bees can defend a nest better than one bee or even fifty bees.

Living together can also help animals find food. Tigers and other animals that hunt alone can usually kill only animals that are smaller than themselves. In contrast, lions, wolves, hyenas, and other predators that hunt cooperatively can kill prey much larger than themselves.

The Downside of Living in a Group Living in groups causes problems as well. Animals living in groups attract predators, so they must always be on the lookout, as shown in **Figure 23.** Groups of animals need more food, and animals in groups compete with each other for food and for mates. Individuals in groups can also give each other diseases.

Figure 23 *When a coyote comes by, a ground squirrel stands up and whistles a loud alarm call. This warns other squirrels that danger is near.*

REVIEW

1. Scientists have discovered pheromones in humans. Name three other types of animal communication used by humans.

2. Why is communication important? Name three reasons.

3. **Applying Concepts** Considering what you have learned about group living, list two advantages and two disadvantages to living in a group of humans.

Chapter Highlights

SECTION 1

Vocabulary

vertebrate *(p. 304)*

invertebrate *(p. 305)*

multicellular *(p. 305)*

embryo *(p. 306)*

tissue *(p. 306)*

organ *(p. 306)*

consumer *(p. 307)*

Section Notes

- Animals with skulls and backbones are vertebrates. Animals without a backbone are invertebrates.

- Animals are multicellular. Their cells are eukaryotic and lack a cell wall.

- Most animals reproduce sexually and develop from embryos.

- Most animals have tissues and organs.

- Most animals move.

- Animals are consumers.

SECTION 2

Vocabulary

predator *(p. 308)*

prey *(p. 308)*

camouflage *(p. 309)*

innate behavior *(p. 310)*

learned behavior *(p. 310)*

migrate *(p. 311)*

hibernation *(p. 311)*

estivation *(p. 311)*

biological clock *(p. 312)*

circadian rhythm *(p. 312)*

navigate *(p. 312)*

landmark *(p. 313)*

Section Notes

- Many animals defend themselves against predators by means of camouflage, chemical defenses, or both.

- Behavior may be classified as innate or learned. The potential for innate behavior is inherited. Learned behavior depends on experience.

- Some animals migrate to find food, water, or safe nesting grounds.

- Some animals hibernate in the winter and some estivate in the summer.

☑ Skills Check

Math Concepts

TIME DIFFERENCE Paris time is 6 hours later than New York time. If it is 10 P.M. in Paris, subtract 6 hours to get New York time.

$$10 - 6 = 4$$

It is 4 P.M. in New York. Similarly, when it is 7 A.M. in Paris, it is 1 A.M. in New York.

Visual Understanding

THE DANCE OF THE BEES The illustration on page 316 shows how bees use the waggle dance to communicate the location of a nectar source. Notice the position of the sun in relation to the hive and the nectar source. The bee communicates this information by the direction of the center line in the dance.

SECTION 2

- Animals have internal biological clocks to control natural cycles.

- Daily cycles are called circadian rhythms.

- Some biological clocks are regulated by cues from an animal's environment.

- Animals navigate close to home using landmarks and a mental image of their home area.

- Some animals use the positions of the sun and stars or Earth's magnetic field to navigate.

Labs

Wet, Wiggly Worms *(p. 604)*

Aunt Flossie and the Bumblebee *(p. 606)*

SECTION 3

Vocabulary

social behavior *(p. 314)*

communication *(p. 314)*

territory *(p. 314)*

pheromone *(p. 315)*

Section Notes

- Communication must include both a signal and a response.

- Two important kinds of communication are courtship and territorial displays.

- Animals communicate through sight, sound, touch, and smell.

- Group living allows animals to spot both prey and predators more easily.

- Groups of animals are more visible to predators than are individuals, and animals in groups must compete with one another for food, mates, and breeding areas.

Chapter Review

USING VOCABULARY

To complete the following sentences, choose the correct term from each pair of terms listed below:

1. An animal with a skull and a backbone is __?__. An animal with no backbone is __?__. *(an invertebrate* or *a vertebrate)*

2. A behavior that does not depend on experience is __?__. *(innate* or *learned)*

3. In the summer, an animal enters a state of reduced activity. The animal is __?__. *(estivating* or *hibernating)*

4. Daily cycles are known as __?__. *(biological clocks* or *circadian rhythms)*

5. When an egg and a sperm come together, they form __?__. *(an embryo* or *an organ)*

UNDERSTANDING CONCEPTS

Multiple Choice

6. Which characteristic is not true of animals?
   a. They are multicellular.
   b. They usually reproduce sexually.
   c. They make their own food.
   d. They have tissues.

7. Living in groups
   a. attracts predators.
   b. helps prey spot predators.
   c. helps animals find food.
   d. All of the above

8. Warning coloration is
   a. a kind of camouflage.
   b. a way to warn predators away.
   c. always black and white.
   d. always a sign that an animal is poisonous to eat.

9. Some birds use Earth's magnetic field
   a. to attract mates.
   b. to navigate.
   c. to set their biological clocks.
   d. to defend their territory.

10. To defend against predators, an animal might use
    a. camouflage.   c. toxins.
    b. warning coloration. d. All of the above

Short Answer

11. How are pheromones used in communication?

12. What is a territory? Give an example of a territory from your own environment.

13. What landmarks help you navigate your way home from school?

14. What do migration and hibernation have in common?

Concept Mapping

15. Use the following terms to create a concept map: estivation, circadian rhythms, seasonal behaviors, hibernation, migration, biological clocks.

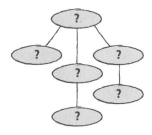

Write one or two sentences to answer the following questions:

16. If you smell a skunk while riding in a car and you shut the car window, has the skunk communicated with you? Explain.

17. Flying is an innate behavior in birds. Is it an innate behavior or a learned behavior in humans? Why?

18. Ants depend on pheromones and touch for communication, but birds depend more on sight and sound. Why might these two types of animals communicate differently?

INTERPRETING GRAPHICS

The pie chart below shows the different phyla of the animal species on Earth. Use the chart to answer the questions that follow.

19. What group of animals has the most species? How is this shown on the chart?

20. How many species of beetles are on Earth? How does that compare with the number of mammal species?

21. How many species of vertebrates are known?

22. Scientists are still discovering new species. Which pie wedges are most likely to increase? Why do you think so?

MATH IN SCIENCE

Use the data from the pie chart to answer the following questions:

23. What is the total number of animal species on Earth?

24. How many different species of moths and butterflies are on Earth?

25. What percentage of all animal species are moths and butterflies?

26. What percentage of all animal species are vertebrates?

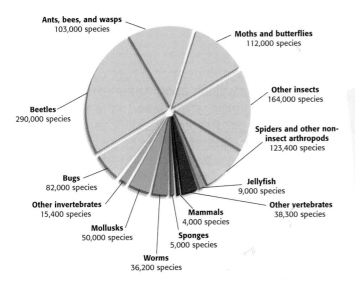

Ants, bees, and wasps
103,000 species

Moths and butterflies
112,000 species

Other insects
164,000 species

Beetles
290,000 species

Spiders and other non-insect arthropods
123,400 species

Bugs
82,000 species

Jellyfish
9,000 species

Other invertebrates
15,400 species

Other vertebrates
38,300 species

Mollusks
50,000 species

Mammals
4,000 species

Sponges
5,000 species

Worms
36,200 species

NOW What Do You Think?

Take a minute to review your answers to the ScienceLog questions found on page 303. Have your answers changed? If necessary, revise your answers based on what you have learned since you began this chapter.

EYE ON THE ENVIRONMENT

Do Not Disturb!

Did you know that bats are the only mammals that can fly? Unlike many birds, most bat species in the northern and central parts of the United States don't fly south for the winter. Instead of migrating, many bat species go into hibernation. But if their sleep is disturbed too often, the bats may die.

Long Winter's Nap

Most bats eat insects, but winter is a time of food shortage. In late summer, many North American bats begin to store up extra fat. These fat reserves help them survive the winter. For the stored fat to last until spring, bats must hibernate. They travel to caves where winter temperatures are low enough—0°C to 9.5°C— and stable enough for the bats to hibernate comfortably.

Hibernating bats go through a major metabolic change. Their body temperature drops to almost the same temperature as the surrounding cave. Their heart rate, normally about 400 beats per minute, slows to about 25 beats per minute. With these changes, the stored-up fat will usually last all winter, unless human visitors wake the bats from their deep sleep. Then the bats may starve to death.

No Admittance!

Even with their slowed metabolism, bats must wake up occasionally. They still need to drink water every so often. Sometimes they move to a warmer or cooler spot in the cave. But bats usually have enough fat stored so that they can wake up a few times each winter and then go back to sleep.

People visiting the caves force the bats to wake up unnecessarily. This causes the bats to use up the fat they have stored faster than they can afford. For example, a little brown bat consumes 67 days worth of stored fat each time it awakes. And with no insects around to eat, it cannot build up its fat reserve again.

▲ *These little brown bats are roosting in a cave.*

Most species of hibernating bats can survive the winter after waking about three extra times. But frequent intrusions can lead to the death of a whole colony of sleeping bats. Thousands of these interesting and extremely beneficial mammals may die when people carelessly or deliberately disturb them as they hibernate.

Increase Your Knowledge

▶ Using the Internet or the library, find out more about bats. Learn how they are beneficial to the environment and what threatens their survival. Discuss with your classmates some ways to protect bats and their habitats.

ANIMAL CANNIBALS

Competing, surviving, and reproducing are all part of life. And in some species, so is *cannibalism* (eating members of one's own species). But how does cannibalism relate to competing, surviving, and reproducing? It turns out that sometimes an animal's choice of food is a factor in whether its genes get passed on or not.

▲ *During mating, male Australian redback spiders offer themselves as food to their mates.*

Picky Eaters

Tiger salamanders start life by eating zooplankton, aquatic insect larvae, and sometimes tadpoles. If conditions in their small pond include intense competition with members of their own species, some of the larger salamanders become cannibals!

Scientists are not sure why tiger salamanders become cannibals or why they usually eat nonrelatives. Scientists hypothesize that this behavior eliminates competition. By eating other salamanders, a tiger salamander reduces competition for food and improves the chances of its own survival. That increases the chances its genes will be passed on to the next generation. And eating nonrelatives helps to ensure that genes coming from the same family are more likely to be passed on to the next generation.

The Ultimate Sacrifice

Male Australian redback spiders take a different approach to making sure their genes are passed on. During mating, the male spider tumbles his body over, does a handstand, and waves his abdomen near the female's mouth, offering himself to her as a meal. The female accepts the dinner invitation if she is hungry. And it seems that about 65 percent of the time she is hungry!

Male spiders want to pass on their genes, so they compete fiercely for the females. A female redback spider wants to make sure that as many of her eggs are fertilized as possible, so she often mates with two different males. If the female eats the first male, studies show that she will not mate with a second male as often as she would if she had not eaten the first suitor. Because eating the male takes some time, more eggs are fertilized by the mate who also becomes dinner. The male spider who offers himself as a meal may then have more of his genes passed to the next generation.

On Your Own

▶ Other animals devour members of their own species. Scientists believe there are a variety of reasons for the behavior. Using the Internet or the library, research cannibalism in different animals, such as praying mantises, blue crabs, stickleback fish, black widow spiders, spadefoot toad tadpoles, and lions. Present your findings to the class.

14 Invertebrates

Amazing but True!

In 1995, researchers in Germany made a computer chip that could send signals to a single nerve cell in a living leech. Even more amazing, the leech's nerve cell could send signals back to the computer chip. What is so amazing about having a "mind link" with a leech? You might be surprised at the answer.

In the United States alone, accidents result in more than 10,000 spinal-cord injuries a year. In severe cases, a person can lose muscle control, particularly in the arms and legs. There is often little or no hope for the person to regain the ability to move. But what does this have to do with leeches?

Giant leeches from South America, like the one shown here on the scientist's arm, have only a few nerve cells, but they are the same as nerve cells from other organisms. By studying leech nerves, biologists are learning how to communicate directly with nerve cells. These scientists hope that communicating with leech nerves using a computer chip will one day help them communicate with human nerve cells. In the future, people with spinal-cord injuries may be able to use computers to communicate with the nerve cells in their body and move their muscles.

Scientists still have a lot to learn before they can apply their work with leeches to humans, but they've made a start. Who would have expected such a breakthrough with an animal that doesn't even have a backbone? In this chapter, you will learn about many spineless critters, the invertebrates.

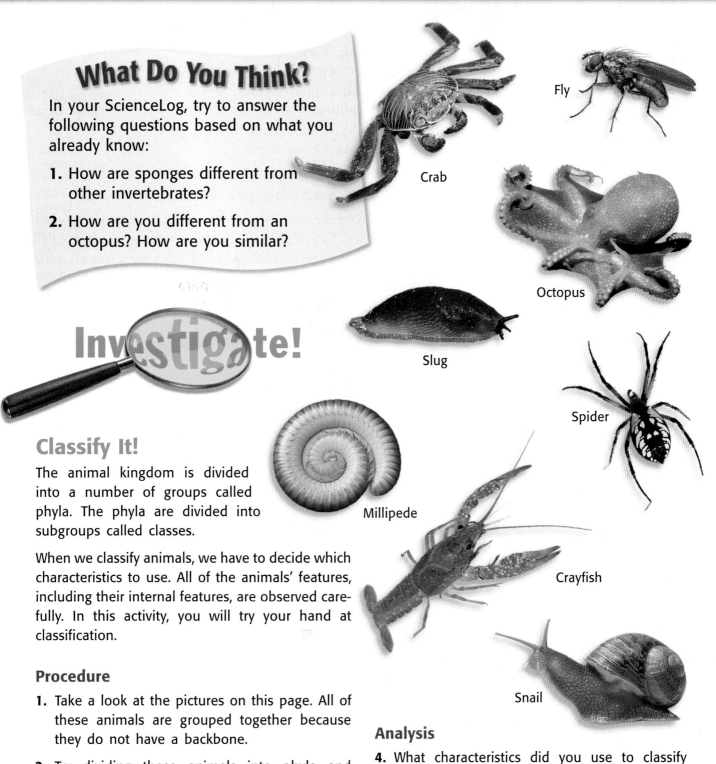

What Do You Think?

In your ScienceLog, try to answer the following questions based on what you already know:

1. How are sponges different from other invertebrates?

2. How are you different from an octopus? How are you similar?

Crab

Fly

Octopus

Slug

Investigate!

Spider

Millipede

Classify It!

The animal kingdom is divided into a number of groups called phyla. The phyla are divided into subgroups called classes.

When we classify animals, we have to decide which characteristics to use. All of the animals' features, including their internal features, are observed carefully. In this activity, you will try your hand at classification.

Crayfish

Snail

Procedure

1. Take a look at the pictures on this page. All of these animals are grouped together because they do not have a backbone.

2. Try dividing these animals into phyla and classes. Which ones are the most similar? Put these in the same phyla. For animals in the same phylum, determine which are the most similar. Put these in classes within the same phylum.

3. Draw a chart to show which animals you have grouped together.

Analysis

4. What characteristics did you use to classify these animals into different phyla? Explain why you think these characteristics are the most important.

5. What characteristics did you use to group these animals into classes?

6. What descriptive names could you give to your phyla and classes?

Simple Invertebrates

NEW TERMS

invertebrate   coelom
bilateral symmetry   medusa
radial symmetry   polyp
asymmetrical   parasite
ganglia   host
gut

OBJECTIVES

- Describe the difference between radial and bilateral symmetry.
- Describe the function of a coelom.
- Explain how sponges are different from other animals.
- Describe the differences in the simple nervous systems of the cnidarians and the flatworms.

Animals without backbones, also known as **invertebrates,** make up an estimated 97 percent of all animal species. So far, more than 1 million invertebrates have been named. Most biologists think that millions more remain undiscovered.

Tiger beetle

No Backbones Here!

Invertebrates come in many different shapes and sizes. Grasshoppers, clams, earthworms, and jellyfish are all invertebrates, and they are all very different from each other. But one thing invertebrates have in common is that they don't have backbones.

The differences and similarities among all animals, including invertebrates, can be compared by looking at several characteristics. These characteristics include the type of body plan, the presence or absence of a head, and the way food is digested and absorbed.

Morpho butterfly

Body Plans Invertebrates have two basic body plans, or types of *symmetry*. Symmetry can be bilateral or radial. Animal body plans are shown on the next page.

Most animals have bilateral symmetry. An animal with **bilateral symmetry** has a body with two similar halves. For example, if you draw an imaginary line down the middle of an ant, you see the same features on each side of the line.

Some invertebrates have radial symmetry. In an animal with **radial symmetry,** the body parts are arranged in a circle around a central point. If you were to draw an imaginary line across the top of a sea anemone, you would see that both halves look the same. But you could draw the line in any direction and still see two similar halves.

The simplest invertebrates, the sponges, have no symmetry at all. Animals without symmetry are **asymmetrical.**

Horned flatworm

Harlequin shrimp

Animal Body Plans

This ant has **bilateral symmetry.** The two halves of its body mirror each other. On each side you see one eye, one antenna, and three legs.

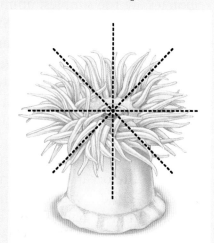

This sea anemone has **radial symmetry.** Animals with radial symmetry have a body organized around the center, like spokes on a wheel.

This sponge is **asymmetrical.** You cannot draw a straight line so that its body is divided into two equal halves.

Getting a Head All animals except sponges have fibers called *nerves* that carry signals to control the movements of their body. Simple invertebrates have nerves arranged in networks or in nerve cords throughout their body. These simple animals have no brain or head.

In some invertebrates, dozens of nerve cells come together in groups called **ganglia.** Ganglia occur throughout the body, controlling different body parts. **Figure 1** shows one of the ganglia, the brain, and nerve cords of a leech.

More-complex animals have a brain and a head, where the brain is stored. The brain controls many different nerves in different parts of the body.

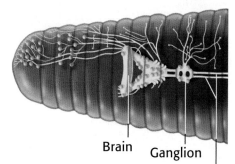

Brain   Ganglion

Nerve cords

Figure 1 *Leeches have a simple brain and ganglia. A pair of nerve cords connects the brain and ganglia.*

Don't You Have Any Guts? Almost all animals digest food in a central gut. The **gut** is a pouch lined with cells that release powerful enzymes. These enzymes break down food into small particles that cells can then absorb. Your gut is your digestive tract.

Complex animals have a special space in the body for the gut. This space is the **coelom** (SEE luhm), shown in **Figure 2.** The coelom allows the gut to move food without interference from the movements of the body. Other organs, such as the heart and lungs, are also in the coelom, but they are separated from the gut.

Coelom   Gut

Figure 2 *This is the coelom of an earthworm. The gut and organs are in this special cavity.*

Sponges

Sponges are the simplest animals. They have no symmetry, no head or nerves, and no gut. Although sponges can move, they are so slow that their movement is very difficult to see. In fact, sponges were once thought to be plants. But plants make their food from sunlight, water, and carbon dioxide. Sponges cannot make their own food and must eat other organisms. That's why they are classified as animals.

Figure 3 *Sponges come in a variety of shapes, sizes, and colors.*

Giant barrel sponge

Kinds of Sponges All sponges live in water, and most are found in the ocean. As shown in **Figure 3,** they come in beautiful colors and a variety of shapes. One of the largest sponges is shaped like a giant pillow and may reach 2 m across.

Most sponges have a skeleton made of needlelike splinters called *spicules,* as shown in **Figure 4.** Spicules come in many shapes, from simple, straight needles to curved rods and complex star shapes. The skeleton supports the body of the sponge and helps protect it from predators.

Sponges are divided into classes according to the type of spicules they have. The largest class of sponges contain spicules made of silicate, the material we use to make glass. Bath sponges are similar to silica sponges, but they lack spicules. Instead of spicules, they have a skeleton made of a special protein called *spongin.* That is why they are soft. Another group of sponges have spicules made of calcium carbonate, the material that makes up the shells of oysters and other shellfish.

Re-form and Replace If a sponge's body is broken apart by being forced through a sieve, the separate cells will come back together and re-form the same sponge. In addition, new sponges can form from pieces broken off another sponge. Unlike most animals, a sponge can also replace its body parts, or *regenerate.*

Tube sponge

Figure 4 *This is the skeleton of a glass sponge.*

How Do Sponges Eat?   Sponges belong to the phylum Porifera. The name refers to the thousands of holes, or *pores*, on the outside of sponges. The sponge sweeps water into its body through these pores. Inside the body, cells called *collar cells* filter food particles and microorganisms from the water. The rest of the water flows into a central cavity and out a hole at the top of the sponge, like smoke going up a chimney. The hole at the top is called the *osculum*. **Figure 5** shows this process.

Sponges don't have a gut. Instead, each collar cell digests its own particles of food. No other animal has anything like collar cells.

Figure 5 *A sponge filters particles of food from water using collar cells and then pumps the water out the osculum. A sponge can filter up to 22 L of water a day.*

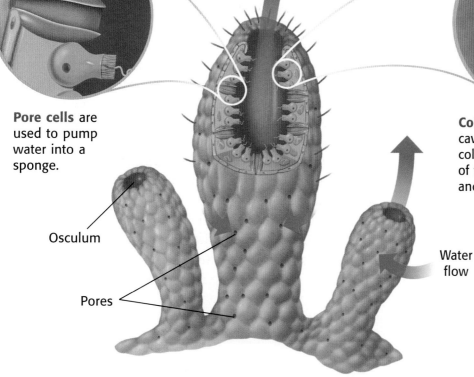

Pore cells are used to pump water into a sponge.

Osculum

Pores

Collar cells line the central cavity of a sponge. Each collar cell filters particles of food from the water and digests them.

Water flow

REVIEW

1. Why are collar cells important in classifying sponges as animals?

2. What is a coelom?

3. **Interpreting Graphics**   Does the animal shown at right have radial symmetry, bilateral symmetry, or no symmetry? Explain your answer.

Jellyfish

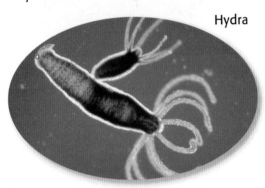
Hydra

Figure 6 *These three organisms are cnidarians. Why are they in the same phylum?*

Sea anemone

Cnidarians

Take a look at the organisms shown in **Figure 6.** They look very different, but all of these animals belong to the phylum Cnidaria (ni DER ee uh).

The word *cnidaria* comes from the Greek word for "nettle." Nettles are plants that release stinging barbs into the skin. Cnidarians do the same. All cnidarians have stinging cells. Do you know anyone who has been stung by a jellyfish? It is a very painful experience!

Cnidarians are more complex than sponges. Cnidarians have complex tissues, a gut for digesting food, and a nervous system. However, some species of cnidarians do share a characteristic with sponges. If the cells of the body are separated, they can come back together to form the cnidarian.

The Medusa and the Polyp Cnidarians come in two forms, the medusa and the polyp. They are shown in **Figure 7.** The **medusa** looks like a mushroom with tentacles streaming down from below. A well-known medusa is the jellyfish. As a medusa's body, or bell, contracts and relaxes, the medusa swims through the water.

The other cnidarian body form is the **polyp.** Polyps are shaped like vases and usually live attached to a surface.

Some cnidarians are polyps and medusas at different times in their life. But most cnidarians spend their life as a polyp.

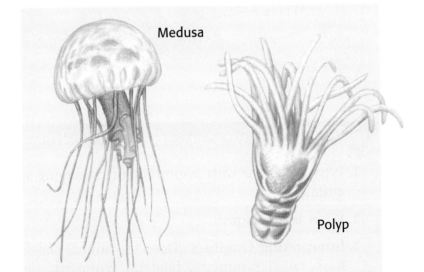
Medusa

Polyp

Figure 7 *Both the medusa and the polyp have radial symmetry. Can you see why?*

Kinds of Cnidarians There are three classes of cnidarians: hydras, jellyfish, and sea anemones and corals. Hydras are common cnidarians that live in fresh water. They spend their entire life in the polyp form. Jellyfish spend most of their life as a medusa.

Sea anemones and corals are polyps all their life. They look like brightly colored flowers. Corals are tiny cnidarians that live in colonies. These colonies build huge skeletons of calcium carbonate. Each new generation of corals builds on top of the last generation. Over thousands of years, these tiny animals build massive underwater reefs. Coral reefs can be found in warm tropical waters throughout the world.

Catching Lunch All cnidarians have long tentacles covered with special stinging cells. When a small fish or other organism brushes against the tentacles of a cnidarian, hundreds of stinging cells fire into the organism and release a paralyzing toxin. Each stinging cell uses water pressure to fire a tiny barbed spear called a *nematocyst* (NEEM uh toh SIST). **Figure 8** shows a nematocyst before and after firing.

Figure 8 *Each stinging cell contains a nematocyst.*

Before firing Coiled inside each stinging cell is a tiny barbed harpoon.

After firing When the nematocyst fires, the long barbed strand ejects into the water. Larger barbs also cover the base of the strand.

You've Got Some Nerve Cnidarians have a simple network of nerve cells called a *nerve net*. The nerve net controls the movements of the body and the tentacles.

A medusa has a *nerve ring* in the center of its nerve net. This ring of nerve cells coordinates the swimming of a jellyfish in the same way that our spinal cord coordinates walking. The nerve ring is not a brain, however. Cnidarians do not think or plan in the way that more-complex animals do.

✓Self-Check

Medusas have a nerve ring, but polyps do not. How does the way medusas move explain their more complex nervous system? *(See page 636 to check your answer.)*

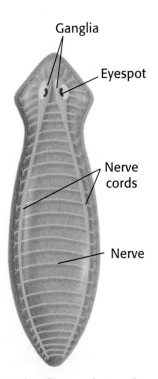

Flatworms

When you think of worms, you probably think of the earthworms that you see in the soil or use to bait fish hooks. But there are many other types of worms, and most of them are too tiny to see. The simplest group of worms are the flatworms.

Look at the flatworm shown in **Figure 9.** Unlike the invertebrates you have studied so far, flatworms have bilateral symmetry. Most flatworms also have a clearly defined head and two large, unblinking eyespots. Even though the eyespots cannot focus, a flatworm knows the direction that light is coming from. A flatworm also has two earlike bumps on each side of its head. These are *sensory lobes* and are used for detecting food.

The flatworm's head, eyespots, and sensory lobes are clues that it has a brain for processing information. **Figure 10** shows a diagram of the nervous system of a flatworm.

Figure 9 *This flatworm is called a planarian. It has a well-developed head with eyespots and sensory lobes.*

Kinds of Flatworms Flatworms are divided into three classes. The big-eyed flatworms we have been discussing are called *planarians*. Most of these flatworms are small; their length is less than the length of a fingernail. They live in water and on land. Most planarians are predators. They eat other animals or parts of other animals. They may actively stalk and attack other tiny animals or eat dead creatures. These flatworms have a working gut, but food and waste go in and out by the same route.

The two other groups of flatworms are *flukes* and *tapeworms*. A fluke is shown in **Figure 11.** These animals are parasites. A **parasite** is an organism that feeds on another living creature, usually without killing it. The victim is called the **host.** Parasites may live outside or inside their host. Most flukes and all tapeworms find their way inside the bodies of other animals, where they live and reproduce. Fertilized eggs pass out of the host's body with the body's waste. If these fertilized eggs end up in drinking water or on food, they can be eaten by another host, where they will develop into a new fluke or tapeworm.

Figure 10 *This figure shows the nervous system of a flatworm. Slender nerves connect two parallel nerve cords. Ganglia in the head make up a primitive brain.*

Ganglia

Eyespot

Nerve cords

Nerve

Figure 11 *Flukes use suckers to attach to their host.*

Flukes and tapeworms look different from planarians. They have a tiny head without eyespots or sensory lobes. They have special suckers and hooks for attaching to the host. Those flatworms that live inside the gut of their host have special skin that resists digestion by the stomach enzymes of the host. Tapeworms are so specialized that they have no gut at all. These creatures simply absorb nutrients from the intestines of their host. **Figure 12** shows a human fish tapeworm.

Roundworms

Roundworms, or nematodes, are round when viewed in cross section and are long and slender. Like other worms, they have bilateral symmetry. Most species of roundworms are tiny. A single rotten apple lying on the ground in an orchard could contain 100,000 roundworms. These tiny creatures break down the dead tissues of plants and animals and help build rich soils. **Figure 13** shows a roundworm.

Roundworms have a simple nervous system, like that of flatworms. A ring of ganglia forms a primitive brain, and parallel nerve cords run the length of their body.

Roundworms have a more complex digestive system than other simple invertebrates. Unlike flatworms, which eat and pass waste from the same opening, roundworms have both a mouth and an anus.

Most roundworms are parasites. Roundworms that infect humans include pinworms and hookworms. Another roundworm, *Trichinella spiralis,* is passed from infected pork to humans and causes trichinosis, a severe illness. Cooking pork thoroughly will kill the roundworms. The most dangerous roundworms live in the tropics.

Figure 12 *Tapeworms can reach enormous sizes. Some can grow up to 13 m long—longer than a school bus!*

Figure 13 *Roundworms have a fluid-filled body cavity.*

REVIEW

1. What characteristic gives cnidarians their name?

2. What are two characteristics of flatworms that make them different from cnidarians?

3. **Analyzing Relationships** Both predators and parasites live off the tissues of other animals. Explain the difference between a predator and a parasite.

Mollusks and Annelid Worms

Have you ever eaten clam chowder or calamari? Have you ever seen worms on the sidewalk after it rains? If you have, then you have encountered the invertebrates discussed in this section—mollusks and annelid worms. These invertebrates are more complex than the invertebrates you have read about so far. Mollusks and annelid worms have a coelom and a circulatory system. And they have more-complex nervous systems than those of the flatworms and roundworms.

Earthworm

Mollusks

The phylum Mollusca includes snails, slugs, clams, oysters, squids, and octopuses. The mollusks are the second largest phylum of animals. Most mollusks are in three classes: *gastropods* (slugs and snails), *bivalves* (clams and other two-shelled shellfish), and *cephalopods* (squids and octopuses). **Figure 14** shows some of the variety of mollusks.

Snails

Clam

Squid

Figure 14 *A snail, a clam, and a squid are all mollusks. Snails are gastropods; clams are bivalves; and squids are cephalopods.*

Most mollusks live in the ocean, but some live in fresh-water habitats. Other mollusks, such as slugs and snails, have adapted to life on land.

Mollusks range in size from 1 mm long snails to the giant squid, which can reach up to 18 m in length. Most mollusks move slowly, but some squids can swim up to 40 km/h and leap more than 4 m above the water.

MATH BREAK

Speeding Squid

If a squid is swimming at 30 km/h, how far can it go in 1 minute?

How Do You Know a Mollusk When You See One? A snail, a clam, and a squid look quite different from one another. Yet on closer inspection, the bodies of all mollusks are almost the same. The body parts shared by mollusks are described in **Figure 15.**

Figure 15 *A mollusk has a soft body, usually covered by a shell. All mollusks also have a foot, a visceral mass, and a mantle.*

Foot The most obvious feature of a mollusk is a broad, muscular *foot.* A mollusk uses its foot to move. In gastropods, the foot secretes mucus that it slides along.

Visceral mass Above the foot is a *visceral mass,* which contains the gills, gut, and other organs. The visceral (VIS uhr uhl) mass is located in a mollusk's coelom.

Mantle The visceral mass, the sides of the foot, and the head are covered by a layer of tissue called the *mantle.* The mantle protects the body of mollusks that do not have a shell.

Shell In most mollusks, the outside of the mantle secretes a *shell.* The shell protects the mollusk from predators and keeps land mollusks from drying out.

How Do Mollusks Eat? Each type of mollusk has its own way of eating. Clams and other bivalves sit in one place and filter tiny plants, bacteria, and other particles from the water around them. Snails and slugs eat with a ribbonlike tongue covered with curved teeth, called a *radula* (RAJ oo luh). **Figure 16** shows a close-up of a slug's radula. Slugs and snails use the radula to scrape algae off rocks, chunks of tissue from seaweed, or pieces from the leaves of plants. Predatory snails and slugs often have large teeth on their radula that they use to attack their prey. And parasitic snails pierce their victims much as a mosquito does. Octopuses and squids use tentacles to grab their prey and place it in their powerful jaws, just as we use our fingers to place food in our mouth.

Figure 16 *Notice the rows of teeth on this slug's radula. The radula is used to scrape food from surfaces.*

Have a Heart Unlike simpler invertebrates, mollusks have a circulatory system. Most mollusks have an **open circulatory system.** In this system, a simple heart pumps blood through blood vessels that empty into spaces in the animal's body called *sinuses.* This is very different from our own circulatory system, which is a **closed circulatory system.** In a closed circulatory system, a heart circulates blood through a network of blood vessels that form a closed loop. Cephalopods (squids and octopuses) also have a closed circulatory system, although it is much simpler than ours.

It's a Brain! Mollusks have complex ganglia. In most mollusks, these ganglia occur throughout the body. Mollusks have ganglia that control breathing, ganglia that move the foot, and ganglia that control digestion.

Cephalopods, like the one in **Figure 17,** have a more complex nervous system than the other mollusks have. In fact, octopuses and squids have the most advanced nervous system of all invertebrates. They have a brain, where all of their ganglia are connected. Not surprisingly, these animals are the smartest of all invertebrates. Octopuses, for example, can learn to navigate a maze and can distinguish between different shapes and colors. If they are given bricks or stones, they will build a cave to hide in.

Figure 17 *An octopus has a large brain. The brain coordinates the movement of its eight long arms.*

Its eyes are as big as basketballs! What is it? Check it out on page 353.

REVIEW

1. What are the four main parts of a mollusk's body?

2. What is the difference between an open circulatory system and a closed circulatory system?

3. **Analyzing Relationships** What two features do cephalopods share with humans that other mollusks do not?

Annelid Worms

You have probably seen earthworms, like the one in **Figure 18.** Earthworms belong to the phylum Annelida. Annelid worms are often called segmented worms because their body has *segments*. **Segments** are identical, or almost identical, repeating body parts. The earthworm in Figure 18 clearly shows segments.

These worms are much more complex than the flatworms and roundworms discussed in the last section. Annelid worms have a coelom and a closed circulatory system. Annelid worms have a nervous system that includes ganglia in each segment and a brain in the head. A nerve cord runs the entire length of the worm and connects the brain and the ganglia.

Kinds of Annelid Worms The annelid worms include three classes: earthworms, bristle worms, and leeches. Annelid worms live in salt water, in fresh water, or on land. They may scavenge anything edible, or they may prey on other organisms as predators or as parasites.

More than Just Bait Earthworms are the most common annelid worms. An earthworm has 100 to 175 segments, most of which are identical. Some segments are specialized for eating and reproduction. Earthworms eat soil. They break down organic matter in the soil and excrete wastes called *castings*. Castings increase the fertility of soil by providing nutrients in a form that plants can use. Earthworms also improve the soil by burrowing tunnels through it. These tunnels allow air and water to reach deep into the soil.

Earthworms have stiff bristles on the outside of their body to help them move. The bristles hold one part of the worm in place while the other part pushes through the soil.

Tail

Figure 18 *Except for the head, tail, and reproductive segments, all the segments of this earthworm are identical. What is the total number of segments?*

Reproductive segments

Head

APPLY

A friend of yours is worried because his garden is full of earthworms. He wants to find a way to get rid of the worms. Do you think this is a good idea? Why? Write a letter to your friend explaining what you think he should do.

Figure 19 *This bristle worm feeds by filtering particles from the water with its bristles. Can you see the segments on this worm?*

Bristles Can Be Beautiful If there were a beauty contest for worms, bristle worms would win. These remarkable worms come in many varieties and in brilliant colors. **Figure 19** shows a bristle worm. All bristle worms live in water. Some burrow through soggy sand and mud, eating whatever small creatures and particles they meet. Others crawl along the bottom, eating mollusks and other small animals.

Blood Suckers and More Leeches are known mostly as parasites that suck other animals' blood. This is true of some leeches, but not all. Other leeches are scavengers that eat dead animals. Still others are predators that prey on insects, slugs, and snails. Leeches that are parasites feed on the blood of other animals.

But leeches aren't all bad. Until the twentieth century, doctors regularly used leeches in medical treatments. Doctors attached leeches to a sick person to drain "bad" blood from the body. Although this practice is not accepted today, leeches are still used in medicine. After surgery, doctors sometimes use leeches to prevent dangerous swelling near a wound, as shown in **Figure 20.** Leeches also make a chemical that keeps blood from forming clots. Modern doctors give heart attack patients medicines that contain this chemical to keep blood clots from blocking arteries.

Explore

Using the library and the Internet, research the use of leeches in medicine. Make a poster describing your findings.

Figure 20
Modern doctors sometimes use leeches to reduce swelling after surgery.

REVIEW

1. Name the three types of annelid worms. How are they alike? How are they different?

2. **Making Inferences** Why would a chemical that keeps blood from clotting be beneficial to leeches?

3. **Analyzing Relationships** How are annelid worms different from flatworms and roundworms? What characteristics do all worms share?

Arthropods

Fiddler crab

They have lived here for hundreds of millions of years and have adapted to nearly all environments. An acre of land contains millions of them. You know them by more common names, such as insects, spiders, crabs, and centipedes. They are *arthropods,* the largest group of organisms on Earth.

Seventy-five percent of all animal species are arthropods. The world population of humans is about 6 billion. Biologists estimate the world population of arthropods to be about a billion billion.

Characteristics of Arthropods

All arthropods share four characteristics: jointed limbs, a segmented body with specialized parts, an exoskeleton, and a well-developed nervous system.

Jointed Limbs Jointed limbs give arthropods their name. *Arthro* means "joint," and *pod* means "foot." Jointed limbs are arms, legs, or other similar body parts that bend at joints. Jointed limbs allow arthropods to move easily.

Segmented and Specialized Like annelid worms, arthropods are s*egmented.* In some arthropods, such as the centipedes, nearly every segment is identical. Only the segments at the head and tail are different from the rest. Most other species of arthropods have segments that include very specialized parts, such as wings, antennae, gills, pincers, and claws. Many of these special parts form during the animal's development, when two or three segments grow together to form a *head,* a *thorax,* and an *abdomen.* These parts are labeled on the grasshopper pictured in **Figure 21.**

Mosquito

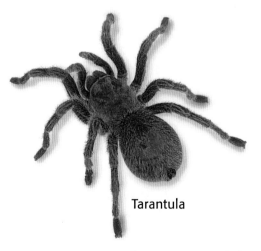
Tarantula

Figure 21 *The segments of this grasshopper fused together as the embryo grew to form a head, a thorax, and an abdomen.*

Head

Thorax

Abdomen

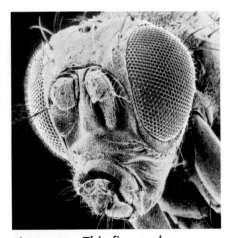

Figure 22 *This figure shows the compound eyes of a fruit fly. A compound eye consists of many individual light-sensitive cells that work together.*

Knights in Shining . . . Chitin? Arthropods have a hard **exoskeleton,** an external skeleton made of protein and a special substance called *chitin* (KIE tin). The exoskeleton does some of the same things an internal skeleton does. It provides a stiff frame that supports the animal's body. The exoskeleton also allows the animal to move. All of the muscles attach to different parts of the skeleton. When the muscles contract, they move the exoskeleton, which moves the parts of the animal.

But the exoskeleton also does things that internal skeletons don't do well. The exoskeleton acts like a suit of armor to protect an arthropod's internal organs and muscles. And the chitinous armor of arthropods allows them to live on land without drying out.

They've Got Smarts All arthropods have a head and a well-developed brain. The brain coordinates information from many sense organs, including eyes and bristles on the exoskeleton. Bristles sense movement, vibration, pressure, and chemicals. The eyes of some arthropods are very simple; they can detect light but cannot form an image. But most arthropods have compound eyes, which allow them to see images, although not as well as we do. A **compound eye** is made of many identical light-sensitive cells, as shown in **Figure 22.**

Kinds of Arthropods

Arthropods are classified according to the kinds of body parts they have. You can also tell the difference between arthropods by looking at the number of legs, eyes, and antennae they have. **Antennae** are feelers that respond to touch, taste, and smell.

Centipedes and Millipedes Centipedes and millipedes have a single pair of antennae, jaws called **mandibles,** and a hard *head capsule.* The easiest way to tell a centipede from a millipede is to count the number of legs per segment. Centipedes have one pair of legs per segment. Millipedes have two pairs of legs per segment. Take a look at **Figure 23.** How many legs can you count?

Figure 23 *Centipedes have one pair of legs per segment. The number of legs can range from 30 to 354. Millipedes have two pairs of legs per segment. The record number of legs on a millipede is 752!*

Crustaceans Crustaceans include shrimps, barnacles, crabs, and lobsters. Nearly all crustaceans are aquatic and have *gills* for breathing underwater. All crustaceans have mandibles and two pairs of antennae. Crustaceans have two compound eyes, usually on the end of stalks. The lobster in **Figure 24** shows all of these traits. The double antennae of crustaceans set them apart from all other arthropods.

✔ **Self-Check**

What is the difference between a segmented worm and a centipede? *(See page 636 to check your answer.)*

Figure 24 *A lobster is a crustacean. Notice the gills, mandibles, two compound eyes on the end of stalks, and two pairs of antennae.*

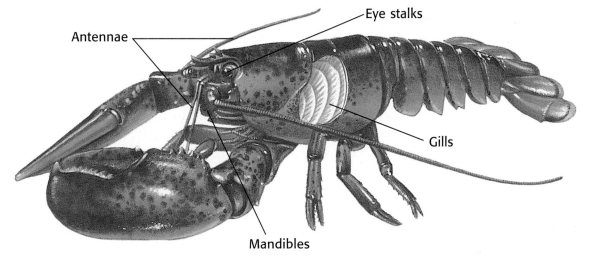

Arachnids Spiders, scorpions, mites, ticks, and daddy long-legs are all arachnids. **Figure 24** shows that an arachnid has two main body parts, the cephalothorax (SEF uh loh THOR aks) and the abdomen. The *cephalothorax* consists of both a head and a thorax and usually has four pairs of walking legs. Arachnids have no antennae and no mandibles. Instead of mandibles, they have special mouthparts called *chelicerae* (kuh LIS uh ree), as illustrated in **Figure 25.** Some chelicerae look like pincers or fangs.

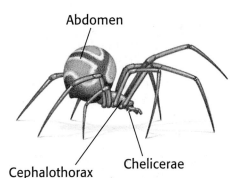

Figure 25 *Arachnids, such as this spider, have two main body parts and special mouthparts called chelicerae.*

The eyes of arachnids are distinctive. While crustaceans and insects have compound eyes, arachnids do not. Spiders, for example, have eight *simple eyes* arranged in two rows at the front of the head. Count the eyes for yourself in **Figure 26.**

Figure 26 *Most people know that spiders have eight legs. But spiders also have eight eyes!*

Several arachnids have painful bites or stings. But the fangs of small garden spiders cannot even pierce human skin. In the United States, just three species of spiders—the black widow and two species of brown spider—have bites poisonous enough to kill a person. However, with proper medical treatment, they are not fatal.

Spiders do not carry diseases and are enormously useful to humans. They kill more insect pests than any other animal, including birds. Spiders eat millions of caterpillars and other pests that ruin crops. They eat moths and beetles, which can ruin our clothes and crops, and they eat flies and mosquitoes, which carry disease.

Ticks live in forests, brushy areas, and even country lawns. **Figure 27** shows an American dog tick. Ticks that bite humans sometimes carry lyme disease, Rocky Mountain spotted fever, encephalitis, and other diseases. Many people wear long pants and hats when going into areas where ticks live, and they check themselves for ticks after being outdoors. Fortunately, most people who are bitten by ticks do not get sick.

Figure 27 American Dog Tick

Insects The largest group of arthropods is insects. If you put all of the insects in the world together, they would weigh more than all other animals combined! **Figure 28** shows some of the wide variety of insects.

Quick **Lab**

Sticky Webs

Some spiders spin webs of sticky silk to trap their prey. Why don't spiders stick to their own webs? This experiment will show you the answer. Place a piece of **tape** on your desk sticky side up. The tape represents a web. Your fingers will represent an insect. Holding the tape in place by the edges, "walk" your fingers across the tape. What happens? Dip your fingers in **cooking oil,** and "walk" them across the tape again. What happens this time? Why? How might this experiment explain why spiders don't get stuck in their webs?

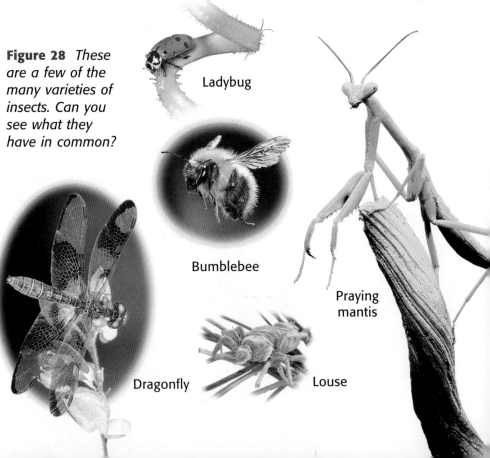

Figure 28 These are a few of the many varieties of insects. Can you see what they have in common?

Atlas silk moth

Ladybug

Bumblebee

Praying mantis

Dragonfly

Louse

Insects Are Everywhere (Almost) Insects live on land, in every freshwater environment, and at the edges of the sea. The only place on Earth insects do not live is in the ocean.

Sixty percent of flowering plant species cannot reproduce without insects. Most flowering plants depend on bees, butterflies, and other insects to carry pollen from one plant to another. Farmers depend on insects to pollinate hundreds of fruit crops, such as apples, cherries, tomatoes, and pumpkins.

Many insects are also pests. Fleas, lice, mosquitoes, and flies burrow into our flesh, suck our blood, or carry diseases. Plant-eating insects consume up to one-third of crops in this country, despite the application of pesticides.

Insect Bodies An insect's body has three parts: the head, the thorax, and the abdomen, as shown in **Figure 29.** On the head, insects have one pair of antennae and two compound eyes. They also have three pairs of mouthparts, including one pair of mandibles. The thorax is made of three segments, each with one pair of legs.

In many insects, the second and third segments of the thorax have a pair of wings. Some insects have no wings, and some have two pairs of wings.

Insect Development As an insect develops from an egg to an adult, it changes form. This process is called **metamorphosis.** There are two main types of metamorphosis, incomplete and complete. Primitive insects, such as grasshoppers and cockroaches, go through incomplete metamorphosis. In this metamorphosis there are only three stages: egg, nymph, and adult, as shown in **Figure 30.**

BRAIN FOOD

A cockroach can live for a week without its head! It finally dies of thirst because it has no mouth to drink water with.

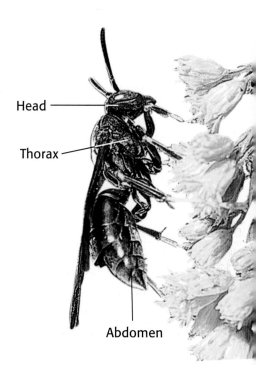

Head

Thorax

Abdomen

Figure 29 *Wasps have the same body parts as all other insects.*

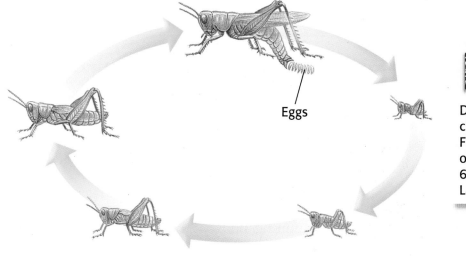

Eggs

Figure 30 *In incomplete metamorphosis, the larvae, called nymphs, look like smaller adults.*

LabBook

Does a cricket like cold climates? Find out on page 609 of your LabBook.

Changing Form—Complete Metamorphosis

In complete metamorphosis, there are four stages: egg, larva, pupa, and adult. Butterflies, beetles, flies, bees, wasps, and ants go through this process. In complete metamorphosis, the larva looks very different from the adult.

4 The adult insect splits open its pupal case and emerges. The adult butterfly pumps blood into its wings until they are full-sized. The butterfly is then strong enough to fly.

1 Eggs are laid by an adult. The embryo forms inside the egg.

3 After its final molt, the caterpillar forms a cocoon and becomes a pupa. During this stage, the butterfly is inactive. All the larval body parts are replaced by adult body parts. Depending on the insect, the pupal stage may last only a few days or several months.

2 A larva hatches from the egg. In butterflies and moths, the larvae are called caterpillars. The caterpillar has special body parts that allow it to eat leaves. It eats constantly and grows rapidly. As the caterpillar grows, it sheds its outer skin several times. This process is called molting.

REVIEW

1. Name the four kinds of arthropods. How are their bodies different?

2. What is the difference between complete metamorphosis and incomplete metamorphosis?

3. **Applying Concepts** Suppose you have found an arthropod in a swimming pool. The creature has compound eyes, antennae, and wings. Is it a crustacean? Why or why not?

Echinoderms

The last major phylum of invertebrates is Echinodermata. All echinoderms (ee KI noh DUHRMS) are marine animals. They include sea stars (starfish), sea urchins, sea lilies, sea cucumbers, brittle stars, and sand dollars. The smallest echinoderms are only a few millimeters across. The largest is a sea star that grows to 1 m in diameter.

Brittle star

Echinoderms live on the sea floor in all parts of the world's oceans. Some echinoderms prey on oysters and other shellfish, some are scavengers, and others scrape algae off rocky surfaces.

NEW TERMS
endoskeleton
water vascular system

OBJECTIVES
- Describe three main characteristics of echinoderms.
- Describe the water vascular system.

Sea star

Feather star

Spiny Skinned

The name *echinoderm* means "spiny skinned." The surface of the animal is not the spiny part, however. The body of the echinoderm contains an **endoskeleton,** an internal skeleton similar to the kind that vertebrates have. The hard, bony skeleton is usually covered with spines. The spines may be no more than sharp bumps, as in many sea stars. Or they may be long and pointed, as in sea urchins. All of the spines are covered by the outer skin of the animal.

Bilateral or Radial?

Adult echinoderms have radial symmetry. But sea stars, sea urchins, sand dollars, and other echinoderms all develop from larvae with bilateral symmetry. **Figure 31** shows a sea urchin larva. Notice how the two sides are similar.

When echinoderm embryos first begin to develop, they form a mouth in the same way the embryos of vertebrates do. This is one of the reasons biologists think that vertebrates are more closely related to echinoderms than to other invertebrates.

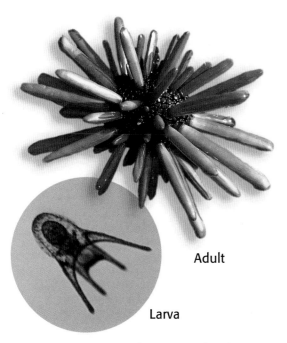

Adult

Larva

Figure 31 *The sea urchin larva has bilateral symmetry. The adult sea urchin has radial symmetry.*

The Nervous System

All echinoderms have a simple nervous system similar to that of a jellyfish. Around the mouth is a circle of nerve fibers called the *nerve ring*. In sea stars, a *radial nerve* runs from the nerve ring to the tip of each arm, as shown in **Figure 32.** The radial nerves control the movements of the sea star's arms.

At the tip of each arm is a simple eye. This is a sea star's only sense organ. The rest of the body is covered with cells that are sensitive to touch and to chemical signals in the water.

Water Vascular System

One system that is unique to echinoderms is the **water vascular system.** This system uses water pumps to help the animal move, eat, breathe, and sense its environment. **Figure 33** shows the water vascular system of a sea star. Notice how water pressure from the water vascular system is used for a variety of functions.

Figure 32 The Nervous System of a Sea Star

Water enters the system through holes in a flat plate on top of the sea star. This plate is called the **sieve plate.**

The water flows through a tube to the **ring canal** around the mouth.

From the ring canal, the water flows into **radial canals** in the arms.

Each tube foot is connected to a bulb called an **ampulla.** The ampulla regulates fluid pressure so that each tube foot may extend or retract, hang on or let go. The movement of the tube feet and of the arm together move a sea star slowly along the bottom of the sea.

Figure 33 *Sea stars and all echinoderms have a water vascular system that allows them to move, eat, and breathe.*

The radial canals connect to dozens of tiny suckers called **tube feet.** These tube feet are used to move and to capture food. Oxygen enters and wastes leave through the thin walls of the tube feet.

Kinds of Echinoderms

Scientists divide echinoderms into several classes. Sea stars are the most familiar echinoderms, and they make up one class. But there are three classes of echinoderms that may not be as familiar to you.

Brittle Stars and Basket Stars The brittle stars and basket stars look like sea stars with long slender arms. These delicate creatures tend to be smaller than sea stars. **Figure 34** shows a basket star.

Sea Urchins and Sand Dollars Sea urchins and sand dollars make up another class of echinoderms. Members of this class are round, and their skeletons form a solid internal shell. They have no arms, but they use their tube feet to move in the same way as sea stars. Some sea urchins also walk on their spines. Sea urchins feed on algae they scrape from the surface of rocks and other objects and chew with special teeth. Sand dollars burrow halfway into soft sand or mud, as shown in **Figure 35,** and eat tiny particles of food they find in the sand.

Sea Cucumbers Like sea urchins, sea cucumbers lack arms. A sea cucumber has a soft, leathery body. Unlike sea urchins, sea cucumbers are long and have a worm-like shape. Like other echinoderms, they move with tube feet. **Figure 36** shows a sea cucumber.

Figure 34 A Basket Star

Figure 35 *Sand dollars burrow in the sand.*

Figure 36 A Sea Cucumber

REVIEW

1. How are sea cucumbers different from other echinoderms?

2. What is the path taken by water as it flows through the parts of the water vascular system?

3. **Applying Concepts** How are echinoderms different from other invertebrates?

Chapter Highlights

SECTION 1

Vocabulary

invertebrate *(p. 326)*

bilateral symmetry *(p. 326)*

radial symmetry *(p. 326)*

asymmetrical *(p. 326)*

ganglia *(p. 327)*

gut *(p. 327)*

coelom *(p. 327)*

medusa *(p. 330)*

polyp *(p. 330)*

parasite *(p. 332)*

host *(p. 332)*

Section Notes

- Invertebrates are animals without a backbone.
- Most animals have radial symmetry or bilateral symmetry.

- Unlike other animals, sponges have no symmetry.
- A coelom is a space inside the body. The gut hangs inside the coelom.
- Ganglia are clumps of nerves that help control the parts of the body.
- Sponges have special cells called collar cells to digest their food.
- Cnidarians have special stinging cells to catch their prey.
- Cnidarians have two body forms, the polyp and the medusa.
- Tapeworms and flukes are parasitic flatworms.

Labs

Porifera's Porosity *(p. 608)*

SECTION 2

Vocabulary

open circulatory system *(p. 336)*

closed circulatory system *(p. 336)*

segment *(p. 337)*

Section Notes

- All mollusks have a foot, a visceral mass, and a mantle. Most mollusks also have a shell.
- Mollusks and annelid worms have both a coelom and a circulatory system.
- In an open circulatory system, the heart pumps blood through vessels into spaces called sinuses. In a closed circulatory system, the blood is pumped through a closed network of vessels.
- Segments are identical or nearly identical repeating body parts.

☑ Skills Check

Math Concepts

SPEED AND DISTANCE If a snail is moving at 30 cm/h, how far can it travel in 1 minute? There are 60 minutes in 1 hour:

$$\frac{30 \text{ cm}}{60 \text{ min}} = 0.5 \text{ cm/min}$$

In 1 minute the snail will travel 0.5 cm.

Visual Understanding

METAMORPHOSIS Some insects go through incomplete metamorphosis, and some go through complete metamorphosis. Look at the illustrations on pages 343 and 344 to see the difference between these two types of metamorphosis.

SECTION 3

Vocabulary

exoskeleton *(p. 340)*

compound eye *(p. 340)*

antennae *(p. 340)*

mandible *(p. 340)*

metamorphosis *(p. 343)*

Section Notes

- Seventy-five percent of all animals are arthropods.

- The four main characteristics of arthropods are jointed limbs, an exoskeleton, segments, and a well-developed nervous system.

- Arthropods are classified by the type of body parts they have.

- The four kinds of arthropods are centipedes and millipedes, crustaceans, arachnids, and insects.

- Insects can undergo complete or simple metamorphosis.

Labs

The Cricket Caper *(p. 609)*

SECTION 4

Vocabulary

endoskeleton *(p. 345)*

water vascular system *(p. 346)*

Section Notes

- Echinoderms are marine animals that have an endoskeleton and a water vascular system.

- Most echinoderms have bilateral symmetry as larvae and radial symmetry as adults.

- The water vascular system allows echinoderms to move around by means of tube feet, which act like suction cups.

- Echinoderms have a simple nervous system consisting of a nerve ring and radial nerves.

---

 internetconnect

go.hrw.com **GO TO:** go.hrw.com

Visit the **HRW** Web site for a variety of learning tools related to this chapter. Just type in the keyword:

KEYWORD: HSTINV

SCILINKS **NSTA** **GO TO:** www.scilinks.org

Visit the **National Science Teachers Association** on-line Web site for Internet resources related to this chapter. Just type in the *sci*LINKS number for more information about the topic:

TOPIC: Sponges   *sci*LINKS NUMBER: HSTL355

TOPIC: Roundworms   *sci*LINKS NUMBER: HSTL360

TOPIC: Mollusks   *sci*LINKS NUMBER: HSTL365

TOPIC: Arthropods   *sci*LINKS NUMBER: HSTL370

Chapter Review

USING VOCABULARY

To complete the following sentences, choose the correct term from each pair of terms listed below:

1. Animals without a backbone are called __?__. (*invertebrates* or *vertebrates*)

2. A sponge uses __?__ to pull water in and releases water out through __?__. (*an osculum* or *pores*)

3. Cnidarians have __?__ symmetry and flatworms have __?__ symmetry. (*radial* or *bilateral*)

4. The shell of a snail is secreted by the __?__. (*radula* or *mantle*)

5. Annelid worms have __?__. (*jointed limbs* or *segments*)

6. An ampulla regulates __?__. (*water pressure in a tube foot* or *blood pressure in a closed circulatory system*)

UNDERSTANDING CONCEPTS

Multiple Choice

7. Invertebrates make up what percentage of all animals?
   a. 4 percent
   b. 50 percent
   c. 85 percent
   d. 97 percent

8. Which of the following describes the body plan of a sponge:
   a. radial symmetry
   b. bilateral symmetry
   c. asymmetry
   d. partial symmetry

9. What cells do sponges have that no other animal has?
   a. blood cells
   b. nerve cells
   c. collar cells
   d. none of the above

10. Which of the following animals do not have ganglia?
    a. annelid worms
    b. cnidarians
    c. flatworms
    d. mollusks

11. Which of the following animals has a coelom?
    a. sponge
    b. cnidarian
    c. flatworm
    d. mollusk

12. Both tapeworms and leeches are
    a. annelid worms.
    b. parasites.
    c. flatworms.
    d. predators.

13. Some arthropods do not have
    a. jointed limbs.
    b. an exoskeleton.
    c. antennae.
    d. segments.

14. Echinoderms live
    a. on land.
    b. in fresh water.
    c. in salt water.
    d. All of the above

15. *Echinoderm* means
    a. "jointed limbs."
    b. "spiny skinned."
    c. "endoskeleton."
    d. "shiny tube foot."

16. Echinoderm larvae have
    a. radial symmetry.
    b. bilateral symmetry.
    c. no symmetry.
    d. radial and bilateral symmetry.

Short Answer

17. What is a gut?

18. How are arachnids different from insects?

19. Which animal phylum contains the most species?

20. How does an echinoderm move?

Concept Mapping

21. Use the following terms to create a concept map: insect, sponges, sea anemone, invertebrates, arachnid, sea cucumber, crustacean, centipede, cnidarians, arthropods, echinoderms.

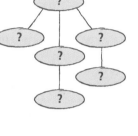

CRITICAL THINKING AND PROBLEM SOLVING

Write one or two sentences to answer the following questions:

22. You have discovered a strange new animal that has bilateral symmetry, a coelom, and nerves. Will this animal be classified in the Cnidaria phylum? Why or why not?

23. Unlike other mollusks, cephalopods can move rapidly. Based on what you know about the body parts of mollusks, why do you think cephalopods have this ability?

24. Roundworms, flatworms, and annelid worms belong to different phyla. Why aren't all the worms grouped in the same phyla?

MATH IN SCIENCE

25. If 75 percent of all animals are arthropods and 40 percent of all arthropods are beetles, what percentage of all animals are beetles?

INTERPRETING GRAPHICS

Below is an evolutionary tree showing how the different phyla of animals may be related to one another. The "trunk" of the tree is on the left. Use the tree to answer the questions that follow.

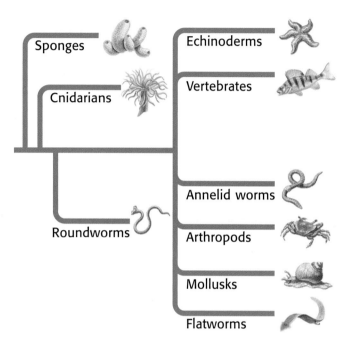

26. Which phylum is the oldest?

27. Are mollusks more closely related to roundworms or flatworms?

28. What phylum is most closely related to the vertebrates?

NOW What Do You Think?

Take a minute to review your answers to the ScienceLog questions on page 325. Have your answers changed? If necessary, revise your answers based on what you have learned since you began this chapter.

WATER BEARS

You're alive and you know it, but how? Well, eating, breathing, and moving around are all pretty sure signs of life. And once something stops eating or breathing, the end is near. Or is it? Oddly enough, this doesn't seem to be the case for one phylum of invertebrates–the water bear.

Grin and Bear It

When conditions get really rough—too hot, too cold, but mostly too dry to survive—a water bear will shut down its body processes. It's similar to a bear going into hiberna- tion, but it is even more extreme. When a water bear can't find water, it dries itself out and forms a sugar that coats its cells. Scientists think this may keep the water bear's cells from breaking down, and it may be the key to its survival.

During this hibernation-like state, called *cryptobiosis* (CRIP toh bie OH sis), the water bear doesn't eat, move, or breathe. And amazingly, it doesn't die either. Once you add water, the water bear will come right back to normal life!

Water Bear

Hard to Put a Finger On

Officially called tardigrades (TAHR di graydz), water bears have been difficult to classify. But the 700 different species of water bears are probably most closely related to arthropods. Most make their homes on wet mosses and lichens. Some water bears feed on nematodes (a tiny, unsegmented worm) and rotifers (a tiny wormlike or spherical animal). Most feed on the fluids from mosses found near their homes.

From the tropics to the Arctic, the world is full of water bears. None are much larger than a grain of sand, but all have a slow, stomping walk. Some tardi- grades live as deep as the bottom of the ocean, more than 4,700 m below sea level. Other water bears live at eleva- tions of 6,600 m above sea level, well above the tree line. It is a wonder how water bears can withstand the range of temperatures found in these places, from 151°C to –270°C.

On Your Own

▶ What do you think people can learn from an organism like the water bear? Write down at least one reason why it is worthwhile to study these special creatures.

EYE ON THE ENVIRONMENT

Sizable Squid

"Before my eyes was a horrible monster . . . It swam crossways in the direction of the *Nautilus* with great speed, watching us with its enormous staring green eyes. The monster's mouth, a horned beak like a parrot's, opened and shut vertically." So wrote Jules Verne in his science-fiction story *Twenty Thousand Leagues Under the Sea.* But what was this horrible monster that was about to attack the submarine *Nautilus*? Believe it or not, it was a creature that actually exists—a giant squid!

▲ *This giant squid was already dead when it was caught in a fishing net off the coast of New Zealand.*

Squid Facts

As the largest of all invertebrates, giant squids range from 8 m to 25 m long and weigh as much as 2,000 kg. It's hard to know for sure, though, because no one has ever studied a living giant squid. Scientists have studied only dead or dying giant squids that have washed ashore or have been trapped in fishing nets.

Giant squids are very similar to their much smaller relatives. They have a torpedo-shaped body, two tentacles, eight arms, a mantle, a funnel, and a beak. All their body parts are much larger, though! A giant squid's eyes, for instance, may be as large as a volleyball! And like adult squids of smaller species, giant squids feed not only on fish but also on smaller squids. Given the size of giant squids, it's hard to imagine that they have any enemies in the ocean, but they do.

A Hungry Enemy

Weighing in at 20 tons, toothed sperm whales eat giant squids. How do we know this? As many as 10,000 squid beaks have been found in the stomach of a single sperm whale. The hard beaks of giant squids are indigestible. It seems that giant squids are a regular meal for sperm whales. Yet this meal can result in some battle scars. Many whales bear ring marks on their forehead and fins that match the size of the suckers found on giant squids.

Fact or Fiction?

▶ Read Chapter 18 of Jules Verne's *Twenty Thousand Leagues Under the Sea,* and then try to find other stories about squids. Write your own story about a giant squid, and share it with the class.

15 Fishes, Amphibians, and Reptiles

Would You Believe...?

In December 1938, a museum curator living on the coast of South Africa made one of her regular visits to a local fishing dock. Marjorie Courtenay Latimer searched the fishermen's catch for interesting fish. There, beneath a pile of rays and sharks, was the shining fin of the most unusual fish she'd ever seen.

The creature was huge—1.5 m long—and the taxicab driver who took Latimer back to the museum was none too happy to have it in his back seat! After checking several books, Latimer decided the fish might be a coelacanth (SEE luh kahnth). Scientists had thought that coelacanths went extinct with the dinosaurs, about 70 million years ago!

Whatever the fish was, it was beginning to rot. To preserve the fish, Latimer had it mounted. But first she drew a quick sketch of the fish and mailed the drawing to a

friend named J.L.B. Smith, an expert on fish. Smith saw right away that the sketch was of a coelacanth.

The preserved fish made Smith and Latimer famous overnight. Latimer's giant fish with thick fins was one of the most fascinating finds of the twentieth century. Smith named the coelacanth *Latimeria* in his friend's honor.

Marjorie Courtenay Latimer discovered a living coelacanth.

What Do You Think?

In your ScienceLog, try to answer the following questions based on what you already know:

1. What does it mean to say an animal is coldblooded?

2. What is the difference between a reptile and an amphibian?

Unscrambling an Egg

The embryos of fish, amphibians, and reptiles all develop in eggs. Fish and amphibians lay their eggs in water or in very moist areas, but most reptiles lay their eggs on dry land. Modern reptiles have eggs with shells. The shells may be hard or leathery, but the eggs are similar to the eggs that birds have. In this activity, you'll uncover the parts of an egg with a shell. What you learn about chicken eggs will also be true for most reptile eggs.

Procedure

1. Get a **hard-boiled chicken egg** from your teacher.

2. Using a **pencil,** draw an outline of your egg on a **piece of paper.**

3. Gently crack the egg, and peel away the shell. Look for a thin membrane between the shell and the white, and look for an air space on the larger end of the egg. Draw all the parts of the egg as you take it apart.

4. Use a **knife** to carefully cut the egg in half lengthwise. Look for a very thin membrane between the white and the yolk. Add the parts you see to your egg diagram.

Analysis

5. Compare your diagram with the illustration below. Did you find all the parts? Label your diagram with the names of the parts.

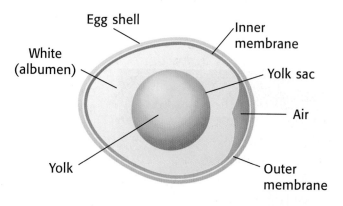

6. Why do you think there is an air space in the egg?

7. Why do you think hard-shelled eggs helped reptiles adapt to life on land?

8. Would the parts be easier or harder to find in a raw egg? Why?

What Are Vertebrates?

NEW TERMS

vertebrate
vertebrae
ectotherm
endotherm

OBJECTIVES

- List the four characteristics of chordates.
- Describe the main characteristics of vertebrates.
- Explain the difference between an ectotherm and an endotherm.

Have you ever seen a dinosaur skeleton at a museum? Fossilized dinosaur bones were put back together to show what the animal looked like. Most dinosaur skeletons are huge compared with the skeletons of the humans who view them. But humans have many of the same kinds of bones that dinosaurs had; ours are just smaller. Your backbone is very much like the one in a dinosaur skeleton, as shown in **Figure 1.** Animals with a backbone are called **vertebrates.**

Figure 1 *Humans and dinosaurs are both vertebrates.*

Chordates

Vertebrates belong to the phylum Chordata. Members of this phylum are called *chordates.* Vertebrates make up the largest group of chordates, but there are two other groups of chordates—lancelets and tunicates. These are shown in **Figure 2.** These chordates do not have a backbone or a well-developed head. They are very simple compared with vertebrates. But all three groups share the chordate characteristics.

At some point in their life, all chordates have four special body parts: a *notochord,* a *hollow nerve cord,* *pharyngeal* (fuh RIN jee uhl) *pouches,* and a *tail.* These are shown in **Figure 3** on the next page.

Figure 2 *Both tunicates, like the sea squirts above, and lancelets, shown at right, are marine organisms.*

A stiff but flexible rod called a **notochord** gives the body support. In most vertebrates, the embryo's notochord disappears and a backbone grows in its place.

A **hollow nerve cord** runs along the back and is full of fluid. In vertebrates, this nerve cord is called the *spinal cord,* and it is filled with *spinal fluid.*

Chordates have a **tail** that begins behind the anus. Some chordates have a tail only in the embryo stage.

Pharyngeal pouches are found in all chordate embryos. These develop into gills or other body parts as the embryo matures.

Figure 3 *The chordate characteristics in a lancelet are shown here. All chordates have these four characteristics at some point in their life.*

Getting a Backbone

Most chordates are vertebrates. Vertebrates have many traits that set them apart from the lancelets and tunicates. For example, vertebrates have a backbone. The backbone is a segmented column of bones. These bones are called **vertebrae** (VUHR tuh BRAY). You can see the vertebrae of a human in **Figure 4.** The vertebrae surround the nerve cord and protect it. Vertebrates also have a well-developed head protected by a skull. The skull and vertebrae are made of either cartilage or bone. *Cartilage* is the tough material that the flexible parts of our ears and noses are made of.

The skeletons of all vertebrate embryos are made of cartilage. But as most vertebrates grow, the cartilage is usually replaced by bone. Bone is much harder than cartilage.

Because bone is so hard, it can easily be fossilized. Many fossils of vertebrates have been discovered, and they have provided valuable information about relationships among organisms.

Vertebrae

Figure 4 *The vertebrae interlock to form a strong but flexible column of bone. The backbone protects the spinal cord and supports the rest of the body.*

Figure 5 *Endotherms, such as this grosbeak, can live in very cold places. Feathers and other adaptations help them maintain their body temperature.*

Are Vertebrates Warm or Cold?

Most animals need to stay warm. The chemical reactions that take place in their body cells occur only at certain temperatures. An animal's body temperature cannot be too high or too low. But some animals control their body temperature more than others.

Staying Warm Birds and mammals warm their body by capturing the heat released by the chemical reactions in their cells. Their body temperature stays nearly constant even as the temperature of their environment changes. Animals that maintain a constant body temperature are called **endotherms.** Endotherms are sometimes called *warmblooded* animals. Because they maintain a constant body temperature, endotherms, like the bird in **Figure 5,** can live in cold environments.

Cold Blood? On sunny days, lizards, like the one in **Figure 6,** bask in the sun. As they become warm, they also become more active. They are able to hunt for food and escape predators. But when the temperature drops, lizards slow down.

Lizards and other animals that do not control their body temperature through the chemical reactions of their cells are called **ectotherms.** Their body temperature fluctuates with the temperature of their environment. Nearly all fishes, amphibians, and reptiles are ectotherms. Ectotherms are sometimes called *coldblooded* animals, but their blood may be warm or cool depending on the external temperature.

Figure 6 *Lizards bask in the sun to absorb heat. When they get too warm, they find some shade.*

REVIEW

1. How are vertebrates the same as other chordates? How are they different?

2. Explain the difference between endotherms and ectotherms.

3. **Applying Concepts** Imagine that you have a pet iguana, a type of lizard. You are afraid it is sick because it is not moving very much. The veterinarian tells you to put a heat lamp in the iguana's cage. Why might this help?

Section 2

Fishes

NEW TERMS

fins
scales
lateral line
  system
gills
external
  fertilization

internal
  fertilization
denticles
swim bladder

OBJECTIVES

- Describe the three classes of living fishes, and give an example of each.
- Describe the function of a swim bladder and an oily liver.
- Explain the difference between internal fertilization and external fertilization.

Find a body of water, and you'll probably find fish. Fishes live in almost every water environment, from shallow ponds and streams to the depths of the oceans. You can find fishes in cold arctic waters and in warm tropical seas. Fishes can be found in rivers, lakes, marshes, and even in water-filled caves.

Fish were the first vertebrates on Earth. Fossil evidence indicates that fish appeared about 500 million years ago. Today Earth's marine and freshwater fishes make up more species than all other vertebrates combined. There are more than 25,000 species of fishes, and more are being discovered. A few are shown in **Figure 7.**

Angel fish

Figure 7 *These are just some of the many species of fishes. Do any look familiar?*

Catfish

Sea horse

Wolf eel

Surgeonfish

across the sciences
CONNECTION

Fish characteristics are being studied to design boats! Check out Robot Fish on page 378.

Fish Characteristics

Although the fishes on this page look very different from each other, they share many characteristics that help them live in water.

Many fishes are predators of other animals. Others are herbivores. Because they must actively search for food, they need a strong body, well-developed senses, and a brain.

Born to Swim Fishes have many body parts that help them swim. Strong muscles attached to the backbone allow fishes to swim vigorously after their prey. Fishes swim through the water by moving their fins. **Fins** are fanlike structures that help fish move, steer, stop, and balance. Many fishes have bodies covered by **scales,** which protect the body and reduce friction as they swim through the water. **Figure 8** shows some of the external features of a typical fish.

Dorsal fin

Lateral line

Pelvic fin

Anal fin

Tail fin

Eye

Gills Gill cover

Pectoral fins

Figure 8 Fishes come in a variety of shapes and sizes, but all have gills, fins, and a tail.

Making Sense of the World Fishes have well-developed vision, hearing, and sense of smell. Most fishes also have a lateral line system. The **lateral line system** is a row or rows of tiny sense organs along each side of the body that often extend onto the head. This system detects water vibrations, such as those caused by another fish swimming by. Fishes have a brain that keeps track of all the information coming in from these senses. A tough skull protects the brain.

Underwater Breathing Fishes breathe with gills. **Gills** are organs that remove oxygen from water. Oxygen in the water passes through the thin membrane of the gills to the blood. The blood then carries oxygen throughout the body. Gills are also used to remove carbon dioxide from the blood.

Making More Fish Most fishes reproduce by **external fertilization.** The female lays unfertilized eggs in the water, and the male drops sperm on them. But some species of fish reproduce by internal fertilization. In **internal fertilization,** the male deposits sperm inside the female. In most cases the female then lays eggs that contain the developing embryos. Baby fish hatch from the eggs. But in some species, the embryos develop inside the mother, and the baby fish are born live.

physics
CONNECTION

When you look at an object through a magnifying glass, you have to move the lens back and forth in front of your eye to bring the object into focus. The same thing happens in fish eyes. Fish have special muscles to change the position of the lenses of their eyes. By moving the eye lenses, fish can bring objects into focus.

Types of Fishes

Fishes include five very different classes of animals. Two classes are now extinct. We know about them only because of fossils. The three classes of fishes living today are *jawless fishes, cartilaginous fishes,* and *bony fishes.*

Jawless Fishes The first fishes did not have jaws. You might think that having no jaws would make it hard to eat and would lead to extinction. But the jawless fishes have thrived for half a billion years. Today there are about 60 species of jawless fishes.

Modern jawless fishes include lampreys, as shown in **Figure 9,** and hagfish. These fishes are eel-like, and they have smooth, slimy skin and a round, jawless mouth. Their skeleton is made of cartilage, and they have a notochord but no backbone. These fishes have a skull, a brain, and eyes.

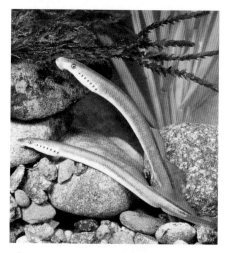

Figure 9 *Lampreys are parasites that live by attaching themselves to other fishes.*

Cartilaginous Fishes Did you know that a shark is a fish? Sharks, like the one in **Figure 10,** belong to a class of fishes called cartilaginous (KART'l AJ uh nuhs) fishes. In most vertebrates, soft cartilage in the embryo is gradually replaced by bone. In sharks, skates, and rays, however, the skeleton never changes from cartilage to bone. That is why they are called cartilaginous fishes.

Figure 10 *Sharks, like this hammerhead, rarely prey on humans. They prefer to eat their regular food, which is fish.*

Sharks are the most well known cartilaginous fishes, but they are not the only ones. Another group includes skates and rays. A sting ray is shown in **Figure 11.**

As any shark lover knows, cartilaginous fishes have fully functional jaws. These fishes are strong swimmers and expert predators. Like most predators, they have keen senses. Many have excellent senses of sight and smell, and they have a lateral line system.

Figure 11 *Rays, like this sting ray, usually feed on shellfish and worms on the sea floor.*

Figure 12 *A shark's denticles and human teeth are made of the same materials.*

The skin of cartilaginous fishes is covered with small tooth-like **denticles** that give it the feel of sandpaper. If you rub your hand on a shark's skin from head to tail, it feels smooth. But if you rub your hand from tail to head, you can get cut! Look at the magnified denticles in **Figure 12.**

To stay afloat, cartilaginous fishes store a lot of oil in their liver. See why in the QuickLab on the next page. Even with oily livers, these fishes are heavier than water. They have to keep moving in order to stay afloat. Once they stop swimming, they gradually glide to the bottom.

Cartilaginous fishes do not swim just to keep from sinking, however. Some must swim to maintain the flow of water over their gills. If these fishes stop swimming, they will suffocate. Others do not have to swim. They can lie on the ocean floor and pump water across their gills.

Bony Fishes When you think of a fish, you probably think of something like the fish shown in **Figure 13.** Goldfish, tuna, trout, catfish, and cod are all bony fishes, the largest class of fishes. Ninety-five percent of all fishes are bony fishes. They range in size from 1 cm long to more than 6 m long.

As their name implies, bony fishes have a skeleton made of bone instead of cartilage. The body of a bony fish is covered by bony scales.

Figure 13 *A goldfish is a bony fish.*

Unlike cartilaginous fishes, bony fishes can float in one place without swimming. This is because they have a swim bladder that keeps them from sinking. The **swim bladder** is a balloon-like organ that is filled with oxygen and other gases from the bloodstream. It gives fish *buoyancy,* or the ability to float in water. The swim bladder and other body parts of bony fishes are shown in **Figure 14.**

A Lot of Bones

If there are 25,000 species of fishes, and 95 percent of all fishes are bony fishes, how many species of bony fishes are there?

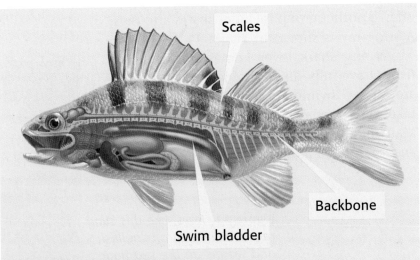

Figure 14 *Bony fishes have a swim bladder, a bony skeleton, and scales.*

Scales

Backbone

Swim bladder

There are two main groups of bony fishes. Almost all bony fishes are *ray-finned fishes*. Ray-finned fishes have paired fins supported by thin rays of bone. Ray-finned fishes include many familiar fishes, such as eels, herrings, trout, minnows, and perch. **Figure 15** shows a ray-finned fish.

Lobe-finned fishes and *lungfishes* make up a second group of bony fishes. Lobe-finned fishes have fins that are muscular and thick. The coelacanths, which were described at the beginning of the chapter, are lobe-finned fishes. There are six known species of modern lungfishes. You can see a lungfish in **Figure 16.** Scientists think that ancient fishes from this group were the ancestors of amphibians.

Figure 15 *Ray-finned fishes are some of the fastest swimmers in the world. A pike, like this one, can swim faster than the fastest human runners can run, about 48 km/h.*

Figure 16 *Lungfishes have air sacs, or lungs, and can gulp air. They are found in Africa, Australia, and South America and live in shallow waters that often dry up in the summer.*

REVIEW

1. What are the three types of fishes? Which type are the coelacanths?

2. Most bony fishes reproduce by external fertilization. What does this mean?

3. What is the lateral line system, and what is its function?

4. **Analyzing Relationships** Compare the ways that cartilaginous fishes and bony fishes maintain buoyancy.

*Quick*Lab

Oil on Troubled Waters

Are you wondering how an oily liver can keep a shark afloat? This experiment will help you understand. Measure out equal amounts of **water** and **cooking oil**. Fill a **balloon** with the water. Fill another balloon with the cooking oil. Tie the balloons so that no air remains inside. Float each balloon in a **bowl** half full of water. What happens? How does the oily liver of a cartilaginous fish keep the fish from sinking?

Amphibians

NEW TERMS

lung

tadpole

metamorphosis

OBJECTIVES

- Understand the importance of amphibians in evolution.
- Explain how amphibians breathe.
- Describe metamorphosis in amphibians.

By the end of the Devonian period, 350 million years ago, fishes lived wherever there was water. But none of these vertebrates could live on land. And the land was a wonderful place for a vertebrate. It had lush green forests, many tasty insects, and few predators. But for vertebrates to adapt to life on land, they needed lungs for breathing and legs for walking. How did these changes occur?

Moving to Land

Most of the amphibians living on Earth today are frogs or salamanders, like those in **Figure 17.** But the early amphibians looked much different. Fossil evidence indicates that the first amphibians evolved from ancient ancestors of modern lungfishes. These fishes developed lungs to get oxygen from the air. A **lung** is a saclike organ that takes oxygen from the air and delivers it to the blood. The fins of these ancient fishes became strong enough to support their body weight and eventually became legs.

Fossils show that the first amphibians looked like a cross between a fish and a salamander, as shown in **Figure 18.** The early amphibians were the first vertebrates to live most of their life on land, and they were very successful. Many were very large—up to 10 m long—and could stay on dry land longer than today's amphibians can. But early amphibians still had to return to the water to keep from drying out, to avoid overheating, and to lay their eggs.

Figure 17 Modern amphibians include frogs and salamanders.

Barred leaf frog

Sierra Nevada salamander

Figure 18 *Ancient amphibians probably looked something like this.*

Characteristics of Amphibians

Amphibian means "double life." Most amphibians have two parts to their life. After they emerge from an egg, they live in the water, like fishes do. Later they develop into animals that can live on land. But even adult amphibians are only partly adapted to life on land, and they must always live near water.

Amphibians are ectotherms. Like the body of a fish, the body of an amphibian changes temperature according to the temperature of its environment.

Thin-Skinned Most amphibians do not have scales. Their skin is thin, smooth, and moist. They do not drink water. Instead, they absorb it through their skin. Amphibians can breathe by gulping air into their lungs. But many also absorb oxygen through their skin, which is full of blood vessels. Some salamanders, like the one in **Figure 19,** breathe only through their skin. Because amphibian skin is so thin and moist, these animals can lose water through their skin and become dehydrated. For this reason, most amphibians live in water or in damp habitats.

Figure 19 *The four-toed salamander has no lungs. It gets all of its oxygen through its skin.*

The skin of many amphibians is brilliantly colored. The colors are often a warning to predators because the skin of many amphibians contains poison glands. These poisons may simply be irritating or they may be deadly. The skin of the dart-poison frog, shown in **Figure 20,** contains one of the most deadly toxins known.

Another kind of frog produces a chemical that causes snakes to yawn. If a snake tries to swallow the frog, the chemical makes the snake yawn, and the frog jumps out of the snake's mouth!

Leading a Double Life Most amphibians start life in water. Frogs usually reproduce by external fertilization. Salamanders reproduce by internal fertilization. Because amphibian eggs do not have a shell and a special membrane to prevent water loss, the embryos must develop in a very wet environment.

Figure 20 *The skin of this dart-poison frog is full of poison glands. In South America, hunters rub the tips of their arrows in the deadly toxin.*

The amphibian embryo usually develops into an aquatic larva called a **tadpole.** The tadpole can live only in wet environments. It obtains oxygen through gills and uses its long tail to swim. Later the tadpole loses its gills and develops lungs and limbs, in a process called metamorphosis. **Figure 21** shows the metamorphosis of a frog. **Metamorphosis** is a change from a larval form to an adult form. Once an amphibian develops into the adult form, it is capable of surviving on land.

Figure 21
Most frogs and salamanders go through metamorphosis. The metamorphosis of a frog is shown here.

Adult frog

The tail and gills disappear, and lungs become functional.

Fertilized eggs

A newly hatched tadpole feeds on yolk stored in its body and breathes with gills.

The tadpole begins to feed and grow legs.

A few amphibians skip the aquatic stage. Their embryos develop directly into adult frogs or salamanders. For example, one species of South American frog lays eggs on moist ground. Groups of male adults guard the developing embryos. When an embryo begins to move, a male frog quickly takes it into its mouth and protects it inside its vocal sacs. When the embryo finishes developing, the adult frog opens its mouth, and a tiny frog jumps out. You can see this frog in **Figure 22.**

Figure 22 *Darwin frogs live in Chile and Argentina. A male frog may carry 5 to 15 embryos in its vocal sacs until the young are about 1.5 cm in length.*

Kinds of Amphibians

It is estimated that there are 4,600 species of amphibians alive today. These belong to three groups: caecilians (see SIL yuhns), salamanders, and frogs and toads.

Caecilians Most people are not familiar with caecilians. These amphibians do not have legs and are shaped like worms or snakes, as shown in **Figure 23.** But they have the thin, moist skin of amphibians. Unlike other amphibians, some caecilians have bony scales. Many caecilians have very small eyes underneath their skin and are blind. Caecilians live in the tropical areas of Asia, Africa, and South America. About 160 species are known.

Figure 23 *Caecilians are legless amphibians that live in damp soil in the tropics. Caecilians eat small invertebrates in the soil.*

Salamanders Of modern amphibians, salamanders are the most like prehistoric amphibians. Although salamanders are much smaller than their ancient ancestors, they have a similar body shape, a long tail, and four strong legs. They range in size from a few centimeters long to 1.5 m long. **Figure 24** shows a salamander.

There are about 390 known species of salamanders. Most of them live under stones and logs in the damp woods of North America. They eat small invertebrates. A few, such as the axolotl (AK suh LAHT 'l), shown in **Figure 25,** do not go through metamorphosis. They live their entire life in the water.

Figure 24 *Salamanders live in moist places, such as under logs and stones in damp woods.*

Figure 25 *This axolotl is an unusual salamander. It retains its gills and never leaves the water.*

Amphibians are often called ecological indicators. When large numbers of amphibians begin to die or show deformities, this may indicate a problem with the environment. Sometimes deformities are caused by parasites, but amphibians are also extremely sensitive to chemical changes in their environment. Based on what you know about amphibians, why do you think they are sensitive to water pollution and air pollution?

Frogs and Toads Ninety percent of all amphibians are frogs or toads. More species of frogs and toads are being discovered all the time. They are found all over the world, from deserts to rain forests. Frogs and toads are very similar to each other, as you can see in **Figure 26.** In fact, toads are a type of frog.

Frog   Toad

Figure 26 Frogs have smooth, moist skin. Toads spend less time in water than frogs do, and their skin is drier and bumpier. They also have shorter hind legs and less webbing in their feet than frogs have.

Frogs and toads are highly adapted for life on land. Adults have powerful leg muscles for jumping. They have well-developed ears for hearing, and they have vocal cords for calling. They also have extendible, sticky tongues, which they use to expertly capture flies and other insects. The tongue is attached to the front of the mouth so that it can be flipped out quickly to catch insects.

Frogs are well known for their nighttime choruses, but many frogs sing in the daytime too. Like humans, they force air from their lungs across vocal cords in the throat. But frogs have something we lack. Surrounding their vocal cords is a thin sac of skin called the *vocal sac.* When frogs vocalize, the sac inflates with air, like a balloon does, and vibrates. You can see this in **Figure 27.** The vibrations of the sac increase the volume of the song so that it can be heard over long distances.

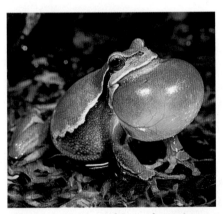
Figure 27 Most frogs that sing are males, and their songs have different meanings. Singing frogs may be defending a territory or trying to attract a female frog.

Examine the princely characteristics of a friendly frog on page 614 of your LabBook.

REVIEW

1. Describe metamorphosis in amphibians.

2. Why do amphibians have to be near water or in a very wet habitat?

3. What adaptations allow amphibians to live on land?

4. Name the three types of amphibians. How are they similar? How are they different?

5. **Analyzing Relationships** Describe the relationship between lungfishes and amphibians. What characteristics do they share? How do they differ?

Reptiles

About 35 million years after the first amphibians colonized the land, some of them evolved special traits that prepared them for life in an even drier environment. These animals developed thick, dry skin that protected them from water loss. Their legs became stronger and more vertical, so they were better able to walk. And they evolved a special egg that could be laid on dry land. These animals were reptiles, the first animals to live completely out of the water.

Reptile History

Fossils show that soon after the first reptiles appeared, they split into groups. This can be shown in a family tree of the reptiles, as illustrated in **Figure 28.**

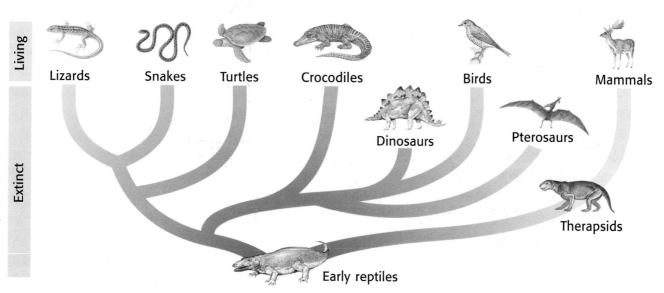

Figure 28 *Early reptiles were the ancestors of modern reptiles, birds, and mammals.*

Many of the most fascinating reptiles are now extinct. When we think of extinct reptiles, we usually think of dinosaurs. But only a fraction of the reptiles living in prehistoric times were land-dwelling dinosaurs. Many were swimming reptiles. A few were flying pterosaurs. And there were turtles, lizards, snakes, and crocodiles. In addition, there was a group of mammal-like reptiles called therapsids. As you can see in Figure 28, **therapsids** (thuh RAP sidz) were the ancestors of mammals.

Characteristics of Reptiles

Reptiles are adapted for life on land. Although crocodiles, turtles, and a few species of snakes live in the water, all of these animals are descended from reptiles that lived on land. All reptiles use lungs to breathe air, just as you do.

Thick-Skinned A very important adaptation for life on land is thick, dry skin, which forms a watertight layer. This thick skin keeps cells from losing water by evaporation. Most reptiles cannot breathe through their skin the way amphibians do. Most depend entirely on their lungs for oxygen and carbon dioxide exchange. Check out the snake skin in **Figure 29.**

Coldblooded? Like fishes and amphibians, reptiles are ectotherms. That means that they usually cannot maintain a constant body temperature. Reptiles are active when their environment is warm, and they slow down when their environment is cool.

A few reptiles can generate some heat from their own body. For example, some lizards in the southwestern United States can keep their body temperature at about 34°C, even when the air temperature is cool. Still, modern reptiles are limited to mild climates. They cannot tolerate the cold polar regions, where many mammals and birds thrive.

The Amazing Amniotic Egg Among reptiles' many adaptations to land life, the most critical is the amniotic (AM nee AH tik) egg. The **amniotic egg** is surrounded by a shell, as shown in **Figure 30.** The shell protects the developing embryo and keeps the egg from drying out. An amniotic egg can be laid under rocks, in the ground, in forests, or even in the desert. The amniotic egg is so well adapted to a dry environment that even crocodiles and turtles return to land to lay their eggs.

Figure 29 *Many people think snakes are slimy, but the skin of snakes and other reptiles is scaly and dry.*

Figure 30 *Compare the amphibian eggs at left with the reptile eggs at right. What differences can you see?*

The shell is just one important part of an amniotic egg. The other parts of an amniotic egg are illustrated in **Figure 31.** The amniotic egg gets its name from the *amniotic fluid* inside the amniotic sac in the egg. This is where the embryo develops. The egg provides protection from predators, bacterial infections, and dehydration.

Figure 31 An Amniotic Egg

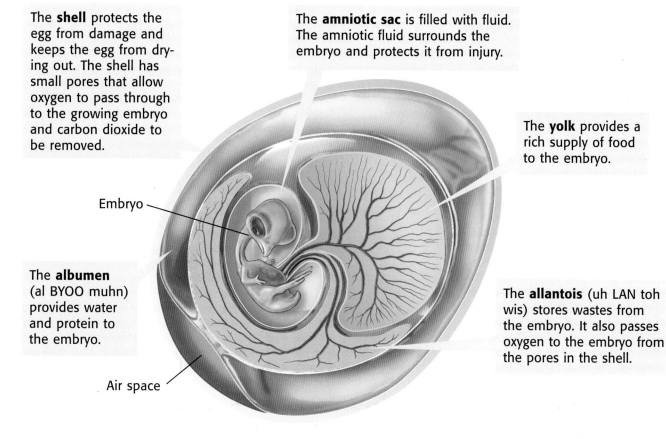

The **shell** protects the egg from damage and keeps the egg from drying out. The shell has small pores that allow oxygen to pass through to the growing embryo and carbon dioxide to be removed.

The **amniotic sac** is filled with fluid. The amniotic fluid surrounds the embryo and protects it from injury.

The **yolk** provides a rich supply of food to the embryo.

Embryo

The **albumen** (al BYOO muhn) provides water and protein to the embryo.

The **allantois** (uh LAN toh wis) stores wastes from the embryo. It also passes oxygen to the embryo from the pores in the shell.

Air space

The amniotic egg is fertilized inside the female. A shell then forms around the egg, and the female lays the egg. Because of the shell, reptiles can reproduce only by internal fertilization.

Most reptiles lay their eggs in soil or sand. A few do not lay eggs. Instead the embryos develop inside the reproductive passages in the mother's body, and the young are born live. In either case, the embryo develops directly into a tiny young reptile. Reptiles do not have a larval stage and do not undergo metamorphosis.

Types of Reptiles

In the age of the dinosaurs, from 300 million years ago until about 65 million years ago, most land vertebrates were reptiles. Today the 6,000 species of living reptiles represent only a handful of the many species of reptiles that once lived.

Modern reptiles include turtles and tortoises, crocodiles and alligators, and lizards and snakes.

Self-Check

1. What adaptations of reptiles are important for living on dry land?

2. Why must animals that lay eggs with shells reproduce by internal fertilization?

(See page 636 to check your answers.)

Figure 32 *The bottom shell of a box turtle is hinged on both ends so the turtle can pull it snug against the top shell. The result is a fortress of bone.*

Turtles and Tortoises The 250 species of turtles and tortoises are only distantly related to the rest of the reptiles.

The trait that makes turtles and tortoises unique is their shell. The shell makes a turtle slow and inflexible, so outrunning its predators is highly unlikely. On the other hand, many turtles can draw their head and limbs into the armorlike shell to protect themselves, as the box turtle shown in **Figure 32** is doing.

Most turtles spend some or all of their life in water. The front legs of sea turtles have evolved into flippers, as shown in **Figure 33.** Female sea turtles come ashore only to lay their eggs on sandy beaches. Desert tortoises are different from other turtles. They live only on land.

Figure 33 *Sea turtles have a streamlined shell to help them swim and turn rapidly.*

Crocodiles and Alligators The 22 species of crocodiles and alligators are all carnivores. They eat water bugs, fish, turtles, birds, and mammals. These reptiles spend most of their time in the water. Because their eyes and nostrils are on the top of their flat head, they can watch their surroundings while most of their body is hidden underwater. This gives them a great advantage over their prey. How can you tell the difference between an alligator and a crocodile? See for yourself in **Figure 34.**

Figure 34 *You can tell an alligator from a crocodile by the shape of its head. An alligator has a broad head and a rounded snout. A crocodile has a narrow head and a pointed snout.*

Alligator

Crocodile

Lizards Most of the species of modern reptiles are lizards and snakes. There are about 4,000 known species of lizards and about 1,600 known species of snakes.

Lizards live in deserts, forests, grasslands, and jungles. Chameleons, geckos, skinks, and iguanas are some of the amazing variety of lizards. Most lizards eat small invertebrates, but many are herbivores. The largest lizard is the 3 m long, 140 kg Komodo dragon of Indonesia, shown in **Figure 35.** But most lizards are less than 30 cm long.

Figure 35 *Komodo dragons eat deer, pigs, and goats. They have even been known to eat humans in rare cases.*

Snakes The most obvious characteristic of snakes is their lack of legs. Snakes move by contractions of their muscular body. On smooth surfaces, scales on their belly grip the surface and help pull the snake forward.

All snakes are carnivores. They eat small animals and eggs. Snakes swallow their prey whole, as shown in **Figure 36.** Snakes have special jaws with five joints that allow them to open their mouth wide and swallow very large prey. Some snakes, such as pythons and boas, kill their prey by squeezing it until it suffocates. Other snakes have poison glands and special fangs for injecting venom into their prey. The venom kills or stuns the prey and contains powerful enzymes that begin digesting it.

Snakes do not see or hear well, but they can smell extremely well. When a snake flicks its forked tongue out of its mouth, it is sampling the air. Tiny particles and molecules stick to the tongue. When the snake pulls its tongue inside its mouth, it places the tips of its tongue into two openings in the roof of its mouth, where the molecules are sensed.

Figure 36 *This common egg eater snake is swallowing a bird's egg.*

REVIEW

1. What characteristics set turtles apart from other reptiles?

2. What special adaptations do snakes have for eating?

3. **Applying Concepts** Like reptiles, mammals have an amniotic egg. But mammals give birth to live young. The embryo develops from a fertilized egg inside the female's body. Which parts of a reptilian amniotic egg do you think a mammal could do without? Explain your answer.

Chapter Highlights

SECTION 1

Vocabulary

vertebrate (p. 356)

vertebrae (p. 357)

endotherm (p. 358)

ectotherm (p. 358)

Section Notes

- At some point during their development, chordates have a notochord, a hollow nerve cord, pharyngeal pouches, and a tail.

- Chordates include lancelets, tunicates, and vertebrates. Most chordates are vertebrates.

- Vertebrates differ from the other chordates in that they have a backbone and skull made of bone or cartilage.

- The backbone is composed of units called vertebrae.

- Vertebrates may be ectotherms or endotherms.

- Endotherms control their body temperature through the chemical reactions of their cells. Ectotherms do not.

SECTION 2

Vocabulary

fins (p. 360)

scales (p. 360)

lateral line system (p. 360)

gills (p. 360)

external fertilization (p. 360)

internal fertilization (p. 360)

denticles (p. 362)

swim bladder (p. 362)

Section Notes

- There are three groups of living fishes: jawless fishes, cartilaginous fishes, and bony fishes.

- The cartilaginous fishes have an oily liver that helps them float.

☑ Skills Check

Math Concepts

HOW MANY SPECIES? If there are 6,000 species of reptiles, and 67 percent of all reptiles are lizards, how many species of lizards are there?

Sixty-seven percent of 6,000 is:

$$6,000 \times 0.67 = 4,020$$

There are 4,020 species of lizards.

Visual Understanding

METAMORPHOSIS Most amphibians go through metamorphosis. They change form as they develop into an adult. Figure 21 on page 366 illustrates the metamorphosis of a frog. Follow the arrows to see how a frog develops from an egg to a tadpole to an adult.

SECTION 2

- Most bony fishes have a swim bladder. The swim bladder is a balloonlike organ that gives bony fishes buoyancy.

- In external fertilization, eggs are fertilized outside the female's body. In internal fertilization, eggs are fertilized inside the female's body.

Labs

Floating a Pipe Fish (p. 612)

SECTION 3

Vocabulary

lung (p. 364)

tadpole (p. 366)

metamorphosis (p. 366)

Section Notes

- Amphibians were the first vertebrates to live on land.

- Amphibians breathe by gulping air into their lungs and by absorbing oxygen through their skin.

- Amphibians start life in water, where they breathe through gills. During metamorphosis, they lose their gills and develop lungs and legs that allow them to live on land.

- Modern amphibians include caecilians, salamanders, and frogs and toads.

Labs

A Prince of a Frog (p. 614)

SECTION 4

Vocabulary

therapsid (p. 369)

amniotic egg (p. 370)

Section Notes

- Reptiles evolved from amphibians by adapting to life on dry land.

- Reptiles have thick, scaly skin that protects them from drying out.

- A tough shell keeps the amniotic egg from drying out and protects the embryo.

- Amniotic fluid surrounds and protects the embryo in an amniotic egg.

- Vertebrates that evolved from early reptiles are reptiles, birds, and mammals.

- Modern reptiles include turtles and tortoises, lizards and snakes, and crocodiles and alligators.

---

internet**connect**

 GO TO: go.hrw.com

Visit the **HRW** Web site for a variety of learning tools related to this chapter. Just type in the keyword:

KEYWORD: HSTVR1

 GO TO: www.scilinks.org

Visit the **National Science Teachers Association** on-line Web site for Internet resources related to this chapter. Just type in the *sci*LINKS number for more information about the topic:

TOPIC: Vertebrates	*sci*LINKS NUMBER: HSTL380
TOPIC: Fishes	*sci*LINKS NUMBER: HSTL385
TOPIC: Amphibians	*sci*LINKS NUMBER: HSTL390
TOPIC: Reptiles	*sci*LINKS NUMBER: HSTL395

Chapter Review

USING VOCABULARY

To complete the following sentences, choose the correct term from each pair of terms listed below:

1. At some point in their development, all chordates have ___?___. (*lungs and a notochord* or *a hollow nerve cord and a tail*)

2. Mammals evolved from early ancestors called ___?___. (*therapsids* or *dinosaurs*)

3. Fish are ___?___. (*endotherms* or *ectotherms*)

4. When a frog lays eggs that are later fertilized by sperm, it is an example of ___?___ fertilization. (*internal* or *external*)

5. The vertebrae wrap around and protect the ___?___ of vertebrates. (*notochord* or *hollow nerve cord*)

UNDERSTANDING CONCEPTS

Multiple Choice

6. Which of the following is not a vertebrate?
   a. tadpole   c. lamprey
   b. lizard   d. tunicate

7. Tadpoles change into frogs by the process of
   a. evolution.
   b. internal fertilization.
   c. metamorphosis.
   d. temperature regulation.

8. The swim bladder is found in
   a. jawless fishes.
   b. cartilaginous fishes.
   c. bony fishes.
   d. lancelets.

9. The amniotic egg first evolved in
   a. bony fishes.   c. reptiles.
   b. birds.   d. mammals.

10. The yolk holds
    a. food for the embryo.
    b. amniotic fluid.
    c. wastes.
    d. oxygen.

11. Both bony fishes and cartilaginous fishes have
    a. denticles.
    b. fins.
    c. an oily liver.
    d. a swim bladder.

12. Reptiles are adapted to a life on land because
    a. they can breathe through their skin.
    b. they are ectotherms.
    c. they have thick, moist skin.
    d. they have an amniotic egg.

Short Answer

13. How do amphibians breathe?

14. What characteristics allow fish to live in the water?

15. How does an embryo in an amniotic egg get oxygen?

Concept Mapping

16. Use the following terms to create a concept map: dinosaur, turtle, reptiles, amphibians, fishes, shark, salamander, vertebrates.

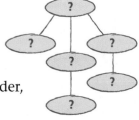

CRITICAL THINKING AND PROBLEM SOLVING

Write one or two sentences to answer the following questions:

17. Suppose you have found an animal that has a backbone and gills, but you can't find a notochord. Is it a chordate? How can you be sure?

18. Suppose you have found a shark that lacks the muscles needed to pump water over its gills. What does that tell you about the shark's lifestyle?

19. A rattlesnake does not see very well, but it can detect a temperature change of as little as three-thousandths of a degree Celsius. How is this ability useful to a rattlesnake?

20. It's 43°C outside, and the normal body temperature of a velociraptor is 38°C. Would you most likely find the raptor in the sun or in the shade? Explain.

MATH IN SCIENCE

21. A Costa Rican viper can eat a mouse that has one-third more mass than the viper. How much can you eat? Write down your mass in kilograms. To find your mass in kilograms, divide your mass in pounds by 2.2. If you were to eat a meal with a mass one-third larger than your mass, what would the mass of the meal be in kilograms?

INTERPRETING GRAPHICS

Examine the graph of body temperatures below, and answer the questions that follow.

Body Temperatures

22. How do the body temperatures of organism A and organism B change with the ground temperature?

23. Which of these organisms is most likely an ectotherm? Why?

24. Which of these organisms is most likely an endotherm? Why?

NOW What Do You Think?

Take a minute to review your answers to the ScienceLog questions on page 355. Have your answers changed? If necessary, revise your answers based on what you have learned since you began this chapter.

Fishes, Amphibians, and Reptiles   **377**

Robot Fish

When is a fish tail not a fish tail? When it's the tail of RoboTuna, a robotic fish designed by scientists at the Massachusetts Institute of Technology.

Something Fishy Going On

There's no doubt about it—fish are quicker and much more maneuverable than most ships and submarines. So why aren't ships and submarines built more like fish—with tails that flap back and forth? This question caught the imagination of some scientists at MIT and inspired them to build RoboTuna, a model of a bluefin tuna. This robot fish is 124 cm long and is composed of six motors, a skin of foam and Lycra, and a skeleton of aluminum ribs and hinges connected by pulleys and strings.

A Tail of Force and Motion

The MIT scientists propose that if ships were designed to more closely resemble fish, the ships would use much less energy and thus save money. A ship moving through water leaves a trail of little whirlpools called *vortices* behind it. These vortices increase the friction between the ship and the water. A fish, however, senses the vortices and responds by flapping its tail, creating vortices of its own. The fish's vortices counteract the effects of the original vortices, and the fish is propelled forward with much less effort.

RoboTuna has special sensors that measure changes in water pressure in much the same way that a living tuna senses vortices. Then the robot fish flaps its vortex-producing tail, allowing it to swim like a living fish. As strange as it may seem, RoboTuna may represent the beginning of a new era in nautical design.

Viewing Vortices

▶ Fill a roasting pan three-quarters full with water. Wait long enough for the water to stop moving. Then tie a 6 cm piece of yarn or ribbon to the end of a pencil. Drag the pencil through the water with the yarn or ribbon trailing behind it. How does the yarn or ribbon respond? Where are the vortices?

▶ *Inner Workings of MIT's RoboTuna*

1. A strut supports the robot, encloses the tendons, and conveys control and sensor information.

3. A skin of foam and Lycra is smooth enough to eliminate wrinkles or bulges and prevent the stray turbulence they cause.

2. Ribs and flexible beams hold the skin in place while allowing the body to flex continuously.

WARM BRAINS IN COLD WATER

Of the world's 30,000 kinds of fish, only a few carry around their own brain heaters. *Brain heaters?* Why would a fish need a special heater just for its brain? Before you can answer that question, you have to think about how fish keep warm in the cold water of the ocean.

A Question of Temperature

Most fish and marine animals are ectotherms. An ectotherm's body temperature closely matches the temperature of its surroundings. Endotherms, on the other hand, maintain a steady body temperature regardless of the temperature of their surroundings. Humans are endotherms. Other mammals, such as dogs, elephants, whales, and birds, are also endotherms. But only a few kinds of fish—tuna, for example—are endotherms. These fish are still coldblooded, but they can heat certain parts of their bodies. Endothermic fish can hunt for prey in extremely chilly water. Yet these fish pay a high price for their ability to inhabit very cold areas—they use a lot of energy.

Being endothermic requires far more energy than being ectothermic. Some fish, such as swordfish, marlin, and sailfish, have adaptations that let them heat only part of their body. Instead of using large amounts of energy to warm the entire body, they warm only their eyes and brain. That's right—they have special brain heaters!

▶ *Why do you think it is important to protect the brain and eyes from extreme cold?*

Warming the Brain

In a "brain-warming" fish, a small mass of muscle attached to each eye acts as a thermostat. It adjusts the temperature of the brain and eyes as the fish swims through different temperature zones. These "heater muscles" help maintain delicate nerve functions that are important to finding prey.

Heater muscles allow the swordfish, for example, to swim in both warm surface waters of the ocean and depths of 485 m, where the temperature drops to near freezing. This adaptation has an obvious advantage: It gives the fish a large range of places to look for food.

Ectotherms in Action

▶ Contact a local pet store that sells various kinds of fish. Find out what water temperature is best for different fish from different regions of the Earth. For example, compare the ideal water temperatures for goldfish, discus fish, and angelfish. Why do you think fish-tank temperatures must be carefully controlled?

Brain
Heater muscles
Eye

16 Birds and Mammals

Would You Believe . . . ?

Would it surprise you to know that the pigeons in your schoolyard are related to velociraptors? A pigeon's waddling gait might not make you think of the fierce prehistoric animal, but most biologists now agree that birds are descendants of dinosaurs.

The first piece of evidence to link reptiles and birds was the fossil of *Archaeopteryx* (ark ee AHP tuhr iks). *Archaeopteryx* fossils were first discovered in Germany almost 150 years ago. Like a dinosaur, *Archaeopteryx* had heavy bones and teeth, but like a bird, it had feathered wings.

Archaeopteryx fossil

Many scientists were skeptical about the link between dinosaurs and birds. For one thing, some research suggested that *Archaeopteryx* wasn't a true dinosaur.

Then in 1998, Chinese scientists discovered fossils of true dinosaurs that had wings and feathers. These feathers share some characteristics of modern bird feathers. So far, no one knows how feathers might have helped the dinosaurs. Their wings were too short for flight. The feathers may have been insulation against cold. Or maybe males used them to attract female dinosaurs.

The discovery of these winged dinosaurs helped to convince some scientists that birds are descendants of dinosaurs. A few scientists go even further. They say the dinosaurs never went extinct because birds *are* dinosaurs.

You'll learn more about birds in this chapter. You'll also learn about another group of vertebrates—mammals.

Winged dinosaur fossils

What Do You Think?

In your ScienceLog, try to answer the following questions based on what you already know:

1. What holds a bird or plane up when it flies?

2. How do kangaroos differ from most other mammals?

3. Can mammals lay eggs? Can they fly?

Archaeopteryx

Investigate!

Let's Fly!

Humans have always been fascinated by birds and their ability to fly. Throughout history, humans have tried to fly too. Leonardo da Vinci designed flying machines in the fifteenth century. And Orville and Wilbur Wright finally got off the ground when they flew the first airplane, in 1903. How do birds and airplanes fly? This Investigate will give you a few hints.

Procedure

1. Carefully fold a **piece of paper** to make a paper airplane. Make the folds symmetrical and the creases sharp.

2. Throw the plane very slowly. What happened?

3. Take the same plane, and throw it more forcefully. Did anything change?

4. Reduce the size of the wings by cutting them with **scissors.** Make sure the two wings are the same size and are symmetrical.

5. Throw the airplane again, both slowly and with more force. What happened each time?

6. Record all your results in your ScienceLog.

Analysis

7. What happened when you threw the original paper airplane slowly? forcefully?

8. What effect does speed have on plane flight? Do you think this is true of bird flight?

9. What happened when the wings were made smaller? Why do you think this happened? Do you think wing size affects the way a bird flies?

10. Based on your experiments, how would you design and throw the perfect paper airplane? Explain your answer.

Birds

NEW TERMS

down feather	brooding
contour feather	precocial chick
preening	altricial chick
lift	

OBJECTIVES

- Name two characteristics that birds share with reptiles.
- Describe the characteristics of birds that make them well suited for flight.
- Explain *lift*.
- List some advantages of migration.

Have you ever fed pigeons in a city park or watched a hawk fly in circles in the sky? Have you heard birds singing on a bright spring day? Humans have always been birdwatchers, perhaps because birds are easier to recognize than almost any other animal. Unlike other animals, all birds have feathers. Birds are also well known for their ability to fly. Birds belong to the class Aves. The word *aves* comes from the Latin word for bird. In fact, the word *aviation*—the science of flying airplanes—comes from the same word.

Birds are found all over the world. They have many different shapes and sizes, as shown in **Figure 1.**

Hummingbird

Road runner

Toucan

Figure 1 *There are almost 9,000 species of birds on Earth today.*

Bird Characteristics

The first birds appeared on Earth about 150 million years ago. As you learned at the beginning of this chapter, birds are thought to be descendants of dinosaurs.

Even today birds share some characteristics with reptiles. Like reptiles, birds are vertebrates. The legs and feet of birds are covered by thick, dry scales, like those of reptiles. Even the skin around their beaks is scaly. Like reptiles, birds have *amniotic eggs,* that is, eggs with an amniotic sac and a shell. However, the shells of bird eggs are generally harder than the leathery shells of turtles and lizards.

Birds also have many characteristics that set them apart from the rest of the animal kingdom. They have beaks instead of teeth and jaws, and they have feathers, wings, and many other adaptations for flight.

Birds of a Feather Birds have two main types of feathers—down feathers and contour feathers. Examples of each are shown in **Figure 2.** Because feathers wear out, birds shed their worn feathers and grow new ones.

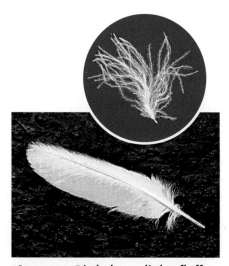

Figure 2 *Birds have light, fluffy down feathers and leaf-shaped contour feathers.*

Down feathers are fluffy, insulating feathers that lie next to a bird's body. To keep from losing heat, birds fluff up their down feathers to form a layer of insulation. Air trapped in the feathers helps keep birds warm. **Contour feathers** are made of a stiff central *shaft* with many side branches, called *barbs*. The barbs link together to form a smooth surface. You can see the structure of a contour feather in **Figure 3.** Contour feathers cover the body and wings of birds to form a streamlined flying surface.

Birds take good care of their feathers. They use their beaks to spread oil on their feathers in a process called **preening.** The oil is secreted by a gland near the bird's tail. The oil helps make the feathers water repellent and keeps them clean.

High-Energy Animals Birds are *endothermic,* which means they maintain a constant body temperature. Birds need a lot of energy from their food in order to fly. To get this energy, they have a high metabolism, and this generates a lot of body heat. In fact, the average body temperature of a bird is 40°C, warmer than yours! If birds are too hot, they lay their feathers flat and pant like dogs do. Birds cannot sweat to cool their bodies.

Eat Like a Bird? Because of their high metabolism, birds eat large amounts of food in proportion to their body weight. Some small birds eat almost constantly to maintain their energy! Most birds eat a high-protein, high-fat diet of insects, nuts, seeds, or meat. This kind of diet requires only a small digestive tract. A few birds, such as geese, eat the leaves of plants.

Birds don't have teeth, so they can't chew their food. Instead, food goes directly from the mouth to the *crop,* where it is stored. Birds also have an organ called a *gizzard,* which often contains small stones. The stones in the gizzard grind up the food so that it can be easily digested by the intestine. The parts of a bird's digestive system are shown in **Figure 4.**

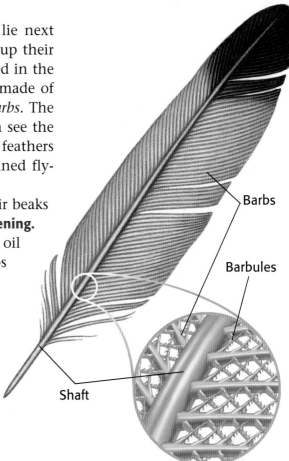

Figure 3 *The barbs of a contour feather have cross branches called barbules. Barbs and barbules give the feather strength and shape.*

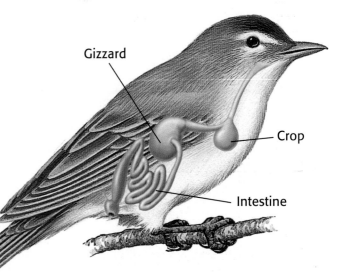

Figure 4 *The digestive system of a bird allows food to be rapidly converted into usable energy.*

Up, Up, and Away

Most birds are flyers. Even flightless birds, such as ostriches, are descended from ancestors that could fly.

Birds have a long list of adaptations for flight. Birds must take in a large amount of energy from the food they eat and a large amount of oxygen from the air they breathe in order to fly. Feathers and wings are also important, as are strong muscles. Birds have lightweight bodies so that they can get off the ground. **Figure 5** on these two pages explains many of the bird characteristics that are important for flight.

Figure 5 Flight Adaptations of Birds

Most birds have large eyes and excellent eyesight. This allows them to see objects and food from a distance. Some birds, like hawks and eagles, can see eight times better than humans!

Air sacs

Lung

The **heart** of a bird beats rapidly. This ensures that the flight muscles get as much oxygen as the blood can carry. In small birds, the heart beats almost 1,000 times a minute! Your heart beats about 70 times a minute.

Birds have special organs called **air sacs** attached to their lungs. The air sacs increase the amount of oxygen that a bird can take in and allow air to flow constantly in one direction through the lungs.

The shape of a bird's wings is related to the kind of flying it does. Short, rounded wings allow rapid maneuvers, like the movements of a fighter plane. Long narrow wings are best for soaring, like the movement of a glider.

Bird skeletons are compact and strong. Some of the vertebrae, ribs, and hip bones are fused together. This makes the skeleton of birds more rigid than that of other vertebrates. The rigid skeleton lets a bird move its wings powerfully and efficiently.

across the sciences
CONNECTION

These characteristics help birds fly, but how do airplanes fly? Find out on page 410.

Keel

Birds that fly have powerful flight muscles attached to a large breastbone called a **keel.** These muscles move the wings.

Bone is a heavy material, but birds have much lighter skeletons than those of other vertebrates because their bones are hollow. But bird bones are still very strong because they have thin cross-supports that provide strength, much like the trusses of a bridge do.

BRAIN FOOD

The cells of a bird's body have less DNA than the cells of any other vertebrate. In most animals, much of the DNA seems to have no function. It's just extra, or "junk," DNA. Birds seem to have dumped much of their extra DNA. Some scientists think this is an adaptation to make birds lighter for flight.

Birds and Mammals   **385**

Getting off the Ground

All of these adaptations make a bird well suited for flight, but how do birds actually overcome gravity and get into the air? Anything that flies needs wings to lift it off the ground. Birds flap their wings to get into the air and to push themselves through the air. Wings provide lift. **Lift** is the upward pressure on the wing that keeps a bird in the air.

When air flows past a wing, some of the air is forced over the top of the wing, and some is forced underneath. A bird's wing is curved on top. As shown in **Figure 6,** the air on top has to move *farther* than the air underneath. As a result, the air on top moves *faster* than the air underneath. The fast-moving air on top creates low pressure in the air. This is called the *Bernoulli effect.* The air pressure under the wing is higher and pushes the wing up.

Figure 6 *A bird's wing is shaped to produce lift. Air moving over the top of the wing moves faster than air moving underneath the wing. This creates a difference in air pressure that keeps a bird in the air.*

Birds generate extra lift by flapping their wings. The faster a bird flies, the greater the lift. Another factor that affects lift is wing size. The larger the wing, the greater the lift. This is why birds with large wings can soar long distances without flapping their wings. An albatross, like the one in **Figure 7,** can glide over the ocean for many hours without flapping its wings.

Figure 7 *The wandering albatross has a wingspan of 3.5 m, the largest of any living bird. Its large wings allow the albatross to glide for very long periods of time. An albatross comes ashore only to lay its eggs.*

Fly Away

It is sometimes said that when the going gets tough, the tough get going. If that's true, birds must be some of the toughest animals in the world. For when times are hard, some birds get going faster and farther than any other animal. Because they are able to fly great distances, birds are able to migrate great distances.

Some birds, like the Canada geese in **Figure 8,** have good reasons to migrate. By migrating, they can find better territories with more food. For example, in the far north in the summer, the Arctic sun is up nearly 24 hours a day. Plants, insects, and other organisms increase explosively, providing lots of food. It's a great place for birds to raise their young. However, the winters are long and harsh, and there is little to eat. So when winter comes, birds fly south to find better feeding grounds.

Figure 8 *These Canada geese are migrating south for the winter.*

Bringing Up Baby

Like reptiles, birds reproduce by internal fertilization and lay amniotic eggs with the developing embryo inside. But unlike most reptiles, birds must keep their eggs warm for the embryo to develop.

Most birds build elaborate nests and lay their eggs inside them. **Figure 9** shows a few of the many different kinds of bird nests. Birds sit on their eggs until the eggs hatch, using their body heat to keep the eggs warm. This is called **brooding.** Some birds, such as gulls, share brooding duties equally between males and females. But among songbirds, the female is in charge of brooding the eggs, and the male brings her food.

Raising young birds is hard work. Some birds, such as cuckoos and cowbirds, have found a way to make other birds do their work for them. A cuckoo lays its eggs in the nest of another species of bird. When the cuckoo egg hatches, the young cuckoo is fed and protected by the foster parents.

Figure 9 *There are many different types of bird nests. Birds use grass, branches, mud, hair, feathers, and many other building materials.*

Figure 10 *Precocial chicks learn to recognize their parents right after they hatch. But if their parents are not there, the chicks will follow the first moving thing they see, even a person.*

Ready to Go Some baby birds hatch from the egg ready to run around and eat bugs. Chicks that hatch fully active are **precocial** (pree KOH shuhl). Chickens, ducks, and shorebirds all hatch precocial chicks. Precocial chicks are covered with downy feathers and follow their parents as soon as they can stand up. You can see some precocial chicks following a stand-in parent in **Figure 10.** Precocial chicks depend on their mother for warmth and protection, but they can walk, swim, and feed themselves.

Help Wanted The chicks of hawks, songbirds, and many other birds hatch weak, naked, and helpless. These chicks are **altricial** (al TRISH uhl). Their eyes are closed when they are born. Newly hatched altricial chicks cannot walk or fly. Their parents must keep them warm and feed them for several weeks. **Figure 11** shows altricial chicks being fed by a parent.

When altricial chicks grow their first flight feathers, they begin learning to fly. This takes days, however, and the chicks often end up walking around on the ground. The parents must work feverishly to distract cats, weasels, and other predators and protect their young.

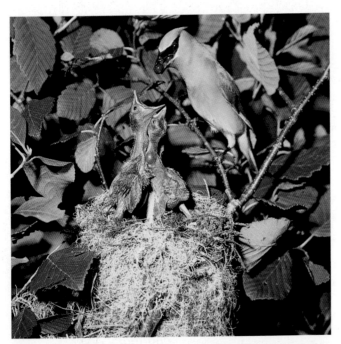

Figure 11 *Both parents of altricial chicks leave the nest in search of food. They return to the nest with food every few minutes, sometimes making 1,000 trips a day between the two of them!*

REVIEW

1. List three ways birds are similar to reptiles and three ways they are different.

2. Explain the difference between precocial chicks and altricial chicks.

3. People use the phrase "eat like a bird" to describe someone who eats very little. Is this saying appropriate? Why or why not?

4. Name some of the adaptations that make bird bodies lightweight.

5. **Understanding Technology** Would an airplane wing that is not curved on top generate lift? Draw a picture to illustrate your explanation.

Kinds of Birds

There are almost 9,000 species of birds on Earth. Birds range in size from the 1.6 g bee hummingbird to the 125 kg North African ostrich. The bodies of birds have different characteristics too, depending on where they live and what they eat. Because of their great diversity, birds are classified into 29 different orders. That can be confusing, so birds are often grouped into four nonscientific categories: flightless birds, water birds, birds of prey, and perching birds. These categories don't include all birds, but they do show how different birds can be.

BRAIN FOOD

An ostrich egg has a mass of about 1.4 kg. A single ostrich egg is big enough to provide scrambled eggs for a family of four every morning for a week.

Flightless Birds

Ostriches, kiwis, emus, and other flightless birds do not have a large keel for flight. Though they cannot fly, many flightless birds are fast runners.

The **kiwi,** of New Zealand, is a forest bird about the size of a chicken. Its feathers are soft and hairlike. Kiwis sleep during the day. At night, they hunt for worms, caterpillars, and berries.

Penguins are unique flightless birds. They have a large keel and very strong flight muscles, but their wings have been modified into flippers. They flap these wings to swim underwater. Although penguins are graceful swimmers, they walk clumsily on land.

The **ostrich** is the largest living bird. Ostriches can reach a height of 2.5 m and a mass of 125 kg. An ostrich's two-toed feet look almost like hoofs, and these birds can run up to 64 km/h (40 mi/h).

Water Birds

Water birds are sometimes called *waterfowl.* These include cranes, ducks, geese, swans, pelicans, loons, and many other species. These birds usually have webbed feet for swimming, but they are also strong flyers.

Male **wood ducks** have beautiful plumage to attract females. Like all ducks, they are strong swimmers and flyers.

The **blue-footed booby** is a tropical water bird. These birds have an elaborate courtship dance that includes raising their feet one at a time.

The **common loon** is the most primitive of modern birds. It can remain underwater for several minutes while searching for fish.

Birds of Prey

Eagles, hawks, falcons, and other birds of prey are meat eaters. They may eat mammals, fish, reptiles, birds, or other animals. The sharp claws on their feet and their sharp, curved beaks help these birds catch and eat their prey. They also have very good vision. Most birds of prey hunt during the day.

Owls, like this **northern spotted owl,** are the only birds of prey that hunt at night. They have a keen sense of hearing to help them find their prey.

Ospreys are fish eaters. They fly over the water and catch fish with their feet.

Perching Birds

Songbirds, like robins, wrens, warblers, and sparrows, are perching birds. These birds have special adaptations for perching on a branch. When a perching bird lands on a branch, its feet automatically close around the branch. So even if the bird falls asleep, it will not fall off.

Parrots are not songbirds, but they have special feet for perching and climbing. Their strong, hooked beak allows them to open seeds and slice fruit.

Chickadees are lively little birds that frequently flock to garden feeders. They often dangle underneath a branch while hunting for insects, seeds, or fruits.

Most tanagers are tropical birds, but the **scarlet tanager** spends the summer in North America. The male is red, but the female is a yellow-green color that blends into the trees.

REVIEW

1. How did perching birds get their name?

2. Birds of prey have extremely good eyesight. Why is good vision important for these birds?

3. **Interpreting Illustrations** Look at the illustrations of bird feet at right. Which foot belongs to a water bird? a perching bird? Explain your answers.

Mammals

Of all the vertebrates, we seem most interested in mammals. Maybe that's because we are mammals ourselves. But with about 4,500 species, mammals are actually a small class of animals. Mollusks, for example, include more than 90,000 species.

Mammals come in many different forms—from the tiniest bats, which weigh less than a cracker, to the largest whales. The blue whale, with a mass of more than 90,000 kg, is the largest animal—vertebrate or invertebrate—that has ever lived. You can find mammals in the coldest oceans, in the hottest deserts, and in every climate in between. You can see some of the variety of mammals in **Figure 12.**

Deer

Mandrill baboon

Figure 12 *Even though they look very different, all of these animals are mammals.*

Rhinoceros

Beluga whale

The Origin of Mammals

Fossil evidence suggests that about 280 million years ago, mammal-like reptiles called therapsids appeared. **Therapsids** (thuh RAP sidz) were the early ancestors of mammals. An artist's rendition of a therapsid is shown in **Figure 13.**

About 200 million years ago, the first mammals appeared in the fossil record. These mammals were about the size of mice. The early mammals were endotherms. Because they did not depend on their surroundings for heat, they could forage at night and avoid their dinosaur predators during the day.

When the dinosaurs became extinct, there was more land and food available for the mammals. Mammals began to diversify and live in many different environments.

Figure 13 *Therapsids had characteristics of both reptiles and mammals and may have looked something like this.*

Characteristics of Mammals

Dolphins and elephants are mammals, and so are monkeys, horses, and rabbits. You are a mammal, too! These animals are very different, but all mammals share many distinctive traits.

Mamma! All mammals have mammary glands; this sets them apart from other animals. **Mammary glands** secrete a nutritious fluid called milk. All female mammals supply milk to their young. Female mammals usually bear live young and care for their offspring, as illustrated in **Figure 14.** Although only mature female mammals make milk, male mammals also have small inactive mammary glands.

Figure 14 *Like all mammals, this calf gets its first meals from its mother's milk.*

All milk is made of water, protein, fat, and sugar. But the milk from different mammals has varying amounts of each nutrient. For example, human milk has half as much fat as cow's milk but twice as much sugar. The milk of seals may be more than one-half fat. At birth, elephant seals have a mass of 45 kg. After drinking this rich milk for just 3 weeks, their mass is 180 kg!

Cozy and Warm If you've ever had a dog fall asleep in your lap, you already know that mammals are really warm! All mammals are endotherms. Like birds, mammals require a lot of energy from the food they eat. Mammals quickly break down food in their bodies and use the energy released from their cells to keep their bodies warm. Usually a mammal keeps its body temperature constant. Only when a mammal is hibernating, estivating, or running a fever does its body temperature change.

Figure 15 *Mammals feel warm to the touch because they are endotherms.*

Figure 16 *The thick fur of this arctic fox keeps its body warm in even the coldest winters.*

Staying Warm Mammals have adaptations to help them keep warm. One way they stay warm is by having a thick coat, and many mammals have luxurious coats of fur. All mammals, even whales, have hair somewhere on their body. This is another trait that sets mammals apart from other animals. Mammals that live in cold climates usually have thick coats of hair, such as the fox in **Figure 16.** But large mammals that live in warm climates, like elephants, have less hair. Gorillas and humans have similar amounts of hair on their bodies, but human hair is finer and shorter.

Most mammals also have a layer of fat under the skin that acts as insulation. Whales and other mammals that live in cold oceans depend on a layer of fat called *blubber* to keep them warm.

Crunch! Another trait that sets mammals apart from other animals is their teeth. Birds don't even have teeth! And although fish and reptiles have teeth, their teeth tend to be all alike. In contrast, most mammals' teeth are specialized. They have different shapes and sizes for different functions.

Let's look at your teeth, for example. The teeth in the front of your mouth are cutting teeth, called *incisors*. Most people have four on top and four on the bottom. The next teeth are stabbing teeth shaped like spears, called *canines*. Canines help you grab food and hold onto it. Farther back in your mouth are flat teeth called *molars* that help grind up food.

The kinds of teeth a mammal has reflect its diet. Dogs, cats, wolves, and other meat-eating mammals have large canines. Molars are better developed in animals that eat plants. **Figure 17** shows the teeth of different mammals.

Unlike other vertebrates, mammals have two sets of teeth. A young mammal's first small teeth are called *milk teeth*. The milk teeth are replaced by a set of permanent adult teeth after the mammal begins eating solid food and its jaw grows larger.

Figure 17 *Mountain lions have sharp canine teeth for grabbing their prey. Donkeys have sharp incisors in front for cutting plants and flat grinding teeth in the back of their mouth.*

Getting Oxygen Just as a fire needs oxygen in order to burn, all animals need oxygen to efficiently "burn," or break down, the food they eat. Like birds and reptiles, mammals use lungs to get oxygen from the air. But mammals also have a large muscle to help bring air into their lungs. This muscle is called the **diaphragm,** and it lies at the bottom of the rib cage.

To get as much oxygen as possible from their lungs to their blood, mammals have a four-chambered heart. This type of heart allows blood with oxygen to be separated from blood without oxygen.

Large Brains The brain of a mammal is much larger than the brain of another animal the same size. This allows mammals to learn, move, and think quickly. A mammal's highly developed brain also helps it keep track of what is going on in its environment and respond quickly. Mammals are among the most coordinated of all animals. Most mammals are swift and responsive animals, whether it's a rabbit disappearing into the bushes or a cheetah springing on a gazelle.

Mammals depend on five major senses to provide them with information about their environment: vision, hearing, smell, touch, and taste. The importance of each sense for any given mammal often depends on the mammal's environment. For example, mammals that are active at night rely more heavily on their ability to hear than on their ability to see.

Mammal Parents All mammals reproduce sexually. Like birds and reptiles, mammals reproduce by internal fertilization. Most mammals give birth to live young, and all mammals nurse their young. Most young mammals are born helpless, and they require a lot of care. Mammal parents are very protective, with one or both parents caring for their young until they are grown. **Figure 18** shows a brown bear caring for its young.

Like all mammals, you have a diaphragm. The diaphragm lies just below the lungs. Place your hand underneath your rib cage. What happens as you breathe in and out? You are feeling the motion of your abdominal muscles, which are connected to your diaphragm. Contract your abdominal muscles. What happens? Now relax them. What happens?

Figure 18 *A mother bear keeps a close eye on her cubs. If anything threatens them, she will attack.*

REVIEW

1. Name three characteristics that are unique to mammals.

2. What is the purpose of a diaphragm?

3. **Making Inferences** Suppose you found a mammal skull on an archaeological dig. How would the teeth give you clues about the mammal's diet?

Kinds of Mammals

Mammals are divided into three groups based on the way their young develop. These groups are monotremes, marsupials, and placental mammals.

Monotremes Mammals that lay eggs are called **monotremes**. Monotremes are the only mammals that lay eggs, and early scientists called them "furred reptiles." But monotremes are not reptiles; they have all the mammal traits. They have mammary glands and a thick fur coat, and they are endotherms.

Monotremes are found only in Australia and New Guinea, and just three species of monotremes are alive today. Two are echidnas (ee KID nuhs), spine-covered animals with long snouts. Echidnas have long sticky tongues for catching ants and termites. You can see an echidna in **Figure 19**.

The third monotreme is the duckbilled platypus, shown in **Figure 20**. The duckbilled platypus is a swimming mammal that lives and feeds in rivers and ponds. It has webbed feet and a flat tail to help it move through the water. It gets its name from the flat, rubbery bill that it uses to dig for worms, crayfish, and other food in the mud. Platypuses are good diggers, and they dig long tunnels in riverbanks to lay their eggs.

A female monotreme lays one or two eggs with thick, leathery shells. Like bird and reptile eggs, monotreme eggs have a yolk and albumen to feed the developing embryo. The female incubates the eggs with her body heat. Newly hatched young are very small embryos and are not fully developed. The mother protects her young and feeds them with milk from her mammary glands. Unlike other mammals, monotremes do not have nipples, and the babies cannot suck. Instead, the tiny monotremes nurse by licking milk from the skin and hair around their mother's mammary glands.

Figure 19 *Echidnas are about the size of a house cat. They have large claws and long snouts that help them dig ants and termites out of their nests.*

Figure 20 *When underwater, a duckbilled platypus closes its eyes and ears. It uses its sensitive bill to find food.*

Marsupials You probably know that kangaroos, like those in **Figure 21,** have pouches. Kangaroos are **marsupials,** mammals with pouches. Like all mammals, marsupials are endotherms. They have mammary glands, fur, and teeth. Unlike the monotremes, marsupials do not lay eggs. They give birth to live young.

Like newly hatched monotremes, marsupial infants are not fully developed. At birth, the tiny embryos of a kangaroo are no larger than bumblebees. Shortly after birth, they drag themselves through their mother's fur until they reach a pouch on her abdomen. Inside the pouch are mammary glands. The young kangaroo climbs in, latches onto a nipple, and drinks milk until it is able to move around by itself and leave the pouch for short periods. Young kangaroos are called joeys.

There are about 280 species of marsupials. The only marsupial in North America north of Mexico is the opossum (uh PAHS suhm), shown in **Figure 22.** Other marsupials include koalas, shown in **Figure 23,** Tasmanian devils, and wallabies. Most marsupials live in Australia, New Guinea, and South America.

Figure 21 After birth, a kangaroo continues to develop in its mother's pouch. Older joeys leave the pouch but return if there is any sign of danger.

Figure 22 When in danger, an opossum will lie perfectly still and pretend to be dead so predators will tend to ignore it.

earth science
CONNECTION

Why do most marsupials live in Australia? Fossils indicate that the first marsupials lived in North America and western Europe about 75 million years ago. Scientists think that the continents were touching each other at that time. So the first marsupials were able to travel to South America, Africa, and Australia. After the continents separated, marsupials died out in Africa and Europe, but they persisted in South America and flourished in Australia. Today Australia has more marsupials than any other place on Earth.

Figure 23 Koalas sleep in trees during the day and are active at night. They eat nothing but eucalyptus leaves.

MATH BREAK

Ants for Dinner!

The giant anteater can stick its tongue out 150 times a minute. Count how many times you can stick out your tongue in a minute. Imagine that you are an anteater and you need 1,800 Calories a day. If you need to eat 50 ants to get 1 Calorie, how many ants would you have to eat per day? If you could catch two ants every time you stuck your tongue out, how many times a day would you have to stick out your tongue? How many hours a day would you have to eat?

Placental Mammals Most mammals are placental mammals. In **placental mammals,** the embryos stay inside the mother's body and develop in an organ called the *uterus*. Placental embryos form a special attachment to the uterus of their mother called a **placenta.** The placenta supplies food and oxygen from the mother's blood to the growing embryo. The placenta also removes wastes from the embryo.

The time during which an embryo develops within the mother is called the **gestation period.** Gestation (jeh STAY shuhn) periods in placental animals range from a few weeks in mice to as long as 23 months in elephants. Humans have a gestation period of about 9 months. After young placental mammals are born, they are fed with milk from the mother's mammary glands.

✓ Self-Check

Explain the difference between a monotreme, a marsupial, and a placental mammal. *(See page 636 to check your answer.)*

Kinds of Placental Mammals

Over ninety percent of all the mammals on Earth are placental mammals. Living placental mammals are classified into 18 orders. Each order has characteristics that help identify it. The characteristics of the most common orders are given on the following pages.

Toothless Mammals

This group includes anteaters, armadillos, aardvarks, pangolins, and sloths. Although these mammals are called "toothless," only the anteaters are completely toothless. The others have small teeth. Most toothless mammals feed on insects they catch with their long sticky tongues.

Not all **armadillos** eat ants. Some species eat other insects, frogs, mushrooms, and roots. When threatened, an armadillo rolls up into a ball and is protected by its tough plates.

The largest anteater is the 40 kg **giant anteater** of South America. Anteaters never destroy the nests of their prey. They open the nests, eat a few ants or termites, and then move on to another nest.

Insect Eaters

Insect eaters, or *insectivores,* live on every continent except Australia. Most insectivores are small, and most have long pointed noses to dig into the soil for food. Compared with other mammals, they have a very small brain and few specialized teeth. Insectivores include moles, shrews, and hedgehogs. The first mammals on Earth looked much like today's insectivores.

The **star-nosed mole** has sensitive feelers on its nose to help it find insects and feel its way while burrowing underground. Although they have tiny eyes, moles cannot see.

Hedgehogs live throughout Europe, Asia, and Africa. Their spines keep them safe from most predators.

Rodents

More than one-third of all mammalian species are rodents, and they can be found on every continent except Antarctica. Rodents include squirrels, mice, rats, guinea pigs, porcupines, and chinchillas. Most rodents are small animals with long, sensitive whiskers. Rodents are chewers and gnawers. All rodents have sharp front teeth for gnawing. Because rodents chew so much, their teeth wear down. So a rodent's incisors grow continuously, just like your fingernails do.

The **capybaras** (KAP i BAH ruhs) of South America are the largest rodents in the world. A female can have a mass of 70 kg—as much as a grown man.

Like all rodents, **beavers** have gnawing teeth. They use these teeth to cut down trees.

Lagomorphs

Rabbits, hares, and pikas belong to a group of placental mammals called lagomorphs. Like rodents, they have sharp gnawing teeth. But unlike rodents, they have two sets of incisors in their upper jaw and short tails. Rabbits and hares have long, powerful hind legs for jumping. To detect their many predators, they have sensitive noses and large ears and eyes.

The large ears of this **black-tailed jack rabbit** help it hear well.

Pikas are small animals that live high in the mountains. Pikas gather plants and mound them in "haystacks" to dry. In the winter, they use the dry plants for food and insulation.

Flying Mammals

Bats are the only mammals that can fly. These mammals have wings made of long finger bones connected by webs of skin. Bats are active at night and sleep in sheltered areas during the day. When they rest, they hang upside down. Most bats eat insects. But some bats eat fruit, and three species of vampire bats drink the blood of other animals. The largest bats are the fruit bats, with a mass of up to 1 kg and wingspans up to 2 m. But most bats have a mass of only a few grams.

Most bats hunt for insects at night. They find their way using echolocation. Bats make clicking noises when they fly. Trees, rocks, insects, and other objects reflect the sound back to the

In many Asian countries, **bats** are symbols of good luck, long life, and happiness.

bat, making an echo. Echoes from a big, hard tree sound very different from those reflecting off a soft, tasty moth. Bats that echolocate often have enormous ears to help them hear the echoes of their own clicks.

APPLY

What do bats have in common with submarines? Submarines use a form of echolocation called sonar to find and avoid objects underwater. Based on what you know about echolocation, what kind of instruments do you think are needed to navigate a submarine with sonar?

Carnivores

Carnivores are a group of mammals that have large canines and special teeth for slicing meat. The name *carnivore* means "meat eater"—the mammals in this group primarily eat meat. Carnivorous mammals include lions, wolves, weasels, otters, bears, raccoons, and hyenas. Carnivores also include a group of fish-eating marine mammals called *pinnipeds.* The pinnipeds include seals, sea lions, and walruses. Some carnivores also eat plants. For example, black bears eat grass, nuts, and berries and only rarely eat meat. But many carnivores eat nothing but other animals.

Coyotes are members of the dog family. They live throughout North America and in parts of Central America.

Cats are divided into two groups, big cats and small cats. All the big cats can roar. The largest of the big cats is the **Siberian tiger,** with a mass of up to 300 kg.

Raccoons have handlike paws that help them catch fish and hold their food. They can handle objects almost as well as monkeys can.

Walruses are pinnipeds. Unlike other carnivores, walruses do not use their canines for tearing food. Instead, they use them to defend themselves, to dig for food, and to climb on ice.

Hoofed Mammals

Horses, pigs, deer, and rhinoceroses are just a few of the many mammals that have thick hoofs. Most hoofed mammals are adapted for swift running. Because they are plant eaters, they have large, flat molars to help them grind plant material. Some also have a modified digestive system that can handle large amounts of cellulose.

Hoofed mammals are divided into groups based on the number of toes they have. Odd-toed hoofed mammals have one or three toes. Horses and zebras have a single large hoof, or toe. Other odd-toed hoofed mammals include rhinoceroses and tapirs. Even-toed hoofed mammals have two or four toes. These mammals include pigs, cows, camels, deer, hippopotamuses, and giraffes.

Giraffes are the tallest living mammals. They have long necks, long legs, and an even number of toes.

Rhinoceroses are huge odd-toed mammals. The horns of a rhinoceros continue to grow throughout its life.

Camels are even-toed mammals. The hump of a camel is a large lump of fat that provides energy for the camel when food is scarce.

Tapirs are large, three-toed mammals that live in forests. Tapirs can be found in Central America, South America, and Southeast Asia.

Trunk-Nosed Mammals

Elephants are the only mammals with a trunk. The trunk is an elongated and muscular combination of the upper lip and nose. Elephants use their trunk the same way we use our hands, lips, and nose. The trunk is powerful enough to lift a tree yet agile enough to pick small fruits one at a time. Elephants use their trunk to place food in their mouth and to spray their back with water to cool off.

There are two species of elephants, African elephants and Asian elephants. African elephants are larger and have bigger ears and tusks than Asian elephants. Both species eat plants. Because they are so large, elephants eat up to 18 hours a day to get enough food.

Elephants are the largest land animals. Male African elephants can reach a mass of 7,500 kg! Elephants are very intelligent and may live more than 60 years.

environmental science CONNECTION

Both species of elephants are endangered. For centuries, humans have hunted elephants for their long teeth, called tusks. Elephant tusks are made of ivory, a hard material used for carving. Because of the high demand for ivory, much of the elephant population has been wiped out. Today elephant hunting is illegal.

Elephants are social animals. They live in herds of related females and their offspring.

Self-Check

1. Why are bats classified as mammals and not as birds?

2. How are rodents and lagomorphs similar? How are they different?

(See page 636 to check your answers.)

Cetaceans

Whales, dolphins, and porpoises make up a group of water-dwelling mammals called cetaceans (see TAY shuhns). At first glance, whales and their relatives may look more like fish than mammals. But like all mammals, cetaceans are endotherms, they have lungs, and they nurse their young. Most of the largest whales are toothless whales that strain tiny, shrimplike animals from sea water. But dolphins, porpoises, sperm whales, and killer whales have teeth, which they use to eat fish and other animals.

Spinner dolphins spin like a football when they leap from the water. Like all dolphins, they are intelligent and highly social.

Like bats, cetaceans use echolocation to "see" their surroundings. **Sperm whales,** like this one, use loud blasts of sound to stun fish, making them easier to catch. .

Sirenia

The smallest group of water-dwelling mammals is called sirenia (sie REE nee uh). It includes just four species—three kinds of manatees and the dugong. These mammals are completely aquatic; they live along coasts and in large rivers. They are quiet animals that eat seaweed and water plants.

Manatees are also called sea cows.

Primates

Prosimians, monkeys, apes, and humans all belong to a group of mammals called **primates.** There are about 160 species of primates. All primates have the eyes facing forward, enabling both eyes to focus on a single point. Most primates have five fingers on each hand and five toes on each foot, with flat fingernails instead of claws. Primates' fingers and opposable thumbs are able to make complicated movements, like grasping objects. Primates have a large brain in proportion to their body size and are considered some of the most intelligent mammals.

Many primates live in trees. Their flexible shoulder joints and grasping hands and feet enable them to climb trees and swing from branch to branch. Most primates eat a diet of leaves and fruits, but some also eat animals.

Orangutans and other apes frequently walk upright. Apes usually have larger brains and bodies than monkeys.

Spider monkeys, like most monkeys, have grasping tails. Their long arms, legs, and tails help them move among the trees.

REVIEW

1. If you saw only the feet of a hippopotamus and a rhinoceros, could you tell the difference between the two animals? Explain your answer.

2. How are monotremes different from all other mammals? How are they similar?

3. To what group of placental mammals do dogs belong? How do you know?

4. **Making Inferences** What is a gestation period? Why do elephants have a longer gestation period than do mice?

Lions and tigers and bears . . . on Mars?! Find out more on page 617 of your LabBook.

Chapter Highlights

Vocabulary

down feather *(p. 383)*

contour feather *(p. 383)*

preening *(p. 383)*

lift *(p. 386)*

brooding *(p. 387)*

precocial chick *(p. 388)*

altricial chick *(p. 388)*

Section Notes

- Like reptiles, birds lay amniotic eggs and have thick, dry scales.

- Unlike reptiles, birds are endotherms and are covered with feathers.

- Because flying requires a lot of energy, birds must eat a high-energy diet and breathe efficiently.

- Birds' wings are shaped so that they generate lift. Lift is air pressure beneath the wings that keeps a bird in the air.

- Birds are lightweight. Their feathers are strong but lightweight, and their skeleton is relatively rigid, compact, and hollow.

- Because birds can fly, they can migrate great distances. They can nest in one habitat and winter in another. Migrating birds can take advantage of food supplies and avoid predators.

Labs

What? No Dentist Bills? *(p. 616)*

☑ Skills Check

Visual Understanding

LIFT The diagram on page 386 helps explain the concept of lift. Looking at this illustration, you can see that air must travel a greater distance over a curved wing than under a curved wing. The air above the wing must move faster than the air underneath in order to cover the greater distance in the same amount of time. Faster-moving air creates lower pressure above the wing. The higher pressure under the wing forces it up, creating lift.

Lift

Air flow

Lift

Vocabulary

therapsid *(p. 392)*

mammary glands *(p. 393)*

diaphragm *(p. 395)*

monotreme *(p. 396)*

marsupial *(p. 397)*

placental mammal *(p. 398)*

placenta *(p. 398)*

gestation period *(p. 398)*

carnivore *(p. 401)*

primate *(p. 405)*

Section Notes

- All mammals have mammary glands; in females, mammary glands produce milk. Milk is a highly nutritious fluid fed to the young.

- Like birds, mammals are endotherms.

- Mammals maintain their high metabolism by eating a lot of food and breathing efficiently.

- Mammals have a diaphragm that helps them draw air into their lungs.

- Mammals have highly specialized teeth for chewing different kinds of food. Mammals that eat plants have incisors and molars for cutting and grinding plants. Carnivores have canines for seizing and tearing their prey.

- Mammals are the only vertebrates that have mammary glands, fur, and two sets of teeth.

- Mammals are divided into three groups: monotremes, marsupials, and placental mammals.

- Monotremes lay eggs instead of bearing live young. Monotremes produce milk but do not have nipples or a placenta.

- Marsupials give birth to live young, but the young are born as embryos. The embryos climb into their mother's pouch, where they drink milk until they are more developed.

- Placental mammals develop inside of the mother for a period of time called a gestation period. Placental mothers nurse their young after birth.

Labs

Wanted: Mammals on Mars
(p. 617)

---

 internetconnect

 GO TO: go.hrw.com

Visit the **HRW** Web site for a variety of learning tools related to this chapter. Just type in the keyword:

KEYWORD: HSTVR2

*SCi***LINKS** **NSTA** **GO TO:** www.scilinks.org

Visit the **National Science Teachers Association** on-line Web site for Internet resources related to this chapter. Just type in the *sci*LINKS number for more information about the topic:

TOPIC: Bird Characteristics	*sci***LINKS NUMBER:** HSTL405
TOPIC: Kinds of Birds	*sci***LINKS NUMBER:** HSTL410
TOPIC: The Origin of Mammals	*sci***LINKS NUMBER:** HSTL415
TOPIC: Characteristics of Mammals	*sci***LINKS NUMBER:** HSTL420

Chapter Review

USING VOCABULARY

To complete the following sentences, choose the correct term from each pair of terms listed below.

1. ___?___ chicks can run after their mother soon after they hatch. ___?___ chicks can barely stretch their neck out to be fed when they first hatch. *(Altricial* or *Precocial)*

2. The ___?___ helps mammals breathe. *(diaphragm* or *air sac)*

3. The ___?___ allows some mammals to supply nutrients to young in the mother's uterus. *(mammary gland* or *placenta)*

4. Birds take care of their feathers by ___?___. *(brooding* or *preening)*

5. A lion belongs to a group of mammals called ___?___. *(carnivores* or *primates)*

6. ___?___ are fluffy feathers that help keep birds warm. *(Contour feathers* or *Down feathers)*

UNDERSTANDING CONCEPTS

Multiple Choice

7. Both birds and reptiles
   a. lay eggs.
   b. brood their young.
   c. are endotherms.
   d. have feathers.

8. Flight requires
   a. a lot of energy and oxygen.
   b. a lightweight body.
   c. strong flight muscles.
   d. All of the above

9. Only mammals
   a. are endotherms.
   b. nurse their young.
   c. lay eggs.
   d. have teeth.

10. Monotremes do not
    a. have mammary glands.
    b. care for their young.
    c. have pouches.
    d. have fur.

11. Lift
    a. is air that travels over the top of a wing.
    b. is provided by air sacs.
    c. is the upward force on a wing that keeps a bird in the air.
    d. is created by pressure from the diaphragm.

12. Which of the following is not a primate?
    a. a lemur   c. a pika
    b. a human   d. a chimpanzee

Short Answer

13. How are marsupials different from other mammals? How are they similar?

14. Both birds and mammals are endotherms. How do they stay warm?

15. What is the Bernoulli effect?

16. Why do some bats have large ears?

Concept Mapping

17. Use the following terms to create a concept map: monotremes, endotherms, birds, mammals, mammary glands, placental mammals, marsupials, feathers, hair.

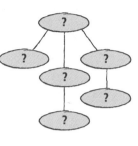

CRITICAL THINKING AND PROBLEM SOLVING

Write one or two sentences to answer the following questions.

18. Unlike bird and monotreme eggs, the eggs of placental mammals and marsupials do not have a yolk. How do developing embryos of marsupials and placental mammals get the nutrition they need?

19. Most bats and cetaceans use echolocation. Why don't these mammals rely solely on sight to find their prey and examine their surroundings?

20. Suppose you are working at a museum and are making a display of bird skeletons. Unfortunately, the skeletons have lost their labels. How can you separate the skeletons of flightless birds from those of birds that fly? Will you be able to tell which birds flew rapidly and which birds could soar? Explain your answer.

MATH IN SCIENCE

21. A bird is flying at a speed of 35 km/h. At this speed, its body consumes 60 Calories per gram of body mass per hour. If the bird has a mass of 50 g, how many Calories will it use if it flies for 30 minutes at this speed?

INTERPRETING GRAPHICS

Endotherms use a lot of energy when they run or fly. The graph below shows how many Calories a small dog uses while running at different speeds. Use this graph to answer the questions below.

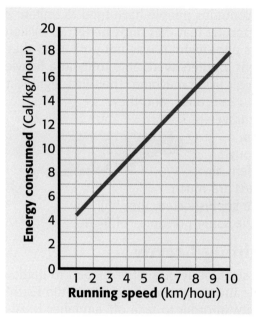

22. As the dog runs faster, how does the amount of energy it consumes per hour change?

23. How much energy per hour will this dog consume if it is running at 4 km/h? at 9 km/h?

24. Energy consumed is given in Calories per kilogram of body mass per hour. If the dog has a mass of 6 kg and is running at 7 km/h, how many Calories per hour will it use?

NOW What Do You Think?

Take a minute to review your answers to the ScienceLog questions on page 381. Have your answers changed? If necessary, revise your answers based on what you have learned since you began this chapter.

The Aerodynamics of Flight

For centuries people have tried to imitate a spectacular feat that birds perfected millions of years ago—flight! It was not until 1903 that the Wright brothers were able to fly in a heavier-than-air flying machine. Their first flight lasted only 12 seconds, and they only traveled 37 m. Although modern airplanes are much more sophisticated, they still rely on the same principles of flight.

Fighting Gravity

The sleek body of a jet is shaped to battle drag, while the wings are shaped to battle Earth's gravity. In order to take off, airplanes must pull upward with a force greater than gravitational force. This upward force is called *lift*. Where does an airplane get lift? The top of an airplane wing is curved, and the bottom is flat. As the wing moves through the air, air must travel farther and faster above the wing than below it. This difference causes the pressure above the wing to be less than the pressure below the wing. This difference pulls the airplane upward.

Push and Pull

The shape of its wing is not enough to get an airplane off the ground. Wings require air to flow past them in order to create lift. Airplanes also rely on *thrust,* the force that gives an airplane forward motion. Powerful engines and propellers provide airplanes with thrust. As airplanes move faster, more air rushes past the wings, and lift increases.

Airplanes usually take off into a head wind, which pushes against the airplane as it travels. Any force that pushes against an airplane's motion, like a head wind, is called *drag* and

can slow an airplane down. The body of an airplane has smooth curves to minimize drag. A tail wind is an airflow that pushes the airplane from the rear and shortens travel time. In order to increase speed, engineers design airplanes with streamlined bodies to reduce drag. Wings can also be designed to increase lift. A rounded and longer wing provides greater lift, but it also produces more drag. Engineers must consider such trade-offs when they design airplanes. Athletes also consider drag when they choose equipment. For example, runners and cyclists wear tight-fitting clothing to reduce drag.

Think About It!

▶ Airplanes have a variety of shapes and sizes and are designed for many purposes, including transport, travel, and combat. Some planes are designed to fly fast, and others are designed to carry heavy loads. Do some research, and then describe how the aerodynamics differ.

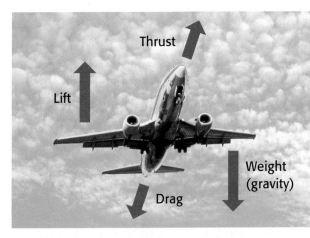

▲ *The design of airplanes got a boost from our feathered friends.*

WEIRD SCIENCE

NAKED MOLE-RATS

What do you call a nearly blind rodent that is 7 cm long and looks like a hot dog that has been left in the microwave too long? A naked mole-rat. For more than 150 years, this mammal—which is native to hot, dry regions of Kenya, Ethiopia, and Somalia—has puzzled scientists by its strange appearance and peculiar habits.

What's Hair Got to Do with It?

Naked mole-rats have such strange characteristics that you might wonder whether they are really mammals at all. Their grayish pink skin hangs loosely, allowing them to maneuver through the narrow underground tunnel systems they call home. At first glance, the naked mole-rats appear to be hairless, and hair is a key characteristic of mammals. However, naked mole-rats are not hairless, but they do lack fur. In fact, they have whiskers to guide them through the dark passages and hair between their toes to sweep up loose dirt like tiny brooms. Believe it or not, they also have hair on their lips to prevent dirt from entering their mouth as their massive teeth dig new passages through the dirt!

Is It Cold in Here?

Naked mole-rats have the poorest endothermic capacity of any mammal. Their body temperature remains close to the temperature of the air in their tunnels—a cool 31°C (more than 5°C cooler than the body temperature of humans). At night these animals minimize heat loss by huddling close together. Fortunately, the temperature does not change very much in their native habitat.

Who's in Charge?

Naked mole-rats are the only mammals known to form communities similar to those formed by social insects, such as honey bees. A community of naked mole-rats is made up of between 20 and 300 individuals that divide up tasks much like bees, wasps, and termites do. Each community has one breeding female, called the queen, and up to three breeding males. All females are biologically capable of reproducing, but only one does. When a female becomes a queen, she actually grows longer!

Think About It!

▶ At first glance, naked mole-rats appear to be missing several key characteristics of mammals. Do further research to find out what characteristics they have that classifies them as mammals.

◀ *Naked mole-rats are so unique that they have become a popular attraction at zoos.*

UNIT 6

Ecology

1661

John Evelyn publishes a book condemning air pollution in London, England.

1771

Joseph Priestley experiments with plants and finds that they use carbon dioxide and release oxygen.

What did you have for breakfast this morning? Whatever you ate, your breakfast was a direct result of living things working together. For example, milk comes from a cow. The cow eats plants to gain energy. Bacteria help the plants obtain nutrients from the soil. And the soil has nutrients because fungi break down dead trees.

All living things on Earth are interconnected. Our actions have an impact on our environment, and our environment has an impact on us. In this unit you will study ecology, the interaction of Earth's living things. This timeline shows some of the ways humans have studied and affected the Earth.

1970

The Environmental Protection Agency (EPA) is formed to set and enforce pollution control standards in the United States.

1973

The U.S. Congress passes the Endangered Species Act.

1990

In order to save dolphins from being caught in fishing nets, United States tuna processors announce that they will not accept tuna caught in nets that can kill dolphins.

Investigate!

A Mini-Ecosystem

In this activity, you will build and observe a miniature ecosystem.

Procedure

1. Place a layer of **gravel** in the bottom of a **large widemouth jar** or a 2 L soda bottle with the top cut off. Add a layer of **soil.**

2. Add a variety of **plants** that require similar growing conditions. Choose small plants that will not grow too quickly.

3. Spray **water** inside the jar to moisten the soil.

4. Cover the jar, and place it in indirect light. Describe the appearance of your ecosystem in your ScienceLog.

5. Observe your mini-ecosystem every week. Record all your observations.

What Do You Think?

In your ScienceLog, try to answer the following questions based on what you already know:

1. What are the main differences between a desert and a rain forest?

2. Where does the water in a lake come from?

3. Which has more species of plants and animals—the open ocean or a swamp? Why?

Analysis

6. List the nonliving factors that make up the ecosystem you have created.

7. How is your mini-ecosystem similar to a real ecosystem? How is it different?

Land Ecosystems

NEW TERMS

abiotic   savanna
biome   desert
deciduous   tundra
conifer   permafrost
diversity

OBJECTIVES

- Define *biome*.
- Describe three different forest biomes.
- Distinguish between temperate grasslands and savannas.
- Describe the importance of permafrost to the arctic tundra biome.

Imagine that you are planning a camping trip. You go to a travel agency, where you find a virtual-reality machine that can let you experience different places before you go. You put on the virtual-reality gear, and suddenly you are transported. At first your eyes hurt from the bright sunlight. The wind that hits your face is very hot and very dry. As your eyes grow accustomed to the light, you see a large cactus to your right and some small, bushy plants in the distance. A startled jack rabbit runs across the dry, dusty ground. A lizard basks on a rock. Where are you?

You may not be able to pinpoint your exact location, but you probably realize that you are in a desert. That's because most deserts are hot and dry. These **abiotic,** or nonliving, factors influence the types of plants and animals that live in the area.

The Earth's Biomes

A desert is one of the Earth's biomes. A **biome** is a geographic area characterized by certain types of plant and animal communities. A biome contains a number of smaller but related ecosystems within it. For example, a tropical rain forest is a biome that contains river ecosystems, treetop ecosystems, forest-floor ecosystems, and many others. A biome is not a specific place. For example, a desert biome does not refer to a particular desert. A desert biome refers to any and all desert ecosystems on Earth. The major biomes of the Earth are shown in **Figure 1.**

Figure 1 *Rainfall and temperature are the main factors that determine what biome is found in a region. What kind of biome do you live in?*

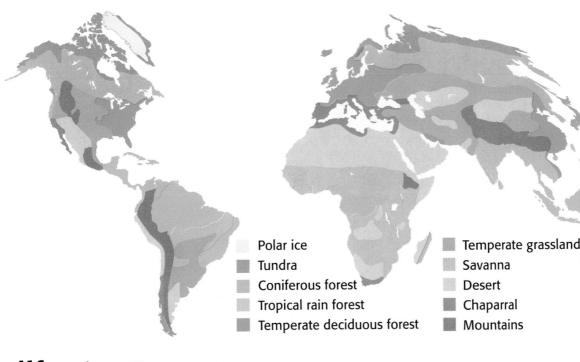

- Polar ice
- Tundra
- Coniferous forest
- Tropical rain forest
- Temperate deciduous forest
- Temperate grassland
- Savanna
- Desert
- Chaparral
- Mountains

Forests

Forest biomes develop where there is enough rain and where the temperature is not too hot in the summer or too cold in the winter. There are three main types of forest biomes—temperate deciduous forests, coniferous forests, and tropical rain forests. The type of forest that develops in a particular area depends on the area's temperature and rainfall.

Temperate Deciduous Forests In the autumn, have you seen leaves that change colors and fall from trees? If so, you have seen trees that are **deciduous,** which comes from a Latin word meaning "to fall off." By losing their leaves in the fall, deciduous trees are able to conserve water during the winter. **Figure 2** shows a temperate deciduous forest. Most of these forests contain several different species of trees. Temperate deciduous forests also support a variety of animals, such as bears and woodpeckers.

Average Yearly Rainfall
75–125 cm (29.5–49 in.)

Average Temperatures
Summer: 28°C (82.4°F)
Winter: 6°C (42.8°F)

Figure 2 *In a temperate deciduous forest, mammals, birds, and reptiles thrive on the abundance of leaves, seeds, nuts, and insects.*

In forests, plant growth occurs in layers. The leafy tops of the trees reach high above the forest floor, where they receive full sunlight.

Beneath the tree layer, woody shrubs and bushes catch the light that filters through the trees.

Grasses, herbs, ferns, and mosses are scattered across the forest floor. Most of the flowering plants bloom, and produce seeds in early spring, before the trees leaf out.

Average Yearly Rainfall
35–75 cm (14–29.5 in.)

Average Temperatures
Summer: 14°C (57.2°F)
Winter: −10°C (14°F)

Coniferous Forests Coniferous forests do not change very much from summer to winter. They are found in areas with long, cold winters. These forests consist mainly of *evergreen* trees, which are trees that don't lose their leaves and stay green all year. Most of these trees are **conifers,** which means that they produce seeds in cones. You have probably seen a pine cone. Pine trees are common conifers.

Most conifers can also be identified by their compact, needlelike leaves. These leaves, or needles, have a thick waxy coating that prevents them from drying out and being damaged during winter.

Figure 3 shows a coniferous forest and some of the animals that live there. Notice that not many large plants grow beneath the conifers, partly because very little light reaches the ground.

Figure 3 *Many animals that live in a coniferous forest survive the harsh winters by hibernating or migrating to a warmer climate for the winter.*

A coniferous forest is home to many insects and to birds that eat them.

Herbivores that live in the coniferous forest include moose, deer, porcupines, and chipmunks.

These conifer leaves are adapted to conserve water.

Carnivores of the coniferous forest include foxes and lynxes.

Tropical Rain Forests The tropical rain forest has more biological **diversity** than any other biome on the planet; that is, it contains more species than any other biome. As many as 100 species of trees may live in an area about one-fourth the size of a football field. Although some animals live on the ground, the treetops, or *canopy,* are the preferred living site. A huge variety of animals live in the canopy. If you counted the birds in the canopy of a rain forest, you would find up to 1,400 species! **Figure 4** shows some of the diversity of the tropical rain forest biome.

Most of the nutrients in a tropical rain forest biome are in the vegetation. The topsoil is actually very thin and poor in nutrients. Farmers who cut down the forest to grow crops must move their crops to freshly cleared land after about 2 years.

Average Yearly Rainfall
Up to 400 cm (157.5 in.)

Average Temperatures
Daytime: 34°C (93°F)
Nighttime: 20°C (68°F)

Figure 4 A Tropical Rain Forest Biome

Trees of various heights form a continuous green roof, called the canopy, that may extend 60 m above the forest floor.

Woody vines climb the tree trunks to reach sunlight.

Little light reaches the ground. Low-growing plants of the rain forest don't require a lot of light.

Grasslands

Plains, steppes, savannas, prairies, pampas—these are names for regions where grasses are the major type of vegetation. Grasslands are found between forests and deserts. They exist on every continent. Most grasslands are flat or have gently rolling hills.

Temperate Grasslands Temperate grassland vegetation is mainly grasses mixed with a variety of flowering plants. There are few trees because fires prevent the growth of most slow-growing plants. The world's temperate grasslands support small, seed-eating mammals, such as prairie dogs and mice, and large herbivores, such as the bison of North America, shown in **Figure 5**.

Average Yearly Rainfall
25–75 cm (10–29.5 in.)

Average Temperatures
Summer: 30°C (86°F)
Winter: 0°C (32°F)

Figure 5 *Bison roamed the temperate grasslands in great herds before they were hunted nearly to extinction.*

Average Yearly Rainfall
150 cm (59 in.)

Average Temperatures
Dry season: 34°C (93°F)
Wet season: 16°C (61°F)

Savanna The **savanna** is a tropical grassland with scattered clumps of trees. During the dry season, the grasses die back, but the deep roots survive even through months of drought. During the wet season, the savanna may receive as much as 150 cm of rain. The savannas of Africa are inhabited by the most abundant and diverse groups of large herbivores in the world, like those shown in **Figure 6**. These include elephants, giraffes, zebras, gazelles, and wildebeests.

Figure 6 *Carnivores, such as lions and leopards, prey on herbivores, such as these zebras and wildebeests. Hyenas and vultures usually "clean up" after the carnivores.*

Self-Check

Use the map in Figure 1 to compare the locations of deciduous and coniferous forests. Explain the differences in location between the two biomes. *(See page 636 to check your answers.)*

Deserts

Deserts are hot, dry regions that support a variety of plants and animals. In a desert, most of the water that falls to the ground evaporates. Organisms have evolved in specialized ways to survive extreme temperatures with very little water. For example, plants are spaced far apart to reduce competition for the limited water supply. Some plants have shallow, wide-spread roots that absorb water quickly during a storm, while others may have very deep roots that reach ground water.

Animals also have adaptations for survival in the desert. Most stay out of the hot sun and are active only at night, when temperatures are cooler. Mosquitoes and some other desert insects get their food and water by sucking the blood of larger animals. Tortoises eat the flowers or leaves of succulent plants and store the water under their shells for months. **Figure 7** shows how some desert plants and animals survive in the heat with little water.

How do animals survive in the heat of the desert? Quite nicely, thank you! See how on page 618 of your LabBook.

Average Yearly Rainfall
Less than 25 cm (10 in.)

Average Temperatures
Summer: 38°C (100°F)
Winter: 7°C (45°F)

Figure 7 *There are many well-adapted residents of the desert biome.*

Cactuses store water in their stems and roots.

Deep-rooted plants can reach down to ground water as deep as 30 m.

Some flowering plants bloom, bear seeds, and die within a few weeks after a heavy rain.

Jack rabbits' huge ears help them get rid of body heat.

Kangaroo rats never need to drink. They recycle water from the foods they eat.

Tundra

In the far north and on the tops of high mountains, the climate is so cold that no trees can grow. A biome called the **tundra** is found there.

Average Yearly Rainfall
30–50 cm (12–20 in.)

Average Temperatures
Summer: 12°C (53.6°F)
Winter: −26°C (−14°F)

Arctic Tundra The major feature of the arctic tundra is permafrost. During the short growing season, only the surface of the soil thaws. The soil below the surface, the **permafrost,** stays frozen all the time. Even though there is little rainfall, water is not in short supply. That's because the permafrost prevents the rain that does fall from draining, and the surface soil stays wet and soggy. Lakes and ponds are common.

The layer of unfrozen soil above the permafrost is too shallow for deep-rooted plants to survive. Grasses, sedges, rushes, and small woody shrubs are common. A layer of mosses and lichens grows beneath these plants on the surface of the ground. Tundra animals, like the one shown in **Figure 8,** include large mammals such as caribous, musk oxen, and wolves, as well as smaller animals, such as lemmings, shrews, and hares. Migratory birds are abundant in summer.

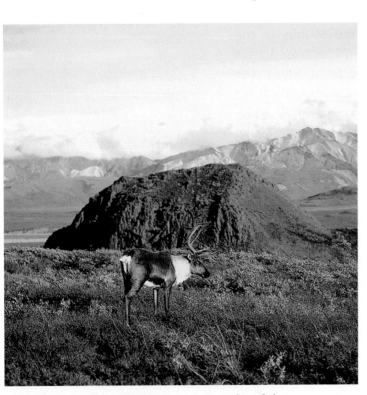

Figure 8 *Caribou migrate to more plentiful grazing grounds during long, cold winters in the tundra.*

Alpine Tundra Another tundra biome is found above the tree line of very high mountains. These areas, called alpine tundra, receive a lot of sunlight and precipitation, mostly in the form of snow.

÷ 5 ÷ Ω ≤ ∞ + Ω √ 9 ∞ ≤ Σ 2

MATH BREAK

Rainfall

In 1 year, how much more rain falls in a tropical rain forest than in a desert? What is the difference in the rainfall amounts in a coniferous forest and a savanna? To compare rainfall amounts, create a bar graph of the rainfall in each biome from the data given in this section.

REVIEW

1. How is the climate of temperate grasslands different from that of savannas?

2. Describe three ways that plants and animals are adapted to the desert climate.

3. Where are most of the nutrients in a tropical rain forest?

4. **Applying Concepts** Could arctic tundra accurately be called a frozen desert? Why or why not?

Section 2

Marine Ecosystems

NEW TERMS

marine
phytoplankton
zooplankton
Sargassum
estuary

OBJECTIVES

- Distinguish between the different areas of the ocean.
- Explain the importance of plankton in marine ecosystems.
- Describe coral reefs and intertidal areas.
- Explain what is unique about polar marine biomes.

They cover almost three-quarters of the Earth's surface. They contain almost 97 percent of the Earth's water supply. The largest animals on Earth inhabit them, along with billions of microscopic creatures, shown in **Figure 9.** Their habitats range from dark, cold, high-pressure depths to warm sandy beaches; from icy polar waters to rocky coastlines. What are they? They are the Earth's oceans and seas. Wherever these salty waters are found, marine ecosystems are found. In fact, a **marine** ecosystem is one that is based on salty water. This abiotic factor has a strong influence on the ecosystems of the oceans and seas.

Abiotic Factors Rule

In Section 1 you learned that rainfall and temperature are the main factors that determine what kind of terrestrial biome is found in a region. In the same way, marine biomes are shaped by abiotic factors, such as temperature, the amount of sunlight penetrating the water, the distance from land, and the depth of the water. These abiotic factors are used to define certain areas of the ocean. As with terrestrial biomes, marine biomes occur all over the Earth and can contain many ecosystems.

Sunny Waters Water absorbs light, so sunlight can penetrate only about 200 m below the ocean's surface, even in the clearest water. As you know, most producers use photosynthesis to make their own food. Because photosynthesis requires light, most producers are found only where light penetrates.

The most abundant producers in the ocean are called **phytoplankton.** Phytoplankton are microscopic photosynthetic organisms that float near the surface of the water. Using the energy of sunlight, these organisms make their own food just as plants that live on land do. **Zooplankton** are the consumers that feed on the phytoplankton. They are small animals that, along with phytoplankton, form the base of the oceans' feeding relationships.

Figure 9 *Marine ecosystems support a broad diversity of life. The humpback whale is one of the Earth's largest mammals. Phytoplankton, such as those shown in the smaller photo below, are very small and are the base of the oceans' food webs.*

The Earth's Ecosystems   **423**

Wonderful Watery Biomes

Unique and beautiful biomes exist in every part of oceans and seas. These biomes are home to many unusually adapted organisms. The major ocean areas and some of the organisms that live in them are shown below in **Figure 10.**

Figure 10 *The life in a particular area depends on how much light the area receives, how far the area is from land, and how far the area is beneath the surface.*

A **The Intertidal Zone** The intertidal zone is the area where the ocean meets the land. This area is above water part of the day, when the tide is out, and is often battered by waves. Mud flats, rocky shores, and sandy beaches are all in the intertidal area.

B **The Neritic Zone** Moving seaward, the water becomes gradually deeper toward the edge of the continental shelf. Water in this area is generally less than 200 m deep and usually receives a lot of sunlight. Diverse and colorful coral reefs exist in the waters over the continental shelf, where the water is warm, clear, and sunny.

A Sea grasses, periwinkle snails, and herons are common in a mud flat intertidal area. You will find sea stars and anemones on the rocky shores, while clams, crabs, and the shells of snails and conchs are common on the sandy beaches.

B Although phytoplankton are the major producers in this area, seaweeds are common too. Animals, such as sea turtles and dolphins, live in the area over the continental shelf. Corals, sponges, and colorful fish contribute to the vivid seascape.

C **The Oceanic Zone** Past the continental shelf, the sea floor drops sharply. This is the deep water of the open ocean. To a depth of about 200 m, phytoplankton are the producers. At greater depths, no light penetrates, so most organisms obtain energy by consuming organic material that falls from the surface.

D **The Benthic Zone** The benthic zone is the sea floor. It extends from the upper edge of the intertidal zone to the bottom of the deepest ocean waters. Organisms that live on the deep-sea floor obtain food mostly by consuming material that filters from above. Some bacteria are *chemosynthetic,* which means they use chemicals in the water near thermal vents to make food. A thermal vent is a place on the ocean floor where heat escapes through a crack in the Earth's crust.

C Many unusual animals are adapted for the darkness and high pressures of great ocean depths. Here you will see whales, squids, and fishes that glow in very deep, dark water.

D Organisms such as bacteria, worms, and sea urchins thrive on the deep-sea floor.

A Closer Look

Marine environments provide most of the water for Earth's rainfall through evaporation and precipitation. Ocean temperatures and currents have major effects on world climates and wind patterns. Humans harvest enormous amounts of food from the oceans and dump enormous amounts of waste into them. Let's take a closer look at some of the special environments that thrive in the ocean.

Coral Reefs In some sunny tropical waters, the sea floor contains coral reefs. Corals live in a close relationship with single-celled algae. The algae produce organic nutrients through photosynthesis. This provides food for the coral. The coral provide a place in the sun for the algae to live. The foundation of the reef is formed from coral skeletons that have built up over thousands of years. Coral reefs, like the one in **Figure 11,** are home to many marine species, including a large variety of brightly colored fish and organisms such as sponges and sea urchins.

The Sargasso Sea In the middle of the Atlantic Ocean is a large ecosystem with no land boundaries. It is called the Sargasso Sea. *Sargassum* is a type of algae usually found attached to rocks on the shores of North America, but it forms huge floating rafts in the Sargasso Sea. Animals adapted to this environment live among the algae. Most of the animals are the same color as the *Sargassum*. Some even look like it! Why do you think this is so? Can you find a fish in **Figure 12**?

Figure 11 *A coral reef is one of the most biologically diverse biomes.*

across the sciences
CONNECTION

Check out deep-sea volcanic vents called black smokers on page 436.

Self-Check

1. List three factors that characterize marine biomes.

2. Describe one way organisms obtain energy at great depths in the open ocean.

(See page 636 to check your answers.)

Figure 12 *The Sargasso Sea is a spawning place for eels and home to a rich diversity of organisms.*

Polar Ice The Arctic Ocean and the open waters surrounding Antarctica make up a very unusual marine biome. Why? Because it includes ice!

The waters are rich in nutrients from the surrounding landmasses. These nutrients support large populations of plankton. The plankton in turn support a great diversity of fish, seabirds, penguins, and sea mammals, such as sea lions, shown in **Figure 13.**

Figure 13 *The shores of Antarctica are breeding grounds for huge numbers of mammals and birds.*

Estuaries An area where fresh water from streams and rivers spills into the ocean is called an **estuary.** The fresh water from the rivers and streams constantly mixes with the salt water of the sea. The amount of salt in an estuary changes frequently. When the tide rises, the salt content of the water rises. When the tide recedes, the water becomes fresher. The fresh water that spills into an estuary is rich in nutrients that are carried by water running off the land. Because estuaries are so nutrient-rich, they support large numbers of organisms. They are crowded with masses of plankton, which provide food for many larger animals.

Intertidal Areas Some amazing adaptations can be found among the organisms that inhabit the intertidal areas. Mud flats are home to many burrowing worms and crabs and the shorebirds that feed on them. Sandy beaches are also home to burrowing worms, clams, crabs, and plankton that live among the sand grains.

On rocky shores, organisms either have tough holdfasts or are able to cement themselves to a rock to avoid being swept away by crashing waves. **Figure 14** shows some animals that can avoid being washed out to sea.

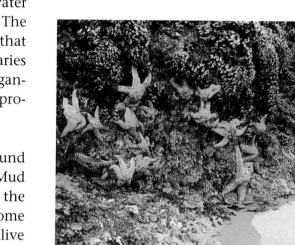

Figure 14 *Anemones "glue" themselves to rocks to keep from being washed out to sea. Sea stars can wedge themselves under a rock. Barnacles lay down a cement foundation!*

REVIEW

1. Explain how a coral reef is both living and dead.

2. Why do estuaries support such an abundance of life?

3. **Analyzing Relationships** Explain how the amount of light an area receives determines the kinds of organisms that live in the open ocean.

The Earth's Ecosystems   **427**

Freshwater Ecosystems

NEW TERMS

tributary   wetland
littoral zone   marsh
open-water zone   swamp
deep-water zone

OBJECTIVES

- List the characteristics of rivers and streams.
- Describe the littoral zone of a pond.
- Explain what happens to a pond as the seasons change.
- Distinguish between two types of wetlands.

A mountain brook bubbles over rocks in its pathway down a mountainside. A mighty river thunders through a canyon. A small backyard pond teems with life. A lake almost as large as a sea tosses boats during a heavy storm. A dense swamp echoes with the sounds of frogs and birds.

What do all of these places have in common? They are freshwater ecosystems. Like other ecosystems, freshwater ecosystems are characterized by abiotic factors, primarily the speed the water is moving.

Water on the Move

Brooks, streams, and rivers are ecosystems based on moving water. The water may begin flowing from melting ice or snow. Or it may come from a spring, where water flows up to the surface of the Earth. Each trickle or stream of water that joins a larger trickle or stream is a **tributary.**

As more tributaries join a stream, the stream becomes larger and wider, forming a river. Aquatic plants line the edge of the river. Bass, perch, and other fishes live in the open waters. In the mud at the bottom, burrowers, such as freshwater clams and mussels, make their home.

Organisms that live in moving water require special adaptations to avoid being swept away with the current. Producers, such as algae, diatoms, and moss, cling to rocks. Consumers, such as immature forms of insects, live under rocks in the shallow water. Some consumers, such as tadpoles, use suction disks to hold themselves to rocks.

As a river grows wider and slower, it may *meander* back and forth across the landscape. Organic material and sediment may be deposited on the bottom, building *deltas*. Dragonflies, water striders, and other invertebrates live in and on slow-moving water. Eventually, the moving water empties into a lake or an ocean. Look at **Figure 15** to see how a river can grow from melted snow.

Melting snow
Stream
Rapids
Waterfall
Tributary
Meander
Marsh
Delta
To lake or ocean

Figure 15 *This figure shows the features of a typical river. Where is the water moving rapidly? Where is it moving slowly?*

Still Waters

Ponds and lakes have different ecosystems than streams and rivers have. Lake Superior, the largest lake in the world, has more in common with a small beaver pond than with a river. **Figure 16** shows a cross section of a typical lake. In looking at this illustration, you will notice that the lake has been divided into three zones. As you read on, you will learn about these zones and the ecosystems they contain.

Where Water Meets Land Look at Figure 16 again, and locate the **littoral zone.** It is the zone closest to the edge of the land. This zone has many inhabitants. Plants that grow in the water closest to the shore include cattails and rushes. Farther from the shore are floating leaf plants, such as water lilies. Still farther out are submerged pond weeds that grow beneath the surface of the water.

The plants of the littoral zone provide a home for small animals, such as snails, small arthropods, and insect larvae. Clams, worms, and other organisms burrow in the mud. Frogs, salamanders, water turtles, various kinds of fishes, and water snakes also live in this area.

Life at the Top Look again at Figure 16. This time locate the **open-water zone.** This zone extends from the littoral zone across the top of the water. The open-water zone only goes as deep as light can reach. This is the habitat of bass, blue gills, lake trout, and other fish. In the open-water zone of a lake, phytoplankton are the most abundant photosynthetic organisms.

Life at the Bottom Now look at Figure 16 and find the **deep-water zone.** This zone is below the open-water zone, where no light reaches. Catfish, carp, worms, insect larvae, crustaceans, fungi, and bacteria live here. These organisms feed off dead organic material that falls down from above.

Quick **Lab**

Pond Food Connections

1. On **index cards**, write the names of the animals and plants that live in a typical freshwater pond or small lake. Write one type of organism on each card.

2. Use **yarn or string** to connect each organism to its food sources.

3. In your ScienceLog, describe the food relationships in the pond.

Figure 16 *Like marine ecosystems, freshwater ecosystems are characterized by abiotic factors that determine which organisms live there.*

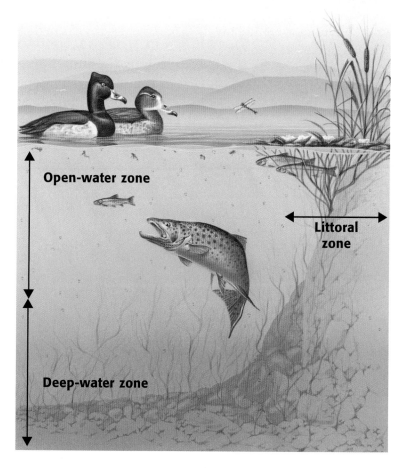

Open-water zone

Littoral zone

Deep-water zone

While exploring in a wetland, you have discovered a new organism. In your ScienceLog, draw the organism. Describe what it looks like and how it is adapted to its environment. Trade with a partner. Is your partner's organism believable?

Wetlands

A **wetland** is an area of land where the water level is near or above the surface of the ground for most of the year. Wetlands support a variety of plant and animal life. They also play an important role in flood control. During heavy rains or spring snow melt, wetlands soak up large amounts of water. The water in wetlands also seeps into the ground, replenishing underground water supplies.

Marshes A **marsh** is a treeless wetland ecosystem where plants such as cattails and rushes grow. A freshwater marsh is shown in **Figure 17.** Freshwater marshes are found in shallow waters along the shores of lakes, ponds, rivers, and streams. The plants in a marsh vary depending on the depth of the water and the location of the marsh. Grasses, reeds, bulrushes, and wild rice are common marsh plants. Muskrats, turtles, frogs, and red-wing blackbirds can be found living in marshes.

Figure 17 *Turtles find a lot of places to escape from predators in a freshwater marsh. Many species raise their young in these protected areas.*

Swamps A **swamp** is a wetland ecosystem where trees and vines grow. Swamps occur in low-lying areas and beside slow-moving rivers. Most swamps are flooded only part of the year, depending on the rainfall. Trees may include willows, bald cypresses, water tupelos, oaks, and elms. Vines such as poison ivy grow up trees, and Spanish moss hangs from the branches. Water lilies and other lake plants may grow in open-water areas. Swamps, like the one in **Figure 18,** provide a home for a variety of fish, snakes, and birds.

Figure 18 *The bases of the trunks of these trees are adapted to give the tree more support in the wet, soft sediment under the water in this swamp.*

From Lake to Forest

How can a lake or pond, like the one in **Figure 19,** disappear? Water entering a standing body of water usually carries nutrients and sediment along with it. These materials then settle to the bottom. Dead leaves from overhanging trees and decaying plant and animal life also settle to the bottom. Gradually, the pond or lake fills in. Plants grow in the newly filled areas, closer and closer toward the center. With time, the standing body of water becomes a marsh. Eventually, the marsh turns into a forest.

Figure 19 *Eventually decaying organic matter, along with sediment in the runoff from land, will fill in this pond.*

REVIEW

1. Describe some adaptations of organisms that live in moving water.

2. Compare the littoral zone with the open-water zone of a pond.

3. Describe how a swamp is different from a marsh.

4. **Interpreting Illustrations** Examine the diagram of a pond at right. Describe the types of organisms that might live in each zone.

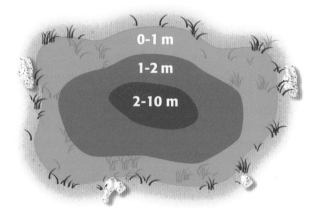

Chapter Highlights

Vocabulary

abiotic *(p. 416)*

biome *(p. 416)*

deciduous *(p. 417)*

conifer *(p. 418)*

diversity *(p. 419)*

savanna *(p. 420)*

desert *(p. 421)*

tundra *(p. 422)*

permafrost *(p. 422)*

Section Notes

- Rainfall and temperature are the main factors that determine what kind of biome is found in a region.

- The three main forest biomes are the temperate deciduous forest and the coniferous forest, which experience warm summers and cold winters, and the tropical rain forest, where temperatures stay warm.

- Grasslands receive more rain than deserts and receive less rain than forests. Temperate grasslands have hot summers and cold winters. Savannas have wet and dry seasons.

- Deserts receive less than 25 cm of rain a year. Plants and animals competing for the limited water supply have developed special adaptations for survival.

- The tundra biome is found mainly in the Arctic region. Arctic tundra is characterized by permafrost.

Labs

Life in the Desert *(p. 618)*

Vocabulary

marine *(p. 423)*

phytoplankton *(p. 423)*

zooplankton *(p. 423)*

Sargassum *(p. 426)*

estuary *(p. 427)*

Section Notes

- The kinds of marine organisms that inhabit an area vary depending on the water depth, the temperature, the amount of light, and the distance from shore.

- The intertidal area is the area where sea and land meet.

- The sea floor is home to biomes as different as coral reefs and thermal vents.

- The open ocean includes unique biomes, including the Sargasso Sea and the cold water oceans around the poles.

✓ Skills Check

Math Concepts

RAINFALL Using a meterstick, measure 400 cm on the floor of your classroom. This distance represents the depth of rainfall a rain forest receives per year. Next measure 25 cm. This measurement represents the amount of rainfall a desert receives per year. Compare these two quantities. Express your comparison as a ratio.

$$\frac{25}{400} = \frac{1}{16}$$

In 1 year, a desert receives $\frac{1}{16}$ the rainfall that a rain forest receives.

Visual Understanding

RAIN FOREST Look at Figure 4, on page 419. There are three layers of a rain forest—the upper story, the middle story, and the ground story. The upper story is the canopy, where most rain forest species live and where there is the most sunlight. The middle story is under the canopy and above the ground. The ground story is dark in most parts of the forest. Most plants in the rain forest grow very tall to compete for light in the canopy. Growth of plants on the ground story is not very dense due to the lack of available light.

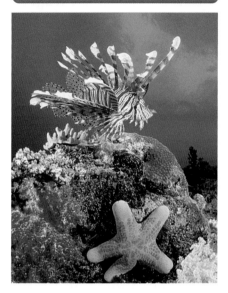

- An estuary is a region where fresh water from rivers spills into the ocean and the fresh and salt water mix with the rising and falling of the tides.

Labs

Discovering Mini-Ecosystems
(p. 619)

Vocabulary

tributary *(p. 428)*

littoral zone *(p. 429)*

open-water zone *(p. 429)*

deep-water zone *(p. 429)*

wetland *(p. 430)*

marsh *(p. 430)*

swamp *(p. 431)*

Section Notes

- Freshwater ecosystems are classified according to whether they have running water or standing water. Brooks, rivers, and streams contain running water. Lakes and ponds contain standing water.

- As tributaries join a stream between its source and the ocean, the volume of water in the stream increases, the nutrient content increases, and the speed decreases.

- The types of organisms found in a stream or river are determined mainly by how quickly the current is moving.

- The littoral zone of a lake is inhabited by floating plants. These plants provide a home for a rich diversity of animal life.

- Wetlands include marshes, which are treeless, and swamps, where trees and vines grow.

Labs

Too Much of a Good Thing?
(p. 620)

internet**connect**

GO TO: go.hrw.com

Visit the **HRW** Web site for a variety of learning tools related to this chapter. Just type in the keyword:

KEYWORD: HSTECO

GO TO: www.scilinks.org

Visit the **National Science Teachers Association** on-line Web site for Internet resources related to this chapter. Just type in the *sci*LINKS number for more information about the topic:

TOPIC: Forests	*sci*LINKS NUMBER: HSTL480
TOPIC: Grasslands	*sci*LINKS NUMBER: HSTL485
TOPIC: Marine Ecosystems	*sci*LINKS NUMBER: HSTL490
TOPIC: Freshwater Ecosystems	*sci*LINKS NUMBER: HSTL495

Chapter Review

USING VOCABULARY

To complete the following sentences, choose the correct term from each pair of terms listed below:

1. At the edge of the ___?___, the open ocean begins. *(continental shelf* or *Sargasso Sea)*

2. ___?___ are tiny consumers that live in water. *(Phytoplankton* or *Zooplankton)*

3. A ___?___ is a treeless wetland. *(swamp* or *marsh)*

4. ___?___ lose their leaves in order to conserve water. *(Deciduous trees* or *Conifers)*

5. The major feature of the ___?___ biome is permafrost. *(desert* or *tundra)*

6. Each major type of plant community and its associated animal communities make up a(n)___?___. *(estuary* or *biome)*

UNDERSTANDING CONCEPTS

Multiple Choice

7. The most numerous organisms in the oceans are the
   a. plankton.
   b. *Sargassum.*
   c. coral animals.
   d. marine mammals.

8. Marine ecosystems at the poles are unusual because
   a. animals spend time both in and out of the water.
   b. plankton are rare.
   c. they contain ice.
   d. the salt content of the water is very high.

9. The major factor that determines the types of organisms that live in a stream or river is
   a. the water temperature.
   b. the speed of the current.
   c. the depth of the water.
   d. the width of the stream or river.

10. Marine ecosystems
    a. contain the largest animals in the world.
    b. exist in all ocean zones.
    c. include environments where organisms survive without light.
    d. All of the above

11. Two major factors that determine what kind of a biome is found in a region are
    a. the amount of rainfall and the temperature.
    b. the depth of water and the distance from land.
    c. the wave action and the salt content of the water.
    d. All of the above

Short Answer

12. Describe how a stream changes as it moves from its source toward the ocean.

13. Describe two adaptations of animals to the desert environment.

14. Are wetlands always wet? Explain.

15. Explain how the salt content in an estuary changes constantly.

Concept Mapping

16. Use the following terms to create a concept map: tropical rain forest, deeprooted plants, coral reef, canopy, biomes, permafrost, desert, continental shelf, tundra, ecosystems.

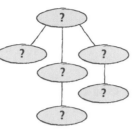

Write one or two sentences to answer the following questions:

17. While excavating a region now covered by grasslands, paleontologists discover the fossil remains of ancient fish and shellfish. What might they conclude?

18. In order to build a new shopping center, developers fill in a wetland. Afterward, flooding becomes a problem in this area. How can this be explained?

19. Explain why most desert flowering plants bloom, bear seeds, and die within a few weeks, while some tropical flowering plants remain in bloom for a much longer time.

MATH IN SCIENCE

20. What is the average difference in rainfall between a temperate deciduous forest and a coniferous forest?

21. An area of Brazilian rain forest received 347 cm of rain in one year. Using the following formula, calculate this amount of rainfall in inches.

    0.394 (the number of inches in a centimeter)
    $\times 347$ cm
    _____?_____ in.

INTERPRETING GRAPHICS

The graphs below illustrate the monthly temperatures and rainfall in a region during 1 year.

22. What kind of biome is probably found in the region represented by these graphs?

23. Would you expect to find coniferous trees in the region represented by these graphs? Why or why not?

NOW What Do You Think?

Take a minute to review your answers to the ScienceLog questions on page 415. Have your answers changed? If necessary, revise your answers based on what you have learned since you began this chapter.

Ocean Vents

▲ *"They're very slim, fuzzy, flattened-out worms. Really hairy," says scientist Bob Feldman about tubeworms.*

Picture the extreme depths of the ocean. There is no light at all, and it is very cold. But in the cracks between the plates on the bottom of the ocean floor, sea water trickles deep into the Earth. On the way back up from these cracks, the heated water collects metals, sulfuric gases, and enough heat to raise the temperature of the chilly ocean to 360°C. That is hot enough to melt lead! This heated sea water blasts up into the ocean through volcanic vents. And when this hot and toxic brew collides with icy ocean waters, the metals and sulfuric gases *precipitate,* that is, settle out of the heated ocean water as solids.

These solids form tubes, called black smokers, that extend up through the ocean floor. To humans, this dark, cold, and toxic environment would be deadly. But to a community of 300 species, including certain bacteria, clams, mussels, and tube worms, it is home. For these species, black smokers make life possible.

Life Without Photosynthesis

For a long time, scientists believed that energy from sunlight was the basis for the Earth's food chains and for life itself. But in the last 15 years, researchers have discovered ecosystems that challenge this belief. We now know of life-forms around black smokers that can live without sunlight. One type of bacteria uses toxic gases from a black smoker in the same way that plants use sunlight. In a process called *chemosynthesis,* these bacteria convert sulfur into energy.

These bacteria are primary producers, and the mussels and clams are the consumers in this deep-sea food web. In fact, the bacteria use the mussels and clams as a sturdy place to live. The mussels and clams, in turn, feed off the bacteria. This kind of relationship between organisms is called *symbiosis.* The closer to the vent the clams and mussels are, the more likely the bacteria are to grow. Because of this, the mussels and clams frequently move to find good spots near the black smokers.

What Do You Think?

▶ Conditions near black smokers are similar to conditions on other planets. Do some research on these extreme environments, both on Earth and elsewhere. Then discuss with your classmates where and how you think life on Earth may have started.

CAREERS

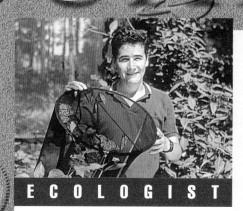

ECOLOGIST

Most winters **Alfonso Alonso-Mejía** climbs up to the few remote sites in central Mexico where about 150 million monarch butterflies spend the winter. He is researching the monarchs because he wants to help preserve their habitat.

onarch butterflies are famous for their long-distance migration. Those that eventually find their way to Mexico come from as far away as the northeastern United States and southern Canada. Some of them travel 3,200 km before reaching central Mexico.

Human Threats to Habitats

Unfortunately, the monarchs' habitat is increasingly threatened by logging and other human activities. Only nine of the monarchs' wintering sites remain. Five of the sites are set aside as sanctuaries for the butterflies, but even those are endangered by people who cut down fir trees for firewood or for commercial purposes.

Research to the Rescue

Alfonso's work is helping Mexican conservationists better understand and protect monarch butterflies. Especially important is Alfonso's discovery that monarchs depend on bushlike vegetation that grows beneath the fir trees, called understory vegetation.

Alfonso's research showed that when the temperature dips below freezing, as it often does at the high-altitude sites where the monarchs winter, some monarchs depend on understory vegetation for survival. This is because low temperatures (−1°C to 4°C) limit the monarchs' movement—the butterflies are not even able to crawl. At extremely cold temperatures (−7°C to −1°C), monarchs resting on the forest floor are in danger of freezing to death. But where there is understory vegetation, the monarchs can slowly climb the vegetation until they are at least 10 cm above the ground. This tiny difference in elevation can provide a microclimate that is warm enough to ensure the monarchs' survival.

The importance of understory vegetation was not known before Alfonso did his research. Now, thanks to Alfonso's work, Mexican conservationists will better protect the understory vegetation.

Get Involved!

▶ If you are interested in a nationwide tagging program to help scientists learn more about the monarchs' migration route, write to Monarch Watch, Department of Entomology, 7005 Howorth Hall, University of Kansas, Lawrence, Kansas 66045.

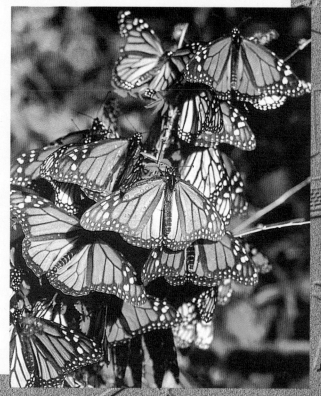

18 Environmental Problems and Solutions

Imagine . . .

Fifteen-year-old Haifa Aldorasi loves science and is concerned about the environment. She knows that today's paper is made by cutting down trees, making them into a pulp, and adding chemicals. Haifa is also fascinated by American history. She knows that the colonists made paper from linen and cotton rags. Their paper had no chemicals, yet some of it is still in good condition today. Haifa knows that today's paper will not last nearly as long as the colonists' paper did.

At age 13, Haifa put her knowledge of history, her love of science, and her concern about the environment together with a variety of vegetables, two years of research and experiments, and a whole lot of patience. The result? Haifa produced good-quality paper without cutting a single branch from a tree or using a single chemical. Her paper will last for centuries.

Haifa hasn't stopped her research. Hoping to develop a process that can be used to manufacture large amounts of paper without cutting any trees, she continues to perfect her technique. She hopes to eventually present her product to major paper companies. In the meantime, Haifa sells a paper-making kit she developed so that other people can make a good quality paper without using wood or chemicals.

In this chapter, you will learn about some environmental problems and what you can do to help, including making your own paper!

Recycling Paper

You can make paper, too. This method doesn't require cutting down trees. Instead, you reuse paper you would otherwise throw away.

Procedure

1. Tear up **two sheets of old newspaper** into small pieces. Put the pieces in a **blender.** Add **1 L of water.** Cover. Blend until you have a soupy pulp. At this point, you may also add small bits of orange peel, carrot peel, or flower petals. Blend again.

2. Cover the bottom of a **large square pan** with **2–3 cm of water.** Place a **wire screen** in the pan. Pour 250 mL of paper pulp onto the screen, as shown below. Spread it evenly into a thin layer with a **spatula** or a **wooden spoon.**

3. To separate the pulp from the water, lift out the screen with the pulp on it. Allow the water to drip off into the pan. Place the screen and the pulp inside a **section of newspaper.**

4. Close the newspaper. Carefully turn it over so that the screen is on top of the pulp. Cover the newspaper with **a flat board.** Press on the board to squeeze out the excess water.

5. Open the newspaper and carefully remove the screen, leaving the layer of pulp behind. Allow the pulp to dry completely. Then carefully peel it off the newspaper, as shown below.

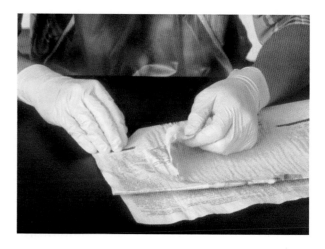

6. Use your recycled paper to write a note to a friend or to draw a picture.

Analysis

7. In what ways is your paper like regular paper? How is it different?

8. What could you do to improve your papermaking methods?

First the Bad News

You've probably heard it before. Perhaps you've even experienced it. The air is unhealthy to breathe. The water is harmful to drink. The soil is filled with poisons. In essence, the message is that our planet Earth is sick and in great danger.

NEW TERMS

pollution
pollutant
toxic
radioactive
waste
renewable
resource
nonrenewable
resource
biodegradable
overpopulation
deforestation
alien
biodiversity

OBJECTIVES

- Describe the major types of pollution.
- Distinguish between renewable and nonrenewable resources.
- Explain how habitat destruction affects organisms.
- Explain why human population growth is a problem.

Pollution

Pollution is the presence of harmful substances in the environment. These harmful substances, known as **pollutants,** take many forms. They may be solid materials, chemicals, noise, or even heat. Often, pollutants damage or kill the plants and animals living in the affected habitat, as shown in **Figure 1.** Pollutants may also harm humans.

Figure 1 *The water poured into the river by this factory is polluted with chemicals and heat. The smoke contains harmful chemicals that pollute the air.*

Piles of Garbage Americans produce more household waste than any other nation. If stacked up, the beverage cans we use in one year could reach the moon 17 times. That's a lot of cans! The average American throws away 12 kg of trash a week, which usually winds up in a landfill like the one in **Figure 2.** Businesses, mines, and industries also produce large amounts of wastes. Billions of kilograms of this waste are classified as *hazardous waste,* which means it's harmful to humans and the environment. Industries that produce paper, plastics, cement, and pesticides produce hazardous wastes. So do nuclear power plants, oil refineries, and metal processing plants. Hospitals, laboratories, and doctors' offices produce hazardous medical wastes. But industry shouldn't get all the blame. Hazardous wastes also come from homes—including yours! Old cars, paints, batteries, medical wastes, and detergents all pollute the environment.

Figure 2 *Every year, we throw away 150 million metric tons of garbage.*

Where Does It All Go? What happens to all our waste? Most of our household waste goes into giant landfills. Many companies bury hazardous wastes in landfills specially designed to contain the wastes. Some companies illegally dispose of their hazardous wastes. They simply dump wastes into rivers and lakes. That certainly causes pollution. Some wastes are burned in incinerators designed to reduce the amount of pollutants that enter the atmosphere. Some wastes are burned improperly, which adds to the pollution of the air.

Chemicals Are Everywhere Chemicals are used to treat diseases from colds to cancer. They are in plastics, thermometers, paints, hair sprays, and preserved foods. In fact, chemicals are everywhere. We can't get along without chemicals. Sometimes, though, we cannot get along *with* them. Chemical pesticides used to kill crop-destroying insects also pollute the soil and water. Rachel Carson, shown in **Figure 3,** wrote about the dangers of pesticides more than three decades ago.

A class of chemicals called CFCs has been widely used in some aerosol sprays, refrigerators, and plastics, but these uses of CFCs have been banned. CFCs rise high into the atmosphere. There they cause the destruction of ozone, a form of oxygen that protects the Earth from harmful ultraviolet light.

Another class of chemicals, called PCBs, was once used as insulation as well as in paints, household appliances, and other products. Then scientists learned that PCBs are **toxic,** or poisonous. PCBs are now banned, but they have not gone away. They break down very slowly in the environment, and they still pollute even the most remote areas on Earth, such as the area shown in **Figure 4.**

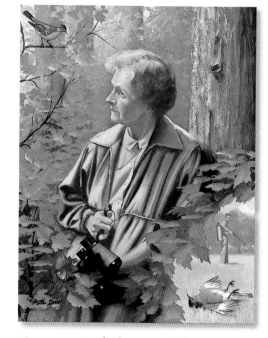

Figure 3 *Rachel Carson's book* Silent Spring, *published in 1962, made people aware of the environmental dangers of pesticides, especially to birds.*

High-Powered Wastes Nuclear power plants produce electricity for millions of homes and businesses. They also produce **radioactive wastes,** special kinds of hazardous wastes that take hundreds or thousands of years to become harmless. These "hot" wastes can cause cancer, leukemia, and birth defects in humans. Radioactive wastes can have harmful effects on all living things.

Figure 4 *No place on Earth is immune to pollution. PCBs and other pollutants have even been found in remote parts of the Arctic.*

Ozone in the stratosphere absorbs most of the ultraviolet light that comes from the sun. Ozone is destroyed by CFCs. The image of the hole in the ozone layer (the gray area in the center) was taken in 1998.

Health effects of increased exposure to ultraviolet light include blindness, rapid aging, skin cancer, and a weakened immune system.

Increased levels of ultraviolet light also contribute to lower crop yields and disruption of the ocean food chain.

Too Much Heat The Earth is surrounded by a mixture of gases, including carbon dioxide, that make up the atmosphere. The atmosphere acts as a protective blanket, keeping the Earth warm enough for life to exist. Since the late 1800s, however, the amount of carbon dioxide in the air has increased by 25 percent. Carbon dioxide and certain pollutants in the air act like a greenhouse. Most scientists think the increase in carbon dioxide and other pollutants has caused a significant increase in global temperatures. If the temperatures continue to rise, the polar icecaps could melt, raising the level of the world's oceans. Some scientists think the sea level could rise 10 cm to 1.2 m by the year 2100. A 1 m rise would flood coastal areas, pollute underground water supplies, and cause present shorelines to disappear.

It's Way Too Noisy! Some pollutants affect the senses. These include bad odors and loud noises. Too much noise is not just annoying; it affects the ability to hear and think. If construction workers and others who work in noisy environments do not protect their ears, they can slowly lose their hearing. The students shown in **Figure 5** are listening to music at a sensible volume so that their hearing will not be damaged.

Figure 5 *Listening to music at a sensible volume will help prevent hearing loss.*

REVIEW

1. Describe two ways pollution can be harmful.

2. Explain how loud noise can be considered pollution.

3. **Applying Concepts** Explain how each of the following can help people but harm the environment: hospitals, refrigerators, and road construction.

Resource Depletion

Another problem for our environment is that we are using up, or depleting, natural resources. Some of the Earth's resources are renewable, and others are nonrenewable. A **renewable resource** is one that can be used again and again or has an unlimited supply. Fresh water and solar energy are renewable resources, as are some kinds of trees. A **nonrenewable resource** is one that can be used only once. Most minerals are nonrenewable. Fossil fuels, such as oil and coal, are also nonrenewable resources.

Some nonrenewable resources, such as petroleum, are probably not in danger of running out in your lifetime. But we use more and more nonrenewable resources every year, and they cannot last forever. Plus, the removal of some materials from the Earth carries a high price tag in the form of oil spills, loss of habitat, and damage from mining, as shown in **Figure 6.**

MATH BREAK

Water Depletion

An underground water supply has a depth of 200 m of water. Water seeps in at the rate of 4 cm/year. Water is pumped out at the rate of 1 m/year. How long will this water supply last?

To find the net water loss from an underground water supply, subtract the amount that seeps into the water supply from the amount removed from the water supply.

How long will the water supply last if water seeps in at the rate of 10 cm/year and is removed at the rate of 10 cm/year?

Figure 6 *This area has been mined for coal using a method called strip mining.*

Nonrenewable or Renewable? Some resources once thought to be renewable are becoming nonrenewable. Ecosystems, such as tropical rain forests, are being polluted and destroyed, resulting in huge losses of habitat. Around the world, rich soil is being eroded away and polluted. A few centimeters of soil takes thousands of years to form and can be washed away in less than a year. Underground water needed for drinking and irrigation is used faster than it is replaced. Several centimeters of water may seep into an underground source each year, but in the same amount of time, *meters* of water are being pumped out.

Self-Check

1. In what ways do you use nonrenewable resources?

2. Why would it not be a good idea to use up a nonrenewable resource?

(See page 636 to check your answers.)

Alien Species

People are constantly on the move. Without knowing it, we take along passengers. Boats, airplanes, and cars carry plant seeds, animal eggs, and adult organisms from one part of the world to another. An organism that makes a home for itself in a new place is an **alien.** One reason alien species often thrive in foreign lands is that they are free from the predators in their native habitats.

Alien species often become pests and drive out native species. The zebra mussel, shown in **Figure 7,** hitched a ride on ships sailing from Europe to the United States in the 1980s. The purple loosestrife arrived long ago from Europe. Today it is crowding out native vegetation and threatening rare plant species in much of North America. Many organisms, such as the dandelion in **Figure 8,** are so common and have been here so long that it is easy to forget they don't belong.

Figure 7 *The zebra mussel (above) is an alien invader that is clogging water treatment plants in the Great Lakes region. The purple loosestrife from Europe (at right) is choking out natural vegetation in North America.*

Figure 8 *Dandelion has been used for more than 1,000 years in China as a medicinal herb. In the United States, it is mostly considered a weed.*

Human Population Growth

In 1800, there were 1 billion people on Earth. In 1990, there were 5.2 billion. By 2100, there may be 14 billion. Today, one out of ten people goes to bed hungry every night, and millions die each year from hunger-related causes. Some people believe that the human population is already too high for the Earth to support.

More people require more resources, and the human population is growing rapidly. **Overpopulation** occurs when the number of individuals becomes so large that they can't get all the food, water, and other resources they need on an ongoing basis.

Figure 9 shows that it took most of human history for the human population to reach 1 billion. Will the planet be able to support 14 billion people?

Human Population Growth

Population (in billions)

5
4
3
2
1
0

8000 B.C.   4000 B.C.   3000 B.C.   2000 B.C.   1000 B.C.   A.D. 1000   A.D. 2000

Figure 9 *The Earth's human population is now doubling every few decades.*

Habitat Destruction

Bio means "life." *Diversity* refers to "variety." The term **biodiversity** means "variety of life." It refers to the many different species found in a particular habitat all across the planet.

Every habitat has its own diverse combination of occupants. Every time a bulldozer digs or a chainsaw buzzes, every time hazardous chemicals or wastes are dumped, every time a dam is built, somewhere on Earth a habitat is damaged, changed, or destroyed. And every time a habitat is destroyed, biodiversity is lost.

Forests Trees give us oxygen, furniture, fuel, fruits and nuts, rubber, alcohol, paper, turpentine, pencils, and telephone poles. Once trees covered twice as much land as they do today. **Deforestation,** such as that in **Figure 10,** is the clearing of forest lands. Tropical forests are cut for mines, dams, and roads. They are cleared to give us wood for paper, fuel, and building materials. But after tropical rain forests are cleared, little can grow on the land. Tropical soil doesn't have many nutrients. The nutrients are mostly in the vegetation. People may try to farm for a few years before abandoning the infertile land.

Wetlands In the past, wetlands were considered unimportant. But as you know, that's not true. Wetlands help control flooding by soaking up the water from overflowing rivers. They filter pollutants from flowing water. They provide breeding grounds for fish, waterfowl, and other animals. They help prevent soil erosion and restore underground water supplies. Yet wetlands are often drained and filled to provide land for farms, homes, and shopping malls. They are dredged to keep passages open for ships and boats. Wetland habitats can also be destroyed by pollution.

Marine Habitats Oil is a major contributor to marine habitat loss. Oil from cities and industries is sometimes dumped into the ocean. Accidental spills and the waste from oil tankers that rinse their empty tanks at sea add more oil to the oceans. Spilled oil contaminates both coastal habitats and open waters, as shown in **Figure 11.** All the oceans are connected, so pollutants from one ocean can be carried around the world.

Figure 10 *Temperate forests are destroyed for many of the same reasons that tropical rain forests are destroyed.*

Explore

Look around the room. How many objects can you find that are made of wood? List them in your ScienceLog. Continue your list. Add all the products you can think of that come from trees.

Figure 11 *Oil from the* Exxon Valdez *damaged more than 2,300 km² of the Alaskan coast.*

Your town is about to celebrate its 200th birthday. A giant birthday party is planned. As part of the celebration, the town plans to release 1,000 helium balloons that say "Happy Birthday to Our Town." Why is this not a good idea? What can you do to convince town officials to change their plans?

Figure 12 *Plastics can harm wildlife at sea. This sea bird has become entangled in a plastic six-pack holder.*

If humans became extinct, other organisms would go on living. But if all the insects became extinct, many plants could not reproduce. Animals would lose their food supply. The organisms we depend on, and eventually all of us, would disappear from the face of the Earth.

Plastics are often dumped into marine habitats. They are lightweight and float on the surface. They are not **biodegradable,** so they are not broken down by the environment. Animals, such as the bird in **Figure 12,** try to eat them and often get tangled in them and die. Dumping plastics into the ocean is against the law, but it is difficult to catch the lawbreakers.

Effects on Humans

Trees and sea creatures are not the only organisms affected by pollution, global warming, and habitat destruction. The damage we do to the Earth affects us too. Sometimes the effect is immediate. If you drink polluted water, you may immediately get sick or even die. But sometimes the damage is not apparent right away. Some chemicals cause cancers 20 or 30 years after a person is exposed to them. Your children or grandchildren may be the ones who have to deal with depleted resources.

Anything that endangers other organisms will eventually endanger us too. Taking good care of the environment requires being concerned about what is happening right now. It also requires looking ahead to the future.

REVIEW

1. Why do alien species often thrive?

2. Explain how human population growth is related to pollution problems.

3. Applying Concepts How can the destruction of wetland habitats affect humans?

The Good News: Solutions

As you've seen, the news is bad. But it isn't *all* bad. In fact, there is plenty of good news. The good news is about what people can do—and are doing—to save the Earth. It is about what *you* can do to save the Earth. Just as people are responsible for damaging the Earth, people can also take responsibility for helping to heal and preserve the Earth.

NEW TERMS
conservation
recycling
resource recovery

OBJECTIVES
- Explain the importance of conservation.
- Describe the three Rs and their importance.
- Explain how habitats can be protected.
- List ways you can help protect the Earth.

Conservation

One major way to help save the Earth is conservation. **Conservation** is the wise use of and the preservation of natural resources. If you ride your bike to your friend's house, you conserve fuel. At the same time, you prevent air pollution. If you use organic compost instead of chemical fertilizer on your garden, you conserve the resources needed to make the fertilizer. You also prevent soil and water pollution.

Practicing conservation means using fewer natural resources. It also means reducing waste. The three Rs, shown in **Figure 13,** describe three ways to conserve resources and reduce damage to the Earth: **R**educe, **R**euse, and **R**ecycle.

Figure 13 *These teenagers are observing the three Rs by using a cloth shopping bag, donating outgrown clothing to be reused, and recycling plastic.*

Reduce — Reuse — Recycle

Reduce

The most obvious way to conserve the Earth's resources is to use less. This will also help reduce pollution and wastes. Some companies have started using a variety of strategies to try to conserve resources. They often save money in the process.

Reducing Waste and Pollution   One-third of the waste from cities and towns is packaging. To conserve resources and reduce waste, products can be wrapped in less paper and plastic. Fast foods can be wrapped in thin paper instead of large plastic containers that are not biodegradable. You can choose to take your purchases without a sack if you don't need one. Scientists, such as the ones in **Figure 14,** are working to make better biodegradable plastics.

Figure 14 *These scientists are studying ways to use waste products to make biodegradable plastics.*

Some companies are searching for less hazardous materials to use in making products. For example, some farmers refuse to use pesticides and chemical fertilizers. They practice organic farming. They use mulch, compost, manure, and natural pesticides. Agricultural specialists are also developing new farming techniques that are better for the environment.

Reducing Use of Nonrenewable Resources Scientists are searching for alternative sources of energy. They want to avoid burning fuels and using nuclear energy. Solar energy already powers some calculators. In some parts of the world it also heats water and powers homes, such as those shown in **Figure 15.** Some engineers are working to make solar-powered cars practical for more people. Other scientists are investigating the use of alternative power sources, such as wind, tides, and falling water.

Reducing the use of resources and the amount of waste is not the job of industry and agriculture alone. Individuals use plenty of manufactured products and plenty of energy too. They also produce large quantities of waste. Each United States citizen produces 40 times more waste than a citizen of a developing country. Why do you think this is so? What could you do to reduce the amount of trash that you produce? Every individual can take responsibility for helping to conserve the Earth's resources.

Figure 15 *Rooftop solar panels provide most of the energy used in this neighborhood in Rotterdam, Holland.*

Reuse

Do you get hand-me-down clothes from an older sibling? Do you try to fix broken sports equipment instead of thowing it away? If so, you are helping preserve the Earth by *reusing* products.

Reusing Products Every time someone reuses a plastic bag, one less bag needs to be made, and one less bag pollutes the Earth. Every time someone uses a rechargeable battery, one less battery needs to be made, and one less battery will pollute the Earth. Reusing is an important way to conserve resources and prevent pollution.

Reusing Water About 85 percent of the water used in homes goes down the drain. Communities with water shortages are experimenting with reclaiming and reusing this waste water. Some use green plants or filter-feeding animals such as clams to clean the water. The water isn't pure enough to drink, but it is fine for watering lawns and golf courses, such as the one shown in **Figure 16.**

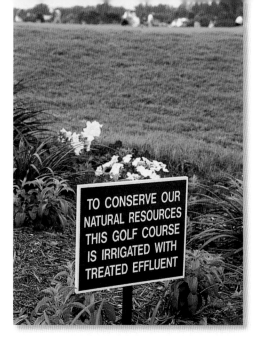

Figure 16 *This golf course is being watered with reclaimed water.*

Recycle

Recycling is a form of reuse. **Recycling** requires breaking down trash and using it again. Sometimes recycled products are used to make the same kind of products. Sometimes they are made into different products. The park bench in **Figure 17** was made from plastic foam cups, hamburger boxes, and plastic bottles that once held detergent, yogurt, and margarine. All of the containers pictured in **Figure 18** can be easily recycled.

Figure 17 *This park bench is made of melted, remolded, and reused plastic.*

Self-Check

1. How can you reduce the amount of electricity you use?

2. List five products that can be reused easily.

(See page 636 to check your answers.)

Figure 18 *These containers are examples of common household trash that can be recycled.*

Figure 19 *Each kind of recycled material is sorted into its own bin in these special trucks. The recycled trash is then delivered to a recycling plant for processing.*

Recycling Trash Plastics, paper, aluminum cans, waste wood, glass, and cardboard are some examples of materials that can be recycled. Every week, half a million trees are needed to make Sunday newspapers. Recycling newspapers could save many trees. Recycling aluminum foil and cans saves 95 percent of the energy needed to change raw ore into aluminum. Glass makes up 8 percent of all our waste. It can be remelted to make new bottles and jars. Lead batteries can be recycled into new batteries.

Some cities, such as Austin, Texas, make recycling easy. Special containers for glass, plastic, aluminum, and paper are provided to each city customer. Each week trash to be recycled is collected in special trucks, such as the one shown in **Figure 19,** at the same time other waste is collected.

Recycling Resources Waste that can be burned can also be used to generate electricity in factories like the one shown in **Figure 20.** The process of transforming garbage to electricity is called **resource recovery.** The waste collected by all the cities and towns in the United States could produce about the same amount of electricity as 15 large nuclear power plants. Some companies are beginning to do this with their own waste. It saves them money, and it is responsible management.

Recycling is not difficult. Yet in the United States, only about 11 percent of the garbage is recycled. This compares with about 30 percent in Europe and 50 percent in Japan.

Figure 20 *A waste-to-energy plant can provide electricity to many homes and businesses.*

Explore

Look around your school or home. How many objects are made of wood or plastic? How many of these items can be reused or recycled? How many are made of recycled material? Make a list of these items in your ScienceLog.

REVIEW

1. Define and explain *conservation.*

2. Describe the three main ways to conserve natural resources.

3. **Analyzing Relationships** How does conservation of resources also reduce pollution and other damage to the Earth?

Maintaining Biodiversity

Imagine a forest with just one kind of tree. If a disease hits that species, the entire forest might be wiped out. Now imagine a forest with 10 different kinds of trees. If a disease hits one kind of tree, nine different species will remain. Look at **Figure 21.** This field is growing a very important crop—cotton. But it is not very diverse. For the crop to thrive, the farmer must carefully manage the crop with weedkillers, pesticides, and fertilizers. Biodiversity helps to keep communities naturally stable.

How much biodiversity is in your part of the world? Investigate by turning to page 622 in your LabBook.

Figure 21 *What could happen if a cotton disease hits this cotton field? Biodiversity is low in fields of crops like this one.*

Species variety is also important because each species makes a unique contribution to an ecosystem. In addition, many species are important to humans. They provide many things, such as foods, medicines, natural pest control, beauty, and companionship, to name just a few.

Species Protection One way to maintain biodiversity is through the protection of individual species. In the United States, the Endangered Species Act is designed to do just that. Endangered organisms are included in a special list. The law forbids activities that would damage a plant or animal on the endangered species list. It also requires the development of programs to help endangered populations recover. Some endangered species are now increasing in number, such as the California condor in **Figure 22.**

Unfortunately, the process of getting a species on the endangered list takes a long time. Many new species need to be added to the list. Many species become extinct even before they are listed!

Figure 22 *The California condor is returning from the verge of extinction thanks to careful captive breeding. The condor is an important scavenger in its environment.*

Figure 23 *Setting aside public lands for wildlife is one way to protect habitats.*

Habitat Protection Waiting until a species is almost extinct to begin protecting it is like waiting until your teeth are rotting to begin brushing them. Scientists want to prevent species from becoming endangered as well as from becoming extinct.

Plants, animals, and microorganisms do not live independently. Each is part of a huge interconnected web of organisms. To protect the entire web and to avoid disrupting the worldwide balance of nature, complete habitats, not just individual species, must be preserved. *All* species, not just those that are endangered, must be protected. All of the species that live in the nature preserve pictured in **Figure 23** are protected because the entire habitat is protected.

Strategies

Laws have been enacted that are designed to conserve the Earth's environment. The purposes of such laws are listed below along with some of the strategies by which citizens can help achieve these goals.

- **Reduce pesticide use.**
  Spray only pesticides that are targeted specifically for harmful insects. Use natural pesticides that interfere with the ways certain insects grow, develop, and live. Develop more biodegradable pesticides that will not injure birds, animals, or plants.

- **Reduce pollution.**
  Regulations prohibit the dumping of toxic substances and solid wastes into rivers, streams, lakes, and oceans and onto farmland and forests.

- **Protect habitats.**
  Conserve wetlands. Reduce deforestation. Practice logging techniques that consider the environment. Use resources at a rate that allows them to be replenished. Protect entire habitats.

- **Enforce the Endangered Species Act.**
  Speed up the process of getting endangered organisms listed.

- **Develop alternative energy sources.**
  Increase the use of solar power, wind power, and other renewable energy sources.

Trash Check

Keep track of all the trash you produce in one day. Classify it into groups. How much is food scraps? What might be considered a hazardous waste? What can be recycled? What can be reused? How can you reduce the amount of trash you produce?

What *You* Can Do

Reduce, reuse, recycle. Protect the Earth. These are jobs for everyone. Children as well as adults can help to save the Earth. The following list offers some suggestions for how *you* can help. How many of these things do you already do? What can you add to the list?

1. Buy things in packages that can be recycled.
2. Give away your old toys.
3. Use recycled paper.
4. Fill up both sides of a sheet of paper.
5. If you can't use permanent dishes, use paper instead of plastic-foam cups and plates.
6. Turn off the water while you brush your teeth.
7. Don't buy anything made from an endangered animal.
8. Use rechargeable batteries.
9. Turn off lights, CD players, and computers when not in use.
10. Wear hand-me-downs.
11. Share books with friends, or use the library.
12. Use cloth napkins and kitchen towels.
13. Carry a reusable cloth shopping bag to the store.
14. Use a lunch box or reuse your paper lunch bags.
15. Recycle glass, plastics, paper, aluminum, and batteries.
16. Make a compost heap.
17. Buy products made from biodegradable plastic.
18. Walk, ride a bicycle, or use public transportation.
19. Buy products with little or no packaging.
20. Repair leaking faucets.

THIS BAG IS BIODEGRADABLE

REVIEW

1. Describe why biodiversity is important.
2. Why is it important to protect entire habitats?
3. **Applying Concepts** In the list above, identify which suggestions involve reducing, reusing, or recycling. Some suggestions will involve more than one of the three Rs.

Chapter Highlights

Vocabulary

pollution *(p. 440)*

pollutant *(p. 440)*

toxic *(p. 441)*

radioactive waste *(p. 441)*

renewable resource *(p. 443)*

nonrenewable resource *(p. 443)*

alien *(p. 444)*

overpopulation *(p. 444)*

biodiversity *(p. 445)*

deforestation *(p. 445)*

biodegradable *(p. 446)*

Section Notes

- The Earth is being polluted by solid wastes, hazardous chemicals, radioactive materials, noise, and heat.

- Some of the Earth's resources renew themselves, and others do not. Some of the nonrenewable resources are being used up.

- Alien species often invade foreign lands, where they may thrive, become pests, and threaten native species.

- The human population is in danger of reaching numbers that the Earth cannot support.

- The Earth's habitats are being destroyed in a variety of ways, including by deforestation, the filling of wetlands, and pollution.

- Deforestation may cause the extinction of species and often leaves the soil infertile.

- Air, water, and soil pollution can damage or kill animals, plants, and microorganisms.

- Humans depend on many different kinds of organisms. Pollution, global warming, habitat destruction—anything that affects other organisms will eventually affect humans too.

☑ Skills Check

Math Concepts

NET WATER LOSS Suppose that water seeps into an underground water supply at the rate of 10 cm/year. The underground water supply is 100 m deep, but it is being pumped out at about 2 m/year. How long will the water last?

First convert all measurements to centimeters.

(100 m = 10,000 cm; 2 m = 200 cm)

Then find the net loss of water per year.

200 cm – 10 cm = 190 cm (net loss per year)

Now divide the depth of the underground water supply by the net loss per year to find out how many years this water supply will last.

10,000 cm ÷ 190 cm = 52.6 years

Visual Understanding

THINGS YOU CAN DO Obviously, the strategies listed on page 452 to help preserve the Earth's habitats are strategies that scientists and other professionals are developing. To help you understand some of the things that you can do now, review the list on page 453.

Vocabulary

conservation *(p. 447)*

recycling *(p. 449)*

resource recovery *(p. 450)*

Section Notes

- Conservation is the wise use of and preservation of the Earth's natural resources. By practicing conservation, people can reduce pollution and ensure that resources will be available to people in the future.

- Conservation involves the three Rs: Reduce, Reuse, and Recycle. Reducing means using fewer resources to begin with. Reusing means using materials and products over and over. Recycling involves breaking down used products and making them into new ones.

- Biodiversity is the variety of life on Earth. It is vital for maintaining stable, healthy, and functioning ecosystems.

- Habitats can be protected by using fewer pesticides, reducing pollution, avoiding habitat destruction, protecting species, and using alternative renewable sources of energy.

- Everyone can help to save the Earth by practicing the three Rs in their daily life.

Labs

Biodiversity—What a Disturbing Thought! *(p. 622)*

Deciding About Environmental Issues *(p. 624)*

---

 internetconnect

go.hrw.com **GO TO:** go.hrw.com

Visit the **HRW** Web site for a variety of learning tools related to this chapter. Just type in the keyword:

KEYWORD: HSTENV

 SCILINKS **NSTA** **GO TO:** www.scilinks.org

Visit the **National Science Teachers Association** on-line Web site for Internet resources related to this chapter. Just type in the *sci*LINKS number for more information about the topic:

TOPIC: Air Pollution	*sci*LINKS NUMBER: HSTL505
TOPIC: Resource Depletion	*sci*LINKS NUMBER: HSTL510
TOPIC: Population Growth	*sci*LINKS NUMBER: HSTL515
TOPIC: Recycling	*sci*LINKS NUMBER: HSTL520
TOPIC: Maintaining Biodiversity	*sci*LINKS NUMBER: HSTL525

Chapter Review

To complete the following sentences, choose the correct term from each pair of terms listed below:

1. __?__ is the presence of harmful substances in the environment. *(Pollution or Biodiversity)*

2. __?__ is a type of pollution produced by nuclear power plants. *(CFC or Radioactive waste)*

3. A __?__ resource can be used only once. *(nuclear or nonrenewable)*

4. __?__ is the variety of forms among living things. *(Biodegradable or Biodiversity)*

5. __?__ is the breaking down of trash and using it to make a new product. *(Recycling or Reuse)*

UNDERSTANDING CONCEPTS

Multiple Choice

6. Habitat protection is important because
   a. organisms do not live independently.
   b. protecting habitats is a way to protect species.
   c. without it the balance of nature could be disrupted.
   d. All of the above

7. The Earth's resources can be conserved
   a. only by the actions of industry.
   b. by reducing the use of nonrenewable resources.
   c. if people do whatever they want to do.
   d. by throwing away all our trash.

8. Endangered species
   a. are those that are extinct.
   b. are found only in tropical rain forests.
   c. can sometimes be brought back from near extinction.
   d. are all protected by the Endangered Species Act.

9. Global warming is a danger
   a. only to people living in warm climates.
   b. to organisms all over the planet.
   c. only to life at the poles.
   d. to the amount of carbon dioxide in the air.

10. Overpopulation
    a. does not occur among human beings.
    b. helps keep pollution levels down.
    c. occurs when a species cannot get all the food, water, and other resources it needs.
    d. occurs only in large cities.

11. Biodiversity
    a. is of no concern to scientists.
    b. helps to keep ecosystems stable.
    c. causes diseases to destroy populations.
    d. is found only in temperate forests.

Short Answer

12. Describe how you can help to conserve resources. Include strategies from all of the three Rs.

13. Describe the connection between alien species and endangered species.

Concept Mapping

14. Use the following terms to create a concept map: pollution, pollutants, CFCs, cancer, PCBs, toxic, radioactive wastes, global warming.

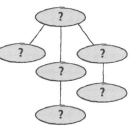

CRITICAL THINKING AND PROBLEM SOLVING

Write one or two sentences to answer the following question:

15. Suppose that the supply of fossil fuels were going to run out in 10 years. What would happen if we ran out without being prepared? What could be done to prepare for such an event?

MATH IN SCIENCE

16. If each person in a city of 150,000 throws away 12 kg of trash every week, how many metric tons of trash does the city produce per year? (There are 52 weeks in a year and 1,000 kg in a metric ton.)

INTERPRETING GRAPHICS

The illustration above shows how people in one home use natural resources.

17. Identify ways in which the people in this picture are wasting natural resources. Describe at least three examples, and tell what could be done to conserve resources.

18. Identify which resources in this picture are renewable.

19. Identify any sources of hazardous waste in this picture.

20. Explain how the girl wearing headphones is reducing pollution in the air. How could such a choice cause her harm?

NOW What Do You Think?

Take a minute to review your answers to the ScienceLog questions on page 439. Have your answers changed? If necessary, revise your answers based on what you have learned since you began this chapter.

CAREERS

BIOLOGIST

Dagmar Werner works at the Carara Biological Preserve, in Costa Rica, protecting green iguanas. Suffering from the effects of hunting, pollution, and habitat destruction, the iguana was nearly extinct. Since the 1980s, Werner has improved the iguanas' chances of survival by breeding them and releasing thousands of young iguanas into the wild. She also trains other people to do the same.

At Werner's "iguana ranch" preserve, female iguanas lay their eggs in artificial nests. After they hatch, the young lizards are placed in a temperature- and humidity-controlled incubator and given a special diet. As a result, the iguanas grow faster and stronger and are better protected from predators than their wild counterparts. Ordinarily, less than 2 percent of all iguanas survive to adulthood, but Werner's iguanas have an 80 percent survival rate. Once the iguanas are released into the wild, Werner tracks and monitors them to determine whether they have successfully adapted to their less-controlled environment.

Chicken of the Trees

Because she knew the iguana was close to extinction, Werner took an immediate and drastic approach to saving the lizards. She combined her captive-breeding program at the preserve with an education program that shows farmers a new way to make money from the rain forest. Instead of cutting down rain forest to raise cattle, Werner encourages farmers to raise iguanas. The iguanas can be released into the wild or sold for food. Known as "chicken of the trees," this lizard has been a favored source of meat among rain-forest inhabitants for thousands of years.

With Werner's methods, farmers can protect iguanas and still earn a living. But convincing farmers hasn't been easy. According to Werner, "Many locals have never thought of wild animals as creatures that must be protected in order to survive." To help, Werner has established the Fundación Pro Iguana Verde (the Green Iguana Foundation), which sponsors festivals and education seminars. These activities promote the traditional appeal of the iguana, increase pride in the animal, and heighten awareness about the iguana's economic importance.

Find Other Solutions

▶ The green iguana is just one animal that is nearing extinction in the rain forest. Research another endangered species and find out what scientists and local communities are doing to protect the species. Does it seem to be working?

▶ *A green Iguana at Carara Biological Preserve in Costa Rica*

Where Should the Wolves Roam?

The U.S. Fish and Wildlife Service has listed the gray wolf as an endangered species throughout most of the United States and has devised a plan to reintroduce the wolf to Yellowstone National Park, central Idaho, and northwestern Montana. The goal is to establish a population of at least 100 wolves at each location. If the project continues as planned, wolves may be removed from the endangered species list by 2002. But some ranchers and hunters are uneasy about the plan, and some environmentalists and wolf enthusiasts think that the plan doesn't go far enough to protect wolves.

Does the Plan Risk Livestock?

Ranchers are concerned that the wolves will kill livestock. These losses could result in a tremendous financial burden to ranchers. There is a compensation program currently established that will pay ranchers if wolves kill their livestock. But this program will end if the wolf is removed from the endangered species list. Ranchers point out that the threat to their livestock will not end when the wolf is removed from the list. In fact, the threat will increase, but ranchers will no longer receive any compensation.

On the other hand, some biologists offer evidence that wolves living near areas with adequate populations of deer, elk, moose, and other prey do not attack livestock. In fact, fewer than five wolf attacks on livestock were reported between 1995 and 1997.

Are Wolves a Threat to Wildlife?

Many scientists believe that the reintroduction plan would bring these regions into ecological balance for the first time in 60 years. They believe that the wolves will eliminate old and weak elk, moose, and deer and help keep these populations from growing too large.

Hunters fear that the wolves will kill many of the game animals in these areas. They cite studies that say large game animal populations can-

not survive hunting by both humans and wolves. Hunting plays a significant role in the economy of the western states.

Are the People Safe?

Some people fear that wolves will attack people. However, there has never been a documented attack on humans by healthy wolves in North America. Supporters say that wolves are shy animals that prefer to keep their distance from people.

Most wolf enthusiasts admit that there are places where wolves belong and places where wolves do not belong. They believe that these reintroduction zones offer places for wolves to thrive without creating problems.

What Do You Think?

▶ Some people argue that stories about "the big, bad wolf" give the wolf its ferocious reputation. Do you think people's fears are based on myth, or do you think that the wolf is a danger to people and livestock living in the reintroduction zones? Do some research and provide examples to support your opinion.

◀ *A Gray Wolf in Montana*

UNIT 7

Human Body Systems

Your body is made up of many systems that all work together like a finely tuned machine. Your lungs take in oxygen. Your heart pumps blood that delivers the oxygen to your tissues. Your brain reacts to things you see, hear, and smell, and sends signals through your nervous system that cause you to react to those things. Your digestive system converts the food you eat into energy that the cells of your body can use. And those are just a few things that your body can do!

In this unit, you will study the systems of your body. You'll discover how the parts of your body work together so that you can complete all your daily activities.

3000 B.C.
Ancient Egyptian doctors are the first to study the human body scientifically.

1824
Prevost and Dumas prove that sperm is essential for fertilization.

1893
Daniel Hale Williams, an African American surgeon, becomes the first to repair a tear in the pericardium, the sac around the heart.

1930
Karl Landsteiner receives a Nobel Prize for his discovery of the four human blood types.

1922
Insulin is discovered.

500 B.C.
Indian surgeon Susrata performs operations to remove cataracts.

1492
Christopher Columbus lands in the West Indies.

1543
Andreas Versalius publishes the first complete description of the structure of the human body.

1766
Albrecht von Haller determines that nerves control muscle movement and that all nerves are connected to the spinal cord or to the brain.

1619
William Harvey discovers that blood circulates and that the heart acts as a pump.

1982
Dr. Robert Jarvik implants an artificial heart in Barney Clark.

1941
During World War II in Italy, Rita Levi-Montalcini is forced to leave her work at a medical school laboratory because she is Jewish. She sets up a laboratory in her bedroom and studies the development of the nervous system.

1998
The first hand transplant is performed in France.

19 Body Organization and Structure

This Really Happened . . .

On April 14, 1912, at 11:40 P.M., the British steamship *Titanic,* the largest and most luxurious steamship ever built, struck an iceberg. Jack Thayer, a 17-year-old from Pennsylvania, felt the impact in his cabin and went on deck to see what had happened. To his horror, he found that the ship was sinking and that there were not enough lifeboats for the 2,207 passengers and crew. Jack watched as the last of the lifeboats, filled with women and children, were launched. Just before the ship slid beneath the icy water, Jack jumped. The pain of the cold felt like knives stabbing every inch of his body. He swam to an overturned lifeboat and climbed on.

Jack Thayer was among the survivors who were able to keep themselves dry enough to survive until help arrived, at 4 A.M. An estimated 1,500 people died. Even those who were wearing life jackets couldn't survive the extreme temperature of the water. The freezing water caused their body systems to fail. Breathing became difficult, and muscles no longer functioned. Finally, they lost consciousness and their hearts stopped.

The water around the *Titanic* was just too cold for human survival.

Under normal circumstances, our bodies are able to maintain a constant internal temperature. Read on to find out about this and other interesting information on how our bodies work.

What Do You Think?

In your ScienceLog, try to answer the following questions based on what you already know:

1. What is the relationship between cells, tissues, and organs?

2. How do your skin, muscles, and bones help to keep you well?

Investigate!

Too Cold for Comfort

Did you know that your nervous system sends you continuous messages about your body's cells? For example, the pain you experience when someone steps on your toe is a message that you need to move your toe to safety. Try the following to see what message you get from your nervous system.

Procedure

1. Clutch **a few pieces of ice** in the palm of one hand. Allow the melting water to drip into **a dish.** Hold the ice until the cold is uncomfortable, and then release the ice into the dish.

2. What message did you receive from your nervous system? Did the sensations make you want to drop the ice and warm your hand?

3. Look at the hand that held the ice, and then look at your other hand. What changes in your skin do you observe? How quickly does the cold hand return to normal?

Analysis

4. What organ systems do you think were involved in restoring homeostasis to your hand?

5. Think of a time in your life when your nervous system sent you a message, such as an uncomfortable feeling of heat or cold or a time when you felt pain. How did your body react? Which organ systems do you think were involved? Share your story with a classmate.

6. The arctic explorer above looks really cold. Use the Internet or library resources to find out how arctic explorers cope with subfreezing temperatures.

Body Organization

Your body has an amazing ability to survive, even in the face of harsh conditions. How did Jack Thayer stay alive even though the environment around him was so cold? A short answer is that his body did not allow its internal conditions to change enough to stop his cells from working properly. The maintenance of a stable internal environment is called **homeostasis.** If homeostasis is disrupted, cells suffer and sometimes die.

Four Types of Tissue

Making sure your internal environment remains stable enough to support healthy cells is not an easy task. Many different "jobs" must be done to maintain homeostasis. Fortunately, not every cell has to do all those jobs because the cells are organized into different teams. Just as each member of a soccer team has a special role in the game, each cell in your body has a specific job in maintaining homeostasis. A group of similar cells working together forms a **tissue.** Your body contains four main types of tissue—epithelial tissue, connective tissue, muscle tissue, and nervous tissue, as shown in **Figure 1.**

NEW TERMS

homeostasis   muscle tissue
tissue   connective tissue
epithelial tissue   organ
nervous tissue   organ system

OBJECTIVES

- Identify the major tissues found in the body.
- Compare an organ with an organ system.
- Describe a major function of each organ system.

Figure 1 *Your body has four types of tissue, and each type has a special function in your body.*

Epithelial tissue covers and protects underlying tissue. When you look at the surface of your skin, you see epithelial tissue. The cells stick tightly and form a continuous sheet.

Nervous tissue sends electrical signals through the body. It is found in the brain, nerves, and sense organs.

Tissues Form Organs

Two or more tissues working together form an **organ.** One type of tissue alone cannot do all the things that several types working together can do. Your stomach, as shown in **Figure 2,** uses several different types of tissue to carry out digestion.

Organs Form Systems

Your stomach does much to help you digest your food, but it doesn't do it all. It works together with other organs, such as the small intestine and large intestine, to digest your food. Organs working together make up an **organ system.** The failure of any part can affect the entire system. Your body has 11 major organ systems, which are illustrated on the next two pages. Are there any that you have not heard of before?

The Stomach Is an Organ

Epithelial tissue lines the inside of the stomach.

Layers of muscle tissue crush and grind stomach contents.

Blood, which supplies the stomach with oxygen, along with a connective tissue called collagen, is found in the wall of the stomach.

The production of acids that aid in the digestion of food is partly controlled by nervous tissue in the stomach. Nervous tissue also sends messages to the brain when the stomach is full.

Figure 2 *The four types of tissue work together so that the stomach can carry out digestion.*

Muscle tissue is made of cells that can contract and relax to produce movement.

Connective tissue joins, supports, protects, insulates, nourishes, and cushions organs. It also keeps organs from falling apart.

Organ Systems

Integumentary system

Your skin, hair, and nails protect underlying tissue.

Muscular system

Your skeletal muscles move your bones.

Skeletal system

Your bones provide a frame to support and protect body parts.

Cardiovascular system

Your heart pumps blood through all your blood vessels.

Respiratory system

Your lungs absorb oxygen and release carbon dioxide.

Urinary system

Your urinary system removes wastes from the blood and regulates the body's fluids.

Reproductive system (male)

The male reproductive system produces and delivers sperm.

Reproductive system (female)

The female reproductive system produces eggs and nourishes and shelters the unborn baby.

Nervous system	Lymphatic system	Digestive system	Endocrine system
It is the role of the nervous system to receive and send electrical messages throughout the body.	Your lymphatic system returns leaked fluids to blood vessels. It also helps you get rid of germs that can harm you.	Your digestive system breaks down the food you eat into nutrients that can be absorbed into your body.	Certain glands regulate body functions by sending out chemical messengers. The ovaries, in females, and testes, in males, are part of this system.

REVIEW

1. Explain the relationship between cells, tissues, organs, and organ systems.

2. Compare the four kinds of tissue found in the human body.

3. **Using Graphics** Make a chart that lists the major organ systems and their functions.

4. **Relating Concepts** Describe a time when homeostasis was disrupted in your body. Which body systems do you think were affected?

Explore

To help you remember the names of these organ sytems, try to make up a sentence in which the first letter of each word stands for one of the eleven systems. Use the following letters in any order: I, M, S, C, R, U, R, E, L, D, N.

The Skeletal System

When you hear the word *skeleton,* you may think of the remains of something that has died. But your skeleton is not dead; it is very much alive. Your bones are not dry and brittle. They are just as alive and active as the muscles that are attached to them. Bones, cartilage, and the special structures that connect them make up your **skeletal system.**

The Burden of Being a Bone

Bones do a lot more than just hold you up. Your bones perform several important functions inside your body. The names of some of your bones are identified in **Figure 3.**

Figure 3 *The adult human skeleton has approximately 206 bones. Several major bones are identified in this skeleton.*

Support Your skeletal system protects and supports you. Your heart and lungs are shielded by your ribs, your spinal cord is protected by your vertebrae, and your brain is protected by your skull.

Storage Bones store minerals such as calcium and release them into the surrounding tissues to help the nerves and muscles function properly. The cavities inside your arm and leg bones also store fat that can be used for energy.

Movement Skeletal muscles, which are attached to bones by tendons, pull on the bones to produce movement. Without bones, you would not be able to sit, stand, walk, or run.

Blood Cell Formation Some of your bones are filled with a special material that makes red and white blood cells.

Skull

Ribs

Radius

Ulna

Clavicle

Humerus

Patella

Femur

Pelvic girdle

Tibia

Fibula

Vertebral column

What's in a Bone?

A bone may seem lifeless, but it is a living organ made of several different tissues. Bone is composed of connective tissue and minerals that are deposited by living cells called *osteoblasts*.

If you look inside a bone, you will notice there are two different kinds of bone tissue. If the tissue does not have any visible open spaces, it is called **compact bone.** Compact bone provides most of the strength and support for a bone. Bone tissue that has many open spaces is called **spongy bone.** Bones contain a soft tissue called *marrow.* Red marrow, sometimes found in spongy bone, produces red blood cells. Yellow marrow, found in the central cavity of long bones, stores fat. Tiny canals within the compact bone contain small blood vessels. **Figure 4** shows a cross section of the longest bone in the body.

Blood vessels

Marrow cavity

Cartilage

Compact bone

Spongy bone

Canal

Blood vessels

Figure 4 *This illustration of a femur, the long bone in the thigh, shows that bone is composed of mineral-filled rings and blood vessels that run through a canal in each group of rings. Marrow fills the center of this type of bone. Blood vessels enter and exit at certain points along the bone.*

A typical femur (thigh bone) can support over 1,000 kg.

Growing Bones

Did you know that most of your skeleton used to be soft and rubbery? Most bones start out as a soft, flexible tissue called **cartilage.** Cartilage contains mostly water, which gives it a rubbery texture. When you were born, you had very little true bone. But as you grew, the cartilage was replaced by bone. During childhood, growth plates of cartilage remain in most bones, providing a place for those bones to continue to grow.

Feel the end of your nose, or bend the top of your ear. Some areas, like these, never become bone. The flexible material beneath your skin in these areas is cartilage. As shown in **Figure 5,** cartilage lacks the mineral density to produce a dark image like the bones of the skull.

Figure 5 *This computer-colored X ray shows the bones in the skull and neck.*

Figure 6 *Joints are shaped according to their function in the body.*

What's the Point of a Joint?

The place where two or more bones connect is called a **joint.** Your joints have special designs that allow your body to move when your muscles contract. Some joints allow a lot of movement, while other joints are fixed, which means they allow little or no movement. For example, the joints in the skull are fixed. Joints that have a wide range of movement tend to be more susceptible to injury than those that are less flexible. Some examples of movable joints are shown in **Figure 6.**

Sliding joint
Sliding joints allow bones in the hand to glide over one another, giving some flexibility to the area.

Ball-and-socket joint
Like a joystick on a computer game, the shoulder enables your arm to move freely in all directions.

Hinge joint
Like a hinge on a door, the knee enables you to flex and extend your lower leg.

BRAIN FOOD

The skeleton of a shark has no bone, only cartilage.

Bone to Bone Joints are kept together with strong elastic bands of connective tissue called **ligaments.** If a ligament is stretched too far, it becomes strained. A strained ligament will usually heal with time, but a torn ligament will not. A torn ligament must be repaired surgically. Cartilage helps cushion the area where two bones meet. If cartilage wears away, the joint becomes arthritic.

Can Levers Lessen Your Load?

You may not think of your limbs as being machines, but they are. The action of a muscle pulling on a bone often works like a type of simple machine called a *lever*. A lever is a rigid bar that moves on a fixed point known as a *fulcrum*. Any force applied to the lever is called the *effort*. A force that resists the motion of the lever, such as the downward force exerted by a weight on the bar, is called the *load* or the *resistance*. **Figure 7** shows how three types of levers are used in the human body.

In each type of lever, notice where the fulcrum is located relative to the effort and the load. In your body, the effort is the force that your muscles apply to the lever. The load is the weight that resists the pull of your muscles. The benefit gained by using a machine is measured by a ratio called **mechanical advantage.**

$$MA = \frac{\text{force applied to the load}}{\text{effort force}}$$

Mechanical advantage is a measure of how many times a simple machine multiplies an effort applied to a load. First-class and second-class levers can have a significant mechanical advantage. Third-class levers increase distance and speed, but they cannot increase force.

REVIEW

1. Describe four important functions of bones.

2. Draw a bone, and label the inside and outside structures. Use colored pencils to color and label spongy bone, blood vessels, marrow cavity, compact bone, and cartilage.

3. Describe and illustrate three types of levers found in your body.

4. **Interpreting Models** Study the models of levers pictured in Figure 7. Use a small box (load), a ruler (bar), and a pencil (fulcrum) to create models of each type of lever.

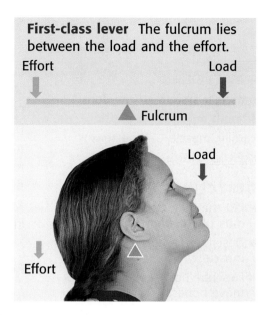

First-class lever The fulcrum lies between the load and the effort.

Second-class lever The load lies between the fulcrum and the effort.

Third-class lever The effort lies between the fulcrum and the load.

Figure 7 *There are three classes of levers, based on the location of the fulcrum, the load, and the effort.*

The Muscular System

Have you ever tried to be perfectly still for just 1 minute? Try as you might, you just can't do it. Somewhere in your body, certain muscles are always working. For example, muscles continuously push blood through your blood vessels. A muscle makes you breathe. And muscles hold you upright. If all your muscles rested at the same time, you would collapse. Your muscles are made of muscle tissue and connective tissue. Muscles that attach to bones and the connective tissue that attaches them make up the **muscular system.**

Types of Muscle

There are three types of muscle tissue that make up the muscles in your body. **Smooth muscle** is found in the digestive tract and the blood vessels. **Cardiac muscle** is a special type of muscle found only in your heart. **Skeletal muscles** are attached to your bones for movement, and they help protect your inner organs. The three types of muscles are shown in **Figure 8.**

Muscle action can be voluntary or involuntary. Muscle action that is under your control is *voluntary.* Muscle action that is not under your control is *involuntary.* The actions of smooth muscle and cardiac muscle are involuntary. The actions of skeletal muscles can be both voluntary and involuntary. For example, you can blink your eyes anytime you want to, but your eyes will also blink automatically if you do not think about it.

Figure 8 *Your body has smooth muscle, cardiac muscle, and skeletal muscle.*

Skeletal muscle enables bones to move.

Cardiac muscle causes the heart to beat.

Smooth muscle moves food through the digestive system.

Making Your Move

Skeletal muscles produce hundreds of different voluntary movements. This is demonstrated by a ballet dancer, a swimmer, or even someone making a funny face, as shown in **Figure 9.** When you want to make a movement, you cause electrical signals to travel from the brain to the skeletal muscle cells. The muscle cells respond to these signals by contracting or getting shorter.

Figure 9 *It takes an average of 13 muscles to smile and an average of 43 muscles to frown.*

Muscles to Bones Strands of tough connective tissue called **tendons** connect your skeletal muscles to your bones. When a muscle gets shorter, a pulling action occurs, bringing the bones closer to each other. For example, the biceps muscle, shown in **Figure 10,** is attached by tendons to a bone in your shoulder and to another bone in your forearm. When the biceps contracts, your arm bends.

Working in Pairs Your skeletal muscles work in pairs to cause smooth, controlled movements. Many basic movements are the result of muscle pairs that cause bending and straightening. If a muscle bends part of your body, then that muscle is called a **flexor.** If the muscle straightens part of your body, then it is called an **extensor.** The flexor muscle of the arm is the biceps. The extensor muscle of the arm is the triceps. Discover some of your own flexor and extensor muscles by doing the QuickLab at right.

Flexor   Extensor

Figure 10 *Skeletal muscles, such as the biceps and triceps muscles in the upper arm, are connected to bones by tendons. When the biceps muscle contracts, the elbow bends. When the triceps muscle contracts, the elbow straightens.*

Power in Pairs

1. While sitting in a chair, place one of your hands palm up under the edge of a **table.** Apply gentle upward pressure, being careful not to strain or overturn the table.

2. With your free hand, feel the front and back of your upper arm.

3. Next place your hand palm down on top of the table. Again apply a gentle pressure, but in a downward direction.

4. Again with your free hand, feel the front and back of your upper arm.

5. What did you notice when you were pressing up? What did you notice when you were pressing down?

chemistry
CONNECTION

Body chemistry is very important for healthy muscle functioning. If there is a chemical imbalance in a muscle due to excessive sweating, poor diet, tension, or illness, spasms or cramping may occur. Sodium, calcium, and potassium—three chemicals called *electrolytes*—must be in proper balance to avoid cramps and spasms. Relaxation and massage usually help the muscle restore its chemical balance.

Use It or Lose It

When someone breaks an arm and has to wear a cast, the muscles surrounding the injured bone change. That's because these muscles are not exercised, and they become smaller and weaker. On the other hand, exercised muscles are stronger and larger. Certain exercises can give muscles more endurance. This means they're able to work longer without getting tired. Strong muscles benefit other systems in your body too. When a muscle contracts, blood vessels in that muscle get squeezed. This helps push blood along, increasing blood flow without demanding more work from the heart.

Resistance Exercises   To develop the size and strength of your skeletal muscles, resistance exercises are the most effective form of exercise. Resistance exercises require muscles to overcome the resistance (weight) of another object. Some resistance exercises, like the bent knee curl-up shown in **Figure 11,** require you to overcome your own weight.

Figure 11 Resistance exercises are tough, but they can really help you build strong muscles.

Aerobic Exercise   Steady, moderate-intensity activity, such as jogging, cycling, skating, swimming laps, or walking, is called aerobic exercise. Aerobic exercise increases the size and strength of your skeletal muscles somewhat, but mostly it strengthens the heart while increasing the endurance of your skeletal muscles. Many people, like the girl in **Figure 12,** enjoy doing aerobic exercise.

Figure 12 Aerobic exercise is a great way to have fun while strengthening your heart.

✓ Self-Check

Which kind of skeletal muscle do you use to perform a curl-up? Which kind do you use to do a push-up? *(See page 636 to check your answers.)*

Muscle Injury

Any exercise program should be started gradually so that the muscles gain strength and endurance without injury. Muscles should also be warmed up gradually to reduce the risk of injury. However, like any system, the muscular system can experience damage. A muscle strain, commonly called a pulled muscle, is the overstretching or even tearing of a muscle. Muscle strain often occurs because the muscle has not been properly conditioned for the work it is doing. Strains can also occur because a muscle is not warmed up or because an exercise is not being done properly.

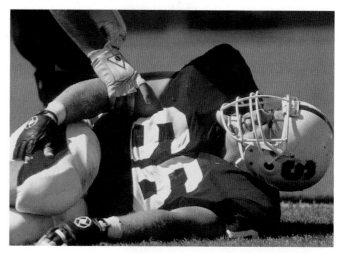

Figure 13 *A pulled hamstring is a tear or strain of one of the muscles or tendons on the back of the thigh.*

As shown in **Figure 13,** tendons, as well as muscles, can get injured from overuse. A damaged tendon can become hot or inflamed as your body tries to repair it. This painful condition is called tendinitis, and an extended period of rest is often required for the tendon to heal.

The Dangers of Anabolic Steroids Some people try to make their muscles larger and stronger by taking hormones called *anabolic steroids.* Anabolic steroids are powerful chemicals that resemble testosterone, a male sex hormone, which you will read about when you study human reproduction. Using anabolic steroids not only gives athletes an unfair advantage in competition but also puts the user at risk for serious long-term health problems. The use of anabolic steroids threatens the heart, liver, and kidneys, and it can cause high blood pressure. If taken before the skeleton is mature, anabolic steroids can cause the bones to stop growing. Competitive athletes, like the ones shown in **Figure 14,** are routinely tested for this type of drug.

Figure 14 *With proper training, athletes can be successful without the use of anabolic steroids.*

REVIEW

1. List three types of muscle tissue, and describe their functions in the body.

2. Compare aerobic exercise with resistance exercise, and give two examples of each.

3. **Applying Concepts** Describe the muscle action required to pick up a book. Make a sketch that illustrates the muscle action.

MATH BREAK

Runner's Time

Jan, who has been a runner for several years, has decided to enter a race. She now runs 5 km in 30 minutes. She would like to decrease her time by 15 percent before the race. What will her time be when she meets her goal?

The Integumentary System

NEW TERMS
integumentary system
sweat glands
melanin
epidermis
dermis
hair follicle

OBJECTIVES

- Describe the major functions of the integumentary system.
- List the major parts of the skin, and discuss their functions.
- Describe the structure and function of hair and nails.
- Describe some common types of damage that can affect skin.

Here's a quiz for you. What part of your body has to be partly dead to keep you alive? Here are some clues: it comes in a variety of colors, it is the largest organ in the body, and it protects you from the outside world. Oh, and guess what—it is showing right now. Did you guess your skin? If you did, you guessed correctly.

Your skin, hair, and nails make up your **integumentary** (in TEG yoo MEN tuhr ee) **system.** (*Integument* means "covering.") Like all organ systems, the integumentary system helps your body maintain a healthy internal environment.

The Skin: More than Just a "Coat"

Why do you need skin? Here are four good reasons:

- Skin protects you by keeping moisture in your body and foreign particles out of your body.

- Skin keeps you "in touch" with the outside world. The nerve endings in your skin allow you to feel what's around you.

- Skin helps regulate your body's temperature. For example, small organs in the skin called **sweat glands** produce sweat, a salty liquid that flows to the surface of the skin. As sweat evaporates, the skin cools.

- Skin helps get rid of wastes. Several types of waste chemicals can leave the bloodstream and be removed in sweat.

What Determines Skin Color? A darkening chemical in skin called **melanin** determines skin color, as shown in **Figure 15.** If a lot of melanin is present, the skin is very dark. If only a little melanin is produced, the skin is very light. Melanin in the upper layer of the skin absorbs much of the harmful radiation from the sun, reducing DNA damage that can lead to cancer. However, *all* skin is vulnerable to cancer and therefore should be protected from sun exposure whenever possible.

Figure 15 *Variety in skin color is caused by the pigment melanin. The amount of melanin varies from person to person.*

A Tale of Two Layers

As you already know, the skin is the largest organ of your body. In fact, the skin of an adult covers an area of about 2 m²! However, there's a lot more to skin than meets the eye. The skin has two main layers: the dermis and the epidermis. The **epidermis** is the thinner layer of the two. It's what you see when you look at your skin. (*Epi* means "on top of.") The deeper, thicker layer is known as the **dermis.**

Epidermis The epidermis is composed of a type of epithelial tissue. Even though the epidermis has many layers of cells, it is only as thick as two sheets of notebook paper over most of the body. It is thicker in the palms of your hands and the soles of your feet. Most epidermal cells are dead and are filled with a protein called keratin, which helps make the skin tough.

Dermis The dermis lies underneath the epidermis. It is mostly connective tissue, and it contains many fibers made of a protein called collagen. The fibers provide strength and allow skin to bend without tearing. The dermis also contains a variety of small structures, as shown in **Figure 16.**

Your epidermis is showing!

✓ **Self-Check**

To what system do the skin's blood vessels belong? (*See page 636 to check your answer.*)

Figure 16 *Beneath the surface, your skin is a complex organ made of blood vessels, nerves, glands, and muscles.*

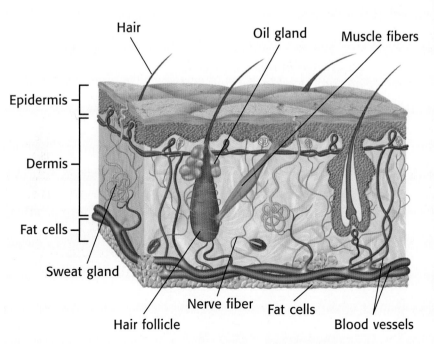

Hair | Oil gland | Muscle fibers
Epidermis
Dermis
Fat cells
Sweat gland
Hair follicle | Nerve fiber | Fat cells | Blood vessels

Blood vessels transport substances and help regulate body temperature.

Nerves carry messages to and from the brain.

Muscle fibers attached to a hair follicle can contract, causing the hair to stand up.

Hair follicles in the dermis produce hair.

Oil glands release oil that keeps hair flexible and helps waterproof the epidermis.

Sweat glands release sweat. As sweat evaporates, heat is removed from the skin, and the body is cooled. Sweat also contains waste materials taken out of the body.

Hair and Nails

A hair, shown in **Figure 17**, is actually several layers of tightly packed, keratin-filled cells. It is formed at the bottom of a tiny sac called a **hair follicle.** The hair grows as new cells are added at the hair follicle and older cells get pushed upward. The only living cells in a hair are in the hair follicle, where the hair is produced.

Hairs protect skin from ultraviolet light and can help keep particles, such as dust and insects, out of your eyes and nose. Like skin, hair gets its color from the pigment melanin. Dark hair contains more melanin than blond hair. In most mammals, hair also helps regulate body temperature. A contraction of a tiny muscle attached to the hair follicle causes the follicle to bend. In humans, the bending follicle pushes up the epidermis to make a goose bump. If the follicle contains a hair, the hair "stands up." When furry animals do this, they become very bushy. The lifted hairs function like a sweater to trap warm air around the body.

The ends of your fingers and toes are protected by nails. Nails protect the tips of your fingers and toes so that they can remain soft and sensitive. This allows you to have a keen sense of touch. Nails form from *nail roots* under the skin at the base and sides of nails. As new cells form, the nail grows longer. The parts of a nail are shown in **Figure 18.**

How fast do your fingernails grow? Find out on page 627.

Figure 17 *A hair is actually layers of dead, tightly packed, keratin-filled cells.*

Hair

Figure 18 *In nails, new cells are produced in the nail root, just beneath the lunula. The new cells push older cells toward the outer edge of the nail.*

Free edge

Nail body

Lunula

Living in Harm's Way

Your skin is the most exposed part of your body. It serves as a protective barrier. Nevertheless, skin is often damaged. The damage may be minor—a blister, an insect bite, or a small cut. Fortunately, your skin has an amazing ability to repair itself, as shown in **Figure 19.**

Figure 19 How Skin Heals
Healing a wound to the skin takes time.

Scab
Blood clot
Bacteria-fighting cells

New cells

1 When you get a cut, a blood clot forms to prevent bacteria from entering the wound. Bacteria-fighting cells then come to the area to kill bacteria.

2 Damaged cells are replaced through cell division. Eventually, all that is left on the surface is a scar.

Other damage to the skin is very serious. Damage to the genetic material in skin cells can result in uncontrolled cell division, producing a mass of skin cells called a tumor. The term *cancer* is used to describe a tumor that invades other tissue. Darkened areas on the skin, such as moles, should be watched carefully for signs of cancer. **Figure 20** shows an example of a mole that has possibly become cancerous.

Your skin may also be affected by changes within your body. During your teens, chemicals called sex hormones cause the oil glands in your skin to produce excess oil. This oil combines with dead skin cells and bacteria to clog hair follicles and cause infections. Proper cleansing and daily skin care can be helpful in decreasing the amount of infections on the skin.

Figure 20 *Moles should be watched for signs of cancer. This mole has two halves that do not match, a characteristic called asymmetry that might indicate skin cancer.*

Are doctors using bandages that are made of real skin? Find out on page 484.

REVIEW

1. Why does skin color vary from person to person?

2. List six structures found in the dermis and the function of each one.

3. **Making Inferences** Why do you feel pain when you pull on your hair or nails but not when you cut them?

Chapter Highlights

SECTION 1

Vocabulary

homeostasis *(p. 464)*

tissue *(p. 464)*

epithelial tissue *(p. 464)*

nervous tissue *(p. 464)*

muscle tissue *(p. 465)*

connective tissue *(p. 465)*

organ *(p. 465)*

organ system *(p. 465)*

Section Notes

• Your body maintains a stable internal environment called homeostasis.

• Four types of tissues work to maintain homeostasis. Each tissue has a special job to do.

• Tissues work together to form organs, such as your stomach.

• Your stomach is part of a group of organs that work to change food into a form that can nourish your body. A group of organs working together for a common purpose is called an organ system.

• There are 11 major organ systems in the human body.

SECTION 2

Vocabulary

skeletal system *(p. 468)*

compact bone *(p. 469)*

spongy bone *(p. 469)*

cartilage *(p. 470)*

joint *(p. 470)*

ligament *(p. 470)*

mechanical advantage *(p. 471)*

Section Notes

• The skeletal system includes bones, cartilage, and ligaments.

• Bones support and protect the body, store minerals and fat, and produce blood cells.

• A typical bone contains marrow, spongy bone, compact bone, blood vessels, and cartilage.

☑ Skills Check

Math Concepts

CALCULATING A PERCENTAGE In the MathBreak on page 475 you were asked to calculate a percentage of a number. To do this, first express the percentage as a decimal or a fraction. Then multiply it by the number. For example, 25 percent can be written as 0.25 or $25 \div 100$. To find 25 percent of 48, multiply by either 0.25 or $25 \div 100$.

$$0.25 \times 48 = 12$$
$$\text{or}$$
$$(25 \div 100) \times 48 = 1{,}200 \div 100 = 12$$

Visual Understanding

MOVING WITH JOINTS Take another look at the three kinds of joints on page 470. Consider how your joints work when you throw a ball or walk up stairs. The hinge joint in your knee can move freely in only two directions. The ball-and-socket joint in your shoulder can move in many directions. The sliding joints in your hand allow bones to glide over one another.

SECTION 2

- A joint is where two bones meet. Some joints allow a lot of movement, and some allow little or no movement.
- Bones are attached to bones by connective tissue called ligaments.
- The action of muscle on bone and joints often works like a simple machine called a lever.

SECTION 3

Vocabulary

muscular system *(p. 472)*

smooth muscle *(p. 472)*

cardiac muscle *(p. 472)*

skeletal muscle *(p. 472)*

tendon *(p. 473)*

flexor *(p. 473)*

extensor *(p. 473)*

Section Notes

- Skeletal muscles and tendons make up the muscular system.
- You have three types of muscle: smooth, cardiac, and skeletal.
- Muscles are attached to bones by tendons.
- Exercise helps keep your muscular system healthy.

Labs

Muscles at Work *(p. 626)*

SECTION 4

Vocabulary

integumentary system *(p. 476)*

sweat glands *(p. 476)*

melanin *(p. 476)*

epidermis *(p. 477)*

dermis *(p. 477)*

hair follicle *(p. 478)*

Section Notes

- Your skin, hair, and nails make up your integumentary system.
- Your skin has two layers that contain a variety of small organs.
- Your hair and nails help protect your body.
- Skin can be damaged, but it has an amazing ability to repair itself.

Labs

Seeing Is Believing *(p. 627)*

---

internetconnect

 GO TO: go.hrw.com

 GO TO: www.scilinks.org

Visit the **HRW** Web site for a variety of learning tools related to this chapter. Just type in the keyword:

KEYWORD: HSTBD1

Visit the **National Science Teachers Association** on-line Web site for Internet resources related to this chapter. Just type in the *sci***LINKS** number for more information about the topic:

TOPIC: Tissues and Organs	*sci***LINKS NUMBER:** HSTL530
TOPIC: Body Systems	*sci***LINKS NUMBER:** HSTL535
TOPIC: The Muscular System	*sci***LINKS NUMBER:** HSTL540
TOPIC: Integumentary System	*sci***LINKS NUMBER:** HSTL545

Chapter Review

To complete the following sentences, choose the correct term from each pair of terms listed below:

1. Electrical signals are sent throughout the body by the __?__ tissue. (*epithelial* or *nervous*)

2. Your __?__ system is made up of skin, hair, and nails. (*integumentary* or *muscular*)

3. Bones are moved by __?__ muscle. (*smooth* or *skeletal*)

4. When __?__ muscles contract, they cause parts of the body to bend. (*extensor* or *flexor*)

5. Most of the skeleton starts out as __?__, which is later replaced by bone. (*cartilage* or *ligaments*)

UNDERSTANDING CONCEPTS

Multiple Choice

6. Which of the following is made up of cells that can contract and relax?
   a. skeletal tissue
   b. muscle tissue
   c. connective tissue
   d. nervous tissue

7. The organ system that provides support and protection for body parts is the
   a. endocrine system.
   b. circulatory system.
   c. skeletal system.
   d. integumentary system.

8. The epidermis is composed of
   a. dermis.
   b. epithelial tissue.
   c. connective tissue.
   d. true skin.

9. The fixed point in a lever is the
   a. effort.
   b. load.
   c. fulcrum.
   d. mechanical advantage.

10. Muscles cause bones to move when
    a. the muscles stretch.
    b. the muscles grow between bones.
    c. the muscles pull on bones.
    d. the muscles push bones apart.

11. Ligaments are the connective tissue that attaches
    a. bones to muscles.
    b. bones to other bones.
    c. muscles to other muscles.
    d. muscles to dermis.

Short Answer

12. Summarize the functions of the four types of tissues, and draw a sketch of each type.

13. How does the skin help protect the body?

14. What is a goose bump?

15. What are two ways skeletal muscle differs from cardiac muscle?

16. How do the functions of the skeletal system relate to the functions of the muscular system?

Concept Mapping

17. Use the following terms to create a concept map: bones, marrow, skeletal system, spongy bone, compact bone, cartilage.

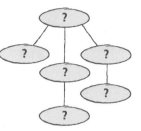

CRITICAL THINKING AND PROBLEM SOLVING

Write one or two sentences to answer the following questions:

18. What would your arm movement be like if you did not have both an extensor and a flexor attached to your lower arm?

19. Unlike human bones, some bird bones have air-filled cavities. What advantage does this give birds?

20. Compare the shapes of the bones of the human skull with the shapes of the bones of the human leg. Why is their shape important?

21. Compare the texture and sensitivity of the skin on your elbows with those of the skin on your fingertips. How can you explain the differences?

MATH IN SCIENCE

22. Your muscles make up about 40 percent of your overall mass. What is the muscle mass of a person whose total body mass is 60 kg?

23. The average person blinks 700 times an hour. How many times would the average person blink in a week if he or she were awake for 16 hours each day?

INTERPRETING GRAPHICS

Look at the picture below, and answer the questions that follow.

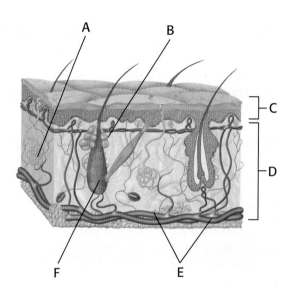

24. What is *D* called? What type of tissue is most abundant in this layer?

25. What is the name and function of *A*?

26. What is the name and function of *B*?

27. What part of the skin is made up of epithelial tissue that contains dead cells?

28. How does skin help regulate body temperature?

NOW What Do You Think?

Take a minute to review your answers to the ScienceLog questions on page 463. Have your answers changed? If necessary, revise your answers based on what you have learned since you began this chapter.

Science, Technology, and Society

Engineered Skin

Your skin is more than just a well-fitting suit—it's your first line of defense against the outside world. Your skin keeps you safe from dehydration and infection, and the oil glands in your skin keep you waterproof. But what happens when a significant portion of skin is damaged?

More Skin Is the Answer

Sometimes doctors perform a skin graft, transferring some of a person's healthy skin to a damaged area of skin. This is because skin is really the best "bandage" for a wound. It protects the wound but still allows it to breathe. And unlike manufactured cloth or plastic bandages, skin can regenerate itself as it covers a wound. Sometimes, though, a person's skin is so severely damaged (as often occurs in burn victims) that the person doesn't have enough skin to spare.

Tissue Engineering

In the past few years, scientists have been studying tissue engineering to learn more about how the human body heals itself naturally. Using a small piece of young, healthy human skin and some collagen from cows, scientists can now engineer human skin. During the engineering process, cells form the dermal and epidermal layers of skin just as they would if they were still on the body. The living human skin that results can even heal itself if it is cut before it is used for a skin graft. Because it is living, the skin must be kept on a medium that provides it with nutrients until it is placed on a wound. Over time, the color of the grafted skin changes to match the color of the skin that surrounds it.

A Woven Dermis

Tissue engineers have also created another kind of skin, except this one has an unusual dermal

▲ *This is a piece of engineered skin used for grafting.*

and epidermal layer. In this skin, the dermis is made of woven collagen fibers. The wounded area digests these fibers and uses them as a guide to create a new dermis. The epidermal layer is a temporary layer of silicone. It shields the body from infection and protects against dehydration while new skin is being made.

After a new dermal layer forms under the protective silicone epidermis, the body is in better condition to accept a skin graft. Doctors can also graft a thinner portion of skin. A thinner graft is better for the body in the long run because it is easier to take from another part of the body. The new dermal layer also gives the body more time to strengthen on its own before the trauma of transplanting healthy skin to other areas.

On Your Own

▶ In the past, doctors have harvested skin from the bodies of people who, before they died, chose to be organ donors. What kinds of problems could arise if this harvested skin were used on burn victims?

Eureka!

Hairy Oil Spills

Oil and water don't mix, right? Oil floats on the surface of water and is clearly visible to the naked eye. Proving this in your kitchen isn't difficult, nor is it dangerous. But what happens when the water is the ocean and the oil is crude oil? You have an environmental disaster that costs millions of dollars to clean up. The worst example in American waters was in 1989 when the *Exxon Valdez* oil tanker spilled nearly 42 million liters of crude oil into the waters of Prince William Sound on the Alaskan coast.

▲ *This otter was drenched with oil spilled from the* Exxon Valdez.

Backyard Testing

A Huntsville, Alabama, hairdresser asked a brilliant question when he saw an otter whose fur was drenched with oil from the *Valdez* spill. If the otter's fur soaked up all the oil, why wouldn't human hair do the same? The hairdresser, Phil McCrory, gathered hair from the floor of his salon and took it home to perform his own experiments. He stuffed 2.2 kg of hair into a pair of his wife's pantyhose and tied the ankles together to form a bagel-shaped bundle. After filling his son's wading pool with water, McCrory floated the bundle in the pool. Next, McCrory poured used motor oil into the center of the ring. When he pulled the ring closed, not a drop of oil remained in the water!

▲ *Phil McCrory among bags of discarded human hair.*

How Does Hair Do This?

What McCrory discovered was that hair *adsorbs* oil instead of *absorbing* it. To adsorb means to collect a liquid or gas in layers on a surface. Because tiny cuticles cover every hair shaft like fish scales, the oil can bind to the surface of hair. Compare this process with the way a sponge works. A sponge completely absorbs a liquid. This means it is wet throughout, not just on the surface.

McCrory approached the National Aeronautics and Space Administration (NASA) with his discovery. In controlled tests performed by NASA, hair proved to be the fastest adsorber around. A little more than 1 kg of hair can adsorb over 3.5 L of oil in just 2 minutes!

It is estimated that within a week, 64 million kilograms of hair in reusable mesh pillows could have soaked up *all* of the oil spilled by the *Valdez*. Unfortunately, the $2 billion spent on the cleanup removed only about 12 percent of the spill. Did you ever think that the hair from your head could have a purpose beyond keeping your head warm?

Compare the Facts

▶ Research how McCrory's discovery compares with the methods currently used to clean up oil spills. Share your findings with the class.

20 Circulation and Respiration

This Really Happened . . .

The human heart is normally a very dependable organ. It may beat more than 100,000 times per day for a person's entire life. During this time it pumps millions of liters of blood through the body. When there is a serious problem with the heart, it is life threatening.

In the past, heart failure resulted in immediate death. But in 1969, Dr. Denton Cooley, of the Texas Heart Institute, kept a patient alive for 5 days after the patient's heart failed. How did he do it? He used an artificial heart that he designed himself.

The design of artificial hearts has improved considerably since Dr. Cooley's first model. The electric artificial heart shown above right

is one of the more recent test models. Its mass is about 680 g—only a little heavier than a real human heart. Newer test models are even smaller and lighter. These artificial hearts have special sensors and microprocessors that regulate the beat and respond to changes in blood pressure.

Currently, there is no artificial heart that can permanently replace the human heart. The human heart is a sophisticated organ that serves the cardiovascular system, one of the body's pathways for circulating fluids. In this chapter you will also read about the lymphatic system and the respiratory system and how all of these systems are related.

In your ScienceLog, try to answer the following questions based on what you already know:

1. What is blood, and what is its function in your body?

2. Why do you need to breathe?

Exercise and Your Heart

How does your heart respond to exercise? You can determine this by measuring how fast your heart beats before and after exercise. Your heart pumps blood through your blood vessels. With each heartbeat, your blood vessels expand and then return to their original position. This produces a throbbing called a *pulse.* You can take your pulse by placing your index and middle fingers on the inside of your wrist just below your thumb.

Procedure

1. Take your pulse while remaining still. Using a **watch with a second hand,** count the number of beats in 15 seconds. Then multiply this number by four to calculate the number of beats in 1 minute.

$$\text{Number of beats in 15 seconds} \times 4 = \text{Number of beats in 1 minute}$$

2. Do jumping jacks or jog in place for 30 seconds, and then stop and calculate your heart rate again.

   Caution: Do not perform this exercise if you have difficulty breathing, have high blood pressure, or get dizzy easily.

3. After resting for 5 minutes, determine your pulse again.

Analysis

4. How did exercise affect your heart rate? Why do you think this happened?

5. Why do you think your heart rate returned to normal after you rested?

The Cardiovascular System

NEW TERMS

cardiovascular system
blood
plasma
platelet
atrium
ventricle
arteries

capillaries
veins
pulmonary circulation
systemic circulation
blood pressure

OBJECTIVES

- Describe the functions of the cardiovascular system.
- Compare and contrast the three types of blood vessels.
- Describe the path that blood travels as it circulates through the body.
- Distinguish between blood types.

When you hear the word *heart*, what do you think of first? Many people think of romance. But the heart is much more than a symbol of love. It's the pump that drives your cardiovascular system. The **cardiovascular system** transports materials to and from your cells. The word *cardio* means "heart," and the word *vascular* means "vessel." The cardiovascular system, which is shown in **Figure 1,** is made up of three parts: blood, the heart, and blood vessels.

What Is Blood?

The human body contains about 5 L of blood. **Blood** is a connective tissue made up of two types of cells, cell parts, and plasma. **Figure 2** shows blood that has been separated into its four main parts. **Plasma** is the fluid part of blood. It is a mixture of water, minerals, nutrients, sugars, proteins, and other substances. Red blood cells, white blood cells, and platelets float in the plasma.

**Figure 1
The Cardiovascular System**

Plasma

White blood cells and platelets

Red blood cells

Figure 2 *Blood is about 55 percent plasma and 45 percent red blood cells, white blood cells, and platelets.*

Red Blood Cells Red blood cells, or RBCs, are the most abundant cells in blood. RBCs, shown in **Figure 3,** supply your cells with oxygen. As you have learned, cells need oxygen to carry out cellular respiration. Each RBC contains a chemical called *hemoglobin.* Hemoglobin, which gives RBCs their red color, clings to the oxygen you inhale. This allows RBCs to transport oxygen throughout the body. The shape of RBCs gives them a large amount of surface area for absorbing and releasing oxygen.

RBCs are made in the bone marrow. Before RBCs enter the bloodstream, they lose their nucleus and other organelles. Without a nucleus, which contains DNA, the RBCs cannot replace worn-out proteins. RBCs therefore can live only about 4 months.

Figure 3
Red blood cells deliver oxygen.

White Blood Cells Sometimes *pathogens*—bacteria, viruses, and other microscopic particles that can make you sick—are able to enter your body. When they do, they often encounter your white blood cells, or WBCs. WBCs, shown in **Figure 4,** help you stay healthy by destroying pathogens and helping to clean wounds.

WBCs fight pathogens in several ways. Some squeeze out of vessels and move around in tissues, searching for pathogens. When they find a pathogen, they engulf it. Other WBCs release chemicals called *antibodies,* which help destroy pathogens. WBCs also keep you healthy by eating body cells that have died or been damaged. WBCs are made in bone marrow. Some of them mature in lymphatic organs, which will be discussed later.

Platelets Drifting among the blood cells are tiny particles called platelets. **Platelets,** shown in **Figure 5,** are pieces of larger cells found in bone marrow. These larger cells remain in the bone marrow, but they pinch off fragments of themselves, which enter the blood. Although platelets last for only 5 to 10 days, they are an important part of blood. When you cut or scrape your skin, you bleed because blood vessels have been opened. As soon as bleeding occurs, platelets begin to clump together in the damaged area and form a plug that helps reduce blood loss, as shown in **Figure 6.** Platelets also release a variety of chemicals that react with proteins in the plasma and cause tiny fibers to form. The fibers create a blood clot.

Figure 4 *White blood cells defend the body against pathogens. These white blood cells have been colored yellow to make their shape easier to see.*

Figure 5 *Platelets help reduce blood loss.*

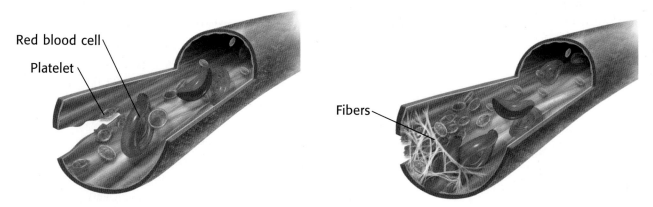

Red blood cell

Platelet

Fibers

Figure 6 *Platelets release chemicals in damaged vessels and cause fibers to form. The fibers make a "net" that traps blood cells and stops bleeding.*

Right atrium

Left atrium

Valves

Valves

Right ventricle

Left ventricle

Figure 7 *The heart is a four-chambered organ that pumps blood through cardiovascular vessels. The vessels carrying oxygen-rich blood are shown in red. The vessels carrying oxygen-poor blood are shown in blue.*

Have a Heart

Your heart is a muscular organ about the size of your fist. It is found in the center of your chest cavity. The heart pumps oxygen-poor blood to the lungs and oxygen-rich blood to the body. Like the hearts of all mammals, your heart has a left side and a right side that are separated by a thick wall. As you can see in **Figure 7,** each side has an upper chamber and a lower chamber. Each upper chamber is called an **atrium** (plural, *atria*). Each lower chamber is called a **ventricle.**

Flaplike structures called *valves* are located between the atria and ventricles and also where large arteries are attached to the heart. As blood moves through the heart, the valves close and prevent blood from going backward. The lub-dub, lub-dub sound that a beating heart makes is caused by the closing of the valves. The flow of blood through the heart is shown in the diagram below.

The Flow of Blood Through the Heart

From body

From lungs

To body

To lungs

Blood from right atrium

Blood from left atrium

❶ Blood enters the atria first. The left atrium receives oxygen-rich blood from the lungs. The right atrium receives oxygen-poor blood from the body.

❷ When the atria contract, blood is squeezed into the ventricles.

❸ While the atria relax, the ventricles contract and push blood out of the heart. Blood from the right ventricle goes to the lungs. Blood from the left ventricle goes to the rest of the body.

Blood Vessels

Blood travels throughout your body through blood vessels. A blood vessel is a hollow tube that transports blood. There are three types of blood vessels—arteries, capillaries, and veins. Their structures and their relationship to each other are shown in **Figure 8.**

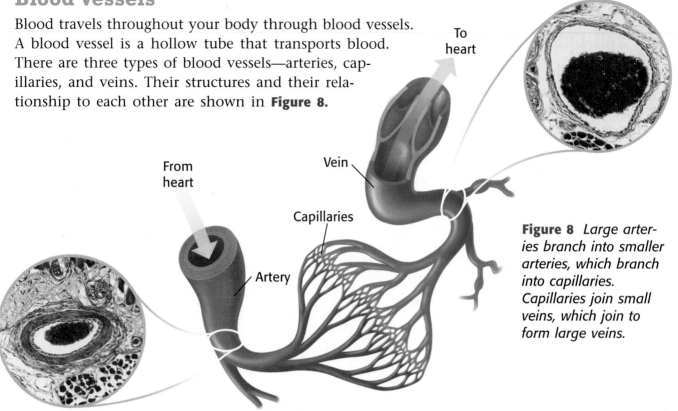

Figure 8 *Large arteries branch into smaller arteries, which branch into capillaries. Capillaries join small veins, which join to form large veins.*

Arteries **Arteries** are blood vessels that direct blood away from the heart. Arteries have thick elastic walls that contain a layer of smooth muscle. Each time the heart beats, blood is pumped out of the heart at high pressure. The thick walls of arteries have the strength to withstand this pressure. The rhythmic change in blood pressure is called a *pulse.* Your pulse can be felt at several places on your body, including the inside of your wrist beneath the thumb.

If all the blood vessels in your body were strung together, the total length would be more than twice the circumference of the Earth.

Capillaries A strand of hair is about 10 times wider than a capillary. **Capillaries** are the smallest blood vessels in your body. Capillary walls are only one cell thick. As shown in **Figure 9,** capillaries are so narrow that blood cells must pass through them in single file. The simple structure of a capillary allows nutrients, oxygen, and many other kinds of substances to diffuse easily through capillary walls to the body's other cells. No cell in the body is more than three or four cells away from a capillary.

Veins After leaving capillaries, the blood enters veins. **Veins** are blood vessels that direct the blood back to the heart. Small veins join to make larger veins. As blood travels through large veins, valves in the veins keep the blood from flowing backward. When skeletal muscles contract, they squeeze nearby veins and help push blood toward the heart.

Figure 9 *These red blood cells are traveling through a capillary.*

Going with the Flow

As you read earlier, one important function of your blood is to supply the cells of your body with oxygen. Where does blood get this oxygen? It gets it from your lungs during pulmonary circulation. **Pulmonary circulation** is the circulation of blood between your heart and lungs.

When oxygen-rich blood returns to the heart from the lungs, it must be pumped to the rest of the body. The circulation of blood between the heart and the rest of the body is called **systemic circulation.** Both types of circulation are diagramed below.

The Flow of Blood Through the Body

The right ventricle pumps oxygen-poor blood into arteries that lead to the lungs. These are the only arteries in the body that carry oxygen-poor blood.

In the capillaries of the lungs, blood absorbs oxygen and releases carbon dioxide. Oxygen-rich blood travels through veins to the left atrium. These are the only veins in the body that carry oxygen-rich blood.

Pulmonary circulation

Oxygen-poor blood travels back to the heart and is delivered into the right atrium by two large veins.

The heart pumps oxygen-rich blood from the left ventricle into arteries and then into capillaries.

Systemic circulation

As blood travels through capillaries, it transports oxygen, nutrients, and water to the cells of the body. At the same time, waste materials and carbon dioxide are carried away.

Blood Flows Under Pressure

When you run water through a hose, you can feel the hose stiffen as the water pushes against the inside of the hose. Blood has the same effect on your blood vessels. The force exerted by blood on the inside walls of a blood vessel is called **blood pressure.**

Like the man shown in **Figure 10,** many people get their blood pressure checked on a regular basis. Blood pressure is reported in millimeters (mm) of mercury, Hg. A blood pressure of 120 mm Hg means the pressure on the vessel walls is great enough to push a narrow column of mercury 120 mm high.

Blood pressure is usually measured at large arteries and is written as two numbers. A normal blood pressure is about 120/80. The first number is called the systolic pressure. *Systolic pressure* is the pressure inside large arteries when the ventricles contract. As you read earlier, the surge of blood causes the arteries to bulge and produce a pulse. The second number is called the diastolic pressure. *Diastolic pressure* is the pressure in the arteries when the ventricles relax.

Figure 10 *This nurse is measuring the blood pressure of a patient. When blood pressure is consistently high or low, something may be wrong with the cardiovascular system.*

Exercise and Blood Flow

When you exercise, your muscles require much more oxygen and nutrients. To solve this problem, the brain sends signals to the heart to make it beat faster. Physical activity causes as much as 10 times more blood to be sent to the muscles than when your body is at rest.

During exercise, some organs do not need as much blood as the skeletal muscles do. Less blood is sent to the kidneys and the digestive system so that more blood can go to the skeletal muscles, brain, heart, and lungs. This is like turning off certain water faucets in a house to allow more water to flow through other faucets. When you finish exercising, blood vessels in other parts of the body open up, and the heart rate slows down.

REVIEW

1. What is the function of the cardiovascular system?

2. What are the three kinds of blood vessels? Compare their functions.

3. **Identifying Relationships** How is the structure of capillaries related to their function?

Explore

Imagine that you are a member of a team of scientists that has been chosen to explore the cardiovascular system. After being shrunk down to the size of red blood cells, you and the team board a miniature submarine and begin your travels through the heart and blood vessels. Describe where you go, what you see, and any problems you might encounter on your journey.

What's Your Blood Type?

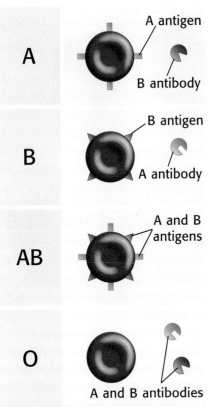

Figure 11 *This table shows which antigens and antibodies may be present in each blood type.*

When a person loses a lot of blood, the person is given blood that has been donated from someone else. The person receiving the blood cannot be given blood from just anyone because people have different blood types. It's safe to mix some blood types, but mixing others causes a person's RBCs to clump together. The clumped cells may form blood clots, which block blood vessels, causing death.

Every person has one of the following blood types: A, B, AB, or O. Your blood type refers to the type of chemicals you have on the surface of your RBCs. These chemicals are called *antigens*. Type A blood has A antigens; type B has B antigens; and type AB has both A and B antigens. Type O blood has neither the A nor B antigen.

To Mix or Not to Mix Different blood types not only have different chemicals on their RBC surfaces but also may have different chemicals in their plasma, the liquid part of blood. These chemicals are *antibodies*. When antibodies bind to RBCs, they cause the RBCs to clump together.

As shown in **Figure 11,** the body makes antibodies against the antigens that are not on its own RBCs. For example, people with type B blood make A antibodies, which attack any blood cell with an A antigen on it. Therefore, people with type B blood can't be given type A or AB blood. Type O blood can be given to anyone because its RBCs don't have any A or B antigens on their surface. A person with type O blood is therefore said to be a *universal donor*. People with type AB blood are *universal recipients*, meaning they can receive any type of blood because they do not make any antibodies against A or B antigens.

APPLY

A young woman is brought into the emergency room and needs a blood transfusion. Her blood type is AB. You call the blood bank to order AB blood, but you are told the bank is out of that type. What other type or types could the blood bank deliver for her transfusion?

Cardiovascular Problems

When something is wrong with a person's cardiovascular system, the person's health will be affected. Some cardiovascular problems involve the heart and the blood vessels, while other problems affect the blood. When there is something wrong with the heart or the blood vessels, the movement of blood through the body is affected.

The leading cause of death in the United States is a cardiovascular disease called *atherosclerosis* (ATH uhr OH skluh ROH sis). Atherosclerosis occurs when fatty materials, such as cholesterol, build up on the inside of blood vessels. The fatty buildup causes the blood vessels to become narrower and less elastic. **Figure 12** shows how the pathway through a blood vessel can become clogged. When a major artery that supplies blood to the heart becomes blocked, a person has a heart attack, and part of the heart can die.

Atherosclerosis also promotes *hypertension,* which is abnormally high blood pressure. Hypertension is dangerous because it overworks the heart and can weaken vessels and make them rupture. If a blood vessel in the brain becomes clogged or ruptures, certain parts of the brain will not receive oxygen and nutrients and may die. This is called a *stroke.*

Cardiovascular problems can be caused by smoking, high levels of cholesterol in blood, stress, and heredity. You may reduce your risk of developing cardiovascular problems by doing the following things: never smoking; eating a diet low in animal fat, palm and coconut oils, and salt; eating plenty of vegetables, fruits, and whole grains; and exercising regularly.

Figure 12 *Atherosclerosis is a common cardiovascular problem. Fatty deposits build up on the inside of blood vessels and block blood flow.*

MATH BREAK

The Beat Goes On

Your heart beats about 100,800 times per day. How many times does it beat per year?

REVIEW

1. Where does blood travel to and from during pulmonary circulation? during systemic circulation?

2. What happens to the oxygen level in blood as it moves through the lungs?

3. **Applying Concepts** Billy has type A blood.

   a. What kind of antigens does he have on his RBCs?

   b. What blood-type antibodies can Billy make?

   c. Which blood types could be given to Billy if he needed a transfusion?

Have blood clots got your goat? Find out on page 507.

The Lymphatic System

NEW TERMS

lymphatic system   lymph nodes
lymph capillaries   thymus
lymph   spleen
lymphatic vessels   tonsils

OBJECTIVES

- Discuss the functions of the lymphatic system.
- Identify the relationship between lymph and blood.
- Describe the organs of the lymphatic system.

Your cardiovascular system is not the only circulatory system in your body. As blood flows through your cardiovascular system, fluid leaks out of the capillaries and mixes with the fluid that bathes your cells. Most of the fluid is reabsorbed by the capillaries, but some is not. To deal with this, your body's **lymphatic system** collects the excess fluid and returns it to your blood.

Like your cardiovascular system, your lymphatic system is a circulatory system. In addition to collecting the excess fluid surrounding your cells and returning it to your blood, your lymphatic system helps your body fight pathogens.

Vessels of the Lymphatic System

The fluid collected by the lymphatic system is transported through vessels. The smallest vessels of the lymphatic system are **lymph capillaries.** From the spaces between cells, lymph capillaries absorb fluid and any particles too large to enter the blood capillaries. Some of these particles are dead cells or cells that are foreign to the body. The fluid and particles absorbed into lymph capillaries are called **lymph.**

As shown in **Figure 13,** lymph capillaries carry lymph into **lymphatic vessels,** which are larger vessels that have valves. Lymph is not pushed by a pump. Instead, the squeezing of skeletal muscles provides the force to move lymph through vessels, and valves help prevent backflow. Lymph travels through your lymphatic system and then drains into large neck veins of the cardiovascular system.

Self-Check

How are the lymphatic system and the cardiovascular system similar? How are they different? *(See page 636 to check your answer.)*

Figure 13 *The white arrows show the movement of lymph into lymph capillaries and through lymphatic vessels. Lymph is composed of fluid from the spaces surrounding cells. This fluid was originally brought to the area by capillaries carrying blood.*

Lymphatic Organs

In addition to vessels and capillaries, a variety of other organs are part of the lymphatic system, as shown in **Figure 14.**

Lymph Nodes As lymph travels through lymphatic vessels, it passes through lymph nodes. **Lymph nodes** are small bean-shaped organs where particles, such as pathogens or dead cells, are removed from the lymph. You have hundreds of lymph nodes scattered along your lymph vessels.

Lymph nodes contain many white blood cells. Some of these cells engulf pathogens. Other WBCs, called *lymphocytes,* produce chemicals that become attached to pathogens and mark them for destruction. When the body becomes infected with bacteria or viruses, the WBCs multiply and the nodes sometimes become swollen and painful.

The Thymus, Spleen, and Tonsils Your **thymus,** which is located just above your heart, releases lymphocytes. The lymphocytes travel to other areas of the lymphatic system.

The largest lymph organ is your spleen, which is located in the upper left side of your abdomen. The **spleen** filters blood and, like the thymus, releases lymphocytes. When red blood cells are squeezed through the spleen's capillaries, the older and more fragile cells rupture. Large white blood cells in the spleen engulf these dead cells and remove them from blood. The RBCs are broken down, and some of their parts are reused. For this reason, the spleen can be thought of as the red-blood-cell recycling center.

Tonsils are made up of groups of lymphatic tissue located at the back of your nasal cavity, on the inside of your throat, and at the back of your tongue. Lymphocytes in the tonsils defend the body against infection. Tonsils sometimes become badly infected and must be removed.

Figure 14 The Lymphatic System

REVIEW

1. What are the main functions of the lymphatic system?

2. Where does lymph go when it leaves the lymphatic system?

3. **Identifying Relationships** How are lymph nodes similar to the spleen?

Section 3

The Respiratory System

Breathing. You do it all the time. You're doing it right now. You hardly ever think about it, though, unless your ability to breathe is suddenly taken away. Then it becomes all too obvious that you must breathe in order to survive. Why is breathing important?

Out with the Bad Air; In with the Good

Your body needs a continuous supply of oxygen in order to obtain energy from the foods you eat. That's where breathing comes in handy. The air you breathe is a mixture of several gases. One of these gases is oxygen. When you breathe, your body takes in air and absorbs the oxygen. Then carbon dioxide from your body is added to the air, and the stale air is exhaled.

The words *breathing* and *respiration* are often thought to mean the same thing. However, breathing is only one part of respiration. **Respiration** is the entire process by which a body obtains and uses oxygen and gets rid of carbon dioxide and water. Respiration is divided into two parts: breathing, which involves inhaling and exhaling, and cellular respiration, which involves the chemical reactions that release energy from food.

NEW TERMS

respiration
respiratory system
pharynx
larynx
trachea
bronchi
alveoli
diaphragm
cellular respiration

OBJECTIVES

- Describe the flow of air through the respiratory system.
- Discuss the relationship between the respiratory system and the circulatory system.
- Identify respiratory disorders.

Breathing: Brought to You by Your Respiratory System

Breathing is made possible by the respiratory system. The **respiratory system** consists of the lungs, throat, and passageways that lead to the lungs. **Figure 15** shows the parts of the respiratory system.

The Nose Your nose is the primary passageway into and out of the respiratory system. Air is inhaled through the nose, where it comes into contact with warm, moist surfaces. Air can also enter and leave through the mouth.

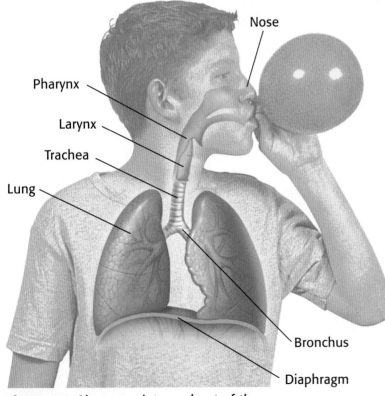

Figure 15 *Air moves into and out of the body through the respiratory system.*

Nose
Pharynx
Larynx
Trachea
Lung
Bronchus
Diaphragm

The Pharynx From the nose, air flows into the **pharynx,** or throat. You can use a mirror to see the walls of your pharynx behind your tongue. In addition to air, food and drink also travel through the pharynx on the way to the stomach. The pharynx branches into two tubes. One leads to the stomach and is called the esophagus. The other leads to the lungs and is called the larynx.

The Larynx Tilt your head up slightly, and rub a finger up and down the front of your throat. The ridges you feel are the outside of the larynx. The **larynx,** or voice box, contains the vocal cords. The vocal cords are a pair of elastic bands that are stretched across the opening of the larynx. Muscles attached to the larynx control how much the vocal cords are stretched. When air flows between the vocal cords, they vibrate and make sound.

The Trachea The larynx guards the entrance to a large tube called the **trachea,** or windpipe. The trachea is the passageway for air traveling from the larynx to the lungs.

The Bronchi The trachea splits into two tubes called **bronchi** (singular, *bronchus*). One bronchus goes to each lung and branches into thousands of tiny tubes called *bronchioles*.

The Lungs Your body has two large spongelike lungs. In the lungs, each bronchiole branches to form thousands of tiny sacs called **alveoli** (singular, *alveolus*). Capillaries surround each alveolus. **Figure 16** shows the arrangement of the tubes in the respiratory system.

When people who live at low elevations travel to the mountains, they usually find that they have difficulty exerting themselves. This is because the concentration of oxygen in the air at high elevations is lower than that at low elevations. Until they become used to the change, people have to take more breaths to supply their bodies with the oxygen they need.

Figure 16 *Inside your lungs, the bronchi branch into bronchioles. The bronchioles lead to tiny sacs called alveoli.*

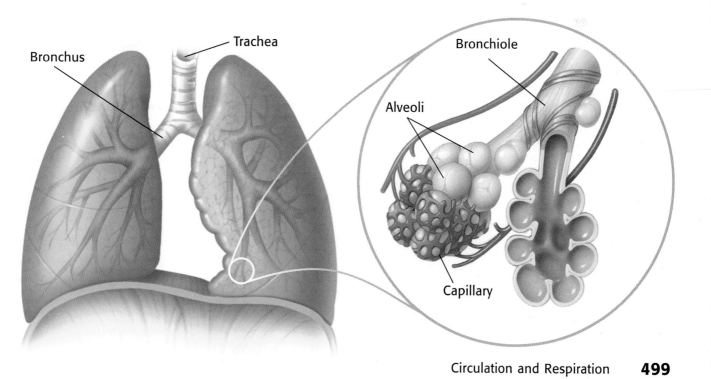

Bronchus — Trachea — Bronchiole — Alveoli — Capillary

Air moves into your lungs.

Your rib cage expands.

Your diaphragm contracts and moves down.

Figure 17 *When your diaphragm contracts, your rib cage expands and creates a vacuum inside your lungs. The vacuum causes air to be sucked in.*

Would you like to linger longer on lungs? Then look at page 630.

How Do You Breathe?

When you breathe, air is sucked in or forced out of your lungs. However, your lungs do not contain muscles that force air in and out. Instead, breathing is done by rib muscles and the **diaphragm,** a dome-shaped muscle underneath the lungs. When the diaphragm contracts, it increases the chest cavity's volume. At the same time, some of your rib muscles contract and lift your rib cage, causing it to expand. To see this diagramed, look at **Figure 17.**

What Happens to the Oxygen? When oxygen has been absorbed by red blood cells, it is transported through the body by the cardiovascular system. Oxygen diffuses inside cells, where it is used in an important chemical reaction known as cellular respiration. During **cellular respiration,** oxygen is used to release energy stored in molecules of carbohydrates, fats, and proteins. When the molecules are broken apart during the reaction, energy is released along with carbon dioxide and water. The carbon dioxide and water leave the cell and return to the bloodstream. The carbon dioxide is carried to the lungs and exhaled. **Figure 18** shows how breathing and blood circulation are related.

Figure 18 *Blood has an important role in respiration.*

O_2 is picked up by blood.

CO_2 enters the air in the alveolus.

Tissues and cells pick up O_2 from the blood.

CO_2 enters the blood.

Respiratory Disorders

Millions of people suffer from respiratory disorders. There are many types of respiratory disorders, including asthma, bronchitis, emphysema, and pneumonia.

In *asthma,* pollen, animal dander, or other irritants cause tissue around the bronchioles to constrict and secrete large amounts of mucus. As the bronchiole tubes get narrower, the person has difficulty breathing. When a person has bronchitis, pneumonia, or asthma, the passageways through the lungs can become clogged with mucus. *Bronchitis* can develop when something irritates the lining of the bronchioles. *Pneumonia* is caused by bacteria or viruses that grow inside the bronchioles and alveoli and cause them to become inflamed and filled with fluid. If there is a significant decrease in the amount of oxygen that can diffuse into the blood, the person may suffocate.

The Hazards of Smoking You probably already know that smoking cigarettes is bad for your health. In fact, smoking is the leading cause of cardiovascular diseases and lung diseases, such as *emphysema* and *lung cancer.* People with emphysema have trouble getting the oxygen they need because their alveoli erode away, as shown in **Figure 19.**

Lung cancer is another dangerous respiratory disorder. Chemicals in tobacco smoke can cause lung cells to become cancerous. The cancerous lung cells divide rapidly and form a mass called a tumor. As the tumor grows, it blocks air flow and hinders the exchange of oxygen and carbon dioxide. Some of the tumor cells may break loose, and the cancer may be carried in blood or lymph to other areas of the body. There, the cells continue to grow and form other tumors.

REVIEW

1. Describe the path that air travels as it moves through the respiratory system.

2. What is the difference between respiration and cellular respiration?

3. What respiratory disorders might a person who smokes cigarettes develop?

4. **Identifying Relationships** How is the function of the respiratory system related to that of the circulatory system?

These are a pair of healthy lungs.

These are the lungs of a person with emphysema.

Figure 19 *Emphysema is a respiratory disease that can be caused by smoking cigarettes.*

Chapter Highlights

Vocabulary

cardiovascular system (*p. 488*)

blood (*p. 488*)

plasma (*p. 488*)

platelet (*p. 489*)

atrium (*p. 490*)

ventricle (*p. 490*)

arteries (*p. 491*)

capillaries (*p. 491*)

veins (*p. 491*)

pulmonary circulation (*p. 492*)

systemic circulation (*p. 492*)

blood pressure (*p. 493*)

Section Notes

• The cardiovascular system delivers oxygen and nutrients to the body's cells, takes away the cells' waste products, and helps the body stay healthy. The cardiovascular system is made up of blood, the heart, and blood vessels.

• Blood is a connective tissue made of plasma, red blood cells, white blood cells, and platelets. The heart is a muscular organ that pumps blood through blood vessels.

• Blood moves away from the heart through arteries and then enters capillaries. After leaving capillaries, blood is carried back to the heart through veins.

• In pulmonary circulation, blood vessels carry blood from the heart to the lungs and back to the heart. In systemic circulation, blood flows from the heart to the rest of the body and then back to the heart.

• People have different blood types. Blood type is determined by the presence of certain chemicals on red blood cells.

Vocabulary

lymphatic system (*p. 496*)

lymph capillaries (*p. 496*)

lymph (*p. 496*)

lymphatic vessels (*p. 496*)

lymph nodes (*p. 497*)

thymus (*p. 497*)

spleen (*p. 497*)

tonsils (*p. 497*)

Section Notes

• The lymphatic system returns excess fluid to the cardiovascular system and helps the body fight infections.

• The lymphatic system includes lymph, lymph capillaries, lymphatic vessels, lymph nodes, the spleen, tonsils, and the thymus.

☑ Skills Check

Math Concepts

A CONTINUOUS BEAT Your heart beats about 100,800 times per day. That means that your heart beats about 4,200 times every hour.

100,800 beats ÷ 24 hours = 4,200 beats

That also means that your heart beats about 70 times every minute.

4,200 beats ÷ 60 minutes = 70 beats

Visual Understanding

AIR PASSAGEWAYS Take another look at Figure 15 on page 498. With your finger, trace the path air takes to reach the lungs. As you do this, reconsider what roles the nose, pharynx, trachea, bronchi, lungs, and diaphragm play in respiration.

Vocabulary

respiration *(p. 498)*

respiratory system *(p. 498)*

pharynx *(p. 499)*

larynx *(p. 499)*

trachea *(p. 499)*

bronchi *(p. 499)*

alveoli *(p. 499)*

diaphragm *(p. 500)*

cellular respiration *(p. 500)*

Section Notes

- The respiratory system moves air into and out of the body. The respiratory system includes the nose, the mouth, the pharynx, the larynx, the trachea, and the lungs.

- Air enters the lungs through bronchi and travels to the alveoli, which are gas-filled sacs surrounded by capillaries of the cardiovascular system.

- The blood in the capillaries of the lungs absorbs oxygen and releases carbon dioxide. The carbon dioxide is exhaled. The oxygen is carried by the blood to the h...

- ...

Cells types

Tissue - 2 or more tissue work together it is an organ

- I...

Labs

Build a Lung *(p. 630)*

Carbon Dioxide Breath *(p. 631)*

---

 internetconnect

 GO TO: go.hrw.com

Visit the **HRW** Web site for a variety of learning tools related to this chapter. Just type in the keyword:

KEYWORD: HSTBD2

 GO TO: www.scilinks.org

Visit the **National Science Teachers Association** on-line Web site for Internet resources related to this chapter. Just type in the *sci*LINKS number for more information about the topic:

TOPIC: The Cardiovascular System	*sci*LINKS NUMBER: HSTL555
TOPIC: Cardiovascular Problems	*sci*LINKS NUMBER: HSTL560
TOPIC: The Lymphatic System	*sci*LINKS NUMBER: HSTL565
TOPIC: The Respiratory System	*sci*LINKS NUMBER: HSTL570
TOPIC: Respiratory Disorders	*sci*LINKS NUMBER: HSTL575

Chapter Review

USING VOCABULARY

To complete the following sentences, choose the correct term from each pair of terms listed below:

1. Oxygen is delivered to the cells of the body by __?__. *(white blood cells* or *red blood cells)*

2. Blood is carried away from the heart in __?__. *(arteries* or *veins)*

3. Lymphocytes are a kind of __?__. *(lymphatic vessel* or *white blood cell)*

4. The __?__ contains the vocal cords. *(trachea* or *larynx)*

5. The pathway of air through the respiratory system ends at the tiny sacs called __?__. *(alveoli* or *bronchi)*

UNDERSTANDING CONCEPTS

Multiple Choice

6. Blood from the lungs enters the heart at the
   a. left ventricle.
   b. left atrium.
   c. right atrium.
   d. right ventricle.

7. Blood cells are made
   a. in the heart.
   b. from plasma.
   c. from lymph.
   d. in the bones.

8. Which of the following is not part of the lymphatic system?
   a. trachea
   b. lymph node
   c. thymus
   d. spleen

9. Alveoli are surrounded by
   a. veins.
   b. muscles.
   c. capillaries.
   d. lymph nodes.

10. What prevents blood from flowing backward in veins?
    a. platelets
    b. valves
    c. muscles
    d. cartilage

11. Air moves into the lungs when the diaphragm muscle
    a. contracts and moves down.
    b. contracts and moves up.
    c. relaxes and moves down.
    d. relaxes and moves up.

Short Answer

12. What is the difference between pulmonary circulation and systemic circulation in the cardiovascular system?

13. Walton has a blood pressure of 110/65. What do the two numbers mean?

14. What body process produces the carbon dioxide you exhale?

Concept Map

15. Use the following terms to create a concept map: blood, oxygen, alveoli, capillaries, carbon dioxide.

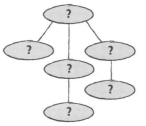

CRITICAL THINKING AND PROBLEM SOLVING

Write one or two sentences to answer the following questions:

16. Why do you think there are hairs in your nose?

17. When a person is not feeling well, sometimes a doctor will examine samples of the person's blood to see how many white blood cells are present. Why would this information be useful?

18. How is the function of the lymphatic system related to the function of the cardiovascular system?

MATH IN SCIENCE

19. After a person donates blood, the blood is stored in one-pint bags until it is needed for a transfusion. A healthy person normally has 5 million RBCs in each cubic millimeter (1 mm^3) of blood.

    a. How many RBCs are there in 1 mL of blood? One milliliter is equal to 1 cm^3 and to 1,000 mm^3.

    b. How many RBCs are there in 1 pt? One pint is equal to 473 mL.

INTERPRETING GRAPHICS

The diagram below shows how the human heart would look in cross section. Examine the diagram, and then answer the questions that follow:

20. Which letter identifies the chamber that receives blood from systemic circulation? What is this chamber's name?

21. Which letter identifies the chamber that receives blood from the lungs? What is this chamber's name?

22. Which letter identifies the chamber that pumps blood to the lungs? What is this chamber's name?

NOW What Do You Think?

Take a minute to review your answers to the ScienceLog questions on page 487. Have your answers changed? If necessary, revise your answers based on what you have learned since you began this chapter.

CATCHING A LIGHT SNEEZE

Do you sneeze when you come out of a dark movie theater into bright sunlight? If not, look around you next time. Chances are several people will sneeze.

Reflex Gone Wrong

For some reason, about one in five people sneeze when they step from a dimly lit area into a brightly lit area. In fact, some may sneeze a dozen times or more! Fortunately, the sneezing usually stops after a few times. This reaction is called a *photic sneeze reflex.* No one knows for certain why it happens.

Normal sneezing is a reflex, which means you do it without thinking about it. Most people sneeze when something tickles the inside of their nose. They sneeze, and moving air pushes the tickling intruder out. For instance, if you get dust in your nose, sneezing pushes the dust out. In the case of people with the photic sneeze, it's a reflex gone wrong.

ACHOO!

A few years ago, some geneticists studied the photic sneeze reflex. They named it the Autosomal Dominant Compelling Helio-ophthalmic Outburst syndrome, or the ACHOO syndrome. Scientists know that the ACHOO syndrome runs in families. So the photic sneeze can be passed from parent to child. Sometimes even the number of times in a row that each person sneezes is the same throughout a family.

Possible Answers

Some scientists have offered a possible explanation for the ACHOO syndrome. First, everyone's pupils contract when they

▲ *Do you sneeze when you see bright light after exiting a dark room?*

encounter bright light. And the nerves from the eyes are right next to the nerves from the nose. Thus, people with the ACHOO syndrome may have their wires slightly crossed: bright light triggers the pupil reflex, and it also triggers the sneeze reflex!

Sneeze Fest

Sunlight is not the only strange trigger for sudden sneezes. Some people sneeze when they rub the inner corner of their eye. Others sneeze when tweezing their eyebrows or brushing their hair. In rare individuals, even eating too much has been known to cause sneezing fits!

Research the Facts

▶ Yawning is also a reflex. Do some research to find out why we yawn.

Health

Goats to the Rescue

They're called transgenic (tranz JEHN ik) goats because their cells contain a human gene. They look just like any other goats, but because of their human gene they produce a chemical that can save lives.

Lifesaving Genes

Heart attacks are the number one cause of death in the United States. Many heart attacks are triggered when large blood clots interfere with the flow of blood to the heart. Human blood cells produce a chemical called *tissue plasminogen activator* (TPA) that dissolves small blood clots. If TPA is given to a person having a heart attack, it can often dissolve the blood clot, stop the attack, and save the person's life. But TPA is difficult to produce in large quantities in the laboratory. This is where the goats come in. Researchers at Tufts University in, Grafton, Massachusetts, have genetically engineered goats to produce this lifesaving drug.

Hybrid Goats

Producing transgenic goats is a complicated process. First, fertilized eggs are surgically removed from normal female goats. The eggs are then injected with hybrid genes that consist of human TPA genes "spliced" into genes from the mammary glands of a goat. Finally, the altered eggs are surgically implanted into female goats, where they develop into young goats, or kids. Some of the kids actually carry the hybrid gene. When the hybrid kids mature, the females' milk contains TPA. Technicians then separate the TPA from the goats' milk for use in heart-attack victims.

The Research Continues

Transgenic research in farm animals such as goats, sheep, cows, and pigs may someday produce drugs faster, cheaper, and in greater quantities than are possible using current methods. The way we view the barnyard may never be the same.

Find Out for Yourself

▶ Using chemicals produced by transgenic animals is just one of many gene therapies. Do some research to find out more about gene therapy, how it is used, and how it may be used in the future.

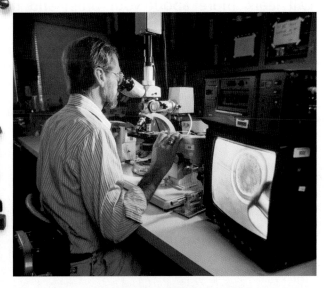

▲ *A scientist at Tufts University injects human TPA genes into fertilized goat eggs.*

21 Communication and Control

Gage's skull showing the path of the tamping rod

This Really Happened . . .

About 150 years ago, a bizarre accident changed the way scientists view the role of the brain. The accident involved a railroad worker named Phineas Gage. One day in 1848, Gage was using a long metal rod to pack explosives into a hole to clear a path for some railroad track. A spark caused an explosion that blew the rod through Gage's head. The rod entered through his left cheek and exited at the top of his skull. You would expect this injury to be fatal, but Gage stood up and was able to speak.

In a little over 2 months, Gage's wounds were healed, but he was not quite the same. The Phineas Gage people knew before the accident was calm, responsible, and considerate of others. But after the accident he become irresponsible and quick to anger. Scientists who studied Gage's change in behavior learned that the brain is responsible for much more than just movement and senses. In this chapter you will learn more about your brain and the rest of your nervous system. You will also learn how the nervous system and the endocrine system control all of the other systems in your body.

What Do You Think?

In your ScienceLog, try to answer the following questions based on what you already know:

1. What are your senses? How do senses help us survive?

2. Why does your heart beat faster when something frightens you?

3. How do eyeglasses and contact lenses help some people see better?

Investigate!

How Fast Do You React?

When you want to move your hand, your brain must send a message all the way to the muscles in your arms. How long does that take? In this exercise, you will work with a partner to see how quickly you can react.

Procedure

1. Sit in a chair and have a partner stand facing you while holding a **meterstick** in a vertical position, as shown at right. Hold your thumb about 3 cm from your fingers near the bottom end of the stick. The meterstick should be positioned to fall between your thumb and fingers.

2. Tell your partner to let go of the meterstick without warning. When you see this happen, catch the stick by pressing your thumb and fingers together. Your partner should be ready to catch the top of the meterstick if it begins to tip over. Record the number of centimeters the stick dropped before you caught it. The distance that the meterstick falls before you catch it can be used to evaluate your reaction time.

3. Repeat the procedure several times, and calculate the average number of centimeters. Next try this procedure with the hand that you do not use for writing.

4. Exchange places with your partner, and repeat the procedure.

Analysis

5. Compare your results with those of your partner. What factors might influence a person's ability to react quickly?

6. How does your reaction time when using one hand compare with that when using your other hand?

7. Make a list of situations in which a quick reaction time is important.

The Nervous System

What do the following events have in common: you hear a knock at the door, you write a book report, you feel your heart pounding after a run, you work a math problem, you are startled by a loud noise, and you enjoy eating a sweet mango. These events are all activities of your *nervous system*. The **nervous system** gathers and interprets information about the body's internal and external environments and responds to that information. The nervous system keeps your organs working properly and allows you to speak, smell, taste, hear, see, move, think, and experience emotions.

Two Systems Within a System

Your nervous system controls and coordinates many things that happen in your body. It acts as a central command post, collecting and processing information and making sure appropriate information gets sent to all parts of the body. These tasks are accomplished by two subdivisions of the nervous system, the *central nervous system (CNS)* and the *peripheral nervous system (PNS)*.

The **central nervous system** includes your brain and spinal cord. It processes all incoming and outgoing messages. The **peripheral nervous system** consists of communication pathways, or *nerves*, that connect all areas of your body to your central nervous system. **Figure 1** shows the major divisions of the nervous system.

Figure 1 *The central nervous system (in orange) acts as the control center for your body. The peripheral nervous system (in purple) carries information toward and away from the central nervous system.*

The Peripheral Nervous System

How long does it take for a light to come on when you flip a light switch? The light seems to come on immediately. In a similar way, specialized cells called **neurons** transfer messages throughout your body in the form of fast-moving electrical energy. A typical neuron is shown in **Figure 2.** The electrical messages that pass along the neurons are called **impulses.** Impulses may travel as fast as 150 m/s or as slow as 1 m/s.

Neuron Structure A neuron consists of a cell body, dendrites, and axons. The enlarged region called the cell body contains a nucleus and cell organelles. Look again at Figure 2. The neuron generally receives information from other cells through short branched extensions called **dendrites.** A neuron may have many dendrites, allowing it to receive impulses from thousands of other cells.

From the cell body, information is transmitted to other cells by a long fiber called an **axon.** Axons can be very short or quite long. You have some really long axons that extend almost 1 m from your lower back to your toes. The end of an axon often has branches that allow information to pass to yet more cells. The tip of each branch is called an *axon terminal.*

MATH BREAK

Time to Travel

To calculate how long it takes for an impulse to travel a certain distance, you can use the following equation:

$$\text{Time} = \frac{\text{distance}}{\text{speed}}$$

If an impulse travels 100 m/s, about how long would it take for an impulse to travel 10 m?

Direction of impulse

Axon

Cell body

Axon terminal

Dendrite

Nucleus

Figure 2 *Neurons are special cells that transfer electrical messages throughout the body.*

BRAIN FOOD

The number of neurons in your brain is about 100 billion, which is about the same as the number of stars in the Milky Way galaxy!

Information Collection Special neurons called **sensory neurons** gather information about what is happening in and around your body and send this information on to the central nervous system for processing. Sensory neurons have specialized dendrites called **receptors** that detect changes inside and outside the body. For example, receptors in your eyes detect the light around you. Receptors in your stomach let your brain know when your stomach is full or empty.

Delivering Orders Neurons that send impulses from the brain and spinal cord to other systems are called **motor neurons.** *Motor* means "to move"; when muscles get impulses from motor neurons, they respond by contracting. For example, motor neurons cause the muscles around your eyes to move when the sensory neurons in your eyes detect bright light. This movement makes you squint, which reduces the amount of light entering the eye. Motor neurons also send messages to your glands, such as sweat glands. These messages tell the sweat glands to release sweat.

Just a Bundle of Axons

The central nervous system is connected to the rest of your body by nerves. **Nerves** are axons bundled together with blood vessels and connective tissue. Nerves extend throughout your body. Most nerves contain the axons of both sensory and motor neurons. **Figure 3** shows the structure of a nerve. The axon in this nerve transmits information from the spinal cord to muscle fibers.

Spinal cord

Muscle fiber

Axon terminal

Axon

Figure 3 *In order for a muscle to contract, a message must travel from the spinal cord to the muscle. The message travels along the axon of a motor neuron inside the nerve.*

Nerve

The Central Nervous System

The central nervous system works closely with the peripheral nervous system. It receives information from the sensory neurons and responds by sending messages to various parts of the body via motor neurons.

Mission Control The **brain,** part of your central nervous system, is the nervous system's largest organ. It has hundreds of different jobs. Many of the processes that the brain controls happen automatically and are referred to as *involuntary*. For example, you couldn't stop digesting the food you have eaten even if you tried. Other activities controlled by your brain are *voluntary*. When you want to move your arm, your brain sends signals along motor neurons to muscles in your arm. This causes the muscles to contract and your arm to move. The brain has three connected parts—the cerebrum, the cerebellum, and the medulla. Each part has its own functions.

Your Thinking Cap The largest part of your brain is called the **cerebrum.** Its shape resembles a mushroom cap over a stalk. This dome-shaped area is where you think and where most memories are stored. It controls voluntary movements and allows you to detect touch, light, sound, odors, taste, pain, heat, and cold.

The cerebrum has two halves called *hemispheres*. The left hemisphere directs the right side of the body, and the right hemisphere directs the left side of the body. This is because axons cross over to the opposite side of the body in the spinal cord. Overall, though, both hemispheres are involved in most brain activities. Look at **Figure 4** to see a general idea of what each hemisphere controls.

Figure 4 The Cerebral Hemispheres

The **left hemisphere** primarily controls activities such as speaking, reading, writing, and solving problems.

$$x = \frac{-b \pm \sqrt{b^2 - 4ac}}{2a}$$

$$e = mc^2$$

$$\pi = 3.14159625$$

Top of Brain

The **right hemisphere** primarily controls activities that involve imagination, appreciation, and creativity.

The Balancing Act The second largest part of your brain is the **cerebellum.** It lies underneath the back of your cerebrum and receives sensory impulses from skeletal muscles and joints. This allows the brain to keep track of your body's position. For example, if you begin to lose your balance, like the girl in **Figure 5,** the cerebellum sends impulses to different skeletal muscles to make them contract, keeping you upright.

The Mighty Medulla The part of your brain that connects to your spinal cord is called the **medulla.** The medulla is only about 3 cm long, but you couldn't live without it. The medulla controls your blood pressure, heart rate, involuntary breathing, and some other involuntary activities.

Your medulla constantly receives sensory impulses from receptors in your blood vessels. It uses this information to regulate your blood pressure. If your blood pressure gets too low, the medulla sends out impulses that tell blood vessels to tighten up to increase the blood pressure. The medulla also sends impulses to the heart to make it beat faster or slower as necessary. **Figure 6** shows the location of each part of the brain and some of the functions associated with each part.

Figure 5 *Your cerebellum causes skeletal muscles to make adjustments in order to keep you upright.*

Figure 6 *Different regions of the brain are responsible for different body functions.*

The Spinal Cord

Your spinal cord, part of the central nervous system, is about as big around as your thumb. It contains neurons and bundles of axons that pass impulses to and from the brain. As shown in **Figure 7,** the spinal cord is surrounded by protective rings of bone called *vertebrae* (VUHR tuh BRAY).

The neuron fibers in your spinal cord enable your brain to communicate with your peripheral nervous system. Sensory neurons in your skin and muscles send impulses along their axons to your spinal cord. The spinal cord then conducts impulses to your brain, where they can be interpreted as pain, heat, cold, or other sensations. Impulses moving from the brain down the cord are relayed to motor neurons, which carry the impulses along their axons to muscles and glands all over your body.

Spinal Cord Injury If the spinal cord is injured, any sensory information coming into it below where the damage occurred may be unable to travel to the brain. Likewise, any motor commands the brain sends to an area below the injury may not get through to the peripheral nerves. Thousands of people each year are paralyzed by spinal cord injuries. Many of these injuries occur in automobile accidents. Among young people, spinal cord injuries are often sports related.

Figure 7 *The spinal cord, shown here in cross section, carries information to and from the brain. It is protected by a long column of vertebrae.*

Self-Check

1. What part of the brain do you use to do your math homework?
2. What part of the brain helps a gymnast maintain balance on the balance beam?
3. What is the function of the vertebrae?

(See page 636 to check your answers.)

Ouch! That Hurt!

Have you ever stepped on something sharp? You probably pulled your foot up without thinking. This quick, involuntary action is called a **reflex.** Reflexes help protect your body from damage.

When you step on a sharp object, the message "pain" travels to your spinal cord, and a message to move your foot travels back to the muscles in your leg. The muscles in your leg respond before the information ever reaches the brain. By the time your brain finds out what happened, your foot has already moved. If you had to wait for your brain to get the message, your foot might be seriously injured! The man in **Figure 8** lifted his foot before he realized he had stepped on a toy.

Figure 8 *When pain impulses from your foot reach your spine, a message is sent immediately to your leg muscles to lift your foot. The pain impulses still travel to your brain, but the cry of pain probably happens after the danger is over.*

Quick **Lab**

Knee Jerks

1. Sit on the edge of a desk or table so your feet don't touch the floor.

2. While your leg is completely relaxed, have a classmate *gently* tap on your knee slightly below the kneecap with the edge of his or her hand. How did your leg respond? Did you have any control over what happened? Explain.

3. Describe the pathway taken by the impulse that started with the tap on the knee.

REVIEW

1. Make a labeled diagram that shows the path of an electrical message from one neuron to another neuron.

2. Explain how the peripheral nervous system connects with the central nervous system.

3. If a spider is crawling up your left arm, which cerebral hemisphere controls the movement that you will use to knock it off?

4. List the three major parts of the brain, and describe their functions.

5. **Applying Concepts** Describe a time when you experienced a reflex.

Responding to the Environment

How do you know when someone taps you on the shoulder or calls your name? How do you feel the touch or hear the sound? Impulses from sensory receptors in your shoulder and in your ears travel to your brain, sending information about your external environment. Your brain depends on this information to make decisions that affect your survival.

Come to Your Senses

Information about your surroundings and the conditions in your body is detected by sensory receptors. This information is converted to electrical signals and sent to your brain for interpretation. Once the signals reach your brain, you become aware of them. This awareness is called a *sensation*. It is in your brain that you have thoughts, feelings, and memories about sensations.

There are many different kinds of sensory receptors in your body. For example, receptors in your eyes detect light. Receptors in your ears detect vibrations called sound waves. The taste buds on your tongue have receptors that detect chemicals in the foods you eat. You have special receptors in your nose that detect tiny particles in the air. Your skin has a variety of receptors as well. Look at **Figure 9** to see some of the different kinds of receptors in the skin.

NEW TERMS

retina   optic nerve
photoreceptors   iris
rods   lens
cones   cochlea

OBJECTIVES

- List four sensations that are detected by receptors in the skin.
- Describe how light relates to vision.
- Explain the function of rods and cones.
- Compare and contrast the functions of photoreceptors, taste buds, and olfactory cells.

I've got to hand it to you—you've gotta lotta nerve. See for yourself on page 632 of your LabBook.

Figure 9 *This diagram shows some of the receptors in your skin and what they detect.*

Light touch

Pressure and heat

Pressure

Light touch and pressure

Deep pressure

Something in My Eye

As you read this sentence, you are using one of your most important senses—*vision*. Vision is your awareness of light energy, your sense of sight. Your eyes have special receptors that detect visible light, a portion of the sun's energy that reaches the Earth. Visible light is composed of all the colors of the rainbow. These colors often become visible to you when sunlight passes through rain droplets. That's when you see a rainbow. Your eyes can also see visible light that reflects off objects around you.

The eye is a complex sensory organ. Examine the parts of the eye shown in **Figure 10.** The outer surface of the eye is covered by the cornea, a transparent membrane that protects the eye but allows light to enter. Visible light that is reflected by objects around you enters through an opening at the front of your eye called the *pupil*. Light is detected by cells at the back of your eye in a light-sensitive layer called the **retina.**

The retina is packed with special neurons called **photoreceptors** (*photo* means "light") that convert light into electrical impulses. There are two types of photoreceptors in the retina—rods and cones. **Rods** can detect very dim light. They are important for night vision. Impulses from rods are perceived in tones of gray. In bright light, the **cones** give you a very colorful view of the world.

Light energy produces changes in photoreceptors that trigger nerve impulses. These impulses travel along axons, leaving the back of each eye through an **optic nerve.**

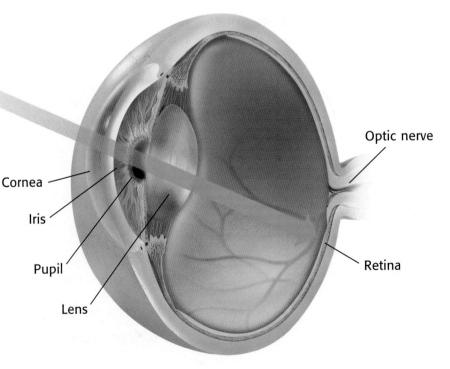

Visible light

Cornea

Iris

Pupil

Lens

Optic nerve

Retina

Figure 10 *The light that reflects off objects around you hits the receptor cells of the retina. The reason carrots look orange is that they absorb all the colors of visible light except orange.*

Seeing the Light Light rays enter the eye through an opening called the *pupil*. Your pupil looks like a black dot in the center of your eye, but it is actually an opening. It is surrounded by the **iris,** the part of the eye that gives the eye color. A ring of muscle fibers causes the iris to open and close, making the pupil change size. This regulates the amount of light that passes to the retina. In bright light, your pupil is small, and in dim light, your pupil is large. Compare the size of the pupils in the eyes in **Figure 11.**

Hocus Focus Light travels in straight lines until it passes through the cornea and the *lens*. A **lens** is a piece of curved material behind the pupil that allows light to pass through but changes its direction. The lens focuses the light entering the eye on the retina. The lens of an eye changes shape to adjust focus. When you look at objects close to the eye, the lens becomes more curved. When you look at objects far away, the lens gets flatter.

In some eyes, the lens focuses the light just in front of the retina (resulting in nearsightedness) or just behind the retina (resulting in farsightedness). Glasses or contact lenses can usually correct these vision problems. Focus on **Figure 12** to see how corrective lenses work.

Figure 11 *The iris surrounds the pupil and gives your eyes their color. Your iris also controls how much light is allowed to pass through your pupil.*

Pupil in normal light

Pupil in dim light

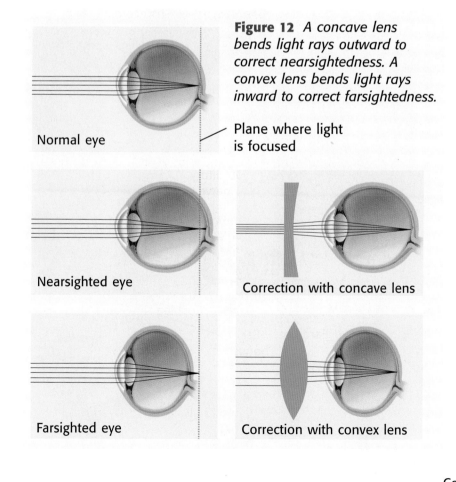

Normal eye

Plane where light is focused

Figure 12 *A concave lens bends light rays outward to correct nearsightedness. A convex lens bends light rays inward to correct farsightedness.*

Nearsighted eye

Correction with concave lens

Farsighted eye

Correction with convex lens

What are some other uses of lenses? Turn to Light on Lenses on page 530 to find out.

Where's the Dot?

1. Hold this book at arm's length and close your right eye. Focus your left eye on the solid dot below.

   ○   ●

2. Slowly move the book toward your face. Stay focused on the solid dot.

3. What happens to the large white dot?

4. Do some research on the optic nerve to find out why this happens.

Did You "Ear" That?

When a guitar string is plucked, what enables you to hear the sound? A sound begins when an object, such as the guitar string, begins to vibrate. The vibrations push on surrounding air particles. These air particles push on other air particles, transferring energy in waves away from the source. Hearing is the sensation experienced in response to these sound waves.

Journey of a Sound Wave   Your ears are organs specialized for hearing. Each ear has an outer, middle, and inner part. The parts of the ear are shown in **Figure 13.** When sound waves reach the outer ear, they are funneled into the middle ear, where they cause the eardrum to vibrate. The vibrating eardrum makes tiny ear bones vibrate. One of the tiny bones vibrates against the **cochlea,** a tiny snail-shaped organ of the inner ear. Inside the cochlea, the vibrations create waves that are similar to the waves you can make by tapping on a glass of water. Neurons in the cochlea convert these waves to electrical impulses and send them to the area of the brain that interprets sound.

Figure 13 *When a sound is heard by the ear, a sound wave travels into the outer ear and is converted to bone vibrations in the middle ear, then to liquid vibrations in the inner ear, and finally to nerve impulses through the auditory nerve.*

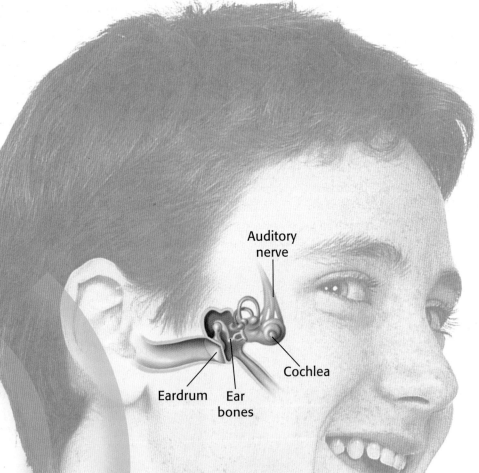

Auditory nerve

Cochlea

Eardrum   Ear bones

Sound waves

Does This Suit Your Taste?

When you put food in your mouth, your sense of what the food tastes like comes mostly from your tongue. Taste is the sensation you feel when the brain is made aware of certain dissolved chemicals in your mouth. The receptors for taste are clustered in the *taste buds*. The tongue is covered with tiny bumps called *papillae* (puh PIL ee), and the taste buds are embedded in the sides of these bumps. As shown in **Figure 14,** there are four types of taste buds. Each type responds to one of the four basic tastes: sweet, sour, salty, and bitter.

Figure 14 *Taste buds in different parts of the tongue respond to different types of chemicals.*

Your Nose Knows

Have you ever noticed that when you have a congested nose you can't taste food very well? Try eating a piece of peppermint while holding your nose. The mint taste is not very intense until you inhale through your nose. That's because smell and taste are closely related. The brain combines information from your taste buds and nose to give you a sense of flavor. The receptors for smell are located on *olfactory cells* in the upper part of your nasal cavity. They react to chemicals that are inhaled and dissolved in the moist lining of the nasal cavity. The woman in **Figure 15** is using her sense of smell to test the effectiveness of underarm deodorants.

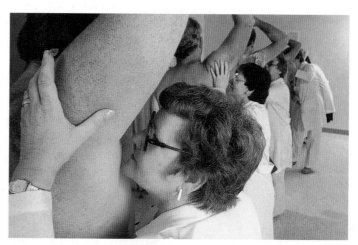

Figure 15 *This woman's nose is detecting chemicals in the sweat and in the underarm deodorants used by these men. Her brain will generate thoughts and opinions about the smells that she will then record in her lab report.*

REVIEW

1. List three sensations that receptors in the skin can detect.

2. Explain why you would have trouble seeing bright colors at a candle-lit dinner.

3. How is your sense of taste similar to your sense of smell?

4. **Applying Concepts** If you can focus on objects close to you but things become blurry when they are far away, would a concave or convex lens correct your vision?

physical science CONNECTION

Sound is produced by vibrating objects. Objects that vibrate more than 20,000 times a second produce sounds too high for humans to hear. Dolphins can detect sounds from objects that vibrate up to 150,000 times per second.

The Endocrine System

NEW TERMS
endocrine system
gland
hormone
feedback control

OBJECTIVES

- Explain the function of the endocrine system.
- List the glands of the endocrine system and describe some of their functions.
- Illustrate the location of some of the endocrine glands in the body.
- Describe how feedback controls stop and start hormone release.

You already know that the job of the nervous system is to communicate with all the other body systems. Your nervous system communicates by using electrical messages called impulses. Its main role is to respond rapidly to stimuli. But it is not the only system that has this role. Your **endocrine system** is involved with the control of much slower, long-term processes, such as fluid balance, growth, and sexual development. Instead of electrical messages, the endocrine system sends messages via chemicals.

Chemical Messengers

The endocrine system controls body functions with the use of chemicals that are released from endocrine glands. A **gland** is a group of cells that makes special chemicals for your body. Chemicals that are produced by the endocrine glands are called **hormones.** The chemicals made by endocrine glands are released into the bloodstream and carried to other places in the body. Because hormones act as chemical messengers, an endocrine gland near your brain can control the actions of an organ located somewhere else in your body.

Endocrine glands often affect many organs at one time. For example, your adrenal glands (also called *adrenals*) prepare your organs to deal with stress. They make the hormone *epinephrine* (ep ih NEF rihn), formerly called *adrenaline.* Epinephrine speeds up your heartbeat and breathing rate to prepare your body either to run from danger or to fight for survival. This hormone effect is often referred to as the "fight-or-flight" response. You may have noticed these effects when you were frightened or angry.

Figure 16 *When you have to move quickly to avoid danger, your adrenal glands help by making more blood glucose available for energy.*

Your body has several other endocrine glands, some with many different functions. For example, your pituitary gland stimulates skeletal growth, helps the thyroid function properly, regulates the amount of water in the blood, and stimulates the birth process in pregnant women. The names and some of the functions of this and other endocrine glands are summarized in **Figure 17.**

Figure 17 *Your endocrine glands produce chemicals called hormones that control many of your body functions.*

Your **thyroid gland** increases the rate at which you use energy.

The **parathyroid glands** (behind the thyroid) regulate calcium levels in the blood.

The **thymus gland** regulates the immune system, which helps your body fight disease.

The **ovaries** produce hormones involved in reproduction.

The **pituitary gland** secretes hormones that affect other glands and organs.

The **adrenal glands** help the body respond to stress and danger.

The **pancreas** regulates blood sugar levels.

The **testes**, in males, produce hormones involved in reproduction.

APPLY

Maria was working late at the library. She was worried about walking home alone. As she started home, she noticed a shadowy figure walking quickly behind her. The figure was gaining on her! She could feel her heart pounding in her chest. She began to run, and then a familiar voice called out her name. It was her father. He had walked to the library to check on her. What a relief!

Maria had a fight-or-flight response. Write a paragraph describing a time when you had a fight-or-flight experience. Include in your story the following terms: *hormones, fight-or-flight,* and *epinephrine.*

Controlling the Controls

How do endocrine glands know when to start and stop hormone release? They know because your body has special systems called **feedback controls** that turn endocrine glands on and off. Feedback controls work something like a thermostat on an air conditioner. Once a room reaches the required temperature, the thermostat sends a message to the air conditioner to stop sending in cold air. Much in the same way, a feedback control sends a message to an endocrine gland to stop sending in a particular hormone. **Figure 18** traces the steps of a feedback control that regulates blood sugar.

Figure 18 *In this feedback-control system, the pancreas produces hormones that help your body maintain the correct blood sugar levels.*

1 After you eat a meal, glucose is absorbed into the bloodstream by the small intestine.

5 To keep your blood sugar level from falling below normal, you must eat again.

Pancreas

Pancreas

2 When glucose levels in the blood are high, the pancreas releases the hormone insulin into the blood.

4 When blood sugar levels return to normal, the pancreas stops releasing insulin.

3 Insulin signals the liver to take in glucose from the body, convert it to glycogen, and store it for future energy needs.

Liver

Hormone Imbalances

Insulin is a hormone made by the pancreas. When the blood glucose level rises after a person has eaten something, insulin triggers the cells to take in glucose and sends a message to the liver to store glucose. A person whose pancreas cannot make enough insulin has a condition called *diabetes mellitus*. A person with diabetes mellitus may need daily injections of insulin to keep his or her blood glucose levels within safe limits. Some patients, like the woman in **Figure 19,** receive their insulin automatically from a small machine they wear next to their body.

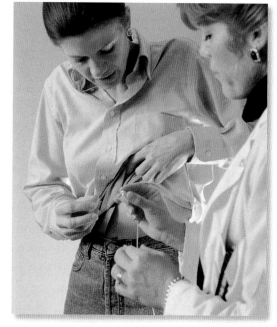

Figure 19 *This young woman has diabetes and must have daily injections of the hormone insulin.*

Growth Hormone Sometimes a child may have a pituitary gland that doesn't make enough growth hormone. This causes the child's growth to be stunted. Fortunately, if this problem is detected soon enough, a doctor can prescribe hormone replacement medication and monitor the child's growth, as shown in **Figure 20.** If the pituitary makes too much growth hormone at an early age, the person becomes much taller than expected.

Thyroxine When a person doesn't get enough iodine in the diet, the thyroid gland cannot make enough of the hormone *thyroxine.* This causes the thyroid to swell up and form a mass called a *goiter.* Since thyroxine increases metabolism, this person's cells are less active than normal, causing fatigue, weight gain, and other problems.

REVIEW

1. What is the function of the endocrine system?

2. Why are feedback controls important?

3. Name four endocrine glands, and tell what each one does in the body.

4. **Applying Concepts** Epinephrine, the fight-or-flight hormone, increases the level of glucose in the blood. Why would this be important in times of stress?

5. **Illustrating Concepts** Look around your house for an example of a feedback control. Draw a diagram explaining how it works to start and stop an action.

Figure 20 *This child receives a growth hormone and is having her height checked by her mother.*

Chapter Highlights

Vocabulary

nervous system *(p. 510)*

central nervous system *(p. 510)*

peripheral nervous system
(p. 510)

neuron *(p. 511)*

impulse *(p. 511)*

dendrite *(p. 511)*

axon *(p. 511)*

sensory neuron *(p. 512)*

receptor *(p. 512)*

motor neuron *(p. 512)*

nerve *(p. 512)*

brain *(p. 513)*

cerebrum *(p. 513)*

cerebellum *(p. 514)*

medulla *(p. 514)*

reflex *(p. 516)*

Section Notes

- The central nervous system includes the brain and spinal cord. The peripheral nervous system includes nerves and sensory receptors.

- A neuron receives information at branched endings called dendrites and passes information to other cells along a fiber called an axon.

- Sensory neurons detect information about the body and its environment. Motor neurons carry messages from the brain and spinal cord to other parts of the body.

- The cerebrum is the largest part of the brain and is involved with thinking, sensations, and voluntary muscle control.

- The cerebellum is the second largest part of the brain. It keeps track of the body's position and helps maintain balance.

- The medulla controls involuntary activities such as heart rate, blood pressure, and breathing.

- Pain signals can trigger a quick involuntary action, called a reflex, in which a motor neuron sends a message to a muscle without first receiving a signal from the brain.

☑ Skills Check

Math Concepts

THE SPEED OF AN IMPULSE An impulse travels very fast. As shown in the MathBreak on page 511, to calculate the amount of time that it takes for an impulse to travel a certain distance, you must first know the speed it is traveling. Then you can divide the distance by the speed to get the time. For example, if an impulse travels 150 m/s, it would take it 0.02 seconds to travel 3 m.

$$\text{time} = \frac{3 \text{ m (distance)}}{150 \text{ m/s (speed)}} = 0.02 \text{ s}$$

Visual Understanding

PATH OF LIGHT Look back at Figure 10 on page 518 to review the path of light entering the eye. The light first passes through the transparent cornea, then through the opening called the pupil, and then through the lens. At the back of the eye, the light is detected by receptors in the retina.

SECTION 2

Vocabulary

retina *(p. 518)*

photoreceptors *(p. 518)*

rods *(p. 518)*

cones *(p. 518)*

optic nerve *(p. 518)*

iris *(p. 519)*

lens *(p. 519)*

cochlea *(p. 520)*

Section Notes

- Different kinds of receptors in the skin are responsible for detecting touch, pressure, temperature, and pain.

- The retina of the eye contains photoreceptors that react to light and cause impulses to be sent to the brain.

- The lens of the eye can change shape to adjust the point of focus so that the image is focused on the retina. Improper focus can usually be corrected with glasses or contact lenses.

- Special receptors inside the cochlea of the ear react to sound waves and send impulses to the brain.

- Receptors for taste are located in taste buds on the bumps of the tongue.

- Receptors for smell are on olfactory cells located in the upper part of the nasal cavity.

Labs

You've Gotta Lotta Nerve *(p. 632)*

SECTION 3

Vocabulary

endocrine system *(p. 522)*

gland *(p. 522)*

hormone *(p. 522)*

feedback control *(p. 524)*

Section Notes

- The endocrine system communicates with other systems using chemicals called hormones.

- Hormones are made in endocrine glands.

- The adrenal glands secrete hormones that help the body cope with stress. Epinephrine is the hormone most associated with "fight-or-flight" situations.

- Feedback control is the body's way of turning glands on and off so that they release hormones only when necessary.

---

 internetconnect

 GO TO: go.hrw.com

Visit the **HRW** Web site for a variety of learning tools related to this chapter. Just type in the keyword:

KEYWORD: HSTBD4

GO TO: www.scilinks.org

Visit the **National Science Teachers Association** on-line Web site for Internet resources related to this chapter. Just type in the *sci*LINKS number for more information about the topic:

TOPIC: The Nervous System	*sci*LINKS NUMBER: HSTL605
TOPIC: The Senses	*sci*LINKS NUMBER: HSTL610
TOPIC: The Eye	*sci*LINKS NUMBER: HSTL615
TOPIC: Hormones	*sci*LINKS NUMBER: HSTL620

Chapter Review

To complete the following sentences, choose the correct term from each pair of terms listed below:

1. Your brain and spinal cord make up your ___?___. (*central nervous system* or *peripheral nervous system*)

2. Sensory receptors in the ___?___ detect vibrations. (*cochlea* or *eardrum*)

3. Epinephrine is produced by the adrenal glands in response to ___?___. (*glucose* or *stress*)

4. The part of a neuron that passes an impulse to other cells is the ___?___. (*dendrite* or *axon terminal*)

5. The medulla is mostly responsible for activities that are ___?___. (*involuntary* or *voluntary*)

6. Receptors that can convert light into impulses are found in the ___?___. (*olfactory cells* or *retina*)

UNDERSTANDING CONCEPTS

Multiple Choice

7. Which of the following has receptors for smelling?
   a. cochlea cells
   b. thermoreceptors
   c. olfactory cells
   d. optic nerve

8. Which of the following gives eyes their color?
   a. iris
   b. cornea
   c. lens
   d. retina

9. Which of the glands is associated with goiters?
   a. adrenal
   b. pituitary
   c. thyroid
   d. pancreas

10. Which of the following are not part of the peripheral nervous system?
    a. spinal cord
    b. axons
    c. sensory receptors
    d. motor neurons

11. Which part of the brain regulates blood pressure?
    a. right cerebral hemisphere
    b. left cerebral hemisphere
    c. cerebellum
    d. medulla

12. Which of the following is associated with the endocrine system?
    a. reflex
    b. salivary gland
    c. fight-or-flight response
    d. voluntary response

Short Answer

13. Describe several situations in which your adrenal glands might release epinephrine, causing you to have a fight-or-flight reaction.

14. What causes the size of your pupils to change?

15. How are the senses of taste and smell similar? How are they different?

16. What is a reflex? How does a reflex enable you to act quickly?

Concept Map

17. Use the following terms to create a concept map: the nervous system, spinal cord, medulla, peripheral nervous system, brain, cerebrum, central nervous system, cerebellum.

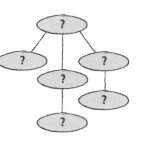

18. Why is it important to have a lens that can change shape inside the eye?

19. What is the function of the middle-ear bones?

20. Why can the nervous system have a much faster effect on the body than the endocrine system?

21. Why is it important that reflexes occur without thought?

22. Using the terms you learned in this chapter, write down a step-by-step sequence for the path taken by an impulse, beginning at a pain receptor in your left big toe. Be sure to mention each kind of neuron and its parts as well as specific organs in the nervous system.

23. List three activities that would involve mostly the right cerebral hemisphere and three activities that would involve mostly the left cerebral hemisphere.

MATH IN SCIENCE

24. Sound travels about 335 m/s (1 km is equal to 1,000 m). How many kilometers would a sound travel in 1 minute?

25. Some axons can send one impulse every 0.4 milliseconds. One second is equal to 1,000 milliseconds. How many impulses could one of these axons send every second?

INTERPRETING GRAPHICS

Look at the drawing below, and answer the following questions:

26. Which letter identifies the gland that regulates blood sugar?

27. Which letter identifies the gland that releases a hormone that stimulates the birth process in pregnant women?

28. Which letter identifies the gland that helps the body fight disease?

NOW What Do You Think?

Take a minute to review your answers to the ScienceLog questions on page 509. Have your answers changed? If necessary, revise your answers based on what you have learned since you began this chapter.

Science, Technology, and Society

Light on Lenses

Can you see in pitch darkness? No, of course not! You need light to see. But there is something else you need in order to see. You need a lens. A **lens** is a curved transparent object that *refracts,* or bends, light.

Lenses are necessary to focus light in all kinds of applications, including in telescopes, microscopes, binoculars, cameras, contact lenses, eyeglasses, and magnifying glasses.

Light Bounces

To learn how lenses work, you must first know something about how light travels. A ray of light travels in a straight path from its source until it strikes an object. When light strikes an object, much of the light bounces off, or is reflected. The light reflects from the object at the same angle that it struck the object in the first place.

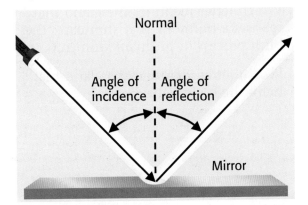

▲ *The angle formed by the incoming light (angle of incidence) always equals the angle of the reflected light (angle of reflection).*

Lenses Bend Light

A lens allows light to travel through it. However, as the light passes through the lens, it is refracted. **Refraction** is the bending of a light ray as it passes from one transparent material into another, such as when light traveling

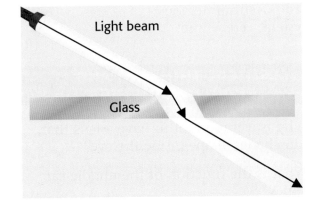

▲ *Light changes speed and direction when it passes from one material into another.*

through air passes through a glass lens.

The type of lens determines how much and in which direction the light is bent. When light waves are absorbed by a substance, light energy is transferred to the substance. The electrons in the substance absorb light energy and re-emit it as heat.

A lens that is thicker in the middle than at its edges is called a **convex lens.** This type of lens bends light toward its center. Convex lenses are used in magnifying glasses, microscopes, and telescopes. The lenses in your eyes are convex lenses.

A lens that is thinner in the middle than at its edges is called a **concave lens.** This type of lens bends light away from its center. Both convex lenses and concave lenses are often used to help correct vision. Convex lenses are also used in combination with concave lenses in cameras to focus light on the film.

Light Your Way

▶ Do some additional research to find out what a photorefractive keratectomy (PRK) is and how it works to correct a person's vision.

Eureka!

Pathway to a Cure

Do you know what would happen if your brain sent out too many impulses to the muscles in your body? First the overload would increase the number of contractions in your muscles, and it would be difficult to carry out simple movements, like scratching your arm or picking up a glass. Even when you wanted to rest, your muscles would continue to tremble. This is what happens to people with Parkinson's disease, and unfortunately, there is still no cure.

The Disease

Parkinson's disease affects the cells in the brain that regulate muscles. These cells require the chemical dopamine, which slows down the activity of nerves so they can function properly. But if the cells that supply the muscle-regulating cells with dopamine are damaged, the brain will send continuous impulses to the muscles. This results in Parkinson's disease.

Parkinson's disease is often diagnosed only after a person has already lost about 80 percent of his or her dopamine-supplying cells. Although there is no known cure for Parkinson's disease, some patients can be treated with chemicals that act like dopamine. Unfortunately, these substitutes are not as good as the real thing. Dopamine itself cannot be given because it cannot pass from the blood into the brain tissue.

Breakthrough

Dr. Bertha Madras studies the effects of drug addiction on the brain. While studying the effects of cocaine addiction, she discovered that a chemical called tropane attaches itself to the same nerves that release dopamine in the brain. This discovery may be used to detect and diagnose Parkinson's disease earlier and at a lower cost to the patient.

A Glow in the Darkness

Madras and her colleagues thought they could use tropane to study the cells that release dopamine. They added a radioactive component to the tropane to make a chemical called altropane. Altropane also attaches to the dopamine-releasing cells. But unlike tropane, altropane glows, so it shows up in a brain scan. Healthy people have large areas where the altropane attaches. Among patients with Parkinson's disease, because of the nerve loss, the altropane attaches to fewer nerves. Therefore, brain scans from these patients do not have as many glowing collections of altropane.

Using this new procedure to diagnose Parkinson's disease could allow doctors to find the disease in people before the neurons are severely damaged or completely lost.

Healthy subject   Parkinson's subject

▲ *Brain scans, such as the ones above, can be used to diagnose Parkinson's disease.*

Activity

▶ Find out what a Single Photon Emission Computed Tomography (SPECT) image is and how it is used to study Parkinson's disease.

22 Reproduction and Development

Strange but True!

A tiny animal is resting peacefully in a warm, dark space. Suddenly it finds itself driven out into the cold and light. The chilly temperature is almost unbearable for its hairless body. The glaring light is disorienting to its blurry vision. Driven by instinct, the animal starts crawling up and up to the promise of warmth and security. If it slips and falls to the ground, it will die. Almost 30 minutes pass before it reaches its destination—a pouch in its mother's abdomen. Inside the pouch, it finds a nipple that will supply milk for several months as the animal grows and develops.

Can you guess what animal has just been born? That's right, a baby kangaroo, called a joey. Joeys are born in a very early stage of development. They continue to develop inside their mother's pouch until they are able to eat solid food such as grasses and other plants.

Like all living things, kangaroos eventually grow old and die. They must reproduce to pass on their genetic heritage. There are many ways of reproducing, as you will discover in this chapter. But reproduction is only part of the story. Development, or the way organisms grow, is also an important part of the cycle of life.

Investigate!

How Grows It?

As you read this, you are aging. Your body is growing into the body of an adult. Look around at your classmates. Their bodies are also growing. But do you and your classmates' bodies have the same proportions as an adult's body? Do this experiment to find out.

Procedure

1. Pair up with a classmate. Have your partner help you measure your total height, head height, and leg length with a **tape measure** and **meterstick.** Your teacher will tell you how to do these measurements.

2. Calculate your head-to-body proportion and leg-to-body proportion. Use the following equations:

$$\left(\frac{\text{head height}}{\text{body height}}\right) \times 100 = \text{head proportion}$$

$$\left(\frac{\text{leg length}}{\text{body height}}\right) \times 100 = \text{leg proportion}$$

3. Your teacher has written his or her head, body, and leg measurements on the board, along with those of two other adults. Calculate their proportions. Record all the measurements and calculations in your ScienceLog.

Analysis

4. How does your head proportion compare with that of adults? How do the leg proportions compare?

Animal Reproduction

The life span of some living things is very short compared with ours. For instance, the fruit fly lives only about 80 days. Other organisms live for a long time. The bristlecone pine can live for 2,000 to 6,000 years. But all living things eventually die. If a species is to survive, its members must reproduce.

NEW TERMS

asexual
  reproduction

budding

fragmentation

sexual
  reproduction

egg

sperm

zygote

external
  fertilization

internal
  fertilization

monotreme

marsupial

placental
  mammal

OBJECTIVES

■ Distinguish between asexual and sexual reproduction.

■ Explain the difference between external and internal fertilization.

■ Describe the three different types of mammalian development.

A Chip off the Old Block

Some animals, particularly simpler ones, reproduce asexually. In **asexual reproduction,** a single parent has offspring that are genetically identical to itself.

One kind of asexual reproduction is called **budding.** This is when a small part of the parent's body develops into an independent organism. The hydra shown in **Figure 1** is reproducing asexually by budding. The young hydra is genetically identical to its parent.

Fragmentation is another type of asexual reproduction. In fragmentation, an organism breaks into two or more parts, each of which may grow into a separate individual. Sea stars are animals that can reproduce by fragmentation. Because sea stars eat oysters, people used to try to kill sea stars by chopping them into pieces and throwing the pieces back into the water. They didn't know that each arm of a sea star can grow into an entire organism! This can be seen in **Figure 2.**

Figure 1 *The young hydra bud will soon separate from its parent. However, buds from other organisms, such as coral, remain attached to the parent.*

Figure 2 *The largest arm on this sea star was a fragment, from which the rest of the sea star has grown. In time, all of the sea star's arms will grow to the same size.*

It Takes Two

Sexual Reproduction produces offspring by combining the genetic material of more than one parent. Most animals, including humans, reproduce sexually. Sexual reproduction most commonly involves two parents, a male and a female. The female parent produces sex cells called **eggs,** and the male parent produces sex cells called **sperm.** When an egg's nucleus joins with a sperm's nucleus, a new kind of cell, called a **zygote,** is created. This joining of an egg and sperm is known as *fertilization.*

Review of Meiosis As you know, DNA contains sets of instructions known as genes within each cell nucleus. Genes are located in *chromosomes.* All human cells except egg and sperm cells contain 46 chromosomes. Eggs and sperm each contain only 23 chromosomes. Eggs and sperm are formed by a process known as *meiosis.*

In humans, meiosis involves the division of one cell with 46 chromosomes into four sex cells with 23 chromosomes each. During the division process, chromosomes are mixed randomly. That means every sex cell can have a different genetic combination.

When an egg and sperm join to form a zygote, the original number of 46 chromosomes is restored. This combination of genes from the father and mother results in a zygote that will grow into a unique individual. **Figure 3** shows how genes are intermixed through three generations.

✓ Self-Check

What is the difference between sexual and asexual reproduction? *(See page 636 to check your answer.)*

MATH BREAK

Chromo-Combos

A cell in an organism is about to undergo meiosis. This cell has 6 chromosomes in 3 pairs. How many chromosomal combinations are possible in the soon-to-be-formed sex cells? To find out, the following formula must be used:

x^y = possible variations where x = the number of chromosomes in a pair and y = the number of pairs.

2^3 (or $2 \times 2 \times 2$) = 8

Therefore, 8 variations are possible.

A typical human cell has 46 chromosomes in 23 pairs. If the cell undergoes meiosis, how many chromosomal combinations are possible in the resulting sex cells?

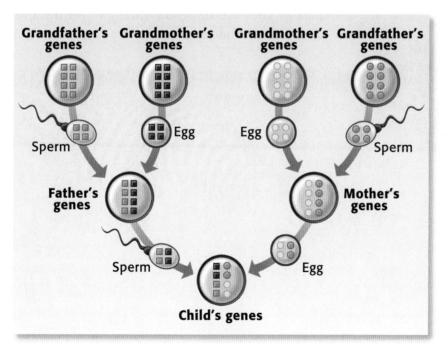

Figure 3 *Eggs and sperm contain genes. You inherit an equal number of genes from each of your parents. Your parents inherited an equal number of genes from their parents.*

Internal and External Fertilization

Depending on the animal, fertilization may occur either outside or inside the female's body. Some fishes and amphibians reproduce by **external fertilization,** in which the sperm fertilize the eggs outside the female's body. External fertilization must take place in a moist environment so the delicate zygotes won't dry out.

Many frogs, such as those pictured in **Figure 4,** mate every spring. The female frog releases her eggs first. The male frog then releases sperm over the eggs to fertilize them. The frogs leave the fertilized eggs to develop on their own. In about two weeks, the eggs hatch into tadpoles.

With **internal fertilization,** eggs and sperm join inside the female's body. Reptiles, birds, mammals, and some fishes reproduce by internal fertilization. Many animals that have internal fertilization lay fertilized eggs. The female penguin in **Figure 5,** for example, usually lays one or two eggs. Instead of leaving them to develop on their own, the parents take turns placing the eggs on their webbed feet and crouching over them. Their body heat keeps the eggs warm. When the chicks hatch, their parents supply them with food until they are large enough to fend for themselves.

In most mammals, internal fertilization is followed by the development of a fertilized egg inside the mother's body. Kangaroos and other marsupials give birth to live young that are in an early stage of development. Other mammals give birth to young that are well developed. Young zebras, like the one in **Figure 6,** can stand up and nurse almost immediately after birth.

Figure 4 *Frogs fertilize their eggs externally. Some species can produce more than 300 offspring in one season.*

Figure 5 *Penguin eggs are fertilized internally, but most of a baby penguin's development takes place outside its mother's body.*

Figure 6 *This zebra has just been born, but he is already able to stand. Within an hour, he will be able to run.*

Making Mammals

All mammals reproduce sexually. All mammals also nurture their young with milk. There are some differences in how mammals produce offspring, but every mammal follows one of three types of development.

Monotremes Mammals that lay eggs are **monotremes.** Two families of monotremes live today—the echidna and the platypus. After these animals lay their eggs, there is an incubation period that lasts up to 2 weeks. When the eggs hatch, the babies are very undeveloped, as can be seen in **Figure 7.** They crawl into a fold of their mother's skin and are nourished by the milk that oozes from her pores.

Figure 7 About 10 days after a female echidna lays an egg, the egg hatches.

Marsupials Mammals that give birth to live young that are only partially developed are **marsupials.** There are about 260 species of marsupials. Most of them have pouches where their young develop, but some South American species do not have this feature. Marsupials with pouches have extra bones to help support the weight of their young, as can be seen in **Figure 8.** When a baby marsupial attaches itself to its mother's nipple, the nipple expands in the baby's mouth to prevent it from separating from its mother.

Placental Mammals There are almost 4,000 different species of placental mammals. These include whales, elephants, armadillos, bats, horses, and humans. **Placental mammals** nourish their young internally before birth. Newborn placental mammals are highly developed compared with newborn marsupials or monotremes.

Figure 8 The skeleton of this opossum has two extra bones extending forward from its pelvis to help support the weight of its young.

REVIEW

1. How many parents are needed to reproduce asexually?

2. What is the difference between monotremes and marsupials?

3. How is a zygote formed?

4. **Applying Concepts** Birds lay eggs, but they are not considered monotremes. Explain why.

Human Reproduction

When a human sperm and egg combine, a new human begins to grow. About 9 months later, a mother gives birth to her baby. But what happens before that? Where do eggs and sperm come from? Many steps must be taken before eggs and sperm become mature.

The Male Reproductive System

The male reproductive system is shown in **Figure 9.** This system produces sperm and delivers it to the female reproductive system. The **testes** (singular, *testis*) make sperm and testosterone. Testosterone is the principal male sex hormone; it regulates the production of sex cells and the development of male characteristics.

Sperm Production The human body is usually around 37°C, but sperm cannot develop properly at such high temperatures. That is why the two testes rest in the **scrotum,** a skin-covered sac that hangs from the body. The scrotum is approximately 3 degrees cooler than body temperature. Inside each testis are masses of tightly coiled tubes called **seminiferous tubules** (SEM uh NIF uhr uhs TOO byoolz), where the sperm cells are produced.

Before sperm leave the testes, they are temporarily stored in the **epididymis** (EP uh DID i mis). Notice the long tube, called a **vas deferens** (vas DEF uh RENZ), that passes from each epididymis into the body. As sperm swim through the vas deferens, they are mixed with fluids from several glands. The mixture of sperm and fluids is called **semen.** A healthy adult male produces several hundred million sperm each day of his life! This massive, continuous sperm production begins at puberty. **Puberty** is the time of life when the sex organs of both males and females become mature.

To leave the body, semen passes through the vas deferens into the **urethra,** the tube that runs through the penis. The **penis** transfers semen into the female's body during sexual intercourse.

Figure 9 The Male Reproductive System

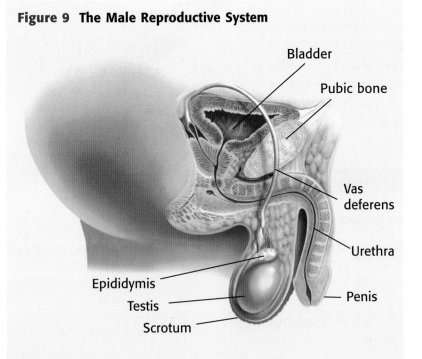

Bladder

Pubic bone

Vas deferens

Urethra

Penis

Epididymis

Testis

Scrotum

The Female Reproductive System

The female reproductive system is shown in **Figure 10.** This system produces eggs, nurtures fertilized eggs, and gives birth. At the center of this system are the **ovaries,** which produce the eggs. The two ovaries also produce sex hormones, such as estrogen and progesterone. These hormones regulate the release of eggs and direct the development of female traits.

The Egg's Journey An ovary is about the size of a large almond and contains eggs in various stages of development. As an egg matures, it becomes a huge cell, growing to almost 200,000 times the size of a sperm. During **ovulation,** a developed egg is ejected through the ovary wall. It passes into a fallopian tube. The **fallopian tubes** lead from each ovary to the uterus. The **uterus** is the organ where a baby grows and develops.

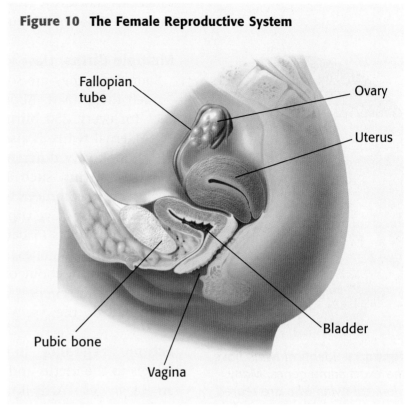

Figure 10 The Female Reproductive System

When a woman is not pregnant, her uterus is folded almost flat. Every month starting at puberty, the lining of the uterus thickens in preparation for pregnancy. If fertilization occurs, the tiny zygote moves down a fallopian tube and embeds in the lining of the uterus. When a baby is born, it passes from the uterus through the vagina. The **vagina** is the same passageway that received the sperm during sexual intercourse.

Menstrual Cycle To prepare for pregnancy, a female's reproductive system goes through several changes. These changes, called the menstrual cycle, usually occur monthly. The first day of the cycle is the beginning of **menstruation,** the monthly discharge of blood and tissue from the uterus. Menstruation lasts about 5 days. As soon as menstruation is over, the uterus's lining begins to build up again in preparation for ovulation. Ovulation typically occurs around the 14th day of the cycle. If the egg isn't fertilized by the time it reaches the uterus, it will deteriorate. Menstruation will flush the egg away, starting the cycle over again. A female's menstrual cycle begins at puberty and continues until late middle age.

MATH BREAK

Counting Eggs

1. The average human female ovulates every month from about age 12 to about age 50. How many mature eggs can she produce during that time period?

2. A female's ovaries typically house 2 million immature egg cells. If she ovulates regularly from age 12 to age 50, what percentage of her eggs will mature?

Irregularities and Disorders

In most cases, the human reproductive system completes its functions flawlessly. However, as with any body system, there can sometimes be irregularities or disorders.

Multiple Births Have you ever seen a pair of identical twins? Sometimes they are so similar that even their parents can't tell them apart. About one pair of identical twins is born for every 250 births. Another type of twins, called fraternal twins, is also born frequently. Fraternal twins can look very different from each other.

Twins, such as those shown in **Figure 11,** are the most common type of multiple births, but humans can also have triplets (3 babies), quadruplets (4 babies), quintuplets (5 babies), and so on. These types of multiple births are extremely rare. For instance, quadruplets occur only about once in every 705,000 births. Do you know what circumstances result in a multiple birth? To find out, do the Apply exercise at the bottom of this page.

Figure 11 *Identical twins have the exact same genes. Many identical twins who are reared apart have similar personalities and interests.*

Ectopic Pregnancy In a normal pregnancy, the fertilized egg travels to the uterus and attaches itself to the uterus's wall. In an *ectopic* (ek TAHP ik) *pregnancy,* the fertilized egg attaches itself to a fallopian tube or another area of the reproductive system. Because the zygote cannot develop correctly outside of the uterus, an ectopic pregnancy can be very dangerous for both the mother and child.

APPLY

Zach and Drew are fraternal twins. Although they are the same age and have the same parents, they don't look much alike. Their friends Emily and Carol are identical twins. They look so similar that Zach and Drew are unable to tell them apart. Why are some twins identical and others fraternal? Consider the two possibilities illustrated at right: In *A*, the mass of cells from a single fertilized egg separates into two halves early in development, and in *B* two eggs are released by an ovary and fertilized by two different sperm cells. Record the answers to the following questions in your ScienceLog:

1. Which instance, *A* or *B*, would produce identical twins? Explain your answer.
2. Could fraternal twins be (a) both boys, (b) both girls, (c) one girl and one boy, or (d) all of the above?

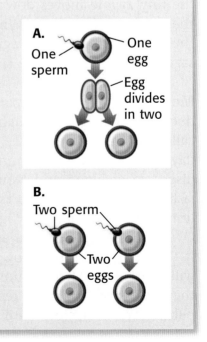

Reproductive System Diseases In the United States, about 15 percent of married couples have difficulty producing offspring. Many of these couples are **infertile,** which means they are unable to have children. Men may be infertile because they cannot produce enough healthy sperm. This is called a low sperm count, and an example can be seen in **Figure 12.** Women may be infertile because they do not ovulate normally.

Female infertility can also be caused by scarred fallopian tubes. The scar tissue, usually caused by a sexually transmitted disease, prevents the passage of eggs into the uterus. **Sexually transmitted diseases** are diseases that can pass from an infected person to an uninfected person during sexual contact. In the United States, the most common sexually transmitted diseases are chlamydia, gonorrhea, and genital herpes.

Acquired immune deficiency syndrome (AIDS) is another common sexually transmitted disease. AIDS can also be transmitted in other ways, including through the shared use of needles, blood transfusions from infected donors, and contact with infected blood. It is not transmitted through casual contact. AIDS is caused by a virus called the human immunodeficiency virus (HIV).

Cancer, the uncontrolled growth of cells, sometimes occurs in the reproductive organs. The testes and the prostate gland, a gland that produces the fluid in semen, are common sites of cancer in men over age 50. In women, the ovaries and breasts are common sites of cancer.

Figure 12 *The micrograph labeled* (a) *shows a low sperm count. The micrograph labeled* (b) *shows a normal sperm count. A low sperm count can be caused by a number of conditions, including a hormone imbalance or a blocked vas deferens.*

BRAIN FOOD

One in four American youths catches a sexually transmitted disease before age 21.

chemistry
CONNECTION

Many chemicals in pollutants are similar to female hormones. Studies are beginning to link these chemicals with early menstruation and low sperm counts.

REVIEW

1. What is the difference between sperm and semen?

2. Can a woman become pregnant at any time of the month? Explain.

3. Define *sexually transmitted diseases,* and give three examples.

4. **Applying Concepts** How are the ovaries similar to the testes? How are they different?

Growth and Development

NEW TERMS

embryo
implantation
placenta

umbilical cord
fetus

OBJECTIVES

■ Summarize the processes of fertilization and implantation.
■ Describe the course of human development.

Every one of us starts out as a single cell that will become a complete person. We are made of millions of cells, each with its own job to do. You, of course, are no exception. You have become a very complex individual, capable of thousands of different thoughts and actions. It is hard to believe that a person as remarkable as you began your life as a single cell, but that is just what happened.

A New Life

The natural process of creating a human baby starts when a man deposits millions of sperm into a woman's vagina during sexual intercourse. Most of the sperm will die because of the vagina's acidic environment, but a few hundred are able to make it through the uterus and into the fallopian tube, as can be seen in **Figure 13.** The surviving sperm cover the egg, releasing enzymes that help dissolve the egg's outer covering. As soon as one sperm gets through, a membrane closes around the fertilized egg. This membrane keeps other sperm cells from entering.

Figure 13 Fertilization and Implantation

2 The egg is fertilized in the fallopian tube by a sperm.

1 The egg is released from the ovary.

3 The embryo implants itself in the uterus's wall.

Implantation The fertilized egg travels down the woman's fallopian tube toward her uterus. The journey takes about 5 days. The zygote undergoes cell division many times during the trip. By the time it reaches the uterus, it is a tiny ball of cells called an **embryo.** During the next few days, the embryo must embed itself in the thick, nutrient-rich lining of its mother's uterus. This process is called **implantation,** and only about 30 percent of all embryos successfully do it. **Figure 14** shows an implanted embryo.

The embryo's actual size is slightly smaller than the period at the end of this sentence.

Embryo

Figure 14 *This embryo has implanted in the wall of its mother's uterus.*

Before Birth

When the embryo implants itself in a woman's uterus, the woman is officially pregnant. For the embryo to survive, a special two-way exchange organ called a **placenta** begins to grow. The placenta contains a network of blood vessels that provide the embryo with oxygen and nutrients from the mother's blood. Wastes that the embryo produces are removed by the placenta and transported to the mother's blood for her to excrete.

About 1 week after implantation, the embryo's blood cells and a heart tube form. Then the heart tube begins to twitch, starting the rhythmic beating that will continue for the individual's entire life. By the fourth week, the embryo is almost 2 mm long. Surrounding the embryo is a thin, fluid-filled membrane called the *amnion,* which is formed to protect the growing embryo from shocks. The **umbilical cord** is another new development. It connects the embryo to the placenta. Through the placenta, the embryo's blood and its mother's blood come into close contact. This allows the exchange of oxygen and nutrients, molecule by molecule. Although the embryo's blood and the mother's blood flow very near each other inside the placenta, they never actually mix. The umbilical cord, amnion, and placenta can be seen in **Figure 15.**

First to Second Month By the time the embryo is 4 weeks old, it has the beginnings of a brain and spinal cord. It also has tiny limb buds that will eventually develop into arms and legs. Its nostrils, eyelids, hands, and feet then begin to form. Its muscles begin to develop, and for the first time in its life, its brain begins to send signals to other parts of its body. Despite all these transformations, the embryo is still only about the size of a peanut. **Figure 16** shows a 5-week-old embryo.

✓ Self-Check

1. How is an embryo nourished?
2. Why is it important that the embryo be implanted in the uterus and not elsewhere?

(See page 636 to check your answers.)

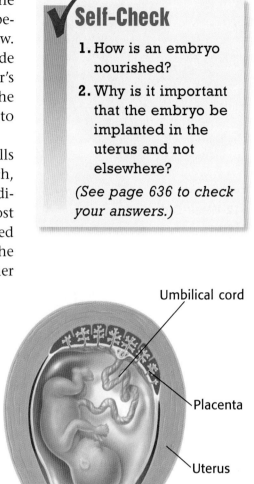

Figure 15 *The placenta, amnion, and umbilical cord are the life support system for the fetus.*

Figure 16 A 5-Week-Old Embryo

Actual size

Figure 17 A 12-Week-Old Fetus

Actual size

The next stage comes as tiny movements begin to flutter through the embryo's body. The embryo stretches its legs and twitches its arms. It is now 8 weeks old and is developed enough to be called a **fetus.** Three more weeks pass, and it continues to grow at a fast rate, doubling and then tripling its size within a month. The fetus's hands are now the size of teardrops, and its body weighs as much as two pieces of paper. A 12-week-old fetus can be seen in **Figure 17.**

Third to Sixth Month The fetus's 13th week of life passes, and suddenly new movement! It can blink its eyes for the first time, swallow, hiccup, make a fist, and curl its toes that now have tiny nails. By the fourth month, the fetus starts to make even bigger movements. The mother now knows when her baby kicks its legs or stretches its arms.

Within the fifth month, the fetus is 20 cm long. Taste buds form on its tongue, and eyebrows form on its face. The fetus begins to hear sounds through the wall of its mother's uterus. Look at the timeline in **Figure 18,** and review the changes that take place during the first 6 months of pregnancy.

Figure 18 Trimester Timeline

The First Trimester Weeks	
1 and 2	The egg is fertilized by a sperm. The fertilized egg makes its way to the uterus, where it burrows into the lining. The fertilized egg is now called an embryo.
3 and 4	Most major organ systems have started to form. The heart starts to beat around day 22. The placenta is completely formed by the fourth week.
5 and 6	Facial features begin to take shape. The skeleton begins to form.
7 and 8	Muscle movement begins. The embryo is now called a fetus.
9 and 10	Arms, legs, hands, and feet have formed.
11 and 12	The internal organs have formed.

The Second Trimester Weeks	
13 and 14	The circulatory system is working.
15 and 16	The mother may start to feel the fetus move.
17 and 18	The fetus responds to sound.
19 and 20	The fetus is now about 20 cm long.
21 and 22	
23 and 24	Eyelashes and eyebrows appear.

The Third Trimester Weeks	
25 and 26	The eyes open.
27 and 28	The fetus can "practice breathe."
29 and 30	
31 and 32	
33 and 34	
35 and 36	The fetus responds to light.
Birth	The baby is born.

Seventh to Ninth Month The seventh month is when the fetus's memories begin to form. During this time, its lungs start to "practice breathe," moving up and down continuously as if breathing real air. If the fetus's mother smokes one cigarette during this stage, the fetus's lung movement will stop for up to an hour. The fetus in **Figure 19** is starting its first lung movement.

By the eighth month, the fetus's open eyes can perceive light through its mother's abdominal wall, and its sleeping pattern starts to be influenced by sunlight. When the fetus is asleep, it dreams. Can you imagine what its dreams might be about?

Actual size of hand

Figure 19 A 21-Week-Old Fetus

Birth

After about 9 months, the fetus is ready to live outside of its mother. The mother goes through a series of muscular contractions called *labor*. During labor, the fetus is usually squeezed headfirst through the vagina. There is little room to spare, and the fetus's head is temporarily squashed out of shape as the fetus passes through its mother's pelvis. Suddenly bright lights and cold air surround the newborn baby. It gasps, fills its lungs with air for the first time, and cries.

The baby in **Figure 20** is still connected to the placenta by its umbilical cord. The doctor or midwife assisting the mother ties and cuts the umbilical cord. The baby's navel is all that will remain of the point where the umbilical cord was attached. After the mother expels the placenta from her body, labor is complete.

Figure 20 *This newborn baby is still attached to its umbilical cord. The average mass of a newborn baby is 3.3 kg. The average length is 50 cm.*

From Birth to Death

Of all the animals on this planet, humans have one of the longest life spans. Human infancy lasts 2 years—the same time it takes for most rabbits to be born, grow old, and die. Our childhood extends over a full decade, longer than many cats or dogs live. Humans can live for more than 100 years!

LabBook

How well does the uterus protect a fetus? Follow the instructions on page 634 of your LabBook to find out.

Reproduction and Development **545**

Infant   **4 years**   **7 years**   **11 years**   **Adult**

Figure 21 *This diagram shows a female in five different stages of development. The stages are shown the same size so you can see how body proportions change as a person develops.*

Infancy What life stages have you gone through since you were born? Probably, you have gone through most of the stages shown in **Figure 21.** You were an infant from birth to 2 years of age. During this time, you grew rapidly. Your teeth began to appear. You also became more coordinated as your nervous system developed. This enabled you to begin to walk.

Childhood Your childhood extends from 2 years to puberty. This is also a period of rapid growth. Your first set of teeth were slowly shed and replaced by permanent teeth. Your muscles became more coordinated, allowing you to do activities such as riding a bicycle and jumping rope. Your intellectual abilities also developed during this time.

Figure 22 *Muscle development is one change that occurs during puberty in males. This boy will soon be as physically developed as his father.*

Adolescence You are considered an adolescent from puberty to adulthood. During puberty, the reproductive systems of young males and females become mature. Puberty occurs in most boys sometime between the ages of 11 and 16. The young male body becomes more muscular, the voice becomes deeper, and body and facial hair appear. The boy in **Figure 22** will soon experience these changes. In most girls, puberty occurs between the ages of 9 and 14. During puberty in females, the amount of fat in the hips and thighs increases, the breasts enlarge, and body hair appears in areas such as the armpits. At this time, the young female also begins to menstruate.

Adulthood From about age 20 to age 40, you will be considered a young adult. You will be at the peak of your physical development. Beginning around age 30, certain changes associated with aging begin. The changes will be gradual and slightly different for everyone. Typically, some of the early signs of aging include decreasing muscle flexibility, deteriorating eyesight and hearing, increasing body fat, and increasing hair loss.

The aging process will continue in a middle-aged adult (someone between 40 and 65). During this period, hair will become gray, athletic abilities will decline, and skin will wrinkle. Any person over 65 years old is considered an older adult. Although aging persists during this period of an individual's life, older adults can still lead full and active lives. Improvements in medical science have allowed many older adults to remain healthy and productive for decades longer than older adults of previous generations. Some of this country's most productive citizens are older adults, as can be seen in **Figure 23**. Furthermore, many people have been able to slow the aging process by exercising and eating a well-rounded, nutritious diet.

Figure 23 John Glenn, the first American to orbit Earth, returned to space at the age of 77.

Quick Lab
Life Grows On

Use Figure 21 on the previous page to complete this activity.

1. Use a **ruler** to measure the infant's head height. Then measure the infant's entire body height, including the head.

2. Calculate the percentage of the infant's head height to the infant's total height.

3. Repeat these measurements and calculations for the other stages shown in the figure.

Answer the following question in your ScienceLog:

   As a baby grows into an adult, does the head grow faster or slower than the rest of the body? Why do you think this is so?

Explore

Create a poster or timeline illustrating the different stages of human growth.

Acne got you down? Page 552 will cheer you up!

REVIEW

1. What is the difference between an embryo and a fetus?

2. Why does a membrane form around an egg once a sperm has entered?

3. What developmental changes take place from birth to puberty?

4. **Applying Concepts** When astronauts work in space, they are sometimes attached to the spacecraft by a line called an umbilical. Why do you think the line has been given this name?

Chapter Highlights

Vocabulary

asexual reproduction *(p. 534)*

budding *(p. 534)*

fragmentation *(p. 534)*

sexual reproduction *(p. 535)*

egg *(p. 535)*

sperm *(p. 535)*

zygote *(p. 535)*

external fertilization *(p. 536)*

internal fertilization *(p. 536)*

monotreme *(p. 537)*

marsupial *(p. 537)*

placental mammal *(p. 537)*

Section Notes

- During asexual reproduction, a single parent produces offspring that are identical to the parent. Budding and fragmentation are examples of asexual reproduction.

- During sexual reproduction, there is a union of an egg and a sperm.

- Each egg and sperm is the product of meiosis and contains half the usual number of chromosomes. The usual number of chromosomes is restored in the zygote.

- Sperm fertilize eggs outside the female's body in external fertilization. Sperm fertilize eggs inside the female's body in internal fertilization.

- Monotremes are egg-laying mammals. Marsupials are mammals that give birth to partially developed young. Placentals are mammals that give birth to well-developed young.

Vocabulary

testes *(p. 538)*

scrotum *(p. 538)*

seminiferous tubules *(p. 538)*

epididymis *(p. 538)*

vas deferens *(p. 538)*

semen *(p. 538)*

puberty *(p. 538)*

urethra *(p. 538)*

penis *(p. 538)*

ovaries *(p. 539)*

ovulation *(p. 539)*

fallopian tubes *(p. 539)*

uterus *(p. 539)*

vagina *(p. 539)*

menstruation *(p. 539)*

infertile *(p. 541)*

sexually transmitted disease *(p. 541)*

☑ Skills Check

Math Concepts

EGGS IN EXILE A woman does not ovulate while she is pregnant. Therefore, if a woman has three children, she will release at least 27 fewer eggs from her ovaries than she would if she never became pregnant.

3 children × 9 months of pregnancy = 27 eggs

Visual Concepts

MALE AND FEMALE REPRODUCTIVE SYSTEMS
The diagrams on pages 538 and 539 show the male and female reproductive systems. Take another look at them, and make sure you recognize all the structures. Also note the similarities between the two systems. For instance, the ovaries have a similar function to the testes, and the fallopian tubes have a similar function to the vas deferens.

Section Notes

- The male reproductive system produces sperm and delivers it to the female reproductive system. Sperm are produced in the seminiferous tubules and stored in the epididymis. Sperm leave the body through the urethra.

- The female reproductive system produces eggs, nourishes the developing embryo, and gives birth. An egg leaves one of two ovaries each month and travels to the uterus. If the egg is not fertilized, it disintegrates and menstruation occurs.

- Reproductive system disorders include infertility, cancer, and sexually transmitted diseases.

Vocabulary

embryo *(p. 542)*

implantation *(p. 542)*

placenta *(p. 543)*

umbilical cord *(p. 543)*

fetus *(p. 544)*

Section Notes

- Fertilization occurs in a fallopian tube. From there, the zygote travels to the uterus and implants itself in the uterus's wall.

- After implantation, the placenta develops. The umbilical cord connects the embryo to the placenta. The amnion surrounds and protects the embryo.

- The embryo grows, developing limbs, nostrils, eyelids, and other features. By the eighth week, the embryo is developed enough to be called a fetus.

- Human life stages are infant (birth to 2 years), child (2 years to puberty), adolescent (puberty to 20 years), young adult (20 to 40 years), middle-aged adult (40 to 65 years), and older adult (older than 65 years).

Labs

It's a Comfy, Safe World *(p. 634)*

My, How You've Grown *(p. 635)*

 internetconnect

GO TO: go.hrw.com

Visit the **HRW** Web site for a variety of learning tools related to this chapter. Just type in the keyword:

KEYWORD: HSTBD5

 GO TO: www.scilinks.org

Visit the **National Science Teachers Association** on-line Web site for Internet resources related to this chapter. Just type in the *sci*LINKS number for more information about the topic:

TOPIC: Reproduction	*sci*LINKS NUMBER: HSTL630
TOPIC: Before Birth	*sci*LINKS NUMBER: HSTL635
TOPIC: Reproductive System Irregularities or Disorders	*sci*LINKS NUMBER: HSTL640
TOPIC: Growth and Development	*sci*LINKS NUMBER: HSTL645

Chapter Review

USING VOCABULARY

To complete the following sentences, choose the correct term from each pair of terms listed below:

1. Reptiles, birds, and mammals reproduce sexually by __?__. (*internal fertilization* or *external fertilization*)

2. Sperm are produced in the __?__ within the testes. (*epididymis* or *seminiferous tubules*)

3. The sperm-containing fluid that exits the male body is known as __?__. (*semen* or *amniotic fluid*)

4. The release of an egg from the ovary occurs once each month and is called __?__. (*ovulation* or *menstruation*)

5. The organ of exchange between the developing embryo and the mother is the __?__. (*amnion* or *placenta*)

UNDERSTANDING CONCEPTS

Multiple Choice

6. The sea star can reproduce asexually by
   a. fragmentation.
   b. budding.
   c. external fertilization.
   d. internal fertilization.

7. The correct path of sperm through the male reproductive system is
   a. testes → epididymis → urethra → vas deferens.
   b. epididymis → urethra → testes → vas deferens.
   c. testes → vas deferens → epididymis → urethra.
   d. testes → epididymis → vas deferens → urethra.

8. If the first day of the menstrual cycle is the onset of menstruation, on what day does ovulation typically occur?
   a. 2nd day   c. 14th day
   b. 5th day   d. 28th day

9. Monotremes are different from placental mammals because they
   a. are mammals.
   b. have hair.
   c. nurture their young with milk.
   d. lay eggs.

10. All of the following are sexually transmitted diseases *except*
    a. chlamydia.   c. infertility.
    b. AIDS.   d. genital herpes.

11. Fertilization occurs in the __?__, and implantation occurs in the __?__.
    a. uterus, fallopian tube
    b. fallopian tube, vagina
    c. uterus, vagina
    d. fallopian tube, uterus

Short Answer

12. What reproductive organs produce sperm? egg cells?

13. Through what structure does oxygen from the mother pass into the fetus's body?

14. What are four stages of human life following birth?

15. What two cells combine to make a zygote?

16. What is the difference between budding and fragmentation?

Concept Mapping

17. Use the following terms to create a concept map: asexual reproduction, budding, external fertilization, fragmentation, internal fertilization, sexual reproduction, reproduction.

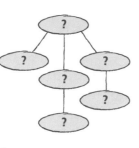

CRITICAL THINKING AND PROBLEM SOLVING

Write one or two sentences to answer the following questions:

18. Explain why the testes are found in the scrotum instead of inside the male body.

19. What is the function of the uterus? How is its function related to the menstrual cycle?

20. How is meiosis important to human reproduction?

MATH IN SCIENCE

21. Hardy Junior High School has 2,750 students. If 1 pair of identical twins is born for every 250 births, about how many pairs of identical twins will be attending the school?

22. Mrs. Schmidt had a baby April 30th. Her baby developed inside her uterus for 9 months. What month was her egg fertilized?

23. In the United States, seven infants die before their first birthday for every 1,000 births. Convert this figure to a percentage. Is your answer greater than or less than 1%?

24. In Haiti, a small country in the Caribbean, 74 infants die before their first birthday for every 1,000 births. Convert this figure to a percentage. Is your answer greater or less than 1%? Why do you think there is such a difference between the United States and Haiti?

INTERPRETING GRAPHICS

The following graph illustrates the cycles of the male hormone, testosterone, and the female hormone, estrogen. The blue line shows the estrogen level in a female over a period of 28 days. The red line shows the testosterone level in a male over a period of 28 days.

25. What is the major difference between the two hormone levels over the 28-day period?

26. What cycle do you think estrogen affects?

27. Why might the level of testosterone stay the same?

NOW What Do You Think?

Take a minute to review your answers to the ScienceLog questions on page 533. Have your answers changed? If necessary, revise your answers based on what you have learned since you began this chapter.

Acne

If you are a teenager, you probably have some firsthand experience with acne. If you don't, you probably will. And contrary to what you may have heard, acne is not caused by greasy foods and candy, though these foods can aggravate the problem. The hormonal fluctuations that occur as young people mature into adults often cause acne.

What Are Pimples?

Skin contains thousands of tiny pores. Each pore contains sebaceous glands that produce sebum, the oil you may have noticed on the surface of your skin. This oil is necessary to maintain healthy skin. Sebum usually escapes from the pores without a problem. But sometimes skin cells do not shed properly, and they clog the pores. The sebum that collects in the pores causes lesions, commonly called pimples. The production and release of sebum is stimulated by androgens, the male sex hormones, which become active in both girls and boys during puberty.

▲ *Acne is caused by the buildup of sebum and dead cells in the pores of the skin.*

Learn Your Lesions

There are two kinds of lesions—noninflamed lesions and inflamed lesions. Noninflamed lesions include blackheads and whiteheads. Some people think blackheads are pores filled with dirt. The dark color of these lesions is actually the result of dark skin pigments or oil trapped in the pores. Whiteheads are white because their contents are hidden under the skin's surface. Inflamed lesions are caused by bacteria and are often red and swollen. Bacteria live in healthy pores, and when pores become clogged, the bacteria are trapped and can cause irritation and infection.

Heredity

Family history appears to be a factor in the development of acne. Unfortunately, if your parents or brothers and sisters had acne, you are likely to have acne too. The causes of hereditary acne remain unclear. Your skin may be genetically programmed to produce more sebum than is produced in other teenagers.

Is There Hope?

Certain over-the-counter products can clean the dead skin cells and sebum out of the pores. Many medications inhibit the production of sebum or encourage the shedding of skin cells. These treatments can help keep the pores clean and prevent acne. Sometimes doctors prescribe antibiotics, such as tetracycline or erythromycin, to treat severe cases of acne. Antibiotics are medicines that kill bacteria, such as the bacteria that irritate inflamed lesions. On the bright side, most acne clears up as people become adults.

On Your Own

▶ Find out what the active ingredient is in an over-the-counter acne medication. Do some research on this ingredient to find out how it works. Report your findings to the class.

Science, Technology, and Society

Technology in Its Infant Stages

Every year thousands of babies are born with life-threatening diseases or severe birth defects. What if medical treatments were available to these babies before they were born? Doctors at San Francisco, Harvard, and Vanderbilt Universities are performing experimental fetal surgery with encouraging results.

When Is Fetal Surgery an Option?

To date, approximately 100 fetal operations have been performed across the country. Corrective treatments can take place between the 18th and 30th weeks of pregnancy. Many factors determine whether fetal surgery is appropriate. Surgery is considered to be an option only if the condition is life threatening. However, fetuses with several defects or chromosomal abnormalities are not eligible for surgery.

Successful surgeries have been performed on fetal patients with spina bifida, diaphragmatic hernias, malformations of the lungs, and urinary tract obstructions. Spina bifida is a defect that leaves the spine exposed. A diaphragmatic hernia is a hole in the diaphragm. This condition causes severe breathing difficulties.

Surgery on a Small Scale

Fetal surgery can fall into one of three categories. The least traumatic type of treatment uses a laser scalpel or an endoscope. The scalpel is used to remove chest tumors. An *endoscope* is a video-guided tool that combines a camera lens and scissors that are less than 0.2 cm wide. The doctor guides the scissors through a tiny cut in the abdominal and uterine walls. The doctor is unable to see the fetus directly during this surgery because the cut is so small. Therefore, he or she must watch the video images provided by the endoscope during the operation.

A more traumatic option is open fetal surgery. In this treatment, the mother's abdomen and uterus are opened, and the fetus is partially exposed.

The third, and relatively new, option is called fetal stem cell transplant. This treatment is essentially a bone marrow transplant for the fetus. It is used to treat genetic diseases and diseases of the immune system.

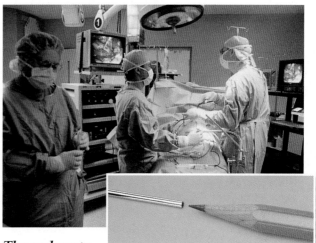

The endoscope shown here is used to perform fetal surgery.

What the Future Holds

Each fetal surgery results in the improvement of techniques and treatments, as well as in the expansion of the types of defects and diseases that can be treated. As the number of fetal surgeries increases, fetal surgery will become much more routine.

Going Further

▶ The endoscopes used in fetal surgery use a technology called fiber optics. Research what items around your home also use fiber optics.

Contents

Exploring, inventing, and investigating are essential to the study of science. However, these activities can also be dangerous. To make sure that your experiments and explorations are safe, you must be aware of a variety of safety guidelines.

You have probably heard of the saying, "It is better to be safe than sorry." This is particularly true in a science classroom where experiments and explorations are being performed. Being uninformed and careless can result in serious injuries. Don't take chances with your own safety or with anyone else's.

Following are important guidelines for staying safe in the science classroom. Your teacher may also have safety guidelines and tips that are specific to your classroom and laboratory. Take the time to be safe.

Safety Rules!

Start Out Right

Always get your teacher's permission before attempting any laboratory exploration. Read the procedures carefully, and pay particular attention to safety information and caution statements. If you are unsure about what a safety symbol means, look it up or ask your teacher. You cannot be too careful when it comes to safety. If an accident does occur, inform your teacher immediately, regardless of how minor you think the accident is.

Safety Symbols

All of the experiments and investigations in this book and their related worksheets include important safety symbols to alert you to particular safety concerns. Become familiar with these symbols so that when you see them, you will know what they mean and what to do. It is important that you read this entire safety section to learn about specific dangers in the laboratory.

If you are instructed to note the odor of a substance, wave the fumes toward your nose with your hand. Never put your nose close to the source.

Eye protection	Clothing protection	Hand safety
Heating safety	Electric safety	Chemical safety
Animal safety	Sharp object	Plant safety

Eye Safety

Wear safety goggles when working around chemicals, acids, bases, or any type of flame or heating device. Wear safety goggles any time there is even the slightest chance that harm could come to your eyes. If any substance gets into your eyes, notify your teacher immediately, and flush your eyes with running water for at least 15 minutes. Treat any unknown chemical as if it were a dangerous chemical. Never look directly into the sun. Doing so could cause permanent blindness.

Avoid wearing contact lenses in a laboratory situation. Even if you are wearing safety goggles, chemicals can get between the contact lenses and your eyes. If your doctor requires that you wear contact lenses instead of glasses, wear eye-cup safety goggles in the lab.

Safety Equipment

Know the locations of the nearest fire alarms and any other safety equipment, such as fire blankets and eyewash fountains, as identified by your teacher, and know the procedures for using them.

Be extra careful when using any glassware. When adding a heavy object to a graduated cylinder, tilt the cylinder so the object slides slowly to the bottom.

Neatness

Keep your work area free of all unnecessary books and papers. Tie back long hair, and secure loose sleeves or other loose articles of clothing, such as ties and bows. Remove dangling jewelry. Don't wear open-toed shoes or sandals in the laboratory. Never eat, drink, or apply cosmetics in a laboratory setting. Food, drink, and cosmetics can easily become contaminated with dangerous materials.

Certain hair products (such as aerosol hair spray) are flammable and should not be worn while working near an open flame. Avoid wearing hair spray or hair gel on lab days.

Sharp/Pointed Objects

Use knives and other sharp instruments with extreme care. Never cut objects while holding them in your hands. Place objects on a suitable work surface for cutting.

Heat

Wear safety goggles when using a heating device or a flame. Whenever possible, use an electric hot plate as a heat source instead of an open flame. When heating materials in a test tube, always angle the test tube away from yourself and others. In order to avoid burns, wear heat-resistant gloves whenever instructed to do so.

Electricity

Be careful with electrical cords. When using a microscope with a lamp, do not place the cord where it could trip someone. Do not let cords hang over a table edge in a way that could cause equipment to fall if the cord is accidentally pulled. Do not use equipment with damaged cords. Be sure your hands are dry and that the electrical equipment is in the "off" position before plugging it in. Turn off and unplug electrical equipment when you are finished.

Chemicals

Wear safety goggles when handling any potentially dangerous chemicals, acids, or bases. If a chemical is unknown, handle it as you would a dangerous chemical. Wear an apron and safety gloves when working with acids or bases or whenever you are told to do so. If a spill gets on your skin or clothing, rinse it off immediately with water for at least 5 minutes while calling to your teacher.

Never mix chemicals unless your teacher tells you to do so. Never taste, touch, or smell chemicals unless you are specifically directed to do so. Before working with a flammable liquid or gas, check for the presence of any source of flame, spark, or heat.

Animal Safety

Always obtain your teacher's permission before bringing any animal into the school building. Handle animals only as your teacher directs. Always treat animals carefully and with respect. Wash your hands thoroughly after handling any animal.

Plant Safety

Do not eat any part of a plant or plant seed used in the laboratory. Wash hands thoroughly after handling any part of a plant. When in nature, do not pick any wild plants unless your teacher instructs you to do so.

Glassware

Examine all glassware before use. Be sure that glassware is clean and free of chips and cracks. Report damaged glassware to your teacher. Glass containers used for heating should be made of heat-resistant glass.

Does It All Add Up?

Your math teacher won't tell you this, but did you know that sometimes 2 + 2 does not equal 4?! (Well, it really does, but sometimes it doesn't *appear* to equal 4.) In this experiment, you will use the scientific method to predict, measure, and observe by mixing two unknown liquids. You will learn that a scientist does not set out to prove a hypothesis, but rather to test it, and sometimes the results just don't seem to add up!

Materials

- 75 mL of liquid A (water)
- 75 mL of liquid B (rubbing alcohol)
- Celsius thermometer
- 7 identical 100 mL graduated cylinders
- glass-labeling marker
- protective gloves

SCIENTIFIC METHOD

Make Observations

1. Put on goggles, protective gloves, and an apron, and wear them throughout the lab. Examine the two liquids in the graduated cylinders given to you by your teacher. **Caution:** Do not taste, touch, or smell any unknown chemicals.

2. In your ScienceLog, write down as many observations as you can about each liquid. Are the liquids bubbly? What color are they? What is the exact volume of each liquid? Touch the graduated cylinders. Are they hot or cold?

3. Pour exactly 25 mL of liquid A into each of two graduated cylinders. Add these samples together in one of the graduated cylinders, and record the final volume in your ScienceLog. Repeat this step for liquid B.

Form a Hypothesis

4. Based on your observations and on prior experience, form a hypothesis about how volumes are affected when liquids combine.

Make a Prediction

5. Make a prediction based on your hypothesis using an "if-then" format. Explain why you have made your prediction.

Test the Hypothesis

6. In your ScienceLog, make a data table similar to the one below to record your observations.

	Contents of cylinder A	Contents of cylinder B	Mixing results: predictions	Mixing results: observations
Volume				
Appearance				
Temperature				

DO NOT WRITE IN BOOK

7. Carefully pour exactly 25 mL of Liquid A (water) into a 50 mL cylinder. Mark this cylinder "A." Record its appearance, volume, and temperature in the data table. Your teacher will demonstrate how to measure volume with a graduated cylinder and how to measure temperature with a lab thermometer.

8. Carefully pour exactly 25 mL of Liquid B (rubbing alcohol) into another 50 mL cylinder. Mark this cylinder "B." Record its appearance, volume, and temperature in the data table.

9. Mark the empty third cylinder "A + B."

10. In the "Mixing results: predictions" column in your table, record the prediction you made earlier. Each classmate may have made a different prediction.

11. Carefully pour the contents of both cylinders into the third cylinder.

12. Observe and record the appearance, total volume, and temperature in the "Mixing results: observations" column of the table.

13. Put away the materials as directed by your teacher.

Analyze the Results

14. Discuss your predictions as a class. How many different predictions were there? Which predictions were supported by testing? Did any of your measurements surprise you?

Draw Conclusions

15. Was your hypothesis supported? If your hypothesis was not supported, can you explain the data?

16. Explain the value of incorrect predictions.

Graphing Data

When performing an experiment it is usually necessary to collect data. To understand the data, it is often good to organize your data into a graph. Graphs can show trends and patterns that you might not notice in a table or list. In this exercise, you will practice collecting data and organizing the data into a graph.

Materials

- 400 mL beaker
- water
- ice
- Celsius thermometer with a clip
- hot plate
- graph paper
- heat-resistant gloves
- clock

Procedure

1. Pour 200 mL of water into a 400 mL beaker. Add ice to the beaker until the water line is at the 400 mL mark.

2. Place a Celsius thermometer into the beaker. Use a thermometer clip to prevent the thermometer from touching the bottom of the beaker. Record the temperature of the ice water in your ScienceLog.

3. Place the beaker and thermometer on a hot plate. Turn on the hot plate on medium heat and, in your ScienceLog, record the temperature every minute until the water temperature reaches 100°C.

4. Using heat-resistant gloves, remove the beaker from the hot plate. Turn off the hot plate. Continue to record the temperature of the water each minute for 10 more minutes.

5. On a piece of graph paper, create a graph similar to the one below. Label the horizontal axis (the *x*-axis) "Time (min)," and mark the axis in increments of 1 minute as shown. Label the vertical axis (the *y*-axis) "Temperature (°C)," and mark the axis in increments of ten as shown.

6. Find the 1-minute mark on the *x*-axis, and move up the graph to the temperature you recorded at 1 minute. Place a dot on the graph at that point. Plot each temperature in the same way. When you have plotted all your data, connect the dots with a smooth line.

Analysis

7. Examine the shape of your graph. Do you think the water heated faster than it cooled? Explain.

8. Estimate what the temperature of the water was 2.5 minutes after putting the beaker on the hot plate. Explain how you can make a good estimate of temperature between those you recorded.

9. Explain how a graph can often give more information than the same data in a list or a chart.

A Window to a Hidden World

Have you ever noticed that objects underwater appear closer than they really are? That's because light waves change speed when they travel from air into water. Anton van Leeuwenhoek, a pioneer of microscopy in the late seventeenth century, used a drop of water instead of a piece of glass to magnify objects. That drop of water brought a hidden world closer into view. How did Leeuwenhoek's microscope work? In this investigation, you will build a model of it to find out.

Materials

- metric ruler
- 3 × 10 cm piece of poster board
- hole punch
- eyedropper
- newsprint
- tape
- clear plastic wrap
- water

Procedure

1. Punch a hole in the center of the poster board with a hole punch, as shown in (a) at right.

2. Tape a small piece of clear plastic wrap over the hole, as shown in (b) at right. Be sure the plastic wrap is large enough so that the tape you use to secure it does not cover the hole.

3. Use an eyedropper to put one drop of water over the hole. Check to be sure your drop of water is dome-shaped (convex), as shown in (c) at right.

4. Hold the microscope close to your eye and look through the drop. Be careful not to disturb the water drop.

5. Hold the microscope over a piece of newsprint and observe the image.

Analysis

6. Describe and draw the image you see. Is the image larger or the same size as it was without the microscope? Is the image clear or blurred? Is the shape of the image distorted?

7. How do you think your model could be improved?

Going Further

Robert Hooke and Zacharias Janssen contributed much to the field of microscopy. Find out who they were, when they lived, and what they did.

Roly-Poly Races

Have you ever watched a bug run? Did you wonder why it was running? The bug you saw running was probably reacting to a stimulus. In other words, something happened that made it run! One of the characteristics of living things is the ability to respond to stimuli. In this activity, you will study the movement of roly-polies. Roly-polies are also called pill bugs. They are not really bugs at all; they are land-dwelling crustaceans called isopods. Isopods live in dark, moist areas under rocks or wood. You will provide stimuli to determine how fast your isopod can move and what affects its speed and direction. Remember that isopods are living things and must be treated with gentleness and respect.

Materials

- small plastic container with lid
- 1 or 2 cm of soil for the container
- small slice of raw potato
- piece of chalk
- 4 isopods
- metric ruler
- stopwatch or watch with a second hand
- protective gloves

Procedure

1. Choose a partner and decide together how you will run your roly-poly race. Discuss some gentle ways you might be able to stimulate your isopods to move. Choose five or six things that might cause movement, such as a change in temperature, sound, light, or gentle nudging. Check your choices with your teacher.

2. In your ScienceLog, make a data table similar to the one below. Label your columns across the top with the kinds of stimuli you want to try. Label the rows down the left side "Isopod 1," "Isopod 2," "Isopod 3," and "Isopod 4."

Isopod Responses		
Stimulus 1: ?	**Stimulus 2:** ?	**Stimulus 3:** ?
Isopod 1		
Isopod 2		
Isopod 3		
Isopod 4		

DO NOT WRITE IN BOOK

3. Put on your gloves and wear them through step 7. Place 1 or 2 cm of soil in a small plastic container. Add a small slice of potato and a piece of chalk. Your isopods will use these things for food.

4. Obtain four isopods from your teacher. Place them in your container. Observe them for a minute or two before you perform your tests. In your ScienceLog, write what you observe.

5. You and your partner will each choose two of the isopods to test. You should each choose at least two of the stimuli you have planned that have been approved by your teacher.

6. Carefully arrange the isopods at the "starting line." The starting line can be an imaginary line on one side of the container.

7. Try the methods you chose earlier to get your isopods to move. Record in your data table the response caused by each stimulus. Be sure to take careful measurements of the distances your isopods travel. Use a stopwatch or a watch with a second hand to time the race.

Analysis

8. How do isopods move? Do their legs move together? Describe the pattern of leg movement.

9. During your observation of the isopods before the race, did you see any movement? Did the movement seem to have a purpose or seem to result from a stimulus? Explain.

10. Did any one of the stimuli you chose make the isopod move faster or go farther? Did a combination of stimuli affect the isopod's movement?

Going Further

Bugs may not run for the joy of running like humans and other mammals do. But humans, like all living things, do react to stimuli. Describe three stimuli that might cause humans to run.

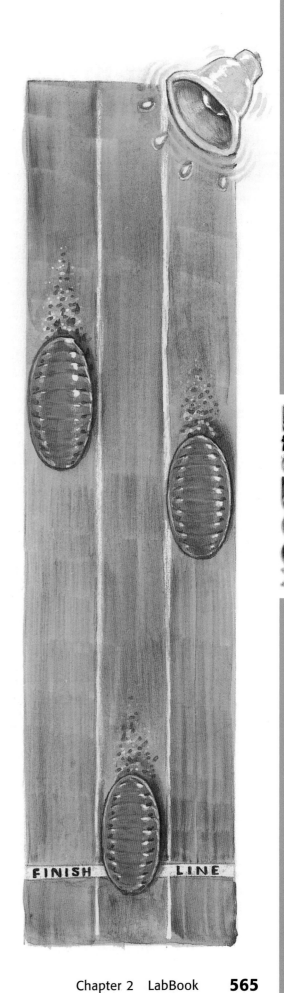

FINISH   LINE

The Best-Bread Bakery Dilemma

The chief baker at the Best-Bread Bakery thinks that the yeast the bakery received may be dead. Yeast is a central ingredient in the baking of bread. Thousands of dollars may be lost if the yeast is dead. As you know, yeast is a living organism, a member of the kingdom Fungi, and it undergoes the same life processes as other living organisms. When yeast grows in the presence of oxygen and other nutrients, it produces carbon dioxide, which appears as bubbles that cause the dough to rise.

The Best-Bread Bakery has requested that you test the yeast to see if it is dead or alive. The bakery has furnished samples of live yeast and some samples of the yeast suspected of being dead. Your teacher will supply you with samples of yeast, necessary nutrients, and equipment necessary to conduct your test.

Materials

- yeast samples (live, A, and B)
- water
- sugar
- flour
- magnifying lens
- test tubes or clear plastic cups
- test-tube rack
- 3 wooden stirring sticks
- graduated cylinder
- hot plate
- scoopula or small spoon
- 250 mL beaker
- Celsius thermometer with clip

Procedure

1. Make a data table similar to the one shown below. Leave plenty of room to fill in your observations.

2. Put on your gloves, goggles, and apron and wear them throughout the lab. Examine each yeast sample with a magnifying lens. You may want to sniff the samples to determine the presence of an odor. (Your teacher will demonstrate the appropriate way to detect odors in the laboratory.) Write your observations in the data table under the column labeled "Observations."

3. Label three containers (test tubes or plastic cups) "Live Yeast," "Sample A Yeast," and "Sample B Yeast."

4. Fill a 250 mL beaker with 125 mL of water, and place the beaker on a hot plate. Use a thermometer to be sure the water does not get warmer than 32°C. Attach the thermometer to the side of the beaker with a clip so the thermometer doesn't touch the bottom of the beaker. Turn off the hot plate when the temperature reaches 32°C.

	Observations	0 min	5 min	10 min	15 min	20 min	25 min	Dead or alive?
Live yeast								
Sample A yeast								
Sample B yeast								

DO NOT WRITE IN BOOK

5. Add a small scoop (about 1/2 tsp) of each yeast sample to the correctly labeled container. Add a small scoop of sugar to each container.

6. Using a graduated cylinder, add 10 mL of the water you heated to each container, and stir with a wooden stick.

7. Add a small scoop of flour to each container, and stir again. The flour will help make the process more visible but is not necessary as food for the yeast.

8. Observe the samples carefully. Look for formation of bubbles. Make observations at 5-minute intervals. Write your observations in the data table under the appropriate time column.

9. In the last column of the data table, write "alive" or "dead" based on your observations during the experiment.

Analysis

10. List and explain any differences in the yeast samples before the experiment.

11. Describe the appearance of the yeast samples at the conclusion of the experiment.

12. Why was a sample of live yeast included in the experiment?

13. Why was sugar added to the sample?

14. Based on your observations, which sample(s) of yeast is alive?

15. Write a letter to the Best-Bread Bakery stating your recommendation to use or not use the yeast samples. Give reasons for your recommendation.

Going Further

Based on your observations of the nutrient requirements of yeast, design an experiment in which you vary the amount of nutrients or examine different energy sources.

Mixing Colors

When you mix two colors, like red and green, you create a different color. But what color do you create? And is that new color brighter or darker? The color and brightness you see depend on the light that reaches your eye, and that depends on whether you are performing color addition (combining wavelengths by mixing colors of light) or color subtraction (absorbing light by mixing colors of pigments). In this experiment, you will try both types of color formation and see the results firsthand!

Part A—Color Addition

Procedure

1. Place a colored filter over each flashlight lens. Use masking tape to hold the filters in place.

2. In a darkened room, shine the red light on a sheet of clean white paper. Then shine the blue light next to the red light. You should see two circles of light, one red and one blue, next to each other.

3. Move the flashlights so that the circles overlap by about half their diameter. Examine the three areas of color, and record your observations. What color is formed in the mixed area? Is the mixed area brighter or darker than the single-color areas?

4. Repeat steps 2 and 3 with the red and green lights.

5. Now shine all three lights at the same point on the sheet of paper. Examine the results, and record your observations.

Analysis

6. In general, when you mixed two colors, was the result brighter or darker than the original colors?

7. In step 5, you mixed all three colors. Was the resulting color brighter or darker than mixing two colors? Explain your answer in terms of color addition. (Hint: Read the definition of color addition in the introduction.)

8. Based on your results, what do you think would happen if you mixed all the colors of light? Explain.

Materials

Part A
- 3 flashlights
- colored filters—red, green, and blue
- masking tape
- white paper

Part B
- masking tape
- 2 small plastic or paper cups
- water
- paintbrush
- watercolor paints
- white paper
- metric ruler

Red   ?   Green

Part B—Color Subtraction

Procedure

9. Place a piece of masking tape on each cup. Label one cup "Clean" and the other cup "Dirty." Fill both cups approximately half full with water.

10. Wet the paintbrush thoroughly in the "Clean" cup. Using the watercolor paints, paint a red circle on the white paper. The circle should be approximately 4 cm in diameter.

11. Clean the brush by rinsing it first in the "Dirty" cup and then in the "Clean" cup.

12. Paint a blue circle next to the red circle. Then paint half the red circle with the blue paint.

13. Examine the three areas: red, blue, and mixed. What color is the mixed area? Does it appear brighter or darker than the red and blue areas? Record your observations in your ScienceLog.

14. Clean the brush. Paint a green circle 4 cm in diameter, and then paint half the blue circle with green paint.

15. Examine the green, blue, and mixed areas. Record your observations.

16. Now add green paint to the mixed red-blue area, so that you have an area that is a mixture of red, green, and blue paint. Clean your brush.

17. Record your observations of this new mixed area.

Analysis

18. In general, when you mixed two colors, was the result brighter or darker than the original colors?

19. In step 16, you mixed all three colors. Was the result brighter or darker than mixing two colors? Explain your answer in terms of color subtraction. (Hint: Read the definition of color subtraction in the introduction.)

20. Based on your results, what do you think would happen if you mixed all the colors of paint? Explain.

Elephant-Sized Amoebas?

Why can't amoebas grow to be as large as elephants? An amoeba is a one-celled organism. Amoebas, like most cells, are microscopic. In fact, if an amoeba could grow to the size of a quarter, it would starve to death. To understand how this can be true, build a model of a cell and see for yourself.

Materials

- cubic cell patterns
- pieces of heavy paper or poster board
- scissors
- tape
- scale or balance
- fine sand

Procedure

1. Use heavy paper to make four cube-shaped cell models from the patterns supplied by your teacher. Cut out each cell model, fold the sides to make a cube, and tape the tabs on the sides. The smallest cell model has sides that are one unit long. The next larger cell has sides of two units. The next cell has sides of three units, and the largest cell has sides of four units. Tape the top of each cell so that it can be opened later. These paper models represent the cell membrane, the part of a cell's exterior through which food and waste pass.

Two-unit cell model

2. In your ScienceLog, make a data table like the Data Table for Measurements at right. Use each formula to calculate the data about your cell models. A key to the formula symbols can be found on the next page. Record your calculations in the table. Calculations for the smallest cell have been done for you.

Data Table for Measurements				
Length of side	Area of one side $(A = S \times S)$	Total surface area of cube cell $(TA = S \times S \times 6)$	Volume of cube cell $(V = S \times S \times S)$	Mass of cube cell
1	1 unit^2	6 unit^2	1 unit^3	
2				
3				
4				

DO NOT WRITE IN BOOK

3. Untape the top of the cube on each cell model. Carefully fill each model with fine sand until the sand is level with the top edge. Find the mass of the filled models using a scale or a balance. What does the sand represent in your model?

4. Record the mass of each cell model in the table. (Always remember to use the appropriate mass unit.)

5. In your ScienceLog, make a data table like the one below.

Data Table for Ratios		
Length of side	Ratio of total surface area to volume	Ratio of total surface area to mass
1		
2		
3		
4		

DO NOT WRITE IN BOOK

6. Find the ratios for each of your cell models by locating the data in your data tables. For example, the total surface area and the volume can be found in the Data Table for Measurements. Fill in the Data Table for Ratios with ratios for each of the cell models.

Analysis

7. As a cell grows larger, does the ratio of total surface area to volume increase, decrease, or stay the same?

8. Which is better able to supply food to all the cytoplasm of the cell—the cell membrane of a small cell or that of a large cell? Explain your answer.

9. As a cell grows larger, does the total surface area to mass ratio increase, decrease, or stay the same?

10. Is the cell membrane of a cell with high mass or the cell membrane of a cell with low mass better able to feed all the cytoplasm of the cell? You may explain your answer in a verbal presentation to the class or you may choose to write a report and illustrate it with drawings of your models.

Key to Formula Symbols
S = the length of one side
A = area
V = volume
TA = total area

Cells Alive!

You have probably used a microscope to look at single-celled organisms such as those shown below. They can be found in pond water. In the following exercise, you will look at *Protococcus*—algae that form a greenish stain on tree trunks, wooden fences, flowerpots, and buildings.

Materials

- *Protococcus* (or other algae)
- microscope
- water
- microscope slide and coverslip

Euglena

Amoeba

Paramecium

Procedure

1. Locate some *Protococcus.* Scrape a small sample into a container. Bring the sample to the classroom, and make a wet mount of it as directed by your teacher. If you can't find *Protococcus* outdoors, look for algae on the glass in an aquarium. Such algae may not be *Protococcus* but will be a very good substitute.

2. Set the microscope on low power to examine the algae. In your ScienceLog, draw the cells that you see.

3. Switch to high power to examine a single cell. In your ScienceLog, draw the single cell that you see.

4. You will probably notice that each cell contains several chloroplasts. Label a chloroplast on your drawing. What is the function of the chloroplast?

5. Another structure that should be clearly visible in all the algae cells is the nucleus. Find the nucleus in one of your cells, and label it on your drawing. What is the function of the nucleus?

6. What does the cytoplasm look like? Describe any movement you see inside the cells.

Analysis

7. Are *Protococcus* one-celled organisms or multicellular organisms?

8. How are *Protococcus* different from amoebas?

Protococcus

Name That Part!

Plant cells and animal cells have many organelles and other parts in common. For example, both plant and animal cells contain a nucleus and mitochondria. Plant cells and animal cells differ in several ways as well. In this exercise, you will investigate the similarities and differences between animal cells and plant cells.

Materials

- colored pencils or markers
- white, unlined paper

Procedure

1. Using colored pencils or markers and white, unlined paper, trace or draw the plant cell and animal cell shown below. Draw each cell on a separate piece of paper. You may color each organelle a different color.

2. Label the parts of each cell.

3. Below each drawing, list all the parts that you labeled and describe their function.

Plant cell   Animal cell

Analysis

4. List at least four structures that plant cells and animal cells have in common.

5. List three structures that plant cells have that animal cells do not have.

The Perfect Taters Mystery

You are the chief food detective at Perfect Taters Food Company. The boss, Mr. Fries, wants you to find a way to keep his potatoes fresh and crisp while they are waiting to be cooked. His workers have tried several methods already, but none have worked. Workers in Group A put the potatoes in very salty water, and the potatoes did something unexpected. Workers in Group B put the potatoes in water with no salt, and the potatoes did something else! Workers in Group C didn't put the potatoes in any water, and that didn't work either. Now you must design an experiment to find out what can be done to make the potatoes come out crisp and fresh.

Materials

Per class:

- potato samples (A, B, and C)
- freshly cut potato pieces
- 1 box of salt
- small, clear-plastic drinking cups
- 4 L of distilled water

SCIENTIFIC METHOD

1. Before you plan your experiment, review what you know. You know that potatoes are made of cells. Plant cells contain a large amount of water. Cells have membranes that hold water and other materials inside and keep some things out. Water and other materials must travel across cell membranes to get into and out of the cell.

2. Mr. Fries has told you that you can obtain as many samples as you need from the workers in Groups A, B, and C. Your teacher will have these samples ready for you to observe.

3. Make a data table like the one below in your ScienceLog to list your observations. Make as many observations as you can about the potatoes tested by workers in Group A, Group B, and Group C.

Observations	
Group A:	
Group B:	
Group C:	

DO NOT WRITE IN BOOK

Ask a Question

4. Now that you have made your observations, state Mr. Fries's problem in the form of a question that can be answered by your experiment.

Form a Hypothesis

5. Form a hypothesis based on your observations and your questions. The hypothesis should be a statement about what causes the potatoes to shrivel or swell. Based on your hypothesis, make a prediction about the outcome of your experiments. State your prediction in an "if, then" format.

Test the Hypothesis

6. Once you have made a prediction, design your investigation. Check your experimental design with your teacher before you begin. Mr. Fries will give you potato pieces, water, salt, and no more than six containers.

7. Keep very accurate records. Write out your plan and procedure. Make data tables. To be sure of your data, measure all materials carefully and make drawings of the potato pieces before and after the experiment.

Draw Conclusions

8. Explain what happened to the potato cells in Groups A, B, and C in your experiment. Include a discussion of the cell membrane and the process of osmosis.

Communicate Results

9. Write a letter to Mr. Fries that explains your experimental method, your results, and your conclusion. Then make a recommendation about how his employees should handle the potatoes so they will stay fresh and crisp.

Stayin' Alive!

Every second of your life, your body's trillions of cells take in, use, and store energy. They repair themselves, reproduce, and get rid of waste. Together, these processes are called *metabolism.* In many ways, your body's overall metabolism is very similar to that of an individual cell. Each cell needs energy on a small scale so all your cells together require energy on a larger scale. Your cells use the food that you eat to provide the energy you need to stay alive.

Your Basal Metabolic Rate (BMR) is a measurement of the energy that your body needs to carry out all the basic life processes while you are at rest. These processes include keeping your heart beating, breathing, and keeping your body's temperature stable. Your BMR is influenced by your gender, your age, and many other things. Your BMR may be different from everyone else's but it is normal for you. In this activity, you will find the amount of energy, measured in Calories, you need every day in order to stay alive.

Materials

- bathroom scale
- tape measure

Procedure

1. Find your weight on a bathroom scale. If the scale measures in pounds, you must convert your weight in pounds to your mass in kilograms. To convert your weight in pounds (lb) to mass in kilograms (kg), multiply the number of pounds by 0.454.

Example: If Carlos weighs 125 lb, his mass in kilograms is:	125 lb
	× 0.454
	56.75 kg

2. Use a tape measure and the help of a classmate to find your height. If the tape measures in inches, convert your height in inches to height in centimeters. To convert your height in inches (in.) to your height in centimeters (cm), multiply the number of inches by 2.54.

If Carlos is 62 in. tall, his height in centimeters is:	62 in.
	× 2.54
	157.48 cm

3. Now that you know your height and mass, use the appropriate formula below to get a close estimate of your BMR. Your answer will give you an estimate of the number of Calories your body needs each day just to stay alive.

Calculating Your BMR	
Females	**Males**
65 + (10 × your mass in kilograms)	66 + (13.5 × your mass in kilograms)
+ (1.8 × your height in centimeters)	+ (5 × your height in centimeters)
− (4.7 × your age in years)	− (6.8 × your age in years)

4. Your metabolism is also influenced by how active you are. Talking, walking, and playing games all take more energy than being at rest. To get an idea of how many Calories your body needs each day to stay healthy, select the lifestyle that best describes yours from the table at right. Then multiply your BMR by the activity factor.

Analysis

5. In what way could you compare your whole body to a single cell? Explain.

6. Does an increase in activity increase your BMR? Does an increase in activity increase your need for Calories? Explain your answers.

7. If you are moderately inactive, how many more Calories would you need if you began to exercise every day?

Activity Factors	
Activity lifestyle	**Activity factor**
Moderately inactive (normal, everyday activities)	1.3
Moderately active (exercise 3 to 4 times a week)	1.4
Very active (exercise 4 to 6 times a week)	1.6
Extremely active (exercise 6 to 7 times a week)	1.8

Going Further

The best energy sources are those that supply the correct amount of Calories for your lifestyle and also provide the nutrients you need. Research in the library or on the Internet to find out which kinds of foods are the best energy sources for you. How does your list of best energy sources compare with your diet?

List everything you eat and drink in 1 day. Find out how many Calories are in each item, and find the total number of Calories you have consumed. How does this number of Calories compare with the number of Calories you need each day for all your activities?

Bug Builders, Inc.

Imagine that you are a designer for a toy company that makes toy alien bugs. The president of Bug Builders, Inc., wants new versions of the wildly popular Space Bugs, but he wants to use the bug parts that are already in the warehouse. It's your job to come up with a new bug design. You have studied how traits are passed from one generation to another. You will use this knowledge to come up with new combinations of traits and assemble the bug parts in new ways. Model A and Model B will act as the "parent" bugs. The two models currently available are shown below.

Materials

- 14 allele sacks (supplied by your teacher)
- large marshmallows (head and body segments)
- red and green toothpicks (antennae)
- green and blue pushpins (noses)
- pipe cleaners (tails)
- green and black gumdrops (feet)
- map pins (eyes)
- scissors

Model A ("Mom")
- red antennae
- 3 body segments
- curly tail
- 2 pairs of legs
- green nose
- black feet
- 3 eyes

Model B ("Dad")
- green antennae
- 2 body segments
- straight tail
- 3 pairs of legs
- blue nose
- green feet
- 2 eyes

SCIENTIFIC METHOD

Make a Prediction

If there are two forms each of seven characteristics, then there are ___?___ possible combinations.

Collect Data

1. Your teacher will display 14 sacks—2 sacks for each characteristic. The sacks will contain slips of paper with capital or lowercase letters printed on them. Take one piece of paper from each sack. (Remember: Capital letters represent dominant alleles, and lowercase letters represent recessive alleles.) For each characteristic, one allele sack carries the alleles from "Mom" and one carries alleles from "Dad." After you have recorded the alleles you have drawn, place the slips of paper back into the sack.

2. In your ScienceLog, create a table just like the one below. Fill in the first two columns with the alleles that you selected from the sacks. Next fill in the third column with the genotype of the new model ("Baby").

Bug Family Traits

Trait	Model A "Mom" allele	Model B "Dad" allele	New model "Baby" genotype	New model "Baby" phenotype
Antennae color				
Number of body segments				
Tail shape				
Number of leg pairs				
Nose color				
Foot color				
Number of eyes				

DO NOT WRITE IN BOOK

3. Use the information at right to fill in the last column of the table.

4. Now that you have your table filled out, you are ready to pick the parts you need to assemble your bug. (Toothpicks can be used to hold the head and body segments together and as legs to attach the feet to the body.)

Genotypes and Phenotypes

RR or Rr = red antennae	rr = green antennae
SS or Ss = 3 body segments	ss = 2 body segments
CC or Cc = curly tail	cc = straight tail
LL or Ll = 3 pairs of legs	ll = 2 pairs of legs
BB or Bb = blue nose	bb = green nose
GG or Gg = green feet	gg = black feet
EE or Ee = 2 eyes	ee = 3 eyes

Analyze the Results

5. Take a class poll of the traits of the offspring. What are the ratios for each trait?

Draw Conclusions

6. Do any of the new models look exactly like the parents? Explain your findings.

7. What are the possible genotypes of the parents?

8. How many different genotypes are possible in the offspring?

Going Further

Find a mate for your "baby" bug. What are the possible genotypes and phenotypes of the offspring from this match?

Tracing Traits

Have you ever wondered about traits that you inherited from your parents? You know that traits are passed from generation to generation, but do you have a trait that neither of your parents has? In this project, you will develop a family tree, or pedigree, similar to the one shown in the diagram below. You will trace an inherited trait through your own family or another family who can help you with the information you will need. Next you will survey a family to determine some of the traits they share. Finally, you will trace a trait to determine how it has passed from generation to generation.

Materials

- pencil
- paper

Pedigree

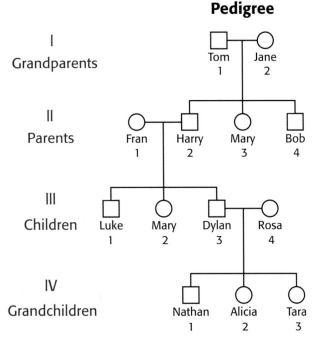

Procedure

1. The diagram at right shows a family history with four generations. On a separate piece of paper, draw a similar diagram of the family you have chosen. Include as many family members as possible, such as grandparents, parents, children, and grandchildren. Use circles to represent the females in the family and squares to represent the males. You may include other information if you wish, such as the family member's name, birthdate, or picture. Other members of the family may be helpful in providing the information you need.

2. Draw a chart similar to the one on the next page. Survey each of the family members shown in your family tree to determine which have the dominant form and which have the recessive form of the trait described in the chart. Ask them if they have hair on the middle segment of their fingers. Write each person's name in the appropriate square. Be sure to explain to each person that it is perfectly normal to have either the dominant or the recessive trait.

Dominant trait	Recessive trait	Family members with the dominant trait	Family members with the recessive trait
Hair present on the middle segment of fingers (H)	Hair absent on the middle segment of fingers (h)	DO NOT WRITE IN BOOK	

3. Trace the trait described in the chart throughout the family tree you diagrammed in step 1. Do this by shading or coloring the square or circle symbols of the family members who demonstrate the dominant form of this trait. Leave the other symbols unshaded.

Analysis

4. What percentage of the family members demonstrate the dominant form of the trait? Calculate this by counting the number of people who have the dominant form of the trait and dividing this number by the total number of family members you surveyed. Then multiply your answer by 100. An example is done for you at right.

Example: Calculating percentage

$$\frac{10 \text{ people with trait}}{20 \text{ people surveyed}} = \frac{1}{2}$$

$$\frac{1}{2} = 0.50 \times 100 = 50\%$$

5. What percentage of the family members demonstrate the recessive form of the trait? Why doesn't every family member have the dominant trait?

6. Compare your percentage calculation for the dominant trait with the calculations of your classmates. Are there some families with a higher percentage of the dominant trait?

7. Choose one of the family members who demonstrates the recessive form of the chosen trait. What must be the genotype of this individual? How did this person get each of the alleles that make up his or her genotype? What are the possible genotypes for the parents of this individual? Are there any brothers or sisters? Do they show the dominant or recessive trait?

8. Draw a Punnett square similar to the one at right. Use it to illustrate how this person might have inherited the recessive trait. Inside the Punnett square, write the genotype of the person you have chosen to study in the bottom right-hand corner. Try to determine the genotypes of the parents. HINT: There may be more than one possible genotype. Which allele (dominant or recessive) must have been passed on from a parent if there is a brother or sister who shows the dominant trait?

	Father	
Mother	?	?
?		
?		

Base-Pair Basics

You have learned that DNA is a molecule shaped something like a twisted ladder. The side rails of the ladder are made of sugar molecules and phosphate molecules. The sides are held together by molecules called nucleotide bases. These bases join in pairs to form the rungs of the ladder. Each nucleotide base can pair with only one other nucleotide base. Each of these pairs is called a base pair. When DNA replicates itself, enzymes cause the base pairs to separate. Then each half attracts the necessary nucleotides available in the nucleus and assembles them to complete a new half. In this activity, you will make and replicate a model of DNA.

Materials

- white paper or poster board
- colored paper or poster board
- scissors
- pencil
- large paper bag

Procedure

1. Use the drawings of the four nucleotide bases below to create a template. Use the template to outline the bases on white paper or poster board. Label the pieces A (for adenine), T (for thymine), C (for cytosine), and G (for guanine), as shown below. Draw the pieces again on colored paper or poster board using a different color for each base. Draw the pieces as large as you want, and draw as many of the white pieces and as many of the colored pieces as time will allow.

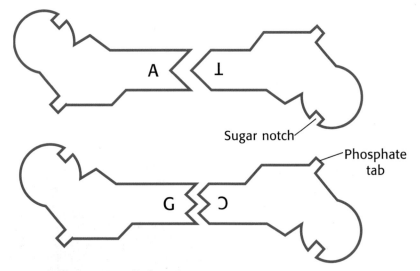

Sugar notch

Phosphate tab

2. Carefully cut out all the pieces.

3. Gather all the colored pieces in the classroom into a large paper bag. Spread all the white pieces in the classroom onto a large work table or lab counter.

4. Withdraw nine pieces at random from the bag containing the colored pieces. Arrange the colored pieces in any order in a straight column so the letters A, T, C, and G are right side up. Be sure to match the sugar and phosphate tabs and notches. Draw this arrangement in your ScienceLog.

5. Find the matching white nucleotide bases for the nine colored bases you drew at random. Remember the base-pairing rules you have studied, and matching will be easy!

6. Fit the pieces together, matching all tabs and notches. You now have one piece of DNA containing nine base pairs. Draw your results in your ScienceLog.

7. Now separate the base pairs, keeping the sugar and phosphate notches and tabs together. Draw this arrangement in your ScienceLog.

8. Next to each separated base you drew in step 7, write the letter of the base that should go there to complete the base pair.

9. Find all the bases you need to complete your replication. Find white pieces to match the bases on the left, and find colored pieces to match the bases on the right.

Be sure all the tabs and notches fit and the sides are straight. You have now replicated DNA. Are the two models identical? Draw your results in your ScienceLog.

Analysis

10. Name the correct base-pairing rules.

11. What happens when you attempt to pair thymine with guanine? Do they fit together? Are the sides straight? Do all the tabs and notches fit? Explain.

Going Further

Construct a 3-D model of the DNA molecule, showing its twisted-ladder structure. Use your imagination and creativity to select your materials. You may want to use licorice whips with gum balls and toothpicks, or pipe cleaners and paper clips! Display your model in your classroom.

Mystery Footprints

Sometimes scientists find clues preserved in rocks that are evidence of the activities of organisms that lived thousands of years ago. Evidence such as preserved footprints can provide important information about an organism. Imagine that your class has been asked by a group of paleontologists to help analyze some human footprints. These footprints were found embedded in rocks in an area just outside of town.

Materials

- large box of slightly damp sand, at least 1 m² (large enough to contain 3 or 4 footprints)
- metric ruler

SCIENTIFIC METHOD

Form a Hypothesis

1. Your teacher will provide you with some mystery footprints in sand. Examine the mystery footprints, and brainstorm about the information you might learn about the people who walked on this patch of sand. As a class, make as many hypotheses as possible about the people who left the footprints.

2. Form research groups of three people, and choose one hypothesis for your group to investigate.

Test the Hypothesis

3. In your ScienceLog, design a table for recording your data. For example, if your hypothesis is that the footprints were made by two adult males who were walking in a hurry, your table would look similar to the one below.

Mystery Footprints		
	Footprint set 1	**Footprint set 2**
Length		
Width		
Depth of toe		
Depth of heel		
Length of stride		

DO NOT WRITE IN BOOK

4. With the help of your group, you may first want to analyze your own footprints to help you draw conclusions about the mystery footprints. For example, how long is your stride when you are running? How long is it when you are walking? Does your weight affect the depth of the footprint? What part of your foot touches the ground first when you are running? What part touches the ground first when you are walking? When you are running, which part of your footprint is deeper? Make a list of the kind of footprint each different activity produces. For example, you might write, "A deep impression in the toe area and a long stride are produced by running."

Analyze the Results

5. Compare the data of your footprints with that of the mystery footprints. What similarities are there? What differences are there?

6. Were the mystery footprints made by one person or more than one person? Explain your reasoning.

7. Is there enough evidence to tell if the mystery footprints were made by men, women, children, or a combination? Explain.

8. Based on your observations of your own footprints, were the people who made the mystery footprints standing still, walking, or running?

Draw Conclusions

9. Does your data support your hypothesis? Explain.

10. How could you improve your experiment?

Communicate Results

11. Outline your group's conclusions in a document addressed to the scientists who asked for your help. Begin by stating your hypothesis. Then outline your method of gathering information from the study of your own footprints. Include the comparisons you made between your footprints and the mystery footprints. Before stating your conclusions, offer some suggestions about how you could improve your method of investigation.

12. Create a poster or chart, or use a computer if one is available, to prepare a presentation of your findings for the class.

Out-of-Sight Marshmallows

An adaptation is a trait that helps an organism survive in its environment. In nature, camouflage is a form of coloration that enables an organism to blend into its immediate surroundings. This is the hypothesis you will be testing: Organisms that are camouflaged have a better chance of escaping from predators and therefore a better chance of survival.

Test the Hypothesis

1. Students should work in pairs.

2. Count out 50 white marshmallows and 50 colored marshmallows. Your marshmallows will represent the prey (food) in this experiment.

3. Place both the white and colored marshmallows randomly on the piece of colored cloth.

4. One student per pair should be the hungry hunter (predator). The other student should record the results of each trial. The hungry hunter should look at the food for a few seconds and pick up the first marshmallow he or she sees. The hungry hunter should then look away.

5. Continue this process without stopping for 2 minutes or until your teacher signals to stop.

Analyze the Results

6. How many white marshmallows did the hungry hunter choose?

7. How many colored marshmallows did the hungry hunter choose?

Draw Conclusions

8. What did the cloth represent in your investigation?

9. Did the color of the cloth affect the color of marshmallows the hungry hunter chose? Explain your answer.

10. Which color of marshmallow represented camouflage?

11. Describe an organism that has a camouflage adaptation.

Materials

- 1 piece of colored cloth (50 cm square). The color of the cloth should closely match one of the marshmallow colors.
- 50 white mini-marshmallows
- 50 colored mini-marshmallows (all one color is preferable)
- stopwatch or clock with a second hand

Survival of the Chocolates

Imagine a world populated with candy, and hold that delicious thought for just a moment. Try to apply the idea of natural selection to a population of candy-coated chocolates. According to the theory of natural selection, individuals who have favorable adaptations are more likely to survive. In the "species" of candy you will study in this experiment, shell strength is an adaptive advantage. Which color of candy do you think will have the highest survival rate? Think like a life scientist, and plan an experiment to find out which color of candy has an advantage over other colors in terms of shell (candy coating) strength.

Materials

- small candy-coated chocolates in a variety of colors (Each student or group will decide how many of each color are needed.)
- other materials as needed, according to the design of your experiment

SCIENTIFIC METHOD

Make a Prediction

1. Write the following sentence in your ScienceLog, and fill in the blanks. If the __?__ colored shell is the strongest, then fewer of the candies with this color of shell will _____?_____ when _____?_____ .

Test Your Hypothesis

2. Design a procedure to determine which color of candy is best suited to survive by not "cracking under pressure." In your plan, be sure to include materials and tools you may need to complete this procedure. Check your experimental design with your teacher before you begin. Your teacher will supply the candy and assist you in gathering materials and tools.

3. Record your results in a data table you have designed in your ScienceLog. Be sure to organize your data in a clear and understandable way.

Analyze the Results

4. Write a report that describes your experiment. Explain how your data either support or do not support your prediction. Include possible errors and ways to improve your procedure.

Going Further

Can you think of another characteristic of these candies that can be tested to determine which candy is best adapted to survive? Explain your choice.

Dating the Fossil Record

You have received nine rock samples from a paleontologist in California. Your job is to arrange the samples in order from oldest to youngest according to their fossil content and to determine their relative ages using the process of relative dating. Results from absolute dating methods will not be available from a laboratory for several weeks, and the paleontologist needs the information immediately. You know from previous work that the rocks of Sample 2 are the oldest.

Materials

- set of nine cards representing rock samples
- pencil and paper
- colored markers
- poster board (61 cm²)

Procedure: Part 1

1. Form teams of three or four students.

2. Arrange the fossil cards from oldest to youngest. Begin with Sample 2 because you know this sample is the oldest. You may need to try several different arrangements to get the cards in order. **HINT:** After an organism becomes extinct, it does not reappear in younger rocks.

Fossil Key

Globus slimius

Circus bozoensis

Fungus amongius

Bogus biggus

Microbius hairiensis

Bananabana bobana

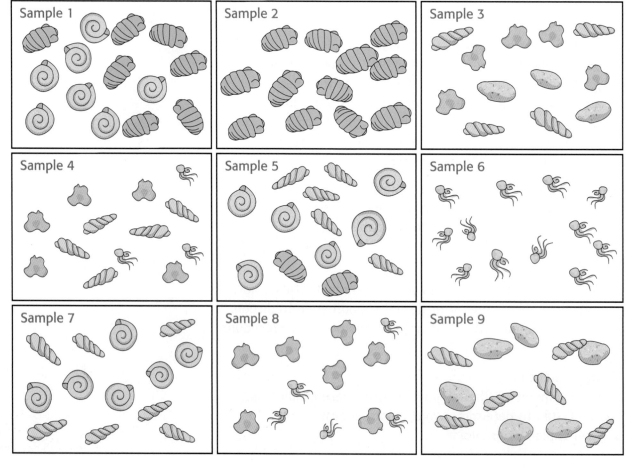

Sample 1 | Sample 2 | Sample 3

Sample 4 | Sample 5 | Sample 6

Sample 7 | Sample 8 | Sample 9

3. Prepare a table similar to the one below. Record the samples in order from bottom to top (oldest to youngest) in the first column. Sample 2 is done for you.

Name of Fossil Organism					
Order of samples	*Globus slimius*				
Sample 2	**X**				

DO NOT WRITE IN BOOK

4. Write the fossil names in order by age from left to right in the top row of the table. **HINT:** Examine your fossil cards carefully to determine where each fossil appears in the rock record. Write an *X* in the appropriate column to indicate which fossil or fossils are present in each sample.

Analysis: Part 1

5. Do the letters make a certain pattern across the table? What would you conclude if there were an *X* outside the pattern?

6. Based on the information in your table, which fossil is the youngest?

7. From the information you have, are you able to tell exactly how old a certain fossil is? Why or why not?

8. What information does relative dating provide to paleontologists?

Procedure: Part 2

1. You are planning to prepare a timeline for the paleontologist in California. But when the results, shown at right, come in from the geology lab, you discover that the dates have become separated from the appropriate rock samples. Absolute dating is very expensive, and you can't have it done again. But wait! You have already determined the relative ages of the samples. All you have to do is arrange the dates from oldest to youngest and label your table from bottom to top. Add these dates to your data table.

2. Your table now contains all the information you need to make a timeline for the paleontologist in California. Use colored markers and poster board to make your timeline. You may want to draw a rock wall showing several layers. To do this, label each layer with a date and the names of the fossils found there. Or you may want to draw a line with the dates labeled on the line and the fossils sketched above the appropriate date. Be creative!

Fossil Ages

The dates provided by the geology lab are as follows: 28.5 mya, 30.2 mya, 18.3 mya, 17.6 mya, 26.3 mya, 14.2 mya, 23.1 mya, 15.5 mya, and 19.5 mya.

Analysis: Part 2

3. Based on absolute dating, which fossil organism lived for the longest period of time? Which fossil organism lived for the shortest period of time? Explain your answers.

4. Based on the information in your timeline, what age range would you assign to the fossil of *Circus bozoensis*? **HINT:** Measure from the year that the fossil first appeared in the rock record to the first year it was absent in the rock record.

5. Determine the age ranges of all of your fossil species.

Going Further

Using the library or an on-line data base, investigate whether the absolute dating of rock surrounding fossils is the most reliable method of dating. Find out what circumstances prevent absolute dating.

The Half-life of Pennies

Imagine existing more than 5,000 years and still having more than 5,000 to go! That is exactly what the unstable element carbon-14 does. Carbon-14 is a special unstable element used in the absolute dating of material that was once alive, such as fossil bones. Every 5,730 years, half of the carbon-14 in a fossil specimen decays or breaks down into a more stable element. In the following experiment you will see how pennies can show the same kind of "decay."

Materials

- 100 pennies
- large container with a cover

Procedure

1. Place 100 pennies in a large, covered container. Shake the container several times, and remove the cover. Carefully empty the container on a flat surface making sure the pennies don't roll away.

2. Remove all the coins that have the "head" side of the coin turned upward. Record the number of pennies removed and the number of pennies remaining in a data table similar to the one at right.

3. Repeat the process until no pennies are left in the container. Remember to remove only the coins showing "heads."

4. In your ScienceLog, draw a graph similar to the one at right. Label the x-axis "Number of shakes," and label the y-axis "Pennies remaining." Using data from your data table, plot the number of coins remaining at each shake on your graph.

Shake number	Number of coins remaining	Number of coins removed
1		
2	DO NOT WRITE IN BOOK	
3		

Half-life of Pennies

Half-life of Pennies graph: y-axis labeled "Pennies remaining" with values 25, 50, 75, 100; x-axis labeled "Number of shakes" with values 0 1 2 3 4 5. (DO NOT WRITE IN BOOK)

Analysis

5. Examine the Half-life of Carbon-14 graph at right. Compare the graph you have made for pennies with the one for carbon-14. Explain any similarities that you see.

6. Recall that the probability of landing "heads" in a coin toss is $\frac{1}{2}$. Use this information to explain why the remaining number of pennies is reduced by about half each time they are shaken and tossed.

Half-life of Carbon-14

Half-life of Carbon-14 graph: y-axis labeled "Grams of carbon-14" with values 6.25, 12.5, 25, 50, 100; x-axis labeled "Number of half-lives (5,730)" with values 0 1 2 3 4 5.

Chapter 9   LabBook   **591**

Shape Island

You are a biologist exploring uncharted parts of the world looking for new species of animals. You sailed for days across the ocean and finally found Shape Island, hundreds of miles south of Hawaii. This island has some very unusual life-forms. Each of them has some variation of a geometric shape. You have spent more than a year collecting specimens and classifying them according to Linnaeus's system. You have been able to assign a two-part scientific name to most species you have collected. You must assign all the names to the final 12 specimens before you begin your journey home.

Materials

- pencil
- paper

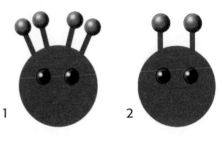

1   2

Procedure

1. In your ScienceLog, draw each of the organisms pictured on this page. Beside each organism, draw a line for its name, as shown on the following page. The first one has been named for you, but you have 12 more to name. Use the glossary of Greek and Latin prefixes, suffixes, and root words below to help you name the organisms. Look at the table and see which ones seem to apply to the organisms shown.

3   4

Greek and Latin roots, prefixes, and suffixes	Meaning
ankylos	angle
antennae	external sense organs
tri-	three
bi-	two
cyclo-	circle
macro-	large
micro-	small
mono-	one
peri-	all around
-plast	body
-pod	foot
quad-	four
stoma	mouth
uro-	tail

5

6

7

8

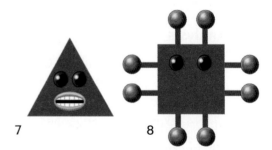

9   10   11   12   13

1. _Cycloplast quadantennae_
   (cyclo + plast quad + antennae)

2. _____

3. _____

DO NOT WRITE IN BOOK

2. One more organism exists on Shape Island, but you have not been able to capture it. However, your supplies are running out, and you must start sailing for home. You have had a good look at the unusual animal and can draw it in detail. In your ScienceLog, draw an animal that is different from all the others, and give it a two-part scientific name.

Analysis

3. If you gave species 1 a common name, such as round-face-no-nose, would any other scientist know which of the newly discovered organisms you were referring to? Explain. How many others have a round face and no nose?

4. Describe two characteristics shared by all your newly discovered specimens.

Going Further

Look up the scientific names listed below. You can use the library, the Internet, a taxonomy index, or field guides.

Mertensia virginica
Porcellio scaber

For each organism answer the following questions: Is the organism a plant or an animal? How many common names does it have? How many scientific names does it have?

Think of the name of your favorite fruit or vegetable. Find out if it has other common names, and find out its two-part scientific name.

Voyage of the USS *Adventure*

You are a crew member on the USS *Adventure*. The *Adventure* has been on a 5-year mission to collect life-forms from outside the solar system. On the voyage back to Earth, your ship went through a meteor shower, which ruined several of the compartments containing the extraterrestrial life-forms. Now it is necessary to put more than one life-form in the same compartment.

You have only three compartments in your starship that are undamaged by the meteor shower. You and your crewmates must stay in one compartment, and that compartment should be used for extraterrestrial life-forms only if absolutely necessary. You and your crewmates must decide which of the life-forms could be placed together. It is thought that similar life-forms will have similar needs. If they are grouped in this way, they will be easier to care for. You can use only observable characteristics to group the life-forms.

Materials

* set of eight drawings of extraterrestrial life-forms (optional)

Life-form 1

Life-form 2

Life-form 3

Procedure

1. Make a data table similar to the one below. Label each column with as many characteristics of the various life-forms as possible. Down the left side, list "Life-form 1," "Life-form 2," and so on, as shown. The life-forms are pictured on this page.

Life-form 4

Life-form Characteristics			
	Color	Shape	Legs	Eyes
Life-form 1				
Life-form 2				
Life-form 3				
Life-form 4				

DO NOT WRITE
IN BOOK

Life-form 5

2. Describe each characteristic as completely as you can. Leave enough space in each square to write what you see. Based on your observations and data table, determine which of the life-forms are most alike.

Life-form 7

Life-form 6

3. Make a data table like the one below. Fill in the table according to the decisions you have made about the similarities among the life-forms. State your reasons for the way you have grouped your life-forms.

Life-form Room Assignments		
Compartment	Life-forms	Reasons
1		
2		
3		

DO NOT WRITE IN BOOK

4. The USS *Adventure* has to make one more stop before returning home. On planet X437 you discover the most interesting life-form ever found outside of Earth—the CC9, shown at right. Make a decision, based on your previous grouping of life-forms, about whether you can safely include CC9 in one of the compartments for the trip to Earth.

CC9

Analysis

5. Describe the life-forms in compartment 1. How are they similar? How are they different?

6. Describe the life-forms in compartment 2. How are they similar? How do they differ from the life-forms in compartment 1?

7. Are there any life-forms in compartment 3? If so, describe their similarities. In which compartment will you and your crewmates remain for the journey home?

8. Are you able to safely transport life-form CC9 back to Earth? Why or why not? If you are able to include CC9, in which compartment will it be placed? How did you decide?

Going Further

In 1831, Charles Darwin sailed from England on a ship called the HMS *Beagle.* You have studied the finches that Darwin observed on the Galápagos Islands. What were some of the other unusual organisms he found there? For example, find out about the Galápagos tortoise.

Leaf Me Alone!

Imagine you are a naturalist all alone on an expedition in a rain forest. You have found several plants that you think have never been seen before. You must contact a botanist, a scientist who studies plants, to confirm your suspicion that the species you've discovered are entirely new to science. Because there is no mail service in the rain forest, you must describe these species completely and accurately by radio. The botanist must be able to draw the leaves of the plants from your description.

In this activity, you will carefully describe five plant specimens using the examples and vocabulary lists in this lab.

Materials

• 5 different leaf specimens

• plant guidebook (optional)

• protective gloves

Procedure

1. To prepare to describe leaves from the plant specimens provided by your teacher, examine each example of leaf characteristics provided in this lab. These examples are provided for you on the following page. You will notice that more than one term is needed to completely describe a leaf. The leaf shown at right has been labeled for you using the examples and vocabulary lists found in this lab.

2. In your ScienceLog, draw a diagram of a leaf from each plant specimen.

3. Next to each drawing, carefully describe each leaf. Include general characteristics, such as relative size and color. For each plant, identify the following: leaf shape, stem type, leaf arrangement, leaf edge, vein arrangement, and leaf-base shape. Use the terms and vocabulary lists in this lab to describe each leaf as exactly as possible and to label your drawings.

Compound Leaf

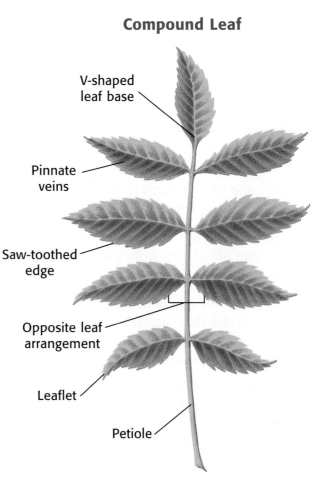

V-shaped leaf base

Pinnate veins

Saw-toothed edge

Opposite leaf arrangement

Leaflet

Petiole

Analyze

4. What is the difference between a simple leaf and a compound leaf?

5. Describe two different vein arrangements in leaves.

6. Based on what you know about adaptation, explain why there are so many different leaf variations.

Going Further

Choose a partner from among your classmates. Using the keys and vocabulary in this lab, describe a leaf, and see if your partner can draw the leaf from your description. Switch roles, and see if you can draw a leaf from your partner's description.

Leaf Shapes Vocabulary List

cordate—heart shaped

lanceolate—sword shaped

lobate—lobed

oblong—leaves rounded at the tip

orbicular—disk shaped

ovate—oval shaped, widest at base of leaf

peltate—shield shaped

reniform—kidney shaped

sagittate—arrow shaped

Stems Vocabulary List

woody—bark or barklike covering on stem

herbaceous—green, nonwoody stems

Leaf Arrangements Vocabulary List

alternate—alternating leaves or leaflets along stem or petiole

compound—leaf divided into segments or several leaflets on a petiole

opposite—compound leaf with several leaflets arranged oppositely along a petiole

palmate—single leaf with veins arranged around a center point

palmate compound—several leaflets arranged around a center point

petiole—leaf stalk

pinnate compound—several leaflets on either side of a petiole

simple—single leaf attached to stem by a petiole

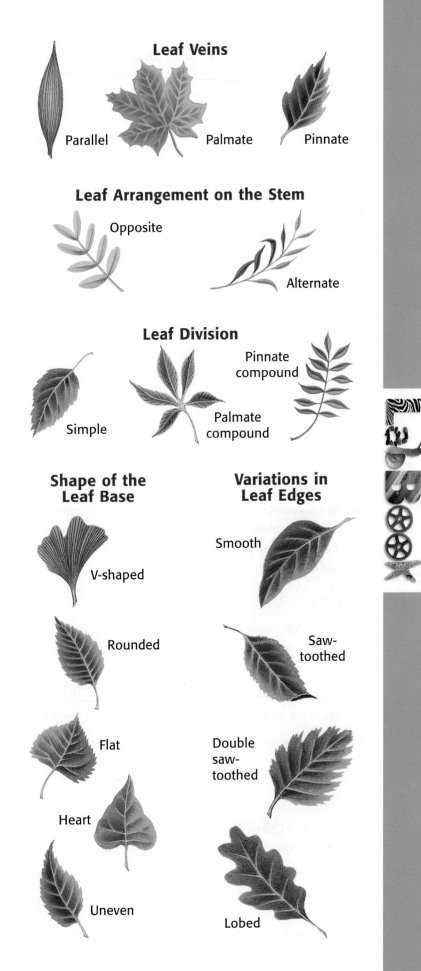

Leaf Veins

Parallel   Palmate   Pinnate

Leaf Arrangement on the Stem

Opposite

Alternate

Leaf Division

Pinnate compound

Simple

Palmate compound

Shape of the Leaf Base

V-shaped

Rounded

Flat

Heart

Uneven

Variations in Leaf Edges

Smooth

Saw-toothed

Double saw-toothed

Lobed

Travelin' Seeds

You have learned from your study of plants that there are some very interesting and unusual plant adaptations. Some of the most interesting adaptations are modifications that allow plant seeds and fruits to be dispersed, or scattered, away from the parent plant. This dispersal enables the young seedlings to obtain the space, sun, and other resources they need without directly competing with the parent plant.

In this activity, you will use your own creativity to disperse a seed.

Materials

- bean seed
- seed-dispersal challenge card
- various household or recycled materials (examples: glue, tape, paper, paper clips, rubber bands, cloth, paper cups and plates, paper towels, cardboard)

Procedure

1. Obtain a seed and a dispersal challenge card from your teacher. In your ScienceLog, record the type of challenge card you have been given.

2. Create a plan for using the available materials to disperse your seed as described on the challenge card. Record your plan in your ScienceLog. Get your teacher's approval before proceeding.

3. Obtain the materials you need to test your seed-dispersal method.

4. With your teacher's permission, test your method. You will need to perform several trials. Make a data table in your ScienceLog, and record the results of your trials.

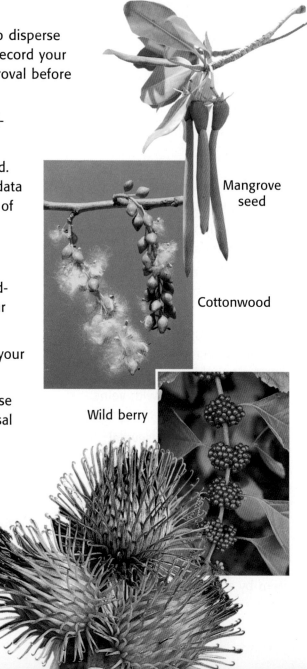

Mangrove seed

Cottonwood

Wild berry

Grass bur

Analyze

5. Were you able to successfully complete the seed-dispersal challenge? Describe the success of your seed-dispersal method.

6. Are there any modifications you could make to your method to improve the dispersal of your seed?

7. Describe any plants you can think of that disperse their seeds in a way similar to your seed-dispersal method.

Going Further
Demonstrate your seed-dispersal method for your classmates.

Build a Flower

Scientists often make models in the laboratory to help them understand processes or structures. In this activity, you will use your creativity and your understanding of the structure of a flower to make a model from recycled materials and art supplies.

Materials

- recycled items (examples: paper plates and cups, yogurt containers, wire, string, beads, buttons, cardboard, bottles)

- art materials (examples: glue, tape, scissors, colored paper, pipe cleaners, yarn)

- 3 × 5 in. card

Procedure

1. In your ScienceLog, draw a flower similar to the one shown below right. Label each of the structures on your drawing. The flower shown has both male and female parts. Not all flowers have this arrangement.

2. Examine the materials available for the construction of your flower. Decide which materials are appropriate for each flower part, and build a three-dimensional model of a flower. The flower you create should contain each of the parts listed below.

Parts of a Flower	
Petals	
Sepals	
Stem	
Pistil	(stigma, style, ovary)
Stamen	(anther, filament)

DO NOT WRITE IN BOOK

3. On a 3 × 5 in. card, draw a diagram key for your flower model. In your key, each of the structures that are represented on your flower must be labeled.

Petal
Stigma
Anther
Filament
Style
Stamen (Anther, Filament)
Sepal
Ovary
Pistil (Stigma, Style, Ovary)
Stem

Analysis

4. List the structures of a flower, and explain the function of each part.

5. Explain how your model flower might attract pollinators. What modifications could you make to increase the number of pollinators?

6. Describe how self-pollination could take place in your model flower.

Going Further

Create a classroom display of all the completed models.

Food Factory Waste

You know that photosynthesis in plants produces food. When plants make food by photosynthesis, they also produce waste that we can't live without.

In this activity, you will observe the process of photosynthesis. You will determine the rate of photosynthesis for two or three sprigs of *Elodea* per day.

Materials

- 600 mL beaker
- 5 percent baking-soda-and-water solution
- glass funnel
- 20 cm long *Elodea* sprigs (2 or 3)
- test tube
- metric ruler
- light source
- protective gloves

Procedure

1. Put on your goggles, gloves, and apron.

2. Add a 5 percent baking-soda-and-water solution to the beaker until the beaker is three-fourths full.

3. Put two or three 20 cm long sprigs of *Elodea* in the beaker. The baking soda will provide the *Elodea* with the carbon dioxide it needs for photosynthesis.

4. Place the wide end of the funnel over the sprigs of *Elodea* so that the end of the funnel with the small opening is pointing up. The *Elodea* and the funnel should be completely under the solution, as shown at right.

5. Completely fill the test tube with the 5 percent baking-soda-and-water solution. Place your thumb over the end of the test tube. Turn the test tube upside down, taking care that no air enters the test tube. Hold the opening of the test tube under the solution and place the test tube over the small end of the funnel, as shown at right. Try not to let any water out of the test tube as you do this.

6. Place the beaker setup in a well-lit area near a lamp or in direct sunlight, if possible.

7. In your ScienceLog, prepare a data table similar to the one below.

Amount of Gas Present in the Test Tube		
Days of exposure to light	**Total amount of gas present (mm)**	**Amount of gas produced per day (mm)**
0		
1		
2		
3		
4		
5		

8. Record in your ScienceLog that there was 0 gas in the test tube on day 0. (If you were unable to place the test tube without getting air in the tube, measure the height of the column of air in the test tube in millimeters using a metric ruler. Record this value for day 0.) Measure the gas in the test tube from the middle of the curve on the bottom of the upside-down test tube to the level of the solution.

9. For days 1 through 5, measure the amount of gas in the test tube. Record the measurements on the appropriate row in your data table under the heading "Amount of gas present (mm)."

10. Calculate the amount of gas produced each day by subtracting the amount of gas present on the previous day from the amount of gas present today. Record these amounts in your data table in the appropriate row under the heading "Amount of gas produced per day (mm)."

11. In your ScienceLog, construct a graph similar to the one at right. Plot the data from your table on the graph.

Amount of Gas Produced by Photosynthesis

DO NOT WRITE IN BOOK

Analysis

12. Using information from your graph, describe what happened to the amount of gas in the test tube.

13. How much gas was produced in the test tube after day 5?

14. Write the formula for photosynthesis in your ScienceLog. Explain each of the parts of the formula. For example, what "ingredients" are necessary for photosynthesis to take place? What substances are produced by photosynthesis? What is the gas we cannot live without that is produced by plants as waste?

15. Write a report describing your experiment, your results, and your conclusions.

Going Further

Hydroponics is the growing of plants in nutrient-rich water, without soil. Research hydroponic techniques, and try to grow a plant without soil.

Weepy Weeds

Imagine that you are a scientist trying to find a way to drain an area that is flooded with water polluted with fertilizer. You know that a plant releases water through the stomata in its leaves. As the water evaporates from the leaves, more water is pulled up from the roots through the stem and into the leaves. By this process, called transpiration, water and nutrients are pulled into the plant from the soil. In fact, about 90 percent of the water a plant takes up through it roots is released into the atmosphere as water vapor through transpiration. Your idea is to add plants to the flooded area that will transpire the water but will also take up the fertilizer in their roots.

How much water can a plant take up and release in a certain period of time? In this activity, you will observe the process of transpiration. You will determine the rate of transpiration for one plant stem.

Materials

- coleus or other plant stem cutting
- metric ruler
- 2 test tubes
- test-tube rack
- clock
- graph paper
- water
- glass-marking pen

Procedure

1. In your ScienceLog, make a data table similar to the one below for recording your measurements.

Height of Water in Test Tubes		
Time	Test tube with plant	Test tube without plant
Initial		
After 10 min		
After 20 min		
After 30 min		
After 40 min		
Overnight		

DO NOT WRITE IN BOOK

2. Fill each test tube approximately three-fourths full of water. Place both test tubes in a test-tube rack.

3. Follow your teacher's instructions to obtain your plant stem. Place the plant stem so that it stands upright in one of the test tubes. Your test tubes should look like the ones in the photograph at right.

4. Use the glass-marking pen to mark the water level in each of the test tubes. Be sure you have the plant stem in place in its test tube before you mark the water level. Why is this necessary?

5. Use the metric ruler to measure the height of the water in each test tube. Be sure to hold the test tube level, and measure from the waterline to the bottom of the curve at the bottom of the test tube. Record these measurements in your data table on the row labeled "Initial."

6. Wait 10 minutes, and measure the height of the water in each test tube again. Record these measurements in your data table on the row labeled "After 10 min."

7. Repeat step 6 three more times. Record your measurements in the appropriate row on your data table each time.

8. Wait 24 hours, and measure the height of the water in each test tube. Record these measurements in your data table on the row labeled "Overnight."

9. Using graph paper, construct a graph similar to the one below, plotting only your results from the first day of the experiment. There will be two lines, one for each test tube. Use different colors for each line, and make a key below your graph, as shown in the example below.

Rate of Transpiration

red–test tube without plant
blue–test tube with plant

10. Calculate the rate of transpiration for your plant by using the following operations:

Test tube with plant:
Initial height
− Overnight height
Difference in height of water **(A)**

Test tube without plant:
Initial height
− Overnight height
Difference in height of water **(B)**

Water height difference due to transpiration:
Difference **A**
− Difference **B**
Water lost due to transpiration (in millimeters) in 24 hours

Analysis

11. What was the purpose of the test tube that held only water?

12. What caused the water to go down in the test tube containing the plant stem and water? Did the same thing happen in the test tube with water only? Explain your answer.

13. What was the calculated rate of transpiration per day?

14. Using your graph, compare the rate of transpiration with the rate of evaporation alone in your test tubes.

15. Prepare a presentation of your experiment for your class using your data tables, graphs, and calculations as visual aids.

Going Further

How many leaves did your plant sprigs have? Use this number to estimate what the rate of transpiration might be for a plant with 200 leaves. When you have your answer in millimeters of height in a test tube, pour this amount into a graduated cylinder to measure it in milliliters.

Wet, Wiggly Worms!

Earthworms have been digging in the Earth for more than 100 million years! They live everywhere on Earth except in deserts and on the polar icecaps. They are usually no longer than about 30 cm (1 ft) but have been known to grow 10 times that long! Earthworms fertilize the soil with their waste and loosen the soil when they tunnel through the moist dirt of a garden or lawn. Worms are food for many animals, such as birds, frogs, snakes, rodents, and fish. Some say they are good food for people, too! If someone offers you a casserole of *pois de terre,* be careful. It's full of worms.

In this activity, you will observe the behavior of a live earthworm. Remember that earthworms are living animals that deserve to be handled gently. Be sure to keep your earthworm moist during this activity. The skin of the earthworm must stay moist so that the worm can get oxygen. If the earthworm's skin dries out, the worm will suffocate and die. Use an eyedropper to moisten the earthworm with water.

Materials

- live earthworm
- flashlight
- paper towels
- celery leaves
- dissecting pan
- probe
- soil
- spray bottle
- shoe box
- water
- eyedropper
- poster paper
- colored markers
- metric ruler

Procedure

1. Place a wet paper towel in the bottom of a dissecting pan. Put a live earthworm on the paper towel, and observe how the earthworm moves. Record your observations in your ScienceLog.

2. Use the probe to carefully touch the anterior end (head) of the worm. Gently touch other areas of the worm's body with the probe. Record the kinds of responses you observe.

3. Place celery leaves at one end of the pan. Record how the earthworm responds to the presence of food.

4. Shine a flashlight on the anterior end of the earthworm. Record the earthworm's reaction to the light.

5. Line the bottom of the shoe box with a damp paper towel. Cover half of the shoe box with the box top, and leave the other half uncovered.

6. Place the worm on the uncovered side of the shoe box in the light. Record your observations of the worm's behavior for 3 minutes.

7. Place the worm on the covered side of the box. Record your observations of the worm's behavior for 3 minutes. Steps 6 and 7 should be repeated 3 times. By repeating these steps, you can tell if the worm's behavior might always be the same.

8. Spread some loose soil evenly in the bottom of the shoe box so that it is about 4 cm deep. Place the earthworm on top of the soil. Observe and record the earthworm's behavior for 3 minutes.

9. Dampen the soil on one side of the box, and leave the other side dry. Place the earthworm in the center of the box between the wet and dry soil. Cover the box, and wait 3 minutes. Uncover the box, and record your observations. Repeat this procedure 3 times. Remember to handle the earthworm gently. (You may need to search for the worm!)

Analysis

10. How did the earthworm respond to being touched? Were some areas more sensitive than others? How is the earthworm's behavior influenced by light? Based on your observations, describe how an animal's response to a stimulus might provide protection for the animal.

11. How did the earthworm respond to the presence of food?

12. When the worm was given a choice of wet or dry soil, which did it choose? Explain this result.

Going Further

Based on your observations of an earthworm's behavior, prepare a poster showing where you might expect to find earthworms. Draw a picture with colored markers, or cut out pictures from magazines or other publications. Include all the variables that you used in your experiment, such as soil or no soil, wet or dry soil, light or dark, and food. Write a caption at the bottom of your poster describing where earthworms might be found in nature.

Aunt Flossie and the Bumblebee

Last week Aunt Flossie came to watch the soccer game, but everyone ended up watching her instead. She was being chased by a big yellow-and-black bumblebee. The bee never stung her, but it buzzed around her repeatedly. Everyone tried not to laugh, but Aunt Flossie did look pretty funny. She was running and screaming, all perfumed and dressed in a bright floral dress, shiny jewelry, and a huge hat with a big purple bow. She ran around the bleachers, and when she thought the bee was gone, she sat down until it found her again. No one could understand why the bumblebee tormented Aunt Flossie and left everyone else alone. She said that she would not come to another game until you determine why the bee chased her.

Your job is to design an experiment that will determine why the bee was attracted to Aunt Flossie. You may simulate the situation by using objects that contain the same sensory clues that Aunt Flossie wore that day—bright, shiny colors and strong scents.

Materials

- to be determined by each experimental design and approved by the teacher

SCIENTIFIC METHOD

Ask a Question

1. Use the information in the story above to help you form questions. Make a list of Aunt Flossie's characteristics on the day of the soccer game. What was Aunt Flossie wearing? What do you think she looked like to a bumblebee? What scent was she wearing? Which of those characteristics may have affected the bee's behavior? What was it about Aunt Flossie that affected the bee's behavior?

Form a Hypothesis

2. Write a hypothesis about insect behavior based on your observations of Aunt Flossie and the bumblebee at the soccer game. A possible hypothesis is, "Insects are attracted to strong floral scents." Write your own hypothesis.

Test the Hypothesis

3. Outline a procedure for your experiment. Be sure to follow the steps in the scientific method. Design your procedure to answer specific questions. For example, if you want to know if insects are attracted to different colors, you might want to display cutouts of several colors of paper.

4. Make a list of materials to be used in your experimental design. You may want to include objects of various colors, colored paper, pictures in magazines, or strong perfumes as bait. You may not use living things as bait in your experiment. Your teacher must approve your experimental design before you begin.

5. Determine a place and method for carrying out your procedure. For example, you may want to place things that might attract insects in a box on the ground, or you may want to hang items from a tree branch.
   Caution: Be sure to remain at a safe distance from your experimental setup containing the bait. Do not touch any insects. Have an adult help you release any insects that are trapped or collected.

6. Develop data tables for recording the results of your trials. For example, a data table similar to the one at right may be used to record the results of testing different colors to see which insects are attracted to them. Design your data tables to fit your investigation.

Analyze the Results

7. Describe your experimental procedure. Did your results support your hypothesis? If not, how would you change your experimental procedure?

Communicate Results

8. Write a letter to Aunt Flossie telling her what you have learned about insect behavior. Tell her what you have concluded was the cause of the bee attack. Invite her to attend another soccer game, and advise her about what she should or should not wear!

Effects of Color

Color	Number of bees	Number of ants	Number of wasps
Red			
Blue			
Yellow			

DO NOT WRITE IN BOOK

Porifora's Porosity

Sponges are aquatic invertebrate animals that make up the phylum Porifera. *Porifera* comes from Latin words meaning "pore bearer." Sponges pump water through many tiny pores into their interior. Food for the sponge is filtered out of the water, and then the water leaves through an opening at the top of the sponge.

Early biologists thought sponges were plants because they resemble plants in many ways. For example, the adults attach to a surface and do not move. They cannot chase their food. Sponges absorb and filter a lot of water to get food. In this activity, you will determine how much water sponges are capable of absorbing.

Materials

- natural sponges
- graduated cylinder
- balance
- calculator
- water
- bowl (large enough for sponge and water)
- additional materials as needed

Procedure

1. Estimate how much water your sponge can hold. Write your predictions in your ScienceLog.

2. In your ScienceLog, make any data tables or sketches you may need for recording your observations.

3. Be sure to measure the mass of your sponge before you add water, and record the result. Why do you think this is a necessary step?

4. Get approval from your teacher before you begin your experiment. Perform your experiment, and record your results.

Analysis

5. How many milliliters of water does your sponge hold per gram of sponge tissue? For example, if your sponge has a dry mass of 12 g and it holds 59.1 mL of water, then your sponge holds 4.9 mL of water per gram. (59.1 mL ÷ 12 g)

6. What feeding advantage does a sponge have because of its ability to hold an enormous amount of water?

Going Further

Repeat this experiment using another kind of absorbent material, such as a paper towel or an artificial sponge. How many milliliters of water does this other absorbent material hold per gram? How does it compare with a natural sponge?

The Cricket Caper

Insects are a special class of invertebrates with more than 750,000 known species. Insects may be the most successful group of animals on Earth. In this activity you will observe a cricket's structure and the simple adaptive behaviors that help make it so successful. Remember, you will be handling a living animal that deserves to be treated with care.

Materials

- crickets (2)
- 600 mL beakers (2)
- plastic wrap
- apple
- hand lens (optional)
- masking tape
- aluminum foil
- sealable plastic bags (2)
- lamp
- crushed ice
- hot tap water

Procedure

1. Place a cricket in a clean 600 mL beaker, and quickly cover the beaker with plastic wrap. The supply of oxygen in the container is enough for the cricket to breathe while you complete your work.

2. While the cricket is getting used to the container, make a data table in your ScienceLog similar to the one below. Be sure to allow enough space to write your descriptions.

Cricket Body Structures	
Number	**Description**
Body segments	
Antennae	
Eyes	
Wings	

DO NOT WRITE IN BOOK

3. Without making much movement, begin to examine the cricket. Fill in your data table with your observations of the cricket's structure.

4. Place a small piece of apple in the beaker. Set the beaker on a table. Sit quietly for several minutes and observe the cricket. Any movement will cause the cricket to stop what it is doing. Record your observations in your ScienceLog.

5. Remove the plastic wrap from the beaker, remove the apple, and quickly attach a second beaker. Join the two beakers together at the mouths with masking tape. Handle the beakers carefully. Remember, there is a living animal inside.

6. Wrap one of the joined beakers with aluminum foil.

7. If the cricket is hiding under the aluminum foil, gently tap the sides of the beaker until the cricket is exposed. Lay the joined beakers on their sides, and shine a bright lamp on the uncovered side. Observe the cricket, and record its location.

8. Observe and record the cricket's location after 5 minutes. Without disturbing the cricket, carefully move the aluminum foil to the other beaker. (This should expose the cricket to the light.) After 5 minutes, observe the cricket and record its location. Repeat this process one more time to see if you get the same result.

9. Fill a sealable plastic bag halfway with crushed ice. Fill another bag halfway with hot tap water. Seal each bag, and arrange them side by side on the table.

10. Remove the aluminum foil from the beakers. Gently rock the joined beakers from side to side until the cricket is in the center. Place the joined beakers on the plastic bags, as shown below.

11. Observe the cricket's behavior for 5 minutes. Record your observations in your ScienceLog.

12. Set the beakers on one end for several minutes to allow them to return to room temperature. Then repeat steps 10 and 11. (Why do you think allowing the beakers to return to room temperature is a necessary step?) Perform this test three times, recording your observations in your ScienceLog each time.

13. Set the beakers on one end. Carefully remove the masking tape, and separate the beakers. Quickly replace the plastic wrap over the beaker containing the cricket. Allow your cricket to rest while you make two data tables in your ScienceLog similar to those at right.

14. Observe the cricket's movement in the beaker every 15 seconds for 3 minutes. Fill in the Cricket (alone) data table using the following codes: 0 = no movement, 1 = slight movement, and 2 = rapid movement.

15. Obtain a second cricket from your teacher, and place this cricket in the container with the first cricket. Every 15 seconds, record the movement of each cricket in the Cricket A and Cricket B data table using the codes given in step 14.

Analyze

16. Do crickets prefer light or dark? Explain.

17. From your observations, what can you infer about a cricket's temperature preferences?

18. Describe crickets' feeding behavior. Are they lappers, suckers, or chewers?

19. Based on your observations of Cricket A and Cricket B, what general statements can you make about the social behavior of crickets?

Going Further

Make a third data table titled "Cricket and Another Species of Insect." Introduce another insect, such as a grasshopper, into the beaker. Record your observations for 3 minutes. Write a short summary of the cricket's reaction to another species.

Cricket (alone)	
15 s	
30 s	
45 s	
60 s	
75 s	
90 s	DO NOT WRITE IN BOOK
105 s	
120 s	
135 s	
150 s	
165 s	
180 s	

Cricket A and Cricket B		
	A	B
15 s		
30 s		
45 s		
60 s		
75 s	DO NOT WRITE IN BOOK	
90 s		
105 s		
120 s		
135 s		
150 s		
165 s		
180 s		

Floating a Pipe Fish

Bony fishes control how deep or shallow they can swim in a lake, river, or ocean with a special structure called a swim bladder. By adding or taking away gases in the swim bladder, they can control how their body rises or sinks in the water. In this activity, you will make a model of a fish with a swim bladder. Then, after the fish is ready, your challenge will be to make the fish float in a container of water so that it is halfway between the top of the water and the bottom of the container. It will probably take several tries and a lot of observing and analyzing along the way. Happy "fishing!"

Materials

- 12 cm length of PVC pipe, 3/4 in. diameter
- slender balloon
- small cork
- rubber band
- water
- container for water at least 15 cm deep

Procedure

1. Estimate how much air you will need in the balloon "swim bladder" of your pipe fish so that it will float halfway between the top of the water and the bottom of the container. Will you need to inflate the balloon halfway, just a small amount, or all the way? Remember, it will have to fit inside the pipe, but there will need to be enough air to lift the pipe.

2. Inflate your balloon according to your estimate. While holding the neck of the balloon so that no air escapes, work the cork into the end of the balloon. If the cork is properly placed, no air should leak out when the balloon is held underwater.

3. Place the cork-balloon swim bladder inside the pipe, and place a rubber band along the pipe as shown. The rubber band will keep the swim bladder from coming out of either end.

Cork with balloon attached

Pipe

Rubber band

4. Place your pipe fish in the water, and note where the fish is positioned in the water. Record your observations in your ScienceLog.

5. If the pipe fish does not float where you want it to float, take it out of the water, adjust the amount of air in the balloon, and try again.

6. You can release small amounts of air from the bladder by carefully lifting the neck of the balloon away from the cork. You can add more air by removing the cork and blowing more air into the balloon. Keep adjusting and testing until your fish floats halfway between the bottom of the container and the top of the water.

Analysis

7. Was the estimate you made in step 1 the correct amount of air your balloon needed to float halfway? Explain your answer.

8. In relation to the length and volume of the entire pipe fish, how much air was needed to make the fish float? State your answer in a proportion or percentage.

9. Based on the amount of space the balloon took up inside the pipe in your model, how much space do you estimate is taken up by a swim bladder inside a living fish? Explain.

Going Further

Some fast-swimming fishes, such as sharks, and marine mammals, such as whales and dolphins, do not have a swim bladder. Find out from the library or the Internet how these animals keep from sinking to the bottom of the ocean. Create a poster, and explain your results on 3 × 5 cards. Include drawings on your poster of the fish or marine mammals you have learned about.

A Prince of a Frog

Imagine that you are a scientist interested in amphibians. You have heard in the news about amphibians disappearing all over the world. What a great loss it will be to the environment if all amphibians become extinct. Your job is to learn as much as possible about how frogs normally behave to act as a resource for other scientists who are studying the problem.

In this activity, you will observe a normal live frog in a dry container and in water.

Procedure

1. In your ScienceLog, make a table similar to the one below to note all of your observations of the frog in this investigation.

Materials

- container half-filled with dechlorinated water
- large rock
- live frog in a dry container
- live crickets
- 600 mL beaker
- protective gloves

Observations of a Live Frog	
Characteristic	**Observation**
Breathing	
Eyes	
Legs	
Response to food	
Response to noise	
Skin texture	
Swimming behavior	
Skin coloration	

DO NOT WRITE IN BOOK

2. Observe a live frog in a dry container. Draw the frog in your ScienceLog. Label the eyes, nostrils, front legs, and hind legs.

3. Watch the frog's movements as it breathes air with its lungs. Write a description of the frog's breathing in your ScienceLog.

4. Look closely at the frog's eyes, and note their location. Examine the upper and lower eyelids as well as the transparent third eyelid. Which of these three eyelids actually moves over the eye?

5. Study the frog's legs. Note in your data table the difference between the front and hind legs.

6. Gently tap on the side of the container farthest from the frog, and observe the frog's response.

7. Place a live insect, such as a cricket, in the container. Observe and record how the frog reacts.

8. Wearing gloves and goggles carefully pick up the frog, and examine its skin. How does it feel?
   Caution: Remember that a frog is a living thing and deserves to be handled with respect and gentleness.

9. Place a 600 mL beaker in the container. Place the frog in the beaker. Cover the beaker with your hand, and carry it to a container of dechlorinated water. Tilt the beaker and gently submerge it in the water until the frog swims out of the beaker.

10. Watch the frog float and swim in the water. How does the frog use its legs to swim? Notice the position of the frog's head.

11. As the frog swims, bend down and look up into the water so that you can see the underside of the frog. Then look down on the frog from above. Compare the color on the top and the underneath sides of the frog.

12. Record your observations of the frog's skin texture, swimming behavior, and skin coloration in your data table.

Analysis

13. Use your answers to the questions below to write a report about amphibian anatomy and behavior.

14. From the position of the frog's eyes, what can you infer about the frog's field of vision?

15. How might the position of the frog's eyes benefit the frog while it is swimming?

16. How does a frog hear?

17. How can a frog "breathe" while it is swimming in water?

18. How are the hind legs of a frog adapted for life on land and in water?

19. What differences did you notice in coloration on the frog's top side and its underneath side? What advantage might these color differences provide?

20. How does the frog eat? What senses are involved in helping the frog catch its prey?

Going Further

Observe another type of amphibian, such as a salamander. How do the adaptations of other types of amphibians compare with those of the frog you observed in this investigation?

What? No Dentist Bills?

When you and I eat food, we must chew it well. Our teeth are made for chewing because breaking food down into small bits is the first step in the digestive process. But birds don't have teeth. How do birds make big chunks of food small enough to begin digestion? In this activity, you will design and build a model of a bird's digestive system to find an answer to that question.

Procedure

1. Examine the diagram of a bird's digestive system. Design a model of a bird's digestive system that you can build using the materials provided by your teacher. Include in your model as many of the following parts as possible: esophagus, crop, gizzard, intestine, cloaca.

2. Obtain a plastic bag and the materials you need from your teacher, and build your model.

3. Test your model using the birdseed provided by your teacher.

Analysis

4. How can a bird break down food particles without teeth?

5. Did your bird gizzard grind the food?

6. What are gizzard stones, and what do they do?

7. How full can the gizzard be to work effectively?

8. Describe how you could change your model to make it work better.

Materials

- several sealable plastic bags of various sizes
- birdseed
- aquarium gravel
- water
- string
- drinking straw
- tape
- scissors or other materials as needed

Esophagus

Crop

Gizzard

Cloaca

Intestine

Going Further

Did you know that "gizzard stones" have been found at the sites of fossilized dinosaur skeletons? Look in the library or on the Internet for information about the evolutionary relationship between dinosaurs and birds. List the similarities and differences you find.

Wanted: Mammals on Mars

The year is 2256. There have been colonies on Mars for almost 50 years. Martian water is scarce but available, and temperatures are still extreme but livable. The Martian planet has slowly developed an atmosphere that humans can breathe due to the efforts of many scientists during the last 200 years. The Interplanetary Commission has decreed that mammals from several different habitats on Earth should be sent to Mars. There they will be housed in a zoo so they can become accustomed to the climate before they are released in the wild.

Your job is to prepare a presentation for the Interplanetary Commission that describes at least three mammals that you think might be able to survive in a zoo on Mars. Select one mammal from a water environment, one mammal from a land environment, and one mammal that lives in the air part of the time.

Materials

- colored markers, crayons, pens, or similar drawing equipment
- poster paper, rolls of newsprint, or other drawing paper
- other materials as needed

Procedure

1. Research in the library or on the Internet to obtain information about the Martian environment as it is today. How might an atmosphere change the environment?

2. Research in the library or on the Internet to learn about different species of mammals and their environments on Earth. Use this information to select mammals that you think might be able to live on Mars.

3. Prepare your presentation for the Interplanetary Commission. Your presentation can be a poster, a mural, a diorama, a computer presentation, or any other format that you choose. Make sure your format is approved by your teacher.

Analysis

4. Name and describe the mammals you chose. Explain why you think your choice of mammals would be the right one for a zoo on Mars.

5. Describe what additions or changes should be made at the zoo to accommodate each of your mammals.

Going Further

If the mammals you presented were sent to Mars and eventually released in the wild, what other mammals could be introduced that would compete with them for food, shelter, and other resources?

Life in the Desert

Organisms that live in the desert have some very unusual methods for conserving water. Conserving water is an important function for all organisms that live on land, but it is a special challenge for animals that live in the desert. In this activity you will invent an "adaptation" for a desert animal, represented by a piece of sponge, to find out how much water the animal can conserve over a 24-hour period. You will protect your wet desert sponge so it will dry out as little as possible.

Materials

- 2 pieces of dry sponge (8 × 8 × 2 cm)
- water
- balance
- example profiles of desert plants and animals
- other materials as needed

Procedure

1. Plan a method for keeping your "desert animal" from drying out. Your "animal" must be in the open for at least 4 hours during the 24-hour period. Real desert animals often expose themselves to the dry desert heat in order to search for food. Write your plan in your ScienceLog. Write down your predictions about the outcome of your experiment.

2. Design data tables, if necessary, and draw them in your ScienceLog. Have your teacher approve your plan before you begin.

3. Soak two pieces of sponge in water until they begin to drip. Place each piece on a balance, and record its mass in your ScienceLog.

4. Immediately begin to protect one piece of sponge according to your plan. Place both of the pieces together in an area where they will not be disturbed. You may take your protected "animal" out for feeding as often as you want, for a total of at least 4 hours.

5. At the end of 24 hours, place each piece of sponge on the balance again, and record its mass in your ScienceLog.

Analysis

6. Describe the adaptation you used to help your "animal" survive. Was it effective? Explain.

7. What was the purpose of leaving one of the sponges unprotected? How did the water loss in each of your sponges compare?

Going Further

Conduct a class discussion about other adaptations and results. How can you relate these invented adaptations to adaptations for desert survival among real organisms?

Discovering Mini-Ecosystems

In your study of ecosystems you learned that a biome is a very large ecosystem that includes a set of smaller, related ecosystems. For example, a coniferous forest biome may include a river ecosystem, a wetland ecosystem, and a lake ecosystem. Each of those ecosystems may include several other smaller, related ecosystems. Even cities have mini-ecosystems! You may find a mini-ecosystem on a patch of sidewalk, in a puddle of rainwater, under a leaky faucet, in a shady area, or under a rock. In this activity, you will design a method for comparing two different mini-ecosystems found near your school.

Materials

- paper and pencil for taking notes and making observations
- other materials as needed for each investigation

Procedure

1. Examine the grounds around your school, and select two different areas you wish to investigate. Be sure to get your teacher's approval before you begin.

2. Decide what you want to find out about your mini-ecosystems. For example, you may want to know what kind of living things each area contains. You may want to list the abiotic factors of each mini-ecosystem.

3. For each mini-ecosystem, make data tables for recording your observations. You may choose to observe the mini-ecosystems for an hour. You may choose to observe the mini-ecosystems for a short period of time at several different times during the day or at the same time for several days. Get your plan approved by your teacher, and make the appropriate data tables.

Analysis

4. What factors determine the differences between your mini-ecosystems? Identify the factors that set each mini-ecosystem apart from its surrounding area.

5. How do the populations of your mini-ecosystems compare?

6. Identify some of the adaptations that the organisms living in your two mini-ecosystems have. Describe how the adaptations help the organisms survive in their environment.

7. Write a report describing and comparing your mini-ecosystems with those of your classmates.

Too Much of a Good Thing?

SKILL BUILDER

Plants require nutrients, such as phosphates and nitrates, to survive. Phosphates are often found in detergents. Nitrates are commonly found in animal wastes and in fertilizers. When people release large amounts of these nutrients into rivers and lakes, algae and plant life grow rapidly and then die off and decay. Microorganisms that decompose the algae and plant matter use up oxygen in the water, causing the death of fish and other animals that depend on oxygen for survival. This process often results in a pond or lake filling in unnaturally.

In this activity, you will observe the effect of fertilizers on organisms that live in pond water.

Materials

- 1 qt jars (3)
- wax pencil
- distilled water
- fertilizer
- graduated cylinder
- stirring rod
- pond water containing living organisms
- eyedropper
- microscope
- microscope slides with coverslips
- plastic wrap
- protective gloves

Procedure

1. Use a wax pencil to label one jar "Control," the second jar "Fertilizer," and the third jar "Excess fertilizer."

2. Pour 750 mL of distilled water in each of the three jars. Read the label on the fertilizer container to determine the recommended amount of fertilizer for plants. To the "Fertilizer" jar, add the amount of fertilizer recommended for 1 qt of water or for 1 L of water if the directions are given in metric. To the "Excess fertilizer" jar, add 10 times this amount of fertilizer to 1 qt of water. Stir the contents of each jar thoroughly to dissolve the fertilizer.

3. Obtain a sample of pond water. Stir it gently but thoroughly to make sure that the organisms in it are evenly distributed. Pour 100 mL of pond water into each of the three jars.

4. Observe a drop of pond water from each jar under the microscope. In your ScienceLog, draw at least four of the organisms that you see. Determine whether the organisms you see are algae, which are usually green, or consumers, which are usually able to move. Describe the number and type of organisms that you see.

5. Cover each jar loosely with plastic wrap. Place all three jars in a well-lit location near a sunny window. Do not place the jars in direct sunlight.

Common Pond-Water Organisms

Volvox (producer)

Spirogyra (producer)

Vorticella (consumer)

Daphnia (consumer)

620 Chapter 17 LabBook

6. Based on your understanding of how ponds and lakes eventually fill in to become dry land, make a prediction about how the pond organisms will grow in each of the three jars.

7. Make three data tables in your ScienceLog. Be sure to allow enough space to record your observations. Title one table "Control," as shown below. Title another table "Fertilizer," and title the third table "Excess fertilizer."

Control			
Date	**Color**	**Odor**	**Other observations**

DO NOT WRITE IN BOOK

8. Observe the jars when you first set them up and at least once every 3 days for the next 3 weeks. Note the color, odor, and any visible presence of life-forms. Record your observations in your data tables.

9. When life-forms begin to be visible in the jars, use an eyedropper to remove a sample of organisms from each jar, and observe the sample under the microscope. How have the number and type of organisms changed from when you first looked at the pond water? Record your observations in the data tables under "Other observations."

10. At the end of your 3-week observation period, once again remove a sample from each jar and observe each sample under the microscope. In your ScienceLog, draw at least four of the most abundant organisms and describe how the number and type of organisms have changed since your last microscopic observation.

Analysis

11. After 3 weeks, which jar shows the most abundant growth of algae? What may have caused this growth?

12. Did you observe any effects on organisms (other than the algae) in the jar with the most abundant algal growth? Explain.

13. Did your observations match your prediction? Explain.

14. How might the rapid filling of natural ponds and lakes be prevented or slowed?

Biodiversity—What a Disturbing Thought!

Biodiversity refers to the number of different species living together in a community. This diversity is important for the survival of each organism in each population in the community. Biodiversity refers not only to the diversity of organisms themselves but also to the diversity of their niches and habitats. Producers, consumers, and decomposers all play a cooperative role in an ecosystem, and each species occupies a niche.

Which do you think is more diverse, a forest or an area cleared and replanted with crops? In this activity you will investigate areas outside your school to determine which areas contain the greatest biodiversity. You will use the information you gathered to determine whether a forest or an area planted with crops is more diverse.

Materials

- materials and tools necessary to carry out your investigation with your teacher's approval. Possible materials include a meterstick, binoculars, magnifying lens, twine, and forceps.

Procedure

1. Select an area that is highly disturbed (such as a mowed yard or a well-kept flower bed) and one that is relatively undisturbed or less disturbed (such as an abandoned flower bed or a vacant lot). Make a prediction about which area contains the greater biodiversity. Get your teacher's approval of the locations you have selected.

2. Design a procedure to determine which area contains the greatest biodiversity, and have your plan approved by your teacher before you begin. To discover the smaller organisms, measure off a 1 m² area, set stakes at the corners, and mark the area with twine. Inside the area, use a magnifying lens to observe tiny creepers and crawlers. Don't worry about knowing scientific names of organisms. When you record your observations in your ScienceLog, for example, refer to organisms in the following way: Ant A, Ant B, and so on. Observe each area quietly, and make note of any visits by birds or other larger organisms.

3. In your ScienceLog, create any data tables that you might need for recording your data. If you observe your areas on more than one occasion, be sure to make data tables for each observation period. Organize your data into categories that are clear and understandable.

Analysis

4. Did your data confirm your prediction about the difference in biodiversity between a forest and a field of crops? Explain.

5. What factors did you consider before deciding which habitats outside your school were disturbed or undisturbed? Why were those factors important? Explain.

6. What problems did you find most difficult about making observations and recording data for each habitat? Describe how you solved them.

7. Describe possible errors in your investigation method. Suggest ways to improve your procedure to eliminate those errors.

8. Do you think the biodiversity outside your school has decreased since the school was built? Why or why not?

9. Both areas shown in the photographs at right have growing, healthy plants and are beautiful to observe. One of them, however, is very low in biodiversity. Describe what you see in each photograph, and account for the difference in biodiversity.

Going Further

The tropical rain forest is thought to have the greatest biodiversity of any biome on Earth. Research rain-forest biodiversity in the library or on the Internet. Find out what factors exist in the rain forest that make that biome so diverse. How might the biodiversity of a rain forest compare with that of a forest community near where you live?

Prairie grasses and wildflowers

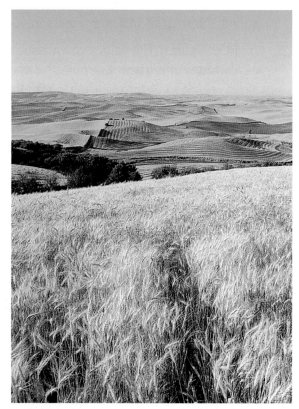
Wheat field

Deciding About Environmental Issues

You make hundreds of decisions every day. Some of them are complicated, but many of them are very simple, such as what to wear or what to eat for lunch. Deciding what to do about an environmental issue can be very difficult. There are many different factors that must be considered. How will a certain solution affect people's lives? How much will it cost? Is it ethically right?

In this activity you will analyze an issue in four steps to help you make a decision about it. Find out about environmental issues that are being discussed in your area. Examine newspapers, magazines, agency publications, and other publications to find out what the issues are. Choose one local issue to evaluate. For example, you could evaluate whether the city should spend the money to provide recycling bins and special trucks for picking up recyclable trash.

Materials

- newspapers, magazines, and other publications containing information about environmental issues

A Four-Step Decision-Making Model

Gather Information

↓

Consider Values

↓

Explore Consequences

↓

Make a Decision

Procedure

1. In your ScienceLog, write a statement about an environmental issue.

2. **Gather information.** Read about your issue in several publications. Summarize important facts in your ScienceLog.

3. **Consider values.** The values of an issue are the things that you consider important. Examine the diagram below. Several values are given. Which values do you think apply most to the environmental issue you are considering? Are there other values that you believe will help you make a decision about the issue? Choose at least four values that you want to consider in making your decision.

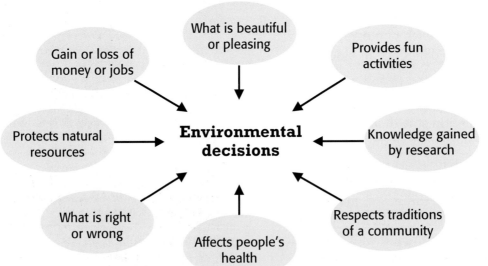

4. **Explore consequences.** Consequences are the things that happen as a result of a certain course of action. In your ScienceLog, create a table similar to the one below. Use your table to organize your thoughts about consequences related to the values of your environmental issue. List your values at the top. Fill in each space with the consequences for each value.

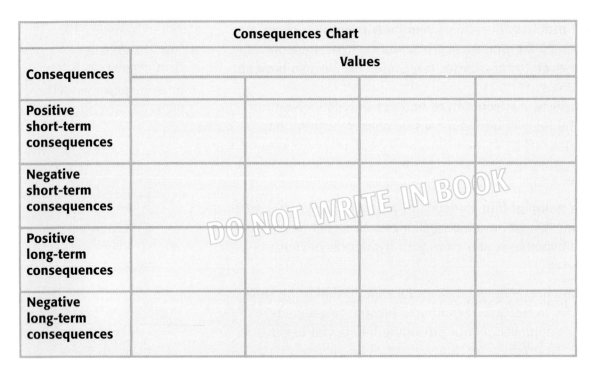

Consequences Chart				
Consequences	**Values**			
Positive short-term consequences				
Negative short-term consequences				
Positive long-term consequences				
Negative long-term consequences				

DO NOT WRITE IN BOOK

5. **Make a decision.** Thoroughly consider all of the consequences you have recorded in your table. Evaluate how important each consequence is. Make a decision about what course of action you would choose on the issue.

Analysis

6. In your evaluation, did you consider short-term consequences or long-term consequences to be more important? Why?

7. Which value or values had the greatest influence on your final decision? Explain your reasoning.

Going Further

Compare your decision-making table with your classmates' tables. Did you all make the same decision about a similar issue? If not, form teams, and organize a formal classroom debate of a specific environmental issue.

Muscles at Work

Have you ever exercised outside on a cold fall day wearing only a thin warm-up suit or shorts? How did you stay warm? The answer is that your muscle cells contracted, and when contraction takes place, some energy is used to do work and the rest is released in the form of heat. This heat helps your body maintain a constant temperature in cold conditions. When you exercise strenuously on a hot summer day, your muscles can cause your body to become overheated.

In this activity, it is your job to find out how the release of energy in the form of heat can cause a change in your body temperature.

Materials

- clock with a second hand or a stopwatch
- small hand-held thermometer
- other materials as approved by your teacher

Procedure

1. Form a group of four students. In your group, discuss several exercises that can produce a change in body temperature. Form a hypothesis, and write your hypothesis in your ScienceLog.

2. Develop an experimental procedure that includes the steps necessary to test your hypothesis. Be sure to get your teacher's approval of your procedure before you begin.

3. Assign tasks to individuals in the group, such as note taking, data recording, and timing. What observations and data will you be recording? Design your data tables in your ScienceLog accordingly.

4. Perform your experiment as planned by your group. Be sure to record all observations made during the experiment in your data tables.

Analysis

5. How did you determine if muscle contractions cause the release of energy as heat? Was your hypothesis supported by your data? Explain your results in a written report. Describe how you could improve your experimental method.

Going Further

Why do humans shiver in the cold? Do all animals shiver? Find out why shivering is one of the first signs that your body is becoming too cold.

Seeing Is Believing

How many times have you seen those advertisements that say "Set of Nails—$25.00," "Tips—$15.00," or "Fill-in—$10.00"? Have you wondered why people pay to have their nails "done"? Regardless of what these advertisements may imply, human nails will grow on their own without expensive treatment. Fingernails are part of your body's integumentary system, which includes the skin that covers your entire body. Nails are a modification of the outer layer of the skin, and they grow continuously throughout your life.

In this activity, you will measure the time it takes for fingernails to grow.

Materials

- permanent marker
- metric ruler
- graph paper (optional)

Procedure

1. In your ScienceLog, use a pencil to trace around each of your hands. Then fill in some of the details, such as the fingernails, which are shown below. Choose one of the fingers you have drawn, and label the parts of the fingernail, as shown at right. Notice that the nail bed is the area where the nail is attached to the finger. The illustration shows a cutaway view so you can see how far inside your finger your fingernail begins.

Left hand   Right hand

2. With your lab partner, take turns measuring the length of each of your fingernails on both hands. Start with your thumb, measuring the distance from the skin at the base of your nail to where the free edge of the fingernail begins. Record the measurement of each nail on your hand drawings in metric units.

Mark

Base of nail

3. Find the center of the nail bed on your right index finger (the finger next to your thumb). Make a mark with the permanent marker on the center of your nail bed, as shown at right. **Caution:** Do not get the permanent marker ink on your clothing. Measure from the mark to the base of your nail. Record this measurement on your hand drawing. Label this measurement "Day 1."

4. Repeat step 3 for your left index finger. Then switch roles with your lab partner.

5. Let your fingernails grow for 2 days including today. Normal, daily activity, such as washing your hands, will not wash away the stain completely. You may need to freshen the mark periodically throughout this lab.

6. After 2 days, measure the distance from the mark on your nail to the base of your nail. Record this distance in metric units on your hand drawing. Label this measurement "Day 3."

7. Continue measuring and recording the growth of your nails every other day for 2 weeks. Refresh the stain mark as necessary. You may continue to file or trim your nails as usual throughout this lab.

8. After you have completed your measurements and recorded them on your hand drawings, prepare a graph similar to the one below to display your findings. Each lab partner will graph his or her own measurements.

Fingernail Growth

Amount of growth (mm) vs. Time allowed for growth (days)

Left index finger
Right index finger

Analysis

9. Which hand had the fastest growing nail? Write two possible explanations for why one fingernail might grow faster than another.

10. Who has the fastest growing nails among your classmates? Who has the slowest growing nails? What is the difference in the total nail growth between these two students?

11. Among your classmates, is there a relationship between nail-growth rates for males and nail-growth rates for females? Is there a relationship between nail growth and other physical characteristics, such as height?

Going Further

Do some research in the library or on the Internet to find answers to the following:

• How are nails important to you? What do they help you do? Give at least three examples to support your findings.

• Are your fingernails an indication of your health or state of nutrition?

Design an experiment to discover the rate of hair growth. How does the rate of hair growth compare to the rate of fingernail growth? Check your experimental design with your teacher before starting your investigation.

Build a Lung

You have learned that when you breathe, you actually pull air into your lungs because your diaphragm muscle causes your chest to expand. You can see this is true by placing your hands on your ribs and inhaling slowly. Did you feel your chest expand?

In this activity, you will build a model of a lung using some common materials. You will see how the diaphragm muscle works to inflate your lungs. Refer to the diagrams at right as you construct your model.

Materials

- top half of a 2 L bottle
- small balloon
- plastic drinking straw
- golf-ball-sized piece of clay
- small plastic trash bag
- 2 rubber bands
- metric ruler
- tape

Procedure

1. Attach the balloon to the end of the straw with a rubber band. Make a hole through the clay, and insert the other end of the straw through the hole. Be sure at least 8 cm of the straw extends beyond the clay. Squeeze the ball of clay gently to seal the clay around the straw.

2. Insert the balloon end of the straw into the neck of the bottle. Use the ball of clay to seal the straw and balloon into the bottle.

3. Turn the bottle gently on its side. Place the trash bag over the cut end of the bottle. Expand a rubber band around the bottom of the bottle to secure the plastic over the end. You may wish to reinforce the seal with tape. Before the plastic is completely sealed, gather the excess material of the bag into your hand, and press toward the inside of the bottle slightly. (You may need to tie a knot about halfway up from the bottom of the bag to take up excess material.) Use tape to finish sealing the bag to the bottle with the bag in this position. This will push the excess air out of the bottle.

Analysis

4. What can you do with your model to make the "lung" inflate?

5. What do the balloon, the plastic wrap, and the straw represent in your model?

6. Using your model, demonstrate to the class how air enters the lung and how air exits the lung.

Going Further

Do some research to find out what an "iron lung" is and why it was used in the past. Find out what is used today to help people who have difficulty breathing.

Carbon Dioxide Breath

Plants take in carbon dioxide and give off oxygen as a byproduct of photosynthesis. Animals, including you, use this oxygen and release carbon dioxide as a byproduct of respiration.

In this activity, you will explore your own carbon dioxide exhalation. The solution you will use—phenol red—turns yellow in the presence of carbon dioxide. You will use it to detect the presence of carbon dioxide in your breath.

Materials

- water
- 150 mL beaker
- 100 mL graduated cylinder
- plastic drinking straw
- phenol red indicator solution
- eyedropper
- clock with a second hand or a stopwatch
- protective gloves

Procedure

1. Put on your gloves, apron, and goggles, and wear them until you complete the lab.

2. Place 100 mL of water into a 150 mL beaker. Using an eye-dropper, carefully place 4 drops of phenol red indicator solution into the water. The phenol red should turn the water orange.

3. Place a plastic drinking straw into the solution of phenol red and water. Carefully blow through the straw into the solution. Drape a paper towel over the beaker to prevent splashing. **Caution:** Do not inhale through the straw. Do not drink the solution. Do not share a straw with anyone.

4. Have your lab partner or another classmate time how long it takes for the solution to change color. Your partner should begin timing when you start blowing. Record this number in your ScienceLog. What color does the solution become?

Analysis

5. Compare your data with those of your classmates. What was the longest length of time it took to see a color change in the phenol red solution? What was the shortest length of time? How do you account for the difference?

6. Is there a relationship between the length of time it takes to change the solution from orange to yellow and the tester's physical characteristics, such as gender or whether the tester has an athletic build?

Going Further

Do jumping jacks or sit-ups for 3 minutes, and then repeat the experiment. Did the timing change? Describe and explain any change.

You've Gotta Lotta Nerve!

Your skin has thousands of nerve receptors that detect sensations, such as heat, cold, and pressure. Your brain is designed to filter out or ignore most of the input it receives from these skin receptors. If that were not the case, simply wearing clothes would trigger so many responses that we couldn't function.

Some areas of the skin, such as the back of your hand, are more sensitive than others. In this activity, you will map the receptors for heat, cold, and pressure on the back of your hand.

Materials

- fine-point washable pens or markers
- metric ruler
- dissecting pin with a small piece of cork or a small rubber stopper stuck on the sharp end
- hot tap water
- very cold water
- eyedropper
- graph paper

Procedure

1. Form groups of three. One of you will volunteer the back of your hand to be tested, one will do the testing, and the third will record the results. Check with your teacher to see if you may switch roles so each of you may play each part.

2. Use a fine-point washable marker or pen and a metric ruler to mark off a 3 × 3 cm square on the back of your partner's hand. Draw a grid within the area, spacing the lines approximately 0.5 cm apart. You will have 36 squares in the grid when you are finished. Examine the photograph below to make sure you have drawn the grid correctly.

3. Mark off three 3 × 3 cm areas on the graph paper. Make a grid in each area exactly as you did on the back of your partner's hand. Label one grid area "Cold," another grid area "Hot," and the third grid area "Pressure."

4. Begin locating receptors in a corner of the grid on your partner's hand. Your partner should not look while his or her hand is being tested! How do you think your partner's looking might influence your results? Use the eye-dropper to apply one small droplet of cold water on each square in the grid. Mark an X on the graph paper in the square that corresponds to where the sensation of cold was felt on the hand. You will need to carefully blot the water off the grid after several drops.

5. Repeat the test using hot-water droplets. The water will cool enough as it drops from the eyedropper so that it will not hurt you. Again mark an X on the graph paper grid to indicate where the sensation of heat was felt on the hand.

6. Repeat the test one more time. This time use the head—not the point!—of the pin to touch the skin to detect pressure receptors. Use a very light touch. Mark an X on the graph-paper grid to indicate where pressure was felt on the hand.

Analysis

7. Count the number of Xs in each grid. How many heat receptors are there per 3 cm^2? How many cold receptors? How many pressure receptors?

8. Do you have areas on the back of your hand where the receptors overlap? Why or why not?

9. How do you think the results of this experiment would be similar or different if you mapped an area of your forearm? the back of your neck? the palm of your hand?

10. Prepare a written report that includes a description of your scientific investigation and a discussion of the questions in the Analysis section of this lab.

Going Further
Find out from your school library or the Internet what happens if a receptor is continuously stimulated. Does it make a difference what kind of receptor it is? Does it make a difference how intense the stimulation is? Explain.

It's a Comfy, Safe World!

Before human babies are born, they have a comfy life. During the third trimester, they just lie around inside their mom, sucking their thumb, blinking their eyes, and perhaps even dreaming. Just how well protected is a baby? Baby birds live inside a hard protective shell until the baby has used up all the food supply. But most mammal moms have soft abdomens where their babies grow, surrounded by fluid and a placenta inside the uterus, a strong muscular organ. Is the internal environment in a placental mammal safer than a baby bird's environment? In this activity your job is to create a model of a placental mammal's uterus and test its effectiveness in protecting a fetus.

Materials

- sealable plastic bags
- soft-boiled chicken eggs, half of them peeled
- water
- mineral oil, cooking oil, syrup, or other thick liquid to represent fluid surrounding the fetus
- cotton, soft fabric, or other soft materials

Procedure

1. Brainstorm several ideas about how you will construct and test your model mammalian uterus. Obtain materials from your teacher, and build your model. A peeled, soft-boiled egg will represent the fetus in your mammalian model.

2. Make a data table similar to the First Model Test at top right in your ScienceLog. Test your model, examine the egg for damage, and record your results.

3. Modify your design as necessary, retest, and record your results. Use the same test you used in step 2.

4. When you are satisfied with the design of your model, obtain another peeled, soft-boiled egg and an egg in the shell.

5. Make another data table in your ScienceLog similar to the Final Model Test at right. Subject your model and the boiled egg in a shell to the same test as in step 2. Record your results in your data table.

First Model Test	
Original model	**Modified model**
	DO NOT WRITE IN BOOK

Final Model Test	
	Test Results
Model	
Egg in shell	DO NOT WRITE IN BOOK

Analysis

6. Explain any differences that you observed in the ability of the model and the egg in a shell to protect the fetus inside.

7. What modification to your model was the most effective in protecting your fetus?

Going Further

Compare the development of placental mammals with that of marsupial mammals and monotremes.

My, How You've Grown!

For human babies, the process of development that takes place between fertilization and birth lasts about 266 days. The new individual grows rapidly from a single fertilized cell to an embryo whose heart is beating and pumping blood in 4 weeks. All of the baby's organ systems and body parts are completely formed by the end of the seventh month. During the last 2 months before birth, the baby grows and its organ systems mature. At birth, the average mass of a newborn baby is about 33,000 times as much as that of an embryo at 2 weeks of development! In this activity you will discover just how fast a fetus grows in a little less than 9 months.

Materials

- graph paper
- colored pencils

Procedure

1. Using graph paper, make two graphs—one titled "Length" and one titled "Mass"—in your ScienceLog. On the length graph, use intervals of 25 mm on the y-axis. Extend the y-axis to 500 mm. On the mass graph, use intervals of 100 g on the y-axis. Extend this y-axis to 3,300 g. Use 2 week intervals for time on the x-axes for both graphs. Both x-axes should extend to 40 weeks.

2. Examine the data table at right. Plot the data in the table on your graphs. Use a colored pencil to draw the curved line that joins the points on each graph.

Analysis

3. Describe the change in mass of a developing fetus. How can you explain this change?

4. Describe the change in length of a developing fetus. How does the change in mass compare to the change in length?

Increase of Mass and Length of Average Human Fetus		
Time (wks)	Mass (g)	Length (mm)
2	0.1	1.5
3	0.3	2.3
4	0.5	5.0
5	0.6	10.0
6	0.8	15.0
8	1.0	30.0
13	15.0	90.0
17	115.0	140.0
21	300.0	250.0
26	950.0	320.0
30	1,500.0	400.0
35	2,300.0	450.0
40	3,300.0	500.0

Going Further

Using the information in your graphs, estimate how tall a child would be at age 3 if he or she continued to grow at the average rate that a fetus grows.

Self-Check Answers

Chapter 1—The World of Life Science

Page 12: 2. Insecticides and fertilizers caused the frog deformities.

Page 15: Jar C is the control group.

Chapter 2—It's Alive!! Or, Is It?

Page 37: Your alarm clock is a stimulus. It rings, and you respond by shutting it off and getting out of bed.

Chapter 3—Light and Living Things

Page 62: The paper will appear blue because only blue light is reflected off the paper.

Page 68: a. the pupil b. the cornea and the lens c. the retina

Chapter 4—Cells: The Basic Units of Life

Page 87: Cells need DNA to control cell processes and to make new cells.

Page 90: 1. The surface-to-volume ratio decreases as the cell size increases. 2. A eukaryotic cell has a nucleus and membrane-covered organelles.

Page 94: Cell walls surround the cell membranes of some cells. All cells have cell membranes, but not all cells have cell walls. Cell walls give structure to some cells.

Chapter 5—The Cell in Action

Page 109: In pure water, the grape would absorb water and swell up. In water mixed with a large amount of sugar, the grape would lose water and shrink.

Page 117: After duplication, there are four chromatids—two from each of the homologous chromosomes.

Chapter 6—Heredity

Page 141: 1. four 2. two 3. They make copies of themselves once. They divide twice. 4. Two, or half the number of chromosomes in the parent, are present at the end of meiosis. After mitosis, there would be four chromosomes, the same number as in the parent cell. 5. The homologous chromosomes separate first.

Chapter 7—Genes and Gene Technology

Page 155: TGGATCAAC

Page 161: 1. 1000 amino acids 2. DNA codes for proteins. Your flesh is composed of proteins, and the way those proteins are constructed and combined influences much about the way you look.

Page 166: The human gene for a particular protein can be inserted into bacteria that can use the gene to produce the needed protein very rapidly and in great quantities. In this way, bacteria are living factories.

Chapter 8—The Evolution of Living Things

Page 191: 1. b 2. a 3. d 4. c

Chapter 9—The History of Life on Earth

Page 205: 5 g, 2.5 g

Page 211: b, c, d, a

Chapter 10—Classification

Page 236: 1. The two kingdoms of bacteria are different from all other kingdoms because bacteria are prokaryotes—single-celled organisms that have no nucleus. 2. The organisms in the kingdom Protista are all eukaryotes.

Chapter 11—Introduction to Plants

Page 252: Plants need a cuticle to keep the leaves from drying out. Algae grow in a wet environment, so they do not need a cuticle.

Page 256: Water transport is very limited for nonvascular plants. They have to stay low to the ground in order to have contact with moisture and soil nutrients. Vascular plants have xylem and phloem to transport nutrients and water throughout the plant; therefore, they can grow to be larger.

Page 268: Stems hold up the leaves so that the leaves can get adequate sunshine for photosynthesis.

Chapter 12—Plant Processes

Page 281: Fruit develops from the ovary, so it can have only one fruit. Seeds develop from the ovules, so there should be six seeds.

Page 285: The sun is the source of the energy in sugar.

Page 288: 1. (See concept map to the right.) 2. During negative phototropism, the plant would grow away from the stimulus (light), so it would be growing to the left.

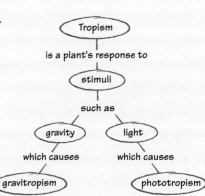

Chapter 13—Animals and Behavior

Page 306: Like other vertebrates, humans have a skull and a backbone.

Page 312: Hibernation is not controlled by a circadian rhythm. Circadian rhythms are daily cycles. Hibernation is a seasonal behavior.

Chapter 14—Invertebrates

Page 331: Because medusas swim through the water by contracting their bodies, they must have a nervous system that can control these actions. Polyps move very little, so they don't need as complex a nervous system.

Page 341: Segmented worms belong to the phylum Annelida. Centipedes are arthropods. Centipedes have jointed legs, antennae, and mandibles. Segmented worms do not.

Chapter 15—Fishes, Amphibians, and Reptiles

Page 366: Amphibians use their skin to absorb oxygen from the air. Their skin is thin, moist, and full of blood vessels, just like a lung.

Page 371: 1. Thick, dry skin and amniotic eggs help reptiles live on dry land. 2. The hard shell prevents fertilization, so the egg must be fertilized before the shell is added.

Chapter 16—Birds and Mammals

Page 384: 1. Down feathers are not stiff and smooth and could not give structure to the wings; they are adapted to keep the bird warm. 2. Birds need tremendous amounts of food for fuel because it takes a lot of energy to fly.

Page 398: Monotremes are mammals that lay eggs. Marsupials bear live young but carry them in pouches or skin folds before they are able to live independently. Placentals develop inside the mother's body and are nourished through a placenta before birth.

Page 403: 1. Bats bear live young, have fur, and do not have feathers. 2. Rodents and lagomorphs both are small mammals with long sensitive whiskers and gnawing teeth. Lagomorphs have two sets of incisors and a short tail.

Chapter 17—The Earth's Ecosystems

Page 421: Deciduous forests tend to exist in mid-latitude or temperate regions, while coniferous forests tend to exist in northern areas, closer to the poles.

Page 426: Answers include: the amount of sunlight penetrating the water, its distance from land, the depth of the water, the salinity of the water, and the water's temperature. 2. There are several possible answers. Some organisms are adapted for catching prey at great depths, some feed on dead plankton and larger organisms that filter down from above, and some, such as the bacteria around thermal vents, make food from chemicals in the water.

Chapter 18—Environmental Problems and Solutions

Page 443: 1. We use nonrenewable resources when we burn fossil fuels when driving or riding in a car or burning coal for heat. When we use minerals that are mined from soil, we are using a nonrenewable resource. The pumping of ground water can also be the use of a nonrenewable resource, if the water is used faster than it is replenished. 2. If a nonrenewable resource is used up, we can no longer rely on that resource to provide something the Earth needs. Certain oil and coal deposits have been building since life began on the planet. It may take hundreds of years to replace a mature forest that can be clear-cut in a day.

Page 449: 1. Turn off lights, CD players, radios, and computers when leaving a room. Set thermostats a little lower in the winter (wear sweaters). Don't stand in front of an open refrigerator while deciding what you want. 2. plastic bags, rechargeable batteries, water, clothing, toys; The difference between reuse and recycle is that a reused article may be cleaned but is basically unchanged. A recycled article has been broken down and re-formed into another usable product.

Chapter 19—Body Organization and Structure

Page 474: Curl-ups use flexor muscles; push-ups use extensor muscles.

Page 477: Blood vessels belong to the cardiovascular system.

Chapter 20—Circulation and Respiration

Page 492: The hollow tube shape of arteries and veins allows blood to reach all parts of the body. Valves in the veins prevent blood from flowing backward.

Page 496: Like blood vessels, lymph capillaries receive fluid from the spaces surrounding cells. The fluid absorbed by lymph capillaries flows into lymph vessels. These vessels drain into large neck veins instead of into an organ, such as the heart. Lymph does not deliver oxygen and nutrients.

Chapter 21—Communication and Control

Page 515: 1. cerebrum 2. cerebellum 3. to protect the spinal cord

Chapter 22—Reproduction and Development

Page 535: In asexual reproduction, one animal produces offspring that are genetically identical to itself. In sexual reproduction, usually the genes of at least two individuals are mixed when sex cells join to form a zygote. This zygote develops into a unique individual.

Page 543: 1. The embryo is nourished by the placenta. Blood vessels inside the umbilical cord absorb oxygen and nutrients from the mother's blood vessels. 2. The uterus provides the nutrients and protection that the embryo needs to continue growing. The uterus is also the only place the placenta will form.

CONTENTS

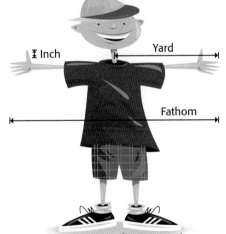

APPENDIX

Concept Mapping: A Way to Bring Ideas Together

What Is a Concept Map?

Have you ever tried to tell someone about a book or a chapter you've just read and found that you can remember only a few isolated words and ideas? Or maybe you've memorized facts for a test, and then weeks later discover you're not even sure what topics those facts cover.

In both cases, you may have understood the ideas or concepts by themselves but not in relation to one another. If you could somehow link the ideas together, you would probably understand them better and remember them longer. This is something a concept map can help you do. A concept map is a way to see how ideas or concepts fit together. It can help you see the "big picture."

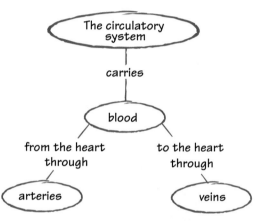

How to Make a Concept Map

1 Make a list of the main ideas or concepts.

It might help to write each concept on its own slip of paper. This will make it easier to rearrange the concepts as many times as necessary to make sense of how the concepts are connected. After you've made a few concept maps this way, you can go directly from writing your list to actually making the map.

2 Spread out the slips on a sheet of paper, and arrange the concepts in order from the most general to the most specific.

Put the most general concept at the top and circle it. Ask yourself, "How does this concept relate to the remaining concepts?" As you see the relationships, arrange the concepts in order from general to specific.

3 Connect the related concepts with lines.

4 On each line, write an action word or short phrase that shows how the concepts are related.

Look at the concept maps on this page, and then see if you can make one for the following terms:

plants, water, photosynthesis, carbon dioxide, sun's energy

One possible answer is provided at right, but don't look at it until you try the concept map yourself.

SI Measurement

The International System of Units, or SI, is the standard measuring system for most scientists. Using the same standards of measurement makes it easier for scientists to communicate with one another.

SI works by combining prefixes and base units. Each base unit can be used with different prefixes to define smaller and larger quantities. The table below lists common SI prefixes.

SI Prefixes

Prefix	Abbreviation	Factor	Example
kilo-	k	1,000	kilogram, 1 kg = 1,000 g
hecto-	h	100	hectoliter, 1 hL = 100 L
deka-	da	10	dekameter, 1 dam = 10 m
		1	meter, liter
deci-	d	0.1	decigram, 1 dg = 0.1 g
centi-	c	0.01	centimeter, 1 cm = 0.01 m
milli-	m	0.001	milliliter, 1 mL = 0.001 L
micro-	µ	0.000001	micrometer, 1 µm = 0.000 001 m

SI Conversion Table

SI units	From SI to English	From English to SI
Length		
kilometer (km) = 1,000 m	1 km = 0.621 mi	1 mi = 1.609 km
meter (m) = 100 cm	1 m = 3.281 ft	1 ft = 0.305 m
centimeter (cm) = 0.01 m	1 cm = 0.394 in.	1 in. = 2.540 cm
millimeter (mm) = 0.001 m	1 mm = 0.039 in.	
micrometer (µm) = 0.000 001 m		
nanometer (nm) = 0.000 000 001 m		
Area		
square kilometer (km^2) = 100 hectares	1 km^2 = 0.386 mi^2	1 mi^2 = 2.590 km^2
hectare (ha) = 10,000 m^2	1 ha = 2.471 acres	1 acre = 0.405 ha
square meter (m^2) = 10,000 cm^2	1 m^2 = 10.765 ft^2	1 ft^2 = 0.093 m^2
square centimeter (cm^2) = 100 mm^2	1 cm^2 = 0.155 $in.^2$	1 $in.^2$ = 6.452 cm^2
Volume		
liter (L) = 1,000 mL = 1 dm^3	1 L = 1.057 fl qt	1 fl qt = 0.946 L
milliliter (mL) = 0.001 L = 1 cm^3	1 mL = 0.034 fl oz	1 fl oz = 29.575 mL
microliter (µL) = 0.000 001 L		
Mass		
kilogram (kg) = 1,000 g	1 kg = 2.205 lb	1 lb = 0.454 kg
gram (g) = 1,000 mg	1 g = 0.035 oz	1 oz = 28.349 g
milligram (mg) = 0.001 g		
microgram (µg) = 0.000 001 g		

Temperature Scales

Temperature can be expressed with three different scales: Fahrenheit, Celsius, and Kelvin. The SI unit for temperature is the kelvin (K).

Although 0 K is much colder than 0°C, a change of 1 K is equal to a change of 1°C.

Three Temperature Scales

	Fahrenheit	Celsius	Kelvin
Water boils	212°	100°	373
Body temperature	98.6°	37°	310
Room temperature	68°	20°	293
Water freezes	32°	0°	273

Temperature Conversions Table

To convert	Use this equation:	Example
Celsius to Fahrenheit °C ⟶ °F	$°F = \left(\dfrac{9}{5} \times °C\right) + 32$	Convert 45°C to °F. $°F = \left(\dfrac{9}{5} \times 45°C\right) + 32 = 113°F$
Fahrenheit to Celsius °F ⟶ °C	$°C = \dfrac{5}{9} \times (°F - 32)$	Convert 68°F to °C. $°C = \dfrac{5}{9} \times (68°F - 32) = 20°C$
Celsius to Kelvin °C ⟶ K	$K = °C + 273$	Convert 45°C to K. $K = 45°C + 273 = 318\ K$
Kelvin to Celsius K ⟶ °C	$°C = K - 273$	Convert 32 K to °C. $°C = 32\ K - 273 = -241°C$

APPENDIX

Measuring Skills

Using a Graduated Cylinder

When using a graduated cylinder to measure volume, keep the following procedures in mind:

1 Make sure the cylinder is on a flat, level surface.

2 Move your head so that your eye is level with the surface of the liquid.

3 Read the mark closest to the liquid level. On glass graduated cylinders, read the mark closest to the center of the curve.

Using a Meterstick or Metric Ruler

When using a meterstick or metric ruler, keep the following procedures in mind:

1 Place the ruler firmly against the object you are measuring.

2 Align one edge of the object exactly with the zero end of the ruler.

3 Look at the other edge of the object to see which of the marks on the ruler is closest to that edge. **Note:** Each small slash between the centimeters represents a millimeter, which is one-tenth of a centimeter.

Using a Triple-Beam Balance

When using a triple-beam balance, keep the following procedures in mind:

1 Make sure the balance is on a level surface.

2 Place all of the countermasses at zero. Adjust the balancing knob until the pointer rests at zero.

3 Place the object you wish to measure on the pan. **Caution:** Do not place hot objects or chemicals directly on the balance pan.

4 Move the largest countermass along the beam to the right until it is at the last notch that does not tip the balance. Follow the same procedure with the next-largest countermass. Then move the smallest countermass until the pointer rests at zero.

5 Add the readings from the three beams together to determine the mass of the object.

6 When determining the mass of crystals or powders, use a piece of filter paper. First mass the paper. Then add the crystals or powder to the paper and remass. The actual mass of the crystals or powder is the total mass minus the mass of the paper. When finding the mass of liquids, first mass the empty container. Then mass the liquid and container together. The mass of the liquid is the total mass minus the mass of the container.

Scientific Method

The steps that scientists use to answer questions and solve problems is often called the **scientific method.** The scientific method is not a rigid procedure. Scientists may use all of the steps or just some of the steps of the scientific method. They may even repeat some of the steps. The goal of a scientific method is to come up with reliable answers and solutions.

Six Steps of a Scientific Method

1 **Ask a Question** Good questions come from careful **observations.** You make observations by using your senses to gather information. Sometimes you may use instruments, such as microscopes and telescopes, to extend the range of your senses. As you observe the natural world, you will discover that you have many more questions than answers. These questions drive the scientific method.

Questions beginning with *what, why, how,* and *when* are very important in focusing an investigation, and they often lead to a hypothesis. (You will learn what a hypothesis is in the next step.) Here is an example of a question that could lead to further investigation.

Question: How does acid rain affect plant growth?

2 **Form a Hypothesis** After you come up with a question, you need to turn the question into a **hypothesis.** A hypothesis is a clear statement of what you expect the answer to your question to be. Your hypothesis will represent your best "educated guess" based on your observations and what you already know. A good hypothesis is one that is testable. If observations and information cannot be gathered or if an experiment cannot be designed to test your hypothesis, it is untestable, and the investigation can go no further.

Here is a hypothesis that could be formed from the question, "How does acid rain affect plant growth?"

Hypothesis: Acid rain causes plants to grow more slowly.

Notice that the hypothesis provides some specifics that lead to methods of testing. The hypothesis can also lead to predictions. A **prediction** is what you think will be the outcome of your experiment or data collection. Predictions are usually stated in an "if . . . then" format. For example, **if** meat is kept at room temperature, **then** it will spoil faster than meat kept in the refrigerator. More than one prediction can be made for a single hypothesis. Here is a sample prediction for the hypothesis that acid rain causes plants to grow more slowly.

Prediction: If a plant is watered with only acid rain (which has a pH of 4), then the plant will grow at half its normal rate.

Ask a Question

Form a Hypothesis

3 **Test the Hypothesis** After you have formed a hypothesis and made a prediction, you should test your hypothesis. There are different ways to do this. Perhaps the most familiar way is to conduct a **controlled experiment.** A controlled experiment tests only one factor at a time. A controlled experiment has a **control group** and one or more **experimental groups.** All the factors for the control and experimental groups are the same except one factor, which is called the **variable.** By changing only one factor (the variable), you can see the results of just that one change.

Sometimes, the nature of an investigation makes a controlled experiment impossible. For example, dinosaurs have been extinct for millions of years, and the Earth's core is surrounded by thousands of meters of rock. It would be difficult if not impossible to conduct controlled experiments on such things. Under such circumstances, a hypothesis may be tested by making detailed observations. Taking measurements is one way of making observations.

Test Your Hypothesis

4 **Analyze the Results** After you have completed your experiments, made your observations, and collected your data, you must analyze all the information you have gathered. Tables and graphs are often used in this step to organize the data.

Analyze the Results

5 **Draw Conclusions** Based on the analysis of your data, you should conclude whether or not your results support your hypothesis. If your hypothesis is supported, you (or others) might want to repeat the observations or experiments to verify your results. If your hypothesis is not supported by the data, you may have to check your procedure for errors. You may even have to reject your hypothesis and make a new one. If you cannot draw a conclusion from your results, you may have to try the investigation again or carry out further observations or experiments.

Draw Conclusions

Do they support your hypothesis?

No

Yes

6 **Communicate Results** After any scientific investigation, you should report your results. By doing a written or oral report, you let others know what you have learned. They may want to repeat your investigation to see if they get the same results. Your report may even lead to another question, which in turn may lead to another investigation.

Communicate the Results

APPENDIX

Scientific Method in Action

A scientific method is not a "straight line" of steps. It contains loops in which several steps may be repeated over and over again, while others may not be necessary. For example, sometimes scientists will find that testing one hypothesis raises new questions and new hypotheses to be tested. And sometimes, testing the hypothesis leads directly to a conclusion. Furthermore, the steps in a scientific method are not always used in the same order. Follow the steps in the diagram below, and see how many different directions a scientific method can take you.

Ask a question

START

Form a hypothesis

Make observations

Test the hypothesis

Perform experiments

YES

NO

Analyze the results

Do Observations and Experiments Support Hypothesis?

YES

NO

Draw conclusions

Was experiment faulty?

Communicate the results

Making Charts and Graphs

Circle Graphs

A circle graph, or pie chart, shows how each group of data relates to all of the data. Each part of the circle represents a category of the data. The entire circle represents all of the data. For example, a biologist studying a hardwood forest in Wisconsin found that there were five different types of trees. The data table at right summarizes the biologist's findings.

Wisconsin Hardwood Trees	
Type of tree	Number found
Oak	600
Maple	750
Beech	300
Birch	1,200
Hickory	150
Total	3,000

How to Make a Circle Graph

1 In order to make a circle graph of this data, first find the percentage of each type of tree. To do this, divide the number of individual trees by the total number of trees and multiply by 100.

$$\frac{600 \text{ Oak}}{3{,}000 \text{ Trees}} \times 100 = 20\%$$

$$\frac{750 \text{ Maple}}{3{,}000 \text{ Trees}} \times 100 = 25\%$$

$$\frac{300 \text{ Beech}}{3{,}000 \text{ Trees}} \times 100 = 10\%$$

$$\frac{1{,}200 \text{ Birch}}{3{,}000 \text{ Trees}} \times 100 = 40\%$$

$$\frac{150 \text{ Hickory}}{3{,}000 \text{ Trees}} \times 100 = 5\%$$

2 Now determine the size of the pie shapes that make up the chart. Do this by multiplying each percentage by 360°. Remember that a circle contains 360°.

$20\% \times 360° = 72°$ $25\% \times 360° = 90°$
$10\% \times 360° = 36°$ $40\% \times 360° = 144°$
$5\% \times 360° = 18°$

3 Then check that the sum of the percentages is 100 and the sum of the degrees is 360.

$20\% + 25\% + 10\% + 40\% + 5\% = 100\%$

$72° + 90° + 36° + 144° + 18° = 360°$

4 Use a compass to draw a circle and mark its center.

5 Then use a protractor to draw angles of 72°, 90°, 36°, 144°, and 18° in the circle.

6 Finally, label each part of the graph and choose an appropriate title.

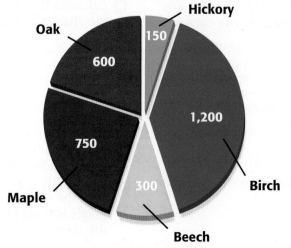

A Community of Wisconsin Hardwood Trees

Population of Appleton, 1900–2000	
Year	Population
1900	1,800
1920	2,500
1940	3,200
1960	3,900
1980	4,600
2000	5,300

Line Graphs

Line graphs are most often used to demonstrate continuous change. For example, Mr. Smith's science class analyzed the population records for their hometown, Appleton, between 1900 and 2000. Examine the data at left.

Because the year and the population change, they are the *variables*. The population is determined by, or dependent on, the year. Therefore, the population is called the **dependent variable**, and the year is called the **independent variable**. Each set of data is called a **data pair**. To prepare a line graph, data pairs must first be organized in a table like the one at left.

How to Make a Line Graph

❶ Place the independent variable along the horizontal (*x*) axis. Place the dependent variable along the vertical (*y*) axis.

❷ Label the *x*-axis "Year" and the *y*-axis "Population." Look at your largest and smallest values for the population. Determine a scale for the *y*-axis that will provide enough space to show these values. You must use the same scale for the entire length of the axis. Find an appropriate scale for the *x*-axis too.

❸ Choose reasonable starting points for each axis.

❹ Plot the data pairs as accurately as possible.

❺ Choose a title that accurately represents the data.

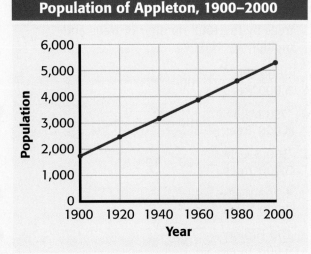
Population of Appleton, 1900–2000

How to Determine Slope

Slope is the ratio of the change in the *y*-axis to the change in the *x*-axis, or "rise over run."

❶ Choose two points on the line graph. For example, the population of Appleton in 2000 was 5,300 people. Therefore, you can define point *a* as (2000, 5,300). In 1900, the population was 1,800 people. Define point *b* as (1900, 1,800).

❷ Find the change in the *y*-axis.
(*y* at point *a*) − (*y* at point *b*)
5,300 people − 1,800 people = 3,500 people

❸ Find the change in the *x*-axis.
(*x* at point *a*) − (*x* at point *b*)
2000 − 1900 = 100 years

❹ Calculate the slope of the graph by dividing the change in *y* by the change in *x*.

$$\text{slope} = \frac{\text{change in } y}{\text{change in } x}$$

$$\text{slope} = \frac{3,500 \text{ people}}{100 \text{ years}}$$

$$\text{slope} = 35 \text{ people per year}$$

In this example, the population in Appleton increased by a fixed amount each year. The graph of this data is a straight line. Therefore, the relationship is **linear**. When the graph of a set of data is not a straight line, the relationship is **nonlinear**.

Using Algebra to Determine Slope

The equation in step 4 may also be arranged to be:

$$y = kx$$

where y represents the change in the y-axis, k represents the slope, and x represents the change in the x-axis.

$$\text{slope} = \frac{\text{change in } y}{\text{change in } x}$$

$$k = \frac{y}{x}$$

$$k \times x = \frac{y \times x}{x}$$

$$kx = y$$

Bar Graphs

Bar graphs are used to demonstrate change that is not continuous. These graphs can be used to indicate trends when the data are taken over a long period of time. A meteorologist gathered the precipitation records at right for Hartford, Connecticut, for April 1–15, 1996, and used a bar graph to represent the data.

Precipitation in Hartford, Connecticut April 1–15, 1996

Date	Precipitation (cm)	Date	Precipitation (cm)
April 1	0.5	April 9	0.25
April 2	1.25	April 10	0.0
April 3	0.0	April 11	1.0
April 4	0.0	April 12	0.0
April 5	0.0	April 13	0.25
April 6	0.0	April 14	0.0
April 7	0.0	April 15	6.50
April 8	1.75		

How to Make a Bar Graph

1 Use an appropriate scale and reasonable starting point for each axis.

2 Label the axes, and plot the data.

3 Choose a title that accurately represents the data.

Precipitation in Hartford, Connecticut, April 1–15, 1996

Math Refresher

Science requires an understanding of many math concepts. The following pages will help you review some important math skills.

Averages

An **average,** or **mean,** simplifies a list of numbers into a single number that *approximates* their value.

> **Example:** Find the average of the following set of numbers: 5, 4, 7, 8.

Step 1: Find the sum.

$$5 + 4 + 7 + 8 = 24$$

Step 2: Divide the sum by the amount of numbers in your set. Because there are four numbers in this example, divide the sum by 4.

$$\frac{24}{4} = 6$$

The average, or mean, is **6.**

Ratios

A **ratio** is a comparison between numbers, and it is usually written as a fraction.

> **Example:** Find the ratio of thermometers to students if you have 36 thermometers and 48 students in your class.

Step 1: Make the ratio.

$$\frac{36 \text{ thermometers}}{48 \text{ students}}$$

Step 2: Reduce the fraction to its simplest form.

$$\frac{36}{48} = \frac{36 \div 12}{48 \div 12} = \frac{3}{4}$$

The ratio of thermometers to students is **3 to 4,** or $\frac{3}{4}$. The ratio may also be written in the form 3:4.

Proportions

A **proportion** is an equation that states that two ratios are equal.

$$\frac{3}{1} = \frac{12}{4}$$

To solve a proportion, first multiply across the equal sign. This is called cross-multiplication. If you know three of the quantities in a proportion, you can use cross-multiplication to find the fourth.

> **Example:** Imagine that you are making a scale model of the solar system for your science project. The diameter of Jupiter is 11.2 times the diameter of the Earth. If you are using a plastic-foam ball with a diameter of 2 cm to represent the Earth, what diameter does the ball representing Jupiter need to be?
>
> $$\frac{11.2}{1} = \frac{x}{2 \text{ cm}}$$

Step 1: Cross-multiply.

$$\frac{11.2}{1} \diagup\!\!\!\!\diagup \frac{x}{2}$$

$$11.2 \times 2 = x \times 1$$

Step 2: Multiply.

$$22.4 = x \times 1$$

Step 3: Isolate the variable by dividing both sides by 1.

$$x = \frac{22.4}{1}$$

$$x = 22.4 \text{ cm}$$

You will need to use a ball with a diameter of **22.4 cm** to represent Jupiter.

Percentages

A **percentage** is a ratio of a given number to 100.

> **Example:** What is 85 percent of 40?

Step 1: Rewrite the percentage by moving the decimal point two places to the left.

$$.85$$

Step 2: Multiply the decimal by the number you are calculating the percentage of.

$$0.85 \times 40 = 34$$

85% of 40 is **34**

Decimals

To **add** or **subtract decimals,** line up the digits vertically so that the decimal points line up. Then add or subtract the columns from right to left, carrying or borrowing numbers as necessary.

> **Example:** Add the following numbers: 3.1415 and 2.96.

Step 1: Line up the digits vertically so that the decimal points line up.

$$\begin{array}{r} 3.1415 \\ + \ 2.96 \\ \hline \end{array}$$

Step 2: Add the columns from right to left, carrying when necessary.

$$\begin{array}{r} {\scriptstyle 1\ 1} \\ 3.1415 \\ + \ 2.96 \\ \hline 6.1015 \end{array}$$

The sum is **6.1015**

Fractions

Numbers tell you how many; **fractions** tell you *how much of a whole*.

> **Example:** Your class has 24 plants. Your teacher instructs you to put 5 in a shady spot. What fraction does this represent?

Step 1: Write a fraction with the total number of parts in the whole as the denominator.

$$\frac{?}{24}$$

Step 2: Write the number of parts of the whole being represented as the numerator.

$$\frac{5}{24}$$

$\frac{5}{24}$ of the plants will be in the shade.

Reducing Fractions

It is usually best to express a fraction in simplest form. This is called *reducing* a fraction.

> **Example:** Reduce the fraction $\frac{30}{45}$ to its simplest form.

Step 1: Find the largest whole number that will divide evenly into both the numerator and denominator. This number is called the greatest common factor (GCF).

factors of the numerator 30: 1, 2, 3, 5, 6, 10, 15, 30

factors of the denominator 45: 1, 3, 5, 9, 15, 45

Step 2: Divide both the numerator and the denominator by the GCF, which in this case is 15.

$$\frac{30}{45} = \frac{30 \div 15}{45 \div 15} = \frac{2}{3}$$

$\frac{30}{45}$ reduced to its simplest form is $\frac{2}{3}$.

Adding and Subtracting Fractions

To **add** or **subtract fractions** that have the **same denominator,** simply add or subtract the numerators.

Examples:

$$\frac{3}{5} + \frac{1}{5} = ? \text{ and } \frac{3}{4} - \frac{1}{4} = ?$$

Step 1: Add or subtract the numerators.

$$\frac{3}{5} + \frac{1}{5} = \frac{4}{} \text{ and } \frac{3}{4} - \frac{1}{4} = \frac{2}{}$$

Step 2: Write the sum or difference over the denominator.

$$\frac{3}{5} + \frac{1}{5} = \frac{4}{5} \text{ and } \frac{3}{4} - \frac{1}{4} = \frac{2}{4}$$

Step 3: If necessary, reduce the fraction to its simplest form.

$$\frac{4}{5} \text{ cannot be reduced, and } \frac{2}{4} = \frac{1}{2}$$

To **add** or **subtract fractions** that have **different denominators,** first find a common denominator (LCD).

Examples:

$$\frac{1}{2} + \frac{1}{6} = ? \text{ and } \frac{3}{4} - \frac{2}{3} = ?$$

Step 1: Write the equivalent fractions with a common demominator.

$$\frac{3}{6} + \frac{1}{6} = ? \text{ and } \frac{9}{12} - \frac{8}{12} = ?$$

Step 2: Add or subtract.

$$\frac{3}{6} + \frac{1}{6} = \frac{4}{6} \text{ and } \frac{9}{12} - \frac{8}{12} = \frac{1}{12}$$

Step 3: If necessary, reduce the fraction to its simplest form.

$$\frac{4}{6} = \frac{2}{3}, \text{ and } \frac{1}{12} \text{ cannot be reduced}$$

Multiplying Fractions

To **multiply fractions,** multiply the numerators and the denominators together, and then reduce the fraction to its simplest form.

Example:

$$\frac{5}{9} \times \frac{7}{10} = ?$$

Step 1: Multiply the numerators and denominators.

$$\frac{5}{9} \times \frac{7}{10} = \frac{5 \times 7}{9 \times 10} = \frac{35}{90}$$

Step 2: Reduce.

$$\frac{35}{90} = \frac{35 \div 5}{90 \div 5} = \frac{7}{18}$$

Dividing Fractions

To **divide fractions,** first rewrite the divisor (the number you divide *by*) upside down. This is called the reciprocal of the divisor. Then you can multiply and reduce if necessary.

Example:

$$\frac{5}{8} \div \frac{3}{2} = ?$$

Step 1: Rewrite the divisor as its reciprocal.

$$\frac{3}{2} \rightarrow \frac{2}{3}$$

Step 2: Multiply.

$$\frac{5}{8} \times \frac{2}{3} = \frac{5 \times 2}{8 \times 3} = \frac{10}{24}$$

Step 3: Reduce.

$$\frac{10}{24} = \frac{10 \div 2}{24 \div 2} = \frac{5}{12}$$

Scientific Notation

Scientific notation is a short way of representing very large and very small numbers without writing all of the place-holding zeros.

> **Example:** Write 653,000,000 in scientific notation.

Step 1: Write the number without the place-holding zeros.

653

Step 2: Place the decimal point after the first digit.

6.53

Step 3: Find the exponent by counting the number of places that you moved the decimal point.

6.53000000

The decimal point was moved eight places to the left. Therefore, the exponent of 10 is positive 8. Remember, if the decimal point had moved to the right, the exponent would be negative.

Step 4: Write the number in scientific notation.

$$6.53 \times 10^8$$

Area

Area is the number of square units needed to cover the surface of an object.

Formulas:
Area of a square = side × side
Area of a rectangle = length × width
Area of a triangle = $\frac{1}{2}$ base × height
Examples: Find the areas.

Triangle
Area = $\frac{1}{2}$ × base × height
Area = $\frac{1}{2}$ × 3 cm × 4 cm
Area = **6 cm²**

4 cm
3 cm

Rectangle
Area = length × width
Area = 6 cm × 3 cm
Area = **18 cm²**

3 cm
6 cm

Square
Area = side × side
Area = 3 cm × 3 cm
Area = **9 cm²**

3 cm
3 cm

Volume

Volume is the amount of space something occupies.

Formulas:
Volume of a cube = side × side × side

Volume of a prism = area of base × height

Examples:
Find the volume of the solids.

Cube
Volume = side × side × side
Volume = 4 cm × 4 cm × 4 cm
Volume = **64 cm³**

4 cm
4 cm
4 cm

4 cm
3 cm
5 cm

Prism
Volume = area of base × height
Volume = (area of triangle) × height
Volume = $\left(\frac{1}{2} \times 3 \text{ cm} \times 4 \text{ cm} \right) \times 5$ cm
Volume = 6 cm² × 5 cm
Volume = **30 cm³**

Periodic Table of the Elements

Each square on the table includes an element's name, chemical symbol, atomic number, and atomic mass.

Atomic number ———————— 6

Chemical symbol ———————— **C**

Element name ———————— Carbon

Atomic mass ———————— 12.0

The background color indicates the type of element. Carbon is a nonmetal.

The color of the chemical symbol indicates the physical state at room temperature. Carbon is a solid.

Background
- Metals
- Metalloids
- Nonmetals

Chemical symbol
- Solid
- Liquid
- Gas

Period 1

1
H
Hydrogen
1.0

	Group 1	Group 2
Period 2	3 **Li** Lithium 6.9	4 **Be** Beryllium 9.0
Period 3	11 **Na** Sodium 23.0	12 **Mg** Magnesium 24.3

	Group 1	Group 2	Group 3	Group 4	Group 5	Group 6	Group 7	Group 8	Group 9
Period 4	19 **K** Potassium 39.1	20 **Ca** Calcium 40.1	21 **Sc** Scandium 45.0	22 **Ti** Titanium 47.9	23 **V** Vanadium 50.9	24 **Cr** Chromium 52.0	25 **Mn** Manganese 54.9	26 **Fe** Iron 55.8	27 **Co** Cobalt 58.9
Period 5	37 **Rb** Rubidium 85.5	38 **Sr** Strontium 87.6	39 **Y** Yttrium 88.9	40 **Zr** Zirconium 91.2	41 **Nb** Niobium 92.9	42 **Mo** Molybdenum 95.9	43 **Tc** Technetium (97.9)	44 **Ru** Ruthenium 101.1	45 **Rh** Rhodium 102.9
Period 6	55 **Cs** Cesium 132.9	56 **Ba** Barium 137.3	57 **La** Lanthanum 138.9	72 **Hf** Hafnium 178.5	73 **Ta** Tantalum 180.9	74 **W** Tungsten 183.8	75 **Re** Rhenium 186.2	76 **Os** Osmium 190.2	77 **Ir** Iridium 192.2
Period 7	87 **Fr** Francium (223.0)	88 **Ra** Radium (226.0)	89 **Ac** Actinium (227.0)	104 **Rf** Rutherfordium (261.1)	105 **Db** Dubnium (262.1)	106 **Sg** Seaborgium (263.1)	107 **Bh** Bohrium (262.1)	108 **Hs** Hassium (265)	109 **Mt** Meitnerium (266)

A row of elements is called a period.

A column of elements is called a group or family.

Lanthanides	58 **Ce** Cerium 140.1	59 **Pr** Praseodymium 140.9	60 **Nd** Neodymium 144.2	61 **Pm** Promethium (144.9)	62 **Sm** Samarium 150.4
Actinides	90 **Th** Thorium 232.0	91 **Pa** Protactinium 231.0	92 **U** Uranium 238.0	93 **Np** Neptunium (237.0)	94 **Pu** Plutonium 244.1

These elements are placed below the table to allow the table to be narrower.

This zigzag line reminds you where the metals, nonmetals, and metalloids are.

Group 18
2 **He** Helium 4.0

Group 13	Group 14	Group 15	Group 16	Group 17
5 **B** Boron 10.8	6 **C** Carbon 12.0	7 **N** Nitrogen 14.0	8 **O** Oxygen 16.0	9 **F** Fluorine 19.0	10 **Ne** Neon 20.2
13 **Al** Aluminum 27.0	14 **Si** Silicon 28.1	15 **P** Phosphorus 31.0	16 **S** Sulfur 32.1	17 **Cl** Chlorine 35.5	18 **Ar** Argon 39.9

Group 10	Group 11	Group 12					
28 **Ni** Nickel 58.7	29 **Cu** Copper 63.5	30 **Zn** Zinc 65.4	31 **Ga** Gallium 69.7	32 **Ge** Germanium 72.6	33 **As** Arsenic 74.9	34 **Se** Selenium 79.0	35 **Br** Bromine 79.9	36 **Kr** Krypton 83.8
46 **Pd** Palladium 106.4	47 **Ag** Silver 107.9	48 **Cd** Cadmium 112.4	49 **In** Indium 114.8	50 **Sn** Tin 118.7	51 **Sb** Antimony 121.8	52 **Te** Tellurium 127.6	53 **I** Iodine 126.9	54 **Xe** Xenon 131.3
78 **Pt** Platinum 195.1	79 **Au** Gold 197.0	80 **Hg** Mercury 200.6	81 **Tl** Thallium 204.4	82 **Pb** Lead 207.2	83 **Bi** Bismuth 209.0	84 **Po** Polonium (209.0)	85 **At** Astatine (210.0)	86 **Rn** Radon (222.0)
110 **Uun** Ununnilium (271)	111 **Uuu** Unununium (272)	112 **Uub** Ununbium (277)					

The names and symbols of elements 110–112 are temporary. They are based on the atomic number of the element. The official name and symbol will be approved by an international committee of scientists.

63 **Eu** Europium 152.0	64 **Gd** Gadolinium 157.3	65 **Tb** Terbium 158.9	66 **Dy** Dysprosium 162.5	67 **Ho** Holmium 164.9	68 **Er** Erbium 167.3	69 **Tm** Thulium 168.9	70 **Yb** Ytterbium 173.0	71 **Lu** Lutetium 175.0
95 **Am** Americium (243.1)	96 **Cm** Curium (247.1)	97 **Bk** Berkelium (247.1)	98 **Cf** Californium (251.1)	99 **Es** Einsteinium (252.1)	100 **Fm** Fermium (257.1)	101 **Md** Mendelevium (258.1)	102 **No** Nobelium (259.1)	103 **Lr** Lawrencium (262.1)

A number in parentheses is the mass number of the most stable isotope of that element.

Physical Science Refresher

Atoms and Elements

Every object in the universe is made up of particles of some kind of matter. **Matter** is anything that takes up space and has mass. All matter is made up of elements. An **element** is a substance that cannot be separated into simpler components by ordinary chemical means. This is because each element consists of only one kind of atom. An **atom** is the smallest unit of an element that has all of the properties of that element.

Atomic Structure

Atoms are made up of small particles called subatomic particles. The three major types of subatomic particles are **electrons, protons,** and **neutrons.** Electrons have a negative electrical charge, protons have a positive charge, and neutrons have no electrical charge. The protons and neutrons are packed close to one another to form the **nucleus.** The protons give the nucleus a positive charge. The electrons of an atom move in a region around the nucleus known as an **electron cloud.** The negatively charged electrons are attracted to the positively charged nucleus. An atom may have several energy levels in which electrons are located.

Atomic Number

To help in the identification of elements, scientists have assigned an **atomic number** to each kind of atom. The atomic number is equal to the number of protons in the atom. Atoms with the same number of protons are all the same kind of element. In an uncharged, or electrically neutral, atom there are an equal number of protons and electrons. Therefore, the atomic number also equals the number of electrons in an uncharged atom. The number of neutrons, however, can vary for a given element. Atoms of the same element that have different numbers of neutrons are called **isotopes.**

Periodic Table of the Elements

In the periodic table, the elements are arranged from left to right in order of increasing atomic number. Each element in the table is in a separate box. Each element has one more electron and one more proton than the element to its left. Each horizontal row of the table is called a **period.** Changes in chemical properties across a period correspond to changes in the elements' electron arrangements. Each vertical column of the table, known as a **group,** lists elements with similar properties. The elements in a group have similar chemical properties because they have the same number of electrons in their outer energy level. For example, the elements helium, neon, argon, krypton, xenon, and radon all have similar properties and are known as the noble gases.

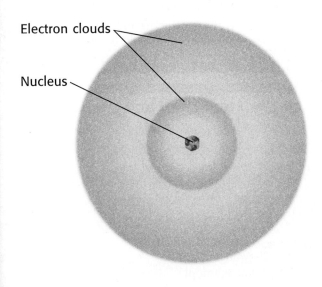

Electron clouds

Nucleus

Molecules and Compounds

When the atoms of two or more elements are joined chemically, the resulting substance is called a **compound.** A compound is a new substance with properties different from those of the elements that compose it. For example, water (H_2O) is a compound formed when atoms of hydrogen (H) and oxygen (O) combine. The smallest complete unit of a compound that has all of the properties of that compound is called a **molecule.** A chemical formula indicates the elements in a compound. It also indicates the relative number of atoms of each element present. The chemical formula for water is H_2O, which indicates that each water molecule consists of two atoms of hydrogen and one atom of oxygen. The subscript number is used after the symbol for an element to indicate how many atoms of that element are in a single molecule of the compound.

Acids, Bases, and pH

An ion is an atom or group of atoms that has an electrical charge because it has lost or gained one or more electrons. When an acid, such as hydrochloric acid (HCl), is mixed with water, it separates into ions. An **acid** is a compound that produces hydrogen ions (H^+) in water. The hydrogen ions then combine with a water molecule to form a hydronium ion (H_3O^+). A **base,** on the other hand, is a substance that produces hydroxide ions (OH^-) in water.

To determine whether a solution is acidic or basic, scientists use pH. The **pH** is a measure of the hydronium ion concentration in a solution. The pH scale ranges from 0 to 14. The middle point, pH = 7, is neutral, neither acidic nor basic. Acids have a pH less than 7; bases have a pH greater than 7. The lower the number is, the more acidic the solution. The higher the number is, the more basic the solution.

Chemical Equations

A chemical reaction occurs when a chemical change takes place. (In a chemical change, new substances with new properties are formed.) A chemical equation is a useful way of describing a chemical reaction by means of chemical formulas. The equation indicates what substances react and what the products are. For example, when carbon and oxygen combine, they can form carbon dioxide. The equation for the reaction is as follows: $C + O_2 \rightarrow CO_2$.

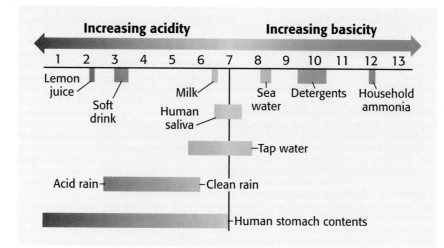

APPENDIX

The Six Kingdoms

Kingdom Archaebacteria

The organisms in this kingdom are single-celled prokaryotes.

Archaebacteria		
Group	**Examples**	**Characteristics**
Methanogens	*Methanococcus*	found in soil, swamps, the digestive tract of mammals; produce methane gas; can't live in oxygen
Thermophiles	*Sulpholobus*	found in extremely hot environments; require sulphur, can't live in oxygen
Halophiles	*Halococcus*	found in environments with very high salt content, such as the Dead Sea; nearly all can live in oxygen

Kingdom Eubacteria

There are more than 4,000 named species in this kingdom of single-celled prokaryotes.

Eubacteria		
Group	**Examples**	**Characteristics**
Bacilli	*Escherichia coli*	rod-shaped; free-living, symbiotic, or parasitic; some can fix nitrogen; some cause disease
Cocci	*Streptococcus*	spherical-shaped, disease-causing; can form spores to resist unfavorable environments
Spirilla	*Treponema*	spiral-shaped; responsible for several serious illnesses, such as syphilis and Lyme disease

Kingdom Protista

The organisms in this kingdom are eukaryotes. There are single-celled and many-celled representatives.

Protists		
Group	**Examples**	**Characteristics**
Sacodines	*Amoeba*	radiolarians; single-celled consumers
Ciliates	*Paramecium*	single-celled consumers
Flagellates	*Trypanosoma*	single-celled parasites
Sporozoans	*Plasmodium*	single-celled parasites
Euglenas	*Euglena*	single-celled; photosynthesize
Diatoms	*Pinnularia*	most are single-celled; photosynthesize
Dinoflagellates	*Gymnodinium*	single-celled; some photosynthesize
Algae	*Volvox*, coral algae	4 phyla; single- or many-celled; photosynthesize
Slime molds	*Physarum*	many-celled decomposers
Water molds	powdery mildew	single- or many-celled, parasites or decomposers

Kingdom Fungi

There are single-celled and many-celled eukaryotes in this kingdom. Like plants, fungi are classified in divisions instead of in phyla. There are four major groups of fungi

Fungi		
Group	**Examples**	**Characteristics**
Threadlike fungi	bread mold	spherical; decomposer
Sac fungi	yeast, morels	saclike; parasites and decomposers
Club fungi	mushrooms, rusts, smuts	club-shaped; parasites and decomposers
Lichens	British soldier	symbiotic with photosynthetic algae

Kingdom Plantae

The organisms in this kingdom are many-celled eukaryotes. They have specialized organ systems for different life processes. They are classified in divisions instead of phyla.

Plants		
Group	**Examples**	**Characteristics**
Bryophytes	mosses, liverworts	reproduce by spores
Club mosses	*Lycopodium*, ground pine	reproduce by spores
Horsetails	rushes	reproduce by spores
Ferns	spleenworts, sensitive fern	reproduce by spores
Conifers	pines, spruces, firs	reproduce by seeds; cones
Cycads	*Zamia*	reproduce by seeds
Gnetophytes	*Welwitschia*	reproduce by seeds
Ginkgos	*Ginkgo*	reproduce by seeds
Angiosperms	all flowering plants	reproduce by seeds; flowers

Kingdom Animalia

This kingdom contains many-celled eukaryotes. They have specialized tissues and complex organ systems.

Animals		
Group	**Examples**	**Characteristics**
Sponges	glass sponges	no symmetry or segmentation; aquatic
Cnidarians	jellyfish, coral	radial symmetry; aquatic
Flatworms	planaria, tapeworms, flukes	bilateral symmetry; organ systems
Roundworms	*Trichina*, hookworms	bilateral symmetry; organ systems
Annelids	earthworms, leeches	bilateral symmetry; organ systems
Mollusks	snails, octopuses	bilateral symmetry; organ systems
Echinoderms	starfish, sand dollars	radial symmetry; organ systems
Arthropods	insects, spiders, lobsters	bilateral symmetry; organ systems
Chordates	fish, amphibians, reptiles, birds, mammals	bilateral symmetry; complex organ systems

Using the Microscope

Parts of the Compound Light Microscope

- The **eyepiece** magnifies the image 10×.

- The **low-power objective** magnifies the image 10×.

- The **high-power objective** magnifies the image either 40× or 43×.

- The **revolving nosepiece** holds the objectives and can be turned to change from one magnification to the other.

- The **body tube** maintains the correct distance between eyepiece and objectives.

- The **coarse-adjustment knob** moves the body tube up and down to allow focusing of the image.

- The **fine-adjustment knob** moves the body tube slightly to bring the image into sharper focus.

- The **stage** supports a slide.

- **Stage clips** hold the slide in place for viewing.

- The **diaphragm** controls the amount of light coming through the stage.

- The **light source** provides light for viewing the slide.

- The **arm** supports the body tube.

- The **base** supports the microscope.

Eyepiece

Fine-adjustment knob

Body tube

Coarse-adjustment knob

Revolving nosepiece

Objective lenses

Arm

Stage clip

Stage

Diaphragm

Light source

Base

Proper Use of the Compound Light Microscope

❶ Carry the microscope to your lab table using both hands. Place one hand beneath the base, and use the other hand to hold the arm of the microscope. Hold the microscope close to your body while moving it to your lab table.

❷ Place the microscope on the lab table at least 5 cm from the edge of the table.

❸ Check to see what type of light source is used by your microscope. If the microscope has a lamp, plug it in, making sure that the cord is out of the way. If the microscope has a mirror, adjust it to reflect light through the hole in the stage.
CAUTION: **If your microscope has a mirror, do not use direct sunlight as a light source. Direct sunlight can damage your eyes.**

❹ Always begin work with the low-power objective in line with the body tube. Adjust the revolving nosepiece.

❺ Place a prepared slide over the hole in the stage. Secure the slide with the stage clips.

❻ Look through the eyepiece. Move the diaphragm to adjust the amount of light coming through the stage.

❼ Look at the stage from eye level. Slowly turn the coarse adjustment to lower the objective until it almost touches the slide. Do not allow the objective to touch the slide.

❽ Look through the eyepiece. Turn the coarse adjustment to raise the low-power objective until the image is in focus. Always focus by raising the objective away from the slide. *Never focus the objective downward.* Use the fine adjustment to sharpen the focus. Keep both eyes open while viewing a slide.

❾ Make sure that the image is exactly in the center of your field of vision. Then switch to the high-power objective. Focus the image, using only the fine adjustment. *Never use the coarse adjustment at high power.*

❿ When you are finished using the microscope, remove the slide. Clean the eyepiece and objectives with lens paper. Return the microscope to its storage area. Remember, you should use both hands to carry the microscope correctly.

Making a Wet Mount

❶ Use lens paper to clean a glass slide and a coverslip.

❷ Place the specimen you wish to observe in the center of the slide.

❸ Using a medicine dropper, place one drop of water on the specimen.

❹ Hold the coverslip at the edge of the water and at a 45° angle to the slide. Position the coverslip so that it is at the edge of the drop of water. Make sure that the water runs along the edge of the coverslip.

❺ Lower the coverslip slowly to avoid trapping air bubbles.

❻ Water might evaporate from the slide as you work. Add more water to keep the specimen fresh. Place the tip of the medicine dropper next to the edge of the coverslip. Add a drop of water. (You can also use this method to add stain or solutions to a wet mount.) Remove excess water from the slide by using the corner of a paper towel as a blotter. Do not lift the coverslip to add or remove water.

Glossary

A

abdomen the body part of an animal that usually contains the gut and other digestive organs (339)

abiotic describes nonliving factors in the environment (416)

absolute dating estimating the age of a sample or event in years, usually by measuring the amount of unstable atoms in the sample (203)

absorption the transfer of energy carried by light waves to particles in matter (60)

active transport the movement of particles through proteins in the cell membrane against the direction of diffusion; requires cells to use energy (110)

adaptation a characteristic that helps an organism survive in its environment (176)

adenine (AD uh NEEN) one of the four bases that combine with sugar and phospate to form a nucleotide subunit of DNA; adenine pairs with thymine (152)

alien an organism that makes a home for itself in a new place (444)

alleles alternative forms of a gene that govern the same characteristics (135)

altricial chick a chick that hatches weak, naked, and helpless (388)

alveoli (al VEE uh LIE) tiny sacs that form the bronchiole branches of the lungs (499)

amnion a thin, fluid-filled membrane surrounding a placental mammal's fetus (543)

amniotic egg (AM nee AH tik) an egg containing amniotic fluid to protect the developing embryo; usually surrounded by a hard shell (370)

amphibian a type of vertebrate ectotherm that usually begins life in the water with gills and later develops lungs (364)

anaerobic without oxygen (209)

angiosperm (AN jee oh SPUHRM) a plant that produces seeds in flowers (253)

Animalia the classification kingdom containing complex, multicellular organisms that lack cell walls, are usually able to move about, and possess nervous systems that help them be aware of and react to their surroundings (239)

antennae feelers on an arthropod's head that respond to touch or taste (340)

Archaebacteria (AHR kee bac TIR ee uh) a classification kingdom containing bacteria that thrive in extreme environments (235)

area the measure of how much surface an object has (24)

arteries blood vessels that carry blood away from the heart (491)

asexual reproduction reproduction in which a single parent produces offspring that are genetically identical to the parent (38, 534)

asymmetrical without symmetry (326)

ATP adenosine triphosphate; a molecule that provides energy for a cell's activities (45)

atrium an upper chamber of the heart (490)

australopithecine (ah STRA loh PITH uh seen) an early hominid that evolved more than 3.6 million years ago (216)

axon a long cell fiber in the nervous system that transfers intercellular messages (511)

B

bacteria extremely small, single-celled organisms without a nucleus; prokaryotic cells (90, 235)

bilateral symmetry a body plan in which two halves of an organism's body are mirror images of each other (326)

binary fission the simple cell division in which one cell splits into two; used by bacteria (116)

biodegradable capable of being broken down by the environment (446)

biodiversity the number and variety of living things (445)

biological clock an internal control of natural cycles (312)

biome a large region characterized by a specific type of climate and certain types of plant and animal communities (416)

blood a type of connective tissue made up of cells, cell parts, and plasma (488)

blood pressure the amount of force exerted by blood on the inside walls of a blood vessel (493)

brain the mass of nerve tissue that is the main organ of the nervous system (513)

bronchi (BRAWNG KEE) the two tubes that connect the lungs with the trachea (499)

brooding when a bird sits on its eggs until they hatch (387)

budding a type of asexual reproduction in which a small part of the parent's body develops into an independent organism (534)

C

camouflage the coloration and/or texture that enables an animal to blend in with the environment (309)

capillaries the smallest blood vessels (491)

carbohydrate a biochemical composed of one or more simple sugars bonded together that is used as a source of energy and to store energy (43)

cardiac muscle the type of muscle found in the heart (472)

cardiovascular system a collection of organs that transport blood to and from your body's cells; the organs in this system include the heart, the arteries, and the veins (488)

carnivore a consumer that eats animals (401)

cartilage a flexible white tissue that gives support and protection but is not rigid like bone (470)

cell a membrane-covered structure that contains all of the materials necessary for life (36)

cell cycle the life cycle of a cell; in eukaryotes it consists of chromosome duplication, mitosis, and cytokinesis (116)

cell membrane a phospholipid layer that covers a cell's surface and acts as a barrier between the inside of a cell and the cell's environment (87)

cell theory the three-part theory about cells that states: (1) All organisms are composed of one or more cells, (2) the cell is the basic unit of life in all living things, and (3) all cells come from existing cells (86)

cell wall a structure that surrounds the cell membrane of some cells and provides strength and support to the cell membrane (93)

cellular respiration the process of producing ATP in the cell from oxygen and glucose; releases carbon dioxide and water (113, 285, 500)

Cenozoic era the period in the geologic time scale beginning about 65 million years ago and continuing until the present day (213)

central nervous system a collection of organs whose primary function is to process all incoming and outgoing messages from the nerves; the organs in this system include the brain and the spinal cord (510)

centromere the region that holds chromatids together when a chromosome is duplicated (117)

cephalothorax (SEF uh loh THOR AKS) the body part of arachnids that consists of both a head and a thorax and that usually has four pairs of legs attached (341)

cerebellum the part of the brain that keeps track of the body's position (514)

cerebrum the part of the brain that detects touch, sight, sound, odors, taste, heat, and cold (513)

chlorophyll a green pigment in chloroplasts that absorbs light energy for photosynthesis (284)

chloroplast an organelle found in plant and algae cells where photosynthesis occurs (95)

chromatids identical chromosome copies (117)

chromosome coiled structure of DNA and protein that forms in the cell nucleus during cell division (116)

circadian rhythm a daily cycle (312)

class the level of classification after phylum; the organisms in all phyla are sorted into classes (229)

classification the arrangement of organisms into orderly groups based on their similarities and presumed evolutionary relationships (228)

closed circulatory system a circulatory system in which a heart circulates blood through a network of vessels that form a closed loop (336)

cochlea (KAHK lee uh) an ear organ that converts sound waves into electrical impulses and sends them to the area of the brain that interprets sound (520)

coelom (SEE luhm) a cavity in the body of some animals where the gut and organs are located (327)

communication a transfer of a signal from one animal to another that results in some type of response (314)

community all of the populations of different species that live and interact in an area (84)

compact bone the type of bone tissue that does not have open spaces (469)

compound eye an eye that is made of many identical units that work together (340)

compound light microscope a microscope that consists of a tube with lenses, a stage, and a light source (19)

concave lens a lens that is thinner in the middle than at the edges (67)

cones photoreceptors that can detect bright light and help you see colors (518)

conifer a tree that produces seeds in cones (418)

connective tissue one of the four main types of tissue in the body; functions include support, protection, insulation, and nourishment (465)

conservation the wise use of and preservation of natural resources (447)

consumer an organism that eats producers or other organisms for energy (40, 307)

contour feather a feather made of a stiff central shaft with many side branches, called barbs (383)

controlled experiment an experiment that tests only one factor at a time (14)

convex lens a lens that is thicker in the middle than at the edges (67)

cotyledon (KAHT uh LEED uhn) a seed leaf inside a seed (263)

Cro-Magnon a species of humans with modern features that may have migrated out of Africa 100,000 years ago and eventually into every continent (218)

cuticle a waxy layer that coats the surface of stems, leaves, and other plant parts exposed to air (251)

cytokinesis (SIET oh ki NEE sis) the process in which cytoplasm divides after mitosis (119)

cytoplasm (SIET oh PLAZ um) cellular fluid surrounding a cell's organelles (87)

cytosine (SIET oh SEEN) one of the four bases that combine with sugar and phosphate to form a nucleotide subunit of DNA; cytosine pairs with guanine (152)

D

deciduous describes trees that have leaves that change color in autumn and fall off in winter (290, 417)

decomposer an organism that gets energy by breaking down the remains of dead organisms and consuming or absorbing the nutrients (40)

deep-water zone the zone of a lake or pond below the open-water zone, where no light reaches (429)

deforestation the clearing of forest lands (445)

dendrite a short, branched extension of a neuron where the neuron receives impulses from other cells (511)

denticles small, sharp toothlike structures on the skin of cartilaginous fishes (361)

dermis the layer of skin below the epidermis (477)

desert a hot, dry biome inhabited by organisms adapted to survive high daytime temperatures and long periods without rain (421)

diaphragm (DIE uh FRAM) the sheet of muscle underneath the lungs of mammals that helps draw air into the lungs (395, 500)

dichotomous key (die KAWT uh muhs KEE) an aid to identifying unknown organisms that consists of several pairs of descriptive statements; of each pair of statements, only one will apply to the unknown organism, and that will lead to another set of statements, and so on, until the unknown organism can be identified (232)

diffusion the movement of particles from an area where their concentration is high to an area where their concentration is low (108)

diversity a measure of the number of species an area contains (419)

DNA deoxyribonucleic (dee AHKS ee RIE boh noo KLAY ik) acid; hereditary material that controls all the activities of a cell, contains the information to make new cells, and provides instructions for making proteins (38, 93, 152)

DNA fingerprinting the analysis of fragments of DNA as a form of identification (166)

dominant trait the trait observed when at least one dominant allele for a characteristic is inherited (133)

dormant an inactive state of a seed (282)

down feather a fluffy, insulating feather that lies next to a bird's body (383)

E

ecosystem a community of organisms and their nonliving environment (84)

ectotherm an animal whose body temperature fluctuates with the environment's temperature (358)

egg a sex cell produced by a female (535)

electromagnetic spectrum the entire range of electromagnetic waves (56)

electromagnetic wave a wave that doesn't require a medium (55)

electron microscope a microscope that uses tiny particles of matter to produce magnified images (20)

embryo an organism in the earliest stage of development (306, 542)

endocrine system a collection of glands that control body-fluid balance, growth, and sexual development (522)

endocytosis (EN doh sie TOH sis) the process in which a cell membrane surrounds a particle and encloses it in a vesicle to bring it into the cell (111)

endoplasmic reticulum (EN doh PLAZ mik ri TIK yuh luhm) a membrane-covered cell organelle that produces lipids, breaks down drugs and other substances, and packages proteins for delivery out of the cell (94)

endoskeleton an internal skeleton (345)

endotherm an animal that maintains a constant body temperature despite temperature changes in its environment (358)

enzyme protein that makes it possible for certain chemical reactions to occur quickly (42)

epidermis the outermost layer of the skin (477); also the outermost layer of cells covering roots, stems, leaves, and flower parts (265)

epididymis (EP uh DID i mis) the area of the testes where sperm are stored before they enter the vas deferens (538)

epithelial tissue One of the four main types of tissue in the body; the tissue that covers and protects underlying tissue (464)

estivation a period of reduced activity that some animals experience in the summer (311)

estuary an area where fresh water from streams and rivers spills into the ocean (427)

Eubacteria a classification kingdom containing mostly free-living bacteria found in many varied environments (235)

eukaryotic cell (eukaryote) (yoo KER ee oht) a cell that contains a central nucleus and a complicated internal structure (91, 210)

evergreen describes trees that keep their leaves year-round (290)

evolution the process by which populations accumulate inherited changes over time (177)

exocytosis (EK soh sie TOH sis) the process used to remove large particles from a cell; during exocytosis, a vesicle containing the particles fuses with the cell membrane (111)

exoskeleton an external skeleton made of protein and chitin found on arthropods (340)

extensor a muscle that straightens part of the body (473)

external fertilization fertilization of an egg by sperm that occurs outside the body of the female (360, 536)

extinct describes a species of organism that has died out completely (205)

F

factor anything in an experiment that can influence the experiment's outcome (14)

fallopian tube the tube that leads from an ovary to the uterus (539)

family the level of classification after order; the organisms in all orders are sorted into families (229)

feedback control a system that turns endocrine glands on or off (524)

fermentation the breakdown of sugars to make ATP in the absence of oxygen (113)

fetus an embryo during the later stages of development within the uterus (544)

fibrous root a type of root in which there are several roots of the same size that spread out from the base of the stem (265)

fins fanlike structures that help fish move, turn, stop, and balance (360)

flexor a muscle that bends part of the body (473)

fossil the solidified remains or imprints of once living organisms (178, 202)

fossil record a historical sequence of life indicated by fossils found in layers of the Earth's crust (178)

fragmentation a type of reproduction where an organism breaks into two or more parts, each of which may grow into a separate individual (534)

frequency the number of waves produced in a given amount of time (56)

Fungi a kingdom of complex organisms that obtain food by breaking down other substances in their surroundings and absorbing the nutrients (238)

G

gametophyte (guh MEET oh FIET) a stage in a plant life cycle during which eggs and sperm are produced (251)

ganglia groups of nerve cells (327)

genes segments of DNA that carry hereditary instructions and are passed from parent to offspring; located on chromosomes (135)

generation time the period between the birth of one generation and the birth of the next generation (190)

genetic engineering manipulation of genes that allows scientists to put genes from one organism into another organism (165)

genotype the inherited combination of alleles (135)

genus the level of classification after family; the organisms in all families are sorted into genera (229)

geologic time scale the division of Earth's history into distinct intervals of time (204)

gestation period the time during which an embryo develops within the mother (398)

gills organs that remove oxygen from the water and carbon dioxide from the blood (360)

gland a group of cells that make special chemicals for the body (522)

Golgi complex the cell organelle that modifies, packages, and transports materials out of the cell (96)

gravitropism (GRAV i TROH piz uhm) a change in the direction of growth of a plant in response to gravity (288)

guanine (GWAH NEEN) one of the four bases that combine with sugar and phosphate to form a nucleotide subunit of DNA; guanine pairs with cytosine (152)

gut the pouch where food is digested in animals (327)

gymnosperm (JIM noh SPUHRM) a plant that produces seeds, but does not produce flowers (253)

H

hair follicle a small organ in the dermis layer of the skin that produces hair (478)

half-life for a particular radioactive sample, the time it takes for one-half the sample to decay (203)

head the body part of animals where the brain is located (339)

heredity the passing of traits from parent to offspring (38, 130)

hibernation a period of inactivity that some animals experience in winter that allows them to survive on stored body fat (311)

homeostasis (HOH mee OH STAY sis) the maintenance of a stable internal environment (37, 464)

hominid family referring specifically to humans and several extinct humanlike species, some of which were human ancestors (215)

homologous (hoh MAHL uh guhs) **chromosomes** chromosomes with matching information (117)

hormone a chemical messenger that carries information from one part of an organism to another; in humans, hormones are made by the endocrine glands (293, 522)

host an organism on which a parasite lives (332)

Human Genome Project a worldwide scientific effort to discover the location of each gene and to create a map of the entire human genome (167)

hypothesis a possible explanation or answer to a question (12)

I

implantation the process in which an embryo imbeds itself in the lining of the uterus (542)

impulse an electrical message that passes along a neuron (511)

infertile the state of being unable to have children (541)

innate behavior behavior that is influenced by genes and does not depend on learning (310)

integumentary system (in TEG yoo MEN tuhr ee) a collection of organs that help the body maintain a stable and healthy internal environment; the organs in this system include skin, hair, and nails (476)

internal fertilization fertilization of an egg by a sperm that occurs inside the body of a female (360, 536)

invertebrate an animal without a backbone (305, 326)

involuntary muscle action that is not under conscious control (472)

iris the colored part of the eye (519)

J

joint the place where two or more bones connect (470)

K

kingdom the most general of the seven levels of classification (229)

L

landmark a fixed object used to determine location during navigation (313)

larynx the area of the throat that contains the vocal cords (499)

lateral line system a row or rows of tiny sense organs along the sides of a fish's body (360)

law of reflection law that states that the angle of incidence is equal to the angle of reflection (59)

learned behavior a behavior that has been learned from experience or observation (310)

lens a curved, transparent object that forms an image by refracting light (67, 519)

lever a simple machine consisting of a bar that pivots at a fixed point, called a fulcrum; there are three classes of levers, based on where the input force, output force, and fulcrum are placed in relation to the load: first-class levers, second-class levers, and third-class levers (471)

life science the study of living things (6)

lift an upward force on an object caused by differences in pressure above and below the object; lift opposes the downward pull of gravity (386)

ligament a strong band of tissue that connects bones to bones (470)

lipid a type of biochemical, including fats and oils, that does not dissolve in water; lipids store energy and make up cell membranes (44)

littoral zone the zone of a lake or pond closest to the edge of the land (429)

lung a saclike organ that takes oxygen from the air and delivers it to the blood (364)

lymph the fluid and particles absorbed into lymph capillaries (496)

lymph capillaries the smallest vessels in the lymphatic system (496)

lymph nodes small, bean-shaped organs that contain small fibers that work like nets to remove particles from the lymph (497)

lymphatic system a collection of organs that collect extracellular fluid and return it to the blood; the organs in this system include the lymph nodes and the lymphatic vessels (496)

lymphatic vessels large vessels in the lymphatic system (496)

lymphocyte a white blood cell that kills pathogens (497)

lysosome a special vesicle in a cell that digests food particles, wastes, and foreign invaders (98)

M

mammary glands glands that secrete a nutritious fluid called milk (393)

mandible a jaw found on some arthropods (341)

marine describes an ecosystem based on salty water (423)

marsh a treeless wetland ecosystem where plants such as cattails and rushes grow (430)

marsupial a mammal that gives birth to live, partially developed young that continue to develop inside the mother's pouch or skin fold (397, 537)

mass the amount of matter that something is made of; its value does not change with the object's location (26)

mass extinction a period when a large number of species die out at the same time (205)

mechanical advantage a measure of how many times a machine multiplies an effort applied to a load; equals force applied to the load/effort force (471)

medulla the part of the brain that connects to the spinal cord (514)

medusa a body form of some cnidarians; resembles a bell with tentacles (330)

meiosis (mie OH sis) cell division that produces sex cells (139)

melanin a darkening chemical in your skin that determines your skin color (476)

menstruation the monthly discharge of blood and tissue from the uterus (539)

Mesozoic era the period in the geologic time scale beginning about 248 million years ago and lasting about 183 million years (212)

metabolism the combined chemical processes that occur in a cell or living organism (38)

metamorphosis the process in which an insect or other animal changes form as it develops from an embryo or larva to an adult (343, 366)

meter the basic unit of length in the SI system (23)

migrate to travel from one place to another in response to the seasons or environmental conditions (311)

mitochondria (MIET oh KAHN dree uh) cell organelles surrounded by two membranes that break down food molecules to make ATP (95)

mitosis nuclear division in eukaryotic cells in which each cell receives a copy of the original chromosomes (117)

monotreme a mammal that lays eggs (396, 537)

motor neuron a neuron that sends impulses from the brain and spinal cord to other systems (512)

multicellular made of many cells (83, 305)

muscle tissue one of the four main types of tissue in the body; contains cells that contract and relax to produce movement (465)

muscular system a collection of organs whose primary function is movement; organs in this system include the muscles and the connective tissue that attaches them to bones (472)

mutagen anything that can damage or cause changes in DNA (162)

mutation a change in the order of the bases in an organism's DNA; deletion, insertion, or substitution (162, 189)

N

natural selection the process by which organisms with favorable traits survive and reproduce at a higher rate than organisms without the favorable trait (188)

navigate to find one's way from one place to another (312)

Neanderthal a species of hominid that lived in Europe and western Asia from 230,000 years ago to about 30,000 years ago (218)

nerve an axon through which impulses travel, bundled together with blood vessels and connective tissue (512)

nervous system a collection of organs that gather and interpret information about the body's internal and external environment and respond to that information; the organs in this system include the brain, nerves, and spinal cord (510)

nervous tissue one of the four main types of tissue in the body; the tissue that sends electrical signals through the body (464)

neuron a specialized cell that transfers messages throughout the body in the form of fast-moving electrical energy (511)

nonrenewable resource a natural resource that cannot be replaced or that can be replaced only over thousands or millions of years (443)

nonvascular plant a plant that depends on the processes of diffusion and osmosis to move materials from one part of the plant to another (252)

nucleic acid a biochemical that stores information needed to build proteins and other nucleic acids; made up of subunits called nucleotides (45)

nucleotide a subunit of DNA consisting of a sugar, a phosphate, and a nitrogenous base (152)

nucleus the membrane-covered organelle found in eukaryotic cells that contains a cell's DNA and serves as a control center for the cell (90)

O

open circulatory system a circulatory system consisting of a heart that pumps blood through spaces called sinuses (336)

open-water zone the zone of a lake or pond that extends from the littoral zone across the top of the water and that is only as deep as light can reach through the water (429)

optic nerve a nerve that transfers electrical impulses from the eye to the brain (518)

order the level of classification after class; the organisms in all the classes are sorted into orders (229)

organ a combination of two or more tissues that work together to perform a specific function in the body (81, 306, 465)

organ system a group of organs working together to perform body functions (82, 465)

organelle (OHR guh NEL) a structure within a cell, sometimes surrounded by a membrane (87)

organism anything that can live on its own (83)

osmosis the diffusion of water across a cell membrane (109)

ovary in animals, an organ in the female reproductive system that produces eggs (539); in flowers, the structure that contains ovules and will develop into fruit following fertilization (271)

overpopulation a condition that occurs when the number of individuals becomes so large that there are not enough resources for all individuals (444)

ovulation the process in which a developed egg is ejected through the ovary wall (539)

ozone a gas molecule made up of three oxygen atoms; absorbs solar ultraviolet radiation (210)

P

paleontologist a scientist who uses fossils to reconstruct the history of life millions of years before humans existed (202)

Paleozoic era the period in the geologic time scale beginning about 570 million years ago and ending about 248 million years ago (211)

Pangaea the single landmass that contained all the present-day continents 200 million years ago (206)

parasite an organism that feeds on another living creature, usually without killing it (332)

passive transport the diffusion of particles through proteins in the cell membrane from areas where the concentration of particles is high to areas where the concentration of particles is low (110)

pedigree a diagram of family history used for tracing a trait through several generations (164)

penis the male reproductive organ that transfers semen into the female's body during sexual intercourse (538)

peripheral nervous system the collection of communication pathways, or nerves, whose primary function is to transfer information from all areas of the body to the central nervous system and from the central nervous system to the rest of the body (510)

permafrost the permanently frozen ground below the soil surface in arctic tundra (422)

petals the often colorful structures on a flower that are usually involved in attracting pollinators (270)

pharynx the upper portion of the throat (499)

phenotype an organism's inherited appearance (135)

pheromone (FER uh MOHN) a chemical produced by animals for communication (315)

phloem (FLOH EM) a specialized plant tissue that transports sugar molecules from one part of the plant to another (264)

phospholipid a type of lipid molecule that forms much of a cell's membrane (44)

photoreceptors specialized neurons in the retina that detect light (518)

photosynthesis the process by which plants capture light energy from the sun and convert it into sugar (112, 210)

phototropism a change in the growth of a plant in response to light (287)

phylum the level of classification after kingdom; the organisms from all the kingdoms are sorted into several phyla (229)

phytoplankton microscopic photosynthetic organisms that float near the surface of the ocean (423)

pigment a material that gives a substance its color by absorbing some colors of light and reflecting others (64)

pistil the female reproductive structure in a flower that consists of a stigma, a style, and an ovary (271)

placenta a special organ of exchange that provides a developing baby with nutrients and oxygen (398, 543)

placental mammal a mammal that nourishes its unborn offspring with a placenta inside the uterus and gives birth to well-developed young (398, 537)

plankton very small organisms floating at or near the oceans' surface that form the base of the oceans' food web (423)

Plantae the kingdom that contains plants—multicellular organisms that use the sun's energy to make sugar by photosynthesis (237)

plasma the fluid part of blood (488)

plate tectonics the study of the forces that drive the movement of pieces of the Earth's crust around the surface of the planet (207)

platelet a cell fragment that helps clot blood (489)

pollen the dustlike particles that carry the male gametophytes of seed plants (258)

pollination the transfer of pollen to the female cone in conifers or to the stigma in angiosperms (261)

pollutant a harmful substance in the environment (440)

pollution the presence of harmful substances in the environment (440)

polyp a body form of some cnidarians; resembles a vase (330)

population a group of individuals of the same species that live together in the same area at the same time (83)

Precambrian time the period in the geologic time scale beginning when the Earth originated, 4.6 billion years ago, and ending when complex organisms appeared, about 540 million years ago (208)

precocial chick a chick that leaves the nest immediately after hatching and is fully active (388)

predator an animal that eats other animals (308)

preening activity in which a bird uses its beak to spread oil on its feathers (383)

prey an organism that is eaten by another organism (308)

primate a group of mammals that includes humans, apes, and monkeys; typically has opposable thumbs and binocular vision (214, 405)

probability the mathematical chance that an event will occur (136)

producer an organism that uses sunlight directly to make sugar (40)

prokaryotic cell (prokaryote) (proh KER ee OHT) a cell that does not have a nucleus or any other membrane-covered organelles; also called a bacterium (90, 209)

prosimian the first primate ancestors; also, a group of living primates that includes lorises and lemurs (216)

protein a biochemical that is composed of amino acids; its functions include regulating chemical reactions, transporting and storing materials, and providing support (42)

Protista a kingdom of eukaryotic single-celled or simple multicellular organisms; kingdom Protista contains all eukaryotes that are not plants, animals, or fungi (236)

puberty the time of life when the sex organs become mature (538)

pulmonary circulation the circulation of blood between the heart and lungs (492)

Punnett square a tool used to visualize all the possible combinations of alleles from parents (135)

pupil the opening to the inside of the eye (519)

radial symmetry body plan in which the parts of the body are arranged in a circle around a central point (327)

radioactive waste hazardous wastes that take hundreds or thousands of years to become harmless (441)

receptor a specialized cell, sometimes a dendrite, that detects changes inside or outside the body (512)

recessive trait a trait that is apparent only when two recessive alleles for the characteristic are inherited (133)

recombinant DNA DNA produced when genes from one organism are put into another using genetic engineering (166)

recycling the process of making new products from reprocessed used products (449)

red blood cell a cell that carries oxygen from the lungs to all cells of the body and carries carbon dioxide back to the lungs to be exhaled (488)

reflection the bouncing back of a wave after it strikes a barrier or object (59)

reflex a quick, involuntary response to a stimulus (516)

refraction the bending of a wave as it passes at an angle from one medium to another (66)

relative dating determining whether an event or object, such as a fossil, is older or younger than other events or objects (203)

renewable resource a natural resource that can be used and replaced over a relatively short time (443)

reptile a type of vertebrate ectotherm that develops from an amniotic egg and is characterized by thick dry skin (369)

resource recovery the process of transforming things normally thrown away into electricity (450)

respiration the exchange of gases between living cells and their environment: includes breathing and cellular respiration (498); see *cellular respiration*

respiratory system a collection of organs whose primary function is to take in oxygen and expel carbon dioxide; the organs of this system include the lungs, the throat, and the passageways that lead to the lungs (498)

retina a layer of light-sensitive cells in the back of the eye (518)

rhizoids small hairlike threads of cells that help hold nonvascular plants in place (254)

rhizome the underground stem of a fern (256)

ribosome a small organelle in cells where proteins are made from amino acids (94, 161)

rock cycle the continuous process by which one rock type changes into another rock type (202)

rods photoreceptors that detect dim light (518)

S

Sargassum an alga that forms huge, floating rafts; basis for the name of the Sargasso Sea, an ecosystem of algae in the middle of the Atlantic Ocean (426)

savanna a tropical grassland biome with scattered clumps of trees (420)

scales bony structures that cover the skin of bony fishes (362)

scattering the release of light energy by particles of matter that have absorbed extra energy (61)

scientific method a series of steps that scientists use to answer questions and solve problems (10)

scrotum a skin-covered sac that hangs from the male body and contains the testes (538)

sediment fine particles of sand, dust, or mud that are deposited over time by wind or water (202)

segment one of many identical or almost identical repeating body parts (337)

selective breeding breeding of organisms that have a certain desired trait (186)

self-pollinating plant a plant that contains both male and female reproductive structures (131)

semen a mixture of sperm and fluids (538)

seminiferous tubules (SEM uh NIF uhr uhs TOO BYOOLZ) coiled tubes inside the testes where sperm cells are produced (538)

sensory neuron a special neuron that gathers information about what is happening in and around the body and sends this information on to the central nervous system (512)

sepals leaflike structures that cover and protect an immature flower (270)

sex cell an egg or sperm; a sex cell carries half the number of chromosomes found in other body cells (138)

sex chromosomes chromosomes that carry genes that determine the sex of offspring (143)

sexual reproduction reproduction in which two sex cells join to form a zygote (38, 535)

sexually transmitted disease a disease that can pass from an infected person to an uninfected person during sexual contact (541)

skeletal muscle the type of muscle that moves your bones and helps protect your inner organs (472)

skeletal system a collection of organs whose primary function is to support and protect the body; the organs in this system include bones, cartilage, ligaments, and tendons (468)

smooth muscle the type of muscle found in the blood vessels and the digestive tract (472)

social behavior the interaction between animals of the same species (314)

speciation the process by which two populations of the same species become so different that they can no longer interbreed (192)

species the most specific of the seven levels of classification; characterized by a group of organisms that can mate with one another to produce fertile offspring (176, 229)

sperm a sex cell produced by a male (535)

spleen an organ that filters blood and produces lymphocytes (497)

spongy bone the type of bone tissue that has many open spaces and contains marrow (469)

sporophyte (SPOH ruh FIET) a stage in a plant life cycle during which spores are produced (251)

stamen the male reproductive structure in the flower that consists of a filament topped by a pollen-producing anther (271)

stigma the flower part that is the tip of the pistil (271)

stimulus anything that affects the activity of an organism, organ, or tissue (37)

stomata openings in the epidermis of a leaf that allow carbon dioxide to enter the leaf and allow water and oxygen to leave the leaf (269)

surface-to-volume ratio the amount of a cell's outer surface in relationship to its volume (88)

swamp a wetland ecosystem where trees and vines grow (430)

sweat glands small organs in the dermis layer of the skin that release sweat (476)

swim bladder a balloon-like organ that is filled with oxygen and other gases; gives bony fish their buoyancy (363)

systemic circulation the circulation of blood between the heart and the body (excluding the lungs) (492)

T

tadpole aquatic larvae of an amphibian (366)

taproot a type of root that consists of one main root that grows downward, with many smaller branch roots coming out of it (265)

taxonomy the science of identifying, classifying, and naming living things (230)

technology the application of knowledge, tools, and materials to solve problems and accomplish tasks; technology can also refer to the objects used to accomplish tasks (18)

temperature a measure of how hot (or cold) something is (26)

tendon a tough connective tissue that connects skeletal muscles to bones (473)

territory an area occupied by one animal or a group of animals from which other members of the species are excluded (314)

testes organs in the male reproductive system that make sperm and testosterone (538)

theory a unifying explanation for a broad range of hypotheses and observations that have been supported by testing (18)

therapsid (thuh RAP sid) a prehistoric reptile ancestor of mammals (369, 392)

thorax the central body part of an arthropod or other animal; where the heart and lungs are located (339)

thymine one of the four bases that combine with sugar and phosphate to form a nucleotide subunit of DNA; thymine pairs with adenine (152)

thymus a lymph organ that releases lymphocytes (497)

tissue a group of similar cells that work together to perform a specific job in the body (306)

tonsils small masses of soft tissue located at the back of the nasal cavity, on the inside of the throat, and at the back of the tongue (497)

toxic poisonous (441)

trachea (TRAY kee uh) the air passageway from the larynx to the lungs (499)

trait a distinguishing quality that can be passed from one generation to another (186)

transmission the passing of light through matter (62)

transpiration the loss of water from leaves through stomata (286)

tributary a small stream or river that flows into a larger one (428)

tropism a change in the growth of a plant in response to a stimulus (287)

true-breeding plant a plant that always produces offspring with the same trait as the parent(s) (132)

tundra a far-northern biome characterized by long, cold winters, permafrost, and few trees (422)

U

umbilical cord a cord that connects the embryo to the placenta (543)

unicellular made of a single cell (83)

urethra in males, a slender tube that carries urine and semen through the penis to the outside (538)

uterus an organ in the female reproductive system where a zygote can grow and develop (539)

V

vacuole (VAK yoo OHL) a large membrane-covered structure found in plant cells that serves as a storage container for water and other liquids (97)

vagina the passageway in the female reproductive system that receives sperm during sexual intercourse (539)

variable the factor in a controlled experiment that changes (14)

vas deferens (vas DEF uh RENZ) a tube in males where sperm is mixed with fluids to make semen (538)

vascular plant a plant that has xylem and phloem, specialized tissues that move materials from one part of the plant to another (253)

veins blood vessels that direct blood to the heart (491)

ventricle a lower chamber of the heart (490)

vertebrae (VUHR tuh BRAY) segments of bone or cartilage that interlock to form a backbone (357)

vertebrate an animal with a skull and a backbone; includes mammals, birds, reptiles, amphibians, and fish (304, 356)

vesicles membrane-covered compartments in a eukaryotic cell that form when part of the cell membrane surrounds an object and pinches off (97)

vestigial structure the remnant of a once-useful anatomical structure (179)

volume the amount of space that something occupies or the amount of space that something contains (24)

voluntary muscle action that is under a person's control (472)

W

water vascular system a system of water pumps and canals found in all echinoderms that allows them to move, eat, and breathe (346)

wave a disturbance that transmits energy through matter or space (54)

wavelength the distance between one point on a wave and the corresponding point on an adjacent wave (56)

wetland an area of land where the water level is near or above the surface of the ground for most of the year (431)

white blood cell a blood cell that protects the body against pathogens (489)

X

xylem (ZIE luhm) a specialized plant tissue that transports water and minerals from one part of the plant to another (264)

Z

zooplankton (ZOH oh PLANGK tuhn) very small animals that, along with the phytoplankton they consume, form the base of the oceans' food web (423)

zygote a fertilized egg (535)

INDEX

Credits

ILLUSTRATIONS

All illustrations, unless otherwise noted below, by Holt, Rinehart and Winston.

Table of Contents Page viii(tr), Morgan Cain & Associates; ix(tl), Marty Roper/Planet Rep; (bl), Frank Ordaz/Dimension; (br), John White/The Neis Group; xv(cl), Christy Krames; xix(tl), Carlyn Iverson.

Unit One Page 2(bl), Kip Carter. **Chapter One** Page 12(cr), Michael Morrow; 13(all), Michael Morrow; 15(c), Ralph Garafola; 16(c), Ross, Culbert and Lavery/The Mazer Corporation Corporation; 18(bl), The Mazer Corporation; 20(tl), Blake Thornton/Rita Marie; 22(tl), Blake Thornton/Rita Marie; (cl, bl), Stephen Durke/Washington Artists/Washington Artists; (b), The Mazer Corporation; 23(c), Susan Johnston Carlson; (c), Frank Ordaz/Dimension; (c), Steve Roberts; (c), Morgan Cain & Associates; (cl), Ross, Culbert and Lavery; 24(bl), Terry Kovalcik; 26(tl), Stephen Durke/Washington Artists; 31(cr), Annie Bissett; (bl), Mark Heine.

Chapter Two Page 39(c), Will Nelson/Sweet Reps; (br), Terry Kovalcik; 42(cl), Morgan Cain & Associates; 43(all), Morgan Cain & Associates; 44(cl), Blake Thornton/Rita Marie; (bl, br), Morgan Cain & Associates; 45(tr), David Merrill/Suzanne Craig; (cr), The Mazer Corporation; (cr), John White/The Neis Group; (cr, br), Morgan Cain & Associates; 47(tr), Morgan Cain & Associates; 48(bl), Morgan Cain & Associates.

Chapter Three Page 55(tl), Will Nelson/Sweet Reps; (br), Blake Thornton/Rita Marie; 56(cl, b), Sidney Jablonski; (cl), Mike Carroll; 57(b), Sidney Jablonski; 58(cl), Blake Thornton/Rita Marie; 59(bl), Dan Stuckenschneider/Uhl Studios/Preface; 60(all), Dan Stuckenschneider/Uhl Studios/Preface; 62(cl), Gary Ferster; 65(bl), Stephen Durke/Washington Artists; 66(b), Stephen Durke/Washington Artists; 67(cr), Keith Kasnot; 68(c), Dan Stuckenschneider/Uhl Studios; 69(all), Dan Stuckenschneider/Uhl Studios; 70(c), Blake Thornton/Rita Marie; 71(cr), Dan Stuckenschneider/Uhl Studios; 72(tr), Stephen Durke/Washington Artists.

Chapter Four Page 82(c), Michael Woods; (br), Christy Krames; 83(c, cl), Morgan Cain & Associates; (cr), Christy Krames; 84(bl), Yuan Lee; 86(bl), David Merrill/Suzanne Craig; 88(tl), Terry Kovalcik; (c, b), Morgan Cain & Associates; 89(cr), Morgan Cain & Associates; (bc), Terry Kovalcik; 90(br), Morgan Cain & Associates; 91(tr), Morgan Cain & Associates; 92(all), Morgan Cain & Associates; 93(all), Morgan Cain & Associates; 94(all), Morgan Cain & Associates; 95(all), Morgan Cain & Associates; 96(all), Morgan Cain & Associates; 97(br), Morgan Cain & Associates; 98(all), Morgan Cain & Associates; 99(c), Morgan Cain & Associates; (br), Blake Thornton/Rita Marie; 103(all), Morgan Cain & Associates.

Chapter Five Page 107(all), Mark Heine; 109(tr), Stephen Durke/Washington Artists; 110(tl), Terry Kovalcik; (bl, br), Morgan Cain and Associates; 111(all), Morgan Cain and Associates; 112(bl), Morgan Cain and Associates; 113(bc), Morgan Cain and Associates; 114(tl), Robin Carter; (tl) The Mazer Corporation; (tr, cl, cr, bl, br), Morgan Cain and Associates; 118, 119(all), Alexander and Turner; 123(cr), Morgan Cain and Associates.

Unit Three Page 127(all), John White/The Neis Group. **Chapter six** Page 131(b), Mike Wepplo/Das Group; 132(tl), Michael Woods; (tl, cl, b), John White/The Neis Group; 133(c), Michael Woods; (cr, bc, br, r), John White/The Neis Group; 134(tl, cl, cr, bl, br), John White/The Neis Group; (tl, tr, cl), Michael Woods; (cr), The Mazer Corporation; 135(tr, cr), John White/The Neis Group; (br), The Mazer Corporation; 136(tl), John White/The Neis Group; 139(r), Alexander and Turner; 140,141(all), Alexander and Turner; 142(cr), Alexander and Turner; 143(bc), Alexander and Turner; (br), Rob Schuster/Hankins and Tegenborg; (br), Blake Thornton/Rita Marie; 144(br), The Mazer Corporation; 145(cr), Blake Thornton/Rita Marie; (cr), Rob Schuster/Hankins and Tegenborg; 146(tr), John White/The Neis Group; 147(bl), John White/The Neis Group.

Chapter Seven Page 150(t), The Mazer Corporation; (c), The Mazer Corporation; (c), Stephen Durke/Washington Artists; 152(b), Rob Schuster/Hankins and Tegenborg; 154(tl), Marty Roper/Planet Rep; (c), Alexander and Turner; 155(cl), Alexander and Turner; 156(c), Morgan Cain & Associates; 157(br) Alexander and Turner; 158(all), John White/The Neis Group; 160,161(c), Rob Schuster/Hankins and Tegenborg; 162(tll), Rob Schuster/Hankins and Tegenborg; 163(cl), Rob Schuster/Hankins and Tegenborg; 166(cl), The Mazer Corporation; 167(cr), The Mazer Corporation; 168(cl) Marty Roper/Planet Rep.

Chapter Eight Page 174(tl), Michael Morrow; (br, l), Will Nelson/Sweet Reps; 177(all), Steve Roberts; 179(tr, tr), Ross, Culbert and Lavery; (b, br), Rob Wood/Wood, Ronsaville, Harlin; 180(all), Rob Wood/Wood, Ronsaville, Harlin; 181(all), Rob Wood/Wood, Ronsaville, Harlin; 182(cl), Christy Krames; 183(tc, c), Sarah Woods; (tr, cr), David Beck; (cr), Frank Ordaz/Dimension; 185(tr, c), Tony Morse/Ivy Glick; (bl, bc, br), John White/The Neis Group; 186(tl), Carlyn Iverson; 187(bl), Ross, Culbert and Lavery; 188(all), Will Nelson/Sweet Reps; 190(cr), Frank Ordaz/Dimension; (bl, bc, br), Carlyn Iverson; 192(c, cl, cr), Mike Wepplo/Das Group; (bl, br), Will Nelson/Sweet Reps; 193(all), Carlyn Iverson; 194(tc), Rob Wood/Wood, Ronsaville, Harlin; 195(cr), Carlyn Iverson; 197(all), Ross, Culbert and Lavery.

Chapter Nine Page 201(all), Michael Morrow; 202(all), Mike Wepplo/Das Group; 203(br), Mike Wepplo/Das Group; (br), The Mazer Corporation; 204(tc, c, bc), Barbara Hoopes-Ambler; (c), The Mazer Corporation; 205(t), John White/The Neis Group; 206(cl), MapQuest.com; 207(t), MapQuest.com; (br), Walter Stuart; 209(c), John White/The Neis Group; 210(cr), Craig Attebery/Jeff Lavaty; 211(all), Barbara Hoopes-Ambler; 212(all), Barbara Hoopes-Ambler; 213(tr, cr), John White/The Neis Group; (br), Terry Kovalcik; 214(bl), Todd Buck; (br), Will Nelson/Sweet Reps; 215(all), Christy Krames; 219(cr), Christy Krames; 220(cr), Barbara Hoopes-Ambler; 223(tr), The Mazer Corporation; (tr), John White/The Neis Group; (bl), The Mazer Corporation; 224(br), Greg Harris.

Chapter Ten Page 227(bl), Terry Kovalcik; 229(c), Michael Woods; (c), David Ashby; (c), Ponde and Giles; (c), Frank Ordaz/Dimension; (c), Will Nelson/Sweet Reps; (c), Graham Allen; (c), Chris Forsey; (c), The Mazer Corporation; 230(tl, cl), Will Nelson/Sweet Reps; (cl), Michael Woods; (cl), Ponde and Giles; (bl), The Mazer Corporation; 231(tr), Blake Thornton/Rita Marie; (b), John White/The Neis Group; 232(c), Marty Roper/Planet Rep; (bl, tl), John White/The Neis Group; 233(t), John White/The Neis Group; (bc), Cy Baker/WAA; (br), The Mazer Corporation; 239(br), Will Nelson/Sweet Reps; (br), Chris Forsey; (br), Michael Woods; (br), Frank Ordaz/Dimension; (br), The Mazer Corporation; 240(cr), John White/The Neis Group; 242(cr), Marty Roper/Planet Rep; 243(tr), Cy Baker/WAA; (tr), The Mazer Corporation; 244(tr), Barbara Hoopes-Ambler; (cl), John White/The Neis Group.

Chapter Eleven Page 248(tc), Marty Roper/Planet Rep; 251(tr), Morgan Cain and Associates; (bl), The Mazer Corporation; 253(c), The Mazer Corporation; (c, cl, cr), John White/The Neis Group; 254(bl), The Mazer Corporation; (bc), Ponde and Giles; 256(bc), The Mazer Corporation; (bc), Ponde and Giles; 259(tl), Sarah Woods; (tr), Keith Locke/Suzanne Craig; (br), James Gritz/Photonica; 261(bc), The Mazer Corporation; (bc), Will Nelson/Sweet Reps; 262(tl), Marty Roper/Planet Rep; 263(tr), The Mazer Corporation; (tc, tr, c, cr), John White/The Neis Group; 264(bl), Will Nelson/Sweet Reps; 265(tc), John White/The Neis Group; 267(all), Will Nelson/Sweet Reps; 269(all), Will Nelson/Sweet Reps; 270(c), Will Nelson/Sweet Reps; 272(br), Sarah Woods; 274(br), John White/The Neis Group; 275(all), Will Nelson/Sweet Reps.

Chapter Twelve Page 278(br), Dan McGeehan/Koralick Associates; 280(all), Will Nelson/Sweet Reps; 281(all), Will Nelson/Sweet Reps; 282(br), Will Nelson/Sweet Reps; 284(all), Stephen Durke/Washington Artists; 285(bl), Ponde and Giles; 286(cr), Ponde and Giles; 287(bl), Carlyn Iverson; 289(cl, bl), Rob Schuster/Hankins and Tegenborg; (cr),

Stephen Durke/Washington Artists, 291(all), Rob Schuster/Hankins and Tegenborg; 294(cl), Will Nelson/Sweet Reps; 296(tr), Will Nelson/Sweet Reps; 297(all), Carlyn Iverson.

Chapter Thirteen Page 302(tr), Tony Morse/Ivy Glick; 305(c), Sidney Jablonski; (c), Barbara Hoopes-Ambler; (c), Sarah Woods; (c), Steve Roberts; (c), Bridgette James; (c), Michael Woods; 306(bl), Kip Carter; 310(cl), Keith Locke/Suzanne Craig; 312(tr), Gary Locke/Suzanne Craig; (bl), Tony Morse/Ivy Glick; 316(all), John White/The Neis Group; 318(br), John White/The Neis Group; 321(bl), Sidney Jablonski.

Chapter Fourteen Page 327(tl), Barbara Hoopes-Ambler; (tc), Sarah Woodward; (tr, cr, br), Alexander and Turner; 329(all), Alexander and Turner; 330(all), John White/The Neis Group; 331(all), Morgan Cain & Associates; 332(cl), Alexander and Turner; 335(tr), The Mazer Corporation; (c, cl, cr), Alexander and Turner; 339(br), Felipe Passalacqua; 341(c), John White/The Neis Group; (cr), Will Nelson/Sweet Reps; 343(bl), Steve Roberts; (br), Marty Roper/Planet Rep; 344(all), Bridgette James; 346(all), Alexander and Turner; 351(cl), The Mazer Corporation; (cr), Barbara Hoopes-Ambler.

Chapter Fifteen Page 355(cr), Kip Carter; 357(tc), Alexander and Turner; 360(cr), Will Nelson/Sweet Reps; 362(br), Kip Carter; 364(br), Peg Gerrity; 366(all), Will Nelson/Sweet Reps; 368(bl), Marty Roper/Planet Rep; 369(c), Barbara Hoopes-Ambler; (c), Chris Forsey; (c), Ponde and Giles; (c), Morgan Cain & Associates; 371(c), Kip Carter; 374(br), Will Nelson/Sweet Reps; 376(bl), Will Nelson/Sweet Reps; 377(tr), Rob Schuster/Hankins and Tegenborg; (bl), Marty Roper/Planet Rep; 378(bc), Ron Kimball; 379(bc), Ka Botz.

Chapter Sixteen Page 381(tr), John White/The Neis Group; 383(tr), Will Nelson/Sweet Reps; (cr, br), Kip Carter; (br), Will Nelson/Sweet Reps; 384(all), Will Nelson/Sweet Reps; 385(all), Will Nelson/Sweet Reps; 386(cr), Will Nelson/Sweet Reps; 391(all), Kip Carter; 392(bl), Howard Freidman; 406(br), Will Nelson/Sweet Reps; 409(cr), Sidney Jablonski.

Chapter Seventeen Page 416(b), MapQuest.com; 417(b), Will Nelson/Sweet Reps; 418(all), Will Nelson/Sweet Reps; 419(all), Will Nelson/Sweet Reps; 421(tr), Marty Roper/Planet Rep; (b), Will Nelson/Sweet Reps; 424(all), Yuan Lee; 425(all), Yuan Lee; 428(all), Will Nelson/Sweet Reps; 429(br), Mark Heine; 431(br), Rob Schuster/Hankins and Tegenborg; 432(tc), Will Nelson/Sweet Reps; 433(cl) Mark Heine; 434(bc), Will Nelson/Sweet Reps; 435(all), Rob Schuster/Hankins and Tegenborg.

Chapter Eighteen Page 444(bl), Morgan Cain & Associates; 457(t), John White/The Neis Group.

Chapter Nineteen: Page 464(all), Morgan Cain & Associates; 465(all), Morgan Cain & Associates; 466(all), Christy Krames; 467(all), Christy Krames; 469(bc), Keith Kasnot; 470(all), John Huxtable/Black Creative; 471(all), Annie Bissett; 473(bl), Christy Krames; 477(tr), Marty Roper/Planet Rep; (bl), Morgan Cain & Associates; 479(all), Morgan Cain & Associates; 480(all) John Huxtable/Black Creative; 482(br), Christy Krames; 483(tr), Morgan Cain & Associates.

Chapter Twenty Page 488(tr), Christy Krames; (cl), Todd Buck; 489(b), Keith Kasnot; 490(all), Kip Carter; 491(tc), Kip Carter; 492(bc), Kip Carter; 494(tl), Jared Schneidman/Wilkinson Studios; (br), Marty Roper/Planet Rep; 496(br), Kip Carter; 497(tr), Christy Krames; 498(bl), Christy Krames; 499(bl), Christy Krames; (br), John Karapelou; 500(tl, br), Christy Krames; (c, bc), Kip Carter; (cl), Eyewire, Inc.; 502(br), Kip Carter; 505(tr), Kip Carter.

Chapter Twenty-One Page 510(bl), Christy Krames; 511(bc), Scott Barrows/The Neis Group; 512(bc), Scott Barrows/The Neis Group; 513(all), Brian Evans; 514(all), Brian Evans; 515(tr), Christy Krames; 517(br), Morgan Cain and Associates; 518(cl), Carlyn Iverson; (br), Keith Kasnot; 519(all), Keith Kasnot; 520(b), Christy Krames; 521(tr), Keith Kasnot; 522(b), Dan McGeehan/Koralick Associates; 523(all), Christy Krames; 524(all), Christy Krames; 526(bc), Keith Kasnot; 527(c), Dan McGeehan/Koralick Associates; 528(tr), Christy Krames; 529(cr), Christy Krames.

Chapter Twenty-Two Page 535(bl), Rob Schuster/Hankins and Tegenborg; 538(bl), Keith Kasnot; 539(tr), Keith Kasnot; 540(br), Rob Schuster/Hankins and Tegenborg; 542(cl), David Fischer; 543(cr), Christy Krames; (bc), Mary Kate Denny; 551(cr), Sidney Jablonski; 552(bl), Morgan Cain and Associates.

LabBook Page 554 (tl), Stephen Durke/Washington Artists; 562(br), The Mazer Corporation; 565(r), Keith Locke/Suzanne Craig; 567(cr), Blake Thornton/Rita Marie; 568(br), Stephen Durke/Washington Artists; 570(tl), David Merrill/Suzanne Craig; (cr), Rob Schuster/Hankins and Tegenborg; 573(all), Morgan Cain & Associates; 580(cr), The Mazer Corporation; (br), Kip Carter; 582(br), Rob Schuster/Hankins and Tegenborg; 584(cr), Frank Ordaz/Dimension; 585(all), John White/The Neis Group; 586(br), Keith Locke/Suzanne Craig; 587(cr), Keith Locke/Suzanne Craig; 591(cr), The Mazer Corporation; (cr, br), Rob Schuster/Hankins and Tegenborg; 592(all), Rob Schuster/Hankins and Tegenborg; 593(tl), The Mazer Corporation; (cr), Keith Locke/Suzanne Craig; 594(cr), Rob Schuster/Hankins and Tegenborg; 595(cr), Rob Schuster/Hankins and Tegenborg; 596(cr), Will Nelson/Sweet Reps; 597(cr), Will Nelson/Sweet Reps; 599(cr), Sarah Woodward; 601(br), John White/The Neis Group; 605(br), Carlyn Iverson; 606(br), Keith Locke/Suzanne Craig; 607(tr), John White/The Neis Group; (cr), The Mazer Corporation; 609(br), Marty Roper/Planet Rep; 611(bc), Keith Locke/Suzanne Craig; 613(tr), John Huxtable/Black Creative; (br), David Merrill/Suzanne Craig; 616(cr), Will Nelson/Sweet Reps; 617(b), Blake Thornton/Rita Marie; 618(cr), John White/The Neis Group; 620(all), Carlyn Iverson; 627(cr), Morgan Cain & Associates; (b), Rob Schuster/Hankins and Tegenborg; 628(tr), Kip Carter; 629(t), Rob Schuster/Hankins and Tegenborg.

Appendix Page 639(cl), Blake Thornton/Rita Marie; 642(t), Terry Guyer; 646(all), Mark Mille/Sharon Langley; 654, 655(all) Kristy Sprott; 656(bl), Stephen Durke/Washington Artists; 657(b), Bruce Burdick.

PHOTOGRAPHY

Cover and Title Page (cl), Frans Lanting/Minden Pictures; (c), Peter Peterson/Tony Stone Images; (cr), Chris Jaffe; (bl), Carr Clifton; (br), Gerry Ellis/ENP Images; owl: (cover, spine, back, title page), Kim Taylor/Bruce Coleman.

Table of Contents Page v(br), Uniphoto; vi(cl), Leonard Lessin/Photo Researchers; vii(tl), Dr. Jeremy Burgess/Science Photo Library/Photo Researchers; (tr), E.R. Degginger/Color-Pic; (cr), Robert Brons/BPS/Tony Stone Images; viii(tl), Frans Lanting/Minden Pictures; ix(tr), Biophoto Associates/Photo Researchers; x(tl), Centre National de Prehistoire, Perigueux, France; (bl), David B. Fleetham/Tom Stack & Associates; xi(tl), SuperStock; (tr), Runk/Schoenberger/Grant Heilman Photography; xii(tl), Richard R. Hansen/Photo Researchers; (bl), Darryl Torckler/Tony Stone Images; xiii(tl), Brian Parker/Tom Stack & Associates; (tr), James Beveridge/Visuals Unlimited; (bl), Tui De Roy/Minden Pictures; (br), Konrad Wothe/Westlight; xiv(tl), Rob & Ann Simpson/Visuals Unlimited; (bl), David Young/Tony Stone Images; xv(tr), Dr. Dennis Kunkel/Phototake; (cr), Enrico Ferorelli; xvi(bl), Lennart Nilsson/Albert Bonniers Forlag AB, A CHILD IS BORN; xxi(bl), S.C. Bisserot/Bruce Coleman.

Feature Borders Unless otherwise noted below, all images copyright ©2001 PhotoDisc/HRW. Pages(104, 124, 224, 378, 410, 436, 552), Across the Sciences: all images by HRW. Pages(32, 225, 277, 437, 458), Careers: sand bkgd and saturn, Corbis Images; DNA, Morgan Cain & Associates; scuba gear, ©1997 Radlund & Associates for Artville. Pages(485, 531), Eureka. Pages(198, 299, 322, 353), Eye on the Environment: clouds and sea in bkgd, HRW; bkgd grass and red eyed frog, Corbis Images; hawks and pelican, Animals Animals/Earth Scenes; rat, John Grelach/Visuals Unlimited; endangered flower, Dan Suzio/PhotoResearchers, Inc. Pages(105, 149, 507), Health Watch: dumbell, Sam Dudgeon/HRW Photo; aloe vera and EKG, Victoria Smith/HRW Photo; basketball, ©1997 Radlund & Associates for Artville; shoes and Bubbles, Greg Geisler. Pages(50, 244, 459), Scientific Debate: Sam Dudgeon/HRW Photo. Pages(33, 51, 125, 199), Science Fiction: saucers, Ian Christopher/Greg Geisler; book, HRW; bkgd, Stock